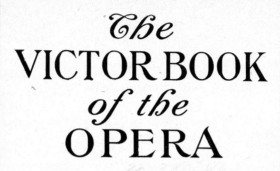

The
VICTOR BOOK
of the
OPERA

Stories of Seventy
Grand Operas with Three
Hundred Illustrations
&. Descriptions of
Seven Hundred Victor
Opera Records

Victor Talking Machine Co.
Camden, New Jersey, U.S.A.

HIS MASTER'S VOICE
REG. U.S. PAT. OFF.

Fourth Edition

INDEX

ALTHOUGH the Opera Stories in this book are in alphabetical order, under the most familiar of the various titles, this index will be found convenient for quick reference. M 475940

(Index continued on page 5)

Famous Opera Houses of Europe

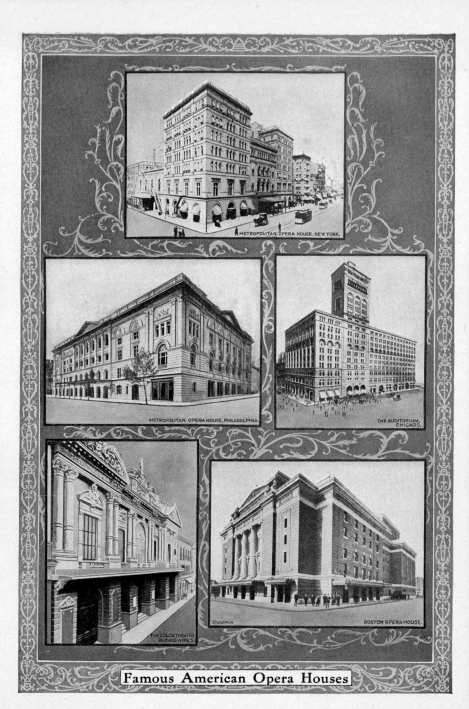

METROPOLITAN OPERA HOUSE, NEW YORK.

METROPOLITAN OPERA HOUSE, PHILADELPHIA.

THE AUDITORIUM, CHICAGO.

THE COLON THEATRE, BUENOS AIRES.

BOSTON OPERA HOUSE.

Famous American Opera Houses

FOREWORD

Opera in America

The opera has at last come into its own in the United States. In former years merely the pastime of the well-to-do in New York City and vicinity, grand opera is now enjoyed for its own sake by millions of hearers throughout the country. Boston, Chicago, Philadelphia, New Orleans, San Francisco and Montreal now have their regular opera season; while many other cities have arranged for occasional performances.

The Victor Responsible for Much of this Awakened Interest

During the recent season several hundred performances of grand opera, at an estimated cost of millions of dollars, were given in the United States. This great outlay for dramatic music alone would not have been possible had it not been for the increased interest aroused in opera by the widespread distribution by the Victor during the past ten years of hundreds of thousands of grand opera records, at widely varying prices—from the double-faced records by well-known Italian and French artists of Europe, at 37½ cents per selection, to the great concerted numbers by famous singers at $6.00 and $7.00.

The Opera-Goer and the Victor

Even though fortunate enough to be able to attend the opera, the lover of operatic music is reminded that with the Victor and the operatic records his enjoyment of the opera may be greatly increased. The favorite singers may be heard at home as often as desired, and their voices will be just as natural as in life.

Do you think Caruso the greatest of tenors? Then do not be satisfied with an occasional hearing of his glorious voice at the opera, but let him sing for you and your friends by means of the Victor.

Is Sembrich, Farrar, Tetrazzini, Gadski, Calvé, Schumann-Heink, Homer or Amato your favorite singer? The Victor makes it possible to hear these voices at any time, no matter where the artists may be singing.

Voices of Absent Singers

Do you regret that Melba is in Australia? There is consolation in the thought that her voice is here in all its loveliness, indelibly impressed on Victor discs.

Have you memories of Tamagno when he was at his best? The Victor will revive these memories for you by bringing the voice of this singer back from the grave. (Foreword continued on page 9)

Interior of Metropolitan Opera House, New York

The Victor an Excellent Substitute for the Opera

For every person who can attend the opera there are a hundred who cannot. However, many thousands of lovers of the opera in the latter class have discovered what a satisfactory substitute the Victor is, for it brings the actual voices of the great singers to the home, with the added advantage that the artist will repeat the favorite aria as many times as may be wished, while at the opera one must usually be content with a single hearing; and even though the scenery and costumes may be lacking, the absence of these accessories will now be atoned for in some measure by the graphic descriptions and numerous illustrations in this catalogue.

The Victor Opera Season Never Ends

In former years, after the close of the opera season and the annual migration of the artists to Europe, no one seemed to think much about grand opera or opera singers. The Victor, however, has changed all this, and operatic records now form a most important part of the musical life in the home; and at all seasons of the year may be heard the voices of the great singers, a consolation and a delight to opera lovers.

This Catalogue the First of Its Kind

This little work is unique in many respects, and while there are many excellent books describing the plots of the operas, we think that in no other book on opera can be found *all* of these features:

¶ Titles in various languages, with pronunciation of each.

¶ Date and place of original production.

¶ Date and place of first performance in America.

¶ Cast of characters and pronunciation of the same when necessary.

¶ Brief and clearly stated synopsis of plots of seventy different operas.

¶ Translations (all or part) of the text of several hundred separate numbers.

¶ Every act and scene indicated, with description of the stage setting.

¶ Every separate number mentioned in its proper place in the opera, and the numbers placed in the order in which they occur.

¶ More than three hundred portraits and pictures, making it the most completely illustrated book on opera ever published.

NOTE—Acknowledgment must be made to Oliver Ditson Co. and G. Schirmer for kind permission to quote occasionally from their copyrighted publications. Both these houses have set new standards with their operatic publications—Schirmer with superbly printed opera scores and collections of opera airs entitled "Operatic Anthology"; and Ditson with the Musicians' Library, masterpieces of music typography.

Caruso as Vasco di Gama

SCENES FROM L'AFRICAINE

Vasco before the Council—Act I
Scene in the Prison—Act II

The Massacre—Act III

The Indian Paradise—Act IV
The Fatal Tree—Act V

(Italian)
L'AFRICANA
(Laf-ree-kah'-nah)

(German)
DIE AFRIKANERIN
(Dee Ah-free-kah'-ner-in)

(French)
L'AFRICAINE
(Laf-ree-kahn)

(English)
THE AFRICAN

OPERA IN FIVE ACTS

Text by Scribe; music by Meyerbeer. First produced at the *Académie*, Paris, April 28, 1865. First London production in Italian, under the French title, at Covent Garden, July 22, 1865; and in English at the Royal English Opera, Covent Garden, October 21, 1865. First New York production December 1, 1865. Revived in 1906 at the Metropolitan, with Caruso, Fremstad, Plançon and Journet.

Characters in the Opera

SELIKA, *(Say-lee'-kah)* a slave, formerly an African princess . . . . Soprano
INEZ, *(Ee'-nez)* daughter of Don Diego . . . . Soprano
ANNA, her attendant . . . . Contralto
NELUSKO, *(Nay-loos'-ko)* a slave, formerly an African chief . . . . Basso
DON PEDRO, *(Don Pay'-dro)* President of the Royal Council . . . . Basso
GRANDE INQUISITORE . . . . Basso
DON DIEGO, *(Don Dee-ay'-go)* Member of the Council . . . . Basso
HIGH PRIEST OF BRAHMA *(Brah'-mah)* . . . . Basso
DON ALVAR, Member of the Council . . . . Tenor
VASCO DI GAMA, *(Vahs'-ko dee Gah'-mah)* an officer in the Portuguese Navy, Tenor

Chorus of Counsellors, Inquisitors, Sailors, Indians and Attendant Ladies.

The action occurs in Portugal, on Don Pedro's ship at sea, and in India.

11

ACT I

The first scene occurs at Portugal, in the King's Council Chamber, whither *Vasco di Gama* has come to announce his discovery of a strange land, producing two of the native slaves, *Selika* and *Nelusko,* as proof.

In this scene is given the noble and stately chorus

Dio che la terra venera (Thou Whom the Universe Adores)

By La Scala Chorus   (*In Italian*) *62614 10-inch, $0.75

in which the voices of the famous male chorus of La Scala are heard to great advantage.

Don Pedro, President of the Council, who wishes to marry *Vasco's* sweetheart, *Inez,* influences that body to discredit the explorer's tale and throw him into prison with his slaves. In the prison scene occurs this duet between *Selika* and *di Gama.*

Sei l'angiol diletto (Oh! Guardian Angel!)

By Tina Farelli, Soprano, and Gino Martinez-Patti,
Tenor   (*In Italian*) *62407 10-inch, $0.75

The slave, seeing her master's grief over his inability to find the route to the unknown country, reveals to him the location of the coveted land. *Vasco,* overcome with gratitude, embraces her.

ACT II

Inez consents to marry *Don Pedro* in order to save *Vasco,* who is released, but too late to prevent his enemy from sailing in search of the unknown land, carrying with him *Vasco's* private papers and maps as well as the two slaves, *Selika* and *Nelusko.* The latter, who loves *Selika,* has discovered her attachment for *Vasco,* and through jealousy offers to guide *Don Pedro* to his country. The young officer secures a ship and goes in pursuit.

ACT III

Preludio (Prelude to Act III)

By La Scala Orchestra   *62614 10-inch, $0.75

Act III shows the decks of *Don Pedro's* vessel. *Nelusko,* who is secretly plotting to destroy the ship, is brooding over his plans; and his gloomy bearing being noticed by the sailors, they ask him to relate the old legend of Adamastor, king of the seas.

FAURE AS NELUSKO, 1865

Adamastor, Re dell' onde profonde (Ruler of Ocean)

By G. Mario Sammarco, Baritone   (*In Italian*) 88310 12-inch, $3.00
By Francesco Cigada, Baritone   (*In Italian*) *62407 10-inch, .75

NELUSKO:

Adamastor, monarch of the pathless deep,
Swift o'er foaming waves
To sound of fierce winds tramping;
When his dark steeds vex the mist covered
   sea,
Beware, mariner! Beware, mariner!

When their breath on the gale rolls o'er the
   deep,
Then beware, then beware!
See, the lightning's flash reveals to thine eye,
How the dark waves seek the storm-laden sky.
All hope now is lost,
For the doomed wretch no tomb,
None, none but a watery grave!

A storm is threatened, and amid the preparations for resisting the elements a ship is seen, which proves to be *di Gama's.* He rashly comes on board, is promptly seized by *Don Pedro* and is about to be executed, when *Selika* draws her dagger and threatens to kill *Inez* unless her lover is released. The tyrant reluctantly yields, but afterward orders *Selika* to be flogged. The storm breaks, and in its midst the ship is boarded by Indians, fellow-country-men of *Nelusko,* and the entire ship's company are either killed or made prisoners.

ACT IV

Act IV represents the Temple of Brahma in the country of *Selika* and *Nelusko.* The act opens with the weird and striking Indian March, played here by the Herbert Orchestra.

Marcia Indiana (Indian March)

By Victor Herbert's Orchestra   70068 12-inch, $1.25
By La Scala Orchestra   *68027 12-inch, 1.25

Double-Faced Record—For title of opposite side see DOUBLE-FACED L'AFRICANA RECORDS, page 13.

The priests, who have crowned *Selika* their Queen, announce the execution of all the prisoners except *Vasco;* and he too is condemned to die. The priests and people disperse and *Vasco* enters, guarded by soldiers. He is entranced with the beauty of this wonderful land, of which he had dreamed, and voices his admiration in the celebrated air, *"O Paradiso."*

O Paradiso! (Oh Paradise!)

By Enrico Caruso, Tenor	(*In Italian*)	88054	12-inch,	$3.00
By Florencio Constantino	(*In Italian*)	74085	12-inch,	1.50
By Evan Williams	(*In English*)	74148	12-inch,	1.50

VASCO:
Hail! fruitful land of plenty, beauteous garden, hail!
An earthly paradise art thou!
Oh Paradise on earth!
Oh azure sky, oh fragrant air
All enchant my heart;
Thou fair new world art mine!
Thee, a radiant gift,
On my native land I'll bestow!
Hail, priceless treasure! Wondrous marvels, hail!
O beauteous country—thine thou art at last!
Yes—land till now unknown, thou'rt mine!
yes, mine!

Caruso's singing of this famous air is a magnificent performance, while two other fine records are offered in both Italian and English.

The soldiers are about to kill *Vasco*, but he is saved by *Selika*, who announces that he is her chosen husband. *Nelusko* is forced to remain silent by threats that *Selika* will destroy herself. *Di Gama*, forgetting *Inez*, yields to the spell and weds the Queen by the native rites.

ACT V—SCENE I

At the beginning of the last act, *Inez*, who had escaped from the prison, is captured and brought before the Queen, who becomes convinced that *di Gama* still loves the Portuguese maiden. In a moment of generosity she sacrifices her own feelings and assists the lovers to escape.

ACT V—SCENE II

The final scene shows a promontory from which *Selika* is watching the ship bearing *Inez* and *di Gama* toward Portugal. As the vessel disappears from view she advances toward the deadly mancanilla tree, the fumes of which are death.

SELIKA:
Aye! here I look upon the mighty sea—boundless—infinite
As is my woe!
Its waves in angry fury break, and then anon their course renew,
As doth my sorrowing heart!
(*Observing the mancanilla tree.*)

Thou leafy temple, thou vault of foliage dark,
That ceaseless wav'st thy deadly branches in the wind,
After life's weary tumult I now come
To seek repose of thee, and find oblivion from my woes,
Yes! thy shade eternal is like the darkness of the tomb!

Gathering the fatal flowers, she inhales their perfume, sadly saying:

Farewell, my Vasco, I forgive thee!
(*To the mancanilla tree*)
'Tis said your dread perfume doth a joy inspire,

Which for a moment yields unearthly joy,
And then doth cause a sleep eternal!

She is overcome and sinks unconscious beneath the tree. *Nelusko*, who has come in search of her, finds her dying; and in a frenzy of grief, also inhales the deadly blossoms and falls lifeless by her side.

DOUBLE-FACED L'AFRICAINE RECORDS

{ Marcia Indiana (Indian March)	By La Scala Orchestra }	68027	12-inch, $1.25
{ *Traviata—Preludio*	*By La Scala Orchestra* }		
{ Adamastor, Re dell onde profonde (Adamaster, Ruler of the Ocean)	By Francesco Cigada, Baritone (*In Italian*) }	62407	10-inch, .75
{ Sei L'angiol di letto (Oh, Guardian Angel!)	By Tina Farelli, Soprano; G. Martinez-Patti, Tenor (*In Italian*) }		
{ Dio che la terra venera	By La Scala Chorus (*In Italian*) }	62614	10-inch, .75
{ Preludio—Atto III	By La Scala Orchestra }		

Homer as Amneris

(Italian)

AIDA

(Ah-ee'-dah)

OPERA IN FOUR ACTS

Text translated from the French of Locle by Antonio Ghislanzoni. Music by Giuseppe Verdi. First produced in Cairo, December 24, 1871; at La Scala, Milan, February 8, 1872; in Paris, April 22, 1876; at Covent Garden, June 22, 1876. First performance in America at the Academy of Music, New York, November 26, 1873, the cast including Torriani, Cary, Campanini and Maurel.

Characters of the Drama

AIDA, an Ethiopian slave...Soprano
THE KING OF EGYPT...Bass
AMNERIS, *(Am-nare'-iss)* his daughter.........................Mezzo-Soprano
RHADAMES, *(Rahd'-ah-maze)* Captain of the Guard.....................Tenor
AMONASRO, *(Am-oh-nahz'-roh)* King of Ethiopia......................Baritone
RAMFIS, *(Rahm'-fiss)* High Priest.....................................Bass
A MESSENGER..Tenor

Priests, Priestesses, Ministers, Captains, Soldiers, Officials, Ethiopian
Slaves and Prisoners, Egyptians, etc.

The scene is laid in Memphis and Thebes, in Pharaoh's time.

This opera was written by request of the Viceroy of Egypt, who wished to celebrate the opening of his new Opera House at Cairo by the production of a work upon an Egyptian subject from the pen of the most popular composer of the time. The story originated with Marietta Bey, the famous Egyptologist, and seems to have inspired Verdi to unusual efforts.

BERT, PARIS

CARUSO AS RHADAMES

Aida, daughter of *Amonasro,* King of Ethiopia, has been captured by the Egyptians and is a slave at the Court of Memphis, where she and the young soldier *Rhadames* have fallen in love with each other. *Rhadames* goes to the Egyptian war, and during his absence the *King's* daughter, *Amneris,* discovers his attachment and is furious, as she herself loves *Rhadames.*

Rhadames returns, covered with glory and bringing many prisoners, among them *Amonasro, Aida's* father. The *King* releases all the prisoners except *Amonasro,* and bestows his daughter on the unwilling *Rhadames.*

In the next scene *Amonasro* forces his daughter to persuade *Rhadames* to become a traitor. The latter's love for *Aida* and his distaste for the approaching union with *Amneris* lead him to consent. *Amneris,* however, has overheard the plot, and after vainly trying to induce *Rhadames* to abandon *Aida,* she denounces him as a traitor, and he is condemned to be buried alive. When the vault is sealed he discovers *Aida,* who had concealed herself there that she might die with him; and the lovers slowly suffocate in each other's arms.

ACT I

SCENE I—*A Hall in the Palace. Through the grand gate at the back may be seen the Pyramids and the Temples of Memphis*

The opera has no overture. The curtain rises, showing a hall in the palace of the King of Memphis, where *Rhadames* and the High Priest, *Ramfis,* are discussing the coming invasion of Ethiopia; and *Ramfis* hints that some young and brave warrior may be chosen to command the expedition. *Rhadames*, left alone, hopes that he himself may gain the coveted honor, and promises to lay his triumphs at the feet of his *Aida*.

Celeste Aida (Heavenly Aida)

By Enrico Caruso, Tenor
(In Italian) 88127 12-inch, $3.00
By Leo Slezak, Tenor
(In German) 64113 10-inch, 1.00

Then occurs the splendid gem of Act I, the *Celeste Aida*, beginning

Ce·le·ste A·i·da, for·ma di vi·na,— mi·sti·co ser·to di lu·ce e fior
Heav'n·ly A·i·da, beau·ty re·splen·dent,—Ra·di·ant flow·er, bloom·ing and bright

COPY'T MISHKIN

SLEZAK AS RHADAMES

in which *Rhadames* chants the praises of the peerless *Aida*. It is seldom enjoyed at the opera, especially in America, as it occurs almost immediately after the rise of the curtain, and is invariably marred by the noise made by late comers. With the Victor, however, it may be heard in all its beauty and the fine renditions by Caruso and Slezak fully appreciated.

RHADAMES:
Heavenly Aida, beauty resplendent,
Radiant flower, blooming and bright;
Queenly thou reignest o'er me transcendent,
Bathing my spirit in beauty's light.

Would that thy bright skies once more beholding,
Breathing the soft airs of thy native land,
Round thy fair brow a diadem folding,
Thine were a throne next the sun to stand!

A fine trio, expressing the emotions of the characters in the scene, then follows.

COPY'T DOVER ST. STUDIOS

MARTIN AS RHADAMES

Ohimé! di guerra fremere (Alas! the Cry of War I Hear)

By Elena Ruszcowska, Soprano; Bianca Lavin de Casas, Mezzo-Soprano; Egidio Cunego, Tenor (In Italian) 88261 12-inch, $3.00

The *King's* daughter, *Amneris*, enters, and seeing the young warrior's glowing enthusiasm, delicately hints of her secret affection for him, saying:

AMNERIS:
What unwonted fire in thy glance!
With what noble pride glows thy face!
Worthy of envy—oh, how much—
Would be the woman whose beloved aspect
Should awaken in thee this light of joy!

Rhadames begins to explain his hope of securing the command of the expedition, when *Aida* enters, and the young soldier's expressive glance reveals to *Amneris* his love for the Egyptian slave.

The *King* and his guards enter and receive a messenger, who reports that Egypt has been invaded by the Ethiopian army, under the command of *Amonasro*. ("My father!" exclaims *Aida* aside.) Amid great excitement *Rhadames* is appointed leader of the army, and is presented with a banner by *Amneris*.

The *King* begins another trio, urging the Egyptian forces to guard with their lives the sacred Nile.

Su! del Nilo (Nilus' Sacred Shores!)

By Elena Ruszcowska, Soprano; Maria Cappiello, Mezzo-Soprano; Tapergi and Davi (*In Italian*) 88266 12-inch, $3.00

Following the trio comes a grand chorus:

> To battle! We'll hunt the invader down.
> On! Rhadames, thy brow may laurels crown!

All depart to prepare for the expedition, while *Aida*, left alone, gives way to her grief and sings the beautiful *Ritorna vincitor*, expressing her conflicting emotions.

Ritorna vincitor (Return Victorious!)
By Johanna Gadski, Soprano
(*In Italian*) 88137 12-inch, $3.00

AIDA:
> Return victorious! And from my lips
> Went forth the impious word! Conqueror
> Of my father—of him who takes arms
> For me—to give me again
> A country; a kingdom; and the illustrious
>   name
> Which here I am forced to conceal!
> The insane word forget, O gods;
> Return the daughter
> To the bosom of her father;
> Destroy the squadrons of our oppressors!. . .
> What am I saying? And my love,
> Can I ever forget
> This fervid love which oppresses and enslaves,
> As the sun's ray which now blesses me?
> Shall I call death on Rhadames—
> On him whom I love so much?
> Ah! Never on earth was heart torn by more
>   cruel agonies!

COPY'T DUPONT

GADSKI AS AIDA

She gives way to her emotion for a brief moment, then sings the lovely and appealing

I sacri nomi (The Sacred Names)
By Celestina Boninsegna, Soprano   88223   (*In Italian*) 12-inch, $3.00

Rousing herself, she calls on her gods for aid and goes slowly out as the curtain falls.

SCENE II—*The Temple of Vulcan—in the centre an altar, illuminated by a mysterious light from above*

Ramfis, the High Priest, and the priests and priestesses have assembled to bless the expedition. The chant in praise of *Ptah* is heard from an invisible choir. *Rhadames* enters and receives the consecrated veil.

RAMFIS:
> Mortal, beloved of the gods, to thee
> Is confided the fate of Egypt. Let the holy
>   sword
> Tempered by the gods, in thy hand become
> To the enemy, terror—a thunderbolt-death!

RHADAMES:
> God, who art leader and arbiter
> Of every human war,
> Protect thou and defend
> The sacred soil of Egypt!

Nume, custode e vindice (God, Guardian and Avenger)
By Antonio Paoli, Tenor; Perello de Segurola, Bass; and Chorus
(*In Italian*) 88268 12-inch, $3.00

COPY'T DUPONT

EAMES AS AIDA

The Return of Rhadames—Act II

LANDE

Ramfis then sings the closing invocation, in which *Rhadames* joins.

He is invested with the sacred armor, and as the priestesses perform the mystic dance the curtain slowly falls.

ACT II

SCENE I—*A hall in Amneris' apartments*

The curtain rises, showing the Princess and her slaves, who are adorning her for the triumphal festival in honor of *Rhadames,* just returned with his victorious army. *Amneris* and the slaves sing the ode to the returned hero.

Chi mai fra (His Glory Now Praise)

By Maria Capiello, Mezzo-Soprano,
and Chorus   (*In Italian*) *55005 12-inch, $1.50

Seeing *Aida* approaching, the Princess dismisses her slaves and prepares to enjoy her revenge.

This scene is expressed in a splendid duet, given here in two records by Mmes. Gadski and Homer, and also by Mmes. Ruszcowska and Lavin de Casas, of the La Scala forces.

Fu la sorte dell' armi ('Neath the Chances of Battle)

By Johanna Gadski, Soprano, and Louise Homer,
Contralto   (*In Italian*) 89024 12-inch, $4.00
By Elena Ruszcowska, Soprano, and Bianca
Lavin de Casas, Mezzo-Soprano
(*In Italian*) 88262 12-inch, 3.00

Alla pompa, che s'appreste (In the Pageant Now Preparing)

By Johanna Gadski, Soprano, and Louise Homer, Contralto
(*In Italian*) 89025 12-inch, $4.00

PHOTO BERT

HOMER AS AMNERIS

Ebben qual nuovo fremito (What New Alarm?)

By Elena Ruszcowska, Soprano, and Bianca
Lavin de Casas, Mezzo-Soprano
(*In Italian*) 88263 12-inch, $3.00

Amneris pretends to sympathize with the afflicted girl, saying:

AMNERIS:
The fate of arms was deadly to thy people.
Poor Aida! The grief
Which weighs down thy heart I share!
I am thy friend;
Time will heal the anguish of thy heart,
And more than time—a powerful god—love.

Amneris, having thus by her pretended sympathy gained *Aida's* confidence, determines to betray her into a declaration of her love for *Rhadames,* and suddenly announces that he has been killed in battle. *Aida,* overcome with grief, reveals plainly that she loves the young soldier.

AMNERIS (*aside*):
This death-like pallor, this strong emotion,
Plainly reveal the fever of love!

Amneris then throws off her mask of friendliness, and gloating in her victory, confesses that she has spoken falsely and that *Rhadames* lives.

Then, stung to fury by *Aida's* joy, she exclaims:

COPY'T MISHKIN

DALMORES AS RHADAMES

* *Double-Faced Record—For title of opposite side see DOUBLE-FACED AIDA RECORDS, page 25.*

AMNERIS:
Tremble! I read thy secret,
Thou lov'st him! lie no longer!
I love him too—dost thou hear?
I am thy rival, daughter of kings Egyptian.

AIDA:
Thou my rival? 'tis well, so be it—
Ah, what have I said? forgive and pity,
Ah, let this my sorrow thy warm heart move.
'Tis true I adore him with boundless love—
Thou art so happy, thou art so mighty,
I cannot live hence from love apart!

AMNERIS:
Tremble, vile minion! be ye heartbroken,
Warrant of death this love shall betoken!
In the pomp which approaches,
With me, O slave, thou shall assist;
Thou prostrate in the dust—
I on the throne beside the King;
Come, follow me, and thou shalt learn
If thou canst contend with me!

AIDA:
Ah, pity! What more remains to me?
My life is a desert;
This love which angers thee
In the tomb I will extinguish!

Always a highly impressive number, this duet is doubly so when rendered by such famous exponents of the parts of *Aida* and *Amneris*. Mme. Gadski's *Aida* is one of her most effective rôles—splendidly acted and vocally perfect; while Mme. Homer's impersonation of the Egyptian Princess is always a thrillingly dramatic one.

The rendition by the two La Scala artists is one of the finest which has come to us from Milan.

SCENE II—*Without the City Walls*

The scene changes to a gate of the city of Thebes. The *King* and his court are assembled on a magnificent throne to receive the conquering army. A splendid chorus is sung by people and priests. The Egyptian troops, preceded by trumpeters, enter, followed by chariots of war, ensigns, statues of the gods, dancing girls carrying treasures, and finally *Rhadames*, under a canopy borne by twelve slaves.

KING (*descending from the throne to embrace Rhadames*):
Saviour of our country, I salute thee.
Come, and let my daughter with her own hand
Place upon you the triumphal crown.

(*Rhadames bows before Amneris, who places the crown upon him.*)
Now ask of me
What thou most wishest. Nothing denied to thee
On such a day shall be—I swear it
By my crown, by the sacred gods!

The prisoners enter, including *Amonasro*, who is dressed as an officer. *Aida* sees him and cries, "What do I see! My father!" All are surprised, and *Amonasro* signals to *Aida* not to betray his rank. *Amonasro* then sings his recital:

Quest' assisa ch'io vesto (This Dress Has Told You)

By Ernesto Badini, Baritone; Sra. Fabris, Soprano; Lavin de Casas, Mezzo-Soprano; Egidio Cunego, Tenor (*In Italian*) 88264 12-inch, $3.00

AMONASRO:
I am her father. I went to war,
Was conquered, and death I sought in vain.
(*Pointing to his uniform*)
This habit I wear may tell you
That I have defended my king and my country.
Fate was hostile to our arms;
Vain was the courage of the brave!
At my feet, in the dust extended,

Lay the King, transfixed by many wounds;
If the love of country is a crime
We are all criminals—all ready to die!
(*Turning to the King with a supplicating accent*)
But thou, O King, thou powerful lord,
Be merciful to these men.
To-day we are stricken by Fate,
To-morrow Fate may smite thee!

The people and prisoners appeal to the *King* for mercy, while the priests demand that the captives be put to death. *Rhadames*, seeing the hesitation of the *King*, reminds him of his vow, and demands life and liberty for the captured Ethiopians. The *King* yields, stipulating only that *Aida* and her father be held as hostages, and then announces that *Rhadames* shall have the hand of *Amneris* as his reward.

The magnificent finale then follows, *Aida* and *Rhadames* gazing at each other in despair, *Amneris* glorying in her triumph, and *Amonasro* swearing secret vengeance against his captors. The curtain falls amid general rejoicing.

ACT III

SCENE I—*A moonlight night on the banks of the Nile—the Temple of Isis can be seen, half concealed by palm trees*

As the curtain rises on this beautiful scene, a chorus within the Temple is heard in a chant of praise.

O tu che sei d'Osiride (Oh, Thou Who Art Osiris)

By Maria Cappiello, Soprano, and Chorus   (*In Italian*) *55005 12-inch, $1.50

A boat approaches, bearing *Rhadames* and *Amneris,* who go into the Temple. *Aida,* veiled, cautiously enters, hoping that *Rhadames* will come thither, and sings a tender and despairing song of that lovely land which she may never see again.

O patria mia (My Native Land)

By Johanna Gadski, Soprano
　　　　　　　　(*In Italian*)　88042　12-inch, $3.00
By Emmy Destinn, Soprano
　　　　　　　　(*In German*)　92058　12-inch,　3.00
By Celestina Boninsegna, Soprano
　　　　　　　　(*In Italian*)　88239　12-inch,　3.00

BERT, PARIS
DESTINN AS AIDA

> AIDA:
> O native land, no more to thee shall I return!
> O skies of tender blue, O soft airs blowing,
> Where calm and peaceful my dawn of life pass'd o'er,
> O hills of verdure, O perfum'd waters flowing,
> O home beloved, I ne'er shall see thee more!
> O fresh and fragrant vales, O quiet dwelling,
> Promise of happy days of love that bore.
> Now hope is banish'd, love and yonder dream dispelling,
> O home beloved, I ne'er shall see thee more!

Three fine renditions of this air, one of the most effective in the opera, are given here by three celebrated prima donnas, all of whom have been seen in America in the part of *Aida.*

Amonasro appears and reproaches his daughter with her love for his enemy *Rhadames,* telling her with significant emphasis that she may behold her native land again if she wishes.

Rivedrai le foreste imbalsamate (Thou Shalt See Again the Balmy Forests)

By Elena Ruszcowska, Soprano, and Giuseppe Maggi, Baritone
　　　　　　　　(*In Italian*)　88267　12-inch, $3.00

LANDE　　DESTINN AND SCOTTI IN AIDA

He tells her that his people have risen again, and proposes that she shall influence *Rhadames* to betray the plans of his army in the new campaign. She at first refuses, but he bids her be true to her country, and pictures the sufferings of her people.

Su, dunque! (Up, Then!)

By Elena Ruszcowska, Soprano, and Ernesto Badini, Baritone
(*In Italian*)　88265　12-inch, $3.00

With growing excitement he describes the consequences of her refusal.

> AMONASRO (*with savage rage*):
> Up, then!
> Rise, Egyptian legions!
> With fire destroy our cities—
> Spread terror, carnage and death.
> To your fury there is no longer check!
> AIDA:
> Ah, father!
> AMONASRO (*repulsing her*):
> My daughter
> Dost thou call thyself?

* Double-Faced Record—For title of opposite side see DOUBLE-FACED AIDA RECORDS, page 25.

AIDA (*terrified and suppliant*):
Pity!

AMONASRO:
Rivers of blood pour
On the cities of the vanquished—
Seeth thou? From the black gulfs
The dead are raised—
To thee they point and cry;
For thee the country dies!

AIDA:
Pity!

AMONASRO:
A horrible ghost
Among the shadows to us approaches—
Tremble! the fleshless arms
Over thy head it raised—

It is thy mother—recognize her—
She curses thee!

AIDA (*in the greatest terror*):
Ah, no! Father!

AMONASRO (*repulsing her*):
Go, unworthy one! Thou'rt not my offspring—
Thou art the slave of the Pharaohs!

AIDA (*yielding*):
Father, their slave I am not—
Reproach me not—curse me not;
Thy daughter again thou canst call me—
Of my country I will be worthy!

AMONASRO:
Courage! he comes—there, I shall hear all.
(*Conceals himself among the palm trees.*)

Rhadames now enters and tries to embrace her, but she repulses him, saying bitterly:

AIDA:
The rites of another love await thee,
Thou spouse of Amneris!

He protests that he loves *Aida* alone, but she bids him prove his affection by fleeing with her.

AIDA:
Ah! fly with me, and leave behind
These deserts bare and blighted;
Some country, new and fresh to find,
Where we may love united.
There, 'mid virgin forest groves,
By fair sweet flow'rs scented,
In quiet joy contented, the world will we forget!

COPY'T MISHKIN

ZEROLA AS RHADAMES

He finally consents, and reveals to her that the army will go by the pass of Napata. *Amonasro*, who has overheard, now enters, and *Rhadames* is horrified at the knowledge that he has betrayed the army to the King of Ethiopia. His scruples are finally overcome, *Amonasro* saying:

AMONASRO:
No; thou art not guilty—
It was the will of fate.
Come; beyond the Nile await

The brave men devoted to us;
There the vows of thy heart
Shall be crowned with love.

Amneris, coming from the temple, pauses behind a pillar and overhears the final words. Mad with jealousy, she rushes in and denounces the guilty trio. *Aida* and *Amonasro* escape but *Rhadames* is taken in custody as a traitor.

ACT IV

SCENE I —*A room in the Palace – on one side a door leading to Rhadames' prison cell*

The curtain rises, disclosing *Amneris* in an attitude of despair. She is torn between her love for *Rhadames* and a desire for vengeance, and finally orders the prisoner brought before her.

AMNERIS (*bitterly musing*):
My rival has escaped me—
And Rhadames awaits from the priests
The punishment of a traitor.
Traitor he is not, though he revealed
The high secret of war. He wished to fly—
To fly with her—traitors all!
To death, to death!
Oh, what am I saying? I love him—
Oh! if he could love me!
I would save him—but how?
Let me try. Guards, Rhadames comes.

PHOTO HALL

RHADAMES DENOUNCED AS A TRAITOR

Rhadames enters, and the first great duet of the act occurs.

Gia i sacerdoti adunansi (The Priests Assemble)
By Louise Homer and Enrico Caruso (*In Italian*) **89050** 12-inch, $4.00
By Pietracewska and Barrera   (*In Italian*) **88269** 12-inch, 3.00

Aida a me togliesti (Aida Thou Hast Taken)
By Louise Homer and Enrico Caruso (*In Italian*) **89051** 12-inch, $4.00

Amneris tells him that *Amonasro* is dead, that *Aida* has disappeared, and offers to save his life if he will renounce his love. He scorns the proposal, resolving to die rather than be false to his Ethiopian Princess.

AMNERIS: Renounce Aida forever
 And thou shalt live!
RHADAMES: I cannot do it!
AMNERIS: Wouldst die, then, madman?
RHADAMES: I am ready to die.

AMNERIS: Who saves thee, O wretch,
 From the fate that awaits thee?
To fury hast thou changed
A love that had no equal.
Revenge for my tears
Heaven will now consummate!

The guards now appear and conduct *Rhadames* to the judgment room. The ensuing scene is a highly dramatic and impressive one.

Ohimè! Morir mi sento (Ah, me! Death Approaches!)
By Lavin de Casas, Mezzo-Soprano; Rizzo Sant' Elia,
 Bass; and Chorus   (*In Italian*) **88270** 12-inch, $3.00

Amneris, seeing *Rhadames* taken out by the Priests, repents her harshness and sinks down desolate on a seat.

AMNERIS (*falling on a chair, overcome*):
 Ah me! Death's hand approaches! who now
 will save him?
He is now in their power.
His sentence I have sealed—Oh, how I curse
 thee,
Jealousy, vile monster, thou who hast doomed
 him
To death, and me to everlasting sorrow!
(*Turns and sees Ramfis and the Priests, who
cross the stage and enter the subterranean
hall.*)
What see I? Behold of death
The ministers fatal, his merciless judges.

Ah, let me not behold those white robed
 phantoms!
(*Covers her face with her hands. The voice
of Ramfis can be heard within.*)
RAMFIS:
 Rhadames, Rhadames: thou hast betrayed
 Of thy country the secrets to aid the foeman:
PRIESTS:
 Defend thyself!
RAMFIS:
 Rhadames, Rhadames: and thou wast absent
 From the camp the very day before the
 combat!

PRIESTS:
 Defend thyself!

RAMFIS:
 Rhadames, Rhadames: and
  thou hast played
 The part of a traitor to King,
  and to honor!

PRIESTS:
 Defend thyself!

RAMFIS:
 He is silent.

ALL:
 Traitor vile!

RAMFIS:
 Rhadames, we thy fate have
  decided,
 Of all traitors the fate shall
  be thine—
 'Neath the altar whose God
  thou'st derided
 Thou a sepulchre living shall
  find.

AMNERIS:
 Find a sepulchre living!
  Hated wretches!
 Ever vengeful, blood-thirsty
  and blind!

SCOMPARINI THE DESPAIR OF AMNERIS—ACT IV

Sacerdoti, compiste un delitto! (Priests, a Crime You Have Enacted!)

By Lavin de Casas, Mezzo-Soprano; F. Rizzi, Bass; and
Chorus   (*In Italian*) 88323 12-inch, $3.00

The priests now enter from the crypt and pass across the hall. The wretched woman denounces them.

Priests of Heaven, a crime you have enacted,
Tigers even in bloodshed exulting,
Earthly justice and Heaven's you are insulting,
On the guiltless your sentence will fall!
PRIESTS: (*Departing slowly.*)
None can his doom recall!

AMNERIS:
Impious priesthood, curses light on ye all!
On your heads Heaven's vengeance will fall!
(*Exit wildly.*)

This is one of the most impressive records of the *Aida* series. The despair of the wretched *Amneris*, and the solemn reply of the unbending priests are wonderfully expressed by Verdi.

SCENE II—*Interior of the Temple of Vulcan—below a Subterranean Apartment*

"*The work finishes in serenity and peace, and such terminations are the most beautiful. Above, the temple full of light, where the ceremonies continue immutable in the sanctuary of the indifferent gods; below, two human beings dying in each other's arms. Their song of love and death is among the most beautiful of all music.*"—*Camille Bellaigue.*

When we hear the expression "the duet from Aida," our thoughts always instinctively turn to this number at the close of the work. There are other duets in the opera, some of them fine numbers, but this is the *great* one—perhaps the most intensely dramatic and melodiously beautiful of all Verdi's writings.

La fatal pietra (The Fatal Stone)

By Johanna Gadski, Soprano, and Enrico Caruso, Tenor
(*In Italian*) 89028 12-inch, $4.00
By Nicola Zerola, Tenor (Part of scene—"To die, so pure and lovely!")
(*In Italian*) 74225 12-inch, 1.50

This last scene is a highly picturesque one. Above we see the splendid Temple of Ptah, where priests and priestesses are chanting their strange songs. Below, a dark vault, in whose depths *Rhadames* is awaiting with patience a slow death by starvation.

RHADAMES (*despairingly*):
The fatal stone upon me now is closing!
Now has the tomb engulf'd me!
The light of day no more shall I see!
No more behold Aida!
Aida, where art thou now?
Whate'er befall me, may'st thou be happy!
Ne'er may my frightful doom be told to thine ear!
(*Then suddenly in the shadows he sees a form—it is Aida, who has secreted herself in the crypt that she may die with her lover.*)
What moan was that?
Is't a phantom, or vision dread?
No! 'tis a human being!
Heaven! Aida!
AIDA: Yes!
RHADAMES (*in great desperation*):
Thou, with me here buried!
AIDA:
My heart foreboded this, thy dreadful sentence,
And to this tomb that shuts on thee its portal,
I crept, unseen by mortal.
Here, free from all,
Where none can more behold us,
Clasp'd in thy arms, love,
I resolved to perish!
RHADAMES: To die! so pure and lovely!
To die! thyself thus dooming,
In all thy beauty blooming,
Fade thus forever!
Thou, whom the gods alone for love created;
Yet to destroy thee, was my love then fated!
Thou shalt not die! so much I love thee,
Thou art too lovely!

AIDA (*transported*):
  See'st thou where death, in angel guise,
  With heavenly radiance beaming,
  Would waft us to eternal joys,
  On golden wings above!

I see heaven's gates are open wide
Where tears are never streaming,
Where only bliss and joy reside,
The bliss and joy of never fading, endless
  love!

The lovers sing their plaintive farewell to earth in hauntingly lovely strains, while in strange contrast the heathen chanting continues above.

O terra addio (Farewell, Oh, Earth)
By Johanna Gadski, Soprano, and Enrico Caruso, Tenor
(*In Italian*) 89029 12-inch, $4.00

AIDA AND RHADAMES:
  Farewell, O earth,
  Farewell, thou dark vale of sorrow,
  Brief dream of joy,
  Condemned to end in woe!

See, brightly opens for us,
Brightly opens now the sky, and endless mor-
  row,
There, all unshadow'd, shall eternal glow!

(*Curtain*)

DOUBLE-FACED AND MISCELLANEOUS AIDA RECORDS

Chi mai fra (His Glory Now Praise) By Maria
  Cappiello, Mezzo-Soprano, and Chorus (*In Italian*)
O tu che sei d'Osiride (Oh, Thou Who Art Osiris)
  By Maria Cappiello, Mezzo-Soprano, and Chorus
  (*In Italian*) } 55005 12-inch, $1.50

Celeste Aida (Heavenly Aida) *Trombone* By Arthur Pryor
Il Guarany Overture By Pryor's Band } 35030 12-inch, 1.25

The Fatal Stone *Cornet-Trombone*
  By Arthur Pryor, Emil Keneke and Pryor's Band
  Serenade (*Titl*) *'Cello-Flute* By Louis Heine and Darius Lyons } 35150 12-inch, 1.25

Aida Fantasia By Police Band of Mexico
  Cascades of Roses Waltz By Police Band of Mexico } 35047 12-inch, 1.25

Aida Selection By Pryor's Band
  Attila—Grand Trio By Kryl's Bohemian Band } 35195 12-inch, 1.25

Aida Selection (Finale, Act II) By Pryor's Orchestra 31359 12-inch, 1.00

Marcha Triunfal (Triumphal March)
  By Garde Republicaine Band
  Tosca—Tosca divina! (*In Italian*)
  By Gustavo Berl-Resky, Baritone } 62409 10-inch, .75

FINAL SCENE OF AIDA

(Italian)

IL BARBIERE DE SIVIGLIA

(Eel Bar-bee-yair' day See-veel'-yah)

(English)

BARBER OF SEVILLE

COMIC OPERA IN TWO ACTS

Text by Sterbini, a Roman poet, founded on the celebrated trilogy of Beaumarchais. Music by Rossini. First presented at the Argentina Theatre in Rome, February 5, 1816. First London production March 10, 1818. First New York production November 29, 1825. The opera was at first called "Almaviva, or the Useless Precaution," to distinguish it from Paisiello's "Barber of Seville."

Cast

COUNT ALMAVIVA (*Al-mah-vee'-vah*) ....Tenor
BARTOLO, (*Bahr'-to-low*) physician...................................Bass
ROSINA, his ward ....Soprano
BASILIO, (*Ba-zee'-lee-oh*) music master.............................Bass
MARCELLINE (*Mar-chel-le'-na*) ....Soprano
FIGARO (*Fee'-gah-row*) ....Baritone
FIORELLO, servant to the Count.......................................Tenor
A Notary, Chorus of Musicians, Chorus of Soldiers

Scene and Period: Seville, the seventeenth century.

Rossini's opera is a marvel of rapid composition, having been composed in about fifteen days! This seems almost incredible, but the fact is well authenticated. The composer had agreed to write two operas for the Roman carnival of 1816, the first of which was produced December 26, 1815, and on that day he was told that the second would be required on January 20, 1816. He agreed to have it completed, although he did not even know what the subject was! The libretto was given to him by Sterbini in sections, and he wrote the music as fast as the verses were furnished. While the opera did not achieve an instantaneous success, it gradually found favor with opera-lovers on account of its brightness and the manner in which the humor of its action is reflected in the music.

The plot of *Barber of Seville* is very simple. The *Count Almaviva* loves *Rosina*, the ward of *Dr. Bartolo*, a crusty old bachelor who secretly wishes to wed her himself. *Almaviva* persuades the village barber, *Figaro*, to arrange a meeting for him, and gains entrance to the house disguised as a dragoon, but is arrested by the guardian.

Not discouraged, he returns, pretending to be a substitute for *Rosina's* music teacher, who, he says, is ill. The appearance of the real *Don Basilio* spoils the plan, and the Count retreats for the second time, having, however, arranged a plan for elopement. *Bartolo* finally arouses *Rosina's* jealousy by pretending that the Count loves another, and she promises to forget him and marry her guardian. When the time for the elopement arrives she meets the Count, intending to reproach him, but he convinces her of the base plot

SETTING OF ACT I, SCENE I, AT LA SCALA

of *Bartolo*, and the lovers are wedded by a notary, just as *Bartolo* arrives with officers to arrest the Count.

Overture

By La Scala Orchestra   68010   12-inch, $1.25

ACT I

SCENE I—*A Street in Seville.   Day is Breaking*

The Count, accompanied by his servant *Fiorello* and several musicians, enters to serenade the beautiful *Rosina*.   Accompanied by the mandolins, he sings his serenade, *Ecco ridente,* considered one of the most beautiful numbers in the opera.

Ecco ridente (Dawn, With Her Rosy Mantle)

By Fernando de Lucia, Tenor (*Piano acc.*)   (*In Italian*)   76000   12-inch, $2.00
By Florencio Constantino, Tenor   (*In Italian*)   74073   12-inch,   1.50

COUNT:

Lo! smiling in the Orient sky,
Morn in her beauty breaking,
Canst thou, my love, inactive lie—
My life, art thou not waking?
Arise, my heart's own treasure,
All that my soul holds dear;
Oh! turn my grief to pleasure!
Awake, my love, appear!

But, hush!—methinks I view that face,
And all my doubts are vanished;
Thine eyes diffuse soft pity's grace.
And all my fears are banished.
Oh, rapturous moment of delight!
All other blisses shaming;
My soul's content, so pure and bright,
On earth no equal claiming!

Even such a lovely serenade as this fails to bring a response from the window, and the Count retires discomfited.   Enter *Figaro,* the jack-of-all-trades of the village and general factotum in the house of *Bartolo,* with his guitar.   He sings that gayest and most difficult of all airs, the joy or despair of baritones the world over, and which has been recorded for the Victor by three famous baritones.

Largo al factotum (Room for the Factotum)

By Pasquale Amato, Baritone
(*In Italian*)   88329   12-inch, $3.00
By Emilio de Gogorza, Baritone
(*In Italian*)   88181   12-inch,   3.00
By Titta Ruffo, Baritone
(*In Italian*)   92039   12-inch,   3.00

Figaro is thoroughly satisfied with himself, and gives a long list of his numerous accomplishments, of which the following is a sample:

FIGARO: Room for the city's factotum here,
La, la, la, la, la, la.
I must be off to my shop, for the dawn is near,
La, la, la, la, la, la.
What a merry life, what pleasure gay,
Awaits a barber of quality.
Ah, brave Figaro; bravo, bravissimo, brave.
La, la, la, la, la, la.
Of men, the happiest, sure, art thou, bravo.
La, la, la, la, la, la, etc.

CAMPANARI AS FIGARO

"Oh! what a happy life," soliloquizes the gay barber, "what pleasure awaits a barber of quality!—Oh, bravo, Figaro, bravo, bravissimo: thou art sure the happiest of men, ready at all hours of the night, and, by day, perpetually in bustle and motion.   What happier region of delight! what nobler life for a barber than mine!   Razors, combs, lancets, scissors—behold them all at my command! besides the snug perquisites of the business, with gay damsels and cavaliers.   All call me! all want me!—dames and maidens—old and young.   My peruke! cries one—my beard! shouts another—bleed me! cries this—this billetdoux! whispers that.   Figaro, Figaro! heavens, what a crowd.   Figaro, Figaro! heavens, what a tumult!   One at a time, for mercy sake!   Figaro here: Figaro there: Figaro above: Figaro below. I am all activity: I am quick as lightning; in a word—I am the factotum of the town.   Oh, what a happy life! but little fatigue—abundant amusement—with a pocket that can always boast a doubloon, the noble fruit of my reputation.   But I must hasten to the shop!"

FROM AN OLD PRINT

THE DISGUISED COUNT AND BARTOLO
IN SCENE II

Three fine records of this great air are given here. Ruffo, in his rendition, proves himself possessed of an admirable sense of humor, and this, with his powerful and flexible voice, enables him to attack this difficult solo in the true opéra-bouffe vein. The result is as fine a performance of the *Largo* as one would wish to hear. The extreme difficulties are made a vehicle for the display of the baritone's ample vocal resources, which sweep everything before them; he is indeed a little free with the text, and sings snatches of the accompaniment out of sheer bravado, while bits of comic characterization peep out at every available opportunity. This rendition is a fine example of how the music of this air should be sung, and is a veritable triumph for the singer.

Signor de Gogorza's version differs from Ruffo's in many respects. It is one of the finest records he has made for the Victor, and exhibits his fine voice and wonderful execution to perfection.

The Count now returns and accosts *Figaro,* asking him to arrange a meeting with *Rosina,* telling him that his rank must not be known and that he has assumed the name of *Lindor.*

Il mio nome? (My Name?)

By Fernando de Lucia, Tenor   (*Piano acc.*)   (*In Italian*)   66000 10-inch, $1.50

Figaro consents to become his ally. *Rosina* and her guardian come on the balcony, and *Rosina*, perceiving the Count, manages to drop a note, which he secures. *Bartolo* leaves the house and orders that no one be admitted.

Figaro now says that he is expecting a military friend to arrive in the village, and suggests the Count dress himself as this soldier and thus gain admittance to the house. He agrees, and retires to assume the disguise.

SCENE II—*A Room in Bartolo's House*

Rosina is discovered holding in her hand a letter from the Count. She is agitated and expresses her feelings in her celebrated entrance song.

Una voce poco fa (A Little Voice I Hear)

By Marcella Sembrich, Soprano
        (*In Italian*)   88097   12-inch, $3.00
By Luisa Tetrazzini, Soprano
        (*In Italian*)   88301   12-inch,   3.00
By Maria Galvany, Soprano
        (*In Italian*)   87060   10-inch,   2.00
By Alice Nielsen, Soprano
        (*In Italian*)   74074   12-inch,   1.50
By Giuseppina Huguet, Soprano
        (*In Italian*) *68144   12-inch,   1.25

MELBA AS ROSINA

The number is in the form to which most Italian composers of the period adhered—a slow opening section (here accompanied by occasional chords for the orchestra) succeeded by a quicker movement culminating in a coda which presents many opportunities for brilliant vocal display. Musically the aria is full of charm, and is deservedly popular with those singers whose method enables them to deliver it with the requisite lightness and bravura.

ROSINA: A little voice I heard just now:
    Oh, it has thrill'd my very heart!
    I feel that I am wounded sore;
    And Lindor 'twas who hurl'd the dart.
    Yes, Lindor, dearest, shall be mine!
    I've sworn it, and we'll never part.

My guardian sure will ne'er consent;
    But I must sharpen all my wit:
Content at last, he will relent,
    And we, oh, joy! be wedded yet.
Yes, Lindor I have sworn to love!
    And, loving, we'll our cares forget.

---

* *Double-Faced Record*—*For title of opposite side see DOUBLE-FACED BARBER OF SEVILLE RECORDS,* page 31.

A bewildering array of artists have essayed this charming song, and Victor audiences can choose whether they will have it sung by an Italian, Polish, Spanish or American prima donna.

Rosina runs out as her guardian and *Don Basilio* come in. *Bartolo* is telling *Basilio* that he wishes to marry his ward, either by love or force. *Basilio* promises to help him, and says that the Count is trying to make *Rosina's* acquaintance. They decide to invent some story that will disgrace him. "A calumny!" says *Basilio*. *Bartolo* asks what that is, and *Basilio*, in a celebrated air gives his famous description, which is a model of its kind.

La calunnia (Slander's Whisper)

By Marcel Journet, Bass

(In Italian) 74104 12-inch, $1.50

COPY'T DUPONT

SEMBRICH AS ROSINA

BASILIO: Oh! calumny is like the sigh
Of gentlest zephyrs breathing by;
How softly sweet along the ground,
Its first shrill voice is heard around.
Then passing on from tongue to tongue,
It gains new strength, it sweeps along
In giddier whirl from place to place,
And gains fresh vigor in its race;
Till, like the sounds of tempests deep,
That thro' the woods in murmurs sweep
And howl amid their caverns drear,
It shakes the trembling soul with fear.
Thus calumny, a simple breath,
Engenders ruin, wreck and death;
And sinks the wretched man forlorn,
Beneath the lash of slander torn,
The victim of the public scorn!
(*They go out.*)

Rosina and *Figaro* return, and the barber tells her that her guardian is planning to marry her. She laughs at the idea, and then asks *Figaro* who the young man was she observed that morning. *Figaro* tells her his name is *Lindor,* and that he is madly in love with a certain young lady, whose name is *Rosina.*

Dunque io son (What! I?)

By Maria Galvany, Soprano, and Titta Ruffo, Baritone

(In Italian) 92501 12-inch, $4.00

ROSINA:
What! I? or dost thou mock me?
Am I, then, the happy being?
(But I all the scheme foreseeing,
Knew it, sir, before yourself);
FIGARO:
Yes, Lindor loves you, lady;
Oft he sighs for his Rosina,
(As a fox she cunning seems,
Ah, by my faith, she sees thro' all).
ROSINA:
Still one word, sir—to my Lindor
How shall I contrive to speak?
FIGARO:
Poor man, he but awaits some sign
Of your affection and assent;
A little note, a single line,
And he himself will soon present.
To this, what say you?
ROSINA:
I do not know.
FIGARO:
Take courage, pray you.

ROSINA:
I could not so—
FIGARO:
A few lines merely.
ROSINA:
I blush to write.
FIGARO:
At what? Why really—may I indite?
Haste, haste, your lover quick invite.
(*Going to the desk.*)
ROSINA:
A letter! Oh, here it is.
(*Calling him, she takes a note from her bosom, which she gives him.*)
FIGARO:
Already written! What a fool (*astonished*)
Was I to think to be her master!
Much fitter that she me should school:
Her wits, than mine, can flow much faster.
Oh, woman, woman, who can find,
Or fathom, all that's in thy mind?
(*Exit Figaro.*)

Bartolo comes in and accuses *Rosina* of dropping a note from the balcony, and when she denies it he shows her ink marks on her finger and calls attention to a cut pen and a missing sheet of paper. She says she wrapped up some sweetmeats to send to a girl friend, and cut the pen to design a flower for her embroidery. *Bartolo* then denounces her in another famous air:

PHOTO JOHNSON, SALT LAKE

NIELSEN AS ROSINA

Manca un foglio (Here's a Leaf Missing)
By Arcangelo Rossi, Bass
(In Italian) *68144 12-inch, $1.25

BARTOLO:
To a doctor of my rank,
These excuses, Signorina,
I advise another time
That you better should invent.
Why is the paper missing?
That I would wish to know.
Useless, ma'am, are all your airs—
Be still, nor interrupt me so.
Another time, sweet Signorina,
When the doctor quits his house
He will carefully provide
For the keeping you inside.
And poor innocent Rosina,
Disappointed, then may pout:
In her room shall she be locked,
Till I choose to let her out.
*(He goes out in a rage, followed by Rosina,
    who is laughing.)*

A loud knocking is heard at the street door,—it is the Count
in his soldier disguise. He pushes his way in, and insists that the
commandant has ordered him to put up in *Bartolo's* house. A long
scene follows, full of comedy, finally ending in the arrest of the
Count, who, however, privately informs the officer who he is; and
the astonished official salutes respectfully and takes his soldiers
away. *Bartolo* is in such a rage that he can hardly speak, and the
act ends with the famous quartet:

Guarda Don Bartolo (Look at Don Bartolo)
By Giuseppina Huguet, Soprano; Antonio Pini-Corsi, Baritone; Gaetano Pini-Corsi, Tenor; Ernesto Badini, Baritone   *63171 10-inch, $0.75

ACT II
SCENE—*A Room in Bartolo's House*

Bartolo is discovered musing on the affair of the soldier, and as he has learned that no
one in the regiment knows the man, he suspects that he was sent by the Count.

A knocking is heard and the Count is ushered in, dressed as a music master. He
greets *Bartolo*, beginning the duet, *Pace e gioia*.

Pace e gioia (Heaven Send You Peace and Joy)
By Antonio Pini-Corsi, Baritone, and Emilio Perea, Tenor
(In Italian) *62105 10-inch, $0.75

Bartolo says he is much obliged for these kind wishes and wonders who this can be.
The Count explains that *Don Basilio* is ill and he has come in the music master's place to
give *Rosina* a lesson. He shows *Bartolo* the note *Rosina* had written, saying he found
it at the inn, and offers to make *Rosina* believe the Count has shown her note to another
lady. *Bartolo* is pleased with the idea and calls *Rosina*. Then occurs the celebrated
"Lesson Scene" in which *Rosina* usually interpolates an air. Rossini wrote a trio for this
scene, but in some manner it was lost.

Figaro now comes in to shave *Bartolo*, and in the course of the scene contrives to secure
the key to the balcony. At this moment all are petrified at the entrance of *Don Basilio*,
who is supposed to be confined to his bed. *Figaro* sees that quick action is necessary and
asks him what he means by coming out with such a fever. "Fever?" says the astonished
music master. "A raging fever," exclaims *Figaro*, feeling his pulse. "You need medicine,"
says the Count, meaningly, and slips a fat purse in his hand. *Don Basilio* partially compre-
hends the situation, looks at the purse and departs.

The shaving is renewed, and *Rosina* and the Count pretend to continue the lesson, but
are really planning the elopement. *Bartolo* tries to watch them, but *Figaro* manages to get
soap in the Doctor's eye at each of his efforts to rise. He finally jumps up and denounces

---

* *Double-Faced Record—For title of opposite side see double-faced list on page 31.*

the Count as an impostor. The three conspirators laugh at him, and go out, followed by *Bartolo*, who is purple with rage. This scene is amusingly pictured in a fresco in the Vienna Opera, which is reproduced on page 26.

Bertha, the housekeeper, enters, and in her air, *Il vecchietto*, complains that she can no longer stand the turmoil, quarreling and scolding in this house.

Il vecchietto cerca moglie (The Old Fool Seeks a Wife)

By Emma Zaccaria   *(Double-Faced—See below)*   *(In Italian)*   62105   10-inch, $0.75

"What kind of thing is this love which drives everybody crazy?" she asks. This air used to be called in Rome *Aria di sorbetto* (sherbet), because the audience used to eat ices while it was being sung!

Don Bartolo now desperately plays his last card, and shows *Rosina* the note, saying that her lover is conspiring to give her up to the *Count Almaviva*. *Rosina* is furious and offers to marry *Bartolo* at once, telling him that he can have *Lindor* and *Figaro* arrested when they arrive for the elopement. *Bartolo* goes after the police, and he is barely out of sight when *Figaro* and the Count enter by means of the key which the barber had secured. *Rosina* greets them with a storm of reproaches, accusing *Lindor* of pretending to love her in order to sacrifice her to the vile *Count Almaviva*. The Count reveals himself and the lovers are soon clasped in a fond embrace, with *Figaro* in a "Bless you, my children," attitude.

Don Basilio, who had been sent for a notary by *Bartolo*, now arrives. The Count demands that the notary shall wed him to *Rosina*. *Basilio* protests, but the sight of a pistol in the Count's hand soon silences him.

This scene is rudely interrupted by the arrival of *Bartolo* and the soldiers. The officer in charge demands the name of the Count, who now introduces *Signor and Signora Almaviva* to the company. *Bartolo* philosophically decides to make the best of the matter. However, he inquires of *Basilio*:

BARTOLO: But you, you rascal—
Even you to betray me and turn witness!

BASILIO: Ah! Doctor,
The Count has certain persuasives
And certain arguments in his pocket,
Which there is no withstanding!

BARTOLO: Ay, ay! I understand you.
Well, well, what matters it?
Go; and may Heaven bless you!

FIGARO: Bravo, bravo, Doctor!
Let me embrace you!

ROSINA: Oh, how happy we are!

COUNT: Oh, propitious love!

FIGARO: Young love, triumphant smiling,
All harsher thoughts exiling,
All quarrels reconciling,
Now waves his torch on high!

COPY'T MISHKIN

SAMMARCO AS FIGARO

(Curtain)

DOUBLE-FACED BARBER OF SEVILLE RECORDS

Barber of Seville Selection Prophete Fantasie	By Pryor's Band By Pryor's Band	35125	12-inch,	$1.25
Overture Don Pasquale—Sinfonia *(Donizetti)*	By La Scala Orchestra By La Scala Orchestra	68010	12-inch,	1.25
Manca un foglio (Here's a Leaf Out) Una voce poco fa	By A. Rossi, Bass By Giuseppina Huguet, Soprano	68144	12-inch,	1.25
Guarda Don Bartolo (Look at Bartolo) By Huguet, A. and G. Pini-Corsi, and Badini *(In Italian)* Fra Diavolo—Agnese la Zietella *By Pietro Lara* *(In Italian)*		63171	10-inch,	.75
Il vecchietto cerca moglie By Emma Zaccaria *(In Italian)* Pace e gioia By A. Pini-Corsi and Perea *(In Italian)*		62105	10-inch,	.75

(French)   (English)
LA BOHÊME   THE BOHEMIANS
(La Bow-haym')

OPERA IN FOUR ACTS

Text by Giacosa and Illica; music by Puccini. First produced at the Teatro Reggio, Turin, February 1, 1896. In English, as "The Bohemians," at Manchester (Carl Rosa Company), April 22, 1897, and at Covent Garden with the same company, October 2d of the same year. In Italian at Covent Garden, July 1, 1899. First American production, November 28, 1899.

Characters

RUDOLPH, a poet..Tenor
MARCEL, a painter..Baritone
COLLINE, a philosopher.......................................Bass
SCHAUNARD, a musician....................................Baritone
BENOIT, an importunate landlord.............................Bass
ALCINDORO, a state councilor and follower of MUSETTA..............Bass
PARPIGNOL...Tenor
MUSETTA, a grisette.......................................Soprano
MIMI, a maker of embroidery...............................Soprano

Students, work-girls, citizens, shopkeepers, street venders, soldiers, restaurant waiters, boys, girls, etc.

Scene and Period: Paris, about 1830.

Puccini's Bohême is an adaptation of part of Mürger's *La Vie Bohême,* which depicts life in the *Quartier Latin,* or the Students' Quarter, in 1830. It being impossible to weave a complete story from Mürger's novel, the librettists have merely taken four of the principal scenes and several of Mürger's characters, and have strung them together without much regard for continuity.

The principal characters in Puccini's delightful opera are the inseparable quartet described by Murger, who with equal cheerfulness defy the pangs of hunger and the landlord of their little garret. In the scenes of careless gaiety is interwoven a touch of pathos; and the music is in turn lively and tender, with a haunting sweetness that is most fascinating.

Rudolph, a poet; *Marcel,* a painter; *Colline,* a philosopher; and *Schaunard,* a musician, are four friends who occupy an attic in the *Quartier Latin,* where they live and work together. Improvident, reckless and careless, these happy-go-lucky Bohemians find a joy in merely living, being full of faith in themselves.

ACT I

SCENE—*A Garret in the Quartier Latin*

The opening scene shows the four friends without money or provisions, yet happy. *Marcel* is at work on a painting, "Passage of the Red Sea," and remarks, beginning a duet with *Rudolph,* that the passage of this supposedly torrid sea seems a very cold affair!

THE FOUR BOHEMIANS

Questo mar rosso (This Red Sea)

By Gennaro de Tura, Tenor, and E. Badini, Baritone

(In Italian)   88233   12-inch, $3.00

CAMPANARI AS MARCEL

Rudolph says that in order to keep them from freezing he will sacrifice the bulky manuscript of his tragedy. *Marcel* holds the landlord at bay until *Schaunard* arrives with an unexpected store of eatables. Having dined and warmed themselves, *Marcel*, *Colline* and *Schaunard* go out, leaving *Rudolph* writing. A timid knock at the door reveals the presence of *Mimi*, a young girl who lives on the floor above. She has come to ask her neighbor for a light for the candle, which has gone out. They enter into conversation, and when *Mimi* artlessly asks *Rudolph* what his occupation is, he sings the lovely air usually termed the "Narrative."

Racconto di Rodolfo (Rudolph's Narrative)

By Enrico Caruso, Tenor
(*In Italian*) 88002 12-inch, $3.00
By John McCormack, Tenor
(*In Italian*) 74222 12-inch, 1.50
By Florencio Constantino, Tenor
(*In Italian*) 74106 12-inch, 1.50
By George Hamlin, Tenor
(*In Italian*) 74185 12-inch, 1.50
By Evan Williams, Tenor
(*In English*) 74129 12-inch, 1.50

Caruso has never done anything more perfect in its way than his superb delivery of this number. It is one of his great scenes in the opera, and always arouses the audience to a high pitch of enthusiasm. He has sung it here with a fervor and splendor of voice which holds one spellbound. The tender sympathy of the opening—"Your little hand is cold"; the bold avowal—"I am a poet"; the glorious beauty of the love motive at the end—all are given with characteristic richness and warmth of style by this admired singer, while the final high note is brilliantly taken.

An entirely different interpretation, though also a very fine one, is given by Mr. McCormack, while three other versions—in Italian by Constantino and Hamlin, and in English by Evan Williams—complete a list in which every lover of this beautiful air can find a record to suit his taste and purse.

Mi chiamano Mimi (My Name is Mimi)

By Nellie Melba, Soprano
(*In Italian*) 88074 12-inch, $3.00
By Alice Nielsen, Soprano
(*In Italian*) 74062 12-inch, 1.50

Then follows the charming *Mi chiamano Mimi*, in which the young girl tells *Rudolph* of her pitifully simple life; of how she works all day making artificial flowers, which remind her of the blossoms and green meadows of the country; of the lonely existence she leads in her chamber up among the housetops.

O soave fanciulla—Duo and Finale, Act I (Thou Sweetest Maiden)

By Nellie Melba, Soprano, and
Enrico Caruso, Tenor 95200 12-inch, $5.00

"*Mimi's delicate perfection enchanted the young poet—especially her little hands, which in spite of her menial work, she managed to keep as white as snow.*"—Mürger's La Vie de la Bohême.

This lovely duet occurs just after the *Mi chiamano Mimi*. The young girl having finished her story, *Rudolph* hears the shouts of his friends in the courtyard below. He opens the window to speak to them, letting in a flood of moonlight which

SEMBRICH AS MIMI

FARRAR AS MIMI

brightens the room. The Bohemians go off singing. As *Rudolph* turns to *Mimi* and sees her in the moonlight, he is struck with her beauty, and tells her how entrancing she appears to him.

Love awakens in the heart of the lonely girl, and in this beautiful duet she pledges her faith to the handsome stranger who has come into her life.

Mme. Melba's singing in this scene is of exquisite beauty, while Caruso's delivery of the passionate phrases of *Rudolph* is superb. The beautiful motive with which the duet begins is associated throughout the opera with the presence of *Mimi*, and is employed with touching effect in the death scene in Act III.

Mimi consents to go to the *Café Momus*, where his friends are to dine, and after a tender scene at the door they go out, and the curtain slowly falls.

ACT II

SCENE—*A Students' Café in Paris*

This act represents the terraces of the *Café Momus*, where the artists are holding a carnival. Puccini has pictured with masterly skill the noisy, bustling activity of this scene, and the boisterous merriment of the gay revelers. The Bohemians of Act I are seated at a table with *Mimi*, when *Musetta*, an old flame of *Marcel's*, appears with her latest conquest, a foolish and ancient beau named *Alcindoro*. *Marcel* pretends not to see her, but *Musetta* is determined on a reconciliation, and soon gets rid of her elderly admirer and joins her old friends.

The gem of this gay scene is the charming waltz of *Musetta*, which Mme. Viafora sings here with spirit and delightful abandon.

Musetta Waltz

By Gina C. Viafora, Soprano

(*In Italian*) 64085 10-inch, $1.00

GLUCK AS MIMI

Mme. Viafora's light soprano is heard to advantage in this pretty waltz, which she sings with fluency and skill.

The fun now becomes fast and furious, and *Musetta* is finally carried off on the shoulders of her friends, while the foolish old banker, *Alcindoro*, is left to pay the bills of the entire party.

ACT III

SCENE—*A City Gate of Paris*

This act begins in the cheerless dawn of a cold morning at the city gates, the bleakness of the scene being well expressed in Puccini's music. The snow falls, workmen come and go, shivering and blowing on their cold fingers. *Mimi* appears, and asks the officer at the gate if

THE CAFÉ MOMUS—ACT II

BOYER, PARIS

THE SCENE OF THE BARRIER—ACT III

he will find *Marcel,* that good and kind-hearted Bohemian painter, now sojourning at the inn on the Orleans Road and painting, not landscapes, but tavern signs, in order to keep body and soul together. *Marcel* enters and is surprised to see *Mimi,* whom he supposes to be in Paris. Noticing that she is melancholy and apparently ill, he kindly questions her and learns her sad story.

Mimi, Io son!
(Mimi, Thou Here!)

By Geraldine Farrar, Soprano, and Antonio Scotti, Baritone
(*In Italian*)
89016 12-inch, $4.00

By Dora Domar, Soprano, and Ernesto Badini, Baritone
88228 12-inch, 3.00

M 475940

By E. Boccolini, Soprano, and E. Badini, Baritone
(*Double-faced—See page 37*) (*In Italian*) 55020 12-inch, 1.50

This duet is one of the finest numbers in Puccini's opera, and Miss Farrar and Mr. Scotti have made a strikingly effective record of it, while other renditions at various prices are furnished by La Scala artists. *Mimi* tells her friend that she can no longer bear the jealous quarrels with *Rudolph,* and that they must separate. *Marcel,* much troubled, goes into the inn to summon *Rudolph,* but before the latter comes, *Mimi* secretes herself, and when he enters she hears him again accuse her of fickleness.

COPY'T DOVER ST. STUDIOS

MARTIN AS RUDOLPH

PHOTO BERT

FARRAR AND SCOTTI AS MIMI AND MARCEL
ACT III

Mimi è una civetta
(Coldhearted Mimi!)

By Laura Mellerio, Soprano; Gennaro de Tura, Tenor; and Ernesto Badini, Baritone
(*In Italian*) 88227 12-inch, $3.00

A distressing fit of coughing reveals her presence, and she appears and sings the sad little air which is one of the features of this act.

Addio (Farewell)

By Nellie Melba, Soprano (*In Italian*) 88072 12-inch, $3.00
By Alma Gluck, Soprano (*In Italian*) 64225 10-inch, 1.00

Most pathetically does the poor girl's "Farewell, may you be happy" come from her simple heart, and she turns to go. *Rudolph* protests, something of his old affection having returned at the sight of her pale cheeks.

Musetta now enters and is accused by *Marcel* of flirting. A furious quarrel follows, which contrasts strongly with the tender passages between *Mimi* and *Rudolph* as the lovers are partially reconciled.

Quartet, "Addio, dolce svegliare" (Farewell, Sweet Love)

By Geraldine Farrar, Soprano; Gina C. Viafora, Soprano; Enrico Caruso, Tenor; and Antonio Scotti, Baritone
(*In Italian*) 96002 12-inch, $6.00

By Dora Domar, Soprano; Annita Santoro, Soprano; Ida Giacomelli, Soprano; and Ernesto Badini, Baritone
(*In Italian*) 89048 12-inch, 4.00

By Sanipoli, Passari, Ciccolini and Badini (*Double-faced—See page 37*) (*In Italian*) 55020 12-inch, 1.50

COPY'T MISHKIN
SAMMARCO AS MARCEL

COPY'T MISHKIN
TRENTINI AS MUSETTA

Like the Rigoletto Quartet, this number is used by the composer to express many different emotions: The sadness of *Mimi's* farewell to *Rudolph;* his tender efforts to induce her to remain; the fond recollections of the bright days of their first meeting— and contrasted to these sentiments is the quarreling of *Musetta* and *Marcel,* which Puccini has skillfully interwoven with the pathetic passages sung by the lovers.

In *Mimi* Miss Farrar has added another rôle to the long list of her successes in America, and her impersonation is a most charming one. She was in superb voice and has given this lovely music most effectively. Caruso sings, as he always does, with a beauty of voice and a sincerity of emotion which cannot fail to excite admiration.

Mme. Viafora, who is always a piquant, gay and interesting *Musetta;* and Signor Scotti, whose admirable *Marcel* is one of his finest impersonations, both vocally and dramatically, round out an ensemble which could not be surpassed.

Truly a brilliantly sung and perfect balanced rendition of one of the greatest of concerted numbers. Two other versions by famous artists of La Scala are also offered.

PAINTED BY BALESTRIERI   THE DEATH OF MIMI

ACT IV

SCENE—*Same as Act I*

"*At this time, the friends for many weeks had lived a lonely and melancholy existence. Musetta had made no sign, and Marcel had never met her, while no word of Mimi came to Rudolph, though he often repeated her name to himself. Marcel treasured a little bunch of ribbons which had been left behind by Musetta, and when one day he detected Rudolph gazing fondly at the pink bonnet Mimi had forgotten, he muttered : 'It seems I am not the only one !'*"—Mürger.

Act IV shows the same garret in which the events of Act I took place. Bereft of their sweethearts, the young men are living sad and lonely lives, each trying to conceal from the other that he is secretly pining for the absent one.

In the opening scene, *Marcel* stands in front of his easel pretending to paint, while *Rudolph*, apparently writing, is really furtively gazing at *Mimi's* little pink bonnet.

COPY'T MISHKIN

CONSTANTINO AS
RUDOLPH

Ah Mimi, tu piu   (Ah, Mimi, False One!)

By Enrico Caruso, Tenor, and Antonio Scotti, Baritone
(*In Italian*)   89006   12-inch, $4.00
By McCormack and Sammarco (*Italian*)   89044   12-inch,   4.00
By Da Gradi and Badini   (*In Italian*) *45013   10-inch,   1.00

Two records of this favorite duet are offered—by Caruso and Scotti, and McCormack and Sammarco—and both are splendidly given.

The friends, however, pretend to brighten up when *Schaunard* and *Colline* enter with materials for supper, and the four Bohemians make merry over their frugal fare. This scene of jollity is interrupted by the unexpected entrance of *Musetta,* who tells the friends that *Mimi,* abandoned by her viscount, has come to die.

The poor girl is brought in and laid on *Rudolph's* bed, while he is distracted with grief. The friends hasten to aid her, *Marcel* going for a doctor, while *Colline,* in order to get money to buy delicacies for the sick girl, decides to pawn his only good garment, an overcoat. He bids farewell to the coat in a pathetic song, which Journet delivers here with much feeling.

Vecchia zimarra   (Coat Song)

By Marcel Journet, Bass   (*In Italian*)   64035   10-inch, $1.00
Colline goes softly out, leaving *Mimi* and *Rudolph* alone, and they sing a beautiful duet.

Sono andati?   (Are We Alone?)

By Maria Bronzoni, Soprano, and Franco de Gregorio, Tenor
(*In Italian*) *45013   10-inch, $1.00

The past is all forgotten and the reunited lovers plan for a future which shall be free from jealousies and quarrels. Just as *Mimi,* in dreamy tones, recalls their first meeting in the garret, she is seized with a sudden faintness which alarms *Rudolph,* and he summons his friends, who are returning with delicacies for *Mimi.* But the young girl, weakened by disease and privations, passes away in the midst of her weeping friends, and the curtain falls to *Rudolph's* despairing cry of "Mimi! Mimi!"

DOUBLE-FACED AND MISCELLANEOUS BOHÊME RECORDS

Quartet, Act III	By Sanipoli, Passari, Ciccolini and		
Badini		(*In Italian*)	55020 12-inch, $1.50
C'e Rodolfo (Where is Rudolph?)	By Boccolini and		
Badini		(*In Italian*)	
Bohême Fantasie ('Cello)	By Victor Sorlin		35132 12-inch, 1.25
Calm Sea and Happy Voyage—Overture	By Pryor's Band		
Bohême Selection	By Pryor's Band		35077 12-inch, 1.25
Jolly Robbers Overture (Suppé)	By Pryor's Band		
Ah, Mimi, tu piu (Ah, Mimi, False One!)			
	By Da Gradi and Badini	(*In Italian*)	45013 10-inch, 1.00
Sono andati?	By Bronzoni and de Gregorio	(*In Italian*)	

* *Double-Faced Record—For title of opposite side see above list.*

© DuPont

Calvé as Carmen

CARMEN'S DEFIANCE—ACT IV

CARMEN

OPERA IN FOUR ACTS

Text by Meilhac and Halévy, founded on the novel of Prosper Mérimée. Music by Bizet. First production at the Opera Comique, Paris, March 3, 1875. First London production June 22, 1878. First New York production October 23, 1879, with Minnie Hauk. Some notable revivals were in 1893, being Calvé's first appearance; in 1905 with Caruso; and the Hammerstein revival of 1906, with Bressler-Gianoli, Dalmores, Gilibert, Trentini and Ancona.

Characters

DON JOSE, (*Don Ho-zay'*) a Brigadier............................Tenor
ESCAMILLO, (*Es-ca-meel'-yo*) a Toreador............................Bass
DANCAIRO (*Dan-ky'-row*) } Smugglers { ....Baritone
REMENDADO (*Rem-en-dah'-dow*) } { ....Tenor
ZUNIGA, (*Zoo-nee'-gah*) a Captain................................Bass
MORALES, (*Moh-rah'-lez*) a Brigadier................................Bass
MICAELA, (*Mih-ky-ay'-lah*) a Peasant Girl........................Soprano
FRASQUITA (*Frass-kee'-tah*) } Gypsies, friends of CARMEN { .... Mezzo-Soprano
MERCEDES (*Mer-chay'-deez*) } { .... Mezzo-Soprano
CARMEN, a Cigarette Girl, afterwards a Gypsy.................Soprano
An Innkeeper, Guide, Officers, Dragoons, Lads, Cigar Girls, Gypsies, Smugglers.

Scene and Period: Seville, Spain ; about 1820.

BIZET

Georges Bizet was a native of Paris, where he was born on October 25, 1838. Like Gounod and Berlioz, he won the *Prix de Rome* (*Pree de Roam'*); in this case in 1857, the year that his first opera, *Docteur Miracle*, was produced. Among other productions came *Les Pecheurs de Perles*, in 1863, an opera recently revived at Covent Garden with Mme. Tetrazzini as *Leila*. Carmen was produced in 1875, and this most Parisian of all operatic works was received at its production with a storm of abuse. It was immoral, it was Wagnerian—the latter at that time being a deadly sin in France! Nevertheless, the supreme merits of Carmen have won it a place among the two or three most popular operas in the modern repertory.

The talents of Bizet are shown by his remarkable lyric gifts; the power of writing short, compact and finished numbers, full of exquisite beauty and convincing style, at the same time handling dramatic scenes with the freedom demanded by modern opera. His music is more virile, concentrated and stimulating than perhaps any other French composer.

It was probably not a little owing to the hostile reception of this, his finest work, that its composer died three months later. The music Bizet has written, however, is likely long to survive him, and chief among the works into which he ungrudgingly poured his life's energy was Carmen.

THE PLOT

I

Carmen has its opening scene in a public square in Seville, showing at one side a guard-house, where *Jose*, a young brigadier, keeps guard. *Micaela*, a peasant girl whom he loved in his village home, comes hither to seek him with a message from his mother. As *Jose* appears, the girls stream out from the cigarette factory hard by, and with them their leading spirit in love and adventure, *Carmen*, the gypsy, reckless and bewitching. Heedless of the pressing throng of suitors, and attracted by the handsome young soldier, *Carmen* throws him a flower, leaving him dazed and bewildered at her beauty and the fascinating flash of her dark eyes. A moment later a stabbing affray with a rival factory girl leads to the gypsy's arrest, and she is placed in the care of *Jose* himself. A few more smiles and softly-spoken words from the fascinating *Carmen*, and he is persuaded to allow her to escape. There is a sudden struggle and confusion—the soldier lets go his hold—and the bird has flown!

II

Act II takes place in the tavern of *Lillas Pastia*, a resort of smugglers, gypsies and questionable characters generally. Here arrives *Escamillo*, the toreador, amid the acclamations of the crowd, and he, like the rest, offers his homage to *Carmen*. Meanwhile, the two smugglers, *Dancairo* and *Remendado*, have an expedition afoot and need *Carmen* to accompany them. But she is awaiting the return of the young soldier, who, as a punishment for allowing her to escape, had gone to prison, and she will not depart until she has seen him. The arrival of *Jose* leads to an ardent love scene between the two. *Carmen* dances her wild gypsy measures before him; yet, in the midst of all, she hears the regimental trumpets sounding the retreat. While *Carmen* bids him remain and join her, the honor of a soldier urges him to return. The arrival of his captain, who orders him back, decides *Jose*. He defies his officer, who is bound by the smugglers, and *Jose* deserts his regiment for *Carmen*.

III

The next scene finds *Jose* with the smugglers in the rocky camp in the mountains. The career of a bandit, however, is one to which a soldier does not easily succumb. His distaste offends *Carmen*, who scornfully bids him return home, she also foreseeing, in gypsy fashion, with the cards, that they will end their careers tragically together. In the midst of this strained situation two visitors arrive: *Escamillo*, the toreador, in the character of a new suitor for *Carmen*; and *Micaela*, with a message from *Jose's* dying mother. The soldier, frustrated in his attempt to kill *Escamillo*, cannot resist the girl's appeal and departs, promising to return later for his revenge.

IV

The final act takes place outside the *Plaza de Toros*, at Seville, the scene of *Escamillo's* triumphs in the ring. *Carmen* has returned here to witness the prowess of her new lover, and is informed by her friends that *Jose*, half crazed with jealousy, is watching, capable of desperate deeds. They soon meet, and the scene between the maddened soldier and the gypsy is a short one. The jealous *Jose* appeals for her to return to him, but she refuses with scorn, although she knows it means death. In a rage *Jose* stabs her, and thus the end comes swiftly, while within the arena the crowd is heard acclaiming the triumph of *Escamillo*.

Prelude (Overture)

By La Scala Orchestra   *68052   12-inch, $1.25
By La Scala Orchestra   *62617   10-inch, .75

The Prelude to Carmen opens with a quick march in 2-4 time, on the following theme:

The march is of an exceedingly virile and fiery description and is taken from the music preceding the bull-fight in the last act. Following this stimulating march comes the "Toreador's Song," leading to the march theme again. These two sections, complete in themselves, are now followed by a short movement in triple time indicating the tragic conclusion of the drama. Here, the appealing notes of the brass, heard beneath the tremolo of the strings, gives poignant expression to the pathos which lies in the jealous love of the forsaken *Jose,* and expresses the menace of the future death of *Carmen.* This movement breaks off on a sudden detached chord of the diminished seventh as the curtain rises.

ACT I

SCENE—*A Public Square in Seville*

The curtain rises on a street in Seville, gay with an animated throng. In the foreground are the military guard stationed in front of their quarters. The cigarette factory lies to the right, and a bridge across the river is seen in the background.

Among the crowd which throngs the stage a young girl may be seen searching for a familiar face. It is *Micaela,* the maiden whom *Jose* has left behind in his native village. The soldiers accost her, and from them she learns of her lover's absence. She declines the invitation to remain, and departs hastily.

The cigarette girls now emerge from the factory, filling the air with the smoke of their cigarettes, and with them *Carmen,* who answers the salutations of her admirers among the men by singing the gay *Habanera.*

MAIRET

SETTING OF ACT I

Habanera (Love is Like a Wood-bird)

By Jeanne Gerville-Réache, Contralto   (*In French*)   88278   12-inch, $3.00
By Emma Calvé, Soprano   (*In French*)   88085   12-inch, 3.00
By Maria Gay, Mezzo-Soprano   (*In Italian*)   92059   12-inch, 3.00

This charming "Habanera" has always been a favorite Carmen number, its entrancing rhythm always being delightful to the ear; and it does not seem strange that *Don Jose* found it irresistible when sung by *Carmen.*

Though often attributed to Bizet, the air was not original with him, but was taken from Yradier's *"Album des Chansons Espagnoles."* The refrain,

L'a-mour est en-fant de Bo - hême   Il n'a ja - mais, ja-mais con-nu de loi,
And Love's a gyp - sy boy so true, He ev - er was a rov-er free as air!

is a particularly fascinating portion of the number.

* *Double-Faced Record—For title of opposite side see DOUBLE-FACED CARMEN RECORDS, page 52.*

CARMEN SINGING "HABANERA"—ACT I

HABANERA.—"Love is Like a Wood-Bird Wild."

CARMEN:

Ah! love, thou art a wilful wild bird,
And none may hope thy wings to tame,
If it please thee to be a rebel,
Say, who can try and thee reclaim?
Threats and prayers alike unheeding;
Oft ardent homage thou'lt refuse,
Whilst he who doth coldly slight thee,
Thou for thy master oft thou'lt choose.

Ah, love!
For love he is the lord of all,
And ne'er law's icy fetters will he wear,
If thou me lovest not, I love thee,
And if I love thee, now beware!
If thou me lovest not, beware!
But if I love you, if I love you, beware!
beware!

To a large number of opera-goers and music-lovers there is but one emotional soprano —but one exponent of such rôles as *Carmen* and *Santuzza.* Calvé's *Carmen,* especially, is almost universally accepted as the greatest of all impersonations of the rôle.

Gerville-Réache's *Carmen* is a fine impersonation, on quite original lines, her conception being based on a careful study of Mérimée's story and on the teachings of her Spanish mother. *Carmen,* according to Mme. Gerville-Réache, was a passionate and fickle woman, but not a vulgar one.

The men invite *Carmen* to choose a new lover, and in reply she flings a flower in the face of the surprised *Jose* and laughingly departs.

Mia madre vedo ancor (My Mother I Behold)

By Fernando de Lucia, Tenor, and Giuseppina Huguet, Soprano (*Piano acc.*)

(*In Italian*) 92052 12-inch, $3.00

Now *Micaela* returns, and finds the soldier she seeks. Her song tells of the message of greeting she brings *Jose* from his mother, and with it a kiss. The innocence of *Micaela* is here a foil to the riper attractions of the gypsy, and the music allotted to the maiden possesses the same simple charm; the conclusion of *Micaela's* air being a broad sustained melody of much beauty. *Jose* takes up the strain, as the memories of his old home crowd upon him, and the beautiful duet follows.

JOSE: Ah! tell me of her—my mother far away.
MICHAELA: Faithful messenger from her to thee,
I bring a letter,
And some money also;
Because a dragoon has not too much.
And, besides that—

GAY AS CARMEN

JOSE:
Something else?

MICHAELA:
Indeed, I know not how to say
It is something more—

COPY'T DUPONT
CALVÉ AS CARMEN

Micaela leaves him after a tender farewell, and *Jose* begins to read his mother's letter, but is interrupted by a commotion within the factory. *Carmen* has stabbed one of her companions, and is arrested and placed under the guard of *Don Jose.* The soldiers drive away the crowd, and *Carmen,* left alone with *Jose,* brings her powers of fascination to bear on the young soldier, partly to facilitate her escape, and partly because she has attracted her attention. Here she sings the *Seguidilla,* a form of Spanish country dance.

Seguidilla (Near the Walls of Seville)

By Maria Gay, Mezzo-Soprano (In Italian)
91085 10-inch, $2.00

The *Seguidilla* is one of Spain's most beloved dances, and its rhythm is most fascinating. Bizet has given us a brilliant example in this dainty number, which he has set to Michael Carre's words.

CARMEN: Near by the ramparts of Seville
There shall I go to find Lillas Pastia.
And the wine-cup we'll share.
We'll dance in the gay seguidille,
There I shall find Lillas Pastia,

JOSE:
Tell me what this may be:
Come, reveal it to me.

MICHAELA:
Yes, I will tell you.
What she has given, I will to thee render.
Your mother with me from the chapel came,
And then, lovingly, she kissed me.
"My daughter," said she, "to the city thou
dost go:
Not long the journey.
When arrived in Seville,
Thou wilt seek out Jose, my beloved son;
Tell him—Thou knowest that thy mother,
By night, by day, thinks of her Jose:
For him she always prays and hopes,
And pardons him, and loves him ever.
And then this kiss, kind one,
Thou wilt to him give for me."

JOSE:
A kiss from my mother?

MICHAELA:
To her son.
Jose, I give it to thee—as I promised.
(*Michaela stands on tip-toe and kisses Jose—
a true mother's kiss.—Jose is moved and
regards Michaela tenderly.*)

JOSE:
My home in yonder valley,
My mother lov'd shall I e'er see?
Ah fondly in my heart I cherish
Mem'ries so dear yet to me.

MICHAELA:
Thy home in yonder valley,
Thy mother lov'd thou yet wilt see,
'Twill strength and courage give thee.
That one sweet hope,
That yet again thou wilt thy home
And thy dear mother once more see.

CARMEN AND ESCAMILLO AT THE INN—ACT II

Yes, but 'tis folly to go alone;
Where there's not two no love can be,
So, to keep me from being dull,
A handsome lad will come with me!

THE INN OF PASTIA—ACT II

Although *Jose* says to himself that the girl is only amusing herself, and whiling away the time with her gypsy songs, the words which fall on his ear—of a meeting-place on the ramparts of Seville—of a soldier she loves—a common soldier, all these play upon the feelings of *Jose* and rouse in him a love for the changeful gypsy, who is fated to be the cause of his downfall.

He unties her hands, and when the soldiers are conducting her to prison she pushes *Jose*, who falls, and in the confusion she escapes.

Between Acts I and II is usually played a charming entr'acte, which has been rendered for this Carmen series by Mr. Herbert.

Intermezzo (1st Entr'acte)
By Victor Herbert's Orch.   60067   10-inch, $0.75

ACT II
SCENE—*A Tavern in the Suburbs of Seville*

The second act opens amid the Bohemian surroundings of the tavern of Lillas Pastia ; the wild tune with which the orchestra leads off depicting the freedom and gaiety with which the mixed characters here assembled are wont to take enjoyment and recreation.

Les tringles des sistres   (Gypsy Song)
By Emma Calvé, Soprano
(*In French*)   88124   12-inch, $3.00

Carmen again leads in with her song, another lively gypsy tune, in the exulting refrain of which all join, a picture of reckless merriment resulting.

CALVÉ SINGING THE GYPSY SONG—ACT II

> Ah! when of gay guitars the sound
> On the air in cadence ringing,
> Quickly forth the gipsies springing,
> To dance a merry, mazy round.
> While tambourines the clang prolong,
> In rhythm with the music beating,
> And ev'ry voice is heard repeating
> The merry burthen of glad song.
>   Tra la la la, etc.

But *Carmen* is thinking of the soldier who went to prison for her sake and who, now at liberty, will shortly be with her. Her musings are interrupted by the arrival of a procession in honor of *Escamillo*, whose appearance is followed by the famous "Toreador Song," the most popular of all Carmen numbers.

Cancion de Toreador (Toreador Song)

By Titta Ruffo, Baritone, and La Scala Chorus
(*In Italian*) 92065 12-inch, $3.00

By Emilio de Gogorza, Baritone, and New York
Opera Chorus (*In Spanish*) 88178 12-inch, 3.00

By Pasquale Amato, Baritone
(*In Italian*) 88327 12-inch, 3.00

By Giuseppe Campanari, Baritone
(*In Italian*) 85073 12-inch, 3.00

By Alan Turner, Baritone
(*In English*) *16521 10-inch, .75

By Francesco Cigada, Baritone; Giuseppina
Huguet, Soprano; Inez Salvador, Mezzo-
Soprano; and La Scala Chorus
(*In Italian*) *62618 10-inch, .75

By Carlos Francisco, Baritone
(*In Spanish*) 4074 10-inch, .60

By Alan Turner, Baritone
(*In English*) 5376 10-inch, .60

COPY'T DUPONT
CARUSO AS DON JOSE

No less than seven renditions of this universal favorite are offered by the Victor for the choice of customers.

After *Escamillo's* departure, *Carmen's* comrades invite her to depart upon a smuggling expedition, but she refuses to stir until she sees the soldier for whom she is waiting. Their efforts to persuade her has been put by Bizet into the form of a brilliant quintet.

Quintet—"Nous avons en tête une affaire" (We Have a Plan)

By Mmes. Lejeune, Soprano; Duchêne, Mezzo-
Soprano; Dumesnil, Soprano; Mm. Leroux,
Tenor; Carlos Gilibert, Baritone
(*In French*) 88237 12-inch, $3.00

This is one of the favorite numbers in Bizet's opera, and at the same time one of the most difficult imaginable. When sung as the tempo indicates, it goes at break-neck speed, and it is only the most capable artists who can do it justice.

For the present reproduction, the Victor has assembled a most competent corps of singers, who were under the direction of the late Charles Gilibert, himself the most famous of *Remendados*.

Jose's voice being heard outside, *Carmen* pushes her companions from the room and greets him with joy. She then tries her fascinations on the stolid soldier to induce him to join the band of smugglers, but without effect, as he is reminded of his duty when he hears the bugle in the distance summoning him to quarters. "Then

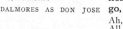

COPY'T MISHKIN
DALMORES AS DON JOSE

go, I hate you!" says *Carmen*, and mocks him, singing

Ah, this is too mortifying!
All to please you, sir, I gaily sang and danced.
(*Aside.*) But now ta ra ta! he hears the trumpet call!
Ta ra ta ra! and then off he flies
Like a guest to a feast!

* *Double-Faced Record*—For title of opposite side see DOUBLE-FACED CARMEN RECORDS, page 52.

Air de la fleur (Flower Song)

By Enrico Caruso, Tenor
(*In French*) 88208   12-inch, $3.00
By Enrico Caruso, Tenor
(*In Italian*) 88209   12-inch, 3.00
By Charles Dalmores, Tenor
(*In French*) 85122   12-inch, 3.00
By Fernando De Lucia, Tenor
(*In Italian*) 76001   12-inch, 2.00
By Evan Williams, Tenor
(*In English*) 74122   12-inch, 1.50
By John McCormack, Tenor
(*In Italian*) 74218   12-inch, 1.50

Desperate at the thought of losing her forever, *Don Jose* shows her the flowers she threw him at their first meeting, and which he had preserved, then sings this lovely romance, beginning:

BRESSLER-GIANOLI AS CARMEN

La fleur que tu ma-vais je - te - e Dans ma pri-son m'e-tait res-té - e
This flow'r you gave to me, de - grad - ed 'Mid pri - son walls I've kept tho' fad - ed

The struggle between love and duty which has been distracting the unfortunate lover is now seemingly forgotten, and he pours out his heart in this romanza, telling only of his great passion for the beautiful but heartless gypsy.

COPY'T DUPONT

DE LUSSAN AS CARMEN

DON JOSE:
This flower you gave to me, degraded
'Mid prison walls, I've kept, tho' faded;
Tho' withered quite, the tender bloom
Doth yet retain its sweet perfume.
Night and day in darkness abiding,
I the truth, Carmen, am confiding;
Its loved odor did I inhale,
And wildly called thee without avail.
My love itself I cursed and hated,
* * * * * * * * * *
Then alone myself I detested,
And naught else this heart interested,
Naught else it felt but one desire,
One sole desire did it retain,
Carmen, beloved, to see thee once again!
   O, Carmen, mine! here as thy slave, love
      binds me fast,
            Carmen, I love thee!

From Schirmer score.   Copy't G. Schirmer

The number might have been written expressly for Caruso, so well does it suit his voice and style. One can but marvel at the masterful ease of phrasing, and the warmth of vocal coloring imparted by the singer. The changing moods of the lover are here indicated with dramatic expression—the regret at the havoc *Carmen* has played with his life mingling with the devotion for her he still feels. This is a remarkable and memorable performance, the whole song being lighted up with that rich vocal beauty and artistic genius which belong only to a Caruso.

McCormack also makes a fine impression in this rôle, and his singing of this famous Flower Song is always greeted with enthusiasm. Dalmores' interpretation is a more vigorous one, his fine voice being shown at its best. Other fine renditions, at varying prices, in both Italian and English, are also offered.

Carmen then paints the joys of the gypsies' life which might be *Jose's,* if he would desert his regiment and follow her.

Las bas dans la montagne (Away to Yonder Mountains)

By Emma Calvé, Soprano, and Carlos Dalmores, Tenor

(*In French*) 89019 12-inch, $4.00

The soldier listens with half-willing ears, his voice joining hers at the close, in a lovely duet passage.

CARMEN:
For roof, the sky—a wandering life;
For country, the whole world;
Thy will thy master;
And above all—most prized of all—
Liberty! freedom!
Up yonder, up yonder, if thou lov'st me,
To the mountains, together we'll go.

JOSE:
Carmen!
CARMEN:
Wilt come with me?
Up yonder, up yonder, thus will we go
Away, if thou lov'st me, together!

However, in spite of *Carmen's* fascinations, *Jose* is about to return to his duty, when the appearance of his superior officer *Zuniga*, who orders him back, decides the matter. *Don Jose* resents the overbearing tone his captain uses and defies him. *Zuniga* is finally overpowered and bound by the gypsies, and the smugglers all depart on their expedition.

Aragonaise (2d Entr'acte)

By Victor Herbert's Orchestra 70067 12-inch, $1.25
By La Scala Orchestra (*Double-faced—See page 52*) 62102 10-inch, .75

The retreat in the mountains is musically described by this pastoral intermezzo. A dreamy melody given to the flute, with a *pizzicato* accompaniment, is taken up by the other instruments in turn, the strings joining in the coda.

This is one of the finest records made by the Herbert Orchestra, who have given an artistic and finished rendering of the interlude.

PHOTO MAIRET

MICAELA PLEADS WITH JOSE—ACT III

BYRON

CARD SCENE—ACT III

ACT III
SCENE—*A Wild and Rocky Pass in the Mountains*

As the curtain rises, the smugglers are seen entering their rocky lair. Here occurs the famous sextette, a portion of which is given in the "Gems from Carmen" (*page 51*).

The smugglers prepare to camp for the night. It is evident that *Jose* is already repenting of his folly, and that *Carmen* is tiring of her latest lover. After a quarrel with *Jose*, she joins *Frasquita* and *M cedes*, who are telling fortunes with cards.

En vain pour eviter (Card Song)
By Jeanne Gerville-Réache, Contralto   (*In French*) **87039** 10-inch, $2.00
By Lavin de Casas, Mezzo-Soprano (*Piano acc.*) (*In Italian*) *62617 10-inch, .75

PHOTO REUTLINGER

THE CARDS PREDICT CARMEN'S DEATH
(EMMA CALVÉ)

Carmen tells her own fate by the cards, reading death, first for herself and then for her lover. In vain she shuffles and re-tries the result; the answer is ever the same.

This highly dramatic air, one of the most impressive numbers in Bizet's opera, is effectively sung by Mme. Gerville-Réache.

The neighboring camp being ready, the smugglers retire, and the stage is once more deserted.

Je dis que rien ne m'epouvante (Micaela's Air, " I am not Faint-Hearted ")

By Emma Eames, Soprano
(*In French*) **88036** 12-inch, $3.00
By Geraldine Farrar, Soprano
(*In French*) **88144** 12-inch, 3.00
By Alma Gluck, Soprano
(*In French*) **74245** 12-inch, 1.50

Into this strange and wild scene now enters *Micaela*, the peasant sweetheart of *Don Jose*, who has forgotten her in his fascination for the wayward *Carmen*. *Micaela* has braved the dangers of the road to the smugglers' retreat, whither *Don Jose* has followed *Carmen*, to carry to the soldier a message from his dying mother. The innocent girl is frightened by the vast and

Double-Faced Record—For title of opposite side see DOUBLE-FACED CARMEN RECORDS, page 52.

lonely mountains, and in her aria appeals to Heaven to protect her, ingenuously confessing her love for *Don Jose* and her detestation of the woman who has led him away from his duty.

MICAELA:
I try not to own that I tremble;
  But I know I'm a coward, altho' bold I appear.
Ah! how can I ever call up my courage,
  While horror and dread chill my sad heart with fear?
Here, in this savage retreat, sad and weary am I,
Alone and sore afraid.
Ah! heav'n, to thee I humbly pray,
  Protect thou me, and guide and aid!
I shall see the guilty creature,
  Who by infernal arts doth sever
From his country, from his duty,
  Him I loved—and shall love ever!
I may tremble at her beauty,
  But her power affrights me not.
Strong, in my just cause confiding,
Heaven! I trust myself to thee.
Ah! to this poor heart give courage,
  Protector! guide and aid now me!

COPY'T MISHKIN

TRENTINI AS FRASQUITA

The young girl, hearing a shot fired, runs into a cave in fright. *Jose,* who is guarding the smugglers' effects, has seen a stranger and fires at him. It proves to be *Escamillo,* the toreador, who has come to join *Carmen.*

Je suis Escamillo (I am Escamillo!)

By Charles Dalmores and Marcel Journet   *(In French)*   85114 12-inch, $3.00
By Léon Beyle, Tenor, and Hector Dufranne, Baritone
  (Double-faced—See page 52) *(In French)* 62750 10-inch, .75

The two men compare notes, and learning that they are rivals, *Jose* challenges the other to a duel with knives, which is interrupted by the timely arrival of *Carmen* herself. This dialogue, with the fiery duet at the close, well depicts this exciting scene.

The Dalmores-Journet record is of especial interest because of the brilliant success Mr. Dalmores has achieved in the part of *Don Jose.* Journet sings *Escamillo's* music splendidly, with that full resonant voice always pleasant to hear. A popular priced rendition by Beyle and Dufranne, of the *Opéra,* is also listed above.

Finale—"Mia tu sei" (You Command Me to Leave You)

By Antonio Paoli, Tenor; Giuseppina Huguet, Soprano;
Inez Salvador, and Francesco Cigada   *(In Italian)*   92035 12-inch, $3.00

A dramatic scene between *Carmen* and *Jose* is interrupted by *Micaela,* who begs *Jose* to return to his mother; and *Carmen,* with fine scorn, echoes her request. Thus to leave his rival in possession of the field is too much for the soldier, who swears never to be parted from the gypsy until death.

CARMEN *(to Jose)*:
  Go, and go quickly; stay not here;
  This way of life is not for thee!
JOSE *(to Carmen)*:
  To depart thou dost counsel me?
CARMEN:
  Yes, thou shouldst go—
JOSE *(fiercely)*:
  Yes, that thou mayst follow
  Another lover—the toreador!
  No, Carmen, I will not depart!

MICAELA:
  Be not deaf to my prayers;
  Thy mother waits thee there.
  The chain that binds thee, Jose,
  Death will break.
JOSE *(to Michaela)*:
  Go from hence;
  I cannot follow thee.
  (To Carmen.)
  Mine thou art, accursed one!
  And I will force thee to know
  And submit to the fate
  That both our lives unites!

The message from his dying mother, however, decides him; he will go, but vows to return. In this wild and tumultuous number the jealous anger of *Jose* gives rise to some highly dramatic singing, delivered with extreme intensity and power by Paoli, the tragic theme at the close being introduced with meaning effect. The Toreador chorus indicates the triumph of *Escamillo* in the gypsy's attentions, and this with the orchestral close slowly sinking to rest brings the powerful act to a finish.

JOSE PLEADING WITH CARMEN—ACT IV

ACT IV

(A Square in Seville, with the walls of the Bull Ring shown at the back)

Prelude

By Victor Herbert's Orchestra
70066 12-inch, $1.25

The fourth act opens with a momentary brightness. Outside the *Plaza de Toros*, in Seville, an animated crowd awaits the procession about to enter the ring. This short movement is a quick bustling one, only the plaintive oboe solo indicating the tragedy which is soon to occur. The playing of this striking prelude is on the same artistic level which marks each of the renditions by this famous orchestra.

This scene, as the orange sellers, hawkers of fans, ices and the rest, press their wares on the waiting crowd, is extremely gay, and affords welcome relief from the intensity of the drama. **Escamillo,** who has returned to take part in the bull-fight, now enters, and all join in the refrain of the Toreador Song in his honor.

Se tu m'ami   (If You Love Me)

By Inez Salvador, Mezzo-Soprano, and Francesco Cigada, Baritone
(Double-faced—See page 52) *(In Italian)* **62102 10-inch, $0.75**

Escamillo takes farewell of *Carmen* before entering the arena. He promises to fight the better for her presence, and she, half conscious of what is coming, avows her readiness to die for him. This number is full of lovely melodies and one of the most beautiful records of the Carmen series.

As the procession passes on, the warning comes to *Carmen* that *Jose* is here, to which she replies that she fears him not.

PHOTO BYRON

THE DEATH OF CARMEN—ACT IV

Duetto e Finale (Duet and Finale)

By Maria Passeri, Mezzo-Soprano;
Antonio Paoli, Tenor; and La Scala
Chorus   92050 12-inch, $3.00

COPY'T DUPONT

MARTIN AS DON JOSE

Jose now enters and makes a last appeal, which is dramatic in its intensity. It takes the form of a swinging melody to an insistent triplet accompaniment. To each request of her lover, *Carmen* adds her disdainful negative, reckless of the danger which threatens her.

JOSE (*in desperation*):
Now thou refusest my prayers,
Inhuman girl! For thy sake am I lost!
And then to know thee shameless, infamous!
Laughing, in his arms, at my despair!
No, no! it shall not be, by Heaven!
Carmen, thou must be mine, mine only!
CARMEN (*proudly*):
No, no, never!
JOSE:
Ah! weary am I of threats.
CARMEN:
Cease then,—or let me pass!
CHORUS (*in bull ring*):
Victory! victory!
Viva Escamillo!
JOSE:
Again I beseech thee, Carmen,
Wilt thou with me depart?

Carmen's last refusal, as she flings him back his ring, rouses the soldier's jealousy to madness and he stabs her to the heart. As she falls the success of the *Toreador* in the arena is announced by the singing of his well-known refrain. The last notes of the opera are a few pitiful tones from the stricken *Jose* addressed to the mute form of his beloved.

This is another truly powerful record by Paoli, worthy of a climax such as this. The music is delivered with the realism and earnestness beyond the reach of all but the very few tenors, and it enables the listener to fully realize the stress and pathos of the moving dramatic picture which thus concludes the last act of Carmen.

DOUBLE-FACED AND MISCELLANEOUS CARMEN RECORDS

Carmen Selection	By Pryor's Band	31562	12-inch, $1.00
Carmen Selection	By Sousa's Band	35000	12-inch, 1.25
Freischutz—Overture	By Sousa's Band		
Carmen Selection	By Pryor's Band	16575	10-inch, .75
Manon—Ah! fuyez douce image!	By M. Rocca, Tenor		

The selection begins with the brilliant and animated Prelude, the first part of which is given, including the refrain of the famous "Toreador Song." Then is heard (as a cornet solo) the quaint "Habanera,"

Allegretto quasi Andantino.

L'a-mour est un - oi - seau re - bel - le Que nul ne - pent ap-pri - vol-ser
Love is like an - y wood-bird wild, That none can cv - er hope to tame,

with its curiously varied rhythm, its chromatic melody and the changes from minor to major which are so effective. With the last note the full band takes up the rollicking chorus of street boys from Act I, and after a few measures there appears suddenly the weird strain from Act IV when *Carmen* hurls at *Don Jose* her last defiance.

Ti bre-elle est née let ti - be ette mour - ral
Free I was born, And free I will die!

The spirited introductory strain returns, closing the selection. A fine record and splendidly played.

Gems from Carmen

By Victor Light Opera Company   (*In English*) 31843 12-inch, $1.00

Chorus, "Here They Are"—Solo and Chorus, "Habanera" (Love is Like a Bird)—Duet, "Again He Sees His Village Home"—Sextette, "Our Chosen Trade" — Solo and Chorus, "Toreador Song"—Finale.

An amazing number of the most popular bits of Bizet's masterpiece have been crowded into this attractively arranged potpourri, which shows both the skill of Mr. Rogers and the remarkable talent of the Opera Company.

Only such an organization as that of the Victor, which stands absolutely alone among record-making bodies, could successfully cope with the difficulties of Bizet's score. The record is one of the most striking and brilliant of the series, including as it does the rollicking chorus of boys in Act I; the favorite *Habanera*, the lovely *Jose-Micaela* duet, the Sextette from the Smuggler Scene, the popular *Toreador Song* and the brilliant finish to Act III.

{Habanera (*Whistling*)	By Guido Gialdini	16752	10-inch,	$0.75
{ The Pretty Maiden (*Xylophone*)	By Peter Lewin			
{Toreador Song By Alan Turner, Baritone (*In English*)		16521	10-inch,	.75
{ Trovatore—Tempest of the Heart By Alan Turner, Baritone (*In English*)				
{Prelude (Overture) By La Scala Orchestra		68052	12-inch.	1.25
{ Damnation of Faust—Hungarian March By Sousa's Band				
{Prelude (Overture) By La Scala Orchestra		62617	10-inch,	.75
{Scena delle carte (Card Song) By Lavin de Casas, Mezzo-				
{ Soprano (*Piano acc.*) (*In Italian*)				
{Canzone del Toreador (Toreador Song) By F. Cigada, Baritone; G. Huguet, Soprano; I. Salvador, Mezzo-Soprano; La Scala Chorus (*In Italian*)		62618	10-inch,	.75
{ Cavalleria Rusticana—Intermezzo By Pryor's Orchestra				
{Intermezzo—Acto III By La Scala Orchestra		62102	10-inch,	.75
{Se tu m'ami (If You Love Me) By Inez Salvador, Mezzo-Soprano; F. Cigada, Baritone (*In Italian*)				
{Je suis Escamillo (I Am Escamillo!) By Léon Beyle, Tenor; Hector Dufranne, Baritone (*In French*)		62750	10-inch,	.75
{ Valse des Roses (*Métra*) By Mlle. Korsoff, Soprano (*In French*)				
{Preludio, Acto IV By La Scala Orchestra		62101	10-inch,	.75
{ Norma—Mira o Norma—By Ida Giacomelli, Soprano; Lina Mileri, Contralto (*In Italian*)				
{Carmen Selection (*Xylophone*) By Wm. Reitz		16892	10-inch,	.75
{ Bohême—Musetta Waltz (*Whistling*) By Guido Gialdini				

A FAMOUS OPEN-AIR PRODUCTION IN FRANCE

THE METROPOLITAN OPERA HOUSE SETTING

(Italian)
CAVALLERIA RUSTICANA
(*Cav-al-leh-ree'-ah Rus-ti-cah'-nah*)

(English)
RUSTIC CHIVALRY

OPERA IN ONE ACT

Libretto adapted from the book of Verga by Targioni-Torzetti and Menasci; music by Mascagni. First production in Rome, May 17, 1890, the opera having won the first prize offered by a music publisher for the best one-act work. First London production at the Shaftesbury Theatre under the direction of Signor Lago, October 19, 1891; and at Covent Garden (under Harris) May 16, 1892. First American production in Philadelphia, September 9, 1891.

Cast

SANTUZZA, (*San-toot'-zah*) a village girl.........................Soprano
LOLA, (*Low'-lah*) wife of Alfio...........................Mezzo-Soprano
TURIDDU, (*Too-ree'-doo*) a young soldier ....Tenor
ALFIO, (*Al'-fee-oh*) a teamster.................................Baritone
LUCIA, (*Loo-chee'-ah*) mother of Turiddu ....Contralto

Chorus of Peasants and Villagers.   Chorus behind the scenes.

The scene is laid in a Sicilian village.

Time—The Present.

THE COMPOSER

Pietro Mascagni, son of a baker in Leghorn, was born December 7, 1863. Destined by his father to succeed him in business, the young man rebelled, and secretly entered the Cherubini Conservatory. He began composing at an early age, but none of his works attracted attention until 1890, when he entered a contest planned by Sonzogno, the Milan publisher. Securing a libretto based on a simple Sicilian tale by Verga, he composed the whole of this opera in eight days, producing a work full of dramatic fire and rich in Italian melody, and easily won the prize. Produced in Rome in 1890, it created a sensation, and in a short time has become one of the most popular of operas.

CARUSO AS TURIDDU

THE STORY

Turiddu, a young Sicilian peasant, returns from the war and finds his sweetheart, *Lola,* has wedded *Alfio,* a carter. For consolation he pays court to *Santuzza,* who loves him not wisely but too well. Tiring of her, he turns again to *Lola,* who seems to encourage him.

Prelude

By La Scala Orchestra *35104 12-inch, $1.25
By Vessella's Italian Band
31831 12-inch, 1.00

The Prelude takes the form of a fantasia on the principal themes of the opera. Mascagni's lovely melodies are played with exquisite tone and expression, while at the climaxes the entry of the brass is most artistically managed. This is band playing of a high order, and certainly the best record of the Prelude we have heard. The La Scala Orchestra record is also a most interesting one.

During the prelude *Turiddu's* voice is heard in the charming *Siciliana,* in which he tells of his love for *Lola* :

O Lo la, bian ca co me fior di spi no,
Oh, Lo · la, with thy lips like crim' son ber · ries!

Siciliana   (Thy Lips Like Crimson Berries)

By Enrico Caruso, Tenor   (*Harp acc.*)   (*In Italian*)   87072   10-inch, $2.00
By Enrico Caruso, Tenor   (*Piano acc.*)   (*In Italian*)   81030   10-inch, 2.00
By Leo Slezak, Tenor   (*In German*)   61202   10-inch, 1.00
By Carlo Caffetto, Tenor   (*Piano acc.*)   (*In Italian*) *62620   10-inch,   .75

It is sung behind the scenes, before the rise of the curtain, making it peculiarly effective. At the close of the number *Turiddu's* voice is heard dying away in the distance. This *decrescendo* passage is exquisitely sung by Caruso. This delightful serenade, one of the most popular of the Caruso records, is almost the only bright spot in Mascagni's passionate and tragic operatic melodrama.

The best of the many translations (Schirmer Edition, copy't 1891) is given here.

TURIDDU :

O Lola, with thy lips like crimson berries,
  Eyes with the glow of love deepening in
  them,
Cheeks of the hue of wild, blossoming cherries,
  Fortunate he who first finds favor to win
  them;

*   *   *   *   *   *   *   *

Yet tho' I died and found Heav'n on me
  beaming,
Wert thou not there to greet me, grief I
  should cherish!

A fine rendition in German by Slezak and one by Caffetto in Italian, at a lower price, are also offered.

SCENE—*A Square in a Sicilian Village*

After the *Siciliana* the chorus of villagers is heard, also behind the scenes, and during this chorus the curtain rises, showing a square in the village, with the church at one side and the cottage of *Turiddu's* mother on the other.

*Double-Faced Record—For title of opposite side see double-faced list, page 58.

Gli aranci olezzano (Blossoms of Oranges)

By New York Grand Opera Chorus	(*In Italian*)	**64048**	10-inch, $1.00
By La Scala Chorus	(*In Italian*)	*68218	12-inch, 1.25

This beautiful chorus is rendered here both by the famous organization of La Scala, Milan, and the New York Grand Opera Chorus.

It is Easter Day and crowds of villagers cross the stage and enter the church. *Santuzza* enters, and knocking at *Lucia's* door, asks her if she has seen *Turiddu*. His mother replies that he is at Francofonte, but the jealous girl refuses to believe it, and suspects that he is watching for *Lola*.

The cracking of a whip and shouts of the villagers announce *Alfio*, who appears and sings a merry song.

Il cavallo scalpita (Gayly Moves the Tramping Horse)

By Renzo Minolfi, Baritone
(*In Italian*) *45003 10-inch, $1.00

He is happy and free, his wife *Lola* loves him and guards his home while he is gone—this is the burden of his air.

The peasants disperse and *Alfio* is left with *Lucia* and *Santuzza*. When he says he has just seen *Turiddu*, *Lucia* is surprised, but at a gesture from *Santuzza* she keeps silent.

After *Alfio* has entered the church, the Easter music is heard within and all kneel and join in the singing.

Regina Coeli (Queen of the Heavens)

By La Scala Chorus
(*In Italian*) *68218 12-inch, $1.25

This great number, given by La Scala Chorus, has been combined with the opening chorus noted above on one double-faced record.

All go into the church except *Lucia* and *Santuzza,* and the agitated girl now sings her touching romanza, beginning:

as she pours out her sad history to the sympathetic *Mamma Lucia*. This is one of the most powerful numbers in Mascagni's work.

Voi lo sapete (Well You Know, Good Mother)

By Emma Calvé, Soprano	(*In Italian*)	**88086**	12-inch, $3.00
By Johanna Gadski, Soprano	(*In Italian*)	**88136**	12-inch, 3.00
By Emma Eames, Soprano	(*In Italian*)	**88037**	12-inch, 3.00

Stung with the remembrance of her great wrong she sings of vengeance, but love overpowers revenge, and in spite of herself, she cries

Then the thought of her rival, *Lola*, returns and she gives way to despair, throwing herself at the feet of the gentle mother of *Turiddu*, who is powerless to aid her and who can only pray for the wretched woman.

*Double-Faced Record—For title of opposite side see double-faced list, page 58

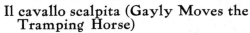

PHOTO BERT, PARIS
AMATO AS ALFIO

GADSKI AS SANTUZZA

SANTUZZA:
Well do you know, good mother,
Ere to the war he departed
Turiddu plighted to Lola his troth,
Like a man true-hearted.
And then, finding her wedded
Loved me!—I loved him!—
She, coveting what was my only treasure—
Enticed him from me!
She and Turiddu love again!
I weep and I weep and I weep still!

Three fine renditions of this dramatic number, by three famous sopranos, are offered to music lovers.

Lucia tries to comfort her and passes into the church just as *Turiddu* appears. He asks *Santuzza* why she does not go to mass. She says she cannot, and accuses him of treachery, which puts him in a rage, and he tells her brutally that she is now nothing to him. This great duet has been recorded in its entirety by two famous artists of Milan.

Tu qui Santuzza (Thou Here, Santuzza!)

By B. Besalù, Soprano, and G. Ciccolini, Tenor
(*In Italian*) *55022 12-inch, $1.50

No, No, Turiddu

By B. Besalù, Soprano, and G. Ciccolini, Tenor
(*In Italian*) *55022 12-inch, 1.50

This scene is now interrupted by *Lola's* voice, heard behind the scenes.

LOLA (*behind the scenes*):
My king of roses,
Radiant angels stand
In Heav'n in thousands;
None like to him so bright
That land discloses,
My king of roses!—

She enters, and divining the situation, shows her power by taking *Turiddu* into the church with her. Frantic with jealousy, *Santuzza* turns to *Alfio*, who now enters, and tells him that his wife is false.

Two records are required to present this powerful scene, and of the first part two versions are offered for a choice.

Turiddu mi tolse (Turiddu Forsakes Me!)

By B. Besalù, Soprano, and E. Badini, Baritone
(*In Italian*) *55021 12-inch, $1.50
By Clara Joanna, Soprano, and Renzo Minolfi, Baritone
(*In Italian*) *45002 10-inch, 1.00

Ad essi non perdono ('Tis They Who Are Shameful)

By Clara Joanna, Soprano, and Renzo Minolfi, Baritone
(*In Italian*) *45002 10-inch, $1.00

Alfio swears vengeance, while *Santuzza* already regrets her disclosure, but is powerless to prevent the consequences of her revelation. They go out, leaving the stage empty, and the beautiful Intermezzo follows.

Intermezzo

By Pryor's Orchestra
*62618 10-inch, $0.75
By Victor Orchestra
4184 10-inch, .60

SANTUZZA PLEADING WITH TURIDDU—ACT I
(DESTINN AND CARUSO)

Double-Faced Record—For title of opposite side see double-faced list, page 58

After the storm and passion of the first scene, this lovely number comes as a blessed relief. The curtain does not fall during the playing of the Intermezzo, although the stage is empty.

A casa, a casa (Now Homeward)

By La Scala Chorus (*In Italian*) *45014 10-inch, $1.00

The services being over, the people now come from the church, and *Turiddu* in a reckless mood invites the crowd to drink with him, and sings his spirited *Brindisi*.

Brindisi (Drinking Song)

By Enrico Caruso, Tenor (*In Italian*) *81062 10-inch, $2.00

In striking contrast to the prevailing tragic tone of Mascagni's opera comes this merry drinking song, which *Turiddu* sings as gaily as if he had not a care in the world, although at that moment the culminating tragedy of the duel was close at hand. *Turiddu* calls to the crowd about the inn:

In - tan - to'a mi - ci, qua, be - via - mone un bic - chie - - re
Come here, good friends, come here, Let's drain a brimming beak

then sings the *Brindisi*, which has a most fascinating swing:

viva il vi - no spu meg gian - te, nel bic - chie - re scin - til - lan - te
Hail the red wine rich - ly flow - ing, In the beak - er spark - ling, glow - ing

At the close of the song occurs a C natural, which is taken by Caruso with consummate ease.

TURIDDU:
Hail the red wine richly flowing,
In the beaker, sparkling, glowing,
I ike young love, with smiles bestowing,
Now our holiday 'twill bless.

Hail the wine that flows and bubbles,
Kills care, banishes all troubles,
Brings peace, pleasure it redoubles,
Causes sweet forgetfulness!

COPY'T DUPONT

TAMAGNO AS TURIDDU

Alfio now enters, and when *Turiddu* offers him a cup refuses, saying:

Thank you! but wine to drink with you
I fear now,
Poison I might be drinking, ere I was
thinking!

Turiddu throws out the wine, saying carelessly:

Very well! suit your pleasure!

The seriousness of this scene is not lost on the peasants, who now leave the young men together. The challenge is quickly given and accepted after the Siciliana fashion, *Turiddu* viciously biting *Alfio's* ear. *Turiddu*, sobered by the deadly earnestness of his neighbor, feels something of remorse, and says to him:

Neighbor Alfio
I own my wrong before you,
But if through you I perish
Poor hapless Santuzza—
Left without her lover—
(*Suddenly changing his tone*)
Yet will I drive my dagger in your heart!
ALFIO (*coldly*):
I will await you behind the garden!

Turiddu now calls his mother from the cottage, and asks for her blessing, bidding her, if he does not return, to be a mother to *Santuzza*.

Addio alla madre (Turiddu's Farewell to His Mother)

By Riccardo Martin, Tenor (*In Italian*) 88277 12-inch, $3.00
By Gennaro de Tura, Tenor (*In Italian*) 76015 12-inch, 2.00
By G. Ciccolini, Tenor (*In Italian*) *55021 12-inch, 1.50
By Leo Slezak, Tenor (*In German*) 61205 10-inch, 1.00
By Giorgio Malesci, Tenor (*Piano acc.*) (*In Italian*) *62620 10-inch, .75

Double-Faced Record—For title of opposite side see double-faced list, page 58.

TURIDDU (*calling*):
Mother!
(*Enter Lucia.*)
Exciting surely that wine was.
I must have taken
Too many cups
While we were drinking!
For a stroll I am going,
But first, I pray you,
Give your son your blessing
As when I left you
To become a soldier!
And listen, mother! This also!
If I return not, if I return not,
You must not falter.

To Santuzza be a mother!
I have sworn to shield her
And lead her to the altar.
LUCIA:
Why speakest thou so strangely?
My son, oh, tell me?
TURIDDU (*nonchalantly*):
Oh, nothing! the wine
Has filled my brain with vapors!
O pray that God forgive me!
One kiss, dear mother!
And yet another!
Farewell now! If I return not
Be a mother to my Santa.
(*He rushes off.*)

Finale to the Opera

By Clara Joanna, Soprano; Sra. Rumbelli, Mezzo-
Soprano; and Chorus (*Double-faced—See below*) (*In Italian*) 45003 10-inch, $1.00

Lucia is distressed and bewildered, and calls after him despairingly. Confused cries are now heard and a woman screams "*Turiddu* is murdered!" *Santuzza* and *Lucia* sink down senseless, and the curtain slowly falls.

DOUBLE-FACED AND MISCELLANEOUS CAVALLERIA RUSTICANA RECORDS

Selection—Part I	By Victor Orchestra	31057	12-inch,	$1.00
Selection—Part II	By Victor Orchestra	31058	12-inch,	1.00
Turiddu, mi tolse (Turiddu Forsakes Me!) By B. Besalù, Soprano, and E. Badini, Baritone (*In Italian*) Mamma, quel vino è generoso (Mother! the Wine Cup too Freely Passes) By G. Coccolini, Tenor (*In Italian*)		55021	12-inch,	1.50
Tu qui Santuzza (Thou Here, Santuzza) By B. Besalù, Soprano, and G. Ciccolini, Tenor (*In Italian*) No, No, Turiddu By B. Besalù, Soprano, and G. Ciccolini, Tenor (*In Italian*)		55022	12-inch,	1.50
Prelude By La Scala Orchestra Selection By Pryor's Band Opening of Act, "Alfio's Song," "Easter Chorale," "Intermezzo."		35104	12-inch,	1.25
Coro d' Introduzione By La Scala Chorus (*In Italian*) Regina Coeli By La Scala Chorus (*In Italian*)		68218	12-inch,	1.25
Turiddu, mi tolse l'onore (Turiddu Forsakes Me!) By Clara Joanna, Soprano, and Renzo Minolfi, Baritone (*In Italian*) Ad essi io non perdono By Clara Joanna, Soprano, and Renzo Minolfi, Baritone (*In Italian*)		45002	10-inch,	1.00
Finale dell' Opera By Clara Joanna, Soprano; Sra. Rumbelli, Mezzo-Soprano; and La Scala Chorus (*In Italian*) Il cavallo scalpita (Gayly Moves the Tramping Horse) By Renzo Minolfi, Baritone (*In Italian*)		45003	10-inch,	1.00
A casa, a casa (Now Homeward!) By La Scala Chorus (*In Italian*) Guglielmo Ratcliff—Padre Nostro By A. Mussini, Soprano, and E. Molinari, Bass (*In Italian*)		45014	10-inch,	1.00
Intermezzo By Pryor's Orchestra Carmen—Toreador (Bizet) By Francesco Cigada, Baritone; Giuseppina Huguet, Soprano; Inez Salvador, Mezzo-Soprano; and Chorus (*In Italian*)		62618	10-inch,	.75
Addio alla madre (*Piano acc.*) By Giorgio Malesci, Tenor Siciliana (*Piano acc.*) By Carlo Caffetto, Tenor		62620	10-inch,	.75

DAMNATION OF FAUST—FOURTH SCENE—PARIS OPÉRA

(French)

LA DAMNATION DE FAUST

(Lah Dan-nah-see-on' deh Fowst)

(English)

DAMNATION OF FAUST

Hector Berlioz's dramatic legend in four parts; book based on de Nerval's version of Goethe's poem, partly by Gandonniere, but completed by Berlioz himself. First performed December 6, 1846, at the *Opéra Comique*, Paris, in concert form, and in New York under Dr. Leopold Damrosch in 1880. It was given at Monte Carlo as an opera in 1903. First American performance of the opera,

Cast

MARGUERITE (*Mahr-guer-eet'*) . . . . Soprano
FAUST (*Fowst*) . . . . Tenor
MEPHISTOPHELES (*Mef-iss-tof'-el-leez*) . . . . Baritone or Bass
BRANDER . . . . Bass

Place : A German village.

THE COMPOSER

No one to-day doubts the genius of Berlioz, and critics are almost unanimous in praising his originality, his spontaneous force and immense creative power. *Le Damnation de Faust,* his best known work, originally written as an oratorio, but which has since been adapted for the stage, was first produced in 1846 and met with a cold reception. Ten years after his death, however, what a change began! A Berlioz memorial in Paris, at the Hippodrome, where thousands were turned away; Berlioz monuments erected in Grenoble and other cities of France; and finally, the production of Damnation of Faust as an opera at Monte Carlo in 1903, amid scenes of the wildest enthusiasm.

In his "Faust" Berlioz has given us a musical legend which has all the picturesqueness of the original work.

Whatever severe critics may say of its merits in the highest artistic sense, it is nevertheless a wonderful work. Strange eccentricities and rare beauties are found side by side; even the wild orgie of fiends called "Pandemonium," which almost transgresses the license of genius, must be admired for its astounding orchestral effects. On the other hand, there are melodies of purest beauty, such as the numbers for *Marguerite*. However, the most striking numbers

AUERBACH'S BEER CELLAR IN LEIPSIC—ACT II

in the opera are those written by Berlioz for *Mephistopheles*, three of which have been most effectively rendered for the Victor by Plançon.

THE OPERA

Berlioz, disregarding Goethe's poem, located the opening scene on a plain in Hungary simply to excuse the interpolation of the Rakoczy March. We quote Berlioz himself here: "The march on the Hungarian Rakoczy theme, written one night at Vienna, made such a sensation at Pesth that I introduced it into my Faust score, taking the liberty of putting my hero in Hungary and making him witness the passage of a Hungarian troop across the plain where he is wandering in reverie." But Raoul Gunsbourg, who adapted the cantata for the stage, changed the first scene to a room with open windows showing the peasants dancing and the military passing by to the strains of the Hungarian March. Here *Faust* soliloquizes on the vanity of all things, while the people make merry outside, and the march of the soldiers makes an inspiring finish to the scene.

COPY'T MISHKIN

RENAUD'S STRIKING CONCEPTION OF MEPHISTO

Hungarian (Rakoczy) March
By Sousa's Band
31424 12-inch, $1.00

This is Berlioz's treatment of the famous "Rakoczy March," known as a national Hungarian melody for a hundred years. Its stirring measures so fascinated the composer that, contrary to his original intention, he laid the scene of his "Faust" legend in Hungary in order that he might make use of this wild and pulse-quickening melody. His treatment of it is brilliant in the extreme, and it remains one of the most effective portions of his "Faust."

In this connection it is interesting to remember that Liszt, although a warm friend of Berlioz, considered himself aggrieved and wrote in 1882: "My transcription of the Rakoczy March * * * is twice as long as the well-known version of Berlioz, and it was written *before* his. Delicate sentiments of friendship for the illustrious Frenchman induced me to withhold it from publication until after his death. * * * In writing it he made use of one of my earlier transcriptions, particularly in the harmony."

Scene II shows *Faust* alone in his study, as in the Gounod version. He is about to take poison, when the strains of the Easter hymn come from the adjoining church and arrest his purpose. *Mephistopheles* then appears and suggests that they go forth and see the world together, to which *Faust* consents.

In the third scene *Faust* and *Mephistopheles* go to a beer cellar in Leipsic, where students and soldiers are carousing. *Brander* sings his song of the rat, which as in the Gounod opera, meets with but ironical praise from *Mephistopheles,* and he volunteers his famous "Romance of the Flea," a curiosity of music as effective as it is difficult to render.

Chanson de la puce   (Song of the Flea)

By Pol Plançon, Bass
(In French)   81087   10-inch, $2.00

Gounod's *Mephistopheles* is mild and innocent by the side of the strange utterances of the Devil as portrayed by Berlioz.

This is one of the most interesting numbers in the work, for Berlioz has described, by means of clever forms in the accompaniment, the skipping of the flea in various directions. The words are most fantastic—

> Once a king, be it noted, had a fine and lusty flea,
> And on this flea he doted, cherish'd him tenderly,
> So he sent for his tailor, and to the tailor spake:
> "Please to measure this youngster, and coat and breeches make!"

Faust dislikes the scene, and the two vanish from the gaze of the astonished students amid a fiery glow.

Voici des roses   ('Mid Banks of Roses)

By Pol Plançon, Bass
(In French)   85117   12-inch, $3.00
By Mattio Battistini, Baritone
(In Spanish)   92023   12-inch, 3.00

COPY'T DUPONT   PLANÇON

We next discover *Faust* asleep in a lonely forest on the banks of the Elbe, where the demon murmurs a softly penetrating melody into his ear, lulling him to slumber with these seductive words—

> 'Mid banks of roses, softly the light reposes,
> On this fair, fragrant bed, rest, O Faust, rest thy head—
> Here slumber, while lovely visions haunt thy dream
> Of radiant forms, rare lips and eyes that fondly beam!

while the gnomes and sylphs dance through his dreams, and the vision of *Marguerite* is seen for the first time.

The next scene corresponds to the Garden Scene of Gounod, and shows a room in *Marguerite's* cottage. The demon now summons the will-o'-the-wisps in this evocation:

Mephist. Recit.

Ye spir-its of in-constant fire,   Hast-en here,   on the wings of air!

The sprites come flying to *Marguerite's* door to aid in her enchantment, and the demon continues:

> Ye spirits of caprice and of evil, conspire
> To enchant and subdue, and win a maiden soul.
> Now dance, ye sons of Evil, dance in the name of the devil,
> Will-o'-the-wisp and gnome, dance, or away you go!

Then follows the beautiful dance of the will-o'-the-wisps, after which *Mephistopheles* sings—

> "To this lute, I'll sing a serenade . . .
> One that shall please the lady . . . .
> It is moral, her tastes to suit!"

Serenade—Mephistopheles

By Pol Plançon, Bass
(In French)   81034   10-inch, $2.00

Mephistopheles then warbles in his scoffing voice this mocking serenade:

Mephist.

De-vant la mai-son De ce-lui qui t'a do- - - re, de ce lui, de ce-lui qui t'a do re
Dear Kath'rine, why to the door of thy lov- - - - er, to the door, to the door of thy lov-er

in the accompaniment of which Berlioz has reproduced the peculiar effect of the guitar by *pizzicato* crescendos for strings.

BOYER
FOURTH ACT SETTING—DAMNATION OF FAUST

MEPHISTOPHELES:
Dear Katherine, why to the
    door of thy lover,
    Drawest thou nigh?
Why there timidly hover? why
    art there?
Oh, sweet maiden, beware;
    come away do not enter;
It were folly to venture,
    Refrain, nor enter there!

Ah, heed thee well, fair lass,
    Lest thy lover betray thee;
Then good night, alas!
    From ill-hap what shall stay
    thee?
But let thy lover prove the
    truth of his advances;
When the ring brightly
    glances,
Ah! then only, believe his
    love!

Berlioz's *Mephistopheles* is
a much more sardonic and
less gentlemanly devil than the
one we are accustomed to see in Gounod's opera. Plançon interprets this difficult character
admirably, and delivers this sneering serenade with great effectiveness.

While the sprites dance *Marguerite* apparently sleeps, but soon comes from the house in
a kind of trance. She tries to enter the church, but the influence of *Mephistopheles* prevents,
and she returns to the house and falls into the arms of *Faust*.

The last act contains four scenes. Scene I shows a moonlit room where the unhappy
Marguerite sings her lament. This changes to a rocky pass where *Mephistopheles* informs
Faust that *Marguerite* is about to be executed for the murder of her mother. *Faust* demands that
she be saved, but is first required by *Mephistopheles* to sign the fatal contract which pledges
his soul to the Devil. Summoning the infernal steeds *Vortex* and *Giaour*, the wild Ride to
Hell commences, shown by a striking moving panorama, while at the close the angels are
seen hovering above the town to rescue the soul of the pardoned *Marguerite*.

L'ART DU THÉÂTRE
THE RIDE TO HELL—ACT V

DINORAH
(Din-oh'-rah)
OPERA IN THREE ACTS

Libretto by Barbier and Carré.   Music by Giacomo Meyerbeer.   First production Paris,
1859.   First London production July 26, 1859.   First New York production November 24,
1864, with Cordier, Brignoli and Amodio.

Cast

HOËL, a goatherd ....Bass
CORENTINO, bag-piper ....Tenor
DINORAH, betrothed to Hoël..Soprano
HUNTSMAN ....Bass

Place: Breton village of Ploërmel.

FAURE AS HOËL, 1859

Although the name of Meyerbeer is usually associated with *Robert le Diable, Prophéte* and *Huguenots,* his opera, *Pardon de Ploërmel* (afterwards revised and renamed *Dinorah),* was at one time a favorite work with opera-lovers.

The revival of Meyerbeer's sparkling opera during the last Manhattan season was most welcome, not only for its tunefulness, but because it was an ideal medium for the exhibition of Mme. Tetrazzini's marvelous gifts of vocalism.

Old opera-goers in America will remember the productions of the past—that arranged for Marie Van Zandt in 1892; Patti's famous performance a dozen years before; and the fine impersonations of Gerster, di Murska and Marimon.   But it is safe to say that no exponent of the part of the wandering Breton shepherdess has ever excelled Mme. Tetrazzini in the rôle.

The plot is utterly absurd—its demented goat-girl, seeking a runaway lover; the lover himself, who contrary to operatic precedent is a baritone, and who spends a year chasing an imaginary treasure; a weak-kneed bag-piper.   These are the principal characters.

But in the music Meyerbeer has atoned for the triviality of the libretto, and the audience listens to the delightful melodies and pays little attention to the plot.

The action is laid in Brittany.   *Dinorah,* a maiden of he village of Ploërmel, is about to be wedded to *Hoël,* a goat-herd, when a storm destroys the house of the bride's father.   *Hoël* resolves to rebuild it, and goes off to seek treasure in a haunted region, while *Dinorah,* thinking herself deserted, loses her reason, and wanders through the country with her faithful goat, seeking the absent *Hoël.*

As the curtain rises, *Dinorah* enters in her bridal garments, seeking her pet goat, and finding the animal asleep, sings this lullaby to him.   So lovely an air is worthy of a better object.

Si, carina caprettina (Yes, My Beloved One)

By Giuseppina Huguet, Soprano   (*In Italian*)   *35180 12-inch, $1.25

Mme. Huguet has sung this pretty air with charming fluency, and the record is one of the most attractive in her list.   The translation follows:

Slumber, darling, sweetly slumber,
Sleep, my belov'd one, sleep!
Soft the evening breeze is playing,
'Neath the cooling shadows here
Flows a streamlet, fresh and clear,
Swift, among the flowers straying.
Alas! six days has she been away,
Nor yet returns!
Perchance she has wandered on the hills

Amid the thorns!
Ah! wert thou to be seized by the wolf—fear not!
I will be there to defend thee—fear not!
Yes, darling sleep in peace,
Sweet little birds your warbling ceas,
My beauteous one must sleep.
Awake her not!   Yet softer still!

Double-Faced Record—On opposite side is the Mad Scene from Hamlet, by Mme. Huguet.

Corentino, a bag-piper, enters and is terrified at the sight of *Dinorah*, believing her to be an evil fairy about whom he had heard, who causes the runaway traveler to dance till he dies. *Dinorah*, in a spirit of mischief, makes him dance until he is exhausted, and runs away laughing.

Hoël enters, still seeking the treasure, and confides in *Corentino*, telling him that the wizard with whom he had lived for a year had instructed him to seek for a white goat which would guide him to the gold. The bell of *Dinorah's* goat is heard, and *Hoël* pursues it, dragging with him the terrified *Corentino*.

The second act begins with the famous shadow dance, for which Meyerbeer has furnished some most beautiful music. *Dinorah* enters, and seeing her shadow in the moonlight, imagines it is a friend and sings and dances to it.

COPY'T FOLEY

TETRAZZINI AS DINORAH

Ombra leggiera (Shadow Song)

By Luisa Tetrazzini, Soprano 88298 12-inch, $3.00
By Maria Galvany, Soprano 88222 12-inch, 3.00

Ombra Leggiera

(*Light Flitting Shadow*)

Light flitting shadow, companion gay
    Go not away!
Play here beside me, dark fears betide me
When thou dost go far from me!
Ah! go not away, go not away!

Each coming morn I thee would find,
Ah prithee stay and dance with me!
If thou wilt stay, nor go away,
Thou thus shalt hear me sing.

Know'st thou not that Hoël loves me?
That as his bride he claims me!
Love well hath known
Our two hearts to unite!
(*A cloud passes over the moon—the shadow disappears.*)

This dance is accompanied by a waltz, which is full of the most brilliant vocal effects, including a florid cadenza for voice and flute, as in Lucia.

The act closes with the rescue of *Dinorah* by *Hoël* when the bridge, on which she was crossing a ravine, gives away.

Act III opens with the famous "Hunter's Song," long a favorite concert number.

Chant du Chasseur (Hunter's Song)

By Pol Plançon, Bass (*Piano acc.*)
(*In French*) 81065 10-inch, $2.00

On, on to the hunt!
To follow the trace of beast or bird.
The day is awake,
The mist from the lake
Rising, passes over,

The fresh morning breeze
Plays light in the trees,
Like a young, a young and happy lover!
Hunting is jolly, when night is over.

Hoël enters, bearing the form of *Dinorah*, who is still senseless. Thinking her dead, he bitterly reproaches himself in the great air, *Sei vendicata*.

Sei vendicata assai (Thou art Avenged!)

By Mario Ancona, Baritone (*In Italian*) 88169 12-inch, $3.00

HOËL:
'Twas on this self-same spot—a year ago
When from the tempest an asylum my Dinorah
  sought;
Within these arms I pressed her; and now!
Dead!—ah! heaven, I'll not believe it yet!
Look up again, dear angel, thy pardon I im-
  plore!

(*He anxiously watches Dinorah, who gradu-
  ally recovers.*)
Great heaven! my pray'r hath risen unto thee!
Yes! she breathes again; her eyes she opens!
But why thus fixedly they gaze upon me?
O heaven, I had forgotten
That grief of reason had bereft her!

Dinorah now opens her eyes and recognizes *Hoël*, her reason having been restored by the shock. The reunited lovers go to the village, are greeted by their friends, and the curtain falls on preparations for the wedding.

(Italian)
DON GIOVANNI
(Don Jee-oh-vahn'-ee)

(French)
DON JUAN
(Don Wahn')

OPERA IN TWO ACTS

Libretto by Lorenzo da Ponte. Music by Wolfgang Amadeus Mozart. First produced at Prague, October 29, 1787, and at Vienna, May 7, 1788. First London production April 12, 1817; produced in New York May 29, 1826. Some notable revivals occurred in 1898 with Sembrich, Nordica, Eames and Plançon, and in 1909 with Russ, Donalda, Bonci and Renaud.

Cast

DON GIOVANNI, a licentious young nobleman......................Baritone
DON OCTAVIO, (*Oct-tah'-vee-oh*) betrothed to Donna Anna..............Tenor
LEPORELLO, (*Lep-oh-rel'-low*) servant of Don Giovanni...................Bass
DON PEDRO, (*Pay-dro*) the Commandant..............................Bass
DONNA ANNA, his daughter.......................................Soprano
MASETTO, (*Mas-set'-to*) a peasant.................................Bass
ZERLINA, (*Zer-lee'-nah*) betrothed to Masetto.......................Soprano
DON ELVIRA, a lady of Burgos...................................Soprano

Peasants, Musicians, Dancers, Demons.

Scene and Period : Seville, in the middle of the seventeenth century.

Mozart's Don Giovanni was written in 1787 and produced during the same year at Prague. Da Ponte, the librettist, was a Viennese Court dramatist, who had also written Le Nozze di Figaro. The plot of the opera was probably founded upon a play entitled *El Burlador de Sevilla y Convirada de piedra,* attributed to Tirso de Molina, a Spanish monk and prior of a monastery at Madrid. This had also served as a basis for numerous other "Don Juan" plays and operas by Fabrizzi, Gardi, Raimondi, Carnicer and latterly Dargomyszky, the Russian composer.

ACT I

SCENE I—*The Courtyard of the Commandant's Palace at Seville. It is Night*

The wicked *Don Giovanni,* ever pursuing his gay conquests, attempts to enter *Donna Anna's* apartments. She cries for help and he tries to escape, but is pursued by the angry girl, who endeavors to penetrate his disguise. Her father comes to the rescue and is mortally wounded by the *Don,* who makes his escape, followed by *Leporello,* his servant. *Donna Anna* is overcome with grief, and charges her betrothed, *Don Octavio,* to avenge her father's death.

SCENE II—*An Inn in a Deserted Spot Outside Seville*

Don Giovanni and *Leporello* enter and conceal themselves as a lady approaches in a carriage. Hoping for a new conquest, the *Don* comes forward, hat in hand, but is surprised to find that it is *Donna Elvira,* a young woman whom he has lately deceived and deserted. She denounces him for his baseness and he makes his escape, leaving *Leporello* to explain as best he can. *Leporello* rather enjoys the situation, produces his diary, and adds to the lady's anger by reading a list of the mistresses of the *Don.* This list is recited by *Leporello* in the famous *Il catalogo.*

COPY'T DUPONT

SCOTTI AS DON GIOVANNI

65

Madamina, il catalogo (Gentle Lady, this List)

By Marcel Journet, Bass	(*In Italian*)	64150	10-inch, $1.00
By Arcangelo Rossi, (*Double-faced—See page 69*)	(*Italian*)	62623	10-inch, .75

Nella bionda (The Fair One)

By Marcel Journet, Bass   (*In Italian*)   74191   12-inch, 1.50

CLICHÉ DU GUY   LEPORELLO

LEPORELLO:
Ev'ry country, ev'ry township, fully confesses
Those of the sex whom to his rank he presses.
Gentle lady, this my catalogue numbers
All whose charms lent my master beguiling.
'Tis a document of my compiling,
An it please ye, peruse it with me.
In Italia,—six hundred and forty;
Then in Germany,—double fifty seem plenty;
While in old Spain here,—we count thousands
  three!
Some you see are country damsels,
Waiting-maids and city ma'amselles,
Countess', duchess', baronesses,
Viscount'—ev'ry kind of 'esses.
Womenfolk of all conditions,
Ev'ry form and ev'ry state!

Journet's *Leporello* is a unique performance of its kind, and his characterization always stands forth as an admirable foil to the polished villainies of the suave and distinguished *Don*. This great buffo number, usually called the *Catalogue Song*, is full of the broadest humor, and is given by this artist with all the sly humor, gaiety, irony and sentiment which it requires.

Donna Elvira is horrified and drives off, swearing vengeance.

SCENE III—*In the Suburbs of Seville. Don Giovanni's Palace Visible on the Right*

A rustic wedding party comprising *Zerlina*, *Masetto* and a company of peasants are enjoying an outing. *Don Giovanni* and *Leporello* appear, and the *Don* is charmed at the sight of so much youthful beauty. He bids *Leporello* conduct the party to his palace and give them refreshments, contriving, however, to detain *Zerlina*. *Masetto* protests, but the *Don* points significantly to his sword and the bridegroom follows the peasants.

The *Don* then proceeds to flatter the young girl and tells her she is too beautiful for such a clown as *Masetto*. She is impressed and coquettes with him in the melodious duet, *La ci darem*, the witty phrases and delicate harmonies of which make it one of the gems of Mozart's opera.

Là ci darem la mano (Thy Little Hand, Love!)

By Geraldine Farrar, Soprano, and
    Antonio Scotti, Baritone
      (*In Italian*)   89015   12-inch, $4.00

By Emma Eames, Soprano, and Emilio
    de Gogorza, Baritone
      (*In Italian*)   89005   12-inch, 4.00

By Graziella Pareto, Soprano, and Titta
    Ruffo, Baritone
      (*In Italian*)   92505   12-inch, 4.00

By Mattia Battistini, Baritone, and
    Emilia Corsi, Soprano
      (*In Italian*)   92024   12-inch, 3.00

VANDYK, LONDON

NIELSEN AS ZERLINA

JEAN DE RESZKE AS DON GIO-
VANNI. HIS DÉBUT AS A
BARITONE (LONDON, 1875)

This celebrated number, which has been sung by many famous artists during the one hundred and twenty years since its first hearing, is one of the best examples of the many sparkling concerted numbers which Mozart has written. Always interesting, it is wholly delightful when sung by such artists as those who have rendered it for the Victor. Not less than four versions, by famous exponents of the characters of *Zerlina* and *Don Giovanni,* are presented here.

> DON GIOVANNI:
> Nay, bid me not resign, love, coldly the hand
> I press,
> Oh! say thou wilt be mine, love, breathe but
> that one word "yes."
> ZERLINA:
> I would and yet I would not, I feel my heart
> misgive,
> Shouldst thou prove false, I could not, become
> thy scorn and live.
> DON GIOVANNI:
> Come then, oh come then, dearest.
> ZERLINA:
> Yet should thy fondness alter.
> DON GIOVANNI:
> Nay, love, in vain thou fearest.
> BOTH:
> Yes, hand and heart uniting, each other's
> cause requiting,
> Our joy no bounds shall know!

Miss Farrar's *Zerlina* is a dainty and fascinating character, and she sings the music brilliantly. It is hardly necessary to say anything about Scotti's *Don Giovanni,* as it is quite familiar to opera-goers, ranking among his best impersonations. The rendition by Mme. Eames and Mr. de Gogorza is a most delightful one, while two other records by famous European artists are also offered.

Giovanni is about to lead *Zerlina* away, when *Donna Elvira,* who has been watching, rescues the young girl and carries her off, to the chagrin of the *Don. Donna Anna* now enters with *Octavio,* who asks the help of his friend *Don Giovanni* in tracing the murderer of *Donna Anna's* father. The *Don* assures them of his devotion, and goes to his palace, while *Donna Anna* tells her lover that she recognizes by his voice that *Don Giovanni* is the one who slew her father. They depart, and *Leporello* and the *Don* enter. The servant tells his master that when *Donna Elvira* and *Zerlina* arrived at the palace, and *Elvira* attempted to tell the peasants the truth about the *Don,* he led her gently outside the gate and then locked it. He is complimented by his master, who bids him prepare for the feast of the evening. Left alone, the gay *Don* sings his brilliant *Drinking Song,* famous in every land.

ABOTT AND RENAUD AS ZERLINA AND
DON GIOVANNI

Fin ch' han dal vino (Wine, Flow a Fountain)

By Antonio Scotti, Baritone   *(Piano acc.)*
   (In Italian)   85031   12-inch, $3.00

The scene changes to *Don Giovanni's* garden. *Zerlina* is endeavoring to make her peace with *Masetto,* but he is sulky. She then sings her lovely *Batti, batti.*

Batti, batti, o bel Masetto (Scold Me, dear Masetto)

By Geraldine Farrar, Soprano
   (In Italian)   88126   12-inch, $3.00
By Marcella Sembrich, Soprano   *(In Italian)*   88026   12-inch, $3.00

This gentle number is in striking contrast to the brilliant writing in the lighter bits of *Zerlina's* music.

> Chide me, dear Masetto,
> Chide Zerlina at your will;
> Like the patient lamb I'll suffer,
> Meek and mute and loving still.
>
> Ah! I see, love, you're relenting,
> Pardon, kneeling, I implore!
> Night and day, to thee, devoted,
> Here I vow to err no more.

Masetto is only half appeased, but goes in to dance with his bride. *Donna Anna, Donna Elvira* and *Don Octavio*, disguised and masked, enter and sing a trio, in which they pledge themselves to have revenge on the traitor.

The scene changes to the interior of the palace, where the ball is in progress. *Don Giovanni* continues his efforts to get *Zerlina* away from her jealous and watchful lover, and finally succeeds, but *Zerlina* calls for help and *Masetto* and the three conspirators rush to her assistance. They denounce *Don Giovanni*, who defies them with drawn sword, and makes his escape from the palace.

COPY'T DUPONT

MAUREL AS DON GIOVANNI

ACT II

SCENE I—*A Square in Seville. Donna Elvira's Residence on the Left. It is a Moonlight Night*

Don Giovanni, followed by his servant, enters, wrapped in a mantle and carrying a mandolin. He has heard of a pretty servant whom *Donna Elvira* possesses, and is plotting to get the mistress out of the way. As *Elvira* sits at her window, he addresses her, pretending to be repentant, but when she comes out he pushes *Leporello* forward to impersonate him. While they are conversing, the *Don* makes a great outcry and the pair run off in fright. The coast clear, the *Don* sings his famous *Serenade* to the fair waiting maid.

RENAUD AS DON GIOVANNI

Serenata, "Deh vieni alla finestra" (Open Thy Window, Love)

By Antonio Scotti, Baritone
(*In Italian*) 88194 12-inch, $3.00

By M. Hector Dufranne, Baritone
(*In French*) *45011 10-inch, 1.00

By Giuseppè de Luca, Baritone (*Piano acc.*) (*In Italian*) *62623 10-inch, .75

DON GIOVANNI:
> Ope, ope thy casement, dearest,
> Thyself one moment show;
> Oh, if my pray'r thou hearest,
> Wave but that arm of snow.
> Canst thou my ceaseless sighing
> With cold indif'rence greet?
>
> Ah! wouldst thou see me dying
> Despairing, at thy feet?
> Thy lip outvies Hymettian-honied bowers;
> Virtue worthy an angel, thy heart doth cherish;
> Thy sigh were balm amid a heav'n of flowers;
> O, for one kiss, one word, this soul would perish!

Scotti's impersonation of *Don Giovanni* is admirable in every respect. He is the profligate nobleman and irresistible wooer to the life, and sings the difficult score with ease. This famous serenade is given by the baritone with the grace and ease which never fail him.

* *Double-Faced Record—For title of opposite side see DOUBLE-FACED DON GIOVANNI RECORDS, page 69.*

EDOUARD DE RESZKE AS LEPORELLO

His amours are rudely interrupted by *Masetto*, who appears with a company of villagers, all armed with muskets, seeking the villain. The *Don*, pretending to be *Leporello*, offers to put them on the right track. Then follows a series of amusing situations, ending with the capture of the supposed *Don* by the three conspirators, but it proves to be *Leporello*, who takes advantage of the situation to make his escape.

At the close of this scene occurs the beautiful air of *Donna Elvira*, in which she reproaches the *Don* for deserting her.

In quali eccessi (Aria of Donna Elvira)

By Johanna Gadski, Soprano

(*In Italian*)   88253   12-inch, $3.00

Mme. Gadski has long been recognized as one of the foremost exponents of Mozart in this country. The music of this master demands singers of great understanding and feeling, who must possess not only voice but intelligence and taste.

That Gadski possesses these qualifications in ample measure is fully apparent to all who listen to this superb reproduction.

PHOTO BERGER   LEPORELLO

The next scene shows the Cathedral Square, with the statue of the murdered Commandant in the centre. The *Don* and *Leporello* enter, and are discussing the events of the evening, when the statue speaks to them. *Leporello* is terrified, but the *Don* defies all spirits and boldly invites the statue to supper at his palace.

The scene changes to the banquet hall in the palace of the *Don*. In the midst of the festivities a loud knocking is heard. The guests flee in terror, the lights go out, and the gigantic figure of the Commandant appears at the door. *Leporello* cowers in terror under the table, but *Don Giovanni* is defiant until the ghost seizes his hand, when he feels for the first time a terrible fear. The statue sinks, flames appear on all sides, and demons rise and seize the guilty libertine, who utters a fearful cry of agony as he is carried down into the fiery abyss.

DOUBLE-FACED AND MISCELLANEOUS DON GIOVANNI RECORDS

Minuet	By Victor Dance Orchestra	
Forward March—Two Step	By Victor Dance Orchestra	35060 12-inch, $1.25
Sérénade By M. Hector Dufranne, Baritone (*In French*)		
Si j'étais Roi—Un regard de ses yeux!		45011 10-inch, 1.00
By Leon Beyle, Tenor (*In French*)		
Madamina, il catalogo (Gentle Lady, This List)		
By Arcangelo Rossi, Bass (*In Italian*)		
Serenata—Deh! vieni alla finestra (Open Thy		62623 10-inch, .75
Window, Love) By Giuseppè de Luca, Baritone		
(*Piano acc.*) (*In Italian*)		

THE GARDEN—ACT III

(Italian)

DON PASQUALE

(Don Pas-kwah'-lay)

COMIC OPERA IN THREE ACTS

Text and music by Gaetano Donizetti. Libretto adapted from the older Italian opera, *Ser Marc' Antonio,* by Camerano. First presented at the Théâtre des Italiens, Paris, on January 4, 1843. First London production June 30, 1843. First New York production March 9, 1846.

Recently revived at the Metropolitan with Sembrich, Scotti and Rossi; and at the Boston Opera House with Nielsen, Bourrillon, Antonio Pini-Corsi and Fornari.

Characters

DON PASQUALE, an old bachelor....................................Bass
DR. MALATESTA, his friend, a physician ....Baritone
ERNESTO, nephew of Don Pasquale ....Tenor
NORINA, beloved of Ernesto ....Soprano
A NOTARY...Baritone
Chorus of Valets and Chambermaids, Majordomo, Dressmaker and Hairdresser.

Scene and Period :   Rome;   the beginning of the nineteenth century.

This brightest of genuine lyric comedies always appeals to that class of opera-goers who find the present-day comic opera or musical comedy to be cheap, gaudy and lacking in genuine humor. *Don Pasquale* is pure entertainment, nothing else, the true spirit of comedy being found in the music as well as the plot; and both are delightful when the opera is presented by such artists as the Victor has assembled for this series.

ACT I

SCENE—*A Room in Don Pasquale's House*

The *Don* is eagerly awaiting the arrival of *Dr. Malatesta,* who has promised to obtain for him a young and lovely bride.

Son nov'ore ('Tis Nine O'Clock !)

By Antonio Pini-Corsi, Baritone, and Ernesto Badini, Baritone

(*In Italian*) *68273   12-inch, $1.25

The *Doctor* enters, declares he has found the bride, and proceeds to describe the charmer. The *Don* is overjoyed, and insists on seeing the lady at once. When the *Doctor* leaves, *Pasquale* gives vent to his feelings in an amusing air.

Un foco insolito (A Fire All Unfelt Before)

By Antonio Pini-Corsi, Baritone, and Ernesto Badini, Baritone

(*In Italian*) *62104   10-inch, $0.75

PASQUALE:

A fire, all unfelt before,
Burns in my heart's core:
I can resist no more—
I'll strive no longer.
Of old age enfeebling me,
Forgot is the misery,
Feeling still young to be—
Than twenty much stronger.

Ah! hasten speedily,
Sweet little bride, to me!
Yes, I am born again! Now for my nephew,—
By playing thus the careless, heedless hair-
  brain,
See what it is the wise and wary gain!
(*Looking off.*)
Ah! here the very man comes, apropos!

His nephew enters, and is again urged by his uncle to give up *Norina,* whom the uncle calls a vain, coquettish widow. *Ernesto* refuses, and *Don Pasquale* announces his intention of marrying and disinheriting his nephew. The young man, at first incredulous, is finally convinced that his uncle is in earnest and gives way to despair, beginning his first air:

Sogno soave e casto (Fond Dream of Love)

By Giuseppe Acerbi, Tenor   (*In Italian*) *62624   10-inch, $0.75

ERNESTO:

Sweet holy dreams I loved to cherish
Of early youth, adieu! ye vanish!
If I e'er long'd for riches, splendor,
It was but for thee, love;

But now, poor and abandon'd, I,
Reduc'd from my condition high,
Sooner than thee in misery see,
Dearest, I'll renounce thee.

Before leaving his uncle, *Ernesto* begs him to consult *Dr. Malatesta* for advice, but *Don Pasquale* says it was the *Doctor* himself who proposed the plan and offered his own sister as the happy bride. *Ernesto* is astonished to hear that the *Doctor,* who he thought was his friend, had deserted him.

SCENE II—*A Room in Norina's House*

Norina is reading a romance, and at the beginning of her air quotes from the book:

Quel guardo (Glances so Soft)

By Alice Nielsen, Soprano   (*In Italian*)   74087   12-inch, $1.50
By Giuseppina Huguet, Soprano   (*In Italian*) *68272   12-inch, 1.25

NORINA:

"Glances so soft revealing
The flame of truest love,

To that sweet maiden kneeling
He swore he'd faithful prove!"

Cavatina—So anch'io la virtù magica (I, Too, Thy Magic Powers Know)

By Amelia Pollini, Soprano   (*In Italian*) *62103   10-inch, $0.75

She then declares that she too knows the value of a glance and smile.

NORINA:

I, too, thy magic virtues know,
Of glance well tim'd and tender,
A gentle smile, born to beguile,
I know—an old offender!
A hidden tear, a languor near,

I know the mode, oh, dear,
Of love's bewitching wiles,
His facile arts and guiles. . . .
To lure with wanton smiles,
I know the modes, oh, dear!

*Double-Faced Record—For title of opposite side see DOUBLE-FACED DON PASQUALE RECORDS, page 75.

A servant gives her a letter from *Ernesto,* just as the *Doctor* enters and informs her that he has conceived a scheme to force her lover's guardian to consent to the marriage. *Norina* declares she will have nothing to do with it, bidding him to read *Ernesto's* despairing letter, in which the young man tells her he is disinherited and will leave Rome, bidding her a last farewell.

The *Doctor* soothes her, telling her he will induce *Ernesto* to remain, and then reveals the details of the plot against *Don Pasquale,* in which he proposes to play on the vanity of the old bachelor, by pretending to find him a young and lovely wife. They decide that *Norina* shall play the part of this girl, and go through a mock marriage with *Don Pasquale.* *Norina* is delighted and begins to rehearse her new rôle. This takes the form of a charming duet, which ends the first act and which is always greatly admired. Two records of this sprightly duet, at widely varying prices, are cataloged here.

Pronta io son (My Part I'll Play)

By Marcella Sembrich, Soprano, and Antonio Scotti, Baritone
(*In Italian*) 89002 12-inch, $4.00
By Giuseppina Huguet, Soprano, and Ernesto Badini, Baritone
(*In Italian*) *68272 12-inch, 1.25

NORINA:
My part I'll play, if not offending
Against my lover's repose and quiet;
Well the plot with me will fare!
DOCTOR:
Our plot but tends, you may believe,
Don Pasquale to deceive.
NORINA:
We're quite agreed, and I'm enlisted.
Would you have me gay or tearful?
DOCTOR:
Listen, and you'll all be told;—
You must play simplicity.
NORINA:
I'll lessons give—leave that to me.
"I'm so confused—I'm young, you know—
Thank you—Your servant,—Yes, sir,—Oh!"

DOCTOR:
Bravo, bravo, capital!
It can't be better—all goes well!
NORINA:
Head turned aside—"Oh fie! oh fie!"
DOCTOR:
Pursed-up mouth—"Ashamed am I."
NORINA:
"I'm quite confus'd, my thoughts take wing—"
DOCTOR:
Oh, clever creature! Just the thing!
BOTH:
Of this old fool, all sense who spurn'd;—
This time the head will be quite turn'd!

The scene is continued in another sprightly duet, which closes the act.

Vado corro (Haste We!)

By Giuseppina Huguet and Ernesto Badini (*Italian*) *62097 10-inch, $0.75

ACT II

SCENE—*A Richly Furnished Hall in Don Pasquale's House*

Don Pasquale, in the most youthful of wedding garments, enters and struts up and down, admiring himself, until the *Doctor* arrives with *Norina,* who is closely veiled. She pretends to be shrinking and frightened, and the *Doctor,* beginning a delightfully humorous trio, the first of the concerted numbers in this act, begs her to have courage.

The pretended notary now arrives, and another comical scene ensues as the mock ceremony is performed. *Pasquale,* so much in love that his judgment is clouded, is not only induced to sign over one-half his property to his wife, but agrees that she shall be absolute mistress of the house. As *Norina* is signing, *Ernesto's* voice is heard outside demanding admittance, having come to bid his uncle farewell. He is amazed to see *Norina* posing as the *Doctor's* sister and about to be wedded to his uncle, and tries to interfere, but is restrained by *Malatesta.*

The moment *Norina* affixes her signature to the contract her manner changes, and when *Pasquale* attempts to embrace her she coldly asks him not to be so rude. *Pasquale* is astonished and *Ernesto* laughs, which enrages the old man so that he orders his nephew from the room. *Norina* stops him and says that as *Don Pasquale* is too old, fat and feeble to attend a young wife, she must have a young cavalier to attend her, and signifies that *Ernesto* is her choice. *Don Pasquale* is thunderstruck and attempts to protest, but *Norina* warns him that if her words are not sufficient to keep him in his place she will beat him! This is the last straw, and the bewildered old man stands in a daze, his brain refusing to comprehend what has happened!

This tableau is followed by the quartet, *E rimasto.*

Double-Faced Record—For title of opposite side see DOUBLE-FACED DON PASQUALE RECORDS, page 75.

E rimasto la impietrato (He Stands Immovable)

By Linda Brambilla, Soprano; Antonio Pini-Corsi, Baritone; Gaetano Pini-Corsi, Tenor; Agusto Scipioni, Bass

(In Italian) *16566 10-inch, $0.75

PASQUALE:
Dream I? Sleep I? What's amiss?
Kicks—cuffs: good—a fine pretext—
'Tis well she warn'd me now of this—what's
 that mean?
We shall see what's coming next!
I, Don Pasquale, she'd think meet
To trample underneath her feet!
NORINA AND ERNESTO:
He stands petrified, and seems—

To know not if he wakes or dreams!
He's like a man by lightning struck!
No drop of blood runs in his veins.
MALATESTA:
Take heart, Pasquale, my old buck,
Don't be discouraged, use your brains.
NORINA:
Now then, at least, my worthy friend,
You must begin to comprehend.

The great finale to Act II then follows, and the curtain always descends amid a gale of laughter from the audience. *Norina* rings a bell, summoning the servants, and announces that she is now sole mistress of the house. She orders new servants engaged, two carriages, new furniture, etc., planning expenditures on a lavish scale. *Don Pasquale* attempts to protest, but is silenced, and in a voice choked with rage and astonishment begins the finale.

Son tradito (I Am Betrayed!)

By Giuseppina Huguet, Soprano; Antonio Pini-Corsi, Baritone; Gaetano Pini-Corsi, Tenor; Agusto Scipioni, Bass

(In Italian) *62097 10-inch, $0.75

PASQUALE:
I am betray'd, trod down and beat,
A laughing stock to all I meet;
Oh! with mingled rage and spite
I am suffocating quite!
NORINA (to Ernesto):
Now you see, ungrateful heart,
How unjust was your suspicion:
Love, to bring him to submission,
Counsell'd me to play this part.
ERNESTO (to Norina):
You are justified, dear heart;
Momentary my suspicion.
Love, to bring him to submission,
Counsell'd thee to play this part.

ALL (pointing to Don Pasquale):
Don Pasquale, poor, dear wight,
Is nearly suffocated quite!
MALATESTA (to Pasquale):
You're a little heated, really—
Do go to bed, dear Don Pasquale.
(To Norina, in a tone of reproof.)
On my brother-in-law to play
Thus, I'll not endure, I say!
(To the lovers, who are embracing behind Don
 Pasquale's back.)
Silly ones, for Heaven's sake, pray,
Don't, I beg, yourselves betray!

ACT III

(Same as Act I—On the floor and furniture are piled up dresses, bandboxes, furs, etc., in great profusion. Servants are running to and fro with bustle and excitement)

Don Pasquale is seen amid the confusion, looking with utmost consternation at a huge pile of bills. He throws them down in despair, and as *Norina* approaches resolves to make one last attempt to remain master in his own house.

Signorina in tanta fretta (My Lady, Why This Haste?)

By Emilia Corsi, Soprano, and Antonio Pini-Corsi, Baritone

(In Italian) *68273 12-inch, $1.25

She is dressed to go out, and is hastening to her carriage when *Don Pasquale* begins:

PASQUALE:
Prithee, where are you running in such haste,
Young lady, may I beg you will inform me?
NORINA:
Oh! that's a thing that very soon is told:
I'm going to the theatre to divert me.
PASQUALE:
But the husband, with your leave—excuse me
Saying so—may perchance object to it.
NORINA:
The husband sees, and wisely holds his tongue:
For when he speaks there's no one listens to
 him.
PASQUALE (with rising warmth):
Not to put me to the trial, Madame,—
It is for your own good that I advise you—
You'll to your chamber go, this very instant—
Remain content at home—stay in the house.
NORINA (ironically):
Oh, really!

(With great heat.)
Why, you impertinent!
But there—take what you well deserve, sir!
(Boxes his ears.)
PASQUALE:
Ah!
(It is all over with you, Don Pasquale!
All that now remains for you to do
Is quietly to go and drown yourself!)
NORINA:
(I must confess, 'tis rather hard a lesson;
Yet was required to have its due effect.)
(To Don Pasquale):
I'm going now, then—
PASQUALE:
Oh, yes, certainly!
But do not take the trouble to return.
NORINA:
Oh, we shall see each other in the morning.
PASQUALE:
A face of wood—a closed door, you will find.

Double-Faced Record—For title of opposite side see DOUBLE-FACED DON PASQUALE RECORDS, page 75.

As she goes out she intentionally drops a note which *Don Pasquale* seizes and peruses. He is petrified to find that it reads:

"Adored Sophrania—
Between the hours of nine and ten this evening,
I shall be at the bottom of the garden—

By the small grated gate.
'Tis in a song I shall announce my coming;
Thine to command—thine faithfully;—adieu."

This is too much, and the unhappy man runs in search of *Malatesta*. *Ernesto* and the *Doctor* enter, discussing the plot, and the young man, after being instructed to be at the garden rendezvous at nine that evening, goes out.

Pasquale returns, and going solemnly up to the *Doctor*, exclaims:

> PASQUALE:
> Brother-in-law, in me, alas, you see
> A dead man, walking upright!

and tells him of the contents of the note. *Malatesta* pretends to sympathize and proposes that they lie in wait for the guilty lovers that evening and teach them a severe lesson. *Pasquale* gloats over his coming triumph, and begins the duet.

Aspetta aspetta cara esposina (Wait, Wait, Dear Little Wife)

By Antonio Pini-Corsi, Baritone, and Giovanni Polese, Baritone
(Double-Faced—See page 75) (*In Italian*) 62103 10-inch, $0.75

PASQUALE:
Wait, wait, dear little wife,
I soon reveng'd will be:
E'en now 'tis near, my life.
This night, without delay,
Thou must the reckoning pay!
Thou'lt see what little use
Now will be each excuse—
Useless thy tender smiles,
Sighs, and tears—and wiles—
All I have now at stake,
Conquer'd, again I'll take!

MALATESTA *(aside)*:
Oh, the poor fellow!
Vengeance he's prating;
Let the dolt bellow—
He knows not what's waiting!
He knows not he is building rare
Castles in the empty air:
He sees not, the simpleton—
That in the trap, poor elf,
He of his own accord
Now goes to throw himself!
(Exit together.)

SCENE II—*Don Pasquale's Garden—It is Night—Ernesto is Discovered Waiting*

This scene begins with the beautiful *serenade*, the most melodious of the airs in Donizetti's work.

Serenata—Com' e gentil (Soft Beams the Light)

By Enrico Caruso, Tenor (*In Italian*) 85048 12-inch, $3.00
By Aristodemo Giorgini, Tenor, and La Scala Chorus (*In Italian*) 76010 12-inch, 2.00

ERNESTO:
Oh! summer night, thy tranquil light
Was made for those who shun the busy day,
Who love too well, yet blush to tell
The hopes that led their hearts astray!
All now is still, on dale, on hill,

And none are nigh, with curious eye;
Then why, my love, oh, why delay?
Your lattice open to the starry night,
And with your presence make the world more bright!

Two renditions of this exquisite air are listed here, headed by Caruso's, familiar to admirers of the great tenor. A fine record by Giorgini, a tenor now much liked in Italy, follows.

Norina joins *Ernesto*, and they are reconciled in a duet, *Tell Me Again*. *Pasquale* and the *Doctor*, with dark lanterns, enter softly and hide behind the trees, but the irate old man can not contain himself no longer and rushes out to denounce the lovers. *Ernesto* vanishes and *Norina* calmly declares there was no one with her, that she had merely come out to get fresh air. *Pasquale* is so beside himself with rage and chagrin that *Malatesta* considers it time to end the farce, and proposes to rid *Pasquale* of his bride by marrying her to *Ernesto*, revealing that the first marriage was not a real one, and that the lady was not his sister but *Norina*. *Pasquale* is so glad to be rid of such an extravagant termagant that he pardons the deception, consents to the union, and settles an income on the happy pair.

DOUBLE-FACED DON PASQUALE RECORDS

Signorina in tanta fretta (My Lady, Why This Haste?)
By Emilia Corsi and Antonio Pini-Corsi (*In Italian*)
Son nov' ore ('Tis Nine O'clock!)
By Antonio Pini-Corsi and Ernesto Badini (*In Italian*)
68273 12-inch, $1.25

D'un guardo, un sorrisetto (Glances So Soft)
By Giuseppina Huguet, Soprano (*In Italian*)
Pronta io son (My Part I'll Play)
By Giuseppina Huguet and Ernesto Badini (*In Italian*)
68272 12-inch, 1.25

Overture By La Scala Orchestra
Barbiere di Siviglia—Manca un foglio By La Scala Orchestra
68010 12-inch, 1.25

Un foco insolito (A Fire All Unfelt Before)
By Antonio Pini-Corsi and Ernesto Badini (*In Italian*)
Vado, corro (Haste We!) By Emilia Corsi, Soprano, and
Ernesto Badini, Baritone (*In Italian*)
62104 10-inch, .75

E rimasto la impietrato (He Stands Immovable)
By Linda Brambilla, Soprano; Antonio Pini-Corsi,
Baritone; Pini-Corsi, Tenor; Scipioni, Bass (*In Italian*)
Elisir d'amore—Io sonno ricco (*I Have Riches*) *By Passari,
Soprano; A. Pini-Corsi, Baritone; and Chorus* (*In Italian*)
16566 10-inch, .75

Cavatina—So anch'io lo virtù magica (I, Too, Thy Magic
Virtues Know)
By Amelia Pollini, Soprano (*In Italian*)
Aspetta aspetta cara esposina (Wait, Wait, Dear Little
Wife) By Antonio Pini-Corsi, Baritone, and Giovanni
Polese, Baritone (*In Italian*)
62103 10-inch, .75

Sogno soave e casto (Fond Dream of Love)
By Giuseppe Acerbi, Tenor (*In Italian*)
Faust—Coro de soldados (*Soldiers' Chorus*) *La Scala Chorus*
62624 10-inch, .75

Vado corro (Haste We) By Giuseppina Huguet, Soprano,
and Ernesto Badini, Baritone (*In Italian*)
Son tradito By Giuseppina Huguet, Soprano; Antonio
Pini-Corsi, Baritone; Gaetano Pini-Corsi, Tenor; Ernesto
Badini, Baritone (*In Italian*)
62097 10-inch, .75

LANDE

SCENE FOR ACT II AT METROPOLITAN OPERA

L'ELISIR D'AMORE
(Layl-leez -ear' dahm-oh'-ray)
(English)
THE ELIXIR OF LOVE
OPERA IN TWO ACTS

Text by Romani. Music by Gaetano Donizetti. First produced in Milan in 1832. First London production December 10, 1836. First New York production in 1838.

Cast

ADINA, a wealthy and independent young woman .... Soprano
NEMORINO, a young peasant, in love with Adina .... Tenor
BELCORE, sergeant of the village garrison .... Bass
DOCTOR DULCAMARA, a quack doctor .... Buffo
GIANNETTA, a peasant girl .... Soprano
A Landlord, a Notary, Peasants, Soldiers, Villagers.

Scene and Period: A little Italian village; the nineteenth century.

This delightful example of Donizetti's work is a real *opéra bouffe*, and while simple and unconventional in plot, it has always been a favorite because of the lovely songs with which it abounds.

Adina, a lively village beauty and heiress, is loved by a young peasant, *Nemorino*, who although handsome and manly, is afraid to press his suit; but while the beauty treats him rather coolly she is by no means indifferent to him.

ACT I

SCENE—*The Homestead of Adina's Farm*

Adina and her companion are seated under a tree reading. *Nemorino* is near, pensively observing his *innamorata*, and sings his first *Cavatina*.

Quant'e bella! (Ah! How Lovely)

By Emilio Perea, Tenor (*In Italian*) *62626 10-inch, $0.75

> NEMORINO:
> Ah! how lovely! ah! how dear to me!
> While I gaze I adore more deeply;
> Ah! what rapture that soft bosom
> With a mutual flame to move.
> But while reading, studying, improving,
> She hath learning and every attainment,
> While I can nothing do but love!

Adina then reads to her friends a legend of a cruel lady who coldly treated a knight who loved her, and only smiled on him when he gave her a love potion. *Nemorino* wishes he could find the receipt for this potent elixir.

Martial music is heard and *Belcore*, a dashing sergeant stationed near the village, appears with a bouquet for *Adina*. She has but few smiles for the military man, which cheers *Nemorino* somewhat, and when *Belcore* departs he renews his suit, but the fair one tells him that it is useless.

A commotion among the villagers is heard, and *Dulcamara*, a quack doctor, comes on the scene, riding in a splendid carriage. He announces his wonderful medicines in a famous song, *Udite, udite o rustici*, the delight of *buffos* for more than eighty years.

Udite, udite o rustici (Give Ear, Ye Rustics)

By Antonio Pini-Corsi, Baritone (*In Italian*) *68152 12-inch, $1.25
By Emilio Perea, Tenor (*In Italian*) *62626 10-inch, .75

* *Double-Faced Record—For title of opposite side see DOUBLE-FACED ELIXIR OF LOVE RECORDS, page 78.*

After the Doctor has recited the wonderful effects of his medicines, saying:

DULCAMARA:
I cure the apoplectical,
The asthmatical, the paralytical,
The dropsical, the diuretical,
Consumption, deafness, too,
The rickets and the scrofula—
All evils are at once upset
By this new and fashionable mode!

Nemorino exclaims, "Heaven itself must have sent this miraculous doctor to our village!" He draws the quack aside, and asks him if he has an elixir that can awaken love. The Doctor, of course, says that he is the original inventor of the liquid, and soon has *Nemorino's* last coin in exchange for the coveted potion, which is in reality a bottle of strong wine.

This scene is in the form of an amusing duet, *Obbligato*.

Obbligato, obbligato (Thank You Kindly)

By Fernando de Lucia, Tenor, and Ernesto Badini, Baritone
(*In Italian*) 91079 10-inch, $2.00

As soon as the Doctor has departed *Nemorino* drinks the elixir, and at once feels a new courage in his veins. He begins to sing and dance, and *Adina*, coming in, is astonished to see her love-sick swain so merry. Feeling sure that the potion will bring the lady to his feet, he pays no attention to her, which piques her so much that when the sergeant arrives and renews his suit, she consents to wed him in three days. *Nemorino* laughs loudly at this, which further enrages the lady, and she sets the wedding for that very day. This sobers *Nemorino*, who fears that the marriage may take place before the potion works, and he pleads for delay. *Adina* and *Belcore* laugh at him, and the curtain falls as preparations for the wedding are begun.

ACT II

SCENE I—*Interior of the Farmhouse*

The wedding feast is in progress, but the notary has not arrived. *Dulcamara* is present, and produces the latest duet from Venice, which he asks *Adina* to sing with him.

Io sono ricco e tu sei bella (I Have Riches, Thou Hast Beauty)

By Mme. Passari, Soprano; Antonio Pini-Corsi, Baritone; La Scala Chorus
(*In Italian*) 16566 10-inch, $0.60

This amusing dialogue, supposed to occur between a rich old man and a young girl, is given here by two well-known singers of La Scala, supported by the chorus.

The company now goes to an adjoining room to dance; all but the Doctor, who says he doesn't know when another free dinner will come his way, and therefore remains at the feast. *Nemorino* enters, distracted, and tells the Doctor that the elixir has not yet taken effect.

"Take another bottle," says the Doctor, "only twenty crowns." *Nemorino* says he has no money, so the Doctor promptly pockets the bottle and goes in to the dancers, telling the unhappy youth to go out and raise the amount.

Belcore, the sergeant, comes in, and learning that *Nemorino's* distress is caused by lack of money, suggests that he enlist as a soldier and be richer by the fee of twenty crowns. *Nemorino* jumps at the chance, signs the articles, runs in search of the Doctor, and drinks the second bottle!

The peasant girls, having heard that the death of *Nemorino's* uncle has just made him rich, begin to pay him attentions. The Doctor tells *Nemorino* that this popularity is the result of the elixir he has just sold him. *Adina*, woman-like, when she sees her lover in such demand, promptly regrets having treated him so coldly, and runs out on the verge of tears. *Nemorino*, noting her downcast looks, feels compassion for her, and gazing after her sadly, sings the lovely *romanza*, famous in every land.

Una furtiva lagrima (Down Her Cheek a Pearly Tear)

By Enrico Caruso, Tenor	(*Piano acc.*)	(*In Italian*)	81027	10-inch, $2.00
By John McCormack, Tenor		(*In Italian*)	74219	12-inch, 1.50
By Florencio Constantino, Tenor		(*In Italian*)	74065	12-inch, 1.50
By Evan Williams, Tenor		(*In English*)	74150	12-inch, 1.50

Donizetti's delightful little comedy, in spite of the beauty of its music and the opportunities it offers for a colorature soprano, is really a tenor opera, and requires a great artist in the rôle of *Nemorino;* and it was the advent of Caruso which made the revival of this sparkling *opéra bouffe* possible.

Neglected as the opera, as a whole, has been for many years, this lovely romanza, *Una furtiva lagrima,* has proved meanwhile an always welcome contribution to the concert stage, and as a test for tenors is comparable to the *Com e gentil* in Don Pasquale. All but four of Donizetti's fifty operas have lost their popularity, but the song which *Nemorino* sings to the tear that stood in his *Adina's* eye will always keep the opera from being forgotten. This is one of the most famous of the Caruso records, and his exquisite singing of this beautiful number is something to be long remembered.

> Down her soft cheek a pearly tear
>   Stole from her eyelids dark,
> Telling their gay and festive cheer,
>   It pained her soul to mark;
> Why then her dear presence fly?
>   When all her love she is showing?
> Could I but feel her beating heart
>   Pressing against mine own;
> Could I my feeling soft impart, and mingle sigh
>   with sigh,
>   But feel her heart against mine own,
> Gladly I then would die, all her love knowing!

Mr. McCormack's rendition is also a most attractive one. Very few English singers are able to sing an Italian aria in a manner that would be acceptable to Italian audiences, but McCormack is one of these, and his rendering of Donizetti's exquisite air is an example of this mastery of the old school of vocalization. Other renderings, by Constantino in Italian, and a fine one in English by Williams, are also offered.

The crafty *Dulcamara* now suggests to *Adini* that she try the wonderful elixir in order to win back her lover, but she says she needs not such aids.

ADINA:
With respect to your elixir,
One more potent, sir, have I—
Through whose virtues Nemorino,
Leaving all, to me will fly!
DULCAMARA *(aside)*:
Oh! she's far too wise and cunning;
These girls know even more than I.

ADINA:
With a tender look I'll charm him—
With a modest smile invite him—
With a tear or sigh alarm him—
With a fond caress excite him.
Never yet was man so mulish,
That I could not make him yield.
Nemorino's fate's decided!

When *Nemorino* has sung his air *Adina* comes on with the soldier's contract, which she has bought back, and tells him that he must not go away. All misunderstandings are now cleared away, and *Belcore* arrives to find his bride-to-be embracing another. However, he is philosophical and saying, "There are other women!" marches off, while the villagers tell *Adina* and *Nemorino* of the latter's good fortune. The Doctor claims credit for the reconciliation, and the curtain falls as he is relieving the peasants of their wages in return for bottles of his wonderful *Elixir of Love !*

DOUBLE-FACED L'ELISIR D'AMORE RECORDS

Udite, udite o rustici (Give Ear, Rustics!) By A. Pini-Corsi, Baritone *(In Italian)* Una furtiva lagrima (A Furtive Tear) By Emilio Perea, Tenor *(In Italian)*	68152	12-inch,	$1.25
Quant'è bella! (Ah, How Lovely!) By Emilio Perea, Tenor *(In Italian)* Udite, udite o rustici—By Arcangelo Rossi, Bass *(In Italian)*	62626	10-inch,	.75
Io sono ricco e tu sei bella (I Have Riches, Thou Hast Beauty) By Maria Passari, Soprano; Pini-Corsi and Chorus *(In Italian)* Don Pasquale—*Quartet, Act I* By Linda Brambilla, Soprano; Antonio Pini-Corsi, Baritone; Gaetano Pini-Corsi, Tenor; and Augusto Scipioni, Baritone *(In Italian)*	16566	10-inch,	.75

ERNANI RESCUES ELVIRA FROM THE KING—ACT I

(Italian)
ERNANI
(*Er-nah'-nee*)

(French)
HERNANI
(*Her-nah'-nee*)

OPERA IN FOUR ACTS

Libretto adapted by Maria Piave; from Victor Hugo's drama "Hernani;" music by Giuseppe Verdi. First production in Venice, March 9, 1844. First London production at Her Majesty's Theatre, March 8, 1845. First New York production, 1846, at the Astor Place. At its Paris production, January 6, 1846, the libretto was altered at Victor Hugo's request, the characters being made Italians and the name of the opera changed to *Il Proscritto*.

Cast of Characters

DON CARLOS, King of Spain................................Baritone
DON RUY GOMEZ DE SILVA, a Grandee of Spain...................Bass
ERNANI, a bandit chief..Tenor
DON RICCARDO, an esquire of the King..........................Tenor
IAGO, (*Ee-ah'-go*) an esquire of Don Silva.........................Bass
ELVIRA, (*El-vee'-rah*) betrothed to Don Silva......................Soprano
GIOVANNA, (*Gee-oh-vah'-nah*) in attendance upon her.........Mezzo-Soprano

Chorus of mountaineers and bandits, followers of *Don Silva*, ladies of *Elvira*, followers of the King, Spanish and German nobles and ladies, electors and pages.

Scene and Period: Aragon; about 1519.

79

ACT I
SCENE I—*The Mountains of Aragon*

Elvira, a Spanish lady of rank, is about to be married to the elderly *Don Gomez de Silva,* a Grandee of Spain. *Ernani,* a bandit chief (in reality John of Aragon, become a brigand after his estates were confiscated), loves *Elvira* and resolves to prevent this unwelcome marriage. The first scene shows a mountain pass where *Ernani's* men are encamped.

Beviam, beviam (Comrades, Let's Drink and Play)
By La Scala Chorus   (*In Italian*) *35168 12-inch, $1.25

The opera opens with this spirited chorus of bandits and mountaineers, who are drinking and gambling in their stronghold. With reckless satisfaction in their lot they sing:

> "What matters to the bandit
> If hunted and branded
> So wine be his share!"

Ernani, their chief, appears on a neighboring height with a melancholy brow. His men remark at his gloomy appearance, and he tells them that he is powerless to prevent the marriage of his betrothed to the aged *Silva* on the morrow. He describes the peerless *Elvira* in a fine aria, The Sweetest Flow'r.

Come rugiada al cespite (The Sweetest Flow'r)
By Luigi Colazza, Tenor   (*In Italian*) *62627 10-inch, $0.75

The bandits offer their lives, if need be, in the service of their chief, and it is decided to rescue *Elvira* that night.

O tu che l'alma adora (O Thou, My Life's Treasure)
By Martinez Patti, Tenor, and La Scala Chorus   (*In Italian*)
*16567 10-inch, $0.75

Ernani, in this passionate aria, sings of the charms of his beloved.

ERNANI:
> Oh thou, my life's sole treasure,
> Come, come to my arms adoring,
> Death at thy feet were pleasure,
> The joy of heav'n is mine where'er thou art.

> I love thy starry glances,
> Thy smile my heart entrances,
> Most blessed he of mortals
> To whom thou gav'st thy heart!

Ernani and his men depart in the direction of *Silva's* castle and the scene changes.

SCENE II—*Elvira's Apartment in the Castle*

Elvira is discovered alone, brooding over the prospect of the sacrifice, which she seems powerless to prevent.

ELVIRA:
> 'Tis near the dawning, and Silva yet returns not! Ah! would he came no more—with odious words of loving, more deeply confirming my love for Ernani!

Ernani involami (Ernani, Fly with Me)
By Marcella Sembrich   88022   12-inch, $3.00
By Celestina Boninsegna   91074   10-inch,   2.00
By Maria Grisi   *63173   10-inch,   .75

In this beautiful but despairing number she calls on her lover to save her, singing:

> Ernani, fly with me;
> Prevent this hated marriage!
> With thee, e'en the barren desert
> Would seem an Eden of enchantment!

Two brilliant renditions of this famous number are given, by Mme Sembrich and Mme. Boninsegna; while a popular-priced record is contributed by Mme. Grisi, of La Scala.

Elvira's ladies-in-waiting now enter, bringing her wedding gifts, and in the graceful chorus with which this record begins, congratulate her.

COPY'T DUPONT
SEMBRICH AS ELVIRA

---

* *Double-Faced Record—For title of opposite side see DOUBLE-FACED ERNANI RECORDS, page 85.*

THE KING PLEADS HIS LOVE

Quante d'Iberia giovani (Noble Hispania's Blood)

By Ida Giacomelli and La Scala Chorus
(In Italian) *16567 10-inch, $0.75

She thanks them, saying: "Each kindly wish awakes a response in my own heart;" then sings, aside, a second number, *"Tutto sprezzo che d'Ernani,"* in which she tells of her hope of rescue. The chorus joins in the concluding strain.

Da quel di che t'ho veduta (From the Day when First Thy Beauty)

**By Angela de Angelis, Soprano;
Francesco Cigada, Baritone**
(In Italian) *35168 12-inch, $1.25

We come now to one of the greatest scenes in the opera. *Elvira*, who has left the room with the ladies, returns and is amazed to discover in her boudoir the King, who has been secretly in love with her. She appeals to his honor, saying:

"In pity, sire, leave me!"

The record begins with the dramatic dialogue between *Carlos* and *Elvira*. *Carlos* then declares his love in the aria *"Da quel di"* leading up to a dramatic duet, which concludes this sixth number.

Tu se' Ernani! (Thou Art Ernani!)

By Giacomelli, Martinez-Patti and Pignataro *(Italian)* *16568 10-inch, $0.75

The King, maddened by *Elvira's* resistance, is about to carry her away by force. She snatches a dagger from *Carlos'* belt and cries: "Go, or with this dagger I will slay us both!" The King is about to summon his guard, when suddenly a secret panel door opens and *Ernani* appears. *Carlos* recognizes him and exclaims: "Thou art Ernani, the assassin and bandit," and in the spirited trio which follows the rivals declare their hatred, while *Elvira*, almost distracted, endeavors to protect her lover.

Infelice e tu credevi (Unhappy One!)

By Marcel Journet, Bass	*(In Italian)*	74008	12-inch, $1.50
By Perello de Segurola, Bass	*(In Italian)*	55007	12-inch, 1.50
By Marcel Journet, Bass	*(In Italian)*	64077	10-inch, 1.00
By Aristodemo Sillich, Bass	*(In Italian)*	*63421	10-inch, .75

In the midst of this thrilling tableau now appears *Silva*, who does not recognize the King and who is naturally astounded to find two rivals in the apartments of his future bride, quarreling for her possession. He summons his squires and soldiers, then addresses himself to *Elvira* and reproaches her in this well-known and impressive *Infelice*, one of the most beautiful of bass arias. Four records of this favorite number are available—by Journet (in both 10 and 12-inch), by de Segurola and by Sillich.

The editor regrets that he is unable to give satisfactory English translations for the majority of the *Ernani* airs, but most of the available translations of *Ernani* are so distorted as to be almost meaningless. The few extracts which are given have been revised and made somewhat intelligible. "Opera in English," about which we hear so much nowadays, would be simply impossible without new translations for some of the older works. For instance, here is a specimen translation of the text of this very air of *Infelice*.

Ah, to win, to win back summer's blossom
In my breast were tho't too gainless,
Winter lords it within this my bosom.
Far congealing, far congealing to the core,
Far congealing unto the core,

Far congealing unto the core.
Winter lords it in this bosom.
Far congealing, far congealing to the core,
Unto the core, congealing unto the core!

* *Double-Faced Record—For title of opposite side see DOUBLE-FACED ERNANI RECORDS, page 85.*

Now anyone who can tell just what this means is certainly a highly gifted ind. idual!
In this connection, however, it should be stated that several American music publishers are entitled to praise for their efforts to improve opera translations, especially G. Schirmer, with many beautiful new editions of the older operas and collections of opera airs; and Oliver Ditson Company, whose Musicians' Library, a splendid piece of music typography, contains many new translations. The editor of this catalogue is indebted to both these firms for permission to quote from their new translations.

Vedi come il buon vegliardo (Well I Knew My Trusty Vassal)

By Maria Grisi, Soprano; Carlo Ottoboni, Bass; Remo Sangiorgi, Tenor; and Giuseppi Sala, Baritone (*In Italian*) *35169 12-inch, $1.25

Having reproached his bride for her supposed treachery, *Silva* thinks of vengeance, and calling for his armor and a sword, demands that the intruders follow him to combat. Before they can reply, the King's squires enter and salute their sovereign. The astounded *Silva*, though secretly enraged, kneels to his King, saying: "Duty to my King cancels all offences." The great finale then begins with *Carlos'* solo, sung aside to his squires:

"Well I knew my trusty vassal	Would his wrath and love surrender
Fierce in hate, in passion tender	In the presence of his King."

This is one of the most impressive records of the Ernani series.

Finale, Act I

By Maria Grisi, Soprano; Carlo Ottoboni, Bass; Remo Sangiorgi, Tenor; and Giuseppi Sala, Baritone (*In Italian*) *16568 10-inch, $0.75

The finale to Act I is continued in this record. The situation at the close of the act may be understood by these quotations from the words the librettist has given to the various characters:

CARLOS (*to Ernani*):
I will save thee!
(*Aloud to Silva*):
Let this trusty friend depart.
ERNANI:
I thy friend? Never! unto death my vengeance will pursue thee!
ELVIRA:
Fly, Ernani, let love teach thee prudence!

CARLOS:
Power, dominion and love's delights,
All these are mine—all my will must obey!
SILVA:
From my eyes a veil has fallen . . .
I can scarce believe my senses!
COURTIERS:
Well doth Silva hide his anger
But within it still doth smolder!

Ernani yields to *Elvira's* pleadings and in the confusion makes his escape. The curtain falls on an impressive tableau.

ACT II

SCENE—*A Hall in Silva's Castle*

After his escape from the castle, nothing has been seen of *Ernani*. *Elvira* believes the rumors of his death and despairingly consents to wed *Don Silva*.

Esultiam (Day of Gladness)

By La Scala Chorus (*In Italian*) *16569 10-inch, $0.75

The first scene of Act II occurs in a magnificent hall in the castle. The company of knights and pages of *Silva*, and ladies in attendance on *Elvira* sing the opening chorus in praise of the noble *Silva* and his peerless bride.

Oro quant' oro (I am the Bandit Ernani)

By Maria Bernacchi, Soprano; Luisi Colazza, Tenor; and Torres de Luna, Bass (*In Italian*) *16569 10-inch, $0.75

Silva, attired as a Grandee, enters. His squire, *Jago*, announces a holy man, who craves the hospitality of the castle. *Ernani*, disguised as a pilgrim, enters, then throws off his disguise and exclaims, beginning this fine trio:

"I am the bandit Ernani . . . My men are dead or in chains . . . My enemies are without the castle . . . Seize me and deliver me up, for I am weary of life!"

Silva, however, refuses to betray one whom he has received as a guest. The trio, which is one of the great scenes of the opera, then follows.

---

* *Double-Faced Record—For title of opposite side see DOUBLE-FACED ERNANI RECORDS, pages 84 and 85.*

La vedremo, o veglio audace (I Will Prove, Audacious Greybeard)

By Mattia Battistini, Baritone, and Aristodemo Sillich, Bass
(*In Italian*) 92007 12-inch, $3.00
By Ernesto Caronna, Baritone, and Torres de Luna, Bass
(*In Italian*) *16570 10-inch, .75

The retainers bring news that the King and his warriors are without the castle. *Silva* hides *Ernani* in a secret passage and orders that the King be admitted. *Don Carlos* inquires, with irony, why *Silva's* castle is so well guarded, and demands that he surrender *Ernani* or lose his own life. *Silva* refuses. The soldiers are ordered to search the castle. This duet then occurs, beginning:

CARLOS: I will prove, audacious greybeard,
If thou'rt loyal to thy King!
In my wrath I will destroy thee!
SILVA: Oh King, be just; I cannot yield!

Vieni meco (Come, Thou Dearest Maiden)

By Emilia Corsi, Soprano; Mattia Battistini, Baritone; and La Scala
Chorus (*In Italian*) 92008 12-inch, $3.00
By Maria Grisi, Soprano; Francesco Cigada, Baritone; Carlo Ottoboni,
Bass; and La Scala Chorus (*In Italian*) *16570 10-inch, .75

This record begins with a chorus of soldiers, who have explored the castle but have found no trace of *Ernani*. The King is about to torture *Silva* into revealing the secret, when *Elvira* rushes in and begs the mercy of his Majesty. *Carlos* turns to her, and sings consolingly of the bright future before her as his Queen, and in the great trio which follows the conflicting emotions of those in the scene are expressed in Verdi's fiery music.

A te scegli, seguimi (Choose Thy Sword, and Follow!)

By Luigi Colazza, Tenor, and Torres de Luna, Bass
(*In Italian*) *35169 12-inch, $1.25

The King, his followers, and the *Lady Elvira* having retired, *Silva* exclaims: "Hell cannot hate with the hatred I bear thee, vile King!" He then takes down two swords from the armory, and releasing *Ernani* from his hiding place, challenges him to combat. *Ernani* refuses, saying that his life belongs to *Silva*, who has saved it. *Silva* taunts him with cowardice and *Ernani* consents to fight, but asks for one look at *Elvira*. *Silva* replies that the King has taken her away. "Fool!" cries *Ernani* to the astonished Grandee, "the King is our rival!" and agrees to combine with *Silva* against their mutual foe. Once their revenge is accomplished, *Ernani* agrees to yield his life at *Silva's* call, and gives him a hunting horn which shall be the signal for his (*Ernani's*) death. For this magnificent number Verdi has written some of his most dramatic music.

In arcion, cavalieri (To Horse, Ye Warriors)

By Giuseppe Sala, Tenor; Cesare Preve, Baritone;
and La Scala Chorus (*Italian*) *16571 10-inch, $0.75

The act closes with the spirited duet and chorus by *Ernani*, *Silva* and the warriors of the Don, who prepare to pursue the King to the death.

ACT III

SCENE—*A Vault in Aix-la-Chapelle Cemetery*

O de' verd' anni miei (Oh Bright and Fleeting Shadows)

By Giuseppi Campanari, Baritone
(*In Italian*) 85087 12-inch, $3.00
By Mario Ancona, Baritone (*Italian*) 88062 12-inch, 3.00

VAN DYCK AS ERNANI

Double-Faced Record—For title of opposite side see *DOUBLE-FACED ERNANI RECORDS, pages 84 and 85.*

The third act occurs in the Tomb of Charlemagne at Aix-la-Chapelle. *Carlos* conceals himself in the tomb of his ancestor to witness the meeting of the conspirators who are plotting against him. He is depressed and melancholy, and sings this famous *O de verd*, in which he pledges himself to better deeds should the Electors, then in session, proclaim him Emperor.

Si ridesti il leon di Castiglia   (Rouse the Lion of Castile)

By La Scala Chorus   (*In Italian*) *16571 10-inch, $0.75

The conspirators, among whom are *Ernani* and *Silva*, assemble at the tomb. *Ernani* is chosen to assassinate *Carlos*, and greets the decision with joy, exclaiming that his dead father will at last be avenged. The great ensemble then follows.

O sommo Carlo   (Oh Noble Carlos)

By Mattia Battistini, Baritone; Emilia Corsi, Soprano; Luigi Colazza, Tenor; Aristodemo Sillich, Bass; and La Scala Chorus

(*In Italian*) 92046 12-inch, $3.00

By Maria Grisi, Soprano; Remo Sangiorgi, Tenor; Francesco Cigada, Baritone; and La Scala Chorus   (*In Italian*) *35170 12-inch, 1.25

The booming of cannon having announced that *Carlos* is proclaimed Emperor, he comes from the tomb and surprises the conspirators. At the same time the Electors and the King's courtiers enter from a secret door. *Carlos* condemns the plotters to death, when *Elvira* rushes to him and asks for mercy. The Emperor heeds her, pardons them all, and unites *Elvira* and *Ernani*. In this great finale all glorify the Emperor except *Silva*, who still secretly cries for vengeance.

ACT IV
SCENE—*Terrace of a Palace in Aragon*

Festa da ballo   (Hail, Bright Hour of Gladness)

By La Scala Chorus   (*In Italian*) *16572 10-inch, $0.75

The lovers are now happily united, and this scene shows them at *Ernani's* palace, which, with his estates, has been restored to him. A chorus of ladies, masks and pages greets the happy pair.

Ferna crudel, estinguere   (Stay Thee, My Lord!)

By Maria Bernacchi, Soprano; Luigi Colazza, Tenor; and Torres de Luna, Baritone   (*In Italian*) *35170 12-inch, $1.25

Elvira and *Ernani* are alone on the terrace, oblivious to all but each other, when a blast from a horn is heard. *Ernani* awakes from his dream of bliss and recognizes the sound of his own hunting horn, which he had given to *Silva* as a pledge to die when the revengeful Don should demand his life. The distracted *Elvira* pleads with *Silva* for her husband, but in vain. After an affecting farewell *Ernani* fulfills his vow, stabs himself and dies, while *Elvira* falls lifeless on his body. The curtain falls as the cruel and remorseless *Silva* is gloating over his terrible revenge.

DOUBLE-FACED ERNANI RECORDS

Infelice e tu credevi By Perelló de Segurola, Bass Puritani—Sorgea la notte By Perelló de Segurola, Bass (*In Italian*)	55007	12-inch,	$1.50
Ferna, crudel By Maria Bernacchi, Soprano; Luigi Colazza, Tenor; and Torres de Luna, Bass (*In Italian*) O sommo Carlo By Maria Grisi, Soprano; Remo Sangiorgi, Tenor; Francesco Cigada, Baritone; and Chorus (*Italian*)	35170	12-inch,	1.25
Ernani Selection By Pryor's Band Meistersinger—Prize Song By Victor Sorlin, 'Cellist	35111	12-inch,	1.25
A te scegli, seguimi By Luigi Colazza, Tenor, and Torres de Luna, Bass (*In Italian*) Vedi come il buon vegliardo By Maria Grisi, Soprano; Remo Sangiorgi, Tenor; Giuseppi Sala, Tenor; and Carlo Ottoboni, Bass (*In Italian*)	35169	12-inch,	1.25

* *Double-Faced Record—For title of opposite side see DOUBLE-FACED ERNANI RECORDS, pages 84 and 85.*

Beviam, beviam By La Scala Chorus (*In Italian*) Da quel dì che t'ho veduta By Angela de Angelis, Soprano, and Francesco Cigada, Baritone (*In Italian*)	35168	12-inch,	$1.25

O tu che l'alma adora   By Martinez-Patti, Tenor,
  and Chorus (*In Italian*)
Quante d'Iberia giovani   By Ida Giacomelli, Soprano,
  and Chorus (*In Italian*)
	16567	10-inch,	.75

Finale, Act I   By Maria Grisi, Soprano; Carlo Ottoboni,
  Bass; Remo Sangiorgi, Tenor; and Giuseppi Sala, Tenor
Tu se' Ernani   By Ida Giacomelli, Soprano; Martinez-
  Patti, Tenor; and Enrico Pignataro, Baritone (*In Italian*)
	16568	10-inch,	.75

Esultiam! By La Scala Chorus (*In Italian*) Oro quant' oro By Maria Bernacchi, Soprano; Luigi Colazza, Tenor; and Torres de Luna, Bass (*In Italian*)	16569	10-inch,	.75

La vedremo   By Ernesto Caronna, Baritone, and
  Torres de Luna, Bass (*In Italian*)
Vieni meco   By Maria Grisi, Soprano; Francesco Cigada,
  Baritone; Carlo Ottoboni, Bass; and Chorus (*In Italian*)
	16570	10-inch,	.75

In arcion, cavalieri! By Giuseppi Sala, Tenor; Cesare Preve, Bass; and Chorus (*In Italian*) Si ridesti il leon di Castiglia By La Scala Chorus (*Italian*)	16571	10-inch,	.75

Festa da ballo "O come felici"   By La Scala Chorus
  (*In Italian*)
Hamlet—O vin, discaccia la tristezza
  By Francesco Cigada, Baritone, and Chorus (*In Italian*)
	16572	10-inch,	.75

Ernani involami (Ernani, Fly with Me)
  By Maria Grisi, Soprano (*In Italian*)
Ballo in Maschera—O Figlio d' Inghilterra
  By Huguet, Salvador, Cigada, Sillich, and Chorus (*In Italian*)
	63173	10-inch,	.75

Infelice e tu credevi (Unhappy One!)
  By Aristodemo Sillich, Bass (*In Italian*)
Manon—Oh, Manon, sempre la stressa
  By Giorgio Malesci, Tenor (*In Italian*)
	63421	10-inch,	.75

Come rugiada al cespite By Luigi Colazza (*In Italian*) O tu che l'alma adora By Martinez-Patti, Tenor, and Chorus (*In Italian*)	62627	10-inch,	.75

VERDI'S BIRTHPLACE (OCTOBER 10, 1813), RONCOLE, DUCHY OF PARMA

FAUST
(*Fowst*)

OPERA IN FIVE ACTS

Words by Barbier and Carre, founded upon Goethe's tragedy. Music by Charles Gounod. First produced at the *Théâtre Lyrique*, Paris, March 19, 1859. First performance in London June 11, 1863; in New York November 26, 1863, at the Academy of Music, with Kellogg, Mazzoleni, Biachi and Yppolito.

Some famous American productions were in 1883, with Nilsson, Scalchi, and Campanini; and the same year with Nordica (début) as *Marguerite*; in 1892 with Eames, the de Reszkes and Lasalle; and recently with Caruso and Farrar.

Characters

FAUST (*Fowst*) . . . . Tenor
MEPHISTOPHELES (*Mef-iss-tof'-el-leez*) Bass
VALENTINE (*Val'-en-teen*) . . . . Baritone
BRANDER, or WAGNER . . . . . Baritone
SIEBEL (*See'-bel*) . . . . Mezzo-Soprano
MARGUERITE (*Mahr-guer-eet'*) . . . . Soprano
MARTHA . . . . Contralto

Students, Soldiers, Villagers,
Sorcerers, Spirits.

The action takes place in Germany.

FAUST

PROGRAM OF A FAMOUS REVIVAL (1869)

Fifty-two years have elapsed since the first production of this masterpiece by Gounod; and it is to-day sung throughout the world more than any other five operas combined. At the Paris Opéra alone it has been given more than 1500 times, and the new setting recently provided for it there cost not less than 150,000 francs, a sum which would not be risked on any other opera whatever.

It seems strange now, in view of the overwhelming success of Faust, to recall that it was received with indifference in Paris, and all but failed in Milan. The London production, however, with Titiens, Giuglini, Trebelli, Gassier and Santley, was quite successful; and in the following June Patti sang *Marguerite* for the first time, the opera receiving a tremendous ovation.

The story is familiar to almost every one and will be but briefly sketched here. The libretto by Barbier and Carre does not attempt to follow the Goethe drama, but merely makes use of the *Faust-Marguerite* incident. This is sufficient, however, to provide an intensely interesting subject for Gounod's lovely music.

Prélude

By L'Orchestre Symphonique, Paris 58016 12-inch, $1.00

The prelude to Faust is a short one, merely giving a clue to the drama which is to follow. The fateful single note of the full orchestra with which it opens and the mysterious chromatic chords stealing in from the strings form a fitting introduction to a drama of such unusual portent.

The tempo is then accelerated and a passage suggesting *Faust's* mental struggles leads to the lovely melody in F major (*Dio possente*). The prelude closes with sustained chords, solemn and impressive.

This number is rarely heard apart from the opera, and so excellent a reproduction as this one by the orchestra will be highly appreciated.

ACT I—The Compact

The first act reveals the studio of *Faust,* an aged philosopher and alchemist, who is seen surrounded by musty parchment rolls and the rude scientific apparatus of the fifteenth century. The fitful light of the expiring lamp is a symbol of the despair in the heart of the aged *Faust,* as after a lifetime spent in the pursuit of learning, he realizes that he knows but little of true knowledge. Tired of the struggle, he resolves to end it with a poisonous draught, and raises the goblet to his lips; but pauses as the songs of the happy peasants float through the open window. He goes to the window, and filled with rage at the sight of human happiness, he curses all earthly things and calls on Satan to aid him.

This scene is given in a most impressive record by De Tura and the La Scala Chorus.

La vaga pupilla

By Gennaro De Tura and La Scala Chorus (*In Italian*) 76019 12-inch, $2.00

CHORUS OF PEASANT GIRLS (*passing without the window*):
Ah! careless, idle maiden,
Wherefore dreaming still?
Day with roses laden
Cometh o'er the hill.
Brooks and bees and flowers
Warble to the grove,
Who has time for sadness?
Awake to love!
FAUST:
Foolish echoes of human gladness,
Go by, pass on your way!
(*His hand trembles.*)
Goblet so often drained by my father's hand
so steady,
Why now dost thou tremble in mine?

CHORUS OF REAPERS (*without*):
Cometh forth, ye reapers, young and hoary!
The earth is proud with harvest glory!
Rejoice and pray.
FAUST:
If I pray there is none to hear—
To give me back my love,
Its believing and its glow.
Accurst be all ye thoughts of earthly pleasure!
Fond dreams of hope! ambitions high,
And their fulfillment so rare!
Accurst, my vaunted learning,
And forgiveness and prayer!
Infernal king, appear!
(*Mephistopheles appears.*)

The Aged Philosopher Wearies of Life

KRELING

FAUST DREAMS OF YOUTH AND BEAUTY

Mephistopheles, attired in the dress of a gallant, promptly appears in response to the call and proposes that the good Doctor shall enter into a compact with him. In return for riches, glory, power, anything he desires, *Faust* shall merely give up his soul. The aged philosopher, spurning gold or power, cries out for youth, only youth!

Io voglio il piacer (The Pleasures of Youth)

By Gaetano Pini-Corsi, Tenor;
Aristodemo Sillich, Bass
(*In Italian*) *63174 10-in., $0.75

The bargain is soon agreed upon and *Faust* is about to pledge his soul in return for youth and love, but as he still hesitates, *Mephisto* says, "See how fair youth invites you! Look!"

O merveille (Heavenly Vision)

By Enrico Caruso, Tenor;
Marcel Journet, Bass
(*In French*) 89039 12-in., $4.00

Then follows the delicate passage for strings which accompanies the vision. *Faust,* gazing rapturously on the beautiful *Marguerite,* sings:

The scroll is signed in letters of fire, *Faust* drains the magic potion and is transformed into a youth. The spirited duet which follows, ending the first act, is sung with fine effect; both of the Victor renditions being most attractive ones.

ACT II—The Fair

(*The scene shows a fair in progress in the public square of a German town*)

A motley crowd of students, soldiers, old men, young women and matrons are disporting themselves—drinking, talking, flirting, quarreling; and this animated chorus, with which the Kermesse Scene begins, graphically pictures the whole.

Kermesse Scene

By New York Grand Opera Chorus   (*In Italian*)   74213   12-inch, $1.50
By La Scala Chorus   (*In Italian*) *68160   12-inch, 1.25

Each group delivers its quota in distinctive fashion, the soldiers' sturdy declaration contrasting with the laughing, chattering passages allotted to the women; the high-pitched falsetto of the gossiping old men always proving a favorite portion of this number. At the close the different groups combine into a chorus of six parts. This wonderful piece of choral writing is reproduced in a striking manner, and gives a most realistic picture of the Kermesse.

**Double-Faced Record—For title of opposite side see DOUBLE-FACED FAUST RECORDS, page 107.*

SOLDIERS:
Red and white liquor, coarse or fine,
What can it matter, so we have wine?

OLD MEN:
Each new feast-day brings the old story,
Danger gone by, how we enjoy it!
While to-day each hot-headed boy
Fights for to-day's little glory!

GIRLS:
Only look how they do eye us,
Yonder fellows gay!
Howsoever they defy us,
Never run away!

STUDENTS:
How those merry girls do eye us
We know what it means—
To despise us, to decoy us,
Like so many queens!

MATRONS:
Only see the brazen creatures
With the men at play;
Had the latter choice in features,
They would turn this way!

SOLDIERS:
Long live the soldier,
The soldier gay!
Be it ancient city, be it maiden pretty,
Both must fall our prey!

Here *Valentine*, the brother of *Marguerite*, is found among the crowd of soldiers just about to depart for the war, and he sings the noble *Dio possente*, a farewell to his sister and his home.

PHOTO BYRON

MEETING OF MARGUERITE AND FAUST—ACT II

Dio possente (Even the Bravest Heart)

By Antonio Scotti, Baritone	(*In Italian*)	88203	12-inch,	$3.00
By Emilio de Gogorza, Baritone	(*In Italian*)	88174	12-inch,	3.00
By Titta Ruffo, Baritone	(*In Italian*)	92043	12-inch,	3.00
By Francesco Cigada (*Double-faced—See page 107*)	(*Italian*)	68275	12-inch,	1.25

In the preceding recitative he speaks of his fears in leaving his sister *Marguerite* alone, and contemplates with affection the amulet she has given him to bring good fortune.

VALENTINE:
Dear gift of my sister,
Made more holy by her pray'r.
However great the danger,
There's naught can do me harm,
Protected by this charm!

The familiar "Cavatina" then follows:

Even bravest heart may swell,
In the moment of farewell,
Loving smile of sister kind,
Quiet home I leave behind;
Oft shall I think of you,
Whene'er the wine-cup passes 'round,
When alone my watch I keep
And my comrades lie asleep

Upon the tented battleground.
But when danger to glory shall call me,
I still will be first in the fray,
As blithe as a knight in his bridal array,
Careless what fate may befall me,
When glory shall call me.
Oft shall I sadly think of you
When far away, far away.

COPY'T DUPONT

JOURNET AS MEPHISTO

This *Dio possente* was not in the original production of the opera, but was written by Gounod especially for Santley in the English production at Her Majesty's Theatre, 1864.

The Victor offers a wide choice to buyers of this fine "Cavatina." Scotti's *Valentine* is always a revelation in dramatic possibilities. This rôle, too often allotted to a mediocre artist, is filled by him with dignity; and he makes a serious and soldierly *Valentine*, singing the music with admirable richness of tone and beauty of expression.

Although Mr. de Gorgoza has not sung the number in opera, it is frequently seen on his concert programs, and he sings it superbly. Other fine renditions in Italian are the ones by Ruffo and Cigada, two famous European baritones, who have not yet visited America.

Le veau d'or (The Calf of Gold)

By Pol Plançon, Bass   *(In French)*   81038   10-inch, $2.00
By Marcel Journet, Bass *(In French)*   64036   10-inch, 1.00

We are now in the full bustle of the Fair Scene, where in front of an inn a crowd of drinkers are listening to one of their number, *Wagner*, singing a some what coarse ditty concerning a rat. *Mephistopheles* breaks in upon the revelers, and offers to sing a song of his own, "The Song of the Golden Calf." After the diabolically suggestive introduction by the orchestra, with its semi-quavers and descending chromatics, we hear the bold opening passage of this anthem in praise of Mammon, of which the calf is symbolic.

MEPHISTOPHELES:
  Calf of Gold! aye in all the world
  To your mightiness they proffer,
  Incense at your fane they offer
  From end to end of all the world.
  And in honor of the idol
  Kings and peoples everywhere
  To the sound of jingling coins
  Dance with zeal in festive circle,
  Round about the pedestal,
  Satan, he conducts the ball!
  Calf of Gold, strongest god below!
  To his temple overflowing
  Crowds before his vile shape bowing,
  As they strive in abject toil,
  As with souls debased they circle
  Round about the pedestal,
  Satan, he conducts the ball!

Two renditions of this effective bass song are offered by the Victor. Plançon's rendition is a spirited one, the number always being sung by him with a full appreciation of its caustic raillery. Journet's record is also a splendid one in many respects, and shows the magnificent voice of this artist to great advantage.

Mephistopheles now proceeds to astonish the company by his feats of magic, first reading their palms and then drawing wine from the barrel of Bacchus—the inn sign perched up aloft—each man drawing the wine he likes the best.

The scene which follows, a most dramatic one, is given in a splendid record by Amato, Journet and the Metropolitan Chorus.

KRELING

MEPHISTOPHELES AND FAUST VIEW THE WORLD

Faust—Scène des Epées (Scene of the Swords)

By Pasquale Amato, Baritone; Marcel Journet, Bass; and
Metropolitan Opera Chorus
(Giulio Setti, Director)
(*In French*) 89055 12-inch, $4.00

The record begins with the invocation to Bacchus.

> MEPHISTOPHELES:
> I drink to you all!
> (*Throwing it out with a wry face.*)
> Bah! what rubbishy wine.
> Let me see if I cannot find you better!
> (*Striking the image of Bacchus with his
> sword.*)
> What ho, Bacchus! up there! some liquors!
> Come while you can,
> And each one drink the wine he likes the best!

He then affronts *Valentine* by proposing the health of *Marguerite,*
and the soldier draws his sword, only to find that some unforeseen
force has made it powerless in his hand.

> MEPHISTOPHELES:
> I propose the health of the dearest of all
> dears,
> Our Margarita!
> VALENTINE:
> Enough!
> Bridle thy tongue, or thou diest by my hand!
> MEPHISTOPHELES:
> Come on! (*Both draw*)
> CHORUS:
> Come on!
> MEPHISTOPHELES (*mocking*):
> So soon afraid, who so lately defied me?
> VALENTINE:
> My sword! O disgrace! In my hand is
> powerless!

COPY'T MISHKIN

SAMMARCO AS VALENTINE
ACT IV

Valentine, however, turns the handle upwards, thus making the Sign of the Cross, the
soldiers doing likewise, and they now face the Tempter with confidence.

> VALENTINE AND SOLDIERS:
> 'Gainst the powers of evil our arms assailing,
> Strongest earthly might must be unavailing.
> VALENTINE:
> But know thou art powerless to harm us!
> VALENTINE:
> Look hither!
> (*Holds up his sword to form a cross.*)

> SOLDIERS (*imitating him*):
> Look hither!
> ALL:
> Whilst this blest sign we wear
> Thou canst not harm us!
> Whilst this blest sign we wear
> Thou canst not harm us!

Mephistopheles is discomfited, and cowers in terror as the soldiers sing the choral, with its
striking unison passage for male voices, alternated with bursts of harmony.

This is a remarkably fine reproduction, the men's voices being rich and sonorous, and
the dramatic feeling intense.

The delightful waltz, which has been a model of its kind ever since the first performance of Faust, now begins.

Waltz from Kermesse Scene

By Pryor's Band (*Double-Faced—See page 107*) 16552 10-inch, $0.75

This favorite number is played by the band with the absolute precision and daintiness
which are indispensable to its proper performance.

Faust now observes *Marguerite* and approaching her, greets her respectfully, offering
his escort.

> FAUST:
> High-born and lovely maid,
> Forgive my humble duty,
> Let me, your willing slave,
> Attend you home to-day?

She modestly declines, saying:

> MARGUERITE:
> No, my lord, not a lady am I,
> Nor yet a beauty;
> And do not need an arm,
> To help me on my way.

> FAUST (*gazing after her*):
> By my youth! what a charm!
> She knows not of her beauty.
> Oh! darling child, I love thee!

The waltz now re-commences and the act ends in a wild and exciting dance, in which
all join—students, soldiers and women.

ACT III—The Garden Scene

The Garden Scene of Faust is undoubtedly Gounod's finest inspiration; and the sensuous beauty of the music with which the composer has surrounded the story of *Marguerite's* innocence and trust betrayed, has held many millions in rapt attention during the fifty years since it was first heard.

Flower Song—Le parlate d'amor (In the Language of Love)

By Louise Homer, Contralto	(*In Italian*)	87075	10-inch,	$2.00
By Corinne Morgan, Contralto	(*In English*)	*35086	12-inch,	1.25
By Rita Fornia, Soprano	(*In French*)	64162	10-inch,	1.00
By Corinne Morgan, Contralto	(*In English*)	31270	12-inch,	1.00
By Emma Zaccaria, Mezzo-Soprano	(*In Italian*)	*62085	10-inch,	.75

This fresh and dainty song of *Siebel* ushers in the act. The gentle boy enters *Marguerite's* garden, thinking of the dark prophecy of *Mephistopheles*, who had told him (in Act II):

> "Each flower that you touch,
> Every beauty you dote on
> Shall rot and shall wither!"

Siebel now thinks to put this curse to a test, and prepares to send a message of love to *Marguerite* by means of a flower, singing

> "In the language of love, oh gentle flow'r,
> Say to her I adore her."

Then gathering a blossom he exclaims, as he sees it fade:

Son viz - zi, ahi - mè lo stre-go ma - le det - to mel di - ce-va or or. . . .
'Tis with-er'd! Á-las! that dark stran-ger fore - told me What my fate must be. . . .

But the happy thought occurs to him to dip his fingers in the font of holy water by the side of the cottage. He does so, and is delighted to find the spell broken. The first strain then reappears, closing the aria.

This popular number is offered in Italian by Homer and Zaccaria, in French by Fornia and in English by Miss Morgan.

Salut demeure (All Hail, Thou Dwelling)

By Enrico Caruso	(*In French*)	88003	12-inch,	$3.00
By John McCormack	(*In Italian*)	74220	12-inch,	3.00
By George Hamlin	(*In English*)	74139	12-inch,	1.50

Mephistopheles and *Faust*, who have been secretly watching *Siebel*, now appear; the Tempter being in high spirits at the apparent success of his schemes, while *Faust* gazes in rapture at the garden where his beloved one is wont to walk, and sings his lovely cavatina. He thus rhapsodizes the modest dwelling of *Marguerite*:

> All hail, thou dwelling pure and lowly!
> Home of an angel fair and holy,
> What wealth is here, what wealth outbidding gold,
> Of peace and love, and innocence untold!
> Bounteous Nature!
> 'Twas here by day thy love was taught her,
> Here thou didst with care overshadow thy daughter
> In her dream of the night!
> Here, waving tree and flower
> Made her an Eden-bower of beauty and delight.

The Caruso record of this number—already familiar to the public—is one of the finest in his entire list; while other renditions are an Italian one by McCormack and an English version by Hamlin.

While *Faust* is singing his apostrophe to *Marguerite's* dwelling, *Mephistopheles*, with an eye to more practical things, has replaced *Siebel's* humble nosegay with a splendid bouquet, a more fitting accompaniment to the casket of jewels with which *Marguerite* is to be tempted.

COPY'T BURR M'INTOSH

CARUSO AS FAUST

Double-Faced Record—For title of opposite side see DOUBLE-FACED FAUST RECORDS, page 107.

KRÉLING   FAUST AND MEPHISTOPHELES ENTERING
MARGUERITE'S GARDEN

Marguerite enters the garden, pensively dreaming of the handsome stranger she had met in the market place. Her entrance is announced on the clarinets and violins in a lovely strain suggesting the coming song.

She seats herself at the spinning wheel, and murmurs dreamily:

I wish I could but know who was he that addressed me;
If he was noble—or at least what his name is. . . .

Le Roi de Thule (Ballad of the King of Thulé)

By Geraldine Farrar, Soprano
(*French*) 88229 12-in., $3.00

By Emma Eames, Soprano
(*French*) 88045 12-in., 3.00

Then rebuking herself for her idle fancies, she applies herself to her spinning, and begins this plaintive *chanson* :

"Once there was a king in Thulé
Who was until death always faithful,
And in memory of his loved one
Caused a cup of gold to be made."

Then her thoughts return to *Faust,* and breaking off the song, she sings as if to herself:

Adagio.

Il a - vait bon - ne grà - ce, à ce - qu'il me sem - blé
He was so gen - tle in bear - ing his voice was so kind.

Again impatient with her wandering mind, she finishes the ballad.

Miss Farrar sings this beautiful folk-song with surpassing loveliness of voice, and in the dreamy sentimental style which it requires, while Mme. Eames' rendition is a fine example of the consummate art of this singer—vocally perfect and sung with exquisite feeling.

Finding herself in no humor to spin, *Marguerite* moves toward the house and sees the flowers, which she stops to admire, thinking them from *Siebel.* The box of jewels then catches her eye, and after some misgivings she opens it. Then follows the bright and sparkling "Jewel Song," or *Air des bijoux,* in which childish glee and virginal coquettishness are so happily expressed.

"Oh Heav'n! what brilliant gems!
Can they be real?
Oh never in my sleep did I dream of aught
so lovely!"

exclaims the delighted *Marguerite.*

Air des bijoux (Jewel Song)

By Nellie Melba, Soprano	(*In French*)	88066	12-inch, $3.00
By Marcella Sembrich, Soprano	(*In French*)	88024	12-inch, 3.00
By Geraldine Farrar, Soprano	(*In French*)	88147	12-inch, 3.00
By Giuseppina Huguet (*Double-faced—See page 107*)	(*Italian*)	68160	12-inch, 1.25

FARRAR AS MARGUERITE

No less than four fine records of this well-known and popular air are presented for the choice of Victor opera lovers.

Melba's rendition is a most delightful one, her voice exhibiting the most entrancing smoothness; in its loveliness, flexibility and brilliancy it seems absolutely without a flaw.

Sembrich's *Marguerite* was always a fine impersonation, and her delivery of the number is exceedingly artistic, being one of the cleanest and most finished bits of colorature singing ever heard in opera.

Miss Farrar's brilliant *Marguerite* has been much admired during the past few seasons, and this number shows well the loveliness and flexibility of her voice. A fine record at a lower price is contributed by Mme. Huguet, doubled with the Kermesse record described in Act II.

Quartet—Seigneur Dieu! (Saints Above, What Lovely Gems!)

By Geraldine Farrar, Soprano; Enrico Caruso, Tenor; Marcel Journet, Bass; and Mme. Gilibert, Mezzo-Soprano

(In French) **95204** 12-inch, **$5.00**

The first of the great quartet records begins with the entrance of *Martha*, a susceptible matron who is companion to the motherless girl. The duenna is struck with astonishment at the sight of the jewels, and begins to question *Marguerite*, when she is interrupted by *Mephistopheles*, who appears with *Faust*; and to excuse his entrance tells *Martha* that her husband is dead. This announcement is received with cries of grief and sympathy from the women, and the impressive pause which ensues is followed by the beautiful quartet, in which Gounod expresses the various emotions of the characters.

Mephistopheles then begins to flatter the vain matron and pay her mock attentions, so that *Faust* may have an opportunity to plead his cause without interruption. This dialogue with the susceptible duenna furnishes the only touch of comedy in the opera.

> MEPHISTOPHELES: Happy will be the man
> Whom you choose for your next!
> I trust he may be worthy!

Faust urges the timid girl to take his arm, at which she demurs, while the crafty Tempter continues his flattering attentions to *Martha*. The second quartet bit then follows, closing the record.

Quartet—Eh quoi toujours seule ? (But Why So Lonely ?)

By Geraldine Farrar, Soprano; Enrico Caruso, Tenor; Marcel Journet, Bass; and Mme. Gilibert, Mezzo-Soprano

(In French) **95205** 12-inch, **$5.00**

The second part of the scene begins with the beautiful dialogue between *Marguerite* and *Faust*. She confides to him her loneliness, and in an exquisite passage speaks of her dead sister.

> MARGUERITE: My mother is gone;
> At the war is my brother;
> One dear little sister I had,
> But the darling, too, is dead!

Faust is tender and sympathetic, and the impressionable girl's heart turns more and more toward the handsome stranger, who seems all that a lover should be.

The record closes with the final quartet passage, by far the most effective bit of concerted writing in the opera. It is magnificently sung here, the balance of the voices being absolutely perfect.

Marguerite's Surrender

The recording of so complex and varied a piece of concerted music as is contained in these two records is a marvelous piece of work, and one of the most amazing achievements in the reproduction of operatic music yet heard. The solo, duet, and quartet parts which constitute it, the short pieces of dialogue between various persons, not forgetting the important orchestral interludes—all these are portrayed with the utmost fidelity, making a marvelous musical picture of one of the most interesting pages of Gounod's charming score.

Mephistopheles has succeeded in getting rid of *Martha,* who vainly looks for him in the garden, and he now watches with satisfaction the lovers, who are wandering among the trees in the moonlight.

The Tempter now sings the famous Incantation, in which he calls upon night and the flowers to aid him in his diabolical plot against the soul of *Marguerite.*

QUARTET—ACT III

Invocation Mephistopheles (Oh Night, Draw Thy Curtain!)
By Marcel Journet, Bass
(In French) 64119 10-inch, $1.00

Stretching out his arms, he invokes the powers of Night, that its mysterious scents and seductive charms may aid him in his work of the lovers' undoing. In this stately passage the singer drops for a time the satirical vein of the previous quartet, and gives the invocation with befitting solemnity and grandeur.

MEPHISTOPHELES:
It was high time—
See, 'neath the balmy linden,
Our lovers devoted approaching; 'tis well!
Better leave them alone,
With the flow'rs and the moon.

O night! draw around them thy curtain!
Let naught waken alarm, or misgivings ever!
Ye flowers, aid the enchanting charm,
Her senses to bewilder; till she knows not
Whether she be not already in Heaven!

This is the most impressive passage in the whole part of *Mephistopheles,* and it is magnificently sung by Journet.

The lovers appear again, and *Mephistopheles* discreetly retires from view. The first part of the exquisite duet then follows.

Tardi si fa! (The Hour is Late!)
By Geraldine Farrar, Soprano, and Enrico Caruso, Tenor
(In French) 89032 12-inch, $4.00
By Giuseppina Huguet, Soprano, and Fernando de Lucia, Tenor
Piano Acc. (In Italian) 92053 12-inch, 3.00

Marguerite, finding herself alone with *Faust,* looks in vain for *Martha,* and not seeing her, endeavors to bid farewell to her lover.

MARGUERITE:
The hour is late! Farewell!

FAUST:
Oh, never leave me, now, I pray thee!
Why not enjoy this lovely night a little longer?
Let me gaze on the form before me!
While from yonder ether blue
Look how the star of eve,

Bright and tender, lingers o'er me!
To love thy beauty too!

MARGUERITE:
Oh! how strange, like a spell,
Does the evening bind me!
And a deep languid charm
I feel without alarm,
With its melody enwind me,
And all my heart subdue!

The second part of the duet begins with the lovely *Sempre amar,* in which *Marguerite* and *Faust* pledge their love.

Dammi ancor (Let Me Gaze on Thy Beauty)

By Alice Nielsen, Soprano, and Florencio Constantino, Tenor

(*In Italian*) **74076** 12-inch, **$1.50**

Eternelle (Forever Thine)

By Geraldine Farrar, Soprano, and Enrico Caruso, Tenor

(*In French*) **89031** 12-inch, **$4.00**

And now the lovers plight their troth in the fateful word "Eternelle," which, with the solemn chords in the wood wind, sounds like a true lover's sigh.

Faust, in an exquisite strain, calls on Heaven, the moon and stars to witness that his love is true.

COPY'T MISHKIN

CONSTANTINO AS FAUST

FAUST:
　　O tender moon, O starry Heav'n
　　Silent above thee where angels are enthron'd,
　　Hear me swear how dearly do I love thee!
(*Struck with a sudden fear, the timid girl begs Faust to depart*):
MARGUERITE:
　　Ah! begone! I dare not hear!
　　Ah! how I falter! I faint with fear!
　　Pity, and spare the heart of one so lonely!
FAUST (*tenderly protesting*):
　　Oh, dear one, let me remain and cheer thee,
　　Nor drive me hence with brow severe!
　　Marguerite, I implore thee!
MARGUERITE:
　　By that tender vow that we have sworn,
　　By that secret torn from me,
　　I entreat you only in mercy to be gone!
FAUST:
　　Oh, fair and tender child!
　　Angel, so holy, thou shalt control me.
　　I obey—but at morn?
MARGUERITE (*eagerly*):
　　Yes, at morn, very early!
　　At morn, all day!
FAUST:
　　One word at parting! Thou lov'st me?
(*She hastens toward the house, but stops at the door and wafts a kiss to Faust*) I love thee!
FAUST (*in rapture*):
　　Were it already morn! Now away!

Elle ouvre sa fenêtre (See! She Opens the Window!)

By Geraldine Farrar, Soprano, and Marcel Journet, Bass

(*In French*) **89040** 12-inch, **$4.00**

Ei m'ama (He Loves Me!)

By Celestina Boninsegna, Soprano

(*In Italian*) **88256** 12-inch, **3.00**

(This is the same selection as 89040 with the short dialogue between Faust and Mephistopheles omitted)

Hurrying away full of thoughts of the morrow, when he will see his *Marguerite* again, *Faust* is confronted by the sneering *Mephistopheles,* who bars his way.

MEPHISTOPHELES (*contemptuously*):
　　Thou dreamer!
FAUST:
　　Thou hast overheard?
MEPHISTOPHELES:
　　I have. Your parting with its modest word!
　　Go back, on the spot, to your school again!

FAUST:
　　Let me pass!
MEPHISTOPHELES:
　　Not a step; you shall stay and overhear
　　That which she telleth the stars!
　　See! She opens the window!

Marguerite had entered the house, but returns to the window, looks out at the night and stars, and pours forth her soul in song.

MARGUERITE (*leaning out in the moonlight*):
　　He loves me! He loves me!
　　Repeat it again, bird that callest!
　　Soft wind that fallest!
　　He loves me! Ah, our world is glorious,

And more than Heaven above! The air is balmy
With the very breath of love!
How the bows embrace and murmur!
Ah, speed, thou night, away!

KRELING

MARGUERITE LONGS FOR FAUST'S RETURN

One of the most original and beautiful of the Faust melodies, this makes a fitting termination of the exquisitely beautiful Garden Scene. A lovely melody in 9/8 time, divided between flute and clarionet, forms the basis of the movement, and in this the soprano joins in short dreamy phrases.

Her longing for the passing of night and the return of *Faust*, expressed in the last ecstatic phrase, is answered by the cry of her lover, and *Mephistopheles*, who has been holding *Faust* back, now releases him.

FAUST (*rushing to the window*):
  Marguerite!
MARGUERITE:
  Ah! (*she faints in his arms*).
MEPHISTOPHELES (*with sardonic laughter*):
  There! Ha, ha, ha! ha!
    (*The curtain slowly falls.*)

Fantasie from Garden Scene

By Mischa Elman, Violinist
(Piano acc.)
64122 10-inch, $1.00

For those who wish to enjoy some of the exquisite melodies of this act in an instrumental form only, the *potpourri* by Elman is included here.

In this record the young artist does not show us feats of execution, but brings out all the sensuous beauty of the music which Gounod composed for this immortal scene. It is one of the loveliest bits of violin playing imaginable.

ACT IV—The Desertion

Quando a te lieta (When All Was Young)

By Louise Homer, Contralto (*In Italian*) 88200 12-inch, $3.00

The opening of the fourth scene shows the unhappy *Marguerite* seated at her spinning wheel, brooding over the sorrows which have overtaken her young life. *Siebel*, her faithful friend, enters and talks of vengeance against the absent *Faust*, but *Marguerite* defends him and sadly goes into the house. Left alone, *Siebel*, with gentle melancholy, sings this exquisite romance, beginning:

> When all was young and pleas-ant, May, was bloom-ing.

This song has long been a favorite number with many famous contraltos, and its lovely melody is frequently used in our churches as a setting to "Come Unto Me," and other sacred words.

SIEBEL:
When all was young and pleasant May was blooming,
  I, thy poor friend, took part with thee in play;
Now that the cloud of Autumn dark is glooming,
  Now is for me, too, mournful the day!

Hope and delight have pass'd from life away!
  We were not born with true love to trifle!
Nor born to part because the wind blows cold:
  What tho' storm the summer garden rifle,
O Marguerite! Still on the bough is left a leaf of gold!

From Ditson libretto, copy't 1896.

The scene abruptly changes to the square in front of the cathedral, with the house of *Marguerite* shown at one side. The victorious soldiers, returning from the war, enter, accompanied by delighted wives and sweethearts, and sing their famous Soldiers' Chorus, a jubilant inspiring number, and one of the finest marches ever composed.

Deponiam il brando (Soldiers' Chorus)

By New York Grand Opera Chorus	(In Italian)	74214	12-inch, $1.50
By Pryor's Band		16502	10-inch, .75
By La Scala Chorus	(Double-Faced—See page 107) (Italian)	62624	10-inch, .75
By Mountain Ash Party of Wales	(In English)	5689	10-inch, .60

SOLDIERS' CHORUS—ACT IV

This number was written for a previous opera by Gounod, but was taken bodily and added to Faust, a happy thought which added another splendid touch to a successful work.

Several renditions of this great chorus are offered, both vocal and instrumental, and a complete translation of the words is given.

Fold the flag, my brothers,
Fold the flag, my brothers,
Lay by the spear!
We come from the battle once more;
Our pale praying mothers,
Our wives and sisters dear,
Our loss need not deplore,
Yes! 'tis a joy for men victorious,
To the children by the fire, trembling in our arms,
To old age of old time glorious,
To talk of war's alarms!

Glory and love to the men of old,
Their sons may copy their virtues bold,
Courage in heart and sword in hand,
Ready to fight or ready to die, for Fatherland!
Who needs bidding to dare, by a trumpet blown?

Who lacks pity to spare, when the field is won?
Who would fly from a foe, if alone, or last?
And boast he was true, as cowards might do
When peril is past?
Glory and love to the men of old, etc.

Now to home again we come,
The long and fiery strife of battle over;
Rest is pleasant after toil as hard as ours
Beneath a stranger sun.
Many a maiden fair is waiting here
To greet her truant soldier lover,
And many a heart will fail and brow grow pale,
To hear the tale of peril he has run!
Glory and love to the men of old, etc.

The unhappy *Marguerite*, shunned by her companions and deserted by all save the faithful *Siebel*, is brooding within the cottage, fearing to meet her brother, who has just returned from the war. *Mephistopheles*, not content with the evil he has already wrought, returns to taunt the maiden with her fault, and sings this insulting and literally infernal song, each verse of which ends with a mocking laugh.

Serenade—Mephistopheles

By Pol Plançon, Bass	(In French)	85100	12-inch, $3.00
By Pol Plançon, Bass	(In French)	81040	10-inch, 2.00
By Marcel Journet, Bass	(In French)	74036	12-inch, 1.50
By Marcel Journet, Bass	(In French)	64137	10-inch, 1.00

After the second verse occurs this famous passage—

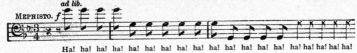

Ha! ha! ha! ha! ha! ha! ha! ha! ha! ha! ha! ha! ha! ha! ha! ha! ha! ha! ha!

with its beginning on a high G and its octave jumps to the low G, concluding with a peal of Mephistophelean laughter.

Two versions, by two famous exponents of the part of *Mephistopheles*, are offered for your choice.

SAMMARCO AS VALENTINE

MEPHISTOPHELES:
Thou who here art soundly sleeping,
Close not thus thy heart,
Close not thus thy heart!
Caterina! wake thee! wake thee!
Caterina! wake! 'tis thy lover near!
Hearken to my love-lorn pleading;
Let thy heart be interceding,
Awake, love, and hear!
Ha, ha, ha, ha, ha! ha! ha! ha! ha! ha!
Don't come down until, my dear,
The nuptial ring appear
On thy finger sparkling clearly—
The wedding-ring—the ring shineth clear.
Ha! ha! ha! ha! etc.

Caterina! cruel, cruel!
Cruel to deny to him who loves thee—
And for thee doth mourn and sigh—
A single kiss from thy rosy lips.
Thus to slight a faithful lover,
Who so long hath been a rover,
Too bad, I declare!
Ha, ha, ha, ha, ha!
Not a single kiss, my dear,
Unless the ring appear!
Ha, ha, ha, ha! etc.

Plancon's *Mephistopheles* was invariably a finished performance—witty, elegant, debonaire and sonorous. It is a polished Devil that he pictured; yet beneath the polish we could see the sinister Satan ever present. In his record of this mocking serenade he is at his best, and it is sung with the brilliancy and vocal finish to be expected of this fine artist.

Journet's impersonation has also been highly praised, and he sings the music superbly, acting with freedom and with an elegance that exhibits the Prince of Darkness as a gentleman, though we never lose sight of his inner nature. The famous serenade is given with much spirit by this artist.

Que voulez-vous, messieurs? (What is Your Will?) (Duel Scene)

By Enrico Caruso, Tenor; Antonio Scotti, Baritone; and Marcel Journet, Bass
(*In French*) 95206 12-inch, $5.00
By Ellison Van Hoose, Tenor; Marcel Journet, Bass; and Emilio de Gogorza, Baritone
(*In French*) 74004 12-inch, 1.50

Valentine, smarting with shame of his sister's disgrace, comes from the house and exclaims, "What is your will with me?" *Mephistopheles* replies in his most mocking voice that their "serenade" was not meant for him. "For my sister, then!" cries *Valentine* in a rage, and draws his sword. The great trio then follows, leading up to a splendid climax.

This thrilling trio forms one of the most effective scenes in the opera, and is closely followed by the duel, in which *Valentine* is wounded.

MELBA AS MARGUERITE—
CHURCH SCENE

101

The Death of Valentine

KRELING   MARGUERITE AT THE SHRINE

Morte di Valentino (Death of Valentine)

By Antonio Scotti, Baritone, and Grand Opera Chorus

(*In French*) 88282 12-inch, $3.00

Leaving the wounded *Valentine* on the ground, the assailants rapidly depart, and the crowd of soldiers and women assemble around the dying soldier, the chorus here crying out in accents of pity, in which *Marguerite* joins. *Valentine*, seeing his sister, utters curses upon her, the solemnity of which is enhanced by the sustained trumpet tones in the accompaniment. The throng endeavor to mitigate the dying man's anger, and *Marguerite* begs forgiveness, but *Valentine* dies with the curse upon his lips.

This dramatic scene is vividly pictured in the wonderful painting by Kreling, reproduced on the opposite page.

Scene de L'Église (I) (Church Scene, Part I)

By Geraldine Farrar, Soprano, and Marcel Journet, Bass

(*In French*) 89035 12-inch, $4.00

We now come to the impressive and almost terrible scene outside the church.

Marguerite, cursed by her dying brother, abandoned by all but the faithful *Siebel*, is kneeling at a small altar. Fearing to enter, and endeavoring to seek consolation in prayer, she supplicates Heaven to accept her repentance.

MARGUERITE:
  Oh, Thou who on Thy throne
  Giv'st an ear for repentance!
  Here, before Thy feet, let me pray!
MEPHISTOPHELES (*invisible*):
  No! thou shalt pray no more!
  Let her know ere she prayeth,
  Demons of ill, what is in store!
CHORUS OF DEMONS:
  Marguerite!
MARGUERITE (*faintly*):
  Who calls me?
DEMONS:
  Marguerite!
MARGUERITE (*terrified*):
  I falter—afraid!
  Oh! save me from myself!
  Has even now the hour of torture begun!

MEPHISTOPHELES (*taunting her*):
  Recollect the old time, when the angels, caressing,
  Did teach thee to pray.
  Recollect how thou camest to ask for a blessing
  At the dawn of the day!
  When thy feet did fall back, and thy breath it did falter
  As though to ask for aid;
  Recollect thou wast then of the rite and the altar
  In thine innocence afraid!
  And now be glad and hear
  Thy playmates do claim thee from below, to their home!
  The worm to welcome thee, the fire to warm thee,
  Wait but till thou shalt come!

As this terrible prophecy is heard from the invisible Evil Spirit, *Marguerite* is overcome with terror and sinks down almost fainting.

Scene de L'Église (II) (Church Scene, Part II)

By Geraldine Farrar, Soprano; Marcel Journet, Bass; and Metropolitan Opera Chorus   (*In French*) 89037 12-inch, $4.00

The unhappy girl, beside herself with terror, cries out wildly

  Ah! what sound in the gloom,
  Is beneath me, around me?
  Angels of wrath? is this your sentence of cruel doom?

MARGUERITE AND THE TEMPTER

Then as the chorale is heard from within the church, she endeavors to break the encircling Satanic spell and kneels again in prayer.

CHOIR (*within the church*):
When the book shall be unsealed,
When the future be revealed,
What frail mortal shall not yield?
MARGUERITE:
And I, the frailest of the frail,
Have most need of Thy forgiveness!
MEPHISTOPHELES:
No! Let them pray, let them weep!
But thy sin is deep, too deep,
To hope forgiveness! No!
CHOIR:
Where shall human sinner be,
How lie hid in earth and sea,
To escape eternity?
MARGUERITE (*wildly*):
Ah, the hymn is around and above me,
It bindeth a cord 'round my brow!
MEPHISTOPHELES:
Farewell, thy friends who love thee!
And thy guardians above thee!
The past is done! the payment now!
MARGUERITE AND CHOIR:
O Thou! on Thy throne, who dost hear me,
Let a tear of mercy fall near me,
To pity and save!
MEPHISTOPHELES:
Marguerite! Mine art thou!
MARGUERITE: Ah!

Tormented beyond further endurance, the unhappy girl's reason gives way, and with a terrible cry she falls lifeless before the church.

Words are pitiful things in describing such a scene as this, given as these two artists render it. The conflict in the soul of *Marguerite*, the taunting apostrophe of *Mephistopheles* as he strives to prevent his victim from praying, while the sombre strains of the *Dies irae* issue from the church, form a musical picture which cannot be adequately described.

The two records on which this great scene have been impressed are among the most effective in the Faust series.

THE WALPURGIS NIGHT

At the period of the first production of Faust, a ballet was an absolutely essential part of an opera, if it were to be given at the Paris Opera, though to-day it is seldom performed.

Gounod placed his ballet between the death of *Valentine* and the Prison Scene; called it a Walpurgis Night, set it in a mountain fastness amid ruins, and called to the scene the classic queens, *Helen, Phryne* and *Cleopatra,* who danced to weird and distorted versions of melodies from the opera.

Ballet Music (Part I—Valse, "Les Nubiennes")

By L'Orchestre Symphonique, Paris   58015 12-inch, $1.00

The first part, which in the opera accompanies the dance of the Nubian Slaves, is a most striking portion, beginning with introductory chords, followed by the violins in this delicious melody:
afterward repeated with bassoon obbligato.

Ballet Music No. 2—Adagio (Cleopatra and the Golden Cup)

By L'Orchestre Symphonique, Paris   58018 12-inch, $1.00

The second part is the *adagio* movement accompanying the scene in which the Nubian Slaves drink from golden cups the poisons of *Cleopatra,* who herself moistens her lips from a vase in which she has dissolved her most precious pearls.

Ballet Music Nos. 5 and 6 (Les Troyennes et Variation)
By L'Orchestre Symphonique, Paris   58020   12-inch, $1.00

These two parts are heard during the appearance of the goddess *Phryne*, who rises, a veiled apparition, and commands the dance to recommence.

Ballet Music—Finale, " Danse de Phryne "
By L'Orchestre Symphonique, Paris   58021   12-inch, $1.00

The finale is brisk in movement, rising to a wild climax and ending suddenly with a crashing chord. It is a most effective and exciting bit of ballet composition, and accompanies the dance of *Phryne*, who surpasses all her rivals and wins the favor of *Faust*, arousing the anger and jealousy of the courtesans—*Helen, Cleopatra, Aspasia* and *Lais*—and the dance develops into a bacchanalian frenzy, graphically pictured in Gounod's music.

ACT V
SCENE—*The Prison Cell of Marguerite*

The short final act of Faust is truly one of the grandest of operatic compositions, Goethe's story giving Gounod ample opportunity for some most dramatic writing. *Marguerite's* reason is gone—grief and remorse have driven her insane, and in a frenzy she has destroyed her child. Condemned to death, she lies in prison, into which *Mephistopheles* and *Faust*, defying bolts and bars, have entered.

"Mon coeur est pénétré d'épouvante!" My Heart is Torn with Grief)
By Geraldine Farrar and Enrico Caruso   (*In French*) 89033   12-inch, $4.00

Gazing at the unhappy girl, who is sleeping on a pallet of straw, *Faust* cries:

Penetran è il mio cor di spa - ven - to! O tor - tu ra!
My heart is torn with grief and re-pent - ance! O, what an - guish!

and, as the full measure of his own guilt comes to him, continues:

FAUST:
Oh, what anguish! She lies there at my feet
A young and lovely being, imprisoned here
As if herself, not I, were guilty!
No wonder that her fright has reason ta'en away!
Marguerite! Marguerite!

MARGUERITE (*awaking*):
Ah, do I hear once again, the song of time gone by—
'Twas not the cry of the demons—
'Tis his own voice I hear!

She forgets all but that her loved one is before her, and sings in a transport of love

MARGUERITE:
Ah! I love thee only!
Since thou cam'st to find me
No tears more, shall blind me!
Take me up to Heaven,
To Heaven by thy aid!

FAUST (*supporting her tenderly*):
Yes, I love thee only!
Let who will, now goad
Or mock me, or upbraid.
Earth will grow as Heaven.
By thy beauty made!

Attends! voici la rue (This is the Fair)
By Geraldine Farrar and Enrico Caruso   (*In French*) 89034   12-inch, $4.00

Marguerite's mind wandering, she sings dreamily of the Fair, where first *Faust* appeared to her

'Tis the Fair!
Where I was seen by you, in happy days gone by,
The day your eye did not dare
To meet my eye!

Marguerite now rehearses the first meeting with *Faust*, his respectful greeting, and her modest and dignified reply

"High born and lovely maid, forgive my humble duty;
Let me your willing slave, attend you home to-day?"
"No my lord! not a lady am I, nor yet a beauty,
Not a lady, not a beauty,
And do not need an arm to help me on my way!"
FAUST (*in despair*):
Come away! If thou lov'st me!
MARGUERITE (*dreamily, her thoughts in the past*):
How my garden is fresh and fair!

Every flower is incense breathing,
And through the still evening air
A cloud of dew, with perfume wreathing;
Hark! how the nightingale above
To every glowing crimson rose
Fondly murmurs thy love!
FAUST (*urging her*):
Yes! but come! They shall not harm thee!
Come away!
There is yet time to save thee!
Marguerite! Thou shalt not perish!
MARGUERITE (*listlessly*):
'Tis all too late! Here let me die!
Farewell! My memory live to cherish!

KRELING

The Redemption of Marguerite

The impassioned duet then follows, *Faust* endeavoring to persuade her to escape; but the poor weak mind cannot grasp the idea of safety. The duet is interrupted by the impatient *Mephistopheles,* whose brutal *"Alerte"* begins the final trio.

Trio—Alerte! ou vous êtes perdus! (Then Leave Her!)

By Farrar, Caruso and Journet   (In French)   95203   12-inch, $5.00
By Giuseppina Huguet, Soprano; Pietro Lara, Tenor; and Torres
De Luna, Baritone   (*Double-faced—See below*)   (In Italian)   62085   10-inch,   .75

Mephistopheles, fearing the coming of the jailers, and uncertain of his own power, cries out:

Then leave her, then leave her, or remain to your shame;
If it please you to stay, mine is no more the game!

MARGUERITE (*in horror, recognizing the Evil One, the cause of all her woes*):
Who is there! Who is there!
Dost thou see, there in the shadow
With an eye like a coal of fire!

What does he here! He who forbade me to pray!

MEPHISTOPHELES (*to Faust*):
Let us go, ere with dawn
Doth justice come on;
Hark! the horses panting in the courtyard below,
To bear us away!
Come, ere 'tis day; or stay and behold her undone!

As he sings, the tramping and neighing of horses are heard in the accompaniment.

MARGUERITE (*with fresh courage, defying him*):
Away, for I will pray! (*in rapture*)
Holy Angels, in Heaven bless'd
My spirit longs with thee to rest!
FAUST: Come, mine own,
Ere 'tis too late to save thee!

The inspiring trio, perhaps the most thrilling and moving of all operatic compositions, then commences; *Marguerite* continuing her prayer, *Faust* urging her to follow him, while *Mephistopheles,* in desperation, repeats his warning to *Faust*.

MEPHISTOPHELES:
Let us leave her! Come or be lost, for the day is near!
Come away! the dawn is grey,
Come, ere they claim thee!
FAUST:
Come with me! Come, wilt thou not hear?
Lean on my breast. The early dawn is grey.
O come! I'm here to save thee!

MARGUERITE:
Holy angels, in Heaven bless'd,
My spirit longs with thee to rest!
Great Heaven, pardon grant, I implore thee,
For soon shall I appear before thee!
O save me! ere I perish forever;
To my despair give ear, I pray thee!
Holy angels, in Heaven bless'd,
My spirit longs with thee to rest! (*She dies.*)

At the close of the trio, *Mephistopheles* is about to triumph over the soul of his victim, when a company of angels appear and announce that *Marguerite* is saved. The Evil One, dragging *Faust* with him, disappears in a fiery abyss.

DOUBLE-FACED AND MISCELLANEOUS FAUST RECORDS

Selection from Faust	By Sousa's Band	31104	12-inch,	$1.00
Selection from Faust	By Victor Band	35016	12-inch,	1.25
Crown Diamonds Overture	By Victor Band			
Flower Song By Corinne Morgan (In English)		35086	12-inch,	1.25
Drink To Me Only With Thine Eyes	By Harry Macdonough			
Aria dei gioielli (Jewel Song) By Huguet (In Italian)		68160	12-inch,	1.25
La Kermesse (Kermesse Scene) By La Scala Chorus (In Italian)				
Dio possente By Francesco Cigada (In Italian)		68275	12-inch,	1.25
Favorita—Quando le soglie By Mileri and Minolfi (In Italian)				
Alerte! ou vous êtes perdus! Huguet, Lara and De Luna		62085	10-inch,	.75
Le parlate d'amor (Flower Song) By Emma Zaccaria				
Deponiam il brando (Soldiers' Chorus) By La Scala Cho		62624	10-inch,	.75
Don Pasquale—Sogno soave e casto By Acerbi, Tenor (In Italian)				
Io voglio il piacer By Pini-Corsi and Sillich (In Italian)		63174	10-inch,	.75
Forza del Destino—Solenne in quest' ora Colazza and Caronna				
Soldiers' Chorus	Pryor's Band	16502	10-inch,	.75
Devil's March (von Suppe)	Pryor's Band			
Waltz from Kermesse Scene	Pryor's Band	16552	10-inch,	.75
In Happy Moments (from Maritana)	Alan Turner			

(German)
DIE FAVORITIN
(Dee Fah-ve-ree'-tin)

(Italian)
LA FAVORITA
(Lah Fah-vo-ree'-tah)

(English)
THE FAVORITE

OPERA IN FOUR ACTS

Text by Alphonse Royer and Gustave Waez, adapted from a drama of Baculard-Darnaud, "*Le Comte de Comminges*." Music by Gaetano Donizetti. In its present form it was first produced at the *Académie*, Paris, December 2, 1840. First London production February 16, 1847. Produced in America July 29, 1853.

Cast

ALPHONSO XI, King of Castile.....................................Baritone
FERDINAND, a young novice of the Convent of St. James of Compostella,
   afterwards an officer..Tenor
DON GASPAR, the King's Minister...................................Tenor
BALTHAZAR, Superior of the Convent of St. James...................Bass
LEONORA DI GUSMANN, the King's favorite......................Soprano
INEZ, her confidante...Soprano

Courtiers, Guards, Monks, Attendants, etc.

Scene and Period: The action is supposed to take place in Castile, about the year 1340.

Favorita so abounds with charming airs, fine music and striking dramatic situations that it is difficult to account for the neglect of it in America. The opera was revived, it is true, in 1905, with Caruso, Walker, Scotti and Plançon, but has not since been given.

However, for the consolation of those who admire Verdi's beautiful work, the Victor has rendered all the best airs and several of the stirring concerted numbers, so that the opera, given by famous artists, may be enjoyed in the comfort and seclusion of the home.

ACT I

SCENE—*The Monastery of St. James*

The rise of the curtain discloses a Spanish cloister with its secluded garden and weather-stained wall, while in the distance is a glimpse of the tiled roofs of the city. *Ferdinand,* a novice in the monastery, confesses to the Prior, *Balthazar,* that he has seen a beautiful woman and has fallen in love with her. He describes his meeting with the fair one in a lovely song, *Una vergine.*

Una vergine (Like An Angel)
By Florencio Constantino, Tenor
                              (In Italian) **64090 10-inch, $1.00**

The good Prior is horrified and urges him to confess and repent.

Non sai tu che d'un giusto (Know'st Thou)
By Gino Martinez-Patti, Tenor, and Cesare Preve, Bass
(Double-Faced—See page 112)   *(In Italian)* **62635 10-inch, $0.75**

BALTHAZAR:
Ah, my son, my life's latest solace,
May thy innocence rescue thee still!
Thou, thou who shouldst be my successor,
And all my solemn duties fill.
FERDINAND:
Ah, father, I love her!
BALTHAZAR:
This woman, wretched one! oh, knowest thou
Who has lur'd thee thus to shame?
Knowest thou her, for whom thy holiest vow
Is forfeit? Her rank—her name?
FERDINAND:
I know her not; but I love her!
BALTHAZAR:
Begone! too profane! Fly these cloisters
Far, far from hence!—avoid my sight.

FERDINAND *(in rapture)*:
Yes, ador'd one! this heart's dearest idol!
For thee I will break ev'ry tie!
To thee all my soul I surrender—
At thy dear feet content to die!
Forgive me! Father, I go!
BALTHAZAR:
Hence, audacious! away in madness!
I'll not curse thee! no—depart!
If Heaven spare thee, soon in sadness,
Thou'lt hither bring a broken heart!
FERDINAND:
Ah, dear Idol! this heart so enchaining,
In vain thy spell I strive to break!
To thee only my truth maintaining,
My cloister I forsake!

COPY'T DUPONT

CARUSO AS FERDINAND

The Prior's pleading fails to restore *Ferdinand* to his duty, and he leaves the convent to search for the beautiful unknown. As he goes he turns and stretches out his arms toward *Balthazar,* who averts his head.

The scene changes to the Island of Leon, where *Inez,* an attendant of *Leonora,* and a chorus of maidens are gathering flowers. They sing a melodious chorus,

Bei raggi lucenti (Ye Beams of Gold)

By Ida Roselli, Soprano, and La Scala Chorus   (*In Italian*) *62635 10-inch, $0.75

which tells of the love which their mistress feels for a handsome youth whom she has seen but once, and who is now on his way to the Isle at *Leonora's* request.

Ferdinand, who, shortly after his departure from the monastery, had received a note bidding him come to the Isle of Leon, now arrives in a boat, blindfolded, is assisted to land by the maidens, and the bandage removed. He gazes around him wonderingly, and asks *Inez* the name of the unknown lady who has sent for him. She smilingly refuses, and tells him only her mistress may reveal the secret. *Leonora* now appears, and the maidens depart. A tender love scene follows, but the Favorite is anxious, fearing that *Ferdinand* will learn that she is the King's mistress. She shows him a parchment which she says will insure his future, and then bids him leave her forever.

Fia vero! lasciarti! (Fly From Thee!)

By Clotilde Esposito and Sig. Martinez-Patti *68309 12-inch, $1.25

Ferdinand, beginning the duet, indignantly refuses, saying:

FERDINAND:
Fly from thee! Oh, never!
'Twere madness to try
From thee to sever;
'Twere better to die!
LEONORA:
Farewell! Go; forget me!

Thy vows and thy love!
No longer regret me—
Mine image remove.
The rose tho' she fair be,
A canker that wears,
Can never restor'd be
By anguish or tears!

Inez enters and whispers to *Leonora* that the King has arrived at the villa. *Leonora* gives *Ferdinand* the parchment and exits hastily. He reads it and is delighted to find that it is a captain's commission, and declares that he will win great honors to lay at the feet of his love.

ACT II

SCENE—*Gardens of the Alcazar Palace*

The King enters and admires the beauty of the palace, which he has just acquired from the Moors by the victory of his army, led by the young captain, *Ferdinand.* A message comes from *Balthazar,* the King's father-in-law, who is at the head of the powerful Church party, and *Alfonso* is threatened with the wrath of the Church if he does not give up *Leonora.* In a fine air he declares he will not submit.

Vien Leonora (Leonora, Thou Alone)

By Francesco Cigada, Baritone   (*In Italian*) *68061 12-inch, $1.25

Leonora enters and the King tenderly asks the cause of her melancholy. She tells him her position is intolerable, and asks that she be allowed to leave the Court. She begins the duet, *Quando le soglie.*

Quando le soglie (From My Father's Halls)

By Lina Mileri, Contralto, and Renzo Minolfi, Baritone
(*In Italian*) *68275 12-inch, $1.25

Leonora recalls the circumstances connected with her departure from her father's home.

Double-Faced Record—For title of opposite side see DOUBLE-FACED LA FAVORITA RECORDS, page 112.

LEONORA:
When from the halls of my father you
  bore me,
A poor simple maiden, betray'd, deceived,
Alas! within these walls I hop'd, fulfilled
Would be those vows , so sworn, and so
  believ'd!
KING (with tender remorse):
No more! No more!
LEONORA:
Silent and alone, shunned by the world,
Live I in the dark: the mistress of the King.
Vainly glitter these jewels,
Vainly bloom these flowers around me.
God knows my afflictions!
E'en if the lip may smile, the heart is
  weeping!
KING:
But tell me the first cause of your grief.

LEONORA:
Ah! ask not to know it.
Permit me, sir, to leave this court!
KING:
No man can love thee more than I;
Thou shalt see how my heart adores thee!
LEONORA:
I dare not look so high as thee.
KING (aside):
Oh, love! soft love! her bosom filling,
With sweet response each fibre thrilling,
Inspire her heart!
LEONORA (aside):
Oh, love, alas! this bosom filling,
With secret woe each fibre thrilling!
KING:
Disperse this gloom; enjoy the feasts
Spread 'round thee by my tender love!

They are interrupted by the entrance of *Balthazar,* who brings the mandate from the
Pope. The King defies him, saying:

KING:
My will is sacred! On my brow
Rests the royal diadem!

This lady I shall wed, and whoever
Doubts my right shall feel
The anger of a monarch!

Balthazar then begins the great finale, one of the most impressive of the concerted
numbers.

Ah! paventa il furore (The Wrath of Heaven)
By Amelia Codolini, Mezzo-Soprano; Francesco Cigada, Baritone;
Aristodemo Sillich, Bass; La Scala Chorus
(*In Italian*) *16536 10-inch, $0.75

BALTHAZAR:
Do not call the wrath of God,
Avenging upon thee;
For it visiteth terribly
Those who do not bow to His will.
Hasten, pacify Heaven
Before the curse descendeth!
LEONORA:
I tremble with fear
In my inmost heart,
Lest this terrible blow
Should crush my fondest hopes.
KING:
Still this sudden tempest

Shall not bend me nor break me;
Calm thee, my Leonora,
Bright is thy destiny.
CHORUS:
We tremble with fear
In our inmost hearts,
Lest he call down upon himself
The wrath of Heaven!
BALTHAZAR (denouncing Leonora):
All ye that hear me
Shun the adultress;
Avoid the outcast,
Accurs'd of Heaven is she!

The curtain falls on a dramatic tableau,—*Leonora* weeping with shame, the King hesita-
ting between love and ambition, while the terrible *Balthazar* thunders the papal curse down
upon the guilty pair.

ACT III
SCENE—*A Room in the Palace*
Ferdinand is received by the King, who praises him for his great victories, and asks him
to name his own reward. The young captain asks for the hand of a noble lady to whom
he owes all his renown, and when the King asks her name he points to *Leonora. Alfonso*
gazes at her coldly and sternly and sings his ironical air.

A tanto amor (Thou Flow'r Beloved)
By Mario Ancona, Baritone
By Mattia Battistini, Baritone
By Francesco Cigada, Baritone

(*In Italian*) 88063 12-inch, $3.00
(*In Italian*) 92045 12-inch, 3.00
(*In Italian*) *16536 10-inch, .75

ALFONSO:
Thou flow'r belov'd,
And in hope's garden cherish'd,
With sighs and tears refresh'd,

Both night and morn;
Fad'st from my breast,
Thine ev'ry beauty perished,
And in thy stead alone have left a thorn!

He consents to the marriage, however, and announcing that they must prepare to wed in
an hour, goes out with *Ferdinand. Leonora* is distracted with the knowledge that she must
tell her secret to her lover. She calls *Inez,* and bidding her seek out *Ferdinand* and reveal
all, goes to her apartments to prepare for the wedding. *Inez* prepares to obey, but on her
way is arrested by the order of the King.

**Double-Faced Record*—For title of opposite side see DOUBLE-FACED LA FAVORITA RECORDS, page 112.*

The King enters with *Ferdinand,* to whom he gives the title of *Count of Zamora.* *Leonora* appears and is overjoyed to see *Ferdinand* still looking at her lovingly, not knowing that *Inez* has failed in her mission, and that he is yet ignorant of her secret.

The ceremony is performed and the pair are presented to the Court, but are met with cold and averted looks. *Ferdinand,* although not aware of the cause, resents this and is about to draw his sword when *Balthazar* enters and demands peace.

When he learns of the wedding he is horrified, and tells *Ferdinand* he has married the King's mistress. *Ferdinand* is furious and denounces the King, who, seized with sudden remorse, begins the great finale to Act III.

Orsù, Fernando (Stay! Hear Me, Ferdinand!)

By Maria Cappiello, Mezzo-Soprano; Giuseppe Acerbi, Tenor;
Francesco Cigada, Baritone   (*In Italian*)   *62659   10-inch, $0.75

Ferdinand hurls at the King's feet his badge of honor and his broken sword and leaves the Court, followed by *Balthazar.* *Leonora* faints as the curtain falls.

ACT IV

SCENE—*The Cloisters of the Monastery*

The opening number in this act is the impressive *Splendon piu belle,* considered by many critics to be the finest of the Favorita numbers. The scene represents the cloister at the Convent of St. James of Compostella, illumined by the rays of the rising sun. The monks have assembled to welcome back the prodigal *Ferdinand,* who, heartbroken at the falseness of *Leonora,* is returning to renew his vows. The ceremonies are conducted by *Balthazar,* who begins this great number.

Splendon più belle in ciel le stelle (In Heavenly Splendor)

By Marcel Journet and Metropolitan Chorus   74273   12-in., $1.50
By Torres de Luna, Bass, and La Scala Chorus (*In Italian*)   *68061   12-in.,   1.25
By Perello de Segurola, Bass, and La Scala Chorus (*Italian*)   *16551   10-inch.,   .75

Balthazar entreats him to lift his eyes from earthly things and contemplate the stars, which typify a forgiving Heaven.

CHORUS (*to Ferdinand*):
Turn thou to Heaven, where there is no grief!
BALTHAZAR AND CHORUS:
Look at the stars' heavenly splendor above!
Up to them the penitent prayers
Of a purified soul ascend,
And carry back peace and happiness!

The monks now go into the chapel to prepare for the final rites, and *Ferdinand,* left alone, casts a look behind him to the world he has left forever, and sings his lovely *Spirto gentil.*

Spirto gentil (Spirit So Fair)

By Enrico Caruso, Tenor   (*In Italian*)   88004   12-inch, $3.00
By Gennaro de Tura, Tenor   (*In Italian*)   76012   12-inch,   2.00
By Evan Williams, Tenor   (*In English*)   74141   12-inch,   1.50

Caruso's *Spirto gentil,* which was the gem of the recent Metropolitan revival, is given with dazzling brilliancy and with that luscious quality of voice so satisfying to the ear. The record is a supremely beautiful one, while the accompaniment is most delicate and pleasing.

FERDINAND:
Spirit so fair, brightly descending,
Then like a dream all sadly ending,
Hence from my heart, vision deceiving,
Phantom of love, grief only leaving,

In thee delighting, all else scorning,
A father's warning, my country, my fame!
Ah, faithless dame, a passion inviting,
Fair honor blighting, branding my name,
Grief alone thou leav'st, phantom of love!

Signor de Tura furnishes a lower priced Italian version, while Mr. Williams' rendering is also one of beauty and power.

The monks now lead *Ferdinand* to the chapel. *Leonora,* who has come hither disguised as a novice to entreat forgiveness of her lover, hears him take the final vows and despairingly falls at the altar. *Ferdinand* comes from the chapel, and seeing a poor novice, assists him to rise. He is at first horrified to recognize *Leonora,* and bids her begone, but she pleads for mercy.

LEONORA:
Ah, heavenlike, thy mercy showing,
Turn not thy heart away from me,
Whose bitter tears ne'er ceas'd from flowing
When parted, dear, from thee.
FERDINAND (*his love returning*):
From tears thy words persuasion borrow,
Like a spell their softness impart,
Those sighs, the hope of some bright morrow
Waken once more in my heart!

(*Impetuously.*)
I love thee!
Come, ah, come, 'tis vain restraining
Passion's torrent onward that dashes,
O'er my bosom still art thou reigning
And we together will live and die!
One thought on me like lightning flashes,
One voice hear I in thunder speaking,
Fly we hence, some calm shelter seeking,
Loving share we life's care and joy!

Pietoso al par d'un Nume (As Merciful as God)

By Clotilde Esposito, Soprano, and Martinez-Patti, Tenor
(*Double-faced—See below*)   (*In Italian*) 62659 10-inch, $0.75

Again gently reminding him of his vows, she falls from weakness and privation.

LEONORA:
No, no!
'Tis Heaven calls thee!
FERDINAND (*recklessly*):
Yet more power hath love;
Come, could I possess thee
There's naught I would not brave,
Aye, here and hereafter!

LEONORA (*feebly*):
Heav'n forgive me, now I'm dying,
Ferdinand, I am happy,
We shall hereafter meet no more to be parted
Farewell, now, farewell!
(*She dies.*)

(*Curtain*)

DOUBLE-FACED AND MISCELLANEOUS FAVORITA RECORDS

Quando le soglie (From My Father's Halls) By Lina Mileri, Contralto, and Renzo Minolfi, Baritone (*In Italian*)	68275	12-inch, $1.25
Faust—Dio possente (Gounod) By Francesco Cigada, Baritone (*In Italian*)		
Fia vero! lasciarti! (Fly From Thee!) By Clotilde Esposito, Soprano, and Sig. Martinez-Patti, Tenor (*In Italian*)	68309	12-inch, 1.25
Norma—In mia mano alfin tu sei By Ida Giacomelli, Soprano, and Gino Martinez-Patti, Tenor (*In Italian*)		
Vien Leonora (Leonora, Thou Alone) By Francesco Cigada, Baritone (*In Italian*)	68061	12-inch, 1.25
Splendon piu belle in ciel (In Heavenly Splendor) By Torres de Luna, Bass, and La Scala Chorus (*In Italian*)		
A tanto amor (Thou Flow'r Beloved) By Francesco Cigada, Baritone (*In Italian*)	16536	10-inch, .75
Ah! paventa il furore (The Wrath of Heaven) By Amelia Codolini, Mezzo-Soprano; Francesco Cigada, Baritone; Aristodemo Sillich, Bass (*In Italian*)		
Non sai tu che d'un giusto (Know'st Thou) By Gino Martinez-Patti, Tenor, and Cesare Preve, Bass (*In Italian*)	62635	10-inch, .75
Bei raggi lucenti (Ye Beams of Gold) By Ida Roselli, Soprano, and La Scala Chorus (*In Italian*)		
Orsu, Fernando (Stay! Hear Me, Fernando!) By Maria Cappiello, Mezzo-Soprano; Giuseppe Acerbi, Tenor; Francesco Cigada, Baritone (*In Italian*)	62659	10-inch, .75
Pietoso al par d'un Nume (As Merciful as God) By Clotilde Esposito, Soprano, and Gino Martinez-Patti, Tenor (*In Italian*)		
Splendon piu belle in ciel le stelle (In Heavenly Splendor) By Perello de Segurola, Bass, and Chorus (*In Italian*)	16551	10-inch, .75
Manon—Et je sais votre nom (If I Knew But Your Name) By Mlle. Korsoff, Soprano, and Leon Beyle, Tenor (*In French*)		

BEETHOVEN

(German)

FIDELIO

(Fee-day'-lee-o)

or, CONJUGAL LOVE

GRAND OPERA IN TWO ACTS

Words adapted by Joseph Sonnleithner from Bouilly's *Léonore, ou l'Amour Conjugal* (Leonora, or Conjugal Love). Music by Ludwig von Beethoven. First produced at the *Theatre an der Wein,* Vienna, November 20, 1805, in three acts, the cast including Weinkoff, Meier, Demmer, Milder and Rothe. A revised version was given in 1806 and a third production in 1814. Produced in London, at the King's Theatre, May 18, 1832. In English at Covent Garden, June 12, 1835. In Italian at Her Majesty's, May 20, 1851. In Paris at the Theâtre Lyrique, translated by Barbier and Carré, and in three acts, May 5, 1860. First American performance in New York, September 9, 1839, with Giubilei, Manvers and Poole. Other notable productions were in 1857, with Johannsen, Weinlich and Oehrlein; in 1858, with Mme. Caradori and Karl Formes; in 1868, with Mme. Rotter, Habelmann and Formes; the Damrosch production of 1884, with Mme. Brandt, Mlle. Belz and Herr Koegel; and in 1901, with Ternina as *Léonore.*

Characters

DON FERNANDO, Minister .... Baritone

DON PIZARRO, Governor of the State Prison .... Baritone

FLORESTAN, a prisoner... Tenor

LÉONORE, his wife, known as Fidelio............................ Soprano

ROCCO, jailor .... Bass

MARZELLINE, his daughter .... Soprano

JAQUINO, gatekeeper.. Tenor

CAPTAIN OF THE GUARD... Bass

LIEUTENANT .... Bass

Soldiers, Prisoners, People, etc.

Place: A Spanish State prison in the vicinity of Seville.

Fidelio must ever be regarded with great interest as being the only opera written by one of the greatest composers. Originally given as *Fidelio*, it was rewritten and condensed into two acts by Breuning, still a third revision being made in 1814 by Treitschke. At the time of the second production in 1806 the title was changed to *Leonore*, Beethoven writing a new overture, now known as *Leonore No. 3*. A portion of this splendid number has been played here by Pryor's Band.

BEETHOVEN (1770-1827)

Leonore Overture No. 3

By Arthur Pryor's Band (*Double-faced—See below*)
35181 12-inch, $1.25

The action of the opera occurs in a fortress near Seville. *Don Florestan*, a Spanish nobleman, has been imprisoned here for life, and to make his fate certain his mortal enemy, *Don Pizarro*, Governor of the prison, has announced his death, meanwhile putting the unfortunate man in the lowest dungeon, where he is expected to die by gradual starvation, thus rendering unnecessary a resort to violent means.

One of the best numbers in the opera is this fine air in D minor, which has been sung for the Victor by Mr. Goritz.

Ha, welch ein Augenblick (Fateful Moment)

By Otto Goritz, Baritone (*In German*) 64165 10-inch, $1.00

In this the wicked Governor unfolds his hatred and his malignant intentions toward *Florestan*.

GOVERNOR:
Fateful moment! My revenge is near!
Long I've waited for this hour,
Fearful lest he should escape me!
Over my enemy I triumph;
He who would my life have taken!
Oh, fateful moment!
Ah, what a day is this!
My vengeance shall be sated,
And thou, thy doom is fated.
Once in the dust I trembled
Beneath thy conquering steel,
But fortune's wheel is turning
In torments thou art burning
The victim of my hate!

An extremely pleasant and agreeable person this Spanish Governor must have been! Goritz, whose *Pizarro* is one of his greatest impersonations, sings this striking air in a highly effective manner, fairly exuding the spirit of revenge.

Don Florestan, however, has a devoted wife who refuses to believe the report of his death. Disguising herself as a servant, and assuming the name of *Fidelio*, she secures employment with *Rocco*, the head jailor. *Rocco's* daughter falls in love with the supposed handsome youth, and he is soon in such high favor that he is permitted to accompany *Rocco* on his visits to the prisoner.

Hearing that the Minister of the Interior is coming to the prison to investigate the supposed death of *Florestan*, the Governor decides to murder him, and asks *Rocco's* help. *Fidelio* overhears the conversation and gets *Rocco* to allow her to dig the grave. Just as *Don Pizarro* is about to strike the fatal blow, *Fidelio* rushes forward, proclaims herself the wife of the prisoner and shields him. The Governor is astonished for a moment, but recovers himself and is about to sacrifice both, when a flourish of trumpets announces the coming of the Minister, and *Don Pizarro* is soon disgraced, while *Florestan* is pardoned and given back to his faithful wife.

DOUBLE-FACED FIDELIO RECORD

{ Leonore Overture No. 3	Arthur Pryor's Band }	
{ Attila Selection	Arthur Pryor's Band }	35181 12-inch, $1.25

THE PHANTOM SHIP

(German)
DER FLIEGENDE HOLLÄNDER
(Dehr -gen-dih Hol´-lan-der)

(English)
FLYING DUTCHMAN

(Italian)
Il Vascello Fantasma
(Eel Vass-sel-low Fahn-tahz´-mah)

A ROMANTIC OPERA IN THREE ACTS

Text and score by Richard Wagner. First produced at the Royal Opera in Dresden, January 2, 1843, with a Paris production the following year under the title of *Le Vaisseau Fantôme*. First London production July 23, 1870; and in English by Carl Rosa in 1876; first New York production, in English, January 26, 1877; in German, March 12, 1877.

Cast

DALAND, a Norwegian sea captain........Bass
SENTA, his daughter...............Soprano
ERIC, a huntsman...................Tenor
MARY, Senta's nurse...............Contralto
DALAND'S STEERSMAN..............Tenor
THE DUTCHMAN.................Baritone
Sailors, Maidens, Hunters, etc.

Place : On the coast of Norway

115

THE STORY

One of the most melodious of Wagner's operas, and the most popular in Germany to-day, *Fliegende Holländer* is also the one which was most promptly condemned by the critics after its production. Its present vogue is a notable example of the change in musical taste since 1843.

Wagner was led to write the *Flying Dutchman* after reading Heine's legend of the unhappy mariner, who, after trying in vain to pass the Cape of Good Hope, had sworn that he would not desist if he had to sail on the ocean to eternity. To punish his blasphemy he is condemned to the fate of the Wandering Jew, his only hope of salvation lying in his release through the devotion unto death of a woman; and to find such a maiden he is allowed every seven years to go on shore.

Flying Dutchman Overture
By Pryor's Band   31787   12-inch, $1.00

The overture is a complete miniature drama, embodying the events of the opera to follow. Driven by the gale, the Phantom Ship approaches the shore, while amid the fury of the tempest is heard the theme of *The Curse:*

The storm increases and reaches its height in a wonderful piece of writing. No composer ever succeeded in portraying a raging storm with such vivid effect. Amid a lull in the tempest, we hear the melancholy complaint of the *Dutchman* from the great air in the first act, "*Wie oft . . . Mein Grab, es schloss sich nicht?*" (*My grave—I find it not!*) A gleam of hope appears in the Redemption theme, and a joyous strain is heard from the sailors of *Daland's* ship, which is safe in the harbor.

CAST OF THE OPERA IN WAGNER'S HANDWRITING

Thus the various events of the drama are presented in miniature; and the overture is in fact a complete *résumé* of the opera, summarizing the leading *motifs*. It is superbly played by Mr. Pryor's fine organization.

ACT I
SCENE—*The Coast of Norway*

The curtain rises showing a rocky sea coast in Norway, with the ship of *Daland* anchored near the shore. As the crew furl the sails, *Daland* goes ashore, and climbing the cliff, sees that he is only seven miles from home, but as he must wait for a change in the wind, bids the crew go below and rest.

The *Steersman* remains on watch, and to keep awake sings a sailor ballad:

STEERSMAN:
Through thunder and wars of distant seas,
　My maiden, come I near!
Over towering waves, with southern breeze,
　My maiden am I here!
My maiden, were there no south wind,
　I never could come to thee;
O fair south wind, to me be kind!
　My maiden, she longs for me!
　　Ho-yo-ho! Hallo-ho!

From the shores of the south, in far-off lands,
　I oft on thee have thought;
Through thunder and waves from Moorish strands,
　A gift I thee have brought.
My maiden, praise the sweet south wind—
　I bring thee a golden ring.
O. fair south wind, to me be kind!
　My maiden doth spin and sing.
　　Ho-yo-ho! Hallo-ho!

He soon falls asleep, however, and fails to see the *Flying Dutchman*, which now appears, with blood-red sails and black masts, for one of her periodical visits.

Wie oft in Meeres tiefsten Schlund (In Ocean's Deepest Wave)
By Otto Goritz, Baritone   (*In German*)   74230 12-inch, $1.50

The spectral crew furl the blood-red sails and drop the rusty anchor. The *Dutchman* stands on the deck, and delivers his great soliloquy. He gloomily gazes at the land, and sings his preliminary recitative:

The term is past, and once again are ended the seven long years;
The weary sea casts me upon the land.
Ha! haughty ocean!
A little while and thou again wilt bear me!
Though thou art changeful, unchanging is my doom!
Release, which on the land I seek for,
Never shall I meet with!
True, thou heaving ocean, am I to thee
Until thy latest billow shall break,
Until at last thou art no more!

An introduction in 6-8 *allegro molto* leads to the aria:

DUTCHMAN:
Engulf'd in ocean's deepest wave,
Oft have I long'd to find a grave;
But ah! a grave, I found it not!
I oft have blindly rushed along,
To find my death sharp rocks among;
But ah! my death, I found it not.
And oft, the pirate boldly daring,
My death I've courted from the sword,
Here, cried I, work thy deeds unsparing,
My ship with gold is richly stor'd!

Alas, the sea's rapacious son,
But sign'd the cross, and straight was gone
Nowhere a grave, no way of death!
Mine is a curse of living breath.
Thee do I pray
Bright angel sent from Heaven.
Was there a fruitless hope to mock me given,

When thou didst tell me how to gain release?
A single hope with me remaineth,
A single hope still standeth fast;
When all the dead are raised again,
Destruction then I shall attain.
Ye worlds, your curse continue not!
Endless destruction be my lot!

Daland comes on deck and is astonished to see the strange ship. He wakes the *Steersman* and they hail the stranger, who asks *Daland* to give him shelter in his home, offering him treasure from his ship. On hearing that *Daland* has a daughter, he proposes marriage. The simple Norwegian is dazzled by such an honor from a man apparently so wealthy, and freely consents, providing his daughter is pleased with the stranger.

The wind changes and *Daland* sails for his home, the *Dutchman* promising to follow at once.

FIRST ACT SETTING USED IN MUNICH

ACT II

SCENE—*A Room in Daland's Home*

Traft ihr das Schiff (Senta's Ballad)

By Johanna Gadski, Soprano

(In German) 88116 12-inch, $3.00

The maidens are busily spinning—all but *Senta, Daland's* daughter, who is idly dreaming, with her eyes fixed on the fanciful portrait of the *Flying Dutchman* which hangs on the wall.

The legend of the unhappy *Hollander* has made a strong impression on the young girl, and he seems almost a reality to her. The maidens ridicule her, saying that her lover, *Eric,* will be jealous of the *Dutchman. Senta* rouses herself and commences the ballad, which begins with the motive of *The Curse.* With growing enthusiasm she goes on, describing the unhappy lot of the man condemned to sail forever on the sea unless redeemed by the love of a woman. Then with emotion she cries:

Doch kann dem blei-chen Man-ne Er lö-sung ein-stens noch wer - den,
Yet this the spec-tral man from his life - long curse may de - liv er,

Senta and the Maidens   (Mme. Gadski on the right)

This is the theme of *Redemption by Woman's Love,* and as *Senta* sings the beautifully tender and melodious phrase, she runs toward the portrait with outstretched arms, hardly conscious of the now alarmed maidens.

SENTA:
Yo-ho-hoe! Yo-ho-hoe! Yo-ho-hoe! Yo-ho-hoe!
Saw ye the ship on the raging deep
Blood-red the canvas, black the mast?
On board unceasing watch doth keep
The vessel's master pale and ghast!
Hui! How roars the wind! Yo-ho-hoe! Yo-ho-hoe!
Hui! How bends the mast! Yo-ho-hoe! Yo-ho-hoe!
Hui! Like an arrow she flies
Without aim, without goal, without rest!
(*She gazes at the portrait with growing excitement*)
Yet can the spectre seaman
Be freed from the curse infernal,
Find he a woman on earth
Who'll pledge him her love eternal.
Ah! that the unhappy man may find her
Pray, that Heaven may soon
In pity grant him this boon!

Mme. Gadski, whose *Senta* is always a fine impersonation, sings this dramatic number most expressively. The difficult attack on the high G, which occurs several times, is beautifully taken and perfectly recorded.

DUPONT   GADSKI AS SENTA

The maidens are so alarmed at *Senta's* outburst of passion that they run out and call *Eric,* who meets them at the door with news of the *Dutchman's* arrival. They run to the shore while *Eric* remains and reproaches *Senta.* She refuses to listen and the distracted lover runs out.

Suddenly the door opens and the *Dutchman* appears. *Senta* is transfixed with surprise as she involuntarily compares the portrait with the living man. A long silence follows. The *Dutchman,* his eyes fixed on the glowing face of the maiden, advances toward her. *Daland* soon observes that the others pay no attention to him, and well satisfied with the apparent understanding between the stranger and his daughter, leaves them together.

The *Hollander* sees in *Senta* the angel of whom he had dreamed and who is to banish the curse, and she sees the original of the portrait on which the sympathy of her girlish and romantic heart had been lavished. The *Hollander* asks *Senta* if she agrees with her father's choice of a husband. She gladly consents, and a long love duet follows, the final theme of which is "faith above all."

Daland re-enters and is delighted to find such a complete understanding between the two. He invites the *Dutchman* to the fête that evening in celebration of the safe arrival of the Norwegian ship. *Senta* repeats her vow unto death, and a magnificent trio closes the act.

DESTINN AS SENTA

ACT III
SCENE—*Daland's Harbor*

This scene shows the ships anchored in the bay near *Daland's* home. *Daland's* vessel is gay with lanterns, in contrast to the gloom and silence which marks the *Dutchman's* ship. A gay Norwegian chorus is followed by a spirited hornpipe with a most peculiar rhythm. Bits of these numbers are to be heard in the Pryor's Band records of the Overture and Fantasia.

The maidens now appear with baskets of eatables, and are joyfully received by the sailors. Having supplied the wants of their own countrymen, they approach the *Dutchman's* ship and call to the sailors, but only a ghostly silence rewards them. Piqued at this neglect, they turn their remaining baskets over to the Norwegian sailors and return home.

Suddenly the sea around the *Dutchman* begins to rise, and a weird glow lights the ship.

The crew appear and begin a sepulchral chant, which causes the gay Norwegians to cease singing and cross themselves in terror, and finally to go below. With mocking laughter, the crew of the *Dutchman* also disappear and the ship is in darkness.

Senta and *Eric* appear and a stormy scene ensues. He has heard of her engagement to the strange captain, and is beside himself. He kneels and begs her to have pity on him. Suddenly the *Hollander* comes upon the scene and is horror-stricken at the tableau. Believing *Senta* to be false, he cries, "All is lost; *Senta*, farewell!"

The crews of both ships appear and the townsmen rush to the scene. The *Dutchman* reveals his identity and declares himself cursed forever. He springs upon his ship—the crimson sails expand as if by magic and the ship departs, with the crew chanting their weird refrain.

Senta, in wild exaltation, rushes to the highest rock, calling to the departing vessel, "I am faithful unto death," and throws herself into the sea. The *Flying Dutchman* sinks beneath the water, and rising from the wreck can be seen the forms of *Senta* and the *Dutchman* clasped in each other's arms. The curse has been banished—true love has triumphed!

FROM AN OLD PRINT

SENTA IS FAITHFUL UNTO DEATH

MISCELLANEOUS FLYING DUTCHMAN RECORDS

{Flying Dutchman Fantasia	By Pryor's Band }	35158 12-inch, $1.25
{ *Pagliacci—Prologue*	*By Pryor's Band* }	

This brilliant selection contains some of the finest music of this wonderful masterpiece, in which Wagner has portrayed the story of the *Dutchman* condemned to sail forever on the stormy sea unless redeemed by the love of a woman.

Two variations of the exquisite theme representing *Redemption by Woman's Love* are given. We first hear the magnificent strain played by the orchestra in Act III when *Senta* plunges into the sea, after the *Dutchman*, believing her false, has sailed away; then follows the theme first heard in *Senta's* ballad, one of the finest numbers in the opera. Then appears the second of the two principal themes: the *Flying Dutchman* motive:

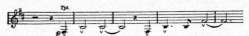

a weird melody representing the restless wanderer. In strong contrast comes the rollicking chorus of *Daland's* sailors, "Steersman, Leave the Watch," and the fantastic dance which follows:

The Fantasia is brought to an effective close with a portion of the great duet between *Senta* and the *Dutchman*, leading up to a splendid climax.

(Italian)
LA FORZA DEL DESTINO
(*La Fort'-zah del Des-tee'*)

(English)
THE FORCE OF DESTINY

OPERA IN FOUR ACTS

Book by Piave; music by Giuseppe Verdi. First produced at St. Petersburg, November 11, 1862; and in London at Her Majesty's Theatre, June 22, 1867. First New York production February 2, 1865, with Carozzi-Zucchi, Massimilliani and Bellini.

CHARACTERS

MARQUIS OF CALATRAVA, (*Kal-ah-trah'-vah*) .... Bass
DONNA LEONORA,⎱ his children .... ⎰Soprano
DON CARLO, ⎰ .... ⎱Baritone
DON ALVARO, (*Ahl-vah'-roh*) .... Tenor
ABBOT OF THE FRANCISCAN FRIARS .... Bass
MELITONE, a friar .... Baritone
CURRA, Leonora's maid ....
TRABUCO, muleteer, afterwards a peddler .... Tenor
A SPANISH MILITARY SURGEON .... Tenor
AN ALCADE .... Bass

Muleteers, Spanish and Italian Peasants and Soldiers,
Friars of the Order of St. Francis, etc.

Scene and Period : Spain and Italy ; about the middle of the eighteenth century.

Verdi's opera of *La Forza del Destino* was never a great success ; its story, which is taken from a drama of the Duke of Rivas, entitled *Don Álvaro o la Fuerzer del Sino,* being doleful and so crowded with horrors that not even the beautiful music could atone for the gloomy plot. Old opera-goers well remember the last production of the opera at the Academy in 1881, with Annie Louise Cary, Campanini, Galassi and Del Puente in the cast.
The only production in America subsequent to that time was that of the Lombardi Opera Company in San Francisco several years ago.
The overture is a most interesting and rather elaborate one.

⎰Overture, Part I   La Scala Orchestra⎱68009   12-inch, $1.25
⎱Overture, Part II   La Scala Orchestra⎰

It opens with a trumpet blast which sufficiently foreshadows the tragic character of the opera, this being followed by an air in the minor, leading up to a striking theme which steals in softly from the strings.

This is the beautiful subject of the *Madre Pietosa,* afterwards heard with such magnificent effect in the opera.
Part II opens with a light and pretty pastoral melody quite in the Italian vein. A notably brilliant passage for strings brings us again to the *Madre Pietosa* melody, this time delivered in a triumphant *fortissimo,* after which the overture works up to a truly animated and powerful finale.

ACT I

SCENE—*Drawing Room in the House of the Marquis of Calatrava*

Don Alvaro, a noble youth from India, becomes enamored with *Donna Leonora,* the daughter of the *Marquis of Calatrava,* who is strongly opposed to the alliance. *Leonora,* knowing her father's aversion, determines to make her escape with *Alvaro,* aided by *Curra,* her confidant.

She is in the act of eloping when her father appears, and is accidentally slain by her lover. *Leonora,* horror-stricken, rushes to her father, who curses her with his dying breath.

ACT II

SCENE I—*An Inn at Hornacuelos*

The second act begins in a village inn, where *Don Carlo,* son of the murdered *Marquis,* is disguised as a student in order to better avenge his father. *Leonora,* who is traveling in male attire, arrives at the inn, and is horror-stricken at seeing her brother, who has sworn to kill her lover *Alvaro* and herself. She flees to the convent of Hornacuelos, arriving at night.

SCENE II—*The Convent of Hornacuelos*

Kneeling in the moonlight, she prays to the Virgin to protect her. This beautiful prayer is splendidly sung here by Mme. Boninsegna, accompanied by the chorus of La Scala.

Madre, pietosa Vergine (Holy Mother, Have Mercy)

By Celestina Boninsegna, Soprano, and La Scala Chorus

(*In Italian*) 92031 12-inch, $3.00

The effect produced by the solo voice with the background of male voices singing the *Venite* in the chapel is powerful and thrilling, and forms one of the finest of the Victor reproductions of Verdi's scenes.

LEONORA:
Oh, Holy Virgin,
Have mercy on my sins!
Send help from Heaven
To erase from my heart
That ungrateful one.
(*The friars are heard in their morning hymn.*)
THE FRIARS:
Venite, adoremus et procelamus
An te Deum, ploremus, ploremus
Coram Domino, coram Domino qui fecit nos.

LEONORA:
O sublime song,
Which like incense,
Ascends heavenward.
It gives faith, comfort,
And quiet to my soul.
I will go to the holy sanctuary.
The pious father cannot refuse to receive me.
O Lord! Have mercy on me,
Nor abandon me.
(*She rings the bell of the convent.*)

Leonora is admitted to the convent by the *Abbot,* to whom she confesses. He procures her a nun's robe and directs her to a cave, assuring her that a curse will rest upon anyone who seeks to know her name or to enter her abode. In her gratitude she sings the second great air.

La Vergine degli angeli (May Angels Guard Thee)

By Celestina Boninsegna, Soprano, and La Scala Chorus

(*In Italian*) 91075 10-inch, $2.00

Again we have the effect of the solemn chant of the priests blending with the prayer of *Leonora.*

THE FRIARS:
La Vergine degli Angeli
Vi copra del suo manto,
E voi protegga vigile
Di Dio l'Angelo santo.

LEONORA:
Let the Holy Virgin
Cover you with her mantle,
And the angels of God
Watch over you!

(*Leonora kisses the hand of the Abbot and goes to her retreat. The monks return to the church.*)

ACT III

SCENE—*A Military Camp near Velletri*

In Act III we are transported to Italy, where we meet *Alvaro,* who has enlisted in the Spanish army. In a sad but beautiful air he recounts his misfortunes, and appeals to heaven for pity.

O tu che in seno agli Angeli (Thou Heavenly One)

By Enrico Caruso, Tenor

(*In Italian*) 88207 12-inch, $3.00

ALVARO:
Life is a misery . . . In vain I seek death. . . . Seville! . . . Leonora! . . . . Oh, memories! Oh, night! Thou hast taken from me all my happiness! I shall ever be unhappy. . . . So it is written. . . . My father tried to make his country free, and to wear a crown by marrying the only daughter of Ineas. He was foiled in his design. . . . I was born in prison. . . . The desert educated me; unknown is my royal descent! My ancestors aspired to a throne. Alas! They were beheaded! Oh, when will my misfortune cease? Thou who hast ascended in heaven, all beautiful and pure from mortal sins, do not forget to look on me, a poor sufferer, who without hope fights eagerly for death against destiny! Leonora, help me and have mercy on my sufferings!

In the next scene he saves the life of *Don Carlo*, whose wanderings in search of vengeance have led him to this region. Both having assumed fictitious names, they do not know each other, and swear eternal friendship.

Shortly afterward, during an engagement, *Don Alvaro*, wounded, is brought in on a stretcher by his soldiers. Thinking himself dying, he sends away the soldiers and requests that he be left alone with *Don Carlo*. The great duet, the finest number in the opera, then occurs.

Solenne in quest'ora (Swear in This Hour)

By Enrico Caruso, Tenor, and Antonio Scotti, Baritone
(*In Italian*)   89001   12-inch, $4.00

By Carlo Barrera, Tenor, and Giuseppe Maggi, Baritone
(*In Italian*)   *68213   12-inch,   1.25

By Luigi Colazza, Tenor, and Ernesto Caronna, Baritone
(*In Italian*)   *63174   10-inch,   .75

The wounded man confides a case of letters to his friend *Don Carlo* to be destroyed, making him swear that he will not look at the contents. *Carlo* swears, and the friends bid each other a last farewell.

ALVARO:
My friend . . . swear that you will grant my last wish.
CARLO: I swear! ALVARO: Look at my breast.
CARLO: A key!
ALVARO:
Open this case and you will find a sealed parcel. . . . I trust it to your honor.
. . . It contains a mystery which must die with me . . . . when I am dead destroy the letters.
CARLO:
So be it.
ALVARO (*feebly*):
Now I die happy . . . . let me embrace you . . . . farewell!
CARLO: Put thy trust in heaven! BOTH: Adieu!

The Caruso and Scotti rendition of this number is considered by many to be one of the most perfect and beautiful of all the Red Seal Records. It is certainly the most wonderfully lifelike reproduction of these two great voices which could be imagined.

Just at this point it may be well to settle a controversy which has been raging ever since the issue of this record in 1906. This argument concerns the identity of the voices in the opening measures, and is the natural result of a remarkable similarity between Caruso's lower register and the medium tones of Scotti's voice. The Victor Catalogue Editor now appoints himself a court of final appeal, and declares that contrary to the usual impression it is Caruso, not Scotti, who begins the record. Here are the opening measures just as sung by the artists:

So - len - ne   in quest' ora   giu - rar - mi   do - ve - te   Far
Swear   in   this   hour   my   last   wish   to   grant   me,   So

pa - go un mio voto   Lo giu - ro lo giu - ro,   Sul co - re cer - ca - te
do   not re - fuse me,   I   swear,   I   swear,   Up - on my heart you'll find

Alvaro, however, does not die, and in the next scene his identity becomes known to *Don Carlo,* who challenges him. They fight, and *Alvaro,* thinking he has killed his enemy, resolves to end his days in a monastery.

ACT IV
SCENE—*Same as Act II, Scene II*

Five years have now elapsed and the last act reveals again the cloister of Hornacuelos, where *Alvaro,* now *Father Raphael,* is discovered by *Don Carlo,* who with a persistence rivaling that of a Kentucky mountaineer, revives the feud and tries to force him to renew the combat. *Alvaro* finally consents, and they agree to fight in a deserted spot near by. This agreement is expressed in a fiery duet.

Invano Alvaro! (In Vain, Alvaro!)
By Enrico Caruso, Tenor, and Pasquale Amato, Baritone
(*In Italian*) 89052 12-inch, $4.00

The host of Victor opera-lovers who are familiar with the wonderful duet from Act III, by Caruso and Scotti, will note with delight the issue of another famous duet from this opera, sung by Caruso and Amato.

This great scene has been recorded in two parts. *Carlo* demands that *Alvaro* renew the feud, but the priest refuses, saying that vengeance is with God. *Don Carlo* taunts him with a terrible persistence, until the monk, goaded past endurance, consents to fight to the death.

CARLOS:
In vain, Alvaro,
Thou hast hid from the world,
And concealed thy coward heart
With the habit of a monk!
My hate and desire for vengeance
Have enabled me to persist
Until I have discovered your retreat!
In this lonely spot
We shall not be disturbed,
And your blood shall wipe out
The stain upon my honor;
That I swear before God!
ALVARO (*recognizing him*):
Don Carlos! Thou livest!

CARLOS:
Yes! and for long years
I have sought and now find thee.
By thy hand I fell,
But God restored my strength
That I may avenge thy crimes!
Here are two swords,
Thy choice now make!
ALVARO:
Leave me! By this holy habit
Thou may'st see my repentance!
CARLOS (*in fury*):
Coward!
Thou shalt not hide behind thy robes!
ALVARO (*agitated*):
Coward! Oh, God
Give me strength to forgive thee!

Le minaccie, i fieri accenti (Thy Menaces Wild!) Part II
By Enrico Caruso, Tenor, and Pasquale Amato, Baritone
(*In Italian*) 89053 12-inch, $4.00
By Titta Ruffo, Baritone, and Emanuele Ischierdo, Tenor
(*In Italian*) 92504 12-inch, 4.00
By Carlo Barrera, Tenor, and Giuseppe Maggi, Baritone
(*Double-faced—See page 125*) (*In Italian*) 68213 12-inch, 1.25

Alvaro recovers his poise and endeavors to appeal to the reason of his enemy, showing him the futility of reopening the feud. Part II begins as follows:

ALVARO (*firmly*):
Thy menaces wild
Be heard only by the winds,
I cannot listen!
Brother, let us submit to fate
And the will of God!
CARLOS:
Thou hast left me
A sister deserted and dishonored!
ALVARO:
No! I swear it!
I adore her with a holy love.
CARLOS (*furiously*):
Thy cowardly pleadings
Cannot move me to pity.
Take thy sword and fight!
ALVARO:
Brother, let me kneel to thee.
(*He kneels.*)
CARLOS:
Ah, by such an act
Thou showest thy base origin!

ALVARO (*rising, unable to control himself*):
My lineage is brighter than a jewel—
CARLOS (*sneeringly*):
A jewel flaw'd and discolored!
ALVARO (*in fury*):
Thou liest!
Give me a sword. Lead on!
CARLOS:
At last!
ALVARO (*recovering himself*):
No, Satan shall not thus triumph.
(*Throws down his sword.*)
CARLOS:
Then coward, I brand thee with dishonor!
(*Strikes him.*)
ALVARO:
Oh, God, no more!
(*To Don Carlos*)
Defend thyself!
BOTH:
We both must die,
Our hatred will be appeased
And Satan will claim us for his own!

ACT V

SCENE—A Wild Spot Near Hornacuelos

The scene changes to the vicinity of *Leonora's* cave. Pale and worn, the unhappy woman comes from the cave, and in another great air implores Heaven to let her die, as she is unable to forget her lover.

Pace mio Dio (Mercy, O My Lord)

By Celestina Boninsegna, Soprano (*In Italian*) 92027 12-inch, $3.00

> LEONORA:
> Mercy, oh Lord!
> My sorrows are too great to bear.
> This fatal love has been my undoing,
> But still do I love him,
> Nor can I blot his image from my heart;
> Yet 'tis Heaven's decree that I shall see him
>   no more!
> Oh Lord, let me die,
> Since death alone can give me peace!

A storm now breaks, and *Leonora* retires within the cave just as *Alvaro* and *Carlo* appear for the final combat. *Alvaro* recognizes the spot as an accursed one, but declares that it is a fitting place for the ending of so deadly a feud.

Don Carlo falls mortally wounded, and desiring to repent his sins asks *Alvaro*, who is known as *Father Raphael*, to confess him, but the monk is under the curse of the cave and cannot. He goes to call the friar who dwells in the cave; *Leonora* rushes forth, sees her brother wounded and embraces him, but true to his vow made in Act I he makes a dying effort and stabs her to the heart.

This dramatic scene has been put by Verdi into the form of a trio.

Non imprecare, umiliati (Swear Not, Be Humble)

By Ida Giacomelli, Soprano; Gino Martinez-Patti, Tenor; Cesare Preve, Bass (*Double-faced—See below*) (*In Italian*) 68026 12-inch, $1.25

Don Alvaro then completes the catalogue of horrors by throwing himself from a cliff just as the monks arrive singing the *Miserere*. The curtain then falls, evidently because, as one critic has said, every member of the cast being dead, there seems to be no reasonable excuse for keeping it up any longer!

DOUBLE-FACED AND MISCELLANEOUS FORZA DEL DESTINO RECORDS

Overture, Part I By La Scala Orchestra		68009	12-inch, $1.25
Overture, Part II By La Scala Orchestra			
Le minaccie, i fieri accenti (Let Your Menaces) By Carlo Barrera, Tenor, and Giuseppe Maggi, Baritone (*In Italian*) Solenne in quest'ora (Swear in This Hour) By Carlo Barrera, Tenor, and Giuseppe Maggi, Baritone (*In Italian*)		68213	12-inch, 1.25
Non imprecare, umiliati By Ida Giacomelli, Soprano; Gino Martinez-Patti, Tenor; Cesare Preve, Bass (*In Italian*) Ballo in Maschera—Ah! qual soave brivido (*Thy Words, Like Dew*) By Ida Giacomelli, Soprano, and Gino Martinez-Patti, Tenor (*In Italian*)		68026	12-inch, 1.25
Solenne in quest'ora (Swear in This Hour) By Luigi Colazza, Tenor, and Ernesto Caronna, Baritone (*Italian*) Faust—Io voglio il piacer (*The Pleasures of Youth*) By G. Pini-Corsi, Tenor, and Aristodemo Sillich, Baritone (*Italian*)		63174	10-inch, .75

THE WOLF'S GLEN SCENE

(German)   (English)

DER FREISCHÜTZ   THE FREESHOOTER

(Der Fry'-shoots)

ROMANTIC OPERA IN THREE ACTS

Words by Friedrich Kind; music by Carl Maria von Weber (his eighth opera); completed as *Die Jägarsbraut,* May 13, 1820. Produced at Berlin, June 18, 1821; in Paris, (as *Robin des Bois,* with new libretto by Blaze and Sauvage, and many changes) at the Odéon, December 7, 1824. Another new version, with accurate translation by Pacini, and recitatives by Berlioz, at the Académie Royale, June 7, 1841, under the title of *Le Franc Archer.* In London as *Der Freischutz* or *The Seventh Bullet,* with many ballads inserted, July 23, 1824; In Italian, as *Il Franco Arciero,* at Covent Garden, March 16, 1850 (recitatives by Costa) in German, at King's Theatre, May 9, 1832. It was revived at Astley's Theatre with a new libretto by Oxenford, April 2, 1866. First New York production, in English, March 12, 1825.

Cast

PRINCE OTTOKAR, Duke of Bohemia............................Baritone
CUNO, head ranger...Bass
MAX,   } two young foresters serving under him.................{ Tenor
CASPAR, }   { Bass
KILIAN, a rich peasant...Tenor
A HERMIT..Bass
ZAMIEL, the fiend huntsman..............................Speaking Part
AGNES, Cuno's daughter......................................Soprano
ANNIE, her cousin..Soprano

Chorus of Hunters, Peasants, Bridesmaids, and invisible Spirits.

Scene and Period: The scene is laid in Bohemia, shortly after the Seven Years' War.

The word *freischutz,* probably better translated as "free marksman," means a *Schütz* or marksman who uses "free bullets," or charmed bullets which do not depend on the aim of the shooter.

Overture

By Sousa's Band	*35000	12-inch, $1.25
By La Scala Orchestra	*62636	10-inch, .75

MAX

The overture presents the story of the opera in a condensed form. An introduction with a tender horn passage leads us into the forest. Night is falling and mysterious sounds are heard. The *allegro*, representing the doubts of the good but vacillating young hunter, begins, and the sound of the magic bullets can be heard as they drop in the melting pot. Next a beautiful melody, portraying love and happiness, appears, but this in turn is succeeded by another mood of distress. At length the triumphant strain indicative of the final victory is sounded, leading up to a splendid climax.

Sousa's Band has given a stirring performance of this brilliant overture, while the rendition by La Scala Orchestra will please those who prefer orchestral music.

The story of the opera is founded on a German tradition, told among huntsmen, that whoever will sell his soul to *Zamiel*, the Demon Hunter, may receive seven magic bullets, which will always hit the mark. For each victim whom he succeeds in securing for the Demon, his own life is extended, and he receives a fresh supply of the charmed missiles.

Cuno, head ranger to *Ottokar*, a Bohemian prince, has two assistants, *Max* and *Caspar*, both excellent marksmen. *Max* is in love with *Agnes*, *Cuno's* daughter, who has promised to be his bride only on condition that he proves himself the best shot at a forthcoming contest. This contest, however, is won by *Kilian*, a peasant. *Max*, in a dramatic air, bitterly bewails his bad luck.

Durch die Wälder (Thro' the Forest)

By Daniel Beddoe, Tenor (*In English*) 74244 12-inch, $1.50

He believes he is cursed by an evil spirit which causes his hand to fail at the critical moment.

MAX: O, I can bear my fate no longer!
E'en hope is banished from my soul!
What unknown grief thus haunts my spirit,
And o'er me works its dark control?
Thro' the forests, thro' the meadows,
Joy was wont with me to stray,
While my rifle, never failing,
Made each bird and beast my prey.
When at length from chase returning,
Ere home rose before my sight,
Agnes, smiling met me,
Cloth'd in beauty's heavenly light.
But now am I by Heaven forsaken
And left—the power of chance to know?
Will hope's long slumber ever waken,
Or am I doomed to endless woe?
Now, methinks, beside her lattice,
I my lovely fair one see;
While her ear seems fondly list'ning,
Every coming sound for me:
See, she fondly waves a welcome,—
Fancy's eye her lover sees;
But her signal gains no answer,
Save the sigh of whispering trees!
What dark'ning power is ruling o'er me?
My anxious bosom fear hath riven,—
Despair hath spread her snares before me:
Does fate rule blindly?
Aid me, Heaven!

PHOTO BOYER

CASPAR

Caspar, who has already put himself in the power of *Zamiel*, sees here an opportunity to extend his own days of grace, and advises *Max* to seek the magician and secure some of the magic bullets.

*Double-Faced Record—For title of opposite side see DOUBLE-FACED DER FREISCHUTZ RECORDS, page 128.

In the meantime *Agnes* is anxiously awaiting her lover and is much alarmed at his non-appearance. *Annie*, her cousin, endeavors to cheer her by singing a gay air, *Comes a Gallant Youth*.

Annie's Air, " Comes a Gallant Youth "

By Marie A. Michailowa, Soprano (*In Russian*) 61134 10-inch, $1.00

She describes playfully the attitude a shy maiden should assume when the right young man happens along.

PHOTO BOYER

AGATHA AND ANNA

ANNIE:
Comes a gallant youth towards me,
  Be he golden hair'd or dark,
Eyes that flash as he regards me,
  Him my captive I will mark!

Eyes bent down to earth for shyness,
  As befits a modest maid,
With a stolen look of slyness
  Yet may ev'rything be said!

And if swift emotion rushes,
  Shot from answ'ring lip and eye,
Nothing worse than maiden blushes
  Need the gallant stranger spy!

Annie begs *Agnes* to retire, but the young girl says she will wait for her lover. Left alone, she draws the curtains aside, revealing a starlight night. She exclaims at the beauty of the night, and folding her hands in prayer she delivers the lovely air which is the gem of the opera.

Preghiera di Agatha (Agatha's Prayer) (Double-faced—See below)

By Emilia Corsi, Soprano (*Piano acc.*)
(*In Italian*) * 62636 10-inch, $0.75

She prays for the safety of her lover, and asks Heaven to watch over them both.

AGNES:
Softly sighing, day is dying,
Soar my prayer heav'nward flying!
Starry splendor shining yonder,
Pour on us thy radiance tender!
How the golden stars are burning
Thro' yon vault of ether blue,
But lo, gath'ring o'er the mountains
Is a cloud, foreboding storm,

Earth has lull'd her care to rest;
Why delays my loitering love?
Fondly beats my anxious breast:
Where, my Rudolph, dost thou rove?
Scarce the breeze among the boughs
Wakes a murmur thro' the silence,
Save the nightingale lamenting,
Not a sound disturbs the night!

Max arrives, followed by *Annie,* but seems embarrassed and says he must go to bring in a stag he has shot near the Wolf's Glen. *Agnes* begs him not to go near that haunted spot, but he disregards her warning and goes out.

The scene changes to the Wolf's Glen, where *Max* meets *Caspar,* and the magic bullets are cast amid scenes of horror, while the demon *Zamiel* hovers near awaiting his prey. *Max* is returning with his prize when he meets the Prince, who asks him to shoot a dove. The hunter complies, just missing *Agnes,* who has come to the wood in search of her lover. *Caspar* is wounded by the very bullet which he had intended should slay *Agnes* at the hands of *Max.* *Zamiel* rises and carries off his victim, while *Max* is forgiven and all ends happily.

DOUBLE-FACED FREISCHUTZ RECORDS

Overture	By Sousa's Band	35000	12-inch, $1.25
Carmen Selection	By Sousa's Band		
Overture	By La Scala Orchestra	62636	10-inch, .75
Preghiera di Agatha (Agatha's Prayer)			
By Emilia Corsi, Soprano (*Piano acc.*) (*In Italian*)			

LANDE

THE BATTLEFIELD OF LEIPZIG—ACT III
(CARUSO, DESTINN AND AMATO)

(Italian)

GERMANIA

(Jer-man'-ee-ah)

A Lyric Drama in a Prologue, Two Scenes and Epilogue

Text by Luigi Illica. Music by Alberto Franchetti. First production at Milan in 1902
First American production, New York, January 22, 1910, with Caruso, Destinn and Amato.

Cast of Characters

GIOVANNI FILIPPO PALM..Bass
FEDERICO LŒWE⎫   ⎧Tenor
CARLO WORMS ⎬Students.....................................⎨Baritone
CRISOGONO   ⎭   ⎩Baritone
RICKE...Soprano
JANE, her sister..Mezzo-Soprano
LENE ARMUTH, an aged beggar-woman....................Mezzo-Soprano
JEBBEL, her nephew...Soprano
STAPPS, Protestant Priest..Bass
LUIGI ADOLFO GUGLIELMO LÜTZOW ....Bass
CARLO TEODORO KÖRNER.......................................Tenor
SIGNORA HEDVIGE...Mezzo-Soprano
PETERS, a herdsman ....Bass
Chief of German Police..Bass

Historical Personages, Students, Soldiers, Police officers, Members and
Associates of the "Tugendbund," "Louise-Bund "
and "Black Knights"; Forest Girls.

Time: 1813.

The opera is the work of an Italian nobleman, who, although a very wealthy man, is
ambitious and makes the writing of operas his hobby. *Germania* is a picturesque and interesting opera, full of local color, describing the Germany of the time of Napoleon, with its
many conspiracies; and for this the Baron has written much effective and agreeable music.
The action takes place in 1813, at the time of the battle of Leipzig.

PROLOGUE
SCENE—*An Abandoned Mill near Nuremberg*

A company of students, under the leadership of *Giovanni Palm,* have occupied an old mill, and are shipping sacks of grain, which really contain political documents intended to rouse the people to revolt. Prominent among the students is *Worms,* who previously had a love affair with *Ricke,* a young girl who is now betrothed to *Loewe,* the poet and warm friend of *Worms. Loewe* is expected to arrive at any moment, and *Ricke* dreads his coming, as she has made up her mind to tell him her guilty secret. *Worms,* however, divines her purpose and bids her keep silent, as in the duel which was sure to occur *Loewe* would likely be the one to die.

Loewe arrives and is joyfully greeted by the conspirators. He encourages them to fresh efforts in his noble aria.

Studenti, udite! (Students, Hear Me!)
By Enrico Caruso, Tenor   (*In Italian*)   87053   10-inch, $2.00

Caruso delivers this inspiring number with splendid effect, showing well the beauty and power of his marvelous voice.

The enthusiasm which follows *Loewe's* great address is rudely interrupted by the arrival of the police, who seize *Palm* and take him away to his death.

ACT I
SCENE—*A Cottage in the Black Forest*

Seven years have elapsed. Hither *Loewe* has come after the disastrous campaign of 1806, which followed the plotting in the old mill. He lives in this hut with his aged mother and the two girls, *Ricke* and her sister *Jane. Worms* has disappeared and is supposed to be dead.

Loewe is about to be married to *Ricke,* and the bridesmaids now arrive to deck the cottage with flowers. *Ricke,* thinking of her past, is melancholy, but the marriage ceremony is performed and the bride and bridegroom are left alone. *Federico* clasps her in his arms and sings his beautiful air to the eyes of his bride.

Non chiuder gli occhi vaghi (Close Not Those Dreamy Eyes)
By Enrico Caruso, Tenor   (*In Italian*)   87054   10-inch, $2.00

Forgetting the past, *Ricke* yields herself to the joy of the moment and tenderly kisses him, when suddenly from the forest is heard a familiar voice singing an old student song. "*Worms!*" joyfully cries *Federico,* and runs out to meet his old friend, who is wasted and battle-scarred.

Worms comes in and is astonished to see *Ricke.* She looks coldly at him and he uneasily says he must be on his way. *Federico* protests, but *Worms* insists and departs. *Ricke,* overcome by this reminder of her past misfortune, resolves to leave her husband, and writes him a note and flees into the forest. *Federico* returns, reads the note, and wrongfully concludes that she has fled with *Worms.*

ACT II
SCENE—*A Cellar in Konigsberg*

In this underground retreat *Worms* is again plotting against *Napoleon.* A meeting of the Council is in progress, when *Federico* appears and demands that *Worms* shall fight with him to the death, but *Worms,* kneeling, asks *Federico* to kill him. *Federico* replies with a violent blow in the face, at which *Worms* decides to fight him, and preparations for the duel are begun. They are interrupted by the entrance of *Queen Louise,* who suggests that such brave men had better be using their swords for their country. Fired with enthusiasm, the enemies embrace each other and swear to die for Germany.

EPILOGUE
SCENE—*The Battlefield of Leipzig*

The awful three days' conflict is over and the field is a mass of ruins, battered wheels and dead and wounded men. *Ricke* searches for the body of *Federico* that she may look upon his face once more. She finds him dying, but he recognizes her, and telling her that the body of *Worms* is nearby, asks her to forgive him as he himself has done. *Ricke* looks on the face of the man who had ruined her life and forgives him. She returns to her husband and when he dies in her arms waits beside his body for her own death, which she feels approaching. As the sun sets the defeated *Napoleon* with the shattered remains of his army is seen retreating.

LA GIOCONDA

(Lah Jee-oh-kon'-dah)

OPERA IN FOUR ACTS

Libretto by Arrigo Boïto; music by Amilcare Ponchielli. It is an adaptation of Victor Hugo's drama, "Angelo," and was first presented at La Scala, Milan, April 8, 1876. First London production in the summer of 1883. First New York production December 20, 1883, with Christine Nilsson, Scalchi, Fursch-Madi, del Puente and Novara.

Characters

LA GIOCONDA, a ballad singer . . . . Soprano
LA CIECA, *(See-ay'-kah)* her blind mother . . . . Contralto
ALVISE, *(Al-vee'-zay)* one of the heads of State Inquisition . . Bass
LAURA, his wife . . . . Mezzo-Soprano
ENZO GRIMALDO, a Genoese noble . . . . Tenor
BARNABA, a spy of the Inquisition . . . . Baritone
ZUANE, a boatman . . . . Bass
ISEPO, public letter-writer . . . . Tenor
A PILOT . . . . Bass

Monks, Senators, Sailors, Shipwrights, Ladies,
Gentlemen, Populace, Masquers, etc.

The action takes place in Venice, in the seventeenth century.

PROGRAM OF FIRST PERFORMANCE
(MILAN)

Gioconda is a work of great beauty, full of wonderful arias, duets and ensembles, with fine choral effects, and a magnificent ballet. The book is founded on Hugo's "Tyrant of Padua," and tells a most dramatic story, which, however, cannot be called inviting, as the librettist has crowded into it nearly all the crimes he could think of!

But the average audience does not concern itself much with these horrors, being engaged in listening to the beautiful music, and admiring the splendid scenes and colorful action. Therefore the story will be but briefly sketched here.

ACT I

SCENE—*Street near the Adriatic Shore, Venice*

Gioconda, a ballad singer who is in love with *Enzo,* a Genoese noble and captain of a ship now in the harbor, supports her blind mother, *La Cieca,* by singing in the streets of Venice. She has attracted the attention of *Barnaba,* an influential police spy, and he plans to gain her affections.

This is the situation at the rise of the curtain. The stage is filled with people: peasants, sailors, masquers, all in holiday attire. *Barnaba* is leaning against a pillar, watching the gay scene. The chorus sing their opening number, *Sports and Feasting.*

Feste! pane! (Sports and Feasting!)

By La Scala Chorus (*In Italian*) *45010   10-inch, $1.00

At the close of this number, *Barnaba* advances and announces the commencement of the Regatta. All hasten to the shore, while *Barnaba* remains to soliloquize on his plot to secure the lovely *Gioconda. Gioconda* enters, leading her mother, *La Cieca,* by the hand, and *Barnaba* hastily hides behind a column to watch them. *La Cieca* sings a beautiful air, blessing her daughter for her tender care, and this leads to a trio.

MUSICAL AMERICA
DESTINN AS GIOCONDA

* *Double-Faced Record—For title of opposite side see DOUBLE-FACED LA GIOCONDA RECORDS, page 137.*

Figlia che reggi tremulo pié (Daughter, My Faltering Steps)

By A. Rossi Murino, Soprano; López Nunes, Soprano;
Ernesto Badini, Baritone   *(In Italian)* *55017   12-inch, $1.50

La Cieca:
Daughter, in thee my faltering steps
Find guidance and protection;
I gratefully bless my loss of sight,
That heightens thy affection!
While thou unto mankind thy songs are singing,
To Heav'n my ceaseless pray'rs their flight are winging,
For thee I pray and render thanks to Fate
That left me sightless,—but not desolate!

Gioconda (*tenderly*):
Place thy dear hand once more in mine
Thy steps I'm safely guiding;
Here recommence thy daily life,
In calm contentment gliding.
Barnaba (*aside*):
With fiercest joy my heart would be enraptured
If in my net she were securely captured!
The wildest ecstasies within me waken!
Beware thee, moth, if in my net thou'rt taken!

LANDE   SCENE—ACT I

Gioconda leaves to seek Enzo, but Barnaba stops her and boldly declares that he loves her. She shudders with an instinctive aversion, and bids him stand aside. He attempts to seize her, but she eludes him and makes her escape, leaving the spy furious and planning revenge.

The people now return from the Regatta, bearing the victor on their shoulders. Barnaba, seeing the defeated combatant, Zuane, conceives a plan to deprive Gioconda of her mother, thus leaving him free to carry out his plans. He takes Zuane aside and tells him that the blind La Cieca is a witch who has cast a spell over him, causing his defeat. The old woman is being roughly handled by Zuane and his friends when Enzo suddenly appears and protects her, holding the mob at bay.

Alvise, Chief of the Council, enters with his wife Laura, formerly betrothed to Enzo. Laura pleads for Cieca, and she is protected by Alvise. The blind woman voices her gratitude in this lovely song, which is familiar to most concert-goers.

Voce di donna (Angelic Voice)

By Louise Homer, Contralto   *(In Italian)*   85104   12-inch, $3.00

Although the part of the blind mother, La Cieca, has never been sung by Mme. Homer, she being usually cast for Laura (the superb lady of Venice and rival of Gioconda), this beautiful air has always appealed to her. It is considered the finest single number in Ponchielli's work, and is undoubtedly one of the loveliest gems in this or any other opera.

Certain it is that no Cieca of present memory has ever delivered this romance with such richness of voice and such touching pathos. This beautiful passage—

which is sung as La Cieca presents the rosary, is perhaps the most effective part of the aria.

Mme. Homer's singing of this Voce di donna makes this record one of the gems of the Victor's fine production of La Gioconda, and it should form part of every opera collection.

COPY'T DUPONT

HOMER AS LAURA

* *Double-Faced Record—For title of opposite side see DOUBLE-FACED LA GIOCONDA RECORDS. page 137.*

La Cieca:
Thanks unto thee, angelic voice,
My fetters asunder are broken;
I cannot see the face of her
By whom those words were spoken.
(*Takes the rosary from her belt.*)

This rosary I offer thee—no richer boon possessing—
Deign to accept the humble gift, 'twill bring
to thee a blessing,
And on thy head may bliss descend; I'll ever
pray for thee!

All go into the church except *Enzo,* who stands gazing after *Laura,* having recognized his former love. *Barnaba* approaches him and tells him that *Laura* plans to visit the Genoese noble's ship that night. *Enzo,* whose love for *Laura* has revived at the sight of her, is delighted at this news, and forgetting *Gioconda,* he returns to his ship.

This scene has been put by Verdi into the form of a dramatic duet, sung here by Conti and Badini, of the La Scala forces.

Enzo Grimaldo (Duet Enzo and Barnaba)
By F. Conti, Tenor, and E. Badini, Baritone (*In Italian*) *45033 10-inch, $1.00

Barnaba (*approaching Enzo*):
Enzo Crimaldo,
Prince of Santa Fior, thou art pensive.
Enzo (*aside*):
I am discovered!
Barnaba:
What magic stupor steals away thy senses?
'Tis of the Lady Laura, Alvise's wife, thou'rt
thinking.
Enzo (*astonished*):
Who art thou?
Barnaba (*impressively*):
I know all;
Can penetrate thy thoughts, however secret.
Thy birthplace was Genoa!
Enzo:
Prince I am not, but sailor. Yonder's my
ship.
I am Dalmatian, Enzo Giordan.
Barnaba:
For others, but not for me. Proscribed thou
wert by Venice,
Yet hither thou art led, by chainless impulse,
Thy life to peril. Thou didst love a maiden
Yonder, in thine own Genoa, but she another's
bride became.

COPY'T DUPONT

CARUSO AS ENZO

Enzo:
I have pledged my faith to Gioconda.
Barnaba:
Poor wand'ring ballad-singer!
Her thou dost love as sister, but Laura as thy
mistress.
Thou hadst all hope abandoned, dreamed not
to see her features,
But here, under her velvet mask, thy beauteous angel saw thee
And recognized thee.
Enzo (*joyfully*):
Oh, happiness!
Barnaba:
Love sees through disguises,
All this night will her husband stay at the
Doge's palace,
With the Great Council. Laura shall be on
board thy vessel.
Love's sweetest consolations await thee!
Enzo:
Ah, with what joy my heart is filled,
Fortune at last is kind!
But who art thou, oh, gloomy messenger of
joy?
Barnaba:
I hate thee! I am the demon-in-chief
Of the Council of Ten. Read this. Beware
thee!

(*Opens his dress and shows the letters "C. X."*
(*Council of Ten*) *embroidered in silver on
his vest.*)
Enzo (*starting back*):
Oh, horror!
Barnaba (*fiercely*):
To thy doom at once I could bring thee, but
I spare thee.
Gioconda loves thee, hates me fiercely;
I have sworn to crush her heart.
Enzo's death would little serve me;
She must learn how false thou art.
Enzo (*aside*):
Kind Heaven, to her thy mercy show,
Save her from grief and pain;
But ah, sweet Laura, my adored,
Bring to my arms again!
Barnaba (*to Enzo*):
Go! not a moment lose,
Spread thy white sails to the skies,
(*Aside*)
I can my triumph read
In each glad glance of thine eyes!
Enzo (*going*):
When the dark night falls,
On board my ship I shall await my Laura.
Barnaba (*sneeringly*):
Good luck attend you!
(*Exit.*)

* *Double-Faced Record—For title of opposite side see DOUBLE-FACED LA GIOCONDA RECORDS, page 137.*

Barnaba then writes to *Alvise* that his wife plans to elope with *Enzo*. He speaks the words aloud as he writes, and is heard by *Gioconda*, who is overcome at this evidence of her lover's faithlessness, and heartbroken, enters the church with her mother.

The act closes with a famous dance, the *Furlana*, played here by the famous Orchestra Sinfonica of La Scala.

Furlana (Finale, Act I)

By Italian Orchestra   *45033 10-inch, $1.00

ACT II

SCENE—*A Lagoon near Venice—it is night.* *Enzo's ship is shown at anchor, with sailors grouped on deck, resting*

Barnaba, disguised as a fisherman, appears in his boat, hails the sailors, and sings them a merry ballad, *Ah, pescator!*

Ah, pescator affonda l'esca (Fisher Boy, Thy Bait Be Throwing!)

By Pasquale Amato, Baritone, and Metropolitan Opera Chorus
                    (*In Italian*)   87093   10-inch, $2.00
By Ernesto Badini, Baritone, and Chorus   (*In Italian*)   *45010   10-inch, 1.00

This is one of the most popular numbers in the opera, its beautiful melody and rhythmical swing being a welcome relief in the midst of so much that is gloomy. It is superbly sung here by Amato, one of the greatest of *Barnabas*, who is assisted by the Metropolitan Opera Chorus. A popular priced rendition is furnished by Badini and the chorus of La Scala.

After taking careful note of the strength of the crew, *Barnaba* sends his aide for the police galleys and leaves in his boat.

Enzo now appears, and is greeted by his men with enthusiasm. He is in a gay humor, thinking of *Laura's* expected visit, and bids the sailors go below while he keeps the watch.

LANDE   ENZO'S VESSEL—ACT II

Left alone, he gives expression to his joy in this great aria, one of the most beautiful in the whole range of opera. Caruso sings the number with exquisite purity of tone and a lavish outpouring of voice.

Cielo e mar (Heaven and Ocean)

By Enrico Caruso, Tenor	(*In Italian*)	88246	12-inch,	$3.00
By Florencio Constantino, Tenor	(*In Italian*)	64070	10-inch,	1.00
By Franco de Gregorio, Tenor	(*In Italian*)	*45027	10-inch,	1.00

Especially noticeable is this fine passage—

vie - ni al ba cio Del - la vi - ta e del l'a - mo - re, del l'a mor!
come to the kiss - es That would make thee all, would make thee all 1 my own!

which the tenor delivers in splendid style, fairly thrilling his hearers.

Other fine records of this effective number, by Constantino and de Gregorio, are also offered.

* *Double-Faced Record—For title of opposite side see DOUBLE-FACED LA GIOCONDA RECORDS, page 137.*

CONSTANTINO AS ENZO

ENZO:
Heaven and ocean! yon ethereal veil
Is radiant as a holy altar,
My angel, will she come from heaven?
My angel, will she come o'er ocean?
Here I await her, I breathe with rapture
The soft zephyrs fill'd with love.
Mortals oft, when fondly sighing,
Find ye a torment, O golden, golden dreams.
Come then, dearest, here I'm waiting;
Wildly panting is my heart.
Come then, dearest! oh come, my dearest!
Oh come, taste the kisses that magic bliss
impart!
Oh come! Oh come! Oh come!

Laura now appears, and after a rapturous embrace, the lovers plan to set sail when the wind rises. *Enzo* goes below to rouse the men, when *Gioconda*, disguised, enters and denounces *Laura*.

They sing a splendid dramatic duet in which each declares her love for *Enzo* and defies the other.

L'amo come il fulgor del creato! (I Adore Him!)

By Elena Ruszcowska, Soprano, and Bianca
Lavin de Casas, Mezzo-Soprano
(In Italian)   88271   12-inch, $3.00

Gioconda is about to stab her rival, when the sight of a rosary worn by her intended victim causes her to repent, and she aids *Laura* to escape just as her husband, summoned by *Barnaba* is approaching.

Enzo appears and is greeted with reproaches by *Gioconda,* who tells him that the war galleys, led by *Barnaba,* are coming to capture the ship. *Enzo,* stung by *Gioconda's* scorn, and heartbroken at the loss of *Laura,* fires his ship to prevent it falling into the hands of *Barnaba.*

ACT III

SCENE—*A Room in the Palace of Alvise. Night*

Alvise is discovered alone, in violent agitation, planning the death of *Laura* because of her attempted elopement with *Enzo.*

He sings a dramatic air, picturing his fearful revenge.

Si! morir ella de'! (To Die is Her Doom!)

By Amleto Galli, Bass   *(In Italian)*   *55019   12-inch, $1.50

ALVISE *(in violent agitation):*
Yes, to die is her doom! My name, my honor,
Shall not with impunity be disgraced.
From Badoers, when betrayed,
Pity 't were vain to hope.
Though yesterday upon the fatal isle
She 'scaped this vengeful hand,
She shall not escape a fearful expiation.
Last night a sharp poniard should have
pierced her bosom;
This night no poniard I'll use; she dies by
poison!
(Pointing to the adjoining room.)
While there the dancers sing and laugh,
In giddy movements flying,
Their mirthful tones shall blend with groans,

Breath'd by a sinner dying.
Shades of my honored forefathers!
Soon shall your blushes disappear;
Soon shall a deadly vengeance prove
Honor to me is dear.
While dance the giddy crowd,
In mirthful movements flying,
Here shall be heard the bitter groans,
The sinner breathes in dying.
Yonder, the nobles of the nation
Are gathered at my invitation;
Here, an insulted husband
For signal vengeance cries!
Exult, in dances and in songs,
While here a faithless one dies!

The guilty woman now enters at his summons and is denounced by him. He orders her to take poison, and leaves her. She is about to obey, when *Gioconda,* who has been concealed in the room, appears, takes the poison from her and gives her a narcotic, which will produce a death-like trance. *Laura* drinks this and *Gioconda* exits just as *Alvise* appears. Seeing the empty phial on the table he believes *Laura* has obeyed his will.

The second scene shows a magnificent hall in the palace, where *Alvise* is giving a masked ball. The famous *Dance of the Hours* is given for the entertainment of the guests.

* *Double-Faced Record—For title of opposite side see DOUBLE-FACED LA GIOCONDA RECORDS, page 137.*

Dance of the Hours

By Victor Orchestra 31443 12-inch, $1.00

This is one of the most beautiful of ballets and symbolizes, like many other modern Italian ballets, the struggle between the conflicting powers of light and darkness, progress and ignorance. The music is fascinating in the extreme, and is one of the most popular parts of the opera.

Enzo is present among the maskers, and when *Barnaba* whispers in his ear that *Laura* is dead, he unmasks and denounces *Alvise,* who causes his arrest. The great finale begins with *Enzo's* solo,

Già ti vedo (I Behold Thee)

**By F. Lotti, Soprano; de Gregorio, Tenor;
Badini, Baritone; and Chorus**
(In Italian) *55019 12-inch, $1.50

The emotions of the various characters may be understood by the quotations below.

ENZO *(aside):*
I behold thee motionless, pallid,
Shrouded in thy snowy veil!
Thou art dead, love! thou art dead, love!
Ah, my darling, hopeless I wail.
The sharp axe for me is waiting,
Opens wide a dark abyss;
But to thee shall torture guide me,
Soon we'll share celestial bliss!

GIOCONDA:
Sadly fall the tear-drops,
In the silence of despair;
Break, oh heart! sad eyes, rain torrents!
Fate, thy sharpest doom prepare!

BARNABA *(aside to Gioconda):*
Yield thee, yield thee! all around thee
See what pow'r I have for ill!
Well may'st thou fear me; pow'rs infernal
To ill deeds attract me still!

GIOCONDA *(aside to Barnaba):*
Do thou save him, bring him safe out there,
Close by the Redentor, and then
Myself I will surrender
To thee, fearfulest of men.

BARNABA *(to Gioconda):*
Though despair may prompt thy offer,
I accept it for my part,
And the bitterest fate will welcome,
Once to press thee to this heart.

LA CIECA:
Thou art weeping, O Gioconda,
Let me fold thee to my breast.
Never love, like love maternal,
Can encounter every test.

ALVISE:
'Mid the splendor this fête surrounding,
Thou art unwelcome, cavalier;
But, ere long, new scenes of horror
Shall from thee attention claim.
Thou shalt soon see if I am watchful
Of the honor of my name!

COPY'T MISHKIN
ANCONA AS BARNABA

To complete his revenge, *Alvise* now draws aside a curtain and shows the guests the body of *Laura,* acknowledging that he took her life. Horror and indignation are expressed by those present, and *Enzo* attempts to kill *Alvise.* He fails, is seized by the guards, and is led away to prison as the curtain falls.

ACT IV

SCENE—*A ruined palace on an island in the Adriatic. Venice visible in the distance*

To this desolate island *Gioconda* has managed to bring the unconscious *Laura,* in an endeavor to save her. As the

THE RUINED PALACE—ACT IV

* Double-Faced Record—For title of opposite side see DOUBLE-FACED LA GIOCONDA RECORDS, page 137.

urtain rises two men are carrying the insensible form into the ruin. *Gioconda* asks the men o seek out her mother, whom she fears never to see again. Left alone, she approaches the able, looks fixedly at a flask of poison, and begins her terrible song, one of the most dramatic of the numbers in Ponchielli's work.

Suicidio (Suicide Only Remains)

By Elda Cavalieri (*Double-Faced—See below*) (*In Italian*) 55015 12-inch, $1.50

For a moment the unhappy girl is tempted to complete *Alvise's* work by giving the poison o *Laura*, but banishes the temptation and throws herself down in a passion of weeping. Gioconda has secured the release of *Enzo*, and has sent for him to come to the ruined palace, ntending, with splendid generosity, to restore the lovers to each other.

Enzo now arrives, thinking that he is only to visit the grave of *Laura*, and a bitter scene occurs between the two, which is interrupted by the voice of *Laura*, who has revived and now calls feebly. *Enzo* rushes forward in a transport of joy, while *Gioconda* makes further preparations for their escape. The lovers express their gratitude and depart, while *Gioconda* prepares for the end. She is about to swallow the poison when *Barnaba* appears, and in terrible accents demands why she has broken her word to him. She pretends to yield to him.

GIOCONDA (*at first terrified, recovers her courage, and retains it to the end*):
Yes, I keep to my compact; we both swore to keep it,

And ne'er will Gioconda be false to her oath.
May Heaven in mercy withhold condemnation,
And pardon us both!

Barnaba is overjoyed and begins the final duet, the most dramatic scene in the opera.

Vo' farmi più gaia (Thou'rt Mine Now!)

By A. Rossi Murino, Soprano, and E. Badini, Baritone
(*In Italian*) 55017 12-inch, $1.50

BARNABA:
Thou'rt mine now! and swift from this desolate heart,
Expelled by love's rays, sombre shadows depart.
GIOCONDA (*to Barnaba, who is approaching her*):
Restrain awhile thy ardent passion!
Thou soon shalt in splendor Gioconda behold!
For thee I am braiding my clustering tresses
With purple and gold!
(*Concealing her terror, she begins to adorn herself.*)
With glittering jewels, the gay tinsel worn nightly
By madcaps theatrical, cover'd I'll be:
Now list to the song that this ardent young siren
Will sing unto thee!
I keep to my compact, no false oath was mine;
(*Changing her tone.*)

Thou claimest Gioconda? Now demon accursed,
Gioconda is thine!
(*She stabs herself in the heart with the dagger that she had secreted while adorning herself, and falls dead at his feet.*)
BARNABA (*in horror*):
Ah, stay thee! 'Tis a jest!
(*With fiendish joy.*)
Well, then, thou shalt hear this,
And die ever damned!
(*Bending over the corpse of Gioconda, and screaming furiously into her ear.*)
LAST NIGHT THY MOTHER DID OFFEND ME:
I HAVE STRANGLED HER!
(*Wildly.*)
She hears me not!
(*With a cry of half-choked rage he rushes from the ruin. The curtain falls.*)

DOUBLE-FACED AND MISCELLANEOUS LA GIOCONDA RECORDS

Figlia che reggi tremulo pié (Daughter, My Faltering Steps) By Murino, Nunes and Badini (*In Italian*) Vo' farmi più gaia (Thou'rt Mine Now) By A. Rossi Murino, Soprano; E. Badini, Baritone	55017	12-inch,	$1.50
Già ti vedi (I Behold Thee) By F. Lotti, Soprano; de Gregorio, Tenor; E. Badini, Baritone (*In Italian*) Sì! morir ella de'! By Amleto Galli, Bass (*In Italian*)	55019	12-inch,	1.50
Suicidio! (Suicide Only Remains) By Elda Cavalieri Mefistofele—L'altra notte By Elda Cavalieri	55015	12-inch,	1.50
Selection By Arthur Pryor's Band	31384	12-inch,	1.00
Opening Chorus—"Feste! pane!" La Scala Chorus Barcarola—"Pescator affonda l'esca" By E. Badini	45010	10-inch,	1.00
Enzo Grimaldo By Conti and Badini (*In Italian*) Furlana (Finale, Act I) By Orchestra Sinfonica	45033	10-inch,	1.00
Cielo e Mar! By Franco de Gregorio (*In Italian*) Manon Lescaut—Ah, Manon! mi tradisce By Franco de Gregorio, Tenor (*In Italian*)	45027	10-inch,	1.00

SIEGFRIED'S DEATH—ACT III

(German)

GÖTTERDÄMMERUNG

(Got-ter-dahm'-er-ung)

(English)

THE DUSK OF THE GODS

MUSIC DRAMA IN THREE ACTS AND A PRELUDE

Words and music by Richard Wagner. First produced at Bayreuth, August 17, 1876, with Materna and Unger. First American production at New York, January 25, 1888, with Lehmann, Seidl-Krauss, Traubman, Niemann and Fischer.

Characters

SIEGFRIED	Tenor
GUNTHER (*Goon'-ter*)	Bass
HAGEN (*Hah'-gen*)	Bass
BRÜNNHILDE	Soprano
GUTRUNE (*Goot-troon'-eh*)	Soprano
WOGLINDA,	Soprano
WELLGUNDA, }Rhine-Nymphs	Soprano
FLOSSHILDE,	Contralto

PRELUDE

SCENE—*The Walkure's Rock*

The Dusk of the Gods, the last part of the tetralogy, consists of three acts and a prelude. In the prelude we once more see *Brünnhilde* on the rock, where she had lain during her magic sleep, and where *Siegfried* had found her and taken her as his bride. *Siegfried,* after a brief period of domestic happiness in a cave near by, decides to leave her for awhile in search of adventures, and gives her the Nibelung's Ring as a pledge of faith. This ring he had obtained when he slew the dragon *Fafner,* and as the opera progresses it will be seen that he is doomed to suffer the consequences of the fatal curse, invoked on every possessor of the Ring by *Alberich,* from whom it was forcibly taken by *Wotan.*

EDOUARD DE RESZKE
AS HAGEN

As the curtain rises *Brünnhilde* and *Siegfried* come out of the cave, *Siegfried* in full armor and the *Valkyrie* leading her horse by the bridle. She begins her tender address of farewell:

Did I not send thee, sweetest hero, to fresh exploits, frail were my love.
But one misgiving fights against it, for fear not wholly thy heart I hold.
I gave to thee all that gods had taught: heavenly runes, the richest hoard; but my restoreless maidenhood's strength snatch'd thou from me, who but seek to serve thee.
My wisdom fails, but good will remains; so full of love, but failing in strength, thou wilt despise perchance the poor one, who having giv'n all, can grant thee no more!

Zu neuen Thaten (Did I Not Send Thee?)

By Johanna Gadski, Soprano

In German 87098 10-inch, $2.00

This lovely air is delivered by Mme. Gadski with tenderness and feeling, and the record is an unusually fine example of the perfect recording of a beautiful soprano voice.

ACT I

SCENE—Castle of King Gunther

Siegfried joyously sets out on his journey and soon comes to the Court of *King Gunther* on the Rhine, where dwells also *Gunther's* sister *Gutrune*, and their half-brother *Hagen*, who is a son of *Alberich*, the dwarf. *Hagen* knows the history of the Ring and is anxious to restore it to his father, so he artfully tries to win the help of *Gunther*. Knowing that the hero is approaching the castle, he outlines this scheme, which is to give *Siegfried* a drink which will make him forget *Brünnhilde* and fall in love with *Gutrune*, after which *Gunther* can win the peerless *Brünnhilde* for himself. *Gunther* is tempted, and when *Siegfried's* horn announces his approach he consents.

Siegfried greets them as friends, and when offered the magic drink he accepts and immediately loses all recollection of *Brünnhilde*. Seeing the lovely *Gutrune*, who stands with lowered eyes, he exclaims:

SIEGFRIED (*gazing on Gutrune with a kindling eye*):
Thou fair one, whose beams
My breast have enflamed,
Why fall thus thine eyes before mine?
(*Gutrune looks up at him, blushing.*)
Ha! sweetest maid!
Screen those bright beams!
The heart in my breast
Burns with their strength.

Gutrune, trembling with emotion, leaves the Hall, and *Siegfried*, gazing after her, asks *Gunther* if he has a wife. The King, prompted by *Hagen*, replies that he knows of one he would wed, but that she is surrounded by a magic fire which he cannot pass. *Siegfried* seems trying to remember his past, but fails, looks confused, then suddenly says:

SIEGFRIED (*with a sudden start*):
I—fear not the fire,
And thy bride fain will I fetch;
For thy own am I
And my arm is thine:
If Gutrune for wife I may gain!

In order that *Brünnhilde* may think that it is *Gunther* who has won her, it is agreed that *Siegfried* shall, by means of the Tarnhelm, change himself into *Gunther's* form. Thinking only of his reward, *Siegfried* eagerly departs.

PAINTED BY ECHTER

ALBERICH AND HAGEN—ACT II

SCENE II—*The Walkure's Rock*

The scene changes to the Valkyrie Rock again, where *Brünnhilde* awaits *Siegfried's* return. She is astonished and alarmed when she sees a stranger approaching, not understanding how he has penetrated through the fiery barrier. It is *Siegfried* in the form of *Gunther.* He announces that he is *Gunther* come to win her for his wife. *Brünnhilde*, in horror and despair, holds up the Ring, exclaiming:

> BRÜNNHILDE:
> Stand back! bow to this token!
> No shame can touch me from thee
> While yet this Ring is my shield.

Siegfried attempts to take it from her and after a struggle, succeeds. As he draws the helpless and despairing *Brünnhilde* into the cave the curtain falls.

COPY'T DUPONT

GADSKI AS BRÜNNHILDE

ACT II

SCENE—*The Rhine near Gunther's Castle*

Hagen and *Alberich* discuss the progress of the plot to regain the Ring. *Hagen* swears to accomplish it, and *Alberich* vanishes. *Siegfried*, in his own form, but wearing the Tarnhelm, arrives, greets him cheerily and says he has gained *Gunther's* wife for him, but that they are returning home more slowly. *Gutrune* comes to meet *Siegfried*, and a long duet follows, after which they go to the Hall. *Hagen* sounds his horn to summon the vassals and bids them prepare for a feast, as *Gunther* has taken a bride.

Gunther now arrives in his boat, leading *Brünnhilde*, who is pale and downcast. *Siegfried* and *Gutrune* come out to meet them and *Brünnhilde* sees *Siegfried* in his rightful form. She recoils in horror at seeing him with another woman, and regarding her as a stranger. She then perceives the Ring on *Siegfried's* finger and demands to know where he obtained it. He seems confused and regards the Ring with a puzzled air. *Brünnhilde*, beginning to comprehend what has occurred, denounces him, and *Gunther,* beginning to doubt whether *Siegfried* had kept his oath to respect *Brünnhilde* as a brother's bride, looks threateningly at him. *Siegfried*, eager to set himself right, swears the oath of the spear.

The vassals make a ring round *Siegfried* and *Hagen*. *Hagen* holds out his spear; *Siegfried* lays two fingers of his right hand on its point.

SIEGFRIED:
Haft of war, hallowed weapon!
Hold thou my oath from dishonor!
On this spotless spear-head
I speak the oath:
Spear-point, aid thou my speech!

Where steel e'er can strike me,
Strike thou at me:
Wher'er death can be dealt me
Deal it to me,
If she is really wronged,—
If I have injured my friend!

Brünnhilde, unable to contain herself at this evidence of *Siegfried's* baseness, repeats his oath and denounces him.

Helle Wehr! Heilige Waffe! (Haft of War! Hallowed Weapon)
By Johanna Gadski, Soprano   (*In German*)   87052 10-inch, $2.00

Siegfried looks at her in pity, thinking her mad, and goes to the Hall with *Gutrune*. *Brünnhilde*, *Hagen* and *Gunther* remain behind, the latter in deep depression. *Hagen* tells *Brünnhilde* that he will avenge her wrongs. "Thou?" says *Brünnhilde*, contemptuously.

> BRÜNNHILDE:
> One angry glance of his glittering eyeball—
> That, e'en through his fraudulent shape,
> Fell unshadowed on me,—
> Would subdue thy most mettlesome daring!

She then tells him that only in his back is he vulnerable, and that no magic protection was placed there because she knew that never would he retreat. *Gunther* now rouses himself and the three decide that *Siegfried* must die for his treachery.

ACT III

SCENE I—*A Wild Valley near the Rhine*

The Rhine nymphs rise to the surface of the water and sing of the Rhinegold. They spy *Siegfried* and ask him to give up the Ring, but he refuses, and they warn him that he shall die that very day. He laughs at the prophecy, and as he watches them swim away, says lightly:

THE RHINE MAIDENS WARN SIEGFRIED—ACT III, SCENE I

SIEGFRIED:
Alike on land and water,
Woman's ways I've learnt to know.
The man who resists their smiles
They seek by threats to frighten.

And when these both are scorned
They bait him with bitter words.
And yet were Gutrune not my wife,
I must have promptly captured
One of those pretty maids!

Hunting horns are heard and *Siegfried* gayly answers with his own. *Gunther, Hagen* and the hunters descend from the hill and greet him. They camp and begin to eat and drink. *Siegfried* tells them of his adventure with *Mime* and the Dragon. *Hagen* gives him a magic drink which brings back his memory and he goes on to tell of the forest bird and his quest of the lovely *Brünnhilde*. *Gunther* begins to listen attentively, but when *Siegfried* reaches this part of his narrative, *Hagen* plunges his spear in *Siegfried's* back and he falls. *Gunther*, in pity for the dying man, leans over him, and *Siegfried* faintly says:

SIEGFRIED:
Brünnhilde! Heavenly bride!—
Look up! Open thine eyelids!
What 'hath sunk thee once more in sleep?
Who drowns thee in slumber so drear?
The wak'ner came, his kiss awoke;—
Again now the bride's bonds he has broken;—

Enchant him Brünnhilde's charms!
Ah! now forever open her eyelids!
Ah! and what od'rous breeze is her breath!
Thrice blessed ending—
Thrill that dismays not—
Brünnhilde beckons to me! (*He dies.*)

SCENE II—*Hall in Gunther's Palace*

Siegfried's body is borne mournfully to the Hall, where the weeping *Gutrune* meets them and clasps her husband's lifeless form. *Hagen* now demands the Ring as his booty, but *Gunther* refuses to yield it and they draw their swords, *Gunther* being killed by *Hagen*.

Hagen now attempts to withdraw the Ring from *Siegfried's* finger, but as he approaches, the arm of the dead hero is raised threateningly. All recoil in terror and *Brünnhilde* approaches. She gazes long and sadly at *Siegfried's* face, then orders a funeral pyre erected to burn the hero's body. The vassals obey and build a huge pyre on the bank of the Rhine, on which the body is laid. *Brünnhilde* summons two ravens from the rocks, and begins her great *Immolation Scene*.

SETTING OF ACT II AT BAYREUTH

Fliegt heim (Immolation Scene)

By Johanna Gadski,
Soprano (*In German*)
88185 12-inch, $3.00

She bids the ravens fly to *Loki*, god of fire, that he may complete the downfall of the gods by burning Valhalla.

BRÜNNHILDE:
Draweth near in gloom
The Dusk of the gods.
Thus, casting my torch,
I kindle Valhalla's tow'rs!

She kindles the pile, which burns rapidly, and the two ravens disappear in the distance. *Brünnhilde's* horse is brought in, and she takes off the bridle.

BRÜNNHILDE (*to the horse*):
Grani, my horse, greet thee again!
Wouldst thou know dear friend,
What journey we follow?
By flame illumined lies there thy lord,
Siegfried, the star of my life.
To meet with thy master neighest thou
merrily?
Lo! how the flame
Doth leap and allure thee!

Feel how my breast too hotly doth burn;
Sparkling fureflame my spirit enfolds.
O, but to clasp him—
Recline in his arms!
In madd'ning emotion
Once more to be his!
Heiajaho! Grano! Greet we our hero!
Siegfried! Siegfried! see!
Sweetly greets thee thy wife!

She swings herself on the steed and rides straight into the burning pile, which flames up mightily, half consuming the Hall itself. The Rhine then rises and puts out the flames, and on the surface are seen the Rhine daughters, who seize the Ring from the embers. *Hagen*, who has been anxiously watching, now rushes into the waters, crying: "The Ring is mine!" The nymphs seize him and drag him down in the flood. An increasing red glow is seen in the sky, and *Valhalla* appears in flames, with the gods and heroes calmly awaiting their doom. As the flames envelop all, the curtain falls.

THE DESTRUCTION OF THE GODS

142

FROM THE PAINTING BY CZACKORSKI   HAMLET AND THE ACTORS—ACT II

HAMLET

OPERA IN FIVE ACTS

Book by Barbier and Carré, based on Shakespeare's play.   Music by Ambroise Thomas.
First production March 9, 1868, at the Paris *Académie*.   First London production June 19, 1869.

Cast

HAMLET	Baritone
CLAUDIUS, King of Denmark	Bass
LAERTES, Polonius' son	Tenor
Ghost of the dead King	Bass
POLONIUS, Chancellor	Bass
GERTRUDE, Hamlet's Mother, Queen of Denmark	Mezzo-Soprano
OPHELIA, daughter of Polonius	Soprano

Lords, Ladies, Officers, Pages, Peasants, etc.

Scene: Elsinore, in Denmark.

The story of *Hamlet, Prince of Denmark*, is so well known that it would seem hardly necessary to describe the plot at any length.   However, for operatic purposes the librettists were obliged to modify and reconstruct certain portions of the tragedy, and the revised version will be briefly sketched here.

The present King of Denmark, *Claudius,* has seized the throne, after having murdered the late King, *Hamlet's* father.   At the opening of the opera *Hamlet* knows nothing of the murder, but is highly incensed at his mother for having married *Claudius* before she had been two months a widow.

ACT I

SCENE I—*A Room of State in the Palace*

The new Queen is being presented to the Court at a public reception.   She is annoyed because *Hamlet* shows his displeasure by absenting himself from the ceremony.   After the presentation is over, *Hamlet* enters slowly, in a melancholy mood.

> HAMLET: Ah! vain indeed is grief!
> Affection, too, doth seem short lived indeed.
> My much-loved father but two months dead;
> And yet, unto another wedlock, my mother hath consented;
> "Frailty, thy name is woman."

His bitter musing is interrupted by the entrance of *Ophelia*, his betrothed.   She has heard that *Hamlet* intends to leave the kingdom and asks if he has ceased to love her.   In the beautiful love duet he reassures her, and tells her why the palace has become intolerable to him.

Nega se puoi la luce (Love Duet)

By Maria Galvany, Soprano, and Titta Ruffo, Baritone (*In Italian*) 92500 12-inch, $4.00

PHOTO DU GUY

RENAUD AS HAMLET

HAMLET:
Celestial maiden, 'tis not thee I chide,
The purity of thy mind doth speak through
those sweet eyes!
"Doubt that the stars are fire,
Doubt that the sun doth move,
Doubt truth to be a liar;
But never doubt my love."

OPHELIA:
It may be so, but such excess of love
Hath no enduring power;
Thou couldst not leave me to my sorrow,
Did thy heart know such love as mine!
Ye heavenly powers,—celestial choir,
That aye surround the eternal throne,
From your bright homes above,
Bear witness to my truthful love.

HAMLET:
Beloved Ophelia!

OPHELIA:
In thee this heart doth trust!

HAMLET:
My heart doth beat for thee alone!

OPHELIA:
Ah! never will we part!

SCENE II—*Esplanade of the Palace. It is Night*

Horatio and *Marcellus* are discovered excitedly discussing the appearance of the spectre of the murdered King. They greet *Hamlet* and tell him of the ghostly visitor, which appeared just at midnight. *Hamlet* is much affected, and suggests that as it is nearly twelve the ghost may come again.

The clock strikes, and the figure of the murdered King appears. *Hamlet* speaks to the spectre:

HAMLET:
Thou spirit dread, thou shade revered,
Hear thou thy hapless son's lament.
In pity answer,—speak to me!
Tell me why the sepulchre,

Wherein we saw thee peacefully entombed,
Hath op'd his ponderous and marble jaws,
To cast thee forth again?

The ghost motions *Horatio* and *Marcellus* to withdraw, and when they are gone he tells *Hamlet* of the murder and bids him become the avenger, and asks him to leave his mother's punishment to God. *Hamlet* is much affected and exclaims:

HAMLET:
Yes! Shade revered! Thy bidding
shall be done.
O light, O sun, O glory, O love to me
so dear,
Farewell! Farewell!

The ghost, before disappearing, pauses at the back of the stage, and stands with one hand extended toward *Hamlet;* at this moment *Horatio* and *Marcellus* re-enter, and appear terror-stricken at the spectacle before them. Trumpets and joyous music are heard without as the curtain falls.

ACT II

SCENE—*Garden of the Palace*

Ophelia enters and is much disturbed because *Hamlet* seems to avoid

PLAY PICTORIAL

HAMLET AND THE GHOST

her. The Queen finds her weeping, and after questioning her says that *Hamlet* has also acted strangely toward his mother and fears his reason is affected.

Hamlet, seeking to entrap the King in some manner into betraying himself, has engaged a troupe of players to present a play which shall enact a similar crime. The King and Queen are delighted that he seems to seek amusement, and gladly accept his invitation to witness the play.

PLAY PICTORIAL

THE KING REVEALS HIS GUILT—ACT II

When the royal pair have departed, the players come on and are instructed by *Hamlet* in the plot he has conceived. The Prince then calls for wine and bids the players be merry, offering to sing them a drinking song.

O vin, discaccia la tristezza (Brindisi) (Wine, This Gloom Dispel)

By Mario Sammarco, Baritone	(*In Italian*)	88312	12-inch, $3.00
By Emilio de Gogorza, Baritone	(*In French*)	88180	12-inch, 3.00
By Titta Ruffo, Baritone, and La Scala Chorus	(*Italian*)	92037	12-inch, 3.00
By Francesco Cigada, Baritone, and La Scala Chorus	*16572	10-inch,	.75

HAMLET:
O wine! the gloom dispel,
That o'er my heart now weighs;
Come grant me thine intoxicating joy;
The careless laugh—the mocking jest!
O wine! Thou potent sorcerer,
Grant thou oblivion to my heart!
Yes, life is short, death's near at hand,

We'll laugh and drink while yet we may.
Each, alas, his burthen bears.
Sad thoughts have all;—grim thoughts and
  sorrows;
But care avaunt, let folly reign,
The only wise man he,
Who wisdom's precepts ne'er obeys!
(*The curtain falls on a scene of merriment.*)

SCENE II—*The Palace Hall. On one side a stage has been erected*

The court assembles and the play begins, *Hamlet* placing himself where he can watch the King closely. As the action proceeds the guilty man shows unmistakable evidence of agitation, and finally in a rage he orders the players away. *Hamlet* rushes forward and denounces the murderer, but the Court believes his accusation to be the ravings of a madman, and all leave the room as he faints in *Horatio's* arms.

ACT III
SCENE—*The Queen's Apartments*
Hamlet enters and sings his farewell soliloquy.

Monologo (Soliloquy)

By Titta Ruffo, Baritone   (*In Italian*)   92042   12-inch, $3.00

This is Thomas' splendid setting of the well-known soliloquy and one of the most conspicuous numbers in the opera. Although the librettists took many liberties with Shakespeare's drama, they did not venture to alter such a well-known excerpt as this. Ruffo sings this famous monologue in a superb manner, delivering it with great dramatic power.

* *Double-Faced Record—For title of opposite side see DOUBLE-FACED HAMLET RECORDS, page 146.*

HAMLET: To be, or not to be, that is the question.
To die, to sleep; perchance to dream;
Ah! were it allowed me to sever
The tie that binds me to mortality,
And seek "the undiscovered country
From whose bourne no traveler returns!"
"Ay! to be, or not to be?
To die, to sleep; perchance to dream."

The Queen and *Ophelia* enter and plead with *Hamlet to* banish his wild imaginings. He sternly rebukes them, advises *Ophelia* to retire to a convent, and accuses his mother of being an accomplice. The ghost again appears, visible only to *Hamlet,* bids him spare his mother, and slowly disappears. The Prince conducts the Queen to the door, urging her to pray and repent.

ACT IV
A rural scene near a lake. Willows line the shore

Ophelia, driven insane by *Hamlet's* desertion of her, has wandered to the lake. She plays with a garland of flowers, and sings her wonderful aria, usually known as the *Mad Scene,* one of the most difficult of all florid compositions.

Ballata d'Ofelia (Mad Scene)

By Nellie Melba	*(In French)*	88251	12-inch, $3.00
By Maria Galvany	*(In Italian)*	88235	12-inch, 3.00
By Giuseppina Huguet	*(Italian)* *35180	12-inch, 1.25

PHOTO ERMINI

RUFFO AS HAMLET

An exquisite introduction by the orchestra is heard as *Ophelia* enters—a strange, wild figure, with flowing hair and torn white dress. She speaks to the wondering peasants and tells them childishly of the lark which she heard at dawn, following with a brilliant display of bird-like trills and staccatos.

COPY'T DUPONT

CALVÉ AS OPHELIA

Ophelia then turns to the shepherds and asks them to listen to her song, a strange, sad melody, which is interrupted at intervals by wild laughter and weeping. Presently she seems to forget, and placidly plays with her flowers, until the magical siren's song is heard luring her to the water's edge, and she plunges in and floats away, singing of *Hamlet's* vow of love.

Mme. Melba fairly surpasses herself in this scene, with its sudden alternations of joy and sorrow, the pathos which overshadows every phrase.

Other fine renditions, that of Mme. Galvany and a popular-priced one by Mme. Huguet, are also offered to opera-lovers.

ACT V—*The Churchyard*

Hamlet comes hither to attend the funeral of *Ophelia.* He sings his beautiful song to her memory and resolves to take his own life upon her grave.

Come il romito fior (As a Lovely Flower)

By Titta Ruffo, Baritone, and La Scala Chorus		
	(In Italian) 92064	12-inch, $3.00
By Enrico Pignataro, Baritone		
	(In Italian) *63424	10-inch, .75

When the cortege has arrived, the ghost again appears and looks reproachfully on *Hamlet,* who stabs the King, and as the curtain falls the people, now convinced of their monarch's guilt, acclaim *Hamlet* as his successor.

DOUBLE-FACED HAMLET RECORDS

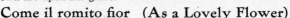

Ballata d'Ofelia (Mad Scene)	By Huguet, Soprano	*(Italian)*	35180	12-inch, $1.25
Dinorah—Si, carina caprettina	By Giuseppina Huguet, Soprano			
Brindisi	By Francesco Cigada and Chorus	*(In Italian)*	16572	10-inch, .75
Ernani—Festa da ballo	By La Scala Chorus	*(In Italian)*		
Come il romito fior	By Enrico Pignataro	*(In Italian)*	63424	10-inch, .75
Pallide Mammole—Romanza	By Lavin de Casas	*(In Italian)*		

(German)
HÄNSEL UND GRETEL
(Hahn'-sel oondt Gray'-tel)

(Italian)
NINO E RITA
(Neen-yo ay Ree'-tah)

(English)
HANSEL AND GRETEL
(Han-sel and Gray'-tel)
(or HANS AND GRETCHEN)

A FAIRY OPERA IN THREE ACTS

Text by Adelheid Wette. Music by Engelbert Humperdinck.
First produced 1893, at Weimar. First American performance at
the Metropolitan Opera House, New York, 1895.

Cast

PETER, a broom-maker	Baritone
GERTRUDE, his wife	Mezzo-Soprano
HÄNSEL, } their children	Mezzo-Soprano
GRETEL, }	Soprano
THE WITCH who eats children	Mezzo-Soprano
SANDMAN, the Sleep Fairy	Soprano
DEWMAN, the Dawn Fairy	Soprano

MUSICAL AMERICA

HUMPERDINCK

It is now some seventeen years since Humperdinck's lovely fairy opera was brought out in America by Augustin Daly, and it has since been firmly established in the repertoire of every producer of grand opera.

Hänsel and Gretel has been called the Peter Pan of grand opera; the audiences who witness it being invariably delighted with the childish joyousness and fairy charm of Humperdinck's work.

This delightful opera is built upon the simple Grimm tale of *Babes in the Woods,* and first suggested itself to the composer to amuse his sister's children. It was afterward elaborated into a complete opera, which has become one of the most important and interesting of modern German works.

COPY'T BURR M'INTOSH

ALTEN AS GRETEL

Two German peasant children, *Hans* and *Gretchen,* are sent to the woods for strawberries and get lost. The *Sandman* finds the babes and sings them to sleep, while angels and fairies watch over them. They are awakened by the *Dew Man,* and go for breakfast to the house of the *Witch,* who plans to eat them; but when she opens the oven to see if it is hot enough to cook *Hans,* she herself is pushed in by *Gretchen.*

GUSSIN

THE CHILDREN AT HOME

BOYER

HÄNSEL AND GRETEL KNOCKING AT THE WITCH'S DOOR

Several numbers from this interesting opera are presented here,—the first being the beautiful Prelude.

Prelude

By Arthur Pryor's Band
31853 12-inch, $1.00

This Prelude is an especially beautiful number. It opens with the *Prayer of the Children*, played by the brass —at first softly, then swelling to the full strength of the band. This is followed by a passage portraying morning in the forest, and upon this pastoral scene there breaks in rudely the *Hocus pocus*, or *Witches' motive*. The Prelude is brought to a close with a return of the *Prayer theme*.

The delicacy and charm of this music is well brought out by the band under Mr. Pryor's masterly baton.

The second number is *Peter's* air in Act I.

Eine Hex' steinalt (The Old Witch)

By Otto Goritz, Baritone   (*In German*) 64164 10-inch, $1.00

This is sung when *Peter* returns to his cottage and finds the children gone after strawberries. In this air he frightens his wife by telling of the witch who lives in a honey-cake house, and who after enticing little children into it, bakes them into gingerbread in her oven.

Mr. Goritz's admirable character study as *Peter*, the tipsy, kind-hearted and superstitious father, is one of the features of the Metropolitan revival, and this odd number is given with much effectiveness.

The third number is the famous *Hexenritt*, or *Witch's Ride*, which occurs in Act III.

Hexenritt (Witch's Ride)

By Albert Reiss, Tenor   (*In German*) 64188 10-inch, $1.00

The curtain rises, showing *Hänsel* and *Gretel* still asleep in the wood. The *Dawn Fairy* shakes dewdrops on the children and wakes them just as the mist clears away, revealing the house of the *Witch*.

The children approach cautiously and begin to nibble at the gingerbread fence, when the *Witch* comes out and casts a spell over them. She makes a good fire in the stove for the purpose of roasting the babes, and in her joy she rides wildly around the room on a broomstick, singing this unique *Hexenritt*.

Mr. Reiss tries his best to conceal his naturally sweet tenor when delivering this number, but only partially succeeds. However, the *Witch's* part is not intended to be sung but "squeaked," and as a humorous performance this rendition is a masterpiece.

LARCHER

THE CHAMBER OF HEROD

(French)
HÉRODIADE
(Her-ro-dee-ah'-d)

OPERA IN FIVE ACTS

Words by Paul Milliet and Henri Grémont, based on Gustave Flaubert's novelette, *Herodias*. Music by Jules Massenet. First production December 19, 1881, at the *Théâtre de la Monnaie*, Brussels. Produced in Paris at the *Théâtre Italien*, February 1, 1884, with Jean and Eduard de Reszke, Maurel, Tremelli and Devriès. Revived at the *Théâtre de la Gaîté* in 1903, with Calvé and Renaud. First German production in Hamburg, 1883, with Sucher, Krauss and Winkelmann. First London production 1904, under the title *Salome,* with the locale changed to Ethiopia by the British censor's orders. First American production at the Manhattan Opera House, New York, November 8, 1909, with Cavalieri, Gerville-Réache, Duchesne, Dalmores and Renaud.

CAST

JOHN THE PROPHET . . . . Tenor
HEROD, King of Galilee . . . . Baritone
PHANUEL, a young Jew . . . . Bass
VITELLIUS, a Roman proconsul . . . . Baritone
THE HIGH PRIEST . . . . Baritone
A VOICE IN THE TEMPLE . . . . Bass
SALOME . . . . Soprano
HERODIAS . . . . Contralto
A YOUNG BABYLONIAN WOMAN . . . .

Merchants, Hebrew Soldiers, Roman Soldiers, Priests, Levites, Temple
Servitors, Seamen, Scribes, Pharisees, Galileans, Samaritans,
Sadducees, Ethiopians, Nubians, Arabs, Romans.

The action takes place in Jerusalem—Time, about 30 A. D.

CAUTIN & BERGER
CALVÉ AS SALOME IN HÉRODIADE

Herodiade was first produced in Brussels in 1881.
The first Paris production of this opera was especially
interesting because of the first appearance of Jean de
Reszke as a tenor (he was formerly a baritone). It was
not until 1904, however, that the opera was brought
out in London (under the title of Salome) with Mme
Calvé, Dalmores and Renaud in the leading rôles. Mr.
Hammerstein's brilliant production of this work was
one of the events of a recent season at the Manhattan.

The opera contains much of the best music
Massenet has written; and several of the most melodious of these airs have been recorded by the Victor.

The plot, while based on the well-known Scrip-
tural story, does not follow the Bible or tradition very
closely, and differs quite largely from Salome.

ACT I

Salome enters and is greeted by *Phanuel*, a young
Jew, who is astonished that she should be in the Palace,
and wonders if she can be ignorant of the fact that
Herodias is her mother. *Salome* tells him she is seeking
John the Prophet, and in this air she describes how
he had saved her from the desert when a child, and
how good and kind he is.

Il est doux, il est bon (He is Kind, He is Good)

By Emma Calvé, Soprano
(*In French*) 88130 12-inch, $3.00

Salome goes out just as *Herod* enters searching for her.
Herodias rushes in and demands *John's* head, saying that he
had insulted her. *John* appears, denounces them both and
drives them out, terrified. *Salome* enters and tells *John* of her
love for him, but he bids her turn to God.

ACT II

Herod lies on his luxurious couch, while attendants sing to
him. He can think of no one but *Salome*, and bids the slaves
dance to distract his mind. A love potion is given him by a
slave, who says it will make him see the face of the one he loves.

He then sings the famous *Vision fugitive*, considered the
most beautiful of the airs in the opera.

Vision fugitive (Fleeting Vision)

By Emilio de Gogorza, Baritone
(*In French*) 88153 12-inch, $3.00

COPY'T MISHKIN
GERVILLE-RÉACHE AS HERODIAS
IN HERODIADE

Herod describes the vision
of *Salome* which haunts him
night and day, and declares that
to possess her he would gladly
surrender his soul. He drinks
the love potion, and falls on the
couch in a delirious sleep.

The scene changes to the
great square at Jerusalem, where
Herod receives messages from
the allies, and denounces Rome.
Herodias enters and announces
that the Roman general, *Vitellius*,
is approaching. The people are

CAUTIN & BERGER
RENAUD AS HEROD

terrified, but *Vitellius* declares that Rome desires the favor of the Jews and will give back the Temple of Israel.

John and *Salome* enter and *Vitellius* is surprised at the honor paid to the *Prophet*. *Herod* gazes with eyes of love at *Salome,* while *Herodias* watches her jealously. *John* denounces *Vitellius* as the curtain falls.

ACT III

The third act begins in *Phanuel's* house. He is gazing at the city, which lies silent under a starry sky, and prophesies the fate which is to overwhelm it.

Air de Phanuel (Oh, Shining Stars)
By Marcel Journet, Bass

(In French)   74152   12-inch, $1.50

COPY'T MISHKIN

DUFRANNE AS PHANUEL

He calls upon the stars to tell him what manner of man is this *John,* who speaks with such authority. "Is he a man or a god?" he cries. *Herodias* enters, much agitated. *Phanuel* inquires what has brought the Queen to his house, and she cries, "Vengeance on the woman who has stolen *Herod's* love!" He reads her fate by the stars, and sees nothing but blood in the horoscope. She asks him about her child, lost so long ago, and he takes her to the window and shows her *Salome,* who is just entering the Temple. Horrified, *Herodias* cries, "My daughter? Never! That is my rival!"

The second scene shows the entrance of the Temple. *Salome* enters half fainting, having heard that *John* has been cast in prison, and falls exhausted at the prison entrance. *Herod* enters, and seeing *Salome,* breaks out into a mad declaration of his love, but she repulses him with horror, and tells him she loves another. He declares he will find this lover and kill him, and goes out as the people enter the Temple.

John is brought in and denounced by the priests, but prays for them as they demand his death. *Salome* runs to *John* and falls at his feet, wishing to die with him. *Herod,* seeing that it is *John* whom *Salome* loves, orders them both put to death, and they are seized and borne out by guards as the curtain falls.

ACT IV

In Act IV *John* and *Salome* are seen in prison. *John* admits that he loves her, and urges her to fly and save her life, but she refuses, declaring she will die with him. Priests appear and order *John* to death, and command *Salome* to be taken to the Palace by *Herod's* commands. She resists desperately, but is dragged away.

In the second scene occurs the great festival in honor of the Roman Empire. *Salome* is brought in and again entreats to be allowed to die with *John.* She appeals to the Queen, saying, "If thou wert ever a mother, pity me." *Herodias* trembles at the word, and gazing on her daughter, seems about to yield, when the executioner appears at the back with a dripping sword and cries, "The *Prophet* is dead." *Salome* gives a terrible cry and tries to kill the Queen, who screams: "Mercy! I am thy mother!" *Salome* recoils in horror, curses her mother and stabs herself.

(Curtain)

MISCELLANEOUS HÉRODIADE RECORD

Hérodiade Selection
By Arthur Pryor's Band

31786   12-inch, $1.25

THE GREAT BALLROOM SCENE—ACT IV

(French)
LES HUGUENOTS
(Leh Hueg'-noh)

(German)
DIE HUGENOTTEN
(Dee Hoo-gen-ott'-en)

(Italian)
GLI UGONOTTI
(Glee Oo-goh-not'-tih)

(English)
THE HUGUENOTS
(Hew-gen'-ahts)

OPERA IN FIVE ACTS

Libretto by Scribe and Émile Deschamps. Score by Giacomo Meyerbeer. First presented at the *Académie* in Paris, February 29, 1836. First London production July 20, 1848. First New York performance June 24, 1850. Some notable American productions were in 1858, with La Grange, Siedenburg, Tiberini and Karl Formes; in 1872, with Parepa-Rosa, Wachtel and Santley; in 1873, with Nilsson, Cary, Campanini and del Puente; in 1892, with Montariol, de Reszke, Lasalle, Albani and Scalchi; in 1905, with Sembrich, Caruso, Walker, Plançon, Scotti and Journet; in 1907, with Nordica, Nielsen, Constantino and de Segurola; and the Manhattan production in 1908, with Pinkert, Russ, Bassi, Ancona and Arimondi.

Cast

COUNT OF ST. BRIS, *(Sah Bree')* ⎫ Catholic noblemen .... ⎰ Baritone
COUNT OF NEVERS, *(Nev-airz')* ⎭ ⎱ Baritone
RAOUL DE NANGIS, *(Rah-ool' day Non-zhee')* a Protestant gentleman ...... Tenor
MARCEL, *(Mahr-chel')* a Huguenot soldier and servant to Raoul .... Bass
MARGARET OF VALOIS, *(Val-ooah')* betrothed to Henry IV .... Soprano
VALENTINE, daughter of St. Bris.................................. Soprano
URBANO, *(Ur-bah'-noh)* page to Queen Margaret .... Mezzo-Soprano
Ladies and Gentlemen of the Court, Pages, Citizens, Soldiers, Students, etc.

Scene and Period: Touraine and Paris; *during the month of August, 1572.*

This opera is considered the composer's masterpiece, and is indeed a wonderfully imposing work, with its splendid scenes, beautiful arias and concerted numbers, and its thrilling dramatic situations. The romance as well as the fanaticism of the period are faithfully pictured, and the whole presented on a magnificent scale. The work, however, is undeniably too long for a single evening's performance, requiring fully five hours when given entire; and it is to be regretted that some courageous *impresario* does not prune and pare it until it becomes of reasonable length. The Victor, however, has been merciful, and has selected only the gems of the work, which have been given by a fine cast headed by Caruso.

The story relates to one of the most dramatic periods in French history, and tells of the massacre of Huguenots in 1572, and of the efforts of *Margaret of Valois*, the betrothed of *Henry IV*, to reconcile the disputes between the Protestants and the Catholics.

ACT I

SCENE I—*House of the Count of Nevers*

The overture is a short one and consists mainly of the Lutheran chorale, which occurs several times in various portions of the opera. The curtain rises, disclosing a magnificent salon in the house of *Nevers*, where a gay party of Catholic noblemen are feasting. The Count explains that he expects another guest, a Huguenot, whom he hopes they will treat with courtesy. *Raoul* arrives and makes a favorable impression on the guests. *Nevers* boasts the ladies, proposing that each relate an adventure with some fair one; *Raoul*, being the latest arrival, is called upon first, and describes his rescue of an unknown beauty (who proves afterward to be *Valentine, St. Bris'* daughter) from some drunken revelers. In this air he tells of her beauty and the deep impression she made on him.

Più bianca—Romanza (Fairer Than the Lily)

| By Enrico Caruso, Tenor | (*In Italian*) | 88210 | 12-inch, $3.00 |
| By M. Gautier, Tenor | (*In French*) | *45007 | 10-inch, 1.00 |

Caruso makes a manly picture as the young nobleman, and sings the music allotted to *Raoul* charmingly, especially this delicate Romanza, in which he describes the vision of the unknown with whom he has fallen in love. In dreamy tones he sings the recitative, after which a short introduction brings us to the romanza, beginning

Più bian - ca, del più bian - co ve - - - - lo.
Fair - er far e'en than fair - est lil - - - - y.

Nothing could be more tender and beautiful than Caruso's singing of this number.

RAOUL:
Fairer far e'en than fairest lily,
Than spring morn more pure and more lovely and bright,
An angel of Heaven born beauty
Burst upon my ravish'd sight.
Sweetly she smiled as I stood by her side,
Sighing the love which e'en her tongue to speak denied;

And in her eyes the love-light gleamed,
Bidding me hope her love to gain.
Oh! she was charming past all expression!
And as before her form divine I bent my knee,
I falter'd forth, "Fair angel, that cometh from Heav'n above,
For evermore shall I love none but thee!"

A French rendition by M. Gautier, of the Paris Opera, is offered at a popular price, and the record is a most excellent one.

The applause which greets this recital is interrupted by the entrance of *Marcel*, who makes no secret of his displeasure at seeing his master dining with Romanists. *Raoul* apologizes, begging indulgence for an old soldier and faithful servant who loves him, and the guests call on *Marcel* for a song. The grim soldier offers to sing an old Huguenot song of warning both against Rome and the wiles of woman.

MARCEL:
Sirs, I will; an old Huguenot song against the snares of Rome and the dark wiles of woman. You, sirs, should know it well—it is our battle song: you heard it at Rochelle, for there 'twas sung, 'mid the din of drums and trumpets; with a full accompaniment—piff, paff, piff, paff,— of bullets from our ranks, thus out it rang:

Double-Faced Record—For title of opposite side see DOUBLE-FACED HUGUENOTS RECORDS, page 158.

PLANÇON AS ST. BRIS

Piff! Paff! (Marcel's Air)
By Marcel Journet, Bass
(*In French*) 74156 12-inch, $1.50

MARCEL:
Old Rome and her revelries,
Her pride and her lust, boys,
The monks and their devilries,
We'll grind them to dust, boys!
Deliver to fire and sword
Their temples of Hell,
Till of the black demons
None live to tell!
Woe to all defilers fair!
I ne'er heed their shrieking—
Woe to the Dalilahs fair,
Who men's souls are seeking!
Deliver to fire and sword
Those children of Hell,
Till of the black demons
None live to tell!

Refrain
Piff, paff, piff; slay them all,
Piff, paff, piff, ev'ry soul!
Piff, paff, piff; paff; piff; piff, paff, piff, paff!
All vainly for aid or for mercy they call;
No pity for them! No they die—slay all!
No, no, no, no, no, no, no; slay all!

Journet's portrayal of the grim, stubborn old serv
ant is a very fine one, and his rendition of the *Piff, Paff* is remarkable in its rugged force
and stern simplicity.

A servant of *Nevers* announces a veiled lady to see him and he retires to an adjoining
room. *Raoul* catches sight of the lady through the window as she lifts her veil, and is
astonished and grieved to recognize the beauty he had saved from the ruffians.

A young page now enters, and in a lovely air, familiarly called the *Page Song*,
announces that she has a message for one of the cavaliers present.

Nobil Signori salute! (Noble Sirs, I Salute You)
By Louise Homer, Contralto   (*In Italian*) 85107 12-inch, $3.00

This gay and brilliant cavatina is considered one of the most difficult of contralto num
bers. It begins with a long and very ornamental cadenza, followed by this graceful melody

No - bil don-na e tan-to o - ne - sta.... che far lie-to un re ..... po - tria,
From a la - dy fair and love - ly.... For whose smiles a king might woo,

worked up with much spirit and reintroduced after a striking series of vocal figures sung
on the word "no." Mme. Homer's execution of this florid air exhibits well the great flexi
bility of her fine voice.

Meyerbeer intended this part for soprano, but it is usually transposed and sung by a
contralto.

URBANO:
A most charming noble lady,
Whom with envy kings might view,
With a message here has charged me,
Cavaliers, cavaliers, to one of you.
I do not name him; but honor be
Unto the good knight, whoe'er be he!
And until now, sirs, there ne'er hath been
Mortal so favor'd by beauty's queen!

The note proves to be for *Raoul*, and bids him consent to come blindfolded in a
carriage, without question, to wherever his guide will take him. The young man is puzzled
but decides to obey, and shows the note to the others. They recognize the seal of *Margaret
of Valois*, and cast looks of envy at him as he follows the page.

ACT II

SCENE—*Castle and Gardens of Chenonceaux*

The Queen is seated on a kind of throne surrounded by her maids, who, with *Urbano*, are assisting in her toilet. She rises and sings her great air in praise of fair Touraine. Two fine records of this florid number, by two famous sopranos, are presented here.

O, vago suol della Turenna (Fair Land of Touraine)

By Maria Galvany, Soprano
(In Italian) 88234 12-inch, $3.00
By Giuseppina Huguet, Soprano
(In Italian) *35123 12-inch, 1.25

QUEEN:
Oh, lovely land of fair Touraine!
Thy vine-clad hills, thy sparkling fountains,
Thy green banks and thy murm'ring zephyrs,
All fill my soul with peace and love!
Yet, for a difference in belief,
This fair scene may by war be stain'd!
Oh, that men would observe the moral,
To love and fear the all-powerful Being!
But hence with sorrow!
Care we will banish;
Quick, let it vanish, far, far away!
In the land where I reign,
From the mount to the main,
All re-echo the strain
That's devoted to love!

COPY'T DUPONT HOMER AS THE PAGE

The maids disperse, and *Valentine* enters and tells the Queen that she has seen the Count de Nevers, who has promised to release her from the engagement which had been arranged. *Margaret* informs her that she has another cavalier in mind—meaning *Raoul*, who is now conducted to the ladies and his mask removed. He is much astonished to find that it is the Queen who has sent for him, and pledges his honor and his sword to her service. He does not, however, perceive *Valentine*, who has retired at the moment of his entrance.

The nobles of the Court, Protestant and Catholic, now enter, having been sent for by *Margaret*. She announces that she is planning a marriage which shall reconcile all their differences, and asks them to swear to live in peace with each other.

MARGARET:
Swear that, by the marriage vow,
Which each this day shall plight,
No more shall enmity prevail,
No more each other's lives assail,
In party feud or right!
(Raoul, Nevers, St. Bris and the Nobles,
gather around the Queen and take the
oath.)
THE NOBLES:
We swear by our forefathers bold,
The Queen and all her powers,
That kindly acts and generous thoughts
Shall evermore be ours!

Valentine is now led in by her father and presented to *Raoul*. He starts in astonishment, having recognized the lady he had rescued, and whom he had seen meeting *Nevers*.

RAOUL *(in a stifled voice)*:
Great Heaven! what do I see?
MARGARET:
Why this astonishment?
RAOUL:
What! is this the bride you would offer to me?
MARGARET:
Yes, to marry and to love.
RAOUL:
What perfidy! what treachery!
I her husband! Never, never!

SCALCHI AS THE PAGE

Double-Faced Record—For title of opposite side see DOUBLE-FACED HUGUENOTS RECORDS, page 158.

A terrible scene follows, *St. Bris* challenging *Raoul,* who is ordered under arrest by the Queen. *Valentine* is overcome with shame, and the Catholics are furious. *Marcel* is delighted that his master has escaped marriage with a Catholic, and the curtain falls as the Lutheran chorale is again heard in the orchestra.

COPY'T MISHKIN

DALMORES AS RAOUL

ACT III
(*A Square in Paris*)

A wedding procession passes on its way to the church; it is for *Valentine,* who has been persuaded to wed *Nevers.* *Valentine* asks that she be permitted to spend the day in the chapel in prayer. While there she overhears a plot to assassinate *Raoul,* and at once goes in search of *Marcel* to inform him of the plan. She meets him in the square and in a great duet tells him of the plot.

NILSSON AS VALENTINE

Nella notte io sol qui veglio (Here By Night Alone I Wander)
By Maria Grisi, Soprano, and Perello De Segurola, Bass
(*In Italian*) *63404 10-inch, $0.75

Marcel thanks her for the warning and goes with his friends to the rescue. A general conflict is threatened but is prevented by the Queen, who appears just in time. She tells *Raoul* that *Valentine* is innocent of wrong, having merely gone to *Nevers'* house to ask him to release her. *Raoul* is overcome with remorse, but the knowledge comes too late, as *Valentine* is already the wife of *Nevers.*

A richly decorated boat approaches, occupied by the nuptial suite. *Nevers* leads *Valentine* to it, and as all salute the bridal couple the boat moves away, while *Raoul,* overcome by grief, is supported by *Marcel.* The curtain falls.

ACT IV
(*A Room in Nevers' Castle*)

Valentine, alone, broods over her sorrows, confessing to herself that although wedded to another, she still loves *Raoul.* She is astounded to see her lover appear, he having braved death and entered the castle to see her again. *Valentine* hears her father's voice, and hastily conceals *Raoul* behind the tapestry. The Catholic nobles enter to discuss the plot outlined by *St. Bris.* They finally agree to his fiendish proposal, and swear to slaughter the Huguenots. *Nevers* is horrified at the bloody scheme to exterminate all Protestants, and refusing to become an assassin, he breaks his sword, and is led away by the guards.

The conference closes with the famous *Benediction of the Swords,* perhaps the greatest and most thrilling of all operatic scenes. A magnificent record of this number has been given by Journet and the Opera chorus.

COPY'T MISHKIN

CONSTANTINO AS RAOUL

Benediction of the Swords
By Marcel Journet, Bass, and Metropolitan

Opera Chorus (*In Italian*)	74275	12-inch,	$1.50
By Sousa's Band	*35118	12-inch,	1.25
By Sousa's Band	31574	12-inch,	1.00

*Double-Faced Record—For title of opposite side see DOUBLE-FACED HUGUENOTS RECORDS, page 154

The number begins with the strain sung by *St. Bris* in his recital of the plan.

Vo - le - te ,yoi, in - sieme a me, col - pi - - re i tra - di - tor? Eb - ben!
Will ye all join with me the trai - lors to de - stroy? 'Tis well!

This is followed by the noble strain of the *Benediction*, one of the best known passages in Meyerbeer's work—

D'un sa - cro zel l'ar do - re cie - le - vie scal - di l'al - ma
On Heav'n's just cause re - ly - ing, This im - pious race de - fy - ing

COPY'T DUPONT

JEAN DE RESZKE AS RAOUL

ST. BRIS:
　Do you wish our dear country to save?
MONKS AND NOBLES:
　It is our wish! our hearts' desire!
ST. BRIS:
　To serve our noble King,
　Will ye the traitors destroy?
MONKS AND NOBLES:
　The King's commands, we will obey!
ST. BRIS:
　'Tis well! now hear the King's decree:
　These Huguenots, whose vile detested race we
　　hate,
　Shall from this day by the sword disappear!
ST. BRIS:
　On Heaven's just cause relying,
　This impious race defying,
　'Mid thousands round thee dying,
　Now swear that no mercy thou'lt show!
　A sacred zeal inspiring,
　All hearts with courage firing,
　To compass Heav'n's desiring,
　Now for vengeance we go!

Then comes the furious and fanatical chorus of priests and lords, one of the most difficult of ensembles.

ALL:
　Strike them down, men and children, all!
　And let no mercy ever be shown!
　By the sword they shall perish,
　And their temples be o'erthrown!

ST. BRIS:
　Be silent, my friends, and breathe not e'en a
　　murmur
　To wake our slumb'ring foe!

ALL:
　Whisper low, not a word,
　Not a breath or sign revealing, while we,
　　silent stealing,
　Strike the impious foe!
　(*With fury.*)
　Now for vengeance! we will go!

The number closes with the famous passage for the basses which finishes on a low E natural, sung very pianissimo, as the company disperses.

The nobles having gone, *Raoul* comes out, horrified at what he has heard, and wishes to warn his friends, when *Valentine*, thinking to save his life, urges him to remain, telling him that she loves him. In a transport of delight he begins the great duet.

LA SALLE AS NEVERS

Dillo ancor (Speak Those Words Again!)
By Ida Giacomelli, Soprano, and Gino Martinez-
Patti, Tenor　　(*In Italian*)　*35123　12-inch, $1.25

RAOUL:
　Ah! say again thou lov'st me!
　From darkness drear I have awakened to bliss!
　Forever now we're united,
　Thou hast link'd thy fate to mine—
　Forever, forever, forever!
　Say once again thou lov'st me!

Double-Faced Record—For title of opposite side see DOUBLE-FACED HUGUENOTS RECORDS, page 158.

The great bell of St. Germain, the signal to prepare for the slaughter, is heard tolling, and *Raoul* makes a fresh effort to go to the aid of his people. He rushes to the window, while *Valentine* clings to him, and shows her that the massacre has already begun; then tears himself from her arms and leaps from the window, while she falls fainting.

In recent productions in America, because of the great length of Meyerbeer's work, the opera has ended with the shooting of *Raoul* by the mob as he leaps from the window; but in the original version a fifth act occurs, in which *Nevers* is killed, and *Valentine*, renouncing her faith, is united by *Marcel* to *Raoul*. *St. Bris* and his party enter the street, and not recognizing *Valentine*, fire upon the three and kill them. The curtain falls as *St. Bris* discovers that he has murdered his daughter. This final tragedy is graphically pictured in the accompanying reproduction from an old drawing.

DOUBLE-FACED AND MISCELLANEOUS LES HUGUENOTS RECORDS

Benediction of the Poignards	By Sousa's Band			
Trovatore—Home to Our Mountains By Corinne Morgan, Contralto, and Harry Macdonough, Tenor (In English)	35118	12-inch,	$1.25
O vago suol della Turenna (Fair Land of Touraine) By Giuseppina Huguet, Soprano (In Italian)			
Dillo ancor (Speak Those Words Again) By Ida Giacomelli, Soprano, and Gino Martinez-Patti, Tenor (In Italian)	35123	12-inch,	1.25
Huguenots Selection By Victor Band			
Norma Overture By Victor Band	35029	12-inch,	1.25
Plus blanche (Fairer Than the Lily) By M. Gautier, Tenor (In French)			
Guillaume Tell—Asile Hereditaire By M. Gautier, Tenor (In French)	45007	10-inch,	1.00
Nella notte io sol qui veglio (Here By Night Alone I Wander) By Maria Grisi, Soprano, and Perello de Segurola, Bass (In Italian)			
Lucrezia Borgia—Vieni la mia vendetta (Haste Thee, To Glut a Vengeance) By Giulio Rossi, Bass (In Italian)	63404	10-inch,	1.00

FROM AN OLD DRAWING   THE FINAL TRAGEDY

(French)

LAKMÉ
(*Lak'-meh*)

OPERA IN THREE ACTS

Book by Goudinet and Gille, taken from the story *Le Mariage de Loti*. Music by Léo Delibes (*Day-leeb'*). First production Paris, April 14, 1883. First London production at the Gaiety Theatre, June 6, 1885. Produced in New York November 28, 1886.

Characters

GERALD, ⎱ officers of the British army in India	⎰ Tenor
FREDERIC, ⎰	⎱ Baritone
NILAKANTHA, a Brahman priest	Bass
HADJI, a Hindoo slave	Tenor
LAKMÉ, daughter of Nilakantha	Soprano
ELLEN, daughter of the Governor	Soprano
ROSE, her friend	Soprano
MRS. BENSON, governess of the young ladies	Mezzo-Soprano
MALLIKA, slave of Lakmé	Mezzo-Soprano
A FORTUNE TELLER	
A CHINESE MERCHANT	
A SEPOY	

Hindoos, Men and Women, English Officers and Ladies, Sailors, Bayaderes, Chinamen, Musicians, Brahman, etc.

Scene and Period : India, at the present time.

This opera, with its graceful music and scenes of Oriental splendor, was first given in America by the American Opera Company in 1886. (The Emma Abbott version in 1883 need not be considered seriously.) Since then it has had three revivals—the Patti production of 1890; that of 1895 for Marie Van Zandt, and the Metropolitan revival of 1906-7. The music of the opera is wholly beautiful, and the principal numbers are exquisite compositions—lovely in idea and execution.

The story resembles in some points both Aida and Africaine; all three are more or less Oriental; *Lakmé*, like *Aida*, loves her country's enemy; *Nilakantha* and *Nelusko* possess similar traits; while *Lakmé* and *Selika* both poison themselves botanically.

The Oriental atmosphere is somewhat spoiled by the introduction of the modern and somewhat commonplace English characters, but the romantic ending atones for any shortcomings.

ACT I

SCENE—*A Garden in India*

Nilankatha, Lakmé's father, hates the English invaders and resists their presence in India. *Gerald* and *Frederic,* English officers, while sauntering with some English ladies, venture on sacred ground near *Nilakantha's* temple, and when rebuked they all depart but *Gerald,* who remains to sketch some Oriental jewels which *Lakmé* had left in the garden. He takes up the trinkets and sings his charming air, *Idle Fancies.*

Fantaisie aux divins mensonges (Idle Fancies)
By M. Rocca, Tenor   (*Double-faced—See page 162*)   (*In French*)   16573   10-inch, $0.75

He is struck with the daintiness and beauty of the gems and tries to picture the unknown beauty to whom they belong.

159

GERALD:
Idle fancy, cradled by delusion,
  You mislead me now as of old.
Go to dreamland, turn back in confusion,
Fair dove fantastic, with wings of gold.
(*Taking up a bracelet.*)
Of some fair maid round her arm folding,
This bracelet rich must oft entwine.
Ah! what delight would be the holding,
The hand that passes there, in mine.
(*Taking up a ring.*)
This ring of gold, my dream supposes,
Oft has followed, wand'ring for hours,

The small foot, that but reposes
  On mossy banks or beds of flowers.
This necklace, too, with her own perfume
  scented,
Embalm'd as yet with sweets from her lips
  that came,
Has felt the true heart, beating, glad, con-
  tented,
Trembling with joy at the one well-loved
  name.
Away, fly, fond illusions,
  Swiftly passing visions that my reason dis-
  turb!
Idle fancy, cradled by delusion, etc.
                    (*From the Ditson Edition.*)

This beautiful air has been sung for the Victor by a brilliant and accomplished young tenor, M. Rocca, of the *Opera Comique*.

Hearing some one approaching, he hides himself in the shrubbery. *Lakmé* enters and lays flowers at the feet of an idol. She is about to go when she pauses and tries to analyze a strange feeling which has come over her, saying:

LAKMÉ:
In my heart now I feel there's a murmur so
  strange,
The flow'rs are more lovely appearing,
And Heaven's more radiant now.
From woods a new song I am hearing,
Fond zephyrs caress my brow.
And a fragrance that's rare is filling,
All my senses with a rapture so thrilling!

She then sings her first lovely song,

Pourquoi dans les grands bois (Why Love I Thus to Stray?)

By Alice Verlet, Soprano (*Double-faced—See page 162*) (*French*) **45006** 10-inch, $1.00

and asks herself why she loves to wander in the forest and why she is both sad and glad.

LAKMÉ:
Why love I thus to stray,
In woods here, day by day,
While tears have sway?
Why doth the dove's note sadden,
And fill my heart with sighing;
As doth a fading flow'ret,
Or a leaf eastward flying?
Yet are these tears most sweet to me,
Tho' sad they be!
And my heart is gladsome,
Tho' I'm sighing, I'm gladsome.

Ah! why?
Why look for reasons here, in the song of
  the stream,
Where roses dream?
In leaves that fall around?
In my heart soft reposes, like a lily at rest,
Sweeter balm than yield roses, by gentle winds
  caressed,
Or by loving lips pressed. Tho' I sigh, I'm
  gladsome,
Ah, why?

She suddenly sees *Gerald* among the trees and utters a cry of fear. Her attendants run in, but some intuition tells her not to reveal *Gerald's* presence, and she sends them away. Going to his hiding place she denounces him for trespassing on sacred ground, and bids him begone. He begs her for a few moments' conversation, and tells her of the impression she has made on his heart.

GERALD: Ah! linger, go not yet, so thoughtful, sweet, unchiding!
        Let blushing charms that mine eyes now have met,
        O'ermantle thy cheek,
        Its lily pallor hiding!

Lakmé looks on the handsome youth with interest, but tells him she fears the return of her father, who would surely seek vengeance for the Englishman's desecration of holy ground. *Gerald* departs just as *Nilakantha*, summoned by *Lakmé's* attendants, enters, and seeing traces of a trespasser, declares that he must die. They go in pursuit of *Gerald*, leaving *Lakmé* motionless with fear.

ACT II

SCENE—*A Street in an Indian City*

Act II shows a public square, lined with Chinese and Indian shops and bazaars. English visitors are strolling about, viewing the scenes with interest. *Nilakantha*, disguised as a beggar, is seeking traces of the intruder, whom he has sworn to kill. *Lakmé* is with him, wearing the dress of a dancing girl. He orders his daughter to sing, hoping that the Englishman will recognize her voice and betray himself. She sings the famous *Bell Song*.

NOTE—Quotations are from the Ditson libretto by permission—Copy't 1890, Oliver Ditson Co.

Où va la jeune Hindoue (Bell Song)

By Luisa Tetrazzini, Soprano	(*In Italian*)	88297	12-inch, $3.00
By Bessie Abott, Soprano	(*In French*)	88084	12-inch, 3.00
By Maria Galvany, Soprano	(*In Italian*)	88219	12-inch, 3.00
By Ellen Beach Yaw, Soprano	(*In French*)	74090	12-inch, 1.50

Delibes has ingeniously used bells to give character to this number, which is a most intricate one, especially in the refrain, where voice, woodwind and bells blend with many charming touches.

PHOTO REUTLINGER

ABOTT AS LAKMÉ

LAKMÉ:
Down there, where shades more deep are
glooming,
What trav'ler's that, alone, astray?
Around him flame bright eyes, dark depths
illuming,
But on he journeys, as by chance, on the way!
The wolves in their wild joy are howling,
As if for their prey they were prowling;
The young girl forward runs, and doth their
fury dare.
A ring in her grasp she holds tightly,
Whence tinkles a bell, sharply, lightly,
A bell that tinkles lightly, that charmers wear!
(*She imitates the bell.*)
Ah! Ah! Ah! Ah!
While the stranger regards her
Stands she dazed, flush'd and glowing,
More handsome than the Rajahs, he!
* * * * * * *
And to heaven she soars in his holding,
It was Vishnu, great Brahma's son!
And since the day in that dark wood,
The trav'ler hears, where Vishnu stood,
The sound of a little bell ringing,
The legend back to him bringing,
A small bell ringing like those the charmers
wear!

Mme. Tetrazzini's rendition of this beautiful air is wholly charming, and the vocal embellishments which she introduces will be something of a novelty to those who are familiar only with the usual cadenzas.

Other fine renditions of this brilliant air are given by Mme. Galvany, who indulges in some quite astonishing cadenzas; by Bessie Abott, whose fresh young voice is heard to great advantage; and by Miss Yaw, who provides a lower-priced version.

As *Nilakantha* had planned, *Gerald* recognizes *Lakmé* and betrays himself. The Brahman goes to collect his Hindoos, intending to kill the Englishman, while *Lakmé* finds *Gerald* and warns him of the plot. She begins the duet:

Dans la forêt, près de nous (In the Forest)

By Mme. Vallandri, Soprano, and M. Rocca, Tenor
(*Double-faced—See page 162*) (*In French*) 45005 10-inch, $1.00

and tells him of a hut in the forest where he may be free from pursuit.

LAKMÉ:
In the forest near at hand,
A hut of bamboo is hiding,
'Neath a shading tree doth stand,
This roof of my providing.
Like a nest of timid birds,
In leafy silence abiding,
From all eyes secret it lies,
And waits it there a happy pair!
Far away from prying sight,
Without there's naught to reveal it,
Silent woods by day and night,
Ever jealously conceal it;
Thither shalt thou follow me!
When dawn earth is greeting,
Thee with smiles I shall be meeting,
For 'tis there thy home shall be.

Gerald at first refuses thus to hide, declaring it unworthy of a British officer, but *Lakmé* pleads with him and he consents; but as he attempts to follow her he is stabbed by *Nila-kantha*, who then escapes. *Lakmé* runs to *Gerald*, and overjoyed to find his wound is not serious, she prepares, with the help of her faithful attendant *Hadji*, to bear him to the forest retreat.

ACT III
SCENE—*An Indian Forest*

Act III shows the hut in the tropical forest. *Gerald* is lying on a bed of leaves while *Lakmé* watches over him, singing soothing melodies. He opens his eyes and greets her with rapture, singing his beautiful *In Forest Depths.*

Vieni al contento profondo (In Forest Depths)

By John McCormack, Tenor   (*In Italian*)   64171   10-inch, $2.00

This lovely *cantilena* is given in delightful style by Mr. McCormack.

GERALD:
I too recall,—still mute, inanimate,—
I saw you bent o'er my lips; while thus lying,
My soul upon your look was attracted and
   fastened;
'Neath your breath life awoke and recovery
   hastened.
O my charming Lakmé;
Through forest depths secluded,
Love's wing above us has passed;
Earth-cares have not been intruded,
And heaven on us falls at last.
These flow'ring vines, with blooms capricious,
Bear o'er our pathway scents delicious;
Which soft hearts, with raptures beset,
While all else we forget!

As the days pass and *Gerald* recovers his strength, he seems to forget all else but his love for the Brahman maiden, but one day, while she is absent, his friend *Frederic* finds him and urges him to return to his duty. When *Lakmé* comes back she finds *Gerald* changed. She asks the reason, but before he can answer the distant sound of bugles calling the regiment together is heard. She sees by his face that he means to go back to his friends, and in despair she eats some flowers of the deadly stramonium tree and dies in his arms.

DOUBLE-FACED AND MISCELLANEOUS LAKMÉ RECORDS

Pourquoi dans les grands bois (Why Love I Thus to Stray?) By Alice Verlet, Soprano (*In French*)		
Mignon—Polonaise By Mlle. Korsoff, Soprano (*In French*)	45006	10-inch, $1.00
Dans la forêt, près de nous (In the Forest) By Mme. Vallandri, Soprano, and M. Rocca, Tenor (*In French*)		
Manon—J'écris à mon père By Mlle. Korsoff, Soprano, and Leon Beyle, Tenor (*In French*)	45005	10-inch, 1.00
Fantaisie aux divins mensonges (Idle Fancies) By M. Rocca, Tenor (*In French*)		
Rigoletto—Cortigiani, vil razza dannata By Renzo Minolfi, Baritone (*In Italian*)	16573	10-inch, .75

NOTE—Quotations from the text of Lakmé are printed by kind permission of Oliver Ditson Company (Copy't 1890).

LINDA DI CHAMOUNIX

OPERA IN THREE ACTS

Words by Rossi; music by Donizetti. First production at the Kärnthnerthor Theatre, Vienna, May 19, 1842; in Paris, November 17, 1842; in London at Her Majesty's, June, 1843.

Cast

MARQUIS OF BOISFLEURY .... Baritone
CHARLES DE SIRVAL, his son .... Tenor
THE PARISH PRIEST .... Bass
ANTONIO LOUSTOLOT, a farmer .... Bass
MADELINE, his wife .... Mezzo-Soprano
LINDA, their daughter .... Soprano

Time and Place : Chamounix and Paris, 1760, during the reign of Louis XV.

The story tells of an aged couple, *Loustolot* and *Madeline,* and their only daughter *Linda,* who dwell in the valley of the Chamounix (in the French Alps). *Linda* loves a young painter, *Charles,* who has come to the valley to paint the mountains. The *Marquis de Sirval,* who holds a mortgage on *Loustolot's* farm, visits the old couple and assures them that he will not press the mortgage; but at the same time he is secretly plotting to effect the ruin of *Linda.*

Linda enters and speaks of her love for *Charles.* She then sings the gem of the first act, a favorite with coloratura sopranos for more than seventy years.

Two renditions of this lovely air, by Sembrich and Huguet, are given here, the Huguet record being doubled with the Trentini-Caffo duet below.

O luce di quest' anima (Guiding Star of Love !)

By Marcella Sembrich, Soprano   *(In Italian)*   88142   12-inch, $3.00
By Giuseppina Huguet, Soprano   *(In Italian)*   62090   10-inch,   .75

LINDA:
Poor are we both in worldly state;
On love we live,—on hope we dream!
A painter yet unknown, is he,
Yet by his genius he will rise,
And I his happy wife shall be! Oh, what joy!

Oh! star that guidest my fervent love,
Thou'rt life and light to me;
On earth, in Heav'n above,
Entwin'd our hearts will be.
Oh, come, then, come, my best belov'd!
My every pulse is thine!

Charles enters, and the lovers sing their charming duet.

A consolarmi affrettati (Oh, That the Blessed Day Were Come)

By Emma Trentini, Soprano, and Alberto Caffo, Tenor   62090   10-inch, $0.75

LINDA AND CHARLES:
Oh! that the blessed day were come,
When standing side by side,
We before God and man shall be
As bridegroom and as bride.

And then, my love, we'll never part,
But each a treasure find
In having brought a faithful heart
To heav'nly love resigned!

The worthy parish priest having warned *Linda's* parents of the dishonorable intention of the *Marquis,* they decide to remove *Linda* from the danger, and send her to Paris. The *Marquis* pursues her to the city and renews his attentions, while *Charles* (who is in reality the son of the *Marquis*) is compelled by his father to transfer his attentions to another. *Linda's* father comes to Paris in disguise, and discovers his daughter. Believing her to be an abandoned woman, he curses her, and she becomes insane through grief.

The last act again shows the little farm at Chamounix. The demented *Linda* has made her way back to her parents, and is found by *Charles,* who has escaped the unwelcome marriage and now brings the release of the farm from debt. The sight of her lover causes *Linda* to fall in a death-like swoon, but when she recovers her reason has returned, and the lovers are united.

LOHENGRIN

(*Low'-en-grin*)

OPERA IN THREE ACTS

Words and music by Richard Wagner. First produced at Weimar, Germany, August 28, 1850, under the direction of Liszt. First London production, 1875; Paris, 1887. First American production in New York, in Italian, March 23, 1874, with Nilsson, Cary, Campanini and Del Puente; in German, in 1885, with Brandt, Krauss, Fischer and Stritt—this being Anton Seidl's American début as a conductor.

Characters

HENRI THE FOWLER, King of Germany..........Bass
LOHENGRIN................................Tenor
ELSA OF BRABANT.......................Soprano
DUKE GODFREY, her brother.........Mute Personage
FREDERICK OF TELRAMUND, Count of Brabant..Baritone
ORTRUD, his wife.....................Mezzo-Soprano
THE KING'S HERALD..........................Bass

Saxon, Thuringian and Brabantian Counts and
Nobles, Ladies of Honor, Pages, Attendants.

Scene and Period: Antwerp, first half of the Tenth Century.

Most of us are familiar with the story of the Knight *Lohengrin,* who comes in his boat, drawn by a swan, to defend *Elsa* from the charge (preferred by *Telramund* and *Ortrud,* who covet *Elsa's* estates) of having murdered her young brother, *Godfrey.*

Telramund is vanquished and disgraced by *Lohengrin,* who wins *Elsa* as his bride. One condition he exacts from her—that she shall never ask who he is or whence he came. By the influence of *Ortrud,* however, she rashly questions him, and in fulfillment of his vow, but in deep grief, he leaves her and departs in his boat drawn by a dove. The ethereal Grail harmonies, the lovely *Swan Motive,* the noble *Prayer of the King* and the *Bridal Chorus* make this one of the most melodious of all the master's operas.

Prelude

By La Scala Orchestra   31779 12-inch, $1.00

The prelude, one of the most beautiful of all Wagner's compositions, symbolizes the descent from Heaven of a group of angels bearing the Holy Grail. The number begins with soft A major chords in the highest register of the violin. The motive of the Grail is then announced:

GADSKI AS ELSA

Coming nearer and nearer, the light of the Grail is seen in the sky, while the air is filled with the blessings dispensed by the holy cup. As the sounds grow louder, the senses are overwhelmed, until at the tremendous climax thundered out by the full orchestra the mystic light of the Grail is seen in all its glory.

164

The mysterious Grail motive then fades away, being played at the end by muted strings; and the number ends with the same A major chords *pianissimo*.

The performance of this wonderful prelude, which is written almost wholly for strings, shows why this organization has become famous for the exquisite playing of its string section.

ACT I

SCENE—*Banks of the Scheldt, near Antwerp*

King Henry of Germany arrives at Antwerp and finds Brabant in almost a state of anarchy. He summons the counts and nobles of Saxony and Brabant to meet under the Oak of Justice, and calls on *Frederick of Telramund* for an explanation, saying:

> KING. Here, to my grief, I meet with naught but strife,
> All in disunion, from your chiefs estranged!
> Confusion, civil warfare meet we here.
> On thee I call, Frederick of Telramund!
> I know thee for a knight as brave as true,
> I charge thee, let me know this trouble's cause.

Frederick now advances and begins his narrative, boldly accusing *Elsa* of the murder of her brother.

GORITZ AS TELRAMUND

Dank, König, dir, dass du zu richten kamst!
(Frederick's Charge Against Elsa)
By Anton Van Rooy, Bass
(In German) 92062 12-inch, $3.00

PANEL BY HUGO BRAUNE

ELSA RELATING HER DREAM

FREDERICK:
> Thanks, gracious King, that thou to judge art come!
> The truth I'll tell thee, falsehood I disdain.
> When death was closing round our valiant Duke,
> 'Twas me he chose as guardian of his children,
> Elsa the maiden, and Gottfried her brother;
> Whose dawning with tender care I guarded,
> Whose welfare I have treasured as my honor.
> My sov'reign, mark now, if I'm aggrieved,
> When of my honor's treasure I am robbed!
> One day, when Elsa had with her brother wandered forth,
> Without the boy, trembling, she returned,
> With feign'd lamenting, questioned of his safety,
> Pretending she had been from him divided,
> And in vain his traces she had sought,
> Fruitless was every search we made to find him;
> And when I questioned her with words severe,
> Her pallor and her falt'ring tongue betray'd her,
> Her crime, in its guilty blackness stood confess'd!
> A horror fell upon me of the maid;
> The claim upon her hand her father had conferr'd
> With willing heart, I straight resigned,
> And chose a wife full pleasant to my sense,

Ortrud, daughter of Radbod, true in death.
I here arraign her, Princess Elsa of Brabant;
Of fratricide be she charged!
I claim dominion o'er this land by right;
My nearest kinsman was the valiant duke,
My wife descended of the race
That gave this land their rulers thro' long ages past.
O King, give judgment! All now thou hast heard!

The host of admirers of this famous Dutch artist, whose
sonorous bass is now at its best, will be greatly pleased by the
issue of this record of the dramatic air of *Telramund.* Mr.
Van Rooy, whose fine impersonations of Wagnerian roles are
familiar to opera goers, is always an effective *Frederick,* acting
the part with the ruggedness it demands and singing the difficult music in the true Wagnerian style.

The *King* is much disturbed, and says:

KING: A dreadful accusation thou hast brought!
A crime so deadly, how can I believe?

Frederick vehemently repeats his accusation, and demands
that the *King* choose between them. The *King* asks that *Elsa*
be sent for, and when she enters timidly with downcast eyes, he says kindly:

KING: Canst thou meet this accusation?
Speak, Elsa, in thy King thou may'st confide!

The young girl seems bewildered and dreamily sings the lovely *Traum,* telling of her
vision of a splendid Knight who came to be her defender.

COPY'T DUPONT

EAMES AS ELSA

Elsa's Traum (Elsa's Dream)

By Johanna Gadski, Soprano

By Emma Juch, Soprano   (*Piano acc.*)

(*In German*) **88038** 12-inch, **$3.00**
(*In German*) **74014** 12-inch, **1.50**

ELSA: Oft when the hours were lonely,
I unto Heav'n have pray'd,
One boon I ask'd for only,
To send the orphans aid;
I pray'd in tears and sorrow,
With heavy heart and sore,
Hoping a brighter morrow
Yet was for us in store.
Away my words were wafted,
I dreamt not help was nigh,
But One on high vouchsaf'd it,
While I in sleep did lie.
(*with growing enthusiasm*)
I saw in splendor shining,
A knight of glorious mien,
On me his eyes inclining,
With tranquil gaze serene.
A horn of gold beside him,
He leant upon his sword,
Thus when I erst espied him,
'Mid clouds of light he soar'd;
His words so low and tender,
Brought life renew'd to me.
(*with rapture*)
My guardian, my defender,
Thou shalt my champion be.

ELSA AND LOHENGRIN

The *King* is much moved, and calls
for a judgment of God after the fashion
of the time. The trumpeters blow the
summons to the four points of the
compass, and the Herald calls:

HERALD:
Who will do battle here on life or
death
For Elsa of Brabant! Let him appear!

At first there comes no response,
and *Elsa* is in despair, but after a
second call a knight in shining armor
is seen approaching in a boat drawn
by a swan.

ARRIVAL OF LOHENGRIN

Nun sei bedankt, mein lieber Schwan! (Thanks, My Trusty Swan!)

By Fernando de Lucia, Tenor
(*In Italian*) 76002 12-inch, $2.00
By Leo Slezak, Tenor
(*In German*) 61203 10-inch, 1.00

Lohengrin steps out, then turning and caressing the swan, sings:

LOHENGRIN:
I give thee thanks, my faithful swan!
Turn thee again and breast the tide,
Return unto that land of dawn
Where joyous we did long abide,
Well thy appointed task is done!
Farewell! farewell! my trusty swan!
(*to the King*)
Hail, gracious sov'reign!
Victory and honor by thy valor's meed!
Thy glorious name shall from the land
That chose thee ruler, ne'er depart.

The knight now announces that he has come to defend the maiden, who is unjustly accused by her enemy.

LOHENGRIN:
Ye knights, nobles and freemen of this land,
Guiltless and true is Elsa of Brabant!
Thy tale was falsehood, Count Telramund,
By Heav'n's assistance all thou shalt recant!

The *King* bids the nobles prepare to fight, and in this noble *Gebet* calls upon Heaven to judge between the combatants.

Mein Herr und Gott— Koenig's Gebet (King's Prayer)

By Marcel Journet, Bass
(*In German*)
64013 10-inch, $1.00

The *King* is one of Journet's best parts, and he always sings it magnificently, his great voice rolling out in tremendous volume. His delivery is always easy and graceful, and his acting dignified and intelligent.

KING HENRY:
O King of kings, on Thee I call;
Look down on us in this dread hour!
Let him in this ordeal fall
Whom Thou know'st guilty, Lord of pow'r!
To stainless knight give strength and might,
With craven heart the false one smite;
Do Thou, O Lord, to hear us deign,
For all our wisdom is but vain!

Frederick is soon stricken to the earth by *Lohengrin*, who is proclaimed a hero. *Elsa* is pronounced innocent, plights her troth to her brave defender, and the curtain falls amid general rejoicing.

PANEL BY HUGO BRAUNE

THE FIGHT BETWEEN LOHENGRIN AND TELRAMUND—ACT I

167

THE PLOT—ACT II

ACT II

SCENE—*Court of the Palace*

This scene shows the inner court of the palace at Antwerp. It is night. *Frederick* and *Ortrud*, disgraced and dressed in sombre garments, are seated on the church steps. They upbraid each other, *Frederick* accusing *Ortrud* of inventing the story of *Elsa's* crime. A long duet follows, ending in a terrible plot for vengeance.

Elsa appears on the balcony of the palace, all unconscious of the wretched and disgraced *Telramund* and *Ortrud,* who are hidden in the shadow. In a blissful reverie, the young girl sings to the soft breezes of the knightly *Lohengrin,* to whom she is now betrothed.

ELSA:
Ye wand'ring breezes heard me,
When grief was all I knew;
Now that delight hath stirred me,
My joy I'll breathe to you!

TELRAMUND AND ORTRUD:
'Tis she! Be near, ye powers of darkness!

ELSA (*continuing dreamily*):
Thro' heaven's azure ye bore him,
Ye wafted him to me;
'Mid stormy waves watched o'er him,
My guide, my love to be!
Where'er thy pinion rusheth,
The mourner's tears are dried;
My cheek that burns and flusheth
With love, oh cool and hide!

Du Aermste (Thou Unhappy One)

By Emma Eames, Soprano, and Louise Homer, Contralto (*In German*)
89021 12-inch, $4.00

Elsa, who has finished her rapturous soliloquy to the wandering breeze, still lingers on the balcony, enjoying the balmy night and dreaming of her betrothal on the morrow. *Ortrud,* pursuing the plot agreed upon with *Frederick,* appears and calls to *Elsa,* who hearing her name, cries:

Who calls? How strangely
My name resoundeth thro' the night!

FROM AN OLD PRINT ORTRUD KNEELING TO ELSA

Ortrud feigns repentance, and *Elsa,* in the flush of her new-found happiness forgives her, saying:

Unhappy one, that thy heart could know the treasure
Of love that knows not fear or doubt!

No child of earth that bliss can measure
Who doth not dwell in faith devout!
Rest thee with me!

THE KING DENOUNCING TELRAMUND—ACT II

Ortrud warns *Elsa* against trusting her husband too blindly, hinting of the mystery in his life, and thus plants a seed of suspicion in the young girl's heart. The duet then follows·

ELSA:
Oh, let me teach thee
How trust doth hallow joy and love.
Turn, then, to our faith, I beseech thee,
Oh, turn unto our faith divine,
For God is love!

ORTRUD (*aside—with fierce joy*):
Oh! pride of heart, I yet will teach thee,
That an illusion is this love,
The gods of vengeance soon shall reach thee,
Their wrath-destroying thou shalt prove!

Elsa enters the palace and the dark plotters renew their vow of imprecation.

Day breaks, and the Herald appears and announces the banishment of *Telramund. Elsa,* attended by her ladies, passes on her way to the minster but is suddenly confronted by *Ortrud,* who has arrayed herself again in splendid garments. She taunts *Elsa* with the fact that her knight has no name.

ORTRUD:
Your stranger, say, as what doth thou
proclaim him?
If I have heard aright, thou canst not
name him!

ELSA (*indignantly*):
Thou slanderer, taunt me no more,
Let my reply all doubts assure—
So pure and noble is his nature,
As none can match in high renown.
Oh, can there live so vile a creature
As to asperse all honor's crown?

SCHUMANN-HEINK AS
ORTRUD

The *King* and *Lohengrin* now enter and *Elsa,* astonished and grieved, goes to *Lohengrin,* saying:

ELSA:
My champion! shelter me against her
wrath!
Blame me, if I obey'd not thy command;
I heard her weeping sore by yonder
portal,

And in compassion harbor'd her this
night,
And now with harsh and bitter words of
hatred
She taunts me for my boundless trust
in thee!

ACT III

SCENE I—*The Bridal Chamber in the Palace*

The act opens with the *Wedding March,* played by the orchestra.

Prelude to Act III—The Wedding March

By La Scala Orchestra   *62693 10-inch, $0.75

This is followed by the beautiful *Bridal Chorus,* one of the loveliest numbers in the opera. As the curtain rises, showing the bridal chamber, the strains of the march continue, but in a softer mood. The great doors at the back open, and the bridal party enters,—the ladies leading *Elsa* and the King and nobles conducting *Lohengrin,*—they come to the front and the chorus begins:

CHORUS:
Faithful and true, we lead thee forth
Where Love, triumphant, shall crown ye with joy!
Star of renown, flow'r of the earth,
Blest, be ye both far from all life's annoy!
Champion victorious, go thou before!
Maid bright and glorious, go thou before!
Mirth's noisy revel ye've forsaken,
Tender delights for you now awaken;
Fragrant abode enshrine ye in bliss;
Splendor and state in joy ye dismiss!

EIGHT LADIES (*passing around the bridal pair*):
As solemn vows unite ye
We hallow ye to joy!
This hour shall still requite ye,
When bliss hath known alloy!

After a striking and effective modulation the first strain is repeated by the full chorus.

Faithful and true, now rest you here.
Where Love, triumphant, etc.

The party goes slowly out, leaving the bridal pair alone, while the strains of the nuptial air die away in the distance.

The full strength of the Victor organization has been used for the vocal rendition, and the result is a record of surpassing beauty. An instrumental record of this number is also offered.

FRAGMENT OF THE BRIDAL CHORUS IN
WAGNER'S OWN HANDWRITING

Bridal Chorus

By Victor Opera Chorus

(*In English*)	31846	12-inch,	$1.00
By Arthur Pryor's Band	31227	12-inch,	1.00
By La Scala Chorus (*In Italian*)	*16537	10-inch,	.75

The bridal pair are left alone and a long duet occurs, part of which is recorded here by two famous artists of La Scala.

Cessero i canti alfin (The Song Has Died Away)

By Giuseppina Huguet, Soprano; Fernando de Lucia, Tenor (*In Italian*) 92055 12-inch, $3.00

The beautiful air which *Lohengrin* sings in the duet, *Dost Thou Breathe the Incense,* is also given here by Dalmores.

Athmest du nicht mit mir die süssen Düfte? (Dost Thou Breathe the Incense Sweet?)

By Charles Dalmores, Tenor

(*In German*) 87088 10-inch, $2.00

COPY'T DUPONT

HOMER AS ORTRUD

This duet is scarcely over when the poison instilled in *Elsa's* mind by *Ortrud* causes her, in violation of her promise, to question

* *Double-Faced Records—For title of opposite side see DOUBLE-FACED LOHENGRIN RECORDS, page 172.*

Lohengrin as to his name and origin. He remonstrates with her, at first gently and then with authority, reminding her that she has promised not to ask his name. She becomes more and more agitated, saying:

ELSA:
No, thou shalt not compel me to trust by words of blame—
No, not unless thou tell me thy country and thy name!

LOHENGRIN: Elsa, oh, I conjure thee!

ELSA:
What fatal spell is thine?
In vain wouldst thou assure me—
Declare thy race and name!

They are interrupted by the entrance of *Frederick* and four associates, who break in with drawn swords. *Elsa* shrieks and hands *Lohengrin* his sword, with which he strikes *Frederick* dead. The nobles surrender, and *Elsa* falls senseless in *Lohengrin's* arms. After a long silence, *Lohengrin* orders the body into the Judgment Hall, and gives *Elsa* in charge of her ladies.

SCENE II—*Same as Act I*

A quick change of scene shows again the banks of the Scheldt at Antwerp, as in Act I. The *King* and his nobles await the coming of *Lohengrin*, who is to accompany them to battle. They are startled by the entrance of the nobles bearing the body of *Telramund*. *Lohengrin* enters and is greeted by the King with warmth:

PANEL BY BRAUNE

TELRAMUND INTERRUPTING THE BRIDAL PROCESSION— ACT II

KING:
Hail, heav'n-sent hero, welcome here!
Thy loyal vassals all are near,
Waiting for thee to give the word,
And fight by thy all-conq'ring sword.

All are surprised when the knight announces that he is forced to decline the command of the expedition, and tells of the attempt on his life.

LOHENGRIN:
My gracious sov'reign, bear me blameless,
Reasons have I that must be nameless,
The destin'd campaign I suspend!
To lead ye forth to battle here I came not;
But judge me, for your leniency I claim not.
Then, firstly, do ye hold that I am guilty?
Your just decree to me is due.
He sought my life despite honor and fealty—
Say, did I right when him I slew?

The King declares *Telramund* to be justly slain, and *Lohengrin* now reveals with reluctance that *Elsa* has broken her promise.

LOHENGRIN:
And further, I declare in face of Heav'n,
Though bitter grief to me it bode,
That from her fair allegiance hath been driven
The wife that Heav'n on me bestow'd.

MEN:
Elsa! say, oh, what hast thou done?
Sentence so stern how hast thou won?

LADIES:
Woe is thine, Elsa!

COPY'T MISHKIN

DALMORES AS LOHENGRIN

LOHENGRIN:
Ye all have heard her give her word in token
That she my name and country ne'er would
  ask:
That promise her impatient heart hath broken—

Vainly I hop'd she would fulfil her task!
Now mark me well, I will no more withhold it,
Nor have I cause to shrink from any test;
When I my name and lineage have unfolded
Ye'll know that I am noble as the best!

Then follows the great narrative of *Lohengrin,* one of the most dramatic declamations in all opera.

Lohengrin's Narrative
By Evan Williams, Tenor
(In English)   74130   12-inch, $1.50

LOHENGRIN:
In distant land, by ways remote and hidden,
There stands a mount that men call Monsalvat;
It holds a shrine, to the profane forbidden:
More precious there is nought on earth than that,
And thron'd in light it holds a cup immortal,
That whoso sees from earthly sin is cleans'd;
'Twas borne by angels thro' the heav'nly portal—
Its coming hath a holy reign commenc'd.
Once every year a dove from Heav'n descendeth,
To strengthen it anew for works of grace;
'Tis called the Grail, the pow'r of Heav'n attendeth
The faithful knights who guard that sacred place.
He whom the Grail to be its servant chooses
Is armed henceforth by high invincible might;
All evil craft its power before him loses,
The spirits of darkness where he dwells take flight.
Nor will he lose the awful charm it blendeth,
Although he should be called to distant lands,
When the high cause of virtue he defendeth:
While he's unknown, its spell he still commands.
By perils dread the holy Grail is girded,
No eye rash or profane its light may see;
Its champion knight from doubtings shall be warded,
If known to man, he must depart and flee.
Now mark, craft or disguise my soul disdaineth,
The Grail sent me to right yon lady's name;
My father, Percival, gloriously reigneth,
His knight am I, and Lohengrin my name!

After this amazing narrative, which causes a great stir among the people, the swan appears to conduct *Lohengrin* away.

LADIES AND MEN:
While I hear him the wondrous tale revealing,
The holy tears adown my cheek are stealing!

ELSA:
'Tis dark around me! Give me air!
Oh, help, help! oh, me, most wretched!

LADIES AND MEN (*in great excitement*):
The swan! the swan! the swan!
The stream he floateth down.
The swan! ah, he comes!

ELSA (*half-fainting*):
Oh, horror! ah, the swan!

LOHENGRIN:
Too long I stay—I must obey the Grail!
My trusty swan! O that this summons ne'er
  had been!
Oh, that this day I ne'er had seen!
I thought the year would soon be o'er
When thy probation would have pass'd;
Then by the Grail's transcendent pow'r,
In thy true shape we'd meet at last!
Oh, Elsa, think what joys thy doubts have
  ended!
Couldst thou not trust in me for one short
  year?

Ortrud, in triumph, now reveals the fact that the swan is really *Elsa's* brother, whom she had transformed by magic. *Lohengrin* kneels in prayer, and as the dove of the Grail is seen descending, the swan sinks, and *Gottfried,* the young Duke, arises, restored to human form. *Lohengrin's* boat is drawn away by the dove as *Elsa* faints in her brother's arms.

DOUBLE-FACED AND MISCELLANEOUS LOHENGRIN RECORDS

Selection, No. 1	By Sousa's Band	31425	12-inch,	$1.00
Selection, No. 1	By Sousa's Band	35114	12-inch,	1.25
Flower Song (Blumenlied)	By Victor Sorlin, 'Cellist			
Selection, No. 2	By Pryor's Band	35147	12-inch,	1.25
Meditation from Thais—Intermezzo Religieuse	By Howard Rattay, Violinist			
Fantasie	By Victor Sorlin, 'Cellist	31785	12-inch,	1.00
Prelude, Act III	By La Scala Orchestra	62693	10-inch,	.75
Walküre—Cavalcata	By La Scala Orchestra			
Coro delle nozze (Bridal Chorus)	By La Scala Chorus	16537	10-inch,	.75
Tannhauser—Pilgrims' Chorus	By Pryor's Band			

LUCIA DI LAMMERMOOR

(Loo-chee'-ah dee Lah'-mair-moor)

(English)

LUCY OF LAMMERMOOR

OPERA IN THREE ACTS

Text by Salvator Cammerano, derived from Scott's novel, "The Bride of Lammermoor."
Music by Gaetano Donizetti. First production at Naples, September 26, 1835. Performed
in London, April 5, 1838; Paris, 1839; New York, in English, at the Park Theatre, 1843; and
in Italian, 1849.

Characters

HENRY ASHTON, of Lammermoor . . . . Baritone
LUCY, his sister . . . . Soprano
SIR EDGAR, of Ravenswood . . . . Tenor
LORD ARTHUR BUCKLAW . . . . Tenor
RAYMOND, chaplain to Lord Ashton . . . . Tenor
ALICE, companion to Lucy . . . . Mezzo-Soprano
NORMAN, Captain of the Guard at Ravenswood . . . . Tenor

Ladies and Knights related to the Ashtons; Inhabitants of Lammermoor;
Pages, Soldiery, and Domestics in the Ashton family.

*Scene and Period: The action takes place in Scotland, part in Ravenswood Castle, part in
the ruined tower of Wolfscrag. The time is the close of the sixteenth century.*

The prolific Donizetti (1797-1848) wrote no fewer than sixty-three operas, the most
popular of these being, of course, Lucia di Lammermoor. It has long been the custom with
a certain class of critics to run down the old Italian school of opera represented by Lucia, and
talk about the artificiality of the music, thinness of the orchestration, etc. But the public in
general pays very little attention to these opinions, because they love the music of Lucia, as
their grandfathers did, and realize that throughout the whole work there runs a current of
tenderness and passion, expressed in simple melody that will ever appeal to the heart and
senses.

Let us now forget the critics and tell the simple and sorrowful story, and listen to the
melodious airs which have given pleasure to many millions in the seventy-six years
since its production.

The plot of Lucia is founded on Sir Walter Scott's novel, The Bride of Lammermoor.
Lord Henry Ashton, Lucy's brother, knowing nothing of her attachment to his enemy, *Edgar
of Ravenswood,* has arranged a marriage between *Lucy* and the wealthy *Lord Arthur,* in order
to retrieve his fallen fortunes. Learning that *Lucy* is in love with *Edgar,* he intercepts her
lover's letters and executes a forged paper, which convinces *Lucy* that *Edgar* is false to her.
Convinced of her lover's perfidy, and urged by the necessities of her brother, she unwillingly
consents to wed *Sir Arthur.*

The guests are assembled for the ceremony, and *Lucy* has just signed the contract,
when *Edgar* appears and denounces *Lucy* for her fickleness. *Edgar* is driven from the castle,
and the shock being too much for the gentle mind of *Lucy,* she becomes insane, kills her
husband and dies. *Edgar,* overcome by these tragic happenings, visits the churchyard of
Ravenswood and stabs himself among the tombs of his ancestors.

ACT I

SCENE I—*A Forest near Lammermoor*

The curtain rises, disclosing *Norman,* and followers of *Sir Henry. Norman* tells the
retainers to watch carefully and ascertain who is secretly meeting *Lucy.* In the opening
chorus they promise to watch with diligence.

Opening Chorus, Act I

By La Scala Chorus (*In Italian*) *62106 10-inch, $0.75

Sir Henry enters and talks with *Norman* of his suspicion that *Lucy* has formed an attachment for some unknown knight. *Norman* suggests that it may be *Edgar*. *Henry* is furious and declares he will have a deadly vengeance.

SCENE II—*A Park near the Castle*

Lucy enters, accompanied by her faithful attendant, *Alice*. She has come from the castle to meet her lover, *Edgar*; and while waiting for him, tells *Alice* of the legend of the fountain, which relates how a Ravenswood lover once slew a maiden on this spot.

Regnava nel silenzio (Silence O'er All)

By Luisa Tetrazzini, Soprano
(*In Italian*) 88303 12-inch, $3.00
By Giuseppina Huguet, Soprano
(*In Italian*) *16539 10-inch, .75

Lucy shudderingly relates how she once saw the spectre of the murdered girl, and fears it is an omen of the future

PHOTO ERMINI
CONSTANTINO AS EDGAR

LUCIA:
Silence o'er all was reigning
Dark was the night and low'ring,
And o'er yon fountain her pallid ray
Yon pale moon was pouring,
Faintly a sharp but stifled sigh
Fell on my startled ear,
And straightway upon the fountain's brink,
The spectre did appear!
But slow on high its skeleton hand,
Threat'ning it did uprear,
Stood for a moment immovable,
Then vanish'd from my view!
(*Despondently.*)
Oh, what horrid omen is this?
I ought to banish from my heart this fatal love,
But I cannot; it is my life,
And comfort to my suff'ring soul!

This graceful number is given by Mme. Tetrazzini with rare charm and pathos; the concluding ornamental passages being sung with especial delicacy, and the beauty of the long sustained A at the close being notable. The popular-priced rendition by Mme. Huguet is also a very attractive one.

This is followed by the second part,—the beautiful *Quando rapita,—*

Quando rapita in estasi (Swift as Thought)

By Graziella Pareto, Soprano
(*In Italian*) 76009 12-inch, $2.00
By Giuseppina Huguet, Soprano
(*In Italian*) *63172 10-inch, .75

also given here by Mme. Huguet and Mme. Pareto. This animated melody is well fitted to display the brilliant tones of these admirable singers.

Edgar appears and tells *Lucy* that he has been summoned to France, and proposes that he seek out *Henry* and endeavor to end the mortal feud which exists between the families. *Lucy*, knowing her brother only too well, entreats him to keep their love secret or they will be forever parted. *Edgar*, roused to fury by this evidence of *Henry's* mortal hate, renews his vow of vengeance, beginning this dramatic duet, *Sulla tomba.*

FROM A PAINTING
LUCY AND EDGAR

* *Double-Faced Record—For title of opposite side see DOUBLE-FACED LUCIA RECORDS, page 179.*

Sulla tomba che rinserra (By My Father's Tomb)

By Emma Trentini, Soprano, and Gino Martinez-Patti, Tenor

(In Italian) *16574 10-inch, $0.75

EDGAR:
By the lone tomb, o'er the cold grave
Where my father's bones lie moulding,
With thy kindred eternal warfare
To the death I swore to wage!
Ah! when I saw thee my heart relented:
Of my dark vow I half repented;
But my oath remains unbroken,
Still I've power to redeem my gage!

LUCY:
Ah! pray calm thee, ah, restrain thee;
Think what misery will soon enthral me;
I can scarce from fear sustain me;
Would'st thou have me die from terror?
Yield thee, yield thee to the dictates of affection,
'Tis a nobler, purer passion,
Let that thought thy rage assuage!

Edgar now says that he must go, and in a tender duet, which closes the act, the lovers bid each other farewell.

Verranno a te sull' aura (Borne on Sighing Breeze)

By Alice Nielsen, Soprano, and Florencio Constantino, Tenor

(In Italian) 74064 12-inch, $1.50

By Emma Trentini, Soprano, and Martinez-Patti, Tenor

(In Italian) *62106 10-inch, .75

COPY'T FOLEY

MCCORMACK AS EDGAR

EDGAR:
My sighs shall on the balmy breeze
That hither wafts thee, be borne, love;
Each murm'ring wave shall echo make.
How I thy absence do mourn, love!
Ah! think of me when far away,
With nought my heart to cheer;
I shall bedew each thought of thee
With many a bitter tear!

LUCY:
The balmy breeze that bears thy sigh,
Will waft one back from me, love;
The murm'ring waves re-echoing still
I'm ever constant to thee, love!
Ah! think of me when far away,
With nought my heart to cheer;
I shall bedew each thought of thee
With many a bitter tear!
Ah! thou wilt not fail to write me,
Many a lonely hour 'twill cheer;

EDGAR:
Fear not! Have no fear, thou shalt hear!

BOTH:
My sighs shall on the balmy breeze
That hither wafts thee be borne, love; etc.

Edgar tears himself from her arms and departs, leaving the half-fainting *Lucy* to be consoled by her faithful *Alice*.

ACT II

SCENE I—*An Ante-room in the Castle*

Sir Henry and his retainer *Norman* are discussing the approaching marriage of *Lucy* to *Arthur*. The events which have occurred since Act I are indicated by this extract from the text:

HENRY:
Should Lucy still persist
In opposing me—

NORMAN:
Have no fear! The long absence
Of him she mourneth, the letters
We've intercepted, and the false news
thou'lt tell her,
Will quench all hope that yet may linger.
Believing Edgar faithless, from her bosom
love will vanish!

HENRY:
See, she approaches! Thou hast that forged
letter,
Give it me. Now haste thee to the northern
entrance,
There keep watch and await
The approach of Arthur, and with all speed,
on his arrival
Conduct him hither!

(*Exit Norman.*)

Lucy enters, pale and listless, and to her brother's greeting:

HENRY:
Draw nearer, my Lucy.
On this fair day accept a brother's greeting!
May this glad day, sacred to Love and
Hymen,

Auspicious prove to thee. Thou hear'st me?
Thou'rt silent!

she answers with a last appeal to him to release her from this hated marriage.

* *Double-Faced Record—For title of opposite side see DOUBLE-FACED LUCIA RECORDS, page 179.*

Il pallor funesto (If My Cheek is Pale)

By Linda Brambilla, Soprano, and Francesco Cigada, Baritone
(*In Italian*) *16574 10-inch, $0.75

LUCY:
See these cheeks so pale and haggard,
See these features so worn with sadness!
Do not they betray too plainly
All my anguish, all my despair?
Pardon may'st thou from Heaven
Not vainly ask for this thy inhuman constraint.
HENRY:
Cease this wild recrimination,
Both to me and thee degrading,
Of the past be thou but silent!
I, thy brother, will no further make complaint!
Flown has my anger! Banish thy dejection!
Buried be all that thine honor could taint.
A noble husband, thou wilt have.

LUCY:
Cease to urge me!
To another true faith have I sworn!
HENRY:
'Tis well!
By this letter thou may'st see
How he keeps his faith with thee!
Read it.
(*Hands her a letter.*)
LUCY:
How beats my flutt'ring heart!
(*Reads*):
Ah! great Heaven!

Henry, in desperation, now tells her that unless she consents to wed *Arthur* he will be disgraced and ruined. This begins another duet, the *Se tradirme.*

Se tradirme tu potrai (I'm Thy Guardian)

By Giuseppina Huguet, Soprano, and Francesco Cigada, Baritone
(*In Italian*) *62089 10-inch, $0.75

HENRY:
I'm thy guardian, dar'st thou brave me?
I'm thy brother—wilt thou save me?
From the hands of thee, my sister,
Must I meet a traitor's doom?
See the axe, by one thread hanging;
Hark! the deep toned deathbell clanging.
Hath affection lost all power?
Wilt consign me unto the tomb?

LUCY:
I'm thy sister, dost thou love me!
I am dying, will that move thee!
From the hands of thee, my brother,
Must I meet now this dreadful doom!
Hopeless misery all surrounding,
E'en while the marriage bell is sounding:
Fear and hate will be my dower;
Better had I wed the tomb!

However, convinced of *Edgar's* falseness, she half consents to the sacrifice, and retires to prepare for the ceremony.

SCENE II—*The Great Hall of the Castle*

The knights and ladies sing a chorus of congratulation to the bride and bridegroom, while *Sir Henry* greets the guests and asks them to pardon *Lucy's* agitated bearing, as she is still mourning for her mother.

Lucy enters and is escorted to the table where the notary is preparing the marriage papers. Believing her lover false, she cares little what becomes of her, and passively signs the contract. Pale as death and almost fainting, she is being supported by her faithful maid and her family adviser, *Raymond,* when suddenly a terrible silence ensues, as *Edgar,* the lover of *Lucy* and the deadly enemy of her brother, appears at the back of the room dressed in a sombre suit of black. The wedding guests are dumb with amazement at the daring of the young noble in thus presenting himself unbidden at the house of his enemy. The great sextette, the most dramatic and thrilling number in the entire range of opera, now begins.

Unlike many operatic ensembles, this sextette is not merely a most remarkable bit of concerted writing, but is so well fitted to the scene in which it occurs that even the enemies of Donizetti, who call Lucia merely a string of melodies, are compelled to admit its extreme beauty and powerful dramatic qualities.

Sextette—Chi mi frena (What Restrains Me)

By Marcella Sembrich, Soprano; Enrico Caruso, Tenor; Antonio Scotti, Baritone; Marcel Journet, Bass; Mme. Severina, Mezzo-Soprano; Francesco Daddi, Tenor (*In Italian*)	96200	12-inch, $7.00
By Victor Opera Sextette (*In Italian*)	70036	12-inch, 1.25
By Victor Band	31020	12-inch, 1.00
By Pryor's Band	31460	12-inch, 1.00

Edgar remains standing, with his eyes steadily fixed on the unhappy *Lucy,* who is unable to meet his glance. This dramatic silence is broken by the commencement of the sextette, as *Edgar* and *Sir Henry,* with suppressed emotion, sing their short duet:

* *Double-Faced Record—For title of opposite side see DOUBLE-FACED LUCIA RECORDS, page 179.*

HENRY AND EDGAR:
  Instant vengeance, what restraineth,
  What thus stays my sword in scabbard?
  Is't affection that still remaineth,
  And each angry tho't enchaineth?
  Of mine own blood { thou'rt | I'm } betrayer,
  And despair { my | her } heart doth wither,
EDGAR:
  Yet, ungrateful one, I love thee still!
HENRY:
  And remorse my breast doth fill!

LUCY (*despairingly*):
  I had hop'd that death had found me,
  And in his drear fetters bound me,
  But he comes not to relieve me!
  Ah! of life will none bereave me?
RAYMOND AND ALICE:
  Ah! like a rose that withers on the stem,
  She now is hovering 'twixt death and life!
  He who for her by pity is not mov'd,
  Has of a tiger in his breast the heart.
ARTHUR:
  Hence, thou traitor, hence betake thee,
  Ere our rage shall o'erwhelm thee!

One by one the characters in the scene take up their portions of the sextette until the great climax, one of the most dramatic moments in opera, is reached.

Several records of this magnificent number are offered to Victor audiences. Besides the splendid Caruso-Sembrich rendition, which made such a sensation on its appearance several years ago, the Victor has recently issued a superb record by the Victor Opera forces at the popular price of $1.25, while for those who prefer an instrumental rendition two fine band records are offered.

Henry and *Edgar,* who have drawn their swords, are separated by *Raymond,* who commands them in Heaven's name to sheath their weapons. *Henry* asks *Edgar* why he has come, and the knight replies:

EDGAR:
  Hither came I
  For my bride—thy sister
  Unto me her faith hath sworn!
RAYMOND:
  Thou must all hope of her relinquish;
  She is another's!

He exhibits the signed contract, but *Edgar* refuses to believe the evidence of his eyes and asks *Lucy* if she had signed it. With her eyes fixed on him she tremblingly nods her head in assent. *Edgar,* in a furious rage, tears the contract in pieces, flings it at the fainting maiden, and rushes from the castle as the curtain falls.

ACT III
SCENE I—*The Tower of Ravenswood Castle*

Edgar is brooding on his misfortunes when a horseman rides up, dismounts and enters the tower. It proves to be *Sir Henry,* who has come to challenge *Edgar* to a duel to the death. They agree to fight the following morning, and in this duet ask the night to hasten away, that their vengeance may be consummated.

COPY'T DUPONT

SALEZA AS EDGARDO

O sole più rapido (Haste, Crimson Morning)
By Giuseppe Acerbi, Tenor, and Renzo Minolfi, Baritone
(*In Italian*) *62644 10-inch, $0.75

Why the gentlemen do not take advantage of the present moment the librettist does not reveal! This scene is so melodramatic that it borders on the absurd, and it is usually omitted in this country, although it is well worth hearing from a musical point of view.

SCENE II—*Hall in Lammermoor Castle*

The peasants and domestics of the castle are making merry at their feast in honor of the marriage when *Raymond* enters, greatly agitated, bearing the fearful news that *Lucy* has become insane and has killed her husband. This gives opportunity for a dramatic air, sung here by Signor Sillich and the La Scala Chorus.

O qual funesto avvenimento (Oh! Dire Misfortune)
By Aristodemo Sillich, Bass, and Chorus (*In Italian*) *62644 10-inch, $0.75

Raymond's tidings have scarcely been spoken when *Lucy* enters, a pale and lovely figure in white, and all unconscious of the horror-stricken servants, begins her famous so-called *Mad Scene.*

* *Double-Faced Record—For title of opposite side see DOUBLE-FACED LUCIA RECORDS, page 179.*

Mad Scene (With Flute Obbligato)

By Luisa Tetrazzini, Soprano	(*In Italian*)	88299	12-inch,	$3.00
By Marcella Sembrich, Soprano	(*In Italian*)	88021	12-inch,	3.00
By Nellie Melba, Soprano	(*In Italian*)	88071	12-inch,	3.00
By Maria Galvany, Soprano	(*In Italian*)	88221	12-inch,	3.00
By Graziella Pareto, Soprano	(*In Italian*)	76006	12-inch,	2.00
By Marie Michailowa, Soprano	(*In Russian*)	61129	10-inch,	1.00

Forgetting her marriage, the demented maiden speaks one moment of the happy day when she will be *Edgar's* wife, and next is terrified by a vague feeling that something has come between them.

This famous number must be judged solely as a brilliant piece of vocalism; it can hardly be considered dramatically, because when the prima donna loses her reason in this style of opera, it only means that the scales become more rapid and the roulades more difficult! The unfortunate *Lucy* in her agony seems inclined and able to sing the most difficult and florid music conceivable, and venture without hesitation on passages at which a sane person would stand aghast! In short, Donizetti forgot his dramatic mission temporarily in his efforts to write a show piece of musical execution.

LUCY:
I hear the breathing of his voice low and tender,
That voice beloved sounds in my heart forever.
My Edgar, why were we parted?
Let me not mourn thee;
See, for thy sake, I've all forsaken!
What shudder do I feel thro' my veins?
My heart is trembling, my senses fail!
(*She forgets her trouble and smiles.*)
Come to the fountain;
There let us rest together,
Ah me! see where yon spectre arises,
Standing between us! Alas! Dear Edgar!

See yon phantom rise to part us!
(*Her mood again changes.*)
Yet shall we meet, dear Edgar, before the altar.
Hark to those strains celestial!
Ah! 'Tis the hymn for our nuptials!
For us they are singing!
The altar for us is deck'd thus,
Oh, joy unbounded!
'Round us the brilliant tapers brightly are shining,
The priest awaits us.
Oh! day of gladness!
Thine am I ever, thou mine forever!
(*She falls fainting into the arms of Raymond.*)

TETRAZZINI AS THE
DEMENTED LUCY

Donizetti's scene seems especially set apart for the display of such a coloratura as Melba possesses, and she sings this florid music with such brilliancy and graceful fluency that the listener is dazzled. Her runs, trills and *staccato* notes glitter and scintillate, and compel a new admiration for the wonderful vocal mechanism over which she has such absolute command.

The rôle of the unhappy *Lucy* is also admirably fitted to Tetrazzini's peculiar talents, and as the heroine of Donizetti's lovely opera she has made quite the greatest success of her career. When she reaches this florid and difficult *Mad Scene*, the listeners are absolutely electrified, and such a torrent of enthusiasm bursts forth that the diva is usually compelled to repeat a portion of the aria.

Mme. Sembrich's rendition proves that the compass of her voice is all but phenomenal, and she sings the difficult music with delightful flexibility and with an intonation which is faultless.

Other renditions of this well-known scene are given by Mme. Galvany and Mme. Pareto, the famous Italian prima donnas, and by Michailowa, the famous Russian singer. Although none of these artists has yet visited America, their beautiful voices are heard in thousands of homes in which the Victor is a welcome entertainer.

The unhappy *Lucy*, after having in this scene again enacted the terrible events of the previous day, falls insensible and is carried to her room by *Alice* and *Raymond*.

SCENE II—*The Tombs of the Ravenswoods*

Edgar, weary of life, has come to the rendezvous arranged with *Henry*, intending to throw himself on his enemy's sword, the last of a doomed race. But he waits in vain, for *Henry*, filled with remorse at the consequences of his schemes, has left England, never to return. *Edgar* sings the first of the two beautiful airs written by Donizetti for this scene.

Fra poco a me ricovero (Farewell to Earth)

By John McCormack, Tenor   (*In Italian*)   74223   12-inch $1.50

His attention is now attracted by a train of mourners coming from the castle, accompanied by *Raymond,* who reveals to the unhappy man that *Lucy* is dying, and even while they converse the castle bell is heard tolling, a signal that the unhappy maiden is no more.

The grief-stricken lover then depicts his emotion in the second air, a lovely number with sadness in every tone.

Tu che a Dio spiegasti l'ali (Thou Hast Spread Thy Wings to Heaven) (O bell' alma innamorata)

By John McCormack, Tenor   (*In Italian*)   74224   12-inch, $1.50
By Florencio Constantino, Tenor   (*In Italian*)   74066   12-inch,   1.50
By Gino Martinez-Patti, Tenor   (*In Italian*)   *62089   10-inch,   .75

The dramatic interest deepens as the air proceeds, until the finale, when *Edgar,* in an excess of penitence, prays that not even the spirit of the wronged *Lucy* may approach so accursed a tomb as that of Ravenswood.

EDGAR:
Tho' from earth thou'st flown before me,
My ador'd, my only treasure;
Tho' from these fond arms they tore thee,
Soon, soon, I'll follow thee,

I'll follow thee above.
Tho' the world frown'd on our union,
Tho' in this life they did part us,
Yet on high, in fond communion,
Shall our hearts be turned to love!

Breaking from *Raymond,* who endeavors to prevent the fatal act, *Edgar* stabs himself, and supported in the good man's arms, he repeats in broken phrases the lovely *O bell' alma innamorata,* and lifting his hands to Heaven, as if to greet the spirit of *Lucy,* he expires.

DOUBLE-FACED AND MISCELLANEOUS LUCIA RECORDS

Regnava nel silenzio (Silence O'er All)
         By Giuseppina Huguet, Soprano   (*In Italian*)
Norma—Casta Diva (Queen of Heaven)
         By Giuseppina Huguet, Soprano   (*In Italian*)
	16539	10-inch, $0.75

Il pallor funesto (If My Cheek is Pale)
   By Linda Brambilla, Soprano, and Francesco Cigada,
     Baritone   (*In Italian*)
Sulla tomba che rinserra (By My Father's Tomb)
   By Emma Trentini, Soprano, and Gino Martinez-Patti,
     Tenor   (*In Italian*)
	16574	10-inch, .75

Se tradirme su potrai (I'm Thy Guardian)
   By Giuseppina Huguet, Soprano, and Francesco Cigada,
     Baritone   (*In Italian*)
Tu che a Dio spiegasti l'ali (Thou Hast Spread Thy Wings
   to Heaven) (O bell' alma innamorata)
     By Gino Martinez-Patti, Tenor   (*In Italian*)
	62089	10-inch, .75

O qual funesto avvenimento
     By Aristodemo Sillich, Bass, and Chorus   (*In Italian*)
O sole piu rapido (Haste, Crimson Morning!)
   By Giuseppe Acerbi, Tenor, and Renzo Minolfi,
     Baritone   (*In Italian*)
	62644	10-inch, .75

Opening Chorus   By La Scala Chorus   (*In Italian*)
Verranno a te sull' aura (Borne on Sighing Breeze)
   By Emma Trentini, Soprano, and Gino Martinez-
     Patti, Tenor   (*In Italian*)
	62106	10-inch, .75

Quando rapita in estasi (Swift as Thought)
     By Giuseppina Huguet, Soprano   (*In Italian*)
Lucrezia Borgia—Rischiarata è la finestra
     By La Scala Chorus   (*In Italian*)
	63172	10-inch, .75

* *Double-Faced Record—For title of opposite side see above list.*

LUCREZIA AND THE SLEEPING GENNARO—ACT I

(Italian)

LUCREZIA BORGIA

(Loo-kray'-tzee-ah Bor'-jee-ah)

OPERA IN THREE ACTS

Text by Felice Romani, taken from a work of the same name by Victor Hugo. Music by Gaetano Donizetti. First presented to the public at La Scala, Milan, in 1834; given at the *Théâtre Italien*, Paris, October 27, 1840. First London production at her Majesty's Theatre, June 6, 1839; in English at the Princess' Theatre, December 30, 1843. Produced in New York at the Astor Place Opera House, 1847.

Characters

LUCREZIA BORGIA	Soprano
MAFFIO ORSINI *(Maf'-fee-oh Or-see'-nee)*	Contralto
GENNARO, *(Jen-nah'-roh)*	Tenor
LIVEROTTO,	Tenor
VITELLOZZO, — Young noblemen in the service of the Venetian	Tenor
PETRUCCI, — Republic	Bass
GAZELLA,	Bass
IL DUCA ALFONSO	Baritone
RUSTIGHELLO, in the service of Don Alfonso	Tenor
GUBETTA, — in the service of Donna Lucrezia	Bass
ASTOLFO,	Bass
BATTISTA	Tenor
LA PRINCIPESSA NEGRONI	Soprano
CHORUS	

Scene and Period: Italy; the beginning of the sixteenth century.

The plot of Donizetti's opera cannot be called a cheerful one—it is, in fact, crowded with horrors. However, it was a great favorite with American audiences for many years, being one of the stock operas of Emma Abott during nearly her whole career. The opera was revived in 1904 for Caruso, but failed to score, and it is quite likely that those who admire its few fine airs must depend on their Victors if they wish to hear them.

COPY'T DUPONT

DE MOSCHI AS LUCREZIA

Lucrezia, the heroine, was a conspicuous member of the notorious patrician family—the *Borgias*—celebrated for their diabolical success as poisoners.

Lucrezia Borgia married as her second husband *Don Alfonso, Duke of Ferrara.* By her former marriage she had a son named *Gennaro,* of whose existence the *Duke* is ignorant. This son had, at birth, been placed in the care of a fisherman who brought him up as his own child.

ACT I

At the opening of the story *Lucrezia,* who in spite of her criminal practices has still the mother's yearning towards her own child, goes in disguise to Venice to visit him.

She finds her son in the company of some gay Venetian gallants. She watches them, and presently *Gennaro,* wearied by the mirth of his companions, draws apart and falls asleep on a seat. *Lucrezia* draws near, and gazing on his youthful beauty, she forgets everything except that she is his mother. She gently presses a kiss on his brow and prepares to depart, when he awakes and asks her who she is. She evades the question, and leads him to talk about his mother, whom he says he has never seen. Feeling drawn toward the beautiful stranger, he tells his story, in the fine *Di pescatore.*

Di pescatore ignoble (In a Fisher's Lowly Cot)

By Francesco Marconi, Tenor	(*In Italian*)	76004 12-inch, $2.00
By Carlo Albani, Tenor	(*In Italian*)	74098 12-inch, 1.50

She bids him farewell, and is about to take her leave when *Orsini* appears, recognizes her, and after brutally reciting her crimes one by one, tells the horror-stricken *Gennaro* that it is the *Borgia.* All turn from him in horror, and *Lucrezia* falls fainting.

ACT II

Gennaro afterwards shows his hatred and contempt for the *Borgias* by tearing down *Lucrezia's* coat of arms from her palace gates, and is imprisoned by the *Duke's* orders. *Lucrezia,* ignorant of the identity of the individual who has insulted her, complains to the *Duke,* who promises that the perpetrator shall be immediately punished. He gives vent to his feelings in his air, *Vieni la mia vendetta.*

Vieni, la mia vendetta (Haste Thee, for Vengeance)

By Giulio Rossi, Bass	(*In Italian*)	*63404 10-inch, $0.75

Gennaro is sent for and *Lucrezia* at once recognizes him. Full of horror, she turns to the *Duke* and begs him to overlook the offense. The *Duke* is relentless and compels *Lucrezia* herself to hand a poisoned cup to her son. She obeys, but afterward contrives to give the youth an antidote. He suspects her of treachery, but she pleads so tearfully with him that he trusts her and drinks the remedy.

ACT III

This act opens with a chorus of bravos, who have been set to watch the dwelling of *Gennaro.*

Rischiarata è la finestra (Yonder Light is the Guiding Beacon)

By La Scala Chorus	(*In Italian*)	*63172 10-inch, $0.75

Gennaro, whose life has been saved by the antidote *Lucrezia* had given him, instead of escaping from the city as she had advised him, accompanies *Orsino* to a banquet which has been secretly arranged by *Lucrezia,* and to which have been invited the young men who had recognized and denounced her in Venice.

In this scene occurs the famous *Brindisi,* or drinking song.

Double-Faced Record—For title of opposite side see DOUBLE-FACED LUCREZIA BORGIA RECORDS, page 182.

Brindisi (It is Better to Laugh)

By Ernestine Schumann-Heink, Contralto (*In German*) 88188 12-inch, $3.00

This air is a very well known one, and has been frequently sung, but Mme. Schumann-Heink puts such brilliant spirit into it, and sings it with such wealth of gayety, such astonishing range and such agility, that the rendition amazes the listener. It is certain that no music-lover of the present generation has ever heard it sung so brilliantly. The high notes are taken with the ease of a soprano, and altogether this familiar drinking song has never been so well delivered.

The rôle of *Maffio Orsini* was always one of Mme. Schumann-Heink's favorites, and she makes a gallant figure as the gay Roman youth. The words are well suited to the gayety of the music, and have been translated as follows:

Brindisi

It is better to laugh than be sighing.
When we think how life's moments are flying;
For each sorrow Fate ever is bringing,
There's a pleasure in store for us springing.
Tho' our joys, like to waves in the sunshine,
Gleam awhile, then are lost to the sight,
Yet, for each sparkling ray
That so passes away,
Comes another as brilliant and light.

In the world we some beings discover,
Far too frigid for friend or for lover;
Souls unblest, and forever repining,
Tho' good fortune around them be shining.
It were well, if such hearts we could banish
To some planet far distant from ours;
They're the dark spots we trace,
On this earth's favored space;
They are weeds that choke up the fair flow'rs!

Then 'tis better to laugh than be sighing;
They are wise who resolve to be gay;
When we think how life's moments are flying,
Enjoy Pleasure's gifts while we may!

In the midst of the feast the door opens, the *Borgia* appears and tells them that they are doomed, as the wine has been poisoned by her.

PHOTO BERT

LUCREZIA DISCOVERS SHE HAS POISONED HER SON

To her horror she sees *Gennaro* among the guests. He, too, has drunk of the fatal wine. She again offers him an antidote, which he refuses, because the amount is insufficient to save the lives of his friends. *Lucrezia* confesses the relationship between them, but *Gennaro* spurns her and dies. The *Duke* now appears, intending to share in *Lucrezia's* hideous triumph, but finds his wife surrounded by her victims—some dead, others dying. *Lucrezia,* a witness to the horrible result of her crime, suffers the keenest remorse, drinks some of her own poison and herself expires.

DOUBLE-FACED AND MISCELLANEOUS LUCREZIA BORGIA RECORDS

Vieni, la mia vendetta   By Giulio Rossi, Bass (*In Italian*)
Gli Ugonotti—Duetto Valentina Marcello
    By Maria Grisi, Soprano, and Perello De Segurola, Bass } 63404 10-inch, $0.75

Rischiarata è la finestra (Yonder Light is the Guiding
    Beacon)   By La Scala Chorus (*In Italian*)
Lucia di Lammermoor—Quando rapita in estasi
    By Giuseppina Huguet, Soprano } 63172 10-inch, .75

THE MARRIAGE SCENE—ACT I

(Italian)
MADAMA BUTTERFLY
(Mah'-dah-mah)

(English)
MADAM BUTTERFLY

OPERA IN THREE ACTS

A Japanese lyric tragedy, founded on the book of John Luther Long and the drama by David Belasco, with Italian libretto by Illica and Giacosa. Music by Giacomo Puccini. First produced at La Scala, Milan, in 1904, it proved a failure. Revived the following year in slightly changed form with much success. First American presentation (in English) occurred in October, 1906, in Washington, D. C., by Savage Opera Company. First representation in Italian at Metropolitan Opera House, February 11, 1907, with Farrar, Caruso, Homer and Scotti.

Characters

MADAM BUTTERFLY (Cho-Cho-San)..........................Soprano
SUZUKI, *(Soo-zu'-key)* Cho-Cho-San's servant...................Mezzo-Soprano
B. F. PINKERTON, Lieutenant in the United States Navy...............Tenor
KATE PINKERTON, his American wife......................Mezzo-Soprano
SHARPLESS, United States Consul at Nagasaki....................Baritone
GORO, a marriage broker...Tenor
PRINCE YAMADORI, suitor for Cho-Cho-San......................Baritone
THE BONZE, Cho-Cho-San's uncle................................Bass
CHO-CHO-SAN'S MOTHER..............................Mezzo-Soprano
THE AUNT...Mezzo-Soprano
THE COUSIN...Soprano
TROUBLE, Cho-Cho-San's child

Cho-Cho-San's relations and friends—Servants.

At Nagasaki, Japan—Time, the present.

The Story

Puccini's opera, which from the first aroused the keenest interest among opera-goers, has become an enduring success. The original Metropolitan production in Italian was under the personal direction of Puccini himself, who refined and beautified it according to his own ideas into one of the most finished operatic productions ever seen here.

The story of the drama is familiar to all through John Luther Long's narrative and the Belasco dramatic version. The tale is the old one of the passing fancy of a man for a woman, and her faithfulness even unto death, which comes by her own hand when she finds herself abandoned.

Puccini has completely identified his music with the sentiments and sorrows of the characters in John Luther Long's drama, and has accompanied the pictorial beauty of the various scenes with a setting of incomparable loveliness. Rarely has picturesque action been more completely wedded to beautiful music.

ACT I

SCENE—Exterior of Pinkerton's house at Nagasaki

At the rise of the curtain *Goro*, the marriage broker who has secured *Pinkerton* his bride, is showing the Lieutenant over the house he has chosen for his honeymoon. *Sharpless*, the American Consul and friend of *Pinkerton*, now arrives, having been bidden to the marriage. Then occurs the fine duet, which Caruso and Scotti have sung here in splendid style.

Amore o grillo (Love or Fancy?)

By Enrico Caruso, Tenor, and Antonio Scotti, Baritone

(*In Italian*)   **89043**   12-inch, $4.00

By Riccardo Martin, Tenor   (*In Italian*)   **87081**   10-inch,   2.00

NOTE.—Mr. Martin sings only *Pinkerton's* solo from above duet.

COPY'T MISHKIN

MARTIN AS PINKERTON

Pinkerton, joyous in the prospect of his marriage with the dainty Japanese girl, and quite careless of the consequences which may result from such a union, describes his bride to the Consul, who gives the young lieutenant some good advice, bidding him be careful, that he may not break the trusting heart of the *Butterfly* who loves him too well.

The number closes with a splendid climax, as *Pinkerton* recklessly pledges the "real American wife" whom he hopes to meet some day; while the Consul gazes at his young friend with some sadness, as if already in the shadow of the tragedy which is to come.

Now is heard in the distance the voice of *Butterfly*, who is coming up the hill with her girl friends; and she sings a lovely song, full of the freshness of youth and the dawning of love.

Entrance of Cio-Cio San

By Geraldine Farrar, Soprano

(*In Italian*)   **87004**   10-inch, $2.00

This dainty little number is given by Miss Farrar with the naïveté and grace of a fascinating child of fifteen, as she pictures the young girl in Act I.

The friends and family having been duly introduced to *Pinkerton,* they go to the refreshment table, while *Butterfly* timidly confides to *Pinkerton,* in this touching number, that she has for his sake renounced her religion, and will in future bow before the God of her husband.

Ieri son salita (Hear Me)

By Geraldine Farrar, Soprano   (*In Italian*)   **87031**   10-inch, $2.00

The contract is signed and the guests are dispersing when *Butterfly's* uncle rushes in and denounces her, having discovered that she has been to the Mission, renounced her religion, and adopted that of her husband.

She is cast off by the family, who flee from the scene in horror. *Butterfly* at first weeps, but is comforted by the Lieutenant, who tells her he cares nothing for her family, but loves her alone.

Then occurs the incomparably beautiful duet which closes the first act, and which is beyond all question the finest of the melodious numbers which Puccini has composed for the opera; and the effect of this exquisite music, given on a darkened stage amid the flashing of fireflies, is wholly beautiful.

O quanti occhi fisi (Oh Kindly Heavens) (Love Duet from Finale, Act I)

By Geraldine Farrar,
Soprano, and Enrico
Caruso, Tenor
(*In Italian*) 89017 12-in., $4.00

Miss Farrar sings all of Puccini's music fluently and gracefully, but is always at her best in this exquisite love duet, while the number is Caruso's finest opportunity in the opera, and he makes the most of it.

The blending of the voices of the artists is remarkably effective, and the ecstatic climax at the end is splendidly given, both singers ending on a high C sharp; the effect being absolutely thrilling.

BUTTERFLY'S UNCLE DENOUNCING HER—ACT I

ACT II

SCENE—Interior of Butterfly's Home—at the back a Garden with Cherries in Bloom

Three years have now elapsed, and *Butterfly*, with her child and faithful maid, *Suzuki*, are awaiting the return of *Pinkerton*. *Suzuki* begins to lose courage, but *Butterfly* rebukes her and declares her faith to be unshaken.

Un bel di vedremo (Some Day He'll Come)

By Geraldine Farrar, Soprano	(*In Italian*)	88113	12-inch,	$3.00
By Emmy Destinn, Soprano	(*In Italian*)	92057	12-inch,	3.00
By Agnes Kimball	(*In English*)	70054	12-inch,	1.25

COPY'T DUPONT

THE LETTER FROM PINKERTON—ACT II
(GERALDINE FARRAR)

This highly dramatic number is sung after *Butterfly* has reproached *Suzuki* for her doubts, and in it she proudly declares confidence in her husband. In the English version this is called the "Vision Song," as it describes her vision of the arrival of *Lieutenant Pinkerton's* ship.

Ora a noi! (Letter Duet)

By Geraldine Farrar, Soprano,
and Antonio Scotti, Baritone
(*In Italian*) 89014 12-inch, $4.00

Butterfly is visited by *Sharpless*, who has received a letter from *Pinkerton*, and has accepted the unpleasant task of informing *Butterfly* that the Lieutenant has deserted her. He finds his task a difficult one, for when he attempts to read *Pinkerton's* letter to her, she misunderstands its purport and continually interrupts the Consul with little bursts of joyful anticipation, thinking that *Pinkerton* will soon come to her. Finally realizing something of his message, she runs to bring her child to prove to *Sharpless* the certainty of her husband's home-coming.

BUTTERFLY AND "TROUBLE"

Sai cos' ebbe cuore (Do You Know, My Sweet One)

By Geraldine Farrar, Soprano
(*In Italian*) 87055 10-in., $2.00
By Emmy Destinn, Soprano
(*In Italian*) 91084 10-in., 2.00

In this pitiful air she asks little "*Trouble*" not to listen to the bad man (*Sharpless*), who is saying that *Pinkerton* has deserted them.

Shocked at the sight of the child, which he knew nothing about, *Sharpless* gives up in despair the idea of further undeceiving her, knowing that she will soon learn the truth, and leaves *Butterfly*, who refuses to doubt *Pinkerton*, in an exalted state of rapture over the idea of her husband's return.

Throughout the duet may be heard the mournfully sweet "waiting motive" played softly by the horns, and accompanied by strings *pizzicati*. This is beautifully given here, and the record is a most impressive one.

The sound of a cannon is heard, and with aid of a glass the two women see *Pinkerton's* ship, the *Abraham Lincoln*, entering the harbor.

Duet of the Flowers

By Geraldine Farrar, Soprano,
and Louise Homer, Contralto
(*In Italian*) 89008 12-in., $4.00

Greatly excited, *Butterfly* bids the maid strew the room with flowers, and they scatter the cherry blossoms everywhere, singing all the while weird harmonies which are hauntingly beautiful.

Miss Farrar's impressive *Cio-Cio-San*, childish and piquant in its lighter aspects and pitifully tragic in its final scenes, and Mme. Homer's *Suzuki*, the patient handmaiden, who loves and protects her mistress through all the weary years of waiting, are two most powerful impersonations. Of the music written for these two rôles, this exquisite duet is especially attractive.

Night is falling, and not expecting *Pinkerton* until morning, *Butterfly*, *Suzuki* and the child take their places at the window to watch for his coming. As the vigil begins, in the orchestra can be heard the "Waiting Motive," with its accompaniment by distant voices of the sailors in the harbor, producing an effect which is indescribably beautiful.

FARRAR AND HOMER IN ACT II

SCENE II—Same as the Preceding

The curtain rises on the same scene. It is daybreak. *Suzuki*, exhausted, is sleeping, but *Butterfly* still watches the path leading up the hill. *Suzuki* awakes and insists on *Butterfly* taking some rest, promising to call her when the Lieutenant arrives.

Sharpless and *Pinkerton* now enter, and question *Suzuki*, the Lieutenant being deeply touched to find that *Butterfly* has been faithful to him, and that a child has been born.

Suzuki, seeing a lady in the garden, demands to know who she is, and *Sharpless* tells her it is the wife of *Pinkerton*, he having married in America.

The introduction by Puccini's librettist of this character has been severely criticised, many considering it of doubtful taste, and forming a jarring note in the opera. So strong is this feeling in France, that the part of *Kate* has been eliminated from the cast.

The faithful maid is horrified, and dreads the effect of this news on her mistress. Weeping bitterly, she goes into *Butterfly's* chamber, while the friends are left to bitter reflections, expressed by Puccini in a powerful duet.

Ve lo dissi ? (Did I Not Tell You ?)

By Enrico Caruso, Tenor, and Antonio Scotti, Baritone
(*In Italian*) 89047 12-inch, $4.00

Pinkerton realizes for the first time the basenes of his conduct, while the Consul reminds him of the warning he had given him in Act I,—to beware lest the tender heart of *Butterfly* be broken.

The part of the Consul is not a great one, but Scotti almost makes it one with his careful portrayal, singing with dignity and tenderness and giving the part its full dramatic value. With the re-entrance of *Suzuki* occurs the trio for *Pinkerton, Sharpless* and *Suzuki*.

Lo so che alle sue pene (Naught Can Console Her)

By Riccardo Martin, Tenor; Rita Fornia, Soprano; Antonio Scotti, Baritone (*In Italian*) 87503 10-inch, $3.00

This trio is dramatically given by Martin, Fornia and Scotti, who have this season made successes in the several rôles of *Pinkerton, Suzuki* and *Sharpless*.

Finale Ultimo (Butterfly's Death Scene)

By Geraldine Farrar, Soprano (*In Italian*) 87030 10-inch, $2.00
By Emmy Destinn, Soprano (*In Italian*) 91086 10-inch, 2.00

Now comes the pathetic death scene at the close of the opera. *Butterfly*, convinced that *Pinkerton* has renounced her, blindfolds her child that he may not witness her suicide, takes down the dagger with which her father committed *hari-kari*, and after reading the inscription on the handle, "To die with honor when one can no longer live with honor," she stabs herself.

In her death struggle she gropes her way to the innocent babe, who, blindfolded and waving his little flag, takes it all in the spirit of play. The tragic intensity of this scene always moves many to tears.

Miss Farrar puts into this final number all the pathetic despair of *Cio-Cio-San's* over-burdened heart; her rendition being a most impressive and wholly pathetic one; while Mme. Destinn gives a most dramatic interpretation of this scene, perhaps the most heart-rending in the entire range of opera.

Pinkerton enters to ask *Butterfly's* forgiveness and bid her farewell, and is horrified to find her dying. He lifts her up in an agony of remorse.

In the orchestra, strangely mingling with the American motive, the tragic death motive may be heard as the curtain slowly falls.

PHOTO HALL THE DEATH OF BUTTERFLY

DOUBLE-FACED AND MISCELLANEOUS MADAM BUTTERFLY RECORDS

Madame Butterfly Selection   By Victor Orchestra 31631 12-inch, $1.00

This selection begins with the entrance music of *Pinkerton,* accompanied by the American theme for which Puccini has utilized the "Star Spangled Banner."

Then in succession are heard the gay air of the thoughtless Lieutenant (as a cornet solo) in which he describes the characteristics of his countrymen; the principal strain of the love duet with which the act closes; the exquisitely poetical "Duet of the Flowers," part of which is given on the orchestra bells; and the beginning of the supremely beautiful scene where *Butterfly,* her maid and little son, take their places at the window to watch until morning for the husband's coming, while in the distance can be heard the faint voices of singers in the night, producing a mournful and indescribable effect.

Then from the last scene we hear the return of *Pinkerton* announced just as *Butterfly* has taken her life; the American *motif* strangely contrasting with the tragic music of the death scene; and a few measures of the final curtain music, with its ancient Japanese melody.

{Madame Butterfly Selection   By Pryor's Band}
{ Bartered Bride Overture   By Pryor's Band} 35148 12-inch, $1.25
Madame Butterfly Selection   By Pryor's Band 31697 12-inch, 1.00

The interest of the public in this exquisite Puccini opera continues to grow, and the fine records the Victor has offered of the music have been much enjoyed and favorably commented upon. This really beautiful twelve-inch fantasia, composed of the most effective portions of the opera, is splendidly played, as usual, by this fine concert band.

Madame Butterfly Fantasie—By Victor Herbert's Orch 70055 12-inch, $1.25
Madame Butterfly Fantasie   By Victor Sorlin 'Cello 31696 12-inch, 1.00

Some of the most beautiful passages in this fascinating Puccini opera have been combined in this attractive fantasie. Among the themes used are the last part of *Butterfly's* "Song of Devotion" in Act II, sometimes called the "Vision Song"; and the mournful but beautiful "Waiting Motive." This motive, which is also sung by a distant chorus with a peculiarly charming and mysterious effect, is one of the composer's happiest inspirations. The *pizzicati* passages on the violin which accompany this strange melody are most effectively given by the orchestra.

BUTTERFLY AND SUZUKI IN THE GARDEN

THE BRILLIANT MAGIC FLUTE REVIVAL OF 1911 IN BERLIN

<table>
<tr><td>(French)</td><td>(English)</td></tr>
</table>

LA FLÛTE ENCHANTÉE   THE MAGIC FLUTE

(Lah Fleut Ahn-shan-tay')

(German)   (Italian)

DIE ZAUBERFLÖTE   IL FLAUTO MAGICO

(Dee Tsow-ber-floe'-teh)   *(Eel Flau'-tow Mah'-jee-ko)*

OPERA IN TWO ACTS

Libretto by Schickaneder, adapted from a tale by Wieland, "Lulu, or the Magic Flute." Music by Wolfgang Amadeus Mozart. First produced in Vienna, September 30, 1791, Mozart directing. First Paris production as *"Les Mystères d'Isis,"* August 20, 1801. First London production, in Italian, in 1811; in German, 1833; in English, 1838. First New York production April 11, 1833.

Characters

SARASTRO, *(Sahr-as-tro)* High Priest of Isis . . . . Bass
TAMINO, *(Tah-mee'-noh)* an Egyptian Prince . . . . Tenor
PAPAGENO, *(Pap-ah-gay'-noh)* a bird-catcher . . . . Baritone
THE QUEEN OF NIGHT . . . . Soprano
PAMINA, *(Pam-ee'-nah)* her daughter . . . . Soprano
MONOSTATOS, *(Moh-no-stat'-oss)* a Moor, chief of the slaves of the Temple
of Isis . . . . Baritone
PAPAGENA, *(Pap-ah-gay-nah)* . . . . Soprano
FIRST LADY, }
SECOND LADY, } attendants on the Queen of Night . . . . { Soprano
THIRD LADY, } { Mezzo-Soprano
{ Alto
FIRST BOY, }
SECOND BOY, } belonging to the Temple, and fulfilling the { Soprano
THIRD BOY, } designs of Sarastro { Mezzo-Soprano
{ Alto

Priests and Priestesses of the Temple of Isis; Male and Female Slaves;
Warriors of the Temple, Attendants, etc.

*The scene is laid in the vicinity of and in the Temple of Isis at Memphis. The action
is represented as taking place about the time of Ramses I.*

"A fantastic fable was the groundwork; supernatural apparitions and a good dose of comic element were to serve as garnish. But what did Mozart build on this preposterous foundation? What godlike magic breathes throughout this work, from the most popular ballad to the noblest hymn! What many-sidedness, what marvelous variety! The quintessence of every noblest bloom of art seems here to blend in one unequaled flower."—*Richard Wagner.*

Strictly speaking, the Magic Flute is not an opera, but rather a fairy extravaganza accompanied by some of the most delightful music imaginable. To fully appreciate Mozart's work it should be heard in some German town on a Sunday evening, where middle-class families and sweethearts find much enjoyment in the mixture of mystery, sentiment, comedy and delightful music which make up the opera. The libretto is, of course, utterly absurd, describing as it does the magic of the pipes of *Tamino* which

PHOTO BERT

PAPAGENA AND PAPAGENO

had the power to control men, animals, birds, reptiles and even the elements, and as the flute is continually playing throughout the work, the results may be imagined.

Overture

By Victor Band		31012	12-inch, $1.00
By Pryor's Band		*35135	12-inch, 1.25
By La Scala Orchestra		*68207	12-inch, 1.25

The overture is not only one of the greatest of its kind, but one of the most generally appreciated. Its wonderful fugue, "in which Mozart sports with fugal counterpoint as though it were mere child's play," is played by the band in a striking manner. This fugue is announced first by the clarinets and a few bars later the cornets take up the theme, followed by every instrument in the band in the marvelous finale.

ACT I

The scene shows a rocky landscape with the Temple of the *Queen of the Night* visible in the background. *Tamino,* an Egyptian prince who is traveling with his friends, becomes separated from them, is pursued by a huge serpent, and finally faints from fright and fatigue. Three veiled ladies, attendants on the *Queen,* come from the Temple to his rescue and stab the snake with their javelins. While they go to tell the *Queen* of the occurrence, *Tamino* revives, sees the dead serpent and hides as he hears a flute.

Ein Vogelfänger bin ich ja (A Bird Catcher Am I)
By Otto Goritz, Baritone
(*In German*) 64163 10-inch, $1.00

Papageno, a bird catcher, admirer of damsels, and all-around rogue, enters and sings a merry lay, piping at every pause. In his song the fowler describes his occupation of snaring birds, but says he would like catching women better!

PAPAGENO:

The fowler comes, in spite of rain,
And sings his song in merry strain;
This merry fowler, too, is known
By young and old, from zone to zone.
Knows how to whistle every sound
That birds may sing the whole year round.
Oh, none can be more blithe than I,
With these sweet warblers of the sky.

The fowler comes, in spite of rain,
And sings his song in merry strain;
This merry fowler, too, is known
By young and old, from zone to zone.
A net for maidens I should like
Would catch the pretty dears by dozens,
I'd shut them safely up at home,
And never let them forth to roam.

In the part of *Papageno* Mr. Goritz has few rivals, and his impersonation was one of the great features of the recent revival at the Metropolitan.

Tamino now comes forward and gives *Papageno* credit for having killed the serpent, an honor which he promptly accepts. The three ladies now return, rebuke *Papageno* and show *Tamino* a photograph of the *Queen of Night's* daughter, the lovely *Pamina,* who has been

*Double Faced Record—For title of opposite side see DOUBLE-FACED MAGIC FLUTE RECORDS, page 192.

taken from her mother by *Sarastro,* the *Priest of Isis,* to save her from evil influences. *Tamino* falls in love with the picture and offers to rescue the maiden. He is given an all-powerful magic flute, and accompanied by *Papageno* sets out for *Sarastro's* palace.

The scene changes to a room in the palace of the High Priest, where *Pamina* is discovered in charge of *Monostatos,* a Moor.

The Moor is betraying his trust by persecuting *Pamina* with his attentions, when *Papageno* enters and frightens him away. The bird catcher then tells *Pamina* of *Tamino's* love for her, and offers to conduct her to this mysterious lover.

La dove prende (Smiles and Tears)

By Emma Eames, Soprano, and Emilio de Gogorza, Baritone
(In Italian) 89003 12-inch, $4.00

This charming duet, with its grace and inimitable gaiety, introduces the melody of an old German song, *Bei Mannern welche Liebe fuhlen.*

Smiles and Tears

The smile, that on the lip is playing,
 How oft 'twill hide a heart's deep woe!
The tear, that down the cheek is straying,
 From purest springs of joy may flow.
And smiles and tears, so legends say,
Make up the sum of Life's brief day.

Yet, whilst that smile the brow is wreathing,
 One word shall change it to a tear,
And one soft sigh's impassion'd breathing
 Shall bid the tear-drop disappear,
When each alike misleads in turn,
Oh, who the heart's deep lore shall learn!

Fair seems false! and false seems fair!
 Still, what bliss, what joy are there!

After many adventures *Tamino* and *Pamina* meet, and by means of the magic flute they are about to escape, but are interrupted by *Sarastro,* who agrees to unite the lovers if they will remain and be purified by the sacred rites; and as the priest separates them and covers their heads with veils, the curtain falls.

ACT II

The first scene shows a noble forest showing the *Temple of Wisdom.* The priests assemble, and *Sarastro* orders the lovers brought before him. He then sings this superb Invocation, one of the most impressive numbers in the opera.

Invocation (Great Isis)

By Pol Plançon, Bass *(Piano acc.)*
(In Italian) 85042 12-inch, $3.00

In the Invocation, *Sarastro* calls on the gods Isis and Osiris to give *Tamino* and *Papageno* strength to bear the trial now at hand.

Great Isis, great Osiris!
 Strengthen with wisdom's strength this tyro pair;
Ye who guide steps where deserts lengthen,
 Brace theirs with nerve, your proof to bear!
Grant them probation's fruit all living;
 Yet, should they find a grave while striving,
Think on their virtues, gracious gods,
 Take them elect to your abodes!

SARASTRO

In the noble rôle of *Sarastro* Plançon is especially effective, and his dignified impersonation of the benignant High Priest, who smooths out all the fantastic tangles in the situations which occur in Mozart's opera, is always singularly impressive.

The lovers are admitted to the Temple and begin their probation.

In the next scene *Pamina* is discovered asleep in a bower of roses. The *Queen* suddenly rises from the earth and gives *Pamina* a dagger, telling her to kill *Sarastro* or *Tamino* can never be hers. *Pamina* hesitates, and her mother, in a terrifying and dramatic song, threatens vengeance on all concerned.

Aria della Regina (The Queen's Air)

By Bessie Abott, Soprano	(*In Italian*)	88051 12-inch, $3.00
By Maria Galvany, Soprano	(*In Italian*)	87059 10-inch, 2.00

The Queen of Night, *Astriflammante*, is one of the most striking characters in Mozart's opera, and the few numbers allotted to her are difficult and florid ones. This great aria is one which the most experienced of sopranos always approaches with misgiving, because of its excessive demands on the vocal powers. Miss Abott and Mme. Galvany completely meet these demands, both singing the air gracefully and with superb execution.

ASTRIFLAMMANTE:

The pangs of hell are raging in my bosom,	I spurn thee and renounce thee,
Death and destruction wildly flame around!	If thou dar'st to brave my wrath;
Go forth and bear my vengeance to Sarastro,	Through thee Sarastro is to perish!
Or as my daughter thou shalt be disown'd!	Hear, gods of vengeance!
I cast thee off forever,	Hear a mother's vow! (*She disappears.*)

Sarastro enters and soothes *Pamina,* saying that he will take a righteous revenge on the *Queen* by obtaining the happiness of her daughter. He then sings the noble Cavatina, considered one of the greatest of bass arias.

Qui sdegno non s'accende (Within These Sacred Walls)

By Pol Plançon, Bass (*Piano acc.*) (*In Italian*) 85077 12-inch, $3.00

In this number the singer is at his best, and the noble strains are delivered in the broad sonorous style which the music requires.

SARASTRO: Within this hallowed dwelling
　　　　　　Revenge and sorrow cease;
　　　Here troubled doubt dispelling,
　　　　　　The weary heart hath peace.
　　　If thou hast stray'd, a brother's hand
　　　Shall guide thee t'ward the better land.
　　　This hallow'd fane protects thee
　　　　　　From falsehood, guile and fear;
　　　A brother's love directs thee,
　　　　　　To him thy woes are dear.

The probationary trials of the lovers continue through many strange scenes, in one of which *Pamina* meets *Tamino,* and not knowing that he has been forbidden to speak to any woman, cries out that he no longer loves her. She then sings this pathetic little air, which Mme. Gadski has interpreted here so beautifully.

Ah lo so (All Has Vanished)

By Johanna Gadski, Soprano
(*In Italian*) 88254 12-inch, $3.00

Mme. Gadski has long been recognized as one of the foremost exponents of Mozart in this country. The music of this master demands singers of great understanding and feeling, who must possess not only voice but intelligence and taste.

That Gadski possesses these qualifications in ample measure is fully apparent to all who listen to her superb Mozart reproductions.

TAMINO AND PAMINA

PAMINA: Wretch that I am, too well I know	Oh, Tamino, if for thee,
Nought is left me but to mourn,	My sighs and bitter tears are vain,
Condemn'd to drain the cup of woe,	Come, kind death, in pity free
Joy to me will ne'er return.	My weary bosom from its pain!

The trials being finally completed, the lovers are united in the sacred Temple. The *Queen* and her accomplices attempt to prevent the ceremony, but the scene suddenly changes to the Temple of the Sun, where *Sarastro* is seen on his throne with *Tamino* and *Pamina* beside him, while the baffled *Queen* and her train sink into the earth.

DOUBLE-FACED MAGIC FLUTE RECORDS

{ Magic Flute Overture	By Pryor's Band }	35135 12-inch, $1.25
{ My Queen Waltz	By Victor Dance Orchestra }	
{ Magic Flute Overture	La Scala Orchestra }	68207 12-inch, 1.25
{ Meistersinger Prelude	La Scala Orchestra }	

(French)

MANON

(*Man-on'*)

OPERA IN FOUR ACTS

Words by Meilhac and Gille, after the novel of Abbé Prévost. Music by Jules Massenet. First production at the *Opéra-Comique*, Paris, January 19, 1884. First London production May 7, 1885; in English by the Carl Rosa Company, at Liverpool, January 17, 1885. In French at Covent Garden, May 19, 1891. First American production at New York, December 23, 1885, with Minnie Hauk, Giannini and Del Puente. Some notable revivals were in 1895 with Sybil Sanderson and Jean de Reszke; in 1899 with Saville, Van Dyk, Dufriche and Plançon; and at the recent production (in 1909) at the Metropolitan, with Caruso, Scotti, Farrar and Note.

Cast

CHEVALIER DES GRIEUX (*Shev-al-yay' deh Gree-ay'*) . . . . Tenor
COUNT DES GRIEUX, his father . . . . Bass
LESCAUT (*Les-koh'*) Manon's cousin, one of the Royal Guard . . . . Baritone
GUILLOT MORFONTEIN, a roué, Minister of France . . . . Bass
DE BRÉTIGNY (*Bray-tee-ynee'*) a nobleman . . . . Baritone
MANON, a school girl . . . . Soprano

People, Actresses, and Students

Time and place : 1721; Amiens, Paris, Havre.

The story of *Manon* is, of course, taken by Massenet's librettists from the famous novel of the Abbé Prévost, but for operatic purposes several changes have been made, notably in the events of the fourth act, which takes place in France instead of America. Although the tale is very well known, a brief sketch will be included here.

Manon is a country girl, gay, pretty and thoughtless, who meets a handsome young cavalier, *des Grieux*, while on her way to a convent to complete her education. He falls in love with her and she with him as far as her nature will allow, and when he tells her of the gaieties and pleasures of Paris, she needs little persuasion to induce her to elope with him to the Capital, to the chagrin of *Guillot*, whose carriage the lovers appropriate.

Soon tiring of love in a cottage, however, the young girl encourages the attentions of a rich nobleman, *de Brétigny*, and when *des Grieux* is taken away forcibly by his father, she siezes the opportunity and leaves with her new lover.

In Act III she learns that *des Grieux*, despondent because of her faithlessness, has resolved to enter a monastery. Her fickle affections turn again to him, and she visits him at the Seminary of St. Sulpice. He at first repulses her, saying his love is dead, but is unable to resist her, and they depart together.

The next act occurs in a gambling house, where *des Grieux* is endeavoring to win money to support *Manon* in the luxury she demands. *Guillot*, in revenge for the trick played on him in Act I, causes their arrest, *des Grieux* for cheating and *Manon* as a dissolute woman.

The last scene occurs on the road to Havre, where *des Grieux* and *Lescaut*, *Manon's* brother, plan to rescue *Manon* as she is being taken to the ship, en route to the prison colony in Louisiana. The soldiers appear, but it is a dying *Manon* they escort, and the unfortunate girl, after repenting and asking forgiveness of *des Grieux*, dies in his arms.

ACT I

SCENE 1—*Courtyard of an Inn at Amiens*

As the curtain rises the crowd of villagers, including *Lescaut,* are waiting the coming of the coach, which presently arrives and d scharges *Manon.* The young girl regards the animated scene with much interest, and soon espies *Lescaut,* her cousin, who was to meet her at this point and escort her to the convent school. He greets her and compliments her on her charming appearance. She blushes and then artlessly tells him of her impressions during the journey from her country home. The scene from this point has been recorded by the Scala singers.

Farrar as Manon

Restate qui (Wait a Moment)

By Elisa Tromben, Soprano; Federico Federici, Tenor; G. Pini-Corsi, Tenor; Riccardo Tegani, Baritone   (*In Italian*) *55000 12-inch, $1.50

Lescaut asks *Manon* to excuse him for a while as he must go to see after her luggage.

LESCAUT (*to Manon*):
Wait a moment.
Be prudent; I am going to find your luggage.

He goes out, and the townspeople desert the square, leaving *Manon* alone. The *roué,* *Guillot,* appears on the balcony of the hotel, crying: "Miserable landlord! Are we never to have any wine?"

He sees *Manon,* and his evil eyes light up at this vision of youth and beauty.

GUILLOT:
Heavens! What do I see?   Young lady!
Ahem! Ahem! Young lady!
(*Aside*)
Really, my head is turning round!

MANON (*aside and laughing*):
What a funny man!

GUILLOT:
Young lady, I am Guillot de Morfontaine. I am rich and would give a good deal to hear a word of love from you. Now, what do you say to that?

MANON:
That I should be ashamed, if I were not more disposed to laugh.

DE BRETIGNY:
Now then, Guillot, what's the game? We are waiting for you.

GUILLOT:
Oh, go to the Devil.

POUSETTE (*to Guillot*):
Are you not ashamed? At your age!

DE BRETIGNY:
This time I swear the dog has by chance found a prize.
Never did sweeter look light up a woman's face!
Now then, Guillot, let the girl alone and come in. We are calling you.

GUILLOT:
Ay, ay, in a moment.
(*To Manon*):
My little one, give me a word.

DE BRETIGNY:
Guillot, let the girl alone.

GUILLOT (*softly to Manon*):
A postillion is coming directly; when you see him, understand that a carriage is at your service. Take it, and afterwards you shall know more.

LESCAUT (*who has just entered*):
What do you say?

GUILLOT (*confused*):
Oh, sir! nothing, sir!

LESCAUT (*boisterously*):
Oh, sir! Did you say—

GUILLOT (*returning to the pavillion*):
Nothing, sir, I said.

Guillot is frightened by the gruff soldier, to the amusement of the bystanders, who laugh at the baffled libertine until he flees in confusion.

Lescaut now warns *Manon* to beware of the men she may meet.

LESCAUT (*to Manon*):
He spoke to you, Manon.

MANON (*lightly*):
Well, can you say 'twas my fault?

LESCAUT:
That's true; and in my eyes you are so good that I won't trouble myself.
(*The two guardsmen enter.*)

FIRST GUARDSMAN (*to Lescaut*):
How now! Thou comest not!

SECOND GUARDSMAN:
Both cards and dice are waiting your pleasure below.

LESCAUT:
I come; but first to this young lady, with your leave, good sirs,
I must speak some words of counsel full of wisdom.

GUARDSMEN (*in mock resignation*):
To his wisdom we'll listen.

Mi raccomando (Wait for Me)

By Elisa Tromben, Soprano; Federico Federici, Tenor; Chorus
(*In Italian*) *55000 12-inch, $1.50

The young girl promises to be prudent and *Lescaut* leaves with the guardsmen.

LESCAUT (*to Manon*):
Give good heed to what I say—
Duty calls me now away,
To consult these comrades here
Upon a point that's not quite clear.
Wait for me, Manon, just a moment, no more.
Make no mistake, but prudent be,
And if, forsooth, some silly man

Should whisper folly in your ear,
Behave as though you did not hear.
For safety's sake adopt that plan.
(*To the Guardsmen, aside*)
Now let us go and see on which of us the goddess of the game will look with loving eyes.
(*They go out.*)

Des Grieux now enters, and seeing *Manon,* is much impressed with her beauty and modest bearing. He addresses her respectfully, beginning the lovely duet, *Et je sais votre nom.*

Double-Faced Record—For title of opposite side see DOUBLE-FACED MANON RECORDS, page 201.

Et je sais votre nom (If I Knew But Your Name)

By Mlle. Korsoff, Soprano, and Léon Beyle, Tenor

(In French) *16551 10-inch, $0.75

The young girl answers simply, but feels herself strangely drawn to the young student. The transition from strangers to lovers is a quick one, as will be seen by the translation.

DES GRIEUX:
If I knew but your name—
MANON (with simplicity):
I am called Manon.
DES GRIEUX (with emotion):
Manon!
MANON (aside):
How tender are his looks,
How delightful his voice to my soul!
DES GRIEUX:
All my fond foolish words,
I pray you forgive!
MANON (naively):
How condemn your words when they charm my heart;
To my ears they are music!
Would to Heav'n such language were mine,
You fit answer to make.
DES GRIEUX (in a transport of joy):
Lovely enchantress, all-conquering beauty,
Manon, from henceforth thou art mistress of my heart!
MANON:
Oh! what joy!
I'm henceforth the mistress of his heart!
DES GRIEUX:
Ah, speak to me!
MANON:
I am only a simple maiden.
(Smiling)
Believe me, I'm not wicked,
But I often am told by those at home,
That I love pleasures too well;

(Sadly)
I am now on my way to a convent,
That, sir, is the story of Manon,
(With simplicity)
Of Manon Lescaut!
DES GRIEUX (with ardor):
No, I will not believe that fate can be so hard!
That one so young and so fair can be destined to dwell in a living tomb.
MANON:
But 'tis, alas! the sovereign will of Heaven,
To whose service I'm devoted,
And no one from this fate can deliver me.
DES GRIEUX (firmly):
No, no! Not from you, Manon, shall hope and joy be torn.
MANON (joyfully):
Oh, Heaven!
DES GRIEUX:
For on my will and power you can safely depend.
MANON (with energy):
Ah! to you I owe far more, far more than life.
DES GRIEUX (passionately):
Ah! Manon, you shall never leave me now!
Since I would gladly roam thro' all the world,
Seeking for you, love, an unknown retreat,
And carry you there in my arms.
MANON:
To you, my life and my soul!
To you I give my life for evermore!
DES GRIEUX:
Light of my soul! Manon,
The mistress of my heart for evermore!

Manon now observes the carriage of Guillot, which had been offered her, and suggests that they take it and fly together. Des Grieux joyfully agrees and they sing their second duet.

Nous vivrons à Paris (We Will Go to Paris)

By Mlle. Korsoff, Soprano, and Léon Beyle, Tenor

(In French) *45009 10-inch, $1.00

MANON AND DES GRIEUX:
We to Paris will go. Heart to heart!
And, though fortune may frown, never part!

Evermore bliss is ours,
And with love's sweetest flow'rs
Will we crown the bright hours!

Hearing Lescaut's voice from within the hotel, where he has been gambling, the lovers hastily enter the carriage and drive off, while Guillot swears revenge and Lescaut bewails his double loss of money and cousin.

ACT II

SCENE—Apartment of Des Grieux and Manon in Paris

Des Grieux is writing at a desk, while Manon is playfully looking over his shoulder.

J'écris à mon père (This Letter's for My Father)

By Mlle. Korsoff, Soprano, and Léon Beyle, Tenor

(In French) *45005 10-inch, $1.00

He tells her he is writing to his father:

DES GRIEUX:
This letter's for my father, and I tremble lest he should read in anger what I write from my heart.
MANON:
You are afraid?

DES GRIEUX:
Yes, Manon, I'm afraid.
MANON:
Ah, well, then we'll read it together.
DES GRIEUX:
Yes, that's the way. Together we'll read.

*Double-Faced Record—For title of opposite side see DOUBLE-FACED MANON RECORDS, page 201.

On l'appelle Manon (She is Called Manon)

By Mlle. Korsoff, Soprano, and Léon Beyle, Tenor

(*In French*) *45009 10-inch, $1.00

Continuing this charming scene, she takes the letter from him and reads with simplicity:

MANON:
"She is called Manon, and is young and fair. In her all charms unite. She has grace, radiant youth and beauty; music flows in a stream from her lips; in her eyes shines the tender light of love."
DES GRIEUX (*ardently*):
In her eyes shines the tender light of love.
MANON:
Is this true? Ah, I knew it not.
(*Tenderly*)
But I know how much I am loved.
DES GRIEUX (*with passion*):
Thou art loved! Manon, I adore thee!
MANON:
Come, come, good sir, there's more to read yet.
DES GRIEUX:
"Like a bird that through all lands follows

the spring, so her young soul to life is ever open. Her lips, like flowers, smile and speak to the zephyrs that kiss them in passing."
MANON (*repeating*):
"To the zephyrs that kiss them in passing."
(*Pensively*)
Do you think your father will give his consent?
DES GRIEUX:
Yes; he will never in such a matter as this oppose me.
MANON:
Dost thou desire it?
DES GRIEUX:
I desire it, with all my soul!
MANON:
Then embrace me, Chevalier. (*They embrace.*) And now, go;—send thy letter.

Des Grieux starts to go, but seeing some beautiful flowers on the table asks who sent them. *Manon* replies evasively, and asks if he does not trust her and if he is jealous. He assures her of his perfect confidence.

A noise is heard outside, and *Lescaut*, accompanied by *de Brétigny*, a French nobleman, enters, the former loudly demanding satisfaction from *des Grieux* for the abduction of his cousin. *Des Grieux* at first defies him, but remembering that he is a member of *Manon's* family, shows him the letter he had written to his father asking her hand in marriage. *Lescaut* engages him in conversation, thus giving *de Brétigny* an opportunity to speak to *Manon* aside. He tells her that *des Grieux* is to be carried off by his father that night, and urges her to fly with him. Tempted by the thoughts of wealth and pleasure, the young girl hesitates. *Lescaut* now loudly expresses satisfaction with the attitude of *des Grieux,* and departs with *de Brétigny.*

Des Grieux goes out to post the letter and *Manon* struggles with the temptation which has come to her; the pathetic air, *Adieu notre petite table,* indicating that she is yielding.

Adieu notre petite table (Farewell Our Little Table)

By Geraldine Farrar, Soprano (*In French*) 88146 12-inch, $3.00
By Mme. Vallandri, Soprano, and Léon Beyle, Tenor
(*In French*) *45008 10-inch, 1.00

NOTE.—In record 45008 Mme. Vallandri sings a portion of the "Farewell" solo and this is followed by the short duet which precedes the "Dream."

She regards the little table at which they had served their simple meals and bids it farewell.

MANON:
Farewell, our pretty little table! So small and yet so large for us. Side by side so often there we've sat. (*With a sad smile.*) I smile as now I call to mind what narrow space we lovers filled. A single glass served both of us, and each, in drinking, sought upon its margin where dear lips had been. Ah! best of friends, how thou hast loved!

Hearing *des Grieux* approaching, she hastily tries to conceal her tears. He observes them, however, and tries to soothe her by relating a dream he has had.

(*Italian*)   (*English*)   (*French*)

Il sogno—The Dream—Le Rêve

By Enrico Caruso, Tenor	(*In Italian*)	81031 10-inch,	$2.00
By Edmond Clement, Tenor,	(*In French*)	74258 12-inch,	1.50
By Fernando de Lucia, Tenor (*Piano acc.*)	(*In Italian*)	66001 10-inch,	1.50
By Léon Beyle, Tenor	(*In French*)	*45008 10-inch,	1.00
By Leo Slezak, Tenor	(*In German*)	61206 10-inch,	1.00

Double-Faced Record—For title of opposite side see DOUBLE-FACED MANON RECORDS, page 201.

"Listen, Manon," he cries, "On my way I dreamed a lovely dream."

DES GRIEUX:
With fancy's eye I saw, Manon,
A sweet and lowly cot,
Its white walls, deck'd with flowers fair,
Gleam'd thro' the wood!
Beneath whose peaceful shadows
Ran clear the babbling brook;
Overhead, 'mid verdant leaves
Sang so sweet and full the joyous birds,

'Tis paradise! Ah, no,
All is sad, so sad and dreary,
For, O my only love, thou art not there.

MANON (*softly*):
'Tis a vision, 'tis but a fancy!

DES GRIEUX:
No! for thus we'll pass our life,
If but thou wilt, O Manon!

A knock is heard and *Manon* exclaims, aside, "Oh, Heaven, already they have come for him!" She tries to prevent him from opening the door, but he insists, and is seized and carried away, while *Manon*, suddenly repenting, is overcome with grief.

ACT III

SCENE—*A Street in Paris on a Fête Day*

Manon enters, accompanied by *de Brétigny* and several gallants. She is in a gay mood and extols youth and love in a fine vocal gavotte, charmingly given here by Miss Farrar.

Gavotte—Obéissons quand leur voix appelle (Hear the Voice of Youth)

By Geraldine Farrar, Soprano   (*In French*)   87023   10-inch, $2.00

MANON:
List to the voice of youth when it calleth,
It bids ye to love for aye!
And ere the pride of beauty falleth,
Love then while you may.
Profit then by the time of youth,
And do not stay to count the days,
Remember well this adage—be merry and gay always!
The heart, alas, to love is e'er willing,
And ever willing to forget,
So while its pulse is thrilling,
Love, ere its day hath set!

Manon, seeing *des Grieux's* father, timidly approaches him and asks if *des Grieux* has forgotten her. She learns that the young man has forgiven her, buried his love, and is planning to enter a monastery. When the Count has departed, the capricious girl resolves to go to St. Sulpice and see for herself if she has been so easily forgotten; and as the curtain falls she is calling to *Lescaut* to conduct her thither.

SCENE II—*Reception Room at St. Sulpice*

At the beginning of this scene the Count pleads with his son not to retire from the world, but *des Grieux* says he is resolved, and his father takes a sorrowful leave.

Left alone, *des Grieux* sings his lovely song of renunciation, which the Victor offers in Italian, French and German by five famous tenors, the Caruso record also including the preceding recitative.

(*French*)   (*Italian*)   (*German*)   (*English*)

Ah, fuyez, douce image!—Dispar, vision—Flieh o flieh! (Depart, Fair Vision!)

NOTE—The Caruso record is preceded by the Recitative, "Je suis seul"

(Alone at Last!)

By Enrico Caruso, Tenor	(*In French*)	88348	12-inch,	$3.00
By Gino Giovannelli, Tenor	(*In Italian*)	*55001	12-inch,	1.50
By Florencio Constantino, Tenor	(*In Italian*)	74174	12-inch,	1.50
By Leo Slezak, Tenor	(*In German*)	64116	10-inch,	1.00
By M. Rocca, Tenor	(*In French*)	*16575	10-inch,	.75

Double-Faced Record—For title of opposite side see DOUBLE-FACED MANON RECORDS, page 201.

He declares he will now seek the peace of mind which only faith in Heaven can give.

> DES GRIEUX: I'm alone at last! The supreme moment now has
> come. From earthly ties I'm free, and only seek the rest
> which faith in heaven can give!
> Ah! depart, image fair,
> Leave me now at rest;
> Have regard to my prayer,
> Ease my poor tortured breast.
> To the dregs I have drain'd
> Life's most bitter cup,
> Nor to Heaven once complain'd,
> Though heart's blood filled it up.
> Dead to me now are love and all that men call glory. I de-
> sire to banish from my memory an evil name—a name
> which haunts me! Oh Heaven! with flame all searching,
> my soul now purge from stain! Oh! let thy pure and glo-
> rious light chase far away the gloom that lays on my heart.

He goes slowly out and *Manon* enters, shuddering at the gloomy walls and wondering if her lover has quite forgotten her. *Des Grieux* soon returns and is astounded to see *Manon*, bidding her begone, saying his love is dead. She says she cannot believe it.

> MANON:
> These eyes that oft thou hast kissed with ardor, do they shine no more, even through my weeping! Am I not myself? Do not turn away, but look on me. Am I not Manon?

Des Grieux is deeply moved, but asks Heaven for strength to resist her. Her pleadings finally have their effect, and he cries: "Ah! Manon! No longer will I struggle against myself!" and they depart together.

THE GAMBLING SCENE—ACT IV

ACT IV

SCENE—*A Gambling Room in Paris*

Des Grieux has been persuaded by *Manon* to come to this place in the hope of winning money to satisfy her desire for luxury. He plays for high stakes and wins large sums from *Guillot*, who leaves in a rage. As *des Grieux* is showing *Manon* the gold he has won, a loud knocking is heard and the police enter with *Guillot*, who denounces *des Grieux* as a swindler and *Manon* as his accomplice. They are arrested and taken to prison, but *des Grieux* is afterward released through his father's influence, while *Manon* is ordered to be deported to America by way of Havre.

ON THE HAVRE ROAD—ACT V

Concertato finale— O dolor

By Aristodemo Giorgini, Tenor; A. Santoro, Soprano; S. Nicolicchia, Baritone; and Chorus
(In Italian)
87083 10-inch, $2.00

ACT V

SCENE—*On the Road to Havre*

Des Grieux and Lescaut are on the Havre road, waiting for the soldiers who are escorting the prisoners to the ship bound for America, *des Grieux* having conceived the mad idea of rescuing *Manon*. Beginning the duet he sings his sad and remorseful air, *Manon in Chains!*

Manon, la catena (Manon in Chains!)

By Remo Andreini, Tenor; Riccardo Tegani, Baritone; and Chorus
(Double-Faced, see page 201) *(In Italian)* 55001 12-inch, $1.50

DES GRIEUX (*discovered seated by the wayside*):
Manon, poor Manon! Must I see thee herded with these wretched beings and be powerless to aid? O Heaven! Merciless Heaven! Must I then despair! (*He sees Lescaut approaching.*) He comes! (*Advancing impetuously to Lescaut.*) Thy fellows now make ready; the soldiers will soon reach this place. Thy men are fully armed; they will rescue Manon and give her back to me! What! can it not be done? Are all my fond hopes vain? Oh! why dost thou keep silence?

Lescaut hesitates and finally says:

LESCAUT:
Sir, I have done my best—
DES GRIEUX (*anxiously*):
Go on!
LESCAUT:
And grieve to say that all is lost.
DES GRIEUX (*piteously*):
Lost!
LESCAUT:
Scarce had the sun shone on the arms of the soldiers ere all our men fled!
DES GRIEUX (*distracted*):
'Tis false! 'Tis false! Great Heaven hath taken pity on my suffering, and at last comes the hour expected! In a moment my Manon shall be free!
LESCAUT (*sadly*):
Since I have told the truth—
DES GRIEUX (*about to strike him*):
Away!
LESCAUT:
Strike if you will. 'Tis soldier's fare. He's by the King ill-paid; and then, whate'er his worth, the good folks shake their head and call him "wretched fellow."
DES GRIEUX (*violently*):
Away!

The voices of the soldiers are now heard in the distance singing as they ride. *Des Grieux* and *Lescaut* listen attentively, and the former, realizing that they are almost at hand, madly tries to rush forward. *Lescaut* dissuades him, saying he has a better plan, as he is well acquainted with the officer in command. When the escort arrives, *Manon* is found to be very ill and is left behind by the officer at *Lescaut's* suggestion. During a heart-rending scene *Manon* asks and receives the forgiveness of *des Grieux*, repents her sins and dies in his arms.

DOUBLE-FACED AND MISCELLANEOUS MANON RECORDS

Restate qui (Wait a Moment) By Elisa Tromben, Soprano; Federico Federici, Tenor; G. Pini-Corsi, Tenor; Riccardo Tegani, Baritone (*In Italian*) Mi raccomando (Wait for Me) By Elisa Tromben, Soprano; Federico Federici, and Chorus (*In Italian*)	55000	12-inch,	$1.50
Io son solo (I'm Alone at Last) By Gino Giovannelli, Tenor (*In Italian*) Manon, la catena (Manon in Chains!) By Remo Andreini, Tenor; Riccardo Tegani, Baritone; Chorus (*In Italian*)	55001	12-inch,	1.50
Nous vivrons à Paris (We Will Go to Paris) By Mlle. Korsoff, Soprano; Léon Beyle, Tenor On l'appelle Manon (She is Called Manon) By Mlle. Korsoff, Soprano; Léon Beyle, Tenor (*In French*)	45009	10-inch,	1.00
Adieu, notre petite table (Farewell, Our Little Table) By Mme. Vallandri, Soprano; Léon Beyle, Tenor (*In French*) Le rêve (The Dream) By Léon Beyle, Tenor (*In French*)	45008	10-inch,	1.00
J'écris à mon père (This Letter's for My Father) By Mlle. Korsoff, Soprano; Léon Beyle (*In French*) Lakme—Dans la forêt, près de nous By Mme. Vallandri, Soprano; M. Rocca, Tenor (*In French*)	45005	10-inch,	1.00
Et je sais votre nom (If I Knew But Your Name) By Mlle. Korsoff, Soprano; Léon Beyle (*In French*) Favorita—Splendon piu belle in ciel le stelle By Perello de Segurola, Bass, and Chorus (*In Italian*)	16551	10-inch,	.75
Ah! fuyez douce image! (Depart Fair Vision) By M. Rocca, Tenor (*In French*) Carmen Selection (Bizet) By Pryor's Band	16575	10-inch,	.75

ACT III—SCENE 1

LANDE   SETTING OF ACT I

(Italian)

MANON LESCAUT

(Man-on' Les-ko')

OPERA IN FOUR ACTS

Music by Giacomo Puccini, the libretto (founded on Abbé Prévost's novel) being the work of the composer and a committee of friends. English version by Mowbray Marras. First presented in Milan in 1893. Produced at the Opéra-Comique, Paris, January 19, 1884; in English by the Carl Rosa Company, at Liverpool, January 17, 1885; at Drury Lane, May 7, 1885. In French at Covent Garden, May 19, 1881. First New York production, January 18, 1907.

Characters

MANON LESCAUT..Soprano
LESCAUT, sergeant of the King's Guards........................Baritone
CHEVALIER DES GRIEUX (*deh Gree-uay'*)...........................Tenor
GERONTE DE RAVOIR, Treasurer-General............................Bass
EDMUND, a student..Tenor

An Innkeeper, a Singer, a Dancing-master, a Sergeant, a Captain. Singers, Old Beaux and Abbés, Girls, Citizens, Villagers, Students, People, Courtezans, Archers, Sailors.

Scene and Period: Paris and vicinity; second half of the eighteenth century.

THE STORY

This early Puccini opera was performed by a struggling opera company in 1898, but the performance was so wholly bad that we have made no mention of it in our chronicle at the top of the page. The real New York *premiere* was of course the Metropolitan production in 1907, when Puccini himself was present. An English version of the opera was given in Philadelphia, however, by Gustav Hinrichs during one of his summer seasons,—August 29, 1894.

The Abbé Prévost romance has been treated operatically by several composers, the first being Halévy, who wrote a ballet on the subject in 1830. Other settings followed—by Balfe, 1836; Auber in 1856 and Massenet in 1884.

Puccini's version consists of four detached scenes selected from the novel, and the hearer should possess some knowledge of the story to fully understand the action of the opera.

The first act shows the courtyard of an inn at Amiens. *Manon's* brother, *Lescaut,* a dissolute soldier, is escorting his pretty little sister to the convent where she is to complete her education. While *Lescaut* is carousing with some chance companions, *Manon* meets a handsome gallant, *des Grieux,* who chances to be dining at the inn, dressed as a student. The prospect of school not appealing strongly to the young girl, she readily agrees to elope with *des Grieux,* thereby spoiling the plans of the old *roué, Geronte,* who had planned to abduct the pretty school girl. *Manon* soon tires of *des Grieux* and his poverty, and leaves him for the wealthy *Geronte;* but even this luxury fails to bring her happiness, and when *des Grieux* appears again she runs away with him.

FARRAR AS MANON

Geronte is furious and denounces *Manon* to the police as an abandoned woman. She is condemned to be deported to the French possessions in Louisiana. *Des Grieux* and *Lescaut* try to rescue her, but the attempt fails, and in desperation the former begs the commandant to permit him to accompany her to America.

In the final scene the lovers are shown in a desert near New Orleans. (The Abbé Prévost's knowledge of American geography was evidently limited!) *Des Grieux* leaves *Manon* to search for water, and returns just in time to see her die in his arms, after a most affecting scene.

ACT I

SCENE—*A Street in front of an Inn at Amiens*

Des Grieux, dressed as a student, strolling among the crowd, meets *Edmund* and a party of students, who warmly greet him. He is in a gay mood and addresses some of the girls who are passing, asking them, in this charming air, if there is one among them who will take pity on his lonely condition.

Tra voi belle brune (Now Among You)

By Franco de Gregorio, Tenor　　　　(*In Italian*)　*45015　10-inch, $1.00

This gay song is effectively given by one of the Victor's new tenors, of the La Scala forces, and the record is doubled with the Madrigale from Act II.

A diligence now arrives, and *Manon* and her brother and *Geronte,* a chance traveling companion, alight. *Des Grieux* is struck with the beauty of the young girl, and when *Lescaut* and *Geronte* have gone into the inn to arrange for quarters, he questions her respectfully. She tells him that she is bound for a convent, but does not wish to go. *Lescaut* now calls to his sister, and she enters the inn after promising to meet *des Grieux* later in the evening.

The young man gazes after her, and says to himself that never has he seen so lovely a picture of youth and innocence. He expresses his emotion in a fine air, one of the loveliest of the numbers allotted to *des Grieux.* (On the reverse side is an air from Tosca.)

Donna non vidi mai (Never Did I Behold)

By Egidio Cunego, Tenor　　　　(*In Italian*)　*45016　10-inch, $1.00

The students now gather round, bantering *des Grieux* on his new conquest, but he is in no mood for joking and goes into the inn. *Lescaut* now joins a crowd of soldiers who are gambling, and soon becomes absorbed in the game. *Geronte,* seeing the brother thus engaged, seeks the landlord and plots to abduct *Manon. Edmund* overhears the scheme and informs *des Grieux,* who finds *Manon* and induces her to elope with him. They take the carriage which *Geronte* had ordered and make their escape, leaving him furious. How-

Double-Faced Record—For title of opposite side see DOUBLE-FACED MANON LESCAUT RECORDS, page 205.

ever, he finds *Lescaut* and suggests that they go to Paris in search of the runaways. *Lescaut*, who has been drinking, consents, delicately hinting that if *Geronte* will admit him into the family group, he will use his influence to induce *Manon* to desert *des Grieux* for the older but wealthier suitor.

ACT II

SCENE—*An Apartment in Geronte's House in Paris*

Since the events of Act I *Manon* is supposed to have left *des Grieux* for the wealthier *Geronte*. She is seen surrounded by the utmost luxury, attended by her hairdresser, dancing master, etc. *Lescaut* enters, evidently much at home, and congratulates her on her change of fortune, taking to himself all the credit for having advised her so cleverly. She says she is happy and contented, but asks *Lescaut* if he has heard any news of *des Grieux*—whether he is grieving or whether he has already forgotten her. *Lescaut* tells her that the young man is gambling in order to get wealth to win her back to him.

Manon gazes pensively at the rich hangings, and in a fine air expresses her longing for the humble cottage she has left.

In quelle trine morbide (In Those Silken Curtains)
By Gina C. Viafora, Soprano (*In Italian*) 64094 10-inch, $1.00

They are interrupted by the entrance of a company of Madrigal singers who have been sent by *Geronte* to amuse *Manon*. They sing a beautiful Madrigal, given here by Signora Lopez-Nunes and La Scala Chorus.

Madrigale—Sulla vetta del monte (Speed O'er Summit)
By Lopez-Nunes, Soprano, and Chorus (*In Italian*) *45015 10-inch, $1.00

When the singers have departed, the dancing master appears to teach *Manon* the minuet. She takes her lesson, while *Geronte* and several friends watch her admiringly. In a gay mood she sings a little song to the air of the minuet.

Minuetto di Manon, "L'ora o Tirsi" (Joyful Hours)
By Frances Alda, Soprano (*In Italian*) 87079 10-inch, $2.00

Des Grieux now enters and reproaches *Manon* bitterly. At the sight of him her love returns, and she begs him to take her away from all this luxury. They sing a passionate duet, followed by a lovely solo for *des Grieux*, who reproaches *Manon* for her fickleness.

MANON IN LUXURY—ACT II

Double-Faced Record—For title of opposite side see DOUBLE-FACED MANON LESCAUT RECORDS, page 205.

Ah! Manon, mi tradisce (Manon, Kind and Gentle)

By Franco de Gregorio, Tenor   (*In Italian*)   *45027   10-inch, $1.00
By Giorgio Malesci, Tenor   (*In Italian*)   *63421   10-inch,   .75

Geronte surprises them, but controls his rage, and sarcastically wishing them a pleasant *tête-à-tête,* goes out. *Lescaut* shortly afterward rushes in and announces that *Geronte* has sent for the police. *Des Grieux* begs *Manon* to escape at once, but she insists on collecting her jewels first. This delay is fatal, and she is arrested and taken to prison, charged with being an abandoned woman.

Intermezzo (Between Acts II and III)

By Arthur Pryor's Band   *35003   12-inch, $1.25

Now comes the exquisite intermezzo, which gives a musical picture of the journey to Havre of *Des Grieux* to secure the release of *Manon,* and of his resolution to follow and protect her wherever she may be sent—"Even to the end of the world!" cries the unhappy lover.

This number exhibits well the genius of this composer in making the orchestra reflect the incidents and passions of the story instead of using it as a mere accompaniment.

ACT III

SCENE—*The Harbor at Havre*

Manon has been banished from France, and is now embarking on the ship for the French colony in Louisiana. *Des Grieux,* unable to secure her release, entreats the officers to permit him to go on board. The captain, touched by the grief of the unhappy lovers, consents, and with a cry of joy *Des Grieux* embarks just as the ship is sailing.

ACT IV

SCENE—*A Desolate Spot in Louisiana*

This act is merely a long duet in which the sad, but very human, tragedy is ended. The music portrays the failing strength of *Manon,* the despair of *Des Grieux* when he is powerless to aid her, the last farewell of the lovers, and the bitter grief of the unhappy young man when *Manon* dies. As she expires, unable to bear more, he falls senseless on her body.

DOUBLE-FACED AND MISCELLANEOUS MANON LESCAUT RECORDS

Intermezzo (Between Acts II and III)	By Pryor's Band	35003 12-inch,	$1.25
Tosca Selection	*By Arthur Pryor's Band*		
Manon Selection	By Arthur Pryor's Band	35052 12-inch,	1.25
El Capitan March (*Sousa*)	*By Sousa's Band*		
Tra voi belle brune (Now Among You)	By Franco de Gregorio, Tenor (*In Italian*)	45015 10-inch,	1.00
Madrigale—Sulla vetta del monte (Speed O'er Summit)	By Lopez-Nunes, Soprano, and Chorus (*In Italian*)		
Donna non vidi mai (Never Did I Behold)	By Egidio Cunego, Tenor (*In Italian*)	45016 10-inch,	1.00
Tosca—Gia mi struggea	*By Ernesto Badini, Baritone* (*In Italian*)		
Ah! Manon, mi tradisce (Manon, Kind and Gentle)	By Franco de Gregorio, Tenor (*In Italian*)	45027 10-inch,	1.00
Gioconda—Cielo e Mar! (*Heaven and Ocean*)	*By Franco de Gregorio, Tenor* (*In Italian*)		
Ah! Manon, mi tradisce	By Giorgio Malesci, Tenor (*In Italian*)	63421 10-inch,	.75
Ernani—Infelice e tu credevi (*Unhappy One!*)	*By Aristodemo Sillich, Bass* (*In Italian*)		

* Double-Faced Record—For title of opposite side see above list.

PAINTED BY BECKER MARRIAGE OF FIGARO AND SUSANNA

(Italian)
NOZZE DI FIGARO
(Not'-zay de Fee'-gar-oh)

(French)
MARIAGE DE FIGARO
(Mah-ree-ahzh' deh Fee'-gah-row)

(English)
THE MARRIAGE OF FIGARO

OPERA IN FOUR ACTS

Text by Lorenza da Ponte, founded on a comedy by Beaumarchais of the same name. Music by Mozart. First production at the National Theatre, Vienna, May 1, 1786. In Paris as *Le Mariage de Figaro*, in five acts, with Beaumarchais' spoken dialogue, at the Academie, March 20, 1793; at the Theatre Lyrique, as *Les Noces de Figaro*, by Barbier and Carré, in four acts, May 8, 1858. In London, in Italian, at the King's Theatre, June 18, 1812. First American production April 8, 1835, in English. Some notable revivals were—in the 70's, with Hersee, Sequin and Parepa-Rosa; in 1889, with Nordica, Eames, de Reszke, Ancona and Arnoldson; in 1902, with Sembrich, Eames, Fritzi Scheff, de Reszke and Campanari; and in 1909, with Sembrich, Eames, Farrar and Scotti.

Cast

FIGARO, *(Fee'-gah--roh)* the Barber, valet to the Count....................Bass
COUNT ALMAVIVA, *(Al-mah-vee'-vah)* a Spanish noble...............Baritone
COUNTESS ALMAVIVA, his wife ....Soprano
SUSANNA, maid of the Countess, betrothed to Figaro...............Soprano
CHERUBINO, *(Chay-rue-bee'-noh)* page to the Countess................Soprano
MARCELLINA, *(Mar-chel-lee'-nah)* servant to Bartolo ....Contralto
BARTOLO, a rejected lover of Susanna ....Bass
BASILIO, *(Bah-zee'-lee-oh)* a busybody..................................Tenor
DON CURZIO ....Tenor
ANTONIO, gardener to the Count....................................Bass

Servants, Country People, Guards.

Scene and Period: Seville; the seventeenth century. The action is a direct continuation of the Barber of Seville.

SETTING OF ACT I AT LA SCALA

Mozart's Marriage of Figaro, with its merry plot and music, is one of the most delightful of musical comedies, and regret must be expressed for the all too infrequent performance of this ever-young and lovely opera, in which the complications of the story, the quick changes of mood, and the sparkling humor are all so well reflected in the music. In no single opera, perhaps, is there such a succession of musical gems as in Figaro. Each is perfect in its way and each seems to enhance the beauty of the others.

This comedy by Beaumarchais, on which the plot is founded, has been utilized by many composers, Mozart's version being written in 1785.

Those who have read the story of *Barber of Seville* will find themselves again making the acquaintance of *Bartolo*, *Almaviva* and *Figaro*, some time after the marriage of the dashing *Count* to *Bartolo's* ward. The *Count* has settled down quietly on his estates, while *Figaro*, as a reward for his services as a match-maker, has been appointed major-domo of the castle. *Figaro* is in love with the *Countess'* maid *Susanna*, and expects to marry her soon, but unfortunately for his plans, had also promised to wed *Marcellina*, the ex-housekeeper of *Bartolo*, on the very same day. Further complications are promised by the fact that the *Count*, already wearying of his wife, is making love to *Susanna* himself.

THE GREAT HALL OF BARTOLO'S PALACE—ACT I, SCENE II

ACT I

SCENE I—*A Room in the Count's Chateau*

Overture

By Arthur Pryor's Band
*35109   12-inch, $1.25

The overture is a most delightful one, written in true Mozartian style, and Mr. Pryor has given a brilliant reading of it, bringing out all its beauties.

Double-Faced Record—For title of opposite side see double-faced list on page 211.

At the opening of the opera *Susanna* tells *Figaro* that the *Count* is trying to flirt with her, and *Figaro* plans revenge. *Marcellina* has confided in *Dr. Bartolo*, and as the portly doctor still harbors a grudge against *Figaro* for robbing him of his ward, he consents to help her. The *Countess*, who seems to be the only one in the castle not engaged in intrigue of some kind, thinks only of her husband, and how to bring him back to her side.

ACT II

SCENE I—*Apartment of the Countess*

At the beginning of Scene II, the *Countess* sings her lovely appeal to Cupid.

Porgi amor (Love, Thou Holy Impulse)

By Johanna Gadski, Soprano	(*In Italian*)	88275	12-inch, $3.00
By Teresa Arkel, Soprano (*Double-faced, see page 211*)	(*Italian*)	63419	10-inch, .75

The *Countess* is one of Mme. Gadski's most effective impersonations, and she makes an imposing figure in her royal garb, singing the Mozart music with a richness of voice which is always a delight to the ear. The *Porgi amor*, with its melancholy undertone, never seems to be heard at its best at the opera, as it is introduced under rather trying conditions—at the very beginning of a scene and without preparatory recitative. Certainly Mme. Gadski has never sung this lovely air better than at this time, it being delivered with much purity of tone and genuine sentiment. The record will be pronounced one of the most satisfactory and appealing interpretations in the artist's entire list.

Susanna tells the *Countess* of her husband's fickleness and they consult *Figaro*, who plans to make the *Count* jealous by telling him that the *Countess* is to meet a lover that evening in the garden. It is planned to send *Marcellina* in the *Countess'* place, and *Cherubino*, dressed as a young girl, to meet the *Count* in *Susanna's* place.

Figaro departs, and *Cherubino* enters. Seeing his mistress, he begins to heave deep sighs, but *Susanna* mocks him and tells the *Countess* he has written a song about his lady love. The *Countess* bids him sing it, and he takes his guitar and describes the delights and torments caused by Cupid's arrow.

GADSKI AND REICELMAN AS COUNTESS AND CHERUBINO

Voi che sapete (What is This Feeling?)

By Nellie Melba, Soprano (*In Italian*)
88067 12-inch, $3.00

By Luisa Tetrazzini, Soprano (*In Italian*)
88300 12-inch, 3.00

The song is in ballad form, to suit the situation, the voice giving out the clear, lovely melody, while the stringed instruments carry on a simple accompaniment *pizzicato*, to imitate the guitar; and this delicate outline is shaded and animated by solo wind instruments.

It is difficult to say which to admire most—the gracefulness of the melodies, the delicacy of disposition of the parts, the charm of the tone-coloring, or the tenderness of expression—the whole is of entrancing beauty.

CHERUBINO:
What is this feeling makes me so sad?
What is this feeling makes me so glad?
Pain that delights me,—How can it be?
Pleasure that pains me.—
Fetter'd though free!
Whence, too, these yearnings,
Strange to myself?
Tell me their meaning, spirit or elf!

Why am I burning? Why do I freeze?
Restless forever, never at ease.
All is so altered, nothing's at rest,
Or are these changes but in my breast?
Gentler the breezes, day is more bright;
Fairer the moonbeams shine on the night:
Greener the forest, greener the hill,
Soft, too, the music flows from each rill.

SCENE—ACT III

The women now dress up the page to represent *Susanna,* and have no sooner finished when the *Count* knocks, and *Cherubino* hides in the closet. The *Count* observes his wife's confusion, and hearing noises in the closet, becomes jealous. He demands that she open the closet door, and when she refuses he goes for a crowbar. The moment he is out *Cherubino,* aided by *Susanna,* slips out and escapes through the window, and *Susanna* enters the closet in his place. When the *Count* returns and opens the door, the maid comes out and the husband is forced to apologize for his suspicions.

Marcellina now enters with her lawyer and demands that *Figaro* shall keep his promise to marry her. The *Count* promises to look into the matter.

ACT III
SCENE I—*A Cabinet in the Count's Residence*

The third act opens with a scene between *Susanna* and the *Count.* He plans to force her to accept his attentions by threatening to make *Figaro* wed the ancient *Marcellina,* while *Susanna* endeavors to gain time. This scene is continued in a charming and graceful duet.

THE COUNT IS JEALOUS—ACT II

Crudel perchè finora (Too Long You Have Deceived Me)
By Geraldine Farrar, Soprano, and Antonio Scotti, Baritone
(In Italian)   89027   12-inch, $4.00

Susanna pretends to encourage the attentions of the *Count*, in furtherance of the plot conceived by the *Countess;* while at the same time she deftly repels his advances. Finally she promises to meet him in the arbor and the *Count* is in ecstasies.

COUNT:
Too long you have deceived me;
Hope, weary, bids farewell.
SUSANNA:
What passes in her bosom
A maiden dreads to tell.
COUNT:
You'll meet me in the grove, then?
SUSANNA:
When sunset's on the lea.
COUNT:
And do not mean it falsely?
SUSANNA:
Oh, no; rely on me!
COUNT (aside):
What transport now is flying
Thro' this enraptured breast!
SUSANNA (aside):
Oh, may the scheme I'm trying,
Bring all to peace and rest!

COUNT:
Then, by the garden bower?
SUSANNA:
At twilight I will be.
COUNT:
You'll not forget the hour?
SUSANNA:
Oh, no, depend on me.
COUNT:
In the garden?
SUSANNA:
Yes!
COUNT:
You'll not forget?
SUSANNA:
No! No! No! Oh, no, depend on me!
COUNT (retiring):
I have won her!
SUSANNA (aside):
Well, cunning as you are, sir,
This time you've met your match!

Of the seven duets in which *Susanna* takes part in the opera, the *Crudel perche* is the most effective, and Miss Farrar and Mr. Scotti, both accomplished Mozart singers, deliver it delightfully. The accompaniment, so all-important in Mozart's works, is perfectly played under Mr. Rogers' direction.

They separate, each satisfied with the interview,—the *Count* believing she has yielded, and *Susanna* convinced that she has him in a trap.

Marcellina, with her lawyer, *Bartolo* and *Figaro* now enter, and *Figaro* is informed that he must wed *Marcellina* or pay damages; but the discovery of a birthmark proves him to be the long lost son of *Marcellina*. He embraces his mother just as *Susanna* comes in, and she, seeing *Figaro* with his arms around the woman he was lately trying to avoid, decides that he has changed his mind. Matters are explained, however, and preparations for the wedding are begun.

Susanna now seeks the *Countess* and tells her mistress that the *Count* wishes to meet her (*Susanna*) in the garden. The *Countess* then dictates a letter in which *Susanna* is to appoint a time and place for the meeting. The writing of this letter is portrayed in the delicate *Letter Duet*.

Che soave zeffiretto (Letter Duet—Song to the Zephyr)
By Marcella Sembrich, Soprano, and Emma Eames, Contralto
(In Italian)   95202   12-inch, $5.00

This number is always greatly enjoyed in representations of the opera, being a fine example of the Mozartian style and full of beauties, not only in the vocal parts, but in the masterly orchestration.

SCENE II—Hall in the Chateau

In this scene *Figaro* and *Susanna* are married, and in the course of the festivities *Susanna* contrives to slip the note to the *Count*, who is overjoyed.

ACT IV
SCENE—The Garden of the Chateau

The last setting shows the garden where the most delightful of the comedy scenes takes place. *Susanna*, disguised as the *Countess*, and the *Countess* disguised as *Susanna*, enter. The mistress conceals herself, while *Susanna*, awaiting the *Count*, and knowing that *Figaro* is listening, sings her famous soliloquy.

Deh vieni non tardar (Oh, Come, My Heart's Delight)
By Marcella Sembrich, Soprano   (In Italian)   88020   12-inch, $3.00

She pours out her whole soul in this address to the imaginary lover, in order to increase the jealousy of *Figaro*, who is hidden near by. This is one of the most exquisite numbers in the opera, and Mme. Sembrich's singing of it always remains long in the memory of those who hear her in *Nozze*.

THE GARDEN—ACT IV

COPY'T DUPONT

DE LUSSAN AS CHERUBINO

SUSANNA:
Ah, why so long delay? speed, speed thee
hither!
While thou'rt away, all nature seems to
wither.
Tho' bright the moon, and bright the stars are
glowing,
Deeper around the wood its shade is throwing.
In ev'ry gentle murmur of the river,
In the rustling reeds that near it quiver,
A voice to love invites, the bosom filling
With love alone, all other passions stilling;—
Come then, my dearest,—the hours are quickly
flying!
Let me with roses bind now thy head!

Cherubino, having an appointment with the maid *Barbarina,*
now enters, and seeing the *Countess,* thinks it is *Susanna* and
kisses her. The *Countess* struggles, and the little rascal says:

CHERUBINO:
Why to me a kiss deny?
With the Count you are not shy!
Come, come, give o'er, then,
And strive no more, then;
One kiss to your little friend!

The *Count* arrives just in time to see this, and giving
Cherubino a box on the ear, sends him flying. He then makes
love to the supposed *Susanna,* the *Countess* disguising her voice
and encouraging him. *Figaro* now sees *Susanna,* whom he
of course takes to be the *Countess,* and tells her that her husband and *Susanna* are together.
Susanna reveals herself and *Figaro* embraces her. The *Count* sees this embrace and his
jealousy making him forget his new conquest, he seizes *Figaro* and calls for help. The
plot is now revealed, and the *Count,* confessing he is conquered, begs the *Countess'* forgiveness
and promises to be a model husband. As the curtain falls the three happy couples are
entering the house to continue the marriage festivities.

DOUBLE-FACED MARRIAGE OF FIGARO RECORDS

{Overture	By Arthur Pryor's Band}	35109 12-inch, $1.25
{ *Fra Diavolo Overture*	By Arthur Pryor's Band}	
{Porgi amor	By Teresa Arkel, Soprano (In Italian)	63419 10-inch, .75
{ *Toglietemi la vita ancor—Romanza*	By Teresa Arkel (In Italian)	

(Italian)

MARTA

(Mahr'-tah)

(English)

MARTHA

(Mahr'-thah)

OPERA IN FOUR ACTS

Libretto by St. George and Friedrich. Music by Friedrich von Flotow. The opera is an elaboration of "Lady Henrietta, or the Servant of Greenwich," a ballet-pantomime, with text by St. George and music by Flotow, Burgmuller and Deldevez, which was suggested by an actual incident and presented in Paris in 1844. *Martha* was first produced at the Court Opera, Vienna, November 25, 1847. First London production July 1, 1858, at Covent Garden, in Italian. First American production 1852, in German.

Characters of the Drama

LADY HARRIET DURHAM, Maid-of-honor to Queen Anne . . . . Soprano
NANCY, her friend . . . . Mezzo-Soprano
SIR TRISTAN MICKLEFORD, Lady Harriet's cousin . . . . Bass
PLUNKETT, a wealthy farmer . . . . Bass
LIONEL, his foster-brother, afterwards Earl of Derby . . . . Tenor
THE SHERIFF OF RICHMOND . . . . Bass
THREE SERVANTS OF LADY HARRIET, ... Tenor and Two Basses
THREE MAIDSERVANTS, ... Soprano and Mezzo-Soprano

Chorus of Ladies, Servants, Farmers, Hunters and Huntresses, Pages, etc.

The scene is laid, at first, in the Castle of Lady Harriet, then in Richmond and environs, during the reign of Queen Anne.

Flotow's melodious opera has always been a most popular one, with its spirited Fair Scene, its beautiful duets and quartet, the famous third act finale and the beloved "Last Rose of Summer."

The composer was of noble birth, a son of Baron von Flotow of Mecklenburg, and was born in 1812. His father destined him for a diplomat, but the boy loved music, and went to Paris to study. His first attempt at opera was *Pierre et Catharine,* followed by *Stradella* and others.

Many great *prima donne* have sung the role of *Martha*—Patti, Nilsson, Kellogg, Gerster, Richings, Parepa Rosa; and in the present day Sembrich, have charmed their audiences with Flotow's beautiful strains.

The fine overture, which contains many of the best known melodies, is splendidly played here by the band. On the reverse side of the double-faced (35133) is a 'cello solo by Sorlin.

LIONEL AND PLUNKETT—ACT I

Overture

By Pryor's Band *35133   12-inch, $1.25
By Pryor's Band   31478   12-inch, 1.00

ACT I

SCENE I—*Boudoir of Lady Harriet*

Lady Harriet, maid-of-honor to Queen Anne, is weary of the monotony of court life. She is bored by her admirers, and jewels and flowers pall upon her. "Why do you weep?" says her faithful maid, *Nancy.* "I do not know," exclaims *Harriet. Nancy,* beginning the duet, ventures to guess.

---

*Double-Faced Record—For title of opposite side see DOUBLE-FACED MARTHA RECORDS, page 217.

Mesta ognor (Ah, These Tears)
By Louise Homer, Contralto, and Bessie Abott, Soprano
(*In Italian*)   89009   12-inch, $4.00

NANCY:
Of the knights so brave and charming
Who surround our gracious queen,
And themselves with wit are arming,
Some one has so lucky been
Your cold and haughty heart to win!
Is there aught in this alarming?
LADY HARRIET:
Vain belief! How can rejoice me
Such insipid, idle love?
For to please and interest me
Flattery is not enough!
NANCY:
Riches heap on you their treasures,
Honor high is offered you.
LADY HARRIET:
In the midst of gold and pleasures
Weariness alone I see.
NANCY:
This is really too distressing;
Her's is called a brilliant lot!
If love does not work a wonder,

This flower fades and blossoms not!
Balls and tournaments are giving,
And your colors win the prize,
Proudly from the banners waving,
While the victor vainly sighs
For a smile from your fair eyes,
Which his armor penetrated!
LADY HARRIET:
All my glowing ardent wishes
Please me not when they're fulfill'd!
What of happiness I dreamed
Always has disgust instill'd.
The homages they offer,
Praise and honor they bestow,
Leave me joyless, once obtained
Make me not with pride to glow.
NANCY:
Then, from ennui to save you,
Nothing is for you remaining
But to let your heart be conquer'd,
Not a particle retaining!

Tristan, Harriet's cousin, a gay but rather ancient beau, is now announced and proposes a long list of diversions for *Harriet's* amusement. She declines them all and teases him unmercifully. The song of the servant maids, on their way to the Richmond Fair, now floats in through the window; and hearing these strains of the happy peasants, *Harriet* conceives a madcap desire to accompany them. *Nancy* and *Tristan* protest, but she orders them to go with her. Dresses are procured and they start for the fair, the ladies in the disguise of servant girls, and *Tristan* garbed as a farmer.

SCENE II—*The Fair at Richmond*

The scene changes to the Richmond Fair, where a motley crowd of men and maidens are looking for positions. Two young farmers, *Plunkett* and *Lionel,* now enter, the latter

THE FAIR SCENE

being an orphan and adopted brother of *Plunkett. Lionel's* father, on his deathbed, had given *Plunkett* a ring, which was to be presented to the *Queen* should the son ever be involved in difficulties.

In this fine duet, one of the gems of Flotow's popular romantic opera, the friends speak of *Lionel's* father and the incident of the ring.

Solo, profugo (Lost, Proscrib'd)

By Enrico Caruso and Marcel Journet   (*In Italian*)   89036   12-inch, $4.00
By Van Hoose and de Gogorza   (*In Italian*)   74005   12-inch, 1.50
By Reinald Werrenrath, Baritone; Harry Macdonough, Tenor
                                     (*In English*)   31769   12-inch, 1.00

Lionel tells the story of his adoption by *Plunkett's* family in the fine aria beginning—

Ne gram-mar sa - per po - tem - mo chi foss' ei, don - de ve - nia
We have nev - er learn'd your sta - tion, nev - er knew your fa ther's rank

This air is universally popular and has been used for many poems, including several hymns. *Plunkett* then sings—

So - lo, pro - fu - go, re jet - to, Di mia vi - ta 'sul mat - tin,.
Lost, pro - scrib'd, a friend-less pil - grim, Sink ing at your cot - tage door.

and tells of the great love he has for his adopted brother.

The duet, which is a very beautiful one, then follows:

PLUNKETT:
We have never learnt his station,
  Never knew your father's rank;
  All he left to tell the secret
  Was the jewel on your hand.
"If your fate should ever darken,"
  Quoth he, "Show it to the Queen;
She will save you, she will guard you
  When no other help is seen."

LIONEL:
Here in peace and sweet contentment
  Have I passed my life with you;
Stronger, daily, grew a friendship
  That forever lasts, when true.
BOTH: Brother, think not wealth and splendor,
  If perchance they e'er be mine,
Can as happy this heart render
  As the friendship fix'd in thine.

The disguised ladies now appear, accompanied by the unwilling and disgusted *Tristan,* who considers the whole affair a joke in very bad taste. The two young farmers spy the girls, and being much taken with their looks, offer to hire them. The ladies, carrying further their mad prank, accept the money which is offered them, not knowing that they are legally bound thereby to serve their new masters for a year. *Tristan* loudly protests, but is hooted off the grounds, and the frightened girls are taken away by the farmers.

ACT II

THE SPINNING WHEEL QUARTETTE

SCENE—*A Farmhouse*

As the curtain rises the farmers enter, dragging with them the unwilling and terrified maidens.

When the ladies have recovered their breath and begin to realize that they are in no immediate danger, the temptation to plague their employers is irresistible, and when the young men endeavor to instruct the new servants in their duties the fun commences.

The maidens determine to lead their captors a strenuous life, and when they are ordered to get supper they promptly refuse.

Spinning Wheel Quartet

By Victor Opera Quartet   (*In English*)   70052   12-inch, $1.25

Astonished at such revolutionary conduct from servants, the young men exclaim:

LIONEL AND PLUNKETT:
Surpris'd I am and astounded,
And I can say no more;
Such impudence unbounded
Was never seen before!

HARRIET AND NANCY:
Surpris'd they are and confounded,
And sorely puzzled is their brain;
This blow has smartly sounded,
May be they'll never try again!

The girls are then requested to show their skill at the spinning wheels. When they confess ignorance of the art the young men offer to teach them:

LIONEL AND PLUNKETT (*spinning*):
When the foot the wheel turns lightly
Let the hand the thread entwine;
Draw and twist it, neatly, tightly,
Then 'twill be both strong and fine.

HARRIET AND NANCY (*sitting at the wheels*):
What a charming occupation
Thus to make the thread entwine;
Gently guided, drawn and twisted,
It becomes both strong and fine!

Nancy leads *Plunkett* a merry chase, causing him to lose his temper, while *Lionel* finds himself falling in love with the beautiful *Martha*. She laughs at him, but is nevertheless impressed with his good looks and manly bearing; so much so that when he asks her to sing she consents, and taking the rose from her bosom she sings the exquisite "Last Rose of Summer."

Last Rose of Summer

By Adelina Patti, Soprano	(*In English*)	95030	12-inch,	$5.00
By Luisa Tetrazzini, Soprano	(*In English*)	88308	12-inch,	3.00
By Marcella Sembrich, Soprano	(*In English*)	88102	12-inch,	3.00
By Alice Nielsen, Soprano	(*In English*)	74121	12-inch,	1.50
By Elizabeth Wheeler, Soprano (*Double-Faced*)	(*In English*)	16813	10-inch,	.75
By Elizabeth Wheeler, Soprano	(*In English*)	5739	10-inch,	.60

SEMBRICH AS MARTHA—ACT I

As is generally known, this air is not by Flotow, but is an old Irish tune, to which Moore fitted his poem. In fact, Martha undoubtedly owes much of its vogue to this ancient Irish air. The melody is a very old one called "The Groves of Blarney." Moore wrote the words about 1813, and they have become the most popular of all his verses.

'Tis the last rose of summer,
Left blooming alone;
All her lovely companions
Are faded and gone;
No flower of her kindred,
No rosebud is nigh
To reflect back her blushes,
Or give sigh for sigh!

I'll not leave thee, thou lov'd one,
To pine on the stem;
Since the lovely are sleeping,
Go sleep thou with them.
Thus kindly I scatter
Thy leaves o'er the bed—
Where thy mates of the garden
Lie scentless and dead!

The farmers, somewhat subdued by the knowledge that they have engaged two most spirited and insubordinate damsels, now bid their new-found servants good night in this beautiful number, one of the gems of Flotow's opera.

Good Night Quartet

By The Lyric Quartet   (*In English*)   5855   10-inch, $0.60

PLUNKETT AND LIONEL:
Midnight sounds!
LADY AND NANCY:
Midnight sounds!
LIONEL (*to Martha*):
Cruel one, may dreams transport thee
To a future rich and blest!
And tomorrow, gently yielding,
Smile upon me! sweetly rest!
PLUNKETT (*to Nancy*):
Sleep thee well, and may thy temper
Sweeter in my service grow;

Still your sauciness is rather
To my liking—do you know?
MARTHA AND NANCY:
Yes, good-night! such night as never
We have lived to see before;
Were I but away, I'd never
Play the peasant any more!
ALL:
Good-night!
(*Harriet and Nancy retire to their chamber, and Plunkett and Lionel leave by the large door, locking it after them.*)

The maidens now peep out from their room and seeing no one, come out, and are excitedly discussing their chances of escape, when *Tristan's* voice is heard outside softly calling to them. Overjoyed, they make their escape through the window, and return to their home in the carriage provided by *Tristan*.

ACT III

SCENE—*A Hunting Park in Richmond Forest*

Act III represents the Forest of Richmond, where the *Queen* is hunting with her attendants. The young farmers, who have sought vainly for their late servants, have come hither to witness the hunting and forget the two maidens who have wrought such havoc with their affections.

The act opens with the spirited apostrophe to porter beer, sung by *Plunkett.*

Canzone del porter (Porter Song)

By Pol Plançon, Bass	(*In Italian*)	81086	10-inch,	$2.00
By Marcel Journet, Bass	(*In Italian*)	64014	10-inch,	1.00
By Carlos Francisco (*Double-Faced, see page 217*)	(*In Italian*)	16812	10-inch,	.75

This most famous of old English beverages is highly praised by the jovial *Plunkett,* who gives it credit for much of Britain's vigorous life.

PLUNKETT:

I want to ask you, can you not tell me,
What to our land the British strand
Gives life and power? say!
It is old porter, brown and stout,
We may of it be justly proud,
It guides John Bull, where'er he be,
Through fogs and mists, through land and sea!

And that explaineth where'er it reigneth
Is joy and mirth! At ev'ry hearth
Resounds a joyous song!
Look at its goodly color here!
Where else can find you such good beer?
So brown and stout and healthy, too!
The porter's health I drink to you!

Yes, hurrah! the hops, and hurrah! the malt,
They are life's flavor and life's salt.
Hurrah! Tra, la, la, la, la, la, la, la!

Three records of this number are offered—the first by Plançon, whose *Plunkett* was a familiar figure to opera-goers a few years ago; while Journet has also made a great success in the part, which suits his robust voice and style admirably. His singing of this "Porter Song" is a fine performance—spirited and magnetic. A lower-priced rendition, and a most excellent one, is furnished by Carlos Francisco.

The farmers disperse, leaving *Lionel* alone, and he sings his famous "M'appari," the melodious air of the broken-hearted lover, in which he tells of his hopeless passion for the fair *Lady Harriet,* whom he knows only as *Martha.*

M'appari (Like a Dream)

By Enrico Caruso, Tenor	(*In Italian*)	88001	12-inch,	$3.00
By Evan Williams, Tenor	(*In English*)	74128	12-inch,	1.50

Caruso sings this lovely air with a glorious outpouring of voice, giving it all the pathos and tenderness which it requires; while Mr. Williams' rendition (in English) is also a very fine one.

LIONEL:

Like a dream bright and fair,
Chasing ev'ry thought of care,
Those sweet hours pass'd with thee
Made the world all joy for me.
But, alas! thou art gone,
And that dream of bliss is o'er.
Ah! I hear now the tone
Of thy gentle voice no more;

Oh! return happy hours fraught with hope
so bright;
Come again, sunny days,
Sunny days of pure delight.
Fleeting vision cloth'd in brightness,
Wherefore thus, so soon depart;
O'er my pathway shed thy lightness
Once again, and cheer my heart.

Lionel suddenly encounters *Lady Harriet,* and although amazed at seeing her in the dress of a lady, warmly pleads his love.

LIONEL:
Yes, 'tis thee!
Once more I do behold thee!
Praised be God; it is no dream!
HARRIET (*aside*):
My heart!
LIONEL:
Lookest down so proudly;
Yet my heart knew thee at once.
HARRIET (*with dignity*):
Knew me? You're mistaken!
LIONEL:
I've hoarded thy fair image
Deep in my breast—No—

This dress does not deceive me—
'Tis thee, thee! Be Heaven blest!
HARRIET:
Madman, you dream!
LIONEL:
Ah! If but a dream,
This, a creation, of my brain,
Then, oh Martha, let me enjoy
This delusion while it lasts!
(*He attempts to seize her hand.*)
HARRIET:
Hold! presumptuous man!
No further! thou hast rav'd too long uncheck'd!

COPY'T DUPONT

CARUSO AS LIONEL

Lady Harriet is forced to call the hunters, to whom she declares that *Lionel* must be mad. He is distracted, while *Plunkett* endeavors to console him. The great finale, a part of which closes the Opera Medley (see below), then occurs. It is a magnificent piece of concerted music.

ACT IV

SCENE I—*Plunkett's Farm House*

Plunkett is discovered alone, musing on the unhappy plight of his foster brother, who, since his rejection by *Harriet,* is inconsolable. He sings his great air, which is often omitted in American presentations of the opera.

Il mio Lionel (My Unhappy Lionel)

By Mattia Battistini, Baritone

(*In Italian*) **92005** **12-inch,** **$3.00**

It is a fine number, superbly sung by Battistini, whose great success in this rôle at Covent Garden is well remembered.

PLUNKETT:
Poor Lionel! he sighs, he laments,
He flies from his friend;
He is beside himself with love
Accursed be the hour
When first we saw that girl,
When first we brought her beneath our roof!
Soon will my Lionel die,

If no aid come from on high;
Fatal the hour,
When first his heart felt love's pow'r;
Weeping, he wanders in grief,
Nought to his pain brings relief;
Merciful God, hear my cry,
Else must my Lionel die!

Nancy now enters, and she and *Plunkett* soon come to an understanding. They decide to present *Lionel's* ring to the *Queen,* hoping thus to clear up the mystery of his birth.

SCENE II—*A Representation of the Richmond Fair*

Lionel's ring has been shown to the *Queen,* who discovers that the young man is really the son of the banished *Earl of Derby.* However, he refuses to accept his rightful rank and continues to brood over the insult offered him in the forest. As a last resort a complete reproduction of the Fair Scene of Act II is arranged, with booths and the crowd of servants all represented. *Harriet, Nancy* and *Plunkett* are dressed in the costumes worn at their first meeting.

Lionel is led in by *Plunkett,* and when he sees *Harriet* in the dress of a servant, the cloud seems to pass from his mind and he embraces her tenderly. The two couples pledge their troth and all ends happily.

DOUBLE-FACED AND MISCELLANEOUS MARTHA RECORDS.

Overture   By Pryor's Band
   Nocturne in E♭ (*Opus 9*)   (*Chopin*)   35133   12-inch, $1.25
               By Victor Sorlin, 'Cellist (*Piano acc.*)

Last Rose of Summer   By Elizabeth Wheeler, Soprano
                        (*In English*)   16813   10-inch,   .75
   Tannhauser—The Evening Star   By Victor Sorlin, 'Cellist

Canzone del porter   (Porter Song)
      By Carlos Francisco, Baritone   (*In Italian*)   16812   10-inch,   .75
   Trovatore—Il balen del suo sorriso   (*The Tempest of the Heart*)
      By Francesco Cigada, Baritone (*In Italian*)

Gems from Martha

Chorus of Servants—Quartet, "Swains So Shy"—"Last Rose of Summer"—"Good Night Quartet"—"May Dreams Transport Thee"—Finale, "Ah, May Heaven Forgive Thee."

By the Victor Light Opera Company   (*In English*)   31797   12-inch, $1.00

Martha Selection

By Victor Orchestra   31029   12-inch,   1.00

(Italian)

BALLO IN MASCHERA

(Mahss'-kay-rah)

(French)   (English)

BAL MASQUÉ   MASKED BALL
(Bahl' Mahs-kay')

OPERA IN THREE ACTS

Text by M. Somma, music by Verdi. First produced in Rome at the Teatro Apollo, February 17, 1859; at Paris, Théâtre des Italiens, January 13, 1861. First London production June 15, 1861. First New York production February 11, 1861.

Characters

RICHARD, Count of Warwick and Governor of Boston.................Tenor
REINHART, his secretary...Baritone
AMELIA, wife of Reinhart.......................................Soprano
ULRICA, a negress astrologer...................................Contralto
OSCAR, a page...Soprano
SAMUEL,⎫ enemies of the Count ....⎧Bass
TOM, ⎭ ....⎩Bass

Scene and Period : In and near Boston, end of the Seventeenth Century.

The opera was composed for the San Carlo, Naples, and first called Gustavo III (after an assassinated Italian monarch), but after the announcement had almost created a riot in Naples, Verdi was forced to change the scene from Stockholm to Boston, and the name to Masked Ball. Finally it was thought best to abandon the Naples premiére altogether, and the opera was taken to Rome.

There are many, of course, who consider this work old-fashioned—and so it is, not pretending at all to be a great music drama; but there are many far more ambitious works with certainly less real music. The familiar *Eri tu* and *Saper vorreste* and the fine concerted numbers in Acts II and III are well worth hearing. The Victor has assembled a very fine collection of the best music in the opera, and presents it with the belief that this revival is the best heard in recent years.

Richard, Count of Warwick and Governor of Boston, falls in love with *Amelia,* the wife of *Reinhart,* his secretary and intimate friend. This love is returned, but the wife's conscience troubles her, and she consults *Ulrica,* a black sorceress, hoping to secure a drug that will cause her to forget *Richard.* *Ulrica* sends her to gather a certain herb which will prove effective. *Richard,* who had also gone to consult the astrologer, overhears the conversation, and follows *Amelia* to the magic spot. *Amelia's* husband, who has come in search of *Richard* to warn him of a conspiracy to assassinate him, now appears, and *Richard* makes his escape, after requesting *Reinhart* to escort the veiled lady to her home without attempting to learn her identity. On the way, however, they are surrounded by the conspirators and *Amelia* is revealed. *Reinhart* swears vengeance on his false friend and joins the plotters.

At the Masked Ball, *Richard* is stabbed by *Reinhart,* but the dying man declares the innocence of *Amelia* and forgives his murderer.

COPY'T DUPONT

CARUSO AS RICHARD

218

ACT I

SCENE I—*A Hall in the Governor's House*

The hall is filled with people—officers, deputies, gentlemen, etc.—waiting for the appearance of the Governor. He enters, is warmly greeted by those assembled, receives their petitions and inspects a list of the guests invited to the Masked Ball. He sees *Amelia's* name, and in an aside sings his rapturous air.

La rivedrà nell'estasi (I Shall Behold Her)

By Nicola Zerola, Tenor

(In Italian)   64167   10-inch, $1.00

This, the first of the lovely gems with which the score of *Ballo in Maschera* is studded, is effectively given by Zerola, whose beautiful voice is shown to great advantage.

COPY'T MISHKIN

ZEROLA AS RICHARD

> RICHARD (*reading aside*):
> Amelia—dear, sweet name!
> Its mere sound fills my heart with joy!
> Her beauteous, charming image
> Inspires my soul with love;
> Here soon shall I behold her
> In all her tender charms.
> No matter what the splendor
> Of night's most brilliant stars,
> I swear none is so brilliant
> As my love's dazzling eyes!

Reinhart enters and tells the Governor of a plot against his life.

Alla vita che t'arride (On the Life Thou Now Dost Cherish)

By Mattia Battistini, Baritone

(In Italian)   88232   12-inch, $3.00

In this fine air he enthusiastically praises *Richard's* noble acts, and tells him his friends and faithful subjects will defeat the plans of the conspirators.

A negro woman, *Ulrica*, is now brought in and accused of being a witch. *Richard* laughs at the accusation and dismisses the woman. He calls his courtiers around him, and suggests that for a lark they go disguised to the hut of the sorceress and consult her. The friends agree, and the plotters, headed by *Samuel* and *Tom*, see a chance to further their plans.

SCENE II—*The Hut of Ulrica*

The hut is crowded with people who have come to have their fortunes told. The sorceress stands over her magic cauldron and sings her incantation.

Re dell' abisso (King of the Shades)

By Carolina Pietracewska, Contralto   *(In Italian)*   76005   12-inch, $2.00

She calls on the abyssmal king to appear and aid in her mystic rites.

ULRICA (*as if inspired*):	The ominous lapwing.
Hasten, O King of the Abyss!	Three times, too, has been hissing
Fly through the ambient air	The venomous red dragon,
And enter my abode.	And three times have been groaning
Three times has been heard screeching,	The spirits from the graves!

The Governor now arrives, dressed as a sailor, and accompanied by his companions. They are conversing with the witch when a knock is heard, and all leave the hut by *Ulrica's* orders except *Richard*, who conceals himself in a corner.

Amelia enters and asks the sorceress to give her peace of mind by banishing a love which she cannot control. The witch promises speedy relief if *Amelia* will gather a certain herb from which can be brewed a magic liquor.

Della città all'occaso (Hard by the Western Portal)

By Ida Giacomelli, Soprano; Lina Mileri, Contralto; Gino Martinez-Patti, Tenor   *(In Italian)*   *68143   12-inch, $1.25

Double-Faced Record—For title of opposite side see DOUBLE-FACED MASKED BALL RECORDS, page 223.

Amelia asks for directions, and the witch proceeds:

ULRICA:
Then pause and listen.
Go from the city eastward,
To where by gloom engirted
Fall the pale moonbeams on the field,

Accurs'd, abhor'd, deserted,
And cull the flowers lowly
From those black rocks unholy,
Where crimes have dark atonement made
With life's departing sigh!

The frightened girl consents to go that very night, and takes her departure. *Ulrica* now admits the people again, and *Richard,* in the character of the sailor, asks her to tell his fortune. His inquiry of the prophetess takes the form of a barcarolle—the favorite measure of a sea-song—and the ballad, vigorous and tuneful, has all the swing of a rollicking song of the sea.

Di tu se fidele (The Waves Will Bear Me)

By Enrico Caruso, Tenor, and Metropolitan Opera Chorus
(In Italian)　87091　10-inch, $2.00

By Nicola Zerola, Tenor　　　　(In Italian)　64166　10-inch, 1.00

This attractive ballad is full of humor, the *staccato* passages towards the close exhibiting the Governor's impatience to learn the future. In a gay mood he banters the woman, asking her to tell him if he will meet with storms on his next voyage.

RICHARD:
Declare if the waves will faithfully bear me;
If weeping the lov'd one from whom I now
　tear me,
Farewell, to me saying, my love is betraying.
With sails rent asunder, with soul in com-
　motion,
I go now to steer thro' the dark waves of
　ocean,
The anger of Heav'n and Hell to defy!
Then haste with thy magic, the future
　exploring,
No power have the thunder or angry winds
　roaring,
Or death, or affection my path to deny!

This famous *Barcarolle* has been a favorite with many great tenors, but no one has ever sung it as Caruso has given it here.

Ulrica rebukes him, and examining his palm, tells him he is soon to die by the sword of that friend who shall next shake his hand. The conspirators, *Samuel* and *Tom,* are uneasy, thinking themselves suspected, but the Governor laughs and asks who will grasp his hand to prove the prophecy false. No one dares to

GORITZ AS REINHART

grant his request.

Reinhart, who has become anxious about his chief and has come in search of him, now enters, and seeing the Governor, shakes him by the hand, calling him by name, to the astonishment of all those not in the secret. *Sir Richard* tells the witch she is a false prophet, as this is his most faithful friend.

RICHARD:
The oracle has lied!
That man who grasped my hand
Is my most faithful friend!

All the people greet the Governor with cheers, and kneeling, sing the hymn:

O figlio d'Inghilterra (O, Son of Glorious England)

By Giuseppina Huguet, Soprano; Ines Salvador, Mezzo-Soprano; Francesco
Cigada, Baritone; Aristodemo Sillich, Bass; La Scala Chorus
(In Italian)　*63173　10-inch, $0.75

This noble concerted number, which closes the first act, is sung in a splendid manner by Huguet, Salvador, Cigada and Sillich of La Scala forces, assisted by the famous chorus of that opera house.

ACT II

SCENE I—*A Field near Boston—on one side a Gallows*

Amelia, much frightened by her lonely surroundings, enters in search of the magic herb. She sings her dramatic air, *Yonder Plant Enchanted.*

---

* Double-Faced Record—For title of opposite side see DOUBLE-FACED MASKED BALL RECORDS, page 223.

Ma dall'arido stelo divulsa (Yonder Plant Enchanted)

By Celestina Boninsegna, Soprano   (*In Italian*)   92000   12-inch, $3.00
By Lucia Crestani, Soprano   (*In Italian*)   *68143   12-inch, 1.25

COPY'T DUPONT

EAMES AS AMELIA

AMELIA:
When at last from its stem I shall sever
Yonder weed of dread virtue enchanted,
From my tempest-torn bosom forever
When that image so ethereal shall perish,
What remains to thee then, oh, my heart!
Ah, tears blind me!
The weight of my sorrow
Chains my steps on their desolate journey!
Heart, have courage;
From these rocks their hardness borrow!
Come, oh, Death, let thy merciful dart,
Still forever my poor throbbing heart!
(*A distant clock strikes.*)
Hark! 'tis midnight! Ah, yon vision!
Moving, breathing, lo! a figure,
All mist-like upward wreathing!
Ha! in those orbits baleful anger is seething;
Fix'd on me they angrily burn!
Deign, oh, Heaven, Thy strength to impart
To this fainting, fear-stricken heart.

The vision resolves itself into *Richard,* who now approaches. The unhappy girl confesses that she loves him, but begs him to leave her. They sing a fine duet.

Ah! qual soave brivido (Like Dew Thy Words Fall on My Heart)

By Ida Giacomelli, Soprano, and Gino Martinez-Patti, Tenor
    (*In Italian*)   *68026   12-inch, $1.25

RICHARD:
Like dew thy words fall on my heart,
Aglow with love's fond passion!
Ah, murmur with compassion those gentle words again!
Bright star that bidst all gloom depart,
My hallow'd love enshrining;
While thus on me thou'rt shining,
Ah, let night forever reign!

AMELIA:
From out the cypress bower,
Where I had thought it laid in death,
Returns with giant power, the love my heart doth fear!
Ah, would by Heaven 'twere granted,
To sigh for him my latest breath,
Or in death's sleep enchanted rest my weary spirit here!

RICHARD:
Amelia! thou lov'st me!
AMELIA:
I love thee,
But thy noble heart will protect me from mine own!

They are interrupted by the appearance of *Reinhart,* who comes to warn *Richard* that his enemies are lying in wait to murder him. *Richard,* unwilling to leave *Amelia,* is forced to ask *Reinhart* to escort the veiled lady to the city without seeking to discover her identity. *Reinhart* swears to obey, and *Richard* makes his escape. The couple start for Boston, but are surrounded by the conspirators, who take *Reinhart* to be the Governor. Disappointed in their prey, they tear the veil from the unknown lady and *Reinhart* is astounded to see that it is his wife. The great finale to Act II now occurs.

Ve' se di notte qui con la sposa (Ah! Here by Moonlight)

By Ida Giacomelli, Soprano; Renzo Minolfi, Baritone; Cesare Preve, Bass;
    Chorus   (*In Italian*)   *35179   12-inch, $1.25

Amelia is overcome with shame, but protests her innocence. *Reinhart* bitterly upbraids her and denounces his false friend *Richard,* while the conspirators depart, anticipating the sensation which the city will enjoy on the morrow.

* *Double-Faced Record—For title of opposite side see DOUBLE-FACED MASKED BALL RECORDS, page 223.*

Reinhart, now bent on revenge, decides to cast his lot with the plotters, and the act closes as he says to *Amelia* with deep meaning:

REINHART (*alone with Amelia*):
I shall fulfill my promise
To take thee to the city!

AMELIA (*aside*):
His voice like a death warrant
Doth sound in my ear!

ACT III

SCENE I—*A Room in Reinhart's House*

Reinhart is denouncing *Amelia* for her supposed crime, and finally decides to kill her. She begs to be allowed to embrace her child once more, and her husband consenting, she goes out. Left alone, the unhappy man repents his resolution, and resolves to spare the guilty woman's life. In the greatest of the airs allotted to *Reinhart* he swears to avenge his wrongs.

Eri tu che macchiavi quell'anima (Is It Thou ?)

By Emilio de Gogorza, Baritone			
(*In Italian*)	88324	12-inch,	$3.00
By Mattia Battistini, Baritone			
(*In Italian*)	92044	12-inch,	3.00
By Antonio Scotti, Baritone			
(*In Italian*)	85044	12-inch,	3.00
By Francesco Cigada, Baritone			
(*In Italian*)	*35179	12-inch,	1.25
By Giuseppe de Luca, Baritone			
(*In Italian*)	*62086	10-inch,	.75

COPY'T MISHKIN
SAMMARCO AS REINHART

Samuel and *Tom* enter and *Reinhart* tells them he knows of their plots, and will assist them, as he desires the Governor's death. They draw lots, and *Reinhart* is chosen to be the assassin. *Amelia* enters in time to realize the state of affairs, and is about to plead for the Governor's life, when *Oscar,* the page, enters bearing an invitation to the Masked Ball. The page, beginning an effective quartet, tells of the brilliancy of the occasion.

Di che fulgor (What Dazzling Light)

By Giuseppina Huguet, Soprano; Francesco Cigada, Baritone; Carlo Ottoboni, Bass; Maria Grisi, Soprano (*In Italian*) *62086 10-inch, $0.75

The varied emotions of the characters are expressed by the librettist as follows:

OSCAR:
What brilliant lights, what music gay, will fill the joyous dwelling!
What crowds of youths and maidens fair—their hearts with rapture swelling!
AMELIA:
And I, myself, ah, hapless me!—the fatal scroll so blindly
Drew from the vase at his command;
Now by his hand the Count must die!
REINHART:
There 'mid the sounds of music light—the coward traitor meeting,
I'll strike the vengeful dagger home—and stay his vile heart's beating!
SAM AND TOM:
Revenge in mask and domino!—'Twill thus be more availing,

Amid the crush of dancers gay—there'll be no chance of failing!
AMELIA (*aside*):
Can I not prevent this crime
Without my husband betraying?
OSCAR (*to Amelia*):
You will be queen of the dance.
AMELIA (*to herself*):
Ulrica can perchance assist me.
SAM AND TOM (*to Reinhart*):
What shall be our style of costume?
REINHART:
A doublet blue,
With crimson scarf
Upon the left side fastened!

The conspirators go out after agreeing on the password, "Death!"

SCENE II—*The Governor's Private Office*

Richard, alone, resolves to tear the unworthy love from his heart and send *Amelia* and *Reinhart* to England. A page brings a note to the Governor from an unknown lady who warns him of the plot, but *Richard* resolves to brave his enemies and attend the ball.

* *Double-Faced Record—For title of opposite side see DOUBLE-FACED MASKED BALL RECORDS, page 223.*

SCENE III—*Grand Ballroom in the Governor's House*

Reinhart, mingling with the guests, meets the page *Oscar,* and attemps to learn how the Governor is dressed. The page teases him, singing his gay air, *Saper vorreste.*

Saper vorreste—Canzone (You Would be Hearing)

By Luisa Tetrazzini, Soprano   (*In Italian*)   88304   12-inch, $3.00

In reply to *Reinhart's* questions the merry page tauntingly sings:

OSCAR:
You'd fain be hearing, what dress he's wearing
When he has bidden, the fact be hidden?
I know right well but may not tell
     Tra la la la, la la la!
Of love my heart feels all the smart,
Yet watchful ever, my secret never
Rank nor bright eyes shall e'er surprise!
     Tra la la la, la la la!

This gay number is brilliantly sung by Tetrazzini, the high B in the *cadenza* being taken with ease.

The page finally reveals to *Reinhart* that the Governor is dressed in black, with a red ribbon on his breast.

Amelia meets the Governor and warns him against the plotters. He bids her farewell and is about to go, when *Reinhart* stabs him. The dying Governor, supported in the arms of his friends, tells *Reinhart* that his wife is guiltless, and that to remove her from temptation he had planned to send *Reinhart* to England to fill an honored post.

The secretary is overcome with remorse, and *Richard* dies, after declaring that *Reinhart* must not be punished.

DOUBLE-FACED MASKED BALL RECORDS

Della citta all'occaso (Hard by the Western Portal)
   By Ida Giacomelli, Soprano; Lina Mileri, Contralto;
     Gino Martinez-Patti, Tenor   (*In Italian*) } 68143   12-inch, $1.25
Ma dall'arido stelo divulsa (Yonder Plant Enchanted)
     By Lucia Crestani, Soprano   (*In Italian*)

Ve' se di notte qui con la sposa (Ah! Here By Moon-
   light) By Ida Giacomelli, Soprano; Renzo Minolfi,
   Baritone; Cesare Preve, Bass; Chorus   (*In Italian*) } 35179   12-inch, 1.25
Eri tu che macchiavi quell' anima (Is it Thou ?)
     By Francesco Cigada, Baritone   (*In Italian*)

Ah! qual soave brivido (Like Dew Thy Words Fall on
   My Heart) By Ida Giacomelli, Soprano, and Gino
   Martinez-Patti, Tenor   (*In Italian*) } 68026   12-inch, 1.25
Forza del Destino—Non imprecare umiliati   *By Ida Giacomelli,*
   Soprano; Gino Martinez-Patti, Tenor; Cesare Preve, Bass
     (*In Italian*)

O figlio d'Inghilterra (Oh, Son of Glorious England)
   By Giuseppina Huguet, Soprano; Inez Salvador, Mezzo-
   Soprano; Francesco Cigada, Baritone; Aristodemo } 63173   10-inch, .75
   Sillich, Bass; La Scala Chorus   (*In Italian*)
Ernani—Ernani involami   *By Maria Grisi, Soprano*   (*In Italian*)

Eri tu che macchiavi quell'anima (Is it Thou ?)
     By Giuseppe de Luca, Baritone   (*In Italian*)
Di che fulgor (What Dazzling Light) By Giuseppina } 62086   10-inch, .75
   Huguet, Soprano; Francesco Cigada, Baritone; Carlo
   Ottoboni, Bass; Maria Grisi, Soprano   (*In Italian*)

SCENE FROM MEFISTOFELE—ACT III

(French)		(English)

MEFISTOFELE

(*May-feess-toh-feh'-lay*)

MEPHISTOPHELES

(*Mef-iss-tof'-e-leez*)

OPERA IN FOUR ACTS

Text and music by Arrigo Boïto; a paraphrase of both parts of Goethe's "Faust," with additional episodes taken from the treatment of the legend by other authorities. The first production at La Scala, Milan, 1868, was a failure. Rewritten and given in 1875 with success. First London production July 6, 1880. First American production at the Academy of Music, November 24, 1880, with Campanini, Cary and Novara. Other productions were in 1896, with Calvé, and in 1901 with McIntyre, Homer and Plançon. Some recent notable revivals: At the Metropolitan, when the opera was brought out for Chaliapine, the cast including Farrar and Martin, and the Boston Opera production of 1910, both noteworthy for their splendid settings.

Characters

MEFISTOFELE . . . . Bass
FAUST . . . . Tenor
MARGARET . . . . Soprano
MARTHA . . . . Contralto
WAGNER . . . . Tenor
HELEN . . . . Soprano
PANTALIS . . . . Contralto
NEREUS . . . . Tenor

Celestial Phalanxes, Mystic Choir, Cherubs, Penitents, Wayfarers, Men-at-arms, Huntsmen, Students, Citizens, Populace, Townsmen, Witches, Wizards, Greek Chorus, Sirens, Naiads, Dancers, Warriors.

FAUST LEAVING HIS STUDIO—ACT I

Arrigo Boïto well deserves a conspicuous place among the great modern composers. His *Mefistofele* ranks with the masterpieces of modern Italy, and contains scenes of great beauty, notably the Garden Scene, with its lovely music, and the Prison Scene, in which the pathos of the demented *Margaret's* wanderings, the beautiful duet and the frenzy of the finale are pictured by a master hand.

Boïto is not only a composer, but a poet of ability and a clever librettist. Notable among his writings are the librettos of Verdi's *Otello* and *Falstaff*, which should rather be called dramas set to music, for it is unfair to class them with the old-fashioned Italian librettos.

The story of Boïto's opera is directly drawn from Goethe's *Faust*, but the composer has chosen episodes from the whole of Goethe's story, not confining himself to the tale of *Gretchen*, but including the episode of *Helen of Troy*. In his *Mefistofele* Boïto has followed the great poet's work more closely than did Gounod's librettist, and the work is a deeper one in many respects.

PROLOGUE

SCENE—*The Regions of Space*

The prologue to Boïto's opera is a most impressive scene, which takes place in the indefinite regions of space. Invisible angels and cherubim, supported by the celestial trumpets, sing in praise of the Ruler of the Universe.

Mefistofele is represented hovering between Hell and Earth, denying the power of God. He addresses the Almighty in his *Hail, Great Lord!*

Ave Signor (Hail, Sovereign Lord)

By Marcel Journet, Bass   (*In Italian*)   64126   10-inch, $1.00

The Devil contends that man is but a weakling, easily cheated of his salvation. Standing on a cloud *Mefistofele* mockingly addresses the Creator:

Hail, Sovereign Lord,
Forgive me if my bawling
Somewhat behind is falling
Those sublime anthems sung
In heavenly places!
Forgive me if my face is
Now wanting the radiance
That, as with a garland,
The cherub legion graces!
Forgive me if in speaking,
Some risk I'm taking of irrev'rent out-
  breaking!
The puny king of puny earth's dominions,
Erreth through wrong opinions
And like a cricket, with a long leap rushing,
'Mid stars his nose is pushing,
Then with superb fatuity tenacious,
Trills with pride contumacious!
Vain, glorious atom!
Proud 'mid confusion!
Phantom of man's delusion!
Ah! in such deep degradation
Is fallen the master,
Lord of the whole creation,
No more have I the will,
While in that station,   From the Ditson Edition
Him to tempt to ill!   Copy't 1880, Oliver Ditson Co.   JOURNET AS MEFISTOFELE

Then, discussing *Faust* with the Mystic Chorus, *Mefistofele* wagers that he can entice the philosopher from the path of virtue. The challenge is accepted, and *Mefistofele* disappears to begin his plots against the soul of *Faust*.

Journet sings this great number splendidly, and it will be pronounced one of the most striking features of his Victor list.

ACT I

SCENE I—*A Square in Frankfort—Easter Sunday*

The aged philosopher, *Faust*, and his pupil *Wagner*, while mingling with the crowd, observe a grey *Friar* who seems to be shadowing their movements. *Faust* is alarmed and says to *Wagner*:

FAUST: Observe him closely. Tell me, who is he?
WAGNER: Some lowly Friar, who begs alms from those he passes.

VICTOR BOOK OF THE OPERA—BOÏTO'S MEFISTOFELE

FAUST: Look more closely. He moves slowly on in lessening circles; and with each spiral, comes ever nearer and nearer. Oh! as I gaze, I see his footprints marked in fire!

WAGNER: No, master, 'tis some idle fancy that thy brain deceives thee; I only see there a poor grey friar. Timidly he ventures to approach us, and we are to him but two passing strangers.

FAUST: Now he seems as though he wove nets about our path. His circles grow smaller! He draweth close! Ah!

WAGNER (carelessly): Look calmly. 'Tis a grey friar, and not a specter. Muttering his prayers, he tells his beads as he journeys. Come hence, good master.

As they leave the square, followed by the *Friar*, the scene changes to *Faust's* laboratory.

SCENE II—*The Studio of Faust. It is Night*

Faust enters, not observing that the *Friar* slips in behind him, and conceals himself in an alcove. The aged philosopher delivers his soliloquy, *Dai campi*.

Dai campi, dai prati (From the Green Fields)
By Alberto Amadi, Tenor (In Italian) *63313 10-inch, $0.75

He speaks of his deep contentment, his love for God and his fellow man.

FAUST:

From the meadows, from the valleys, which lie bathed in moonlight,
And where paths silent sleep, I come returning; my soul filled
With calmness, mysterious and deep,
The passions, the heart rudely trying,
In quiet oblivion are lying;
My spirit knows only its love for its fellows;

Its love for its God!
Ah! From the meadows, from the valleys,
I come to read the blest Evangels;
Who delight me, and fill me with holy fire!
(*Opens a Bible placed upon a high reading desk. As he begins to meditate he is startled by a cry from the Friar in the alcove.*)

The *Friar* appears, and throwing off his disguise, reveals himself as the Devil, singing a splendid aria, *I Am the Spirit*.

Ballata del fischio, "Son lo spirito" (I Am the Spirit)
By Marcel Journet, Bass (In Italian) 74210 12-inch, $1.50

Mefistofele says that he is that great force which forever thinketh ill but doeth well, and then continues:

MEFISTOFELE:

I'm the spirit that denieth all things, always;
Stars or flowers—that by sneers and strife supplieth
Cause to vex the Heavenly powers.
I'm for Naught and for Creation,
Ruin universal, death!
And my very life and breath,
Is what here they call transgression, sin and Death!
Shouting and laughing out this word I throw:
"No!" Sland'ring, wasting, howling, hissing,

On I go, whistling! whistling! Eh!
Part am I of that condition,
Of the whole obscurity.
Child of darkness and ambition,
Shadows hiding, wait for me.
If the light usurps, contending,
On my rebel scepter's right,
Not prolong'd will be the fight,
Over sun and earth is pending,
Endless night!
Shouting and laughing, etc.

This is sometimes called *Ballata del fischio*, or *Whistling Ballad*, because of the peculiar whistles Boïto has introduced in the number. Journet delivers this splendid number with admirable declamatory power, bringing out the strange symbolism of the climax in a thrilling manner.

Mefistofele offers to be *Faust's* servant if he will accompany him. "What is the price?" asks the philosopher. "Up here I will obey thee," says *Mefistofele*, "but below our places will be reversed." *Faust* says he cares nothing for the future, and if *Mefistofele* can give him but one hour of happiness, for that one hour he would sell his soul. The bargain is made and they set forth.

This departure from the laboratory of *Faust* is strikingly pictured in the great painting of Kreling, a reproduction of which is given on page 224.

ACT II
SCENE—*The Garden of Margaret*

Faust (now a handsome young man known as *Henry*) is strolling in the garden with *Margaret*, while *Mefistofele*, as in Gounod's version, makes sarcastic love to *Martha*, whom Boïto has pictured as *Margaret's* mother. *Faust* pleads for a meeting alone with the maiden, but she dares not consent because her mother sleeps lightly. He gives her a sleeping draught, assuring her that it will not harm her mother, but merely cause her to sleep soundly. The four then sing a fine quartet, and the scene suddenly changes to the Brocken.

* Double-Faced Record—For title of opposite side see DOUBLE-FACED MEFISTOFELE RECORDS, page 229
NOTE—Mefistofele quotations are from the Ditson libretto, by permission. (Copy't 1880, Oliver Ditson Company)

SCENE II—*The Summit of the Brocken—The Night of the Witches' Sabbath*

This scene shows a wild spot in the Brocken mountains by moonlight. The wind is whistling in weird gusts. *Mefistofele* is helping *Faust* to climb the jagged rocks, from which flames now and then dart forth. Will-o-the-wisps flutter to and fro, and *Faust* welcomes them, grateful for the light they give.

Folletto, folletto (Sprites of Hades)

By Gennaro de Tura, Tenor, and Gaudio
Mansueto, Bass
(*In Italian*)   87067   10-inch, $2.00

Mefistofele echoes him, ever urging him to climb higher.

MEFISTOFELE:
 Come up higher, and higher, and higher,
 Farther yet 'tis more dreary the road
 That will lead us to Satan's abode,
 Dark the sky is, the ascent grows steeper;
 Come up higher, and higher, and higher!
FAUST:
 Ah! wild-fire, pallid light,
 Now so dim, now so bright,
 Flash o'er us thy ray
 To illumine our way,
 Come nigher, come nigher
 For dark is the ascent
 As higher and higher,
 We're upward advancing,
 Come flame wildly dancing,
 Come nigher, and nigher!

FARRAR AND MARTIN IN ACT II

KRELING   THE VISION OF MARGARET

Arriving at the summit, *Mefistofele* summons the infernal host—demons, witches, wizards, goblins, imps—and presides over the satanic orgies as King. All pay him homage and dance in wildest joy as he breaks into fragments a glass globe, typifying the earth, crying: "On its surface vile races dwell, degraded, toilsome, quarreling among themselves. They laugh at me, but I can laugh also!"

Faust now sees a vision of *Margaret,* on her way to prison for the murder of her mother and her babe. A red stain on her neck horrifies him, but *Mefistofele* laughs and says, "Turn away your eyes." The act closes in a riotous orgy, the demons whirling and dancing in a mad revelry. This wild scene is graphically pictured in the painting by Kreling.

ACT III

SCENE—*The Prison of Margaret*

The demented girl is lying on a straw bed. She rouses herself and sings her sad ballad, *L'altra notte.*

L'altra notte (Last Night in the Deep Sea)

By Geraldine Farrar, Soprano
(*Italian*)   88114   12-inch, $3.00

MELBA AS HELEN

Lontano, lontano (Away From All Strife)

By Giuseppina Huguet, Soprano, and Gennaro de Tura, Tenor
(In Italian)

87056 10-inch, $2.00

MARGARET AND FAUST:
Away, far from strife and commotion,
O'er waves of a wide-spreading ocean,
'Mid perfumes exhaled by the sea,
'Mid palm trees and flow'rs in profusion,
The portal of peace and seclusion,
The blue isle seems waiting for me.
There, skies in their beauty transcendent,
Seem girt with a rainbow resplendent,
Reflecting the sun's loving smile.
The flight of all hearts that are loving,
And hopeful and moving and roving,
Is turned towards that life-giving island.
Away to that island far distant!

The return of *Mefistofele* drives *Margaret* into a frenzy, and she refuses to leave the prison, finally falling into *Faust's* arms in her death agony. Her senses returning for a brief period, she forgives him and dies, while a chorus of celestial beings announce that her soul is saved. *Faust* and *Mefistofele* disappear just as the headsman and jailers come to conduct *Margaret* to execution.

ACT IV

The Night of the Classical Sabbath—A Moonlit View in the Vale of Tempe

We are now transported to distant Greece, where *Mefistofele* has resurrected

She raves of the cruel jailors, whom she says threw her babe into the ocean and now accuse her of the crime.

MARGARET:
To the sea, O night of sadness!
They my babe took and in it threw him!
Now to drive me on to madness,
They declare 'twas I that slew him!
Cold the air is, the dark cell narrow,
And my spirit broken to-day,
Like the timid woodland sparrow,
Longs to fly; ah, to fly off, far, far away,
Father, pity me!
In a deathly slumber falling,
Died my mother, no aid could save her;
And to crown the woe appalling,
They declare I poison gave her!

Mefistofele now enters, followed by *Faust*, who begs the demon to save *Margaret*. The fiend reminds *Faust* that it is his own fault, but promises to try.

MEFISTOFELE:
To this condition, who has bro't her?
I or you? I will do what I can.
Here is the cell key.
Sleeping are all the jailers,
And the coursers infernal for speedy flight
are ready!

However, he promises to try, and goes out.

Faust goes to *Margaret,* who does not know him and is frightened, thinking her jailers have come for her. He urges her to fly with him, and they sing a tender duet, *Far Away.*

MARGARET GOING TO EXECUTION

the beautiful *Helen of Troy* for the further temptation of *Faust*. The scene shows an enchanting spot on the banks of the Peneus, with the moon shedding a golden light upon *Helen, Pantalis* and groups of Sirens. *Helen* begins her enchanting ode to the moon, followed by the trio.

Scena della Grecia—La luna immobile (Moon Immovable!)

By N. Ardoni, Soprano; Lavin de Casas, Mezzo-Soprano; Gaetano
Pini-Corsi, Tenor   (*In Italian*) 87068 10-inch, $2.00

Faust and *Mefistofele* enter and the former soon forgets all else in the love of the fair Grecian. *Mefistofele*, however, feels out of place in this classic neighborhood, and leaving *Faust* in the arms of *Helen*, returns to the Brocken, where he amuses himself with his satanic crew.

EPILOGUE

SCENE—*Faust's Studio*

Faust has returned to his studio, again old and feeble and full of remorse for his past life. He has tasted all the pleasures of the earth and found them empty. He sings his famous epilogue:

Giunto sul passo (Nearing the End of Life)

By Florencio Constantino, Tenor   (*In Italian*)   74084   12-inch, $1.50
By Alberto Amadi (*Double-faced—See below*)   (*In Italian*)   63313   10-inch,   .75

> FAUST:
> Nearing the utmost limit of life's extremest
>   goal,
> In a vision delightful did wander forth my
>   soul.
> King of some placid region, unknown to care
>   and striving,
> I found a faithful people and fain would aid
>   their living.
> Ah! would then that this fair vision could
>   but be my last dream!
> Look you—the crowds now come within my
>   observation!
> Lo, the crowds turn t'wards cities, Heav'n-
>   ward turn the nation!
> Holy songs now I hear.
> Now I bathe in the radiant splendor of
>   Heaven's glorious morning!
> Ideal bliss upon my soul is already dawning!

Mefistofele enters for his final triumph, but *Faust* turns to the Bible and seeks salvation. *Mefistofele*, in desperation, summons the Sirens to his aid, but *Faust*, leaning on the sacred book, prays for forgiveness, and the defeated *Mefistofele* sinks into the ground. A shower of roses, a token of *Faust's* salvation, falls on the dying man as the curtain descends.

DOUBLE-FACED AND MISCELLANEOUS MEFISTOFELE RECORDS

Selection   By Pryor's Band   31458   12-inch, $1.00

Dai campi, dai prati   (From the Green Fields)
                By Alberto Amadi, Tenor   (*In Italian*)   } 63313 10-inch,   .75
Giunto sol passo   (Nearing the End of Life)
                By Alberto Amadi, Tenor   (*In Italian*)

DIE MEISTERSINGER   THE MASTERSINGERS
(Dee My'-ster-singer)

OPERA IN THREE ACTS

Both text and music of *Die Meistersinger von Nürnberg* are by Wagner. The idea of the opera was suggested to the composer in boyhood, as was Tannhäuser, by the reading of one of Hoffmann's novels, and was planned as a kind of burlesque of the *Minnesinger* contest in Tannhauser. First production in Munich, June 21, 1868.

The first performance in England took place under Richter, at Drury Lane, May 30, 1882; an Italian version was given at Covent Garden, July 13, 1889, and an English production by the Carl Rosa Company at Manchester, April 16, 1896.

In 1888 it was given for the first time at Bayreuth; and the first American production took place in New York, January 4, 1886.

Characters

HANS SACHS, cobbler,		Bass
POGNER, goldsmith,		Bass
VOGELGESANG, furrier,		Tenor
NACHTIGAL, buckle maker,		Bass
BECKMESSER, town clerk,		Bass
KOTHNER, baker,		Bass
ZORN, pewterer,	Master-Singers...	Tenor
EISSLINGER, grocer,		Tenor
MOSER, tailor,		Tenor
ORTEL, soap boiler,		Bass
SCHWARZ, stocking weaver,		Bass
FOLZ, coppersmith,		Bass

SIR WALTER VON STOLZING, a young Franconian knight............................Tenor
DAVID, apprentice to Hans Sachs.............Tenor
EVA, Pogner's daughter......................Soprano
MAGDALENA, Eva's nurse....................Soprano
A NIGHT WATCHMAN.......................Bass

Burghers of all Guilds, Journeymen, Apprentices, Girls and People.

FIRST PROGRAM OF MEISTER-
SINGER, MUNICH, 1868

Scene: Nüremberg in the middle of the sixteenth century.

To the opera-going public in general Meistersinger is the most entertaining of all the Wagner operas. Its gaiety and tunefulness are charming, and its story easily understood by an audience, which cannot be said of most of the works by the master.

The humor is essentially German,—an intermingling of playfulness, satire, practical jokes, and underneath all something of seriousness and even sadness, while the romantic element, provided by the lovers, *Eva* and *Walter,* is not lacking.

The opera is a satire on the musical methods of the days of the Reformation, the mediæval burgher's life in Nuremberg being pictured with a master hand. The loves of *Walter* and *Eva;* the noble philosophy of *Sachs,* the cobbler-poet; the envy of the ridiculous *Beckmesser;* and the youthful frolics of *David*—all are surrounded by some of the most glorious music imaginable.

The first act opens in St. Catherine's Church at Nuremberg, where *Eva,* daughter of the wealthy goldsmith *Pogner,* and *Walter,* a

OTTO GORITZ
AS HANS SACHS

young knight, meet and fall in love. When *Walter* learns that *Eva's* hand has been promised by her father to the winner of the song contest, he resolves to compete, and remains

WALTER'S TRIAL—ACT I

for the examination before the meeting of Master-singers. *Beckmesser*, who also wishes to marry *Eva*, is chosen marker, and under the rigid rules of the order gives *Walter* so many bad marks that he is rejected in spite of the influence of *Hans Sachs* in his favor.

Act II shows a street, with the houses of *Hans Sachs* and *Pogner* on opposite sides. The apprentices, who are putting up the shutters, plague *David* on his affection for *Magdalena*, *Eva's* nurse. *Sachs* drives them away and sends *David* to bed, then sits down in his door-way and soliloquizes.

Was duftet doch der Flieder (The Scent of Elder Flowers)

By Herbert Witherspoon, Bass   (*In German*)   74145   12-inch, $1.50

He cannot forget the song which *Walter* delivered before the Mastersingers,—its beauty haunts him.

SACHS:
The elder's scent is waxing
So mild, so full and strong!
Its charm my limbs relaxing:
Words unto my lips would throng.
What boot such thoughts as I can span
I'm but a poor, plain-minded man!
When work's despised altogether,
Thou, my friend, settest me free;
But I'd better stick to my leather
And let all this poetry be!
(*He tries again to work. Leaves off and
    reflects.*)
And yet—it haunts me still.
I feel, but comprehend ill;
Cannot forget it,—and yet cannot grasp it;
I measure it not, e'en when I clasp it.
It seemed so old, yet new in its chime,—
Like songs of birds in sweet May-time:—
Spring's command
And gentle hand
His soul with this did entrust:
He sang because he must!
His power rose as needed;
That virtue well I heeded.
The bird who sang to-day
Has got a throat that rightly waxes;
Masters may feel dismay,
But well content with him Hans Sachs is!

BERT   DAVID AND HANS SACHS

Eva learns of *Walter's* rejection, and is so indignant that she promises to elope with him. The lovers are interrupted and forced to hide by *Beckmesser*, who comes beneath *Eva's* window for the double purpose of serenading her and rehearsing the song he is to sing for the prize on the morrow. *Hans Sachs*, hearing the tinkling of the lute, peeps out, and just as *Beckmesser* begins to sing *Sachs* breaks out into a jolly folk song.

SACHS:
Tooral looral!
Tiddy fol de rol!
Oho! Tralala! Oho!

When mother Eve from Paradise
Was by the Almighty driven,
Her naked feet so small and nice,
By stones were sorely riven!

Beckmesser is greatly annoyed and says *Sachs* must be drunk. After a long altercation with the cobbler, *Beckmesser* finally starts his song, but as *Sachs* continues to hammer on his shoe at each mistake or wrong accent, *Beckmesser* gets badly mixed, and delivers himself of this doggerel:

BECKMESSER:
I see the dawning daylight,
With great plea*sure* I do;
For now my heart takes a right
Cour*age* both fresh and new.
I do not think of dying,
Rather of trying
A young mai*den* to win.
Oh, wherefore doth the weather
Then *to*-day so excel?
I *to* all say together
'Tis *because* a dam*sel*
By her fond father,
At *his* wish rather,
To *be* wed *doth* go in.
    The bold man who
    Would come and view,
May see the maiden there so true,
On whom my hopes I firmly glue,
There*fore* is the sky *so* bright blue,
As I said to begin.

BECKMESSER'S SERENADE

The neighbors now begin to put their heads out the windows and inquire who is bawling there so late. *Magdalena* opens *Eva*'s window and signals to *Beckmesser* to go away; but *David,* thinking she is waving her hand at the marker, becomes jealous and attacks *Beckmesser.* The noise brings everyone into the street, and the curtain falls on something resembling a riot.

Act III opens in *Sachs'* workshop. *Walter,* who had spent the night with *Sachs,* comes in and tells the cobbler of a wonderful melody which had come to him in a dream. They write it down and leave it on the table. *Walter* goes out and *Beckmesser* enters, sees the song, and questions *Sachs* about it. *Sachs* makes him believe it is his own and offers to give it to him, having conceived a plan to force the Mastersingers to consent to the appearance of *Walter.* *Beckmesser* is overjoyed and runs out to learn the song. *Eva* enters to get a shoe fitted, and then occurs the great scene in which the famous quintet, one of the finest numbers in the opera, is sung.

Quintette—Selig wie die Sonne (Brightly as the Sun)

By Johanna Gadski, Soprano; Marie Mattfeld, Soprano; Ellison Van Hoose, Tenor; Marcel Journet, Bass; Albert Reiss, Baritone
(*In German*) 95201 12-inch, $5.00

The young girl, who has just had fully revealed to her the noble character of *Hans Sachs,* turns to the good shoe-maker, and with a grateful heart sings—

EVA:
Through thee life's treasure
I control,
Through thee I measure
First my soul.
And were my choice but free,
'Tis you would please my eyes;
My husband you should be,
None else should win the prize!

RENAUD AS BECKMESSER

Sachs then alludes to the fate of *King Mark* in Tristan, who married *Isolde* only to find too late that she loved another, and says:

SACHS:
To find the man before too late
I sought, or else that had been my fate!

He calls in *Magdalena* and *David*, who are dressed for the festival, and tells them he wishes them for witnesses for a christening. All look amazed, and *Sachs* explains that he wishes to christen *Sir Walter's* Master Song. As no apprentice can be a witness, *Sachs* surprises *David* by creating him a journeyman. *Eva* then commences the *Quintette of Baptism* with a short solo, beginning:

Se - - lig, wie die Son - - ne mei - nes Glü - ckes lacht,
Bright - ly as the sun up - on my for - tune breaks,

In the rapture of her new-found love she sings of the Prize Song:

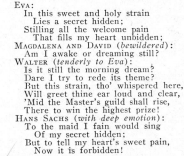

> EVA:
>   In this sweet and holy strain
>   Lies a secret hidden;
>   Stilling all the welcome pain
>   That fills my heart unbidden;
> MAGDALENA AND DAVID (*bewildered*):
>   Am I awake or dreaming still?
> WALTER (*tenderly to Eva*):
>   Is it still the morning dream?
>   Dare I try to rede its theme?
>   But this strain, tho' whispered here,
>   Will greet thine ear loud and clear,
>   'Mid the Master's guild shall rise,
>   There to win the highest prize!
> HANS SACHS (*with deep emotion*):
>   To the maid I fain would sing
>   Of my secret hidden;
>   But to tell my heart's sweet pain,
>   Now it is forbidden!

Mme. Gadski's *Eva* is quite familiar to opera-goers and is one of the most delightful of her impersonations.

COPY'T DUPONT   GADSKI AS EVA

Mr. Van Hoose's delivery of Sir Walter's music is a most artistic one, while the part of *Sachs* is splendidly sung by Journet. Miss Mattfeld, who always makes a pretty, coquettish *Magdalena*, and Herr Reiss, whose clever and amusing *David* is perhaps the best of his impersonations, sing the music of these characters most effectively.

During the *Quintette*, the beautiful theme of the *Preislied* frequently appears.

SCENE II—*A Field on the Shores of the River Pegnitz*

The scene suddenly changes to an open meadow on the banks of the Pegnitz, where the contest is to be held. The spectacle is a brilliant one, with gaily decorated boats discharging the various Guilds, with the wives and families of the members. It is in this scene that the famous March of the Guilds is played. A fine rendition of this number has been given by Sousa's Band.

March of the Guilds

By Sousa's Band
35044 12-inch, $1.25

COPY'T DUPONT

HOMER AS MAGDALENA

The Mastersingers now arrange their procession and march to take their places on the platform.

COPY'T DUPONT

FISCHER AS SACHS IN FIRST AMERICAN PRODUCTION, 1886

When all are assembled, *Sachs* rises, and in a noble address states the terms of the contest.

SACHS:

A Master, noble, rich and wise,
Will prove you this with pleasure:
His only child, the highest prize
With all his wealth and treasure,
He offers as inducement strong
To him who in the art of song
Before the people here
As victor shall appear.
Ye Masters who compete to-day,
To you before all here I say:
Bethink you what a prize this is!
Let each if he would win it,
Be sure a guileless heart is his;
Pure love and music in it.
This crown's of worth infinite,
And ne'er in recent days or olden,
By any hand so highly holden,
As by this maiden tender:
Good fortune may it lend her!
Thus Nuremberg gives honor due
To Art and all her Masters too.
(Great stir among all present. Sachs goes up to Pogner, who presses his hand, deeply moved.)

Beckmesser, who is in an awful state with his efforts to commit *Walter's* song to memory, wipes his heated brow and begins. He confuses his old melody with the new one, loses his place, mixes his lines, and is forced by the laughter of the people to stop. In a towering rage he accuses *Sachs* of plotting his defeat, then flings down the song and rushes off. *Sachs* calmly picks up the scroll and remarks that the song is a very fine one, but that it must be rendered properly. The Mastersingers accuse him of joking, but he declares:

SACHS: I tell you, sirs, the work is fine;
   But it is easy to divine
   That Beckmesser has sung it wrong.
   I swear, though you will like the song
    When someone rehearses
    The rightful tune and verses.
   And he who does will thus make known
    That he composed them, clearly;
   A Master's name, too, he should own
    Were he but judged sincerely.
   I am accused and must defend:
   A witness let me bid attend!
   Is there one here who knows I'm right,
   Let him appear before our sight.
   (Walter advances amid a general stir.)

THE MASTERS: Ah, Sachs! You're very sly indeed!—
   But you may for this once proceed.

SACHS: It shows our rules are of excellence rare
   If now and then exceptions they'll bear.

PEOPLE: A noble witness, proud and bold!
   Methinks he should some good unfold.

SACHS: Masters and people all agree
   To give my witness liberty.
   Sir Walter von Stolzing, sing the song!
   You, Masters, see if he goes wrong.

FROM AN OLD PRINT

HANS SACHS AND EVA

The Mastersingers agree that *Walter* may attempt the air, and he mounts the platform and sings the noble *Prize Song.*

Preislied (Prize Song)

By Evan Williams	*(In English)*	74115	12-inch, $1.50
By Mischa Elman, Violinist		74186	12-inch, 1.50
By Sousa's Band		*35044	12-inch, 1.25
By Victor Sorlin, 'Cellist		*35111	12-inch, 1.25

* Double-Faced Record—For title of opposite side see DOUBLE-FACED MASTERSINGER RECORDS, page 235.

WINKLEMANN AS WALTER

WALTER (*who has ascended to the platform with firm and proud steps*):
Morning was gleaming with roseate light,
The air was filled
With scent distilled
Where, beauty-beaming,
Past all dreaming,
A garden did invite.
(*The Masters here, absorbed, let fall the scroll they are watching to prove that Walter knows the song; he notices it without seeming to do so, and now proceeds in a freer style.*)
Wherein, beneath a wondrous tree
With fruit superbly laden,
In blissful love-dream I could see
The rare and tender maiden,
Whose charms beyond all price,
Entranced my heart—
Eva, in Paradise!
THE PEOPLE (*softly to one another*):
That is quite different! Who would surmise
That so much in performance lies?
WALTER:
Evening fell and night closed around;
By rugged way
My feet did stray
Towards a mountain,

Where a fountain
Enslaved me with its sound;
And there beneath a laurel tree,
With starlight glinting under,
In waking vision greeted me
A sweet and solemn wonder;
She dropped on me the fountain's dews,
That woman fair—
Parnassus's glorious Muse.
(*With great exaltation*):
Thrice happy day,
To which my poet's trance gave place!
That Paradise of which I dreamed,
In radiance before my face
Glorified lay.
To point the path the brooklet streamed:

She stood beside me,
Who shall my bride be,
The fairest sight earth ever gave,
My Muse, to whom I bow,
So angel—sweet and grave.
I woo her boldly now,
Before the world remaining,
By might of music gaining
Parnassus and Paradise.
PEOPLE (*accompanying the close, very softly*):
I feel as in a lovely dream,
Hearing but grasping not the theme!
Give him the prize!
MASTERS:
Yes, glorious singer! Victor, rise!
Your song has won the Master-prize!

Several vocal and instrumental renditions of this lovely song are given. Mr. Williams sings it beautifully in the purest of English, while the instrumental performances by Sousa and Sorlin are most pleasing. Elman gives the arrangement by Wilhelmj of the *Preislied,* which has often been played in America—in fact, as one critic has said, "it has been sawed and scratched almost to annihilation." But Elman recreates it, and plays it with a marvelous softness and purity of tone which will delight every listener.

Eva, who has listened with rapt attention, now advances to the edge of the platform and places on the head of *Walter,* who kneels on the steps, a wreath of myrtle and laurel, then leads him to her father, before whom they both kneel. *Pogner* extends his hands in benediction over them.

Walter and *Eva* lean against *Sachs,* one on each side, while *Pogner* sinks on his knee before him as if in homage. The Mastersingers point to *Sachs,* with outstretched hands, as to their chief, while the 'prentices clap hands and shout and the people wave hats and kerchiefs in enthusiasm.

ALL:
Hail Sachs! Hans Sachs!
Hail Nuremberg's darling Sachs!

(*The curtain falls*)

DOUBLE-FACED AND MISCELLANEOUS MEISTERSINGER RECORDS

Prize Song	By Sousa's Band	35044	12-inch, $1.25
Meistersinger March	By Sousa's Band		
Prize Song	By Victor Sorlin, 'Cellist	35111	12-inch, 1.25
Ernani Selection	By Pryor's Band		

(French)
MIGNON
(*Me-nyon'*)

(English)
MIGNON
(*Min'-yon*)

OPERA IN THREE ACTS

Text by Barbier and Carre, based upon Goethe's *Wilhelm Meister*. Music by Ambroise Thomas. First production at the *Opéra Comique*, Paris, in 1866. In London at Drury Lane, 1870. First New York production November 22, 1872, with Nilsson, Duval and Capoul.

Characters of the Drama

MIGNON, a young girl stolen by gypsies . . . . Mezzo-Soprano
FILINA, (*Fil-ee'-nah*) an actress . . . . Soprano
FREDERICK, a young nobleman . . . . Contralto
WILHELM MEISTER, a student . . . . Tenor
LAERTES, (*Lay-eer'-teez*) an actor . . . . Tenor
LOTHARIO, (*Low-thah'-ree-oh*) an Italian nobleman . . . . Basso Cantante
GIARNO, (*Gee-ahr'-no*) a gypsy . . . . Bass

Townsfolk, Peasants, Gypsies, Actors and Actresses.

The scene of Acts I and II is laid in Germany; of Act III in Italy.

Overture

Part I and Part II	By La Scala Orchestra	*68025	12-inch, $1.25
By Pryor's Band		31336	12-inch, 1.00

The overture is full of the grace and delicacy for which Thomas' music is celebrated, and contains the principal themes, notably *Filina's* dashing "Polonaise." The Pryor record is a fine example of the perfection attained in the playing of this organization. Every detail of the wonderful instrumentation which Thomas has written, and especially the passages for the wood-wind, is clearly brought out. A fine orchestral rendition by the La Scala players, in two parts, is also offered.

ACT I

SCENE—*Courtyard of a German Inn*

COPY'T DUPONT

FARRAR AS MIGNON

Mignon, a daughter of noble parents, was stolen when a child by gypsies, and as the act opens is a girl of seventeen, forced to dance in the public streets by the brutal *Giarno*, chief of the gypsy band.

The first scene shows the courtyard of a German inn, where townspeople and travelers are drinking. After the vigorous opening chorus, sung here by the La Scala forces, *Lothario*, a wandering minstrel, enters and sings, accompanying himself on his harp.

Opening Chorus and Solo, "Fuggitivo e tremante" (A Lonely Wanderer)

By Perelló de Segurola, Bass,
and La Scala Chorus
(*In Italian*) *55004 12-inch, $1.50

Fuggitivo e tremante (A Lonely Wanderer)

By Cesare Preve, Bass (*In Italian*) *62650 10-inch, $0.75

The minstrel is in reality *Mignon's* father, whose mind was affected by his daughter's abduction, and he wanders about seeking her.

> LOTHARIO: A lonely wanderer am I! I stray from door to door,
> As fate doth guide, or as the storm doth hurry me.
> Far, far I'll roam in search of *her!*

* *Double-Faced Record—For title of opposite side see DOUBLE-FACED MIGNON RECORDS, page 241.*

236

The gypsy band appears and *Mignon* is ordered to dance by *Giarno*, who threatens her with his stick when she wearily refuses. *Wilhelm,* a young student, protects her from the gypsy and questions her about her parents. She remembers but little, but tells him of her impression of home in this lovely *Connais-tu le pays,* full of tender beauty.

(French)   (English)

Connais-tu le pays ?   (Knowest Thou the Land ?)

(German)   (Italian)

Kennst du das Land ?   Non conosci il bel suol ?

By Marcella Sembrich, Soprano	(In French)	88098	12-inch,	$3.00
By Ernestine Schumann-Heink, Contralto	(In German)	88090	12-inch,	3.00
By Geraldine Farrar, Soprano	(In French)	88211	12-inch,	3.00
By Emmy Destinn, Soprano	(In German)	91083	10-inch,	2.00
By Giuseppina Huguet, Soprano	(In Italian)	*35178	12-inch,	1.25
By Zelie de Lussan, Soprano (Piano acc.)	(In French)	64005	10-inch,	1.00

Six records of this beautiful air, in French, German and Italian, by six famous singers, ranging in price from $1.00 to $3.00, are listed here for a choice.

This air is one of the happiest inspirations of the composer. It is said that much of its charm comes from Thomas' intimate study of Scheffer's painting, "Mignon." At any rate he has caught the inner sense of Goethe's poem and has expressed it in exquisite tones. The opening passage

gives us an idea of the melody, one of the most beautiful in the entire range of opera. The passionate longing of the orphan child for her childhood home is effectively expressed in this superb climax:

in which *Mignon* seems to pour forth her whole heart in a flood of emotion. The words are most beautiful ones.

Knowest Thou the Land ?

MIGNON:
Knowest thou yonder land where the orange grows,
Where the fruit is of gold, and so fair the rose?
Where the breeze gently wafts the song of birds,
Where the season round is mild as lover's words?
Where so calm and so soft, like Heaven's blessing true,
Spring eternally reigns, with the skies ever blue?
Alas, why afar am I straying, why ever linger here?
'Tis with thee I would fly!
'Tis there! 'Tis there! my heart's love obeying,
'Twere bliss to live and die!
'Tis there my heart's love obeying,
I'd live, I would die!

Wilhelm, full of pity for the helpless girl, offers *Giarno* a sum of money to release her, and goes into the inn to complete the bargain. *Lothario* comes to *Mignon* to bid her farewell, saying he must go south, following the swallows.

Then occurs the beautiful "Swallow Duet," one of the gems of the opera.

Les hirondelles (Song of the Swallows)

By Geraldine Farrar, Soprano; Marcel Journet, Bass   (In French)   89038   12-inch, $4.00

COPY'T DUPONT

ABOTT AS FILINA

* *Double-Faced Record—For title of opposite side see DOUBLE-FACED MIGNON RECORDS, page 241.*

BY HANS PRINTZ

MIGNON AND LOTHARIO

MIGNON: (*accompanying herself on the harp*):
Oh swallows gay and blithe,
Ye joy of every land,
Unfold your gentle wings,
Speed quickly on your way!

LOTHARIO:
The harp, touched by her gentle hand
A melancholy sound mysteriously gives forth.

MIGNON:
Ye blithe and gentle swallows,
Unfold your nimble wings;
Quick, hasten to the land
Where winter never reigns.
Thrice happy bird, thrice happy bird,
Who first the wished-for good
Right joyously shall reach.

The effectiveness of Thomas' exquisite score depends very much on the perfection of its rendering; and this is especially true of the first act music—the *Connais-tu, Lothario's* song, and this serene and beautiful duet, given so charmingly here.

Very little need be said about Miss Farrar's familiar impersonation of *Mignon*. It is always delightful, both to eye and ear. Journet sings the music of *Lothario* with dignity and beauty of voice; while Farrar's every note is exquisite in its loveliness.

Wilhelm is now invited to go to the Castle of *Prince Tieffenbach* with the troupe of players, headed by the lovely *Filina*, who has observed the handsome student with an appreciative eye. He hesitates, thinking of *Mignon*, but she begs to be allowed to accompany him disguised as a servant.

MIGNON:
Stranger! thou didst purchase me—
Dispose of me, henceforth, e'en as thou wilt.

WILHELM:
In this very town, to which Fate hath brought thee,
There lives an aged relative of mine,
Who, to her home, will gladly welcome thee.

MIGNON:
Must I then part from thee?

WILHELM:
My child, thou can'st *not* dwell with me;
Ill could I the part perform,
Of father!

MIGNON:
Could I not disguise myself,
And as thy servant, travel with thee?

WILHELM (*taking her hands*):
And what couldst thou do then?

MIGNON:
With love and gratitude,
My heart is filled.
To follow thee, O master mine,
Indeed were happiness to me!

WILHELM:
Would'st thou anew thy liberty renounce,
And be a slave once more?

MIGNON (*sadly*):
Well since my prayers thou wilt not hear,
(*pointing to Lothario, who approaches*)
I'll e'en depart with *him!*

LOTHARIO (*rushing to Mignon, and encircling her with his arms*):
Come! my footsteps follow;
Through by-paths lone and wild!
(*Attempts to draw Mignon with him.*)

Wilhelm finally yields a reluctant consent, not knowing what else to do, and the act ends with the departure of the players.

PHOTO MANUEL

FARRAR AS MIGNON—ACT II

ACT II

SCENE I—*A Boudoir in Tieffenbach Castle*

Act II represents a room in the Prince's castle. *Filina* is seated in front of her toilet table, musing on the handsome *Wilhelm,* who has made a deep impression on her somewhat volatile affections. *Wilhelm* enters with *Mignon,* who meets with a cool reception from the gay actress. *Wilhelm* makes love to *Filina* while *Mignon* watches them with a sad heart, as she has learned to love her new master. When left alone, she tries by the aid of *Filina's* rouge to make her complexion as beautiful as that of the actress who has dazzled her master, and, noting the effect in the glass, sings a gay song with an odd refrain, called by the composer "Styrienne."

Styrienne, "Je connais" (I Know a Poor Maiden)

By Geraldine Farrar, Soprano   (In French) 88152 12-inch, $3.00

Miss Farrar has given us a charming rendition of this Mignon air, which (next to the well-known *Connais-tu*) is the favorite one in the opera.

Mignon:
Well I know a poor young child,
A sad young child of Bohemia,
On whose pale sunken cheeks joy ne'er rested,
Ah! ah! ah! ah! what a dull story!
I cannot leave the glass,
So much improved I'm seeming,
Am I the same, or dreaming?
Ah! la la.
(*Looking in the glass*):
Am I still Mignon?
Can it be Mignon that I see?
One fine day, the child in play,
A stratagem boldly trying,
To the master's good pleasure applying,
Ah! ah! ah! what a foolish story!

I fain would turn away,
But so improved am seeming,
Am I the same, or dreaming?
Ah! Ah! la la
Am I still Mignon?
No! no! 'tis I no longer!
But then! 'tis not she either!
Some other secrets she must have her charms
  to heighten.
(*Opens the door of the dressing room*):
Is it not there she keeps her gayest dresses?
Yes! alas! were I Filina, would he love me
  as well?
What idle folly!   (From the Ditson score.
'Tis a demon now tempts me!   Copy't 1880.)

Miss Farrar sings this quaint and fascinating "Styrienne" with the child-like gaiety and charm which belong to it; and her voice is as pure and true as a flute when she reaches the high D at the end of the air.

Mignon now goes into the closet, and after *Wilhelm* has returned makes her appearance in one of *Filina's* dresses. He tells her in a beautiful air that he must leave her.

Addio, Mignon (Farewell, Mignon)

By M. Régis, Tenor   (In French) *45023 10-inch, $1.00
By Emilio Perea, Tenor (Piano acc.)   (In Italian) *63420 10-inch,   .75

Mignon utters a cry of grief and begins to weep, while *Wilhelm* tenderly says:

Wilhelm:
Farewell, Mignon, take heart!
Thy tears restrain!
In the bright years of youth no grief doth
  linger long.
Weep not, Mignon!
O'er thee just Heaven will watch with fost'-
  ring care.
Oh, may'st thou thy dear native land once
  more regain!
May fortune on thy fate henceforth benignly
  smile!
It pains me much to leave thee: my stricken
  heart
With thy lone destiny will ever sympathize!
Farewell, Mignon, take heart!
Then dry thy tears.

Mignon refuses money which he offers her, and is about to bid him farewell when *Filina* enters, and seeing *Mignon* in one of her own dresses, eyes her with sarcastic amusement, which puts *Mignon* into a jealous rage and she rushes into the cabinet, tears off the borrowed finery and puts on her gypsy garments.

SCENE II—*The Gardens of the Castle*

The scene changes to the park of the castle. *Mignon,* in despair, attempts to throw herself into the lake, but is prevented by *Lothario,* who consoles her. In a fit of jealousy she

---

Double-Faced Record—For title of opposite side see DOUBLE-FACED MIGNON RECORDS, page 241.

wishes that fire would consume the castle in which *Filina* had won her master's affections. *Lothario* is puzzled by this and goes off muttering to himself.

The actors and guests now issue from the castle proclaiming the beauty and talent of *Filina*. In the flush of her triumph she sings the brilliant *Polonese* or *polacca* (French *Polonaise*), one of the most difficult and showy of all soprano airs.

Polonese, "Io son Titania" (I'm Fair Titania!)

By Luisa Tetrazzini, Soprano	(*In Italian*)	88296	12-inch,	$3.00
By Giuseppina Huguet, Soprano	(*In Italian*)	*35178	12-inch,	1.25
By Mlle. Korsoff, Soprano	(*In French*)	*45006	10-inch,	1.00

The Victor is able to offer three fine renditions of this popular number, headed by the superb Tetrazzini record, one of the most perfect in her list. Mlle. Korsoff, of the *Opéra Comique,* sings the air in French with much brilliancy, while an Italian record is furnished by that gifted Spanish prima donna, Mme. Huguet.

Io son Titania
(*Behold Titania!*)

CHORUS:
She is truly divine, Filina!
At her feet we lay our hearts and our flowers!
What charms, what beauties are hers!
Ah! what success! Bravo! Honor to Titania!
FILINA:
Yes; for to-night I am queen of the fairies!
Observe ye here, my sceptre bright,
(*Raising the wand which she holds in her hand.*)
And behold my num'rous trophies!
(*Pointing to the wreath which has been presented to her.*)
I'm fair Titania, glad and gay,
Thro' the world unfetter'd I blithely stray.
With jocund heart and happy mien,
I cheerily dance the hours away,
Like the bird that freely wings its flight.
Fairies dance around me,
Elfin sprites on nimble toe around me gaily dance.
For I'm fair Titania!
Both night and day. My attendants ever sing,
The achievements of the god of Love!
On the wave's white foam,
'Mid the twilight grey, 'mid hedges, 'mid flowers,
I blithely do dance!
Behold Titania, glad and gay!

Wilhelm now sees *Mignon* and is about to speak to her when *Filina* interposes and asks her to go to the castle on some errand. The young girl, glad to escape meeting *Wilhelm,* obeys, but has no sooner gone than the castle is discovered to be in flames, the half-witted *Lothario* having set fire to it after having heard *Mignon's* jealous wish.

Wilhelm rushes into the burning castle and soon reappears with the unconscious form of *Mignon,* while the curtain falls on a magnificent tableau.

ACT III

SCENE—*Count Lothario's Castle in Italy*

This act takes place in the castle of *Lothario,* to which the old man has instinctively returned with *Mignon,* followed by *Wilhelm,* who now realizes that he loves his youthful ward. The young girl is recovering from a dangerous illness, and as *Lothario* watches outside her sick room, he sings a beautiful lullaby or *berceuse,*

Berceuse (Lullaby) (Ninna nanna)

By Pol Plancon, Bass	(*In Italian*)	85126	12-inch,	$3 00
By Gaudio Mansueto, Bass	(*In Italian*)	*55004	12-inch,	1.50
By Cesare Preve, Bass	(*In Italian*)	*62650	10-inch,	.75

LOTHARIO:
I've soothed the throbbing of her aching heart
And to her lips the smile I have restored.
Her weary eyes at last have closed
In gentle slumber;

By day and night some heav'nly spirit
The maiden doth protect;
On wings celestial, it doth hover round
Protecting her from harm!

---

* *Double-Faced Record—For title of opposite side see DOUBLE-FACED MIGNON RECORDS, page 241.*

Wilhelm takes *Lothario's* place as watcher, and tells of his new-found affection in this beautiful air, given here by M. Regis, of the Paris *Opéra Comique.*

Elle ne croyait pas (Pure as a Flower)

By M. Regis, Tenor　　　　　　　　　　　　(*In French*) *45023 10-inch, $1.00

WILHELM:

In soothing yon poor, hapless maiden
At last I have discovered her secret;
From her sweet lips my name escaped!
Ah! little thought the maid,
In innocence arrayed,
What she in her breast had nurtured,
Would ardent love become,

And thus pervert the peaceful current
Of her peaceful life.
Oh balmy April,
Who to the wither'd flowers restoreth their colors,
Kiss her fair cheek,
And a grateful sigh of love cause to escape!

Mignon now comes with feeble step on the balcony, and seeing *Wilhelm,* is much agitated. He endeavors to soothe her, but she insists that only *Lothario* loves her. *Lothario* now enters, and announces that he is the *Count Lothario,* having been restored to his right mind by the familiar scenes of his ancestral home. He shows them the jewels and prayer book of his lost daughter, and tells them her name was *Sperata. Mignon* starts at the name and murmurs:

Ah, that sweet name to my ear is familiar,
A memory of my childhood
It may be, that's gone forever!

She then begins to read from the book a little prayer, but soon drops the book and continues from memory, her hands clasped and her eyes raised to Heaven. *Lothario* is much agitated and when she has finished, recognizes her as his lost daughter. Father and daughter are reunited, while a blessing is bestowed on the young people by the happy *Lothario.*

DOUBLE-FACED AND MISCELLANEOUS MIGNON RECORDS

Opening Chorus and Solo, "Fuggitivo e tremante" By Andrea Perelló de Segurola, Bass, and La Scala Chorus		55004	12-inch,	$1.50
Ninna nanna　　　　By Gaudio Mansueto, Bass				
Preludio, Parte 2a (Overture, Parte 2) By La Scala Orchestra		68025	12-inch,	1.25
Preludio, Parte 1a (Overture, Parte 1) By La Scala Orchestra				
Polonese—Io Son Titania! (I'm Fair Titania!) By Giuseppina Huguet, Soprano (*In Italian*)		35178	12-inch,	1.25
Non conosci il bel suol? (Dost Thou Know That Fair Land?)　　By Giuseppina Huguet, Soprano (*In Italian*)				
Polonaise—Io Son Titania! By Mlle. Korsoff, Soprano (*In French*)		45006	10-inch,	1.00
Lakmé—Pourquoi dans les grands bois By Alice Verlet, Soprano (*In French*)				
Adieu, Mignon, Courage (Farewell, Mignon) By M. Regis, Tenor (*In French*)		45023	10-inch,	1.00
Elle ne croyait pas (Pure as a Flower) By M. Regis, Tenor (*In French*)				
Fuggitivo e tremante　　By Cesare Preve, Bass		62650	10-inch,	.75
Ninna nanna　　　　By Cesare Preve, Bass				
Gavotte　　　　By Victor String Quartet		16323	10-inch,	.75
Norma Selection (Bellini)　　By Pryor's Band				
Addio, Mignon (Farewell, Mignon) By Emilio Perea, Tenor (*In Italian*)		63420	10-inch,	.75
Stelle d'Oro—Romanza　By Silvano Isalberti, Tenor (*In Italian*)				

NORMA

(*Nor'-mah*)

OPERA IN TWO ACTS

Book by Felice Romani, founded on an old French story.   Score by Vincenzo Bellini.
First production December 26, 1831, at Milan.   First London production at King's Theatre,
in Italian, June 20, 1833.   In English at Drury Lane, June 24, 1837.   First Paris production
December 8, 1835.   First New York production February 25, 1841.

Characters

NORMA, High Priestess of the Temple of Esus ....Soprano
ADALGISA, a Virgin of the Temple...............................Soprano
CLOTILDE, attendant on Norma ....Soprano
POLLIONE, a Roman proconsul commanding the legions of Gaul ...... Tenor
FLAVIO, his lieutenant ....Tenor
OROVESO, the Arch-Druid, father of Norma.......................Bass

Ministering and Attendant Priests and Officers of the Temple, Gallic
Warriors, Priestesses and Virgins of the Temple,
two children of Norma and Pollione

Scene and Period : The scene is laid in Gaul, shortly after the Roman conquest

Norma, although an opera of the old school and seldom performed nowadays, contains
some of the loveliest of the writings of Bellini.   Its beauties are of the old-fashioned kind
which our forefathers delighted in, and which are an occasional welcome relief from the
abundance of "music dramas" with which we are surrounded of late.   Especially charming is the spirited overture, always a favorite on band programs.

Overture

By Arthur Pryor's Band	*35166	12-inch, $1.25
By Victor Band	*35029	12-inch, 1.25

The briskness and sparkle of this fine overture and its inspiring climax are well preserved in Mr. Pryor's vigorous rendering, and in the splendidly played Victor Band record,
made under Mr. Rogers' direction.

The scene is laid among the Druids at the time of the Roman invasion.   *Norma*, the
High Priestess, though sworn to bring about the expulsion of Rome, is secretly married to
a Roman proconsul, *Pollione*, by whom she has two children.   She rebukes the Druids for
wishing to declare war, and after the ceremony of cutting the mistletoe, she invokes peace
from the moon in the exquisite prayer, *Casta Diva*.

Casta Diva (Queen of Heaven)

By Marcella Sembrich, Soprano	(*In Italian*)	88104	12-inch,	$3.00
By Celestina Boninsegna, Soprano	(*In Italian*)	92025	12-inch,	3.00
By Giuseppina Huguet, Soprano	(*In Italian*)	*16539	10-inch,	.75

This lovely air still holds a high place in popular favor, its beauty and tenderness making it well worthy of a place among modern airs.   As evidence of the great popularity of
this number, three famous prima donnas have selected it for their Victor lists.

NORMA:
Queen of Heaven, while thou art reigning
Love upon us is still remaining.
Clad in pureness, alone disdaining
Grosser earth's nocturnal veil.

Queen of Heaven, hallow'd by thy presence,
Let its holier, sweeter essence,
Quelling ev'ry lawless license,
As above, so here prevail!

In the next scene *Norma* discovers that her husband loves *Adalgisa*, and in her rage she
contemplates killing her children; but her mother's heart conquers, and she resolves to

---

* *Double-Faced Record—For title of opposite side see next page.*

yield her husband and children to *Adalgisa* and expiate her offences on the funeral pyre. *Adalgisa* pleads with her, urging her to abandon her purpose, and offers to send *Pollione* back to her.

This scene is expressed in the exquisite *Hear Me, Norma*, familiar to every music-lover.

GRISI AS NORMA

Mira o Norma (Hear Me, Norma)

By Ida Giacomelli, Soprano,
and Lina Mileri, Contralto
(*In Italian*) *62101 10-inch, $0.75
By Arthur Pryor's Band *16323 10-inch, .75

The lovely strains of this melodious number have delighted countless hearers in the eighty years since it was written.

ADALGISA:
Dearest Norma, before thee kneeling,
View these darlings, thy precious treasures;
Let that sunbeam, a mother's feeling,
Break the night around thy soul.

NORMA:
Wouldst win that soul, by this entreating
Back to earth's delusive pleasures,
From the phantoms, far more fleeting,
Which in death's deep ocean shoal?

Pollione refuses to return to *Norma* and attempts to seize *Adalgisa* against her will. *Norma* foils this attempt and reasons with him, telling him he must give up his guilty love or die. This is expressed in a dramatic duet.

In mia mano (In My Grasp)

By Ida Giacomelli, Soprano, and Gino Martinez-Patti, Tenor
(*In Italian*) *68309 12-incn, $1.25

Pollione still refuses, and *Norma* strikes the sacred shield to summon the Druids. She declares war on Rome and denounces *Pollione*, but offers to save his life if he will leave the country. He refuses, and she is about to put him to death, when love overcomes justice and the Priestess denounces herself to save *Pollione*. *Norma's* noble sacrifice causes his love to return and they ascend the funeral pyre together. As the flames mount about them they are declared purified of all sin.

DOUBLE-FACED AND MISCELLANEOUS NORMA RECORDS

{Overture	By Arthur Pryor's Band}	35166	12-inch,	$1.25
{ Oberon Overture (*Weber*)	By Arthur Pryor's Band}			
{Overture	By Victor Band}	35029	12-inch,	1.25
{ Huguenots Selection	By Victor Band}			
{In mia mano alfin tu sei (In My Grasp)				
{ By Ida Giacomelli, Soprano, and Gino Martinez-Patti, Tenor (*In Italian*)				
{ Favorita—Fia vero lasciarti (*Shall I Leave Thee?*)		68309	12-inch,	1.25
{ By Clotilde Esposito, Soprano, and Gino Martinez-Patti, Tenor (*In Italian*)				
{Norma Selection (Hear Me, Norma!)	By Pryor's Band}	16323	10-inch,	.75
{ Mignon—Gavotte	By Victor String Quartet}			
{Casta Diva (Queen of Heaven)				
{ By Giuseppina Huguet, Soprano (*In Italian*)		16539	10-inch,	.75
{ Lucia—Regnava nel silenzio (*Silence O'er All*) By Giuseppina Huguet, Soprano (*In Italian*)				
{Mira o Norma (Hear Me, Norma) By Ida Giacomelli,				
{ Soprano, and Lina Mileri, Contralto (*In Italian*)		62101	10-inch,	.75
{ Carmen—Preludio, Act IV	By La Scala Orchestra}			

* Double-Faced Record—For title of opposite side see above list.

ELYSIUM—ACT II

(Italian)

ORFEO ED EURIDICE

(*Or'-fee-oh ay U-ree-dee'-chee*)

(English)

ORPHEUS AND EURYDICE

(*Or'-fee-us and U-ri-dee'-chee*)

OPERA IN FOUR ACTS

Book by Ramieri De Calzabigi; music by Christoph Willibald von Gluck. First production in Vienna, October 5, 1762. First Paris production, 1764. First London production at Covent Garden, June 26, 1860. Other revivals were during the Winter Garden season of 1863; in 1885 (in German), by the Metropolitan Opera under Walter Damrosch; the English production in 1886 by the National Opera Company, and the Abbey revival in Italian in 1892; and the Metropolitan production of 1910, with Homer, Gadski and Gluck.

Cast

ORPHEUS .... Contralto
EURIDICE .... Soprano
LOVE .... Soprano
A HAPPY SHADE .... Soprano

Shepherds and Shepherdesses, Furies and Demons, Heroes and
Heroines in Hades.

This opera, which has been called "Gluck's incomparable masterpiece," and of which the great Fétis wrote, "it is one of the most beautiful productions of genius," may be properly termed a purely classical music drama. The music is exquisite in its delicacy and

HOMER AND GADSKI AS ORPHEUS AND
EURYDICE

grace, while the story is an interesting and affecting one. Orpheus may be called the grandfather of grand opera, it being the oldest work of its kind to hold its place on the stage, the first representation occurring one hundred and fifty years ago.

The opera has had only one adequate American production previous to the Metropolitan revival, and that was during the American Opera Company season of 1886—the Abbey revival of 1892 meeting with but indifferent success. Such has been the interest aroused by the recent performances, that it is likely to be heard quite frequently in the future.

The story concerns the Greek poet *Orpheus,* who grieves deeply over the death of his wife *Euridice,* and finally declares he will enter the realms of *Pluto* and search for her among the spirits of the departed. The goddess *Love* appears and promises to aid him, on condition that when he has found *Euridice* he will return to earth without once looking back.

Orpheus journeys to the Gates of Erebus, and so softens the hearts of the Demon guards by his grief and his exquisite playing of his lyre, that he is permitted to enter. He finds *Euridice,* and without looking at her, takes her by the hand and bids her follow him. She obeys, but failing to understand his averted gaze, upbraids him for his apparent coldness and asks that he shall look at her.

Su e con me vieni cara (On My Faith Relying)

By Johanna Gadski, Soprano; Louise Homer, Contralto
(*In Italian*) 89041 12-inch, $4.00

Orpheus, knowing that to cast a single look at his loved one means death to her, keeps his face averted. The dialogue portrays the emotions of the characters, while Gluck's music suggests the present perplexity and the tragedy which is to follow.

Unable to endure longer the reproaches of his wife, he clasps her in his arms, only to see her sink down lifeless.

Ach, Ich habe sie verloren (I Have Lost My Eurydice)

By Ernestine Schumann-Heink, Contralto
(*In German*) 88091 12-inch, $3.00

J'ai perdu mon Euridice (I Have Lost My Euridice)

By Jeanne Gerville-Réache, Contralto
(*In French*) 88198 12-inch, 3.00

Che faro senza Euridice (I Have Lost My Euridice)

By Louise Homer, Contralto
(*In Italian*) 88285 12-inch, 3.00

COPY'T DUPONT
HOMER AS ORPHEUS

"Malheureux! qu'ai-je fait? Et dans quel précipice m'a plongé mon funeste amour!" ("Wretched one, what have I done! Into what gulf has my fatal love cast me?") cries the hapless youth, and breaks into his pathetic lamentation, the beauty and pathos of which have never been questioned.

LANDE   THE GATES OF HELL—ACT IV

"I have lost my Eurydice   It is your faithful husband.
My misfortune is without its like.   Hear my voice, which calls you.
Cruel fate! I shall die of my sorrow.   Silence of death! vain hope!
Eurydice, Eurydice, answer me!   What suffering, what torment, wrings my heart!"

Of the many beautiful numbers in Gluck's drama this lovely aria of mourning, (best known by the Italian title *Che faro senza Euridice*) is the most familiar. No fewer than three renditions, in German, French and Italian, by three famous exponents of the part of *Orpheus*, are offered for the choice of opera lovers.

The grief-stricken poet is about to take his own life when the goddess again appears and arrests his arm.

LOVE:
    Hold, Orpheus!
ORPHEUS (*despairingly*):
    What would you with me?
LOVE:
    Thine anguish well doth prove
    Thy constancy and truth.
    'Tis time that the trial be ended!

Eurydice! revive!
To embrace the fond youth
Who dared so much for thee!
ORPHEUS:
    My Eurydice!
EURYDICE (*reviving*):
    My Orpheus! (*They embrace.*)

(**Curtain**)

MAIRET

EURYDICE RESTORED TO ORPHEUS—ACT III

OTELLO AND DESDEMONA

(Italian)		(English)
OTELLO		**OTHELLO**
(*Oh-tel'-low*)		(*Oth-thel'-low*)

OPERA IN FOUR ACTS

Text by Arrigo Boito after the drama of Shakespeare. Music by Giuseppe Verdi. First production February 5, 1887, at La Scala, Milan. First London production May 18, 1889. First American production April 16, 1888, with Campanini as *Otello*. Some notable revivals occurred in 1894, with Tamagno and Maurel; in 1902, with Eames, Alvarez and Scotti; and in 1908 at the Manhattan, with Melba, Zenatello and Sammarco.

Characters

OTELLO, a Moor, general in the Venetian army....................Tenor
IAGO, (*Ee-ah'-go*) his ensign ....Baritone
CASSIO, (*Cass'-ee-oh*) his lieutenant...............................Tenor
RODERIGO, (*Roh-der-ee'-go*) a Venetian gentleman....................Tenor
LODOVICO, ambassador of the Venetian Republic...................Bass
MONTANO, predecessor of Othello in the government of Cyprus.......Bass
A HERALD..Bass
DESDEMONA, wife of Othello....................................Soprano
EMILIA, (*Ay-mee'-lee-ah*) wife of Iago ....Mezzo-Soprano

Soldiers and Sailors of the Republic; Venetian Ladies and Gentlemen; Cypriot Men, Women and Children; Greek, Dalmatian and Albanian Soldiers; an Innkeeper.

Scene and Period: *End of the fifteenth century; a seaport in Cyprus.*

VERDI AND MAUREL AT FIRST
PERFORMANCE OF OTELLO

After having given the world his splendid *Aida,* Verdi rested on his laurels and was silent for sixteen years; then, at the age of seventy-four, he suddenly astonished the world with his magnificent Otello, a masterly music-drama which alone would suffice to make him famous.

The change from the Verdi of 1853 and Il Trovatore, to the Verdi of 1887 and Otello, is amazing. Each opera produced by him shows a steady advance, until something approximating perfection is reached in Otello, the writing of which was an astonishing feat for a man of nearly eighty years of age.

The text, by that accomplished scholar and master librettist, Boito, follows closely the tragedy of Shakespeare.

ACT I

SCENE—*Otello's Castle in Cyprus. A Storm is Raging and the Angry Sea is visible in the Background*

Venetians, soldiers, including *Iago, Roderigo* and *Cassio,* are awaiting the return of *Otello.* His vessel arrives safely, and amid much rejoicing the Moor announces that the war is over, the enemy's ships having all been sunk. He goes into the castle, and *Iago* and *Roderigo* plan the conspiracy against *Cassio* and *Otello,* by which *Roderigo* hopes to secure *Desdemona* for himself and *Iago* to be revenged on *Otello.*

They join the soldiers and try to induce *Cassio* to drink. He refuses, but when *Iago* toasts *Desdemona,* he is compelled to join. *Iago* sings the rousing *Brindisi:*

Brindisi—Inaffia l'ugola (Drinking Song —Let Me the Cannakin Clink)

By Pasquale Amato, Baritone, and Chorus
    (*In Italian*) 88338 12-inch, $3.00
By Antonio Scotti, Baritone
    (*In Italian*) 88082 12-inch, 3.00
By Antonio Scotti, Baritone (*Piano acc.*)
    (*In Italian*) 87040 10-inch, 2.00

during which he continues to fill *Cassio's* glass. When the latter is quite drunk they pick a quarrel with him, and he draws his sword, wounding *Montano,* while *Iago* and *Cassio* rouse a cry of "riot," which brings *Otello* from the castle. He disgraces *Cassio* and orders all to disperse, remaining alone with *Desdemona* for a long love scene. Part of this scene has been recorded here by Mme. Lotti and M. Conti, of Milan. The curtain falls as husband and wife go slowly into the castle.

Quando narravi (When Thou Speakest)

By F. Lotti, Soprano; F. Conti, Tenor
    (*In Italian*) *55023 12-inch, $1.50

SLEZAK AS OTELLO

ACT II

SCENE —*A Room in the Castle*

The crafty *Iago* is advising *Cassio* how to regain the favor of *Otello,* telling him that he must induce *Desdemona* to intercede for him. *Cassio* eagerly goes in search of *Desdemona,* while *Iago* gazes after him, satisfied with the progress of his schemes, and then sings the superb *Credo.*

Double-Faced Record—For title of opposite side see DOUBLE-FACED OTELLO RECORDS, page 251.

Credo (Otello's Creed)

By Antonio Scotti, Baritone	(*In Italian*)	88030	12-inch, $3.00
By Pasquale Amato, Baritone	(*In Italian*)	88328	12-inch, 3.00
By Ernesto Badini, Baritone	(*In Italian*) *55023		12-inch, 1.50

This is a free adaptation of *Iago's* last speech with *Cassio* in Shakespeare, Act II. In his setting Verdi has expressed fully the character of the perfidious *Iago*: cynical, vain, weak and subtle. He declares that he was fashioned by a cruel God who intended him for evil, and that he cares naught for the consequences, as after death there is nothing.

Scotti's singing of this number is a most impressive one; while the wonderful rendition by Amato will be pronounced one of the most striking in his list.

Iago sees *Desdemona* approach and *Cassio* greet her, and as soon as the young officer is earnestly pleading with her to intercede for *Otello*, *Iago* runs in search of *Otello*, and sows the first seeds of jealousy in the heart of the Moor, bidding him watch his wife well. *Otello*, much troubled, seeks *Desdemona* and questions her. She begins to intercede for *Cassio*, but the Moor repulses her, and when she would wipe his perspiring brow, roughly throws down the handkerchief, which is picked up by *Iago*.

Left alone with *Iago*, *Otello* gives way to despair, and expresses his feelings in the bitter *Ora e per sempre*.

Ora e per sempre addio (And Now, Forever Farewell)

By Francesco Tamagno, Tenor

(*In Italian*)	95003	10-inch, $5.00	
By Enrico Caruso	87071	10-inch, 2.00	
By Nicola Zerola	64168	10-inch, 1.00	

PHOTO BERT

AMATO AS IAGO

Now finally convinced that *Desdemona* is deceiving him, he bids farewell to peace of mind, ambition and the glory of conquest.

Caruso delivers the number magnificently, being especially effective in the closing passage. Other renditions are the famous one by Tamagno, and a popular-priced record by Zerola.

Iago further says that he has seen *Desdemona's* handkerchief in *Cassio's* room, at which news *Otello* is beside himself with rage. The act closes with the great scene in which *Iago* offers to help *Otello* secure his revenge, and they swear an awful oath never to pause until the guilty shall be punished.

ACT III
SCENE—*The Great Hall of the Castle*

Otello now seeks *Desdemona* and contrives an excuse to borrow her handkerchief. She offers it, but he says it is not the one, and asks for the one he had given her, with a peculiar pattern. She says it is in her room and offers to bring it, but he at once denounces her, and sends her away astonished and grieved at the sudden jealousy which she cannot understand. He remains looking after her in the deepest dejection, then sings his sorrowful soliloquy, *Dio mi potevi*.

Dio mi potevi scagliare (Had it Pleased Heaven)

By Antonio Paoli, Tenor

(*In Italian*)	88240	12-inch, $3.00	
By Carlo Barrera, Tenor			
(*In Italian*) *55009		12-inch, 1.50	

LE THEATRE

ALDA AS DESDEMONA

Double-Faced Record—For title of opposite side see DOUBLE-FACED OTELLO RECORDS, page 251.

"Had Heaven seen fit to send me sorrow, shame, poverty," he says, "I could have endured it with patience, but this blow is too much to bear."

Iago now tells *Otello* how he had slept in *Cassio's* room lately and had heard *Cassio* talking in his sleep, bemoaning the fate which had robbed him of *Desdemona* and given her to the Moor. This dream is related in a highly dramatic air:

Era la notte (Cassio's Dream)
By Mario Ancona, Baritone   *(In Italian)* 87015 10-inch, $2.00

Cassio enters, and *Iago,* bidding *Otello* watch behind a pillar, goes to the young officer, and with fiendish ingenuity induces him to talk of his sweetheart *Bianca. Otello,* listening, thinks that it is of *Desdemona* that *Cassio* speaks. *Cassio* produces the fatal handkerchief, telling *Iago* he had found it in his room, and wondering to whom it can belong. *Otello,* seeing the handkerchief and not hearing the conversation, has no further doubt of *Desdemona's* guilt, and when *Cassio* departs he asks *Iago* how best can he murder them both. The villain suggests that *Desdemona* be strangled in her bed, and says he will himself kill *Cassio.* In a highly dramatic duet, given here by Barrera and Badini, they swear a solemn oath of vengeance.

Ah! mille vite (A Thousand Lives!)
By Carlo Barrera, Tenor; E. Badini, Baritone *(In Italian)* *55009 12-inch $1.50

Messengers now arrive from the Senate bearing orders for *Otello,* who has been recalled to Venice, and *Cassio* appointed Governor of Cyprus in his stead. He announces his departure on the morrow, and then unable to control his rage and jealousy he publicly insults *Desdemona* and flings her to the ground. As she is being led away by her maids he falls in a fit. The people, considering the summons to Venice an additional honor for the Moor, rush in, shouting "Hail to Otello," when *Iago,* pointing with fiendish triumph to the prostrate body, cries, "Behold your Lion of Venice!"

SCOTTI, WICKHAM, ALDA AND SLEZAK IN OTELLO

ACT IV
SCENE—*Desdemona's Bedroom*

The heartbroken *Desdemona* is preparing to retire, assisted by her maid, *Emilia.* She tells *Emilia* that an old song of her childhood keeps coming into her mind. Then she sings the sad and beautiful *Willow Song.*

Salce, salce (Willow Song)
By Nellie Melba, Soprano   *(In Italian)* 88148 12-inch, $3.00
By Frances Alda, Soprano   *(In Italian)* 88214 12-inch, 3.00

This plaintive song seems like the lamentation of a broken heart, its last words being prophetic of the coming tragedy.

The faithful *Emilia* leaves her, and she kneels before the image of the Madonna and sings the noble *Ave,* one of the most inspired portions of the wonderful fourth act, in which Verdi has risen to his greatest height.

Ave Maria (Hail, Mary)
By Nellie Melba, Soprano   *(In Italian)* 88149 12-inch, $3.00
By Frances Alda, Soprano   *(In Italian)* 88213 12-inch, 3.00

Double-Faced Record—For title of opposite side see DOUBLE-FACED OTELLO RECORDS, page 251.

This prayer occurs in the last act of the opera, and is sung by *Desdemona* as she retires to the couch from which she is fated never to rise. The "Ave Maria" is introduced by a characteristic monotone for the voice, accompanied by some organ-like harmonies which steal in with exquisite effect from the strings of the orchestra.

The portrayal of the mingled apprehension and resignation of *Desdemona* in this scene through the medium of the voice is worthy to rank with Melba's most celebrated operatic creations—her *Marguerita*—her *Juliet*—her *Mimi*. The purity and youthfulness of the feeling imparted, apart from the freshness and delicate perfection of the tones themselves, is amazing, filling the mind with wonder at the perpetual miracle of Melba's perfect art. Mme. Alda, whose *Desdemona* has been one of the finest of her impersonations at the Metropolitan, sings the number beautifully.

At the close of the air *Desdemona* remains kneeling and prays in broken accents, her voice being almost inaudible.

And now we come to the most dramatic scene of the opera, one in which the nerves of the spectators are strained to the breaking point.

LANDE
THE MURDER OF DESDEMONA (ALDA AND SLEZAK)

Otello enters and rushes toward the bed, but stops and gazes at his sleeping wife a long time, then approaches and kisses her. She wakes and speaks his name. He accuses her again of an intrigue with *Cassio,* but she swears that it is false and that the handkerchief was not given by her to *Cassio.* He disregards her cries for mercy and strangles her. *Emilia* knocks at the door and is admitted by *Otello,* who is in a kind of daze, not realizing what he has done. Seeing *Desdemona* lifeless, she accuses him of the crime and calls loudly for help. All rush in and *Emilia,* seeing *Iago,* denounces him as the author of the plot, and tells *Otello* that *Desdemona* was

innocent. The Moor is torn with remorse, and tenderly gazing on his dead wife, sings the passage with which his last air begins.

Morte d'Otello (Death of Otello)

By Francesco Tamagno, Tenor	*(In Italian)*	95002	10-inch, $5.00
By Nicola Zerola, Tenor	*(In Italian)*	74217	12-inch, 1.50

He then draws a dagger and stabs himself, and with a final effort to embrace the *Desdemona* he has so cruelly wronged, he dies.

DOUBLE-FACED AND MISCELLANEOUS OTELLO RECORDS

Dio mi potevi scagliare (Had It Pleased Heaven)
By Carlo Barrera, Tenor *(In Italian)*
Giuramento—Ah! mille vite (A Thousand Lives)
By Carlo Barrera, Tenor; Ernesto Badini, Baritone
(In Italian) } 55009 12-inch, $1.50

Quando narravi (When Thou Speakest)
By F. Lotti, Soprano; F. Conti, Tenor *(In Italian)*
Credo (Otello's Creed)
By Ernesto Badini, Baritone *(In Italian)* } 55023 12-inch, 1.50

I PAGLIACCI   THE PLAYERS

(Ee Pahl-yat'-chee)

Drama in Two Acts. Words and Music by R. Leoncavallo

The English version quoted from is by Henry Grafton Chapman

Quotations from text and music (except the Prologue) by kind permission of G. Schirmer. (Copy't 1906)

LEONCAVALLO

Ruggiero Leoncavallo was born at Naples, March 8, 1858, and was the son of a magistrate, the Chevalier Vincont, president of the tribunal of Potenza. His mother was a daughter of the celebrated artist, Raffaele d'Auria, famous for his decorations in the royal palace at Naples. He took up the pianoforte at an early age with Simonetti, a well-known teacher of Naples, and entered the Neapolitan Conservatoire, where he studied under Cesi, Ruta and Rossi. At sixteen he made a concert tour as a pianist with some success. Leaving the Conservatoire at eighteen he promptly showed his leaning toward operatic composition by beginning to write an opera, the libretto based on de Vigny's well-known drama, Chatterton. Finding an *impressario,* the production of this opera was promised, but at the last moment he was deserted by his manager and the young composer was reduced to poverty. He did not despair, however, and abandoning for a time his operatic pretensions, set to work at anything which would give him a living. He gave lessons and played accompaniments at cafe concerts, finally becoming a concert pianist, the latter occupation taking him to many countries—England, France, Holland, Germany and Egypt. Returning to Italy after several years of these wanderings, he proved that he had not been idle by submitting to the house of Ricordi the first part of a tremen-dous trilogy based on the subject of the Renaissance in Italy.

This monumental work he entitled *Crepusculum* (Twilight), and the three parts were called : I—*Medici;* II—*Girolamo Savonarola;* III—*Cezare Borgia.* This Ricordi accepted, agreeing to produce the first part, and Leoncavallo spent a year in its completion. Three years passed by and the production was not made. In despair he went to the rival firm of Sonzogno, which encouraged him to write the opera which was to make him famous. The young composer went to work and in the space of five months completed his opera, basing the plot on an actual occurrence in the court where his father was presiding as judge.

The production of Pagliacci was made on May 21, 1892, at the Teatro dal Verme, Milan. Its success was overwhelming, and the name of Leoncavallo was heard throughout the world. His fame led to the production, in 1893, of the first section of the great trilogy, *Medici;* but it was not well received. Other operas by Leoncavallo which have been pro-duced with more or less success are: Chatterton (produced 1896); Bohême (1897); Zaza (1900); and finally Roland, written at the request of the German Emperor (1904). He has written also a symphonic poem, *Serafita;* a ballet (*La Vita d'una Marionetta*) and several comic operas.

But it is Pagliacci which will keep the name of Leoncavallo remembered. Its master-fully constructed libretto ; its compelling and moving story ; the orchestration, written with extraordinary skill ; and finally, its moving and intensely dramatic plot, which always holds an audience in rapt attention.

It is indeed a matter for congratulation that the Victor is able to offer such a fine pro-duction of this master work.

ANNOUNCEMENT

The Victor Company takes pleasure in announcing Leoncavallo's famous two-act musical drama, recorded especially for the Victor under the personal direction of the composer. The records in the series were made in the presence of Signor Leoncavallo, and the music conducted by him, a feature which should make this collection ever valuable and unique. Any question arising in future concerning the composer's intentions in regard to the opera may be decided by reference to this performance as he himself conducted it. This advantage would have been priceless with regard to many well-known operas of the past, as it would have settled many controversies. But now, by means of the Victor, the composer's ideas may be imperishably recorded.

The artists selected by Signor Leoncavallo to interpret his great work are well known and most competent ones. Mme. Huguet, one of Italy's most beloved *prima donne,* has a voice of ample range and power, and sings the music of *Nedda* most beautifully. Cigada's *Tonio* is a remarkable performance, the richness and beauty of his voice being especially noticeable in the Prologue and the duet with *Nedda.* As *Canio* a choice of tenors is offered, the more delicate voice of Barbaini being contrasted with the splendid fire and intensity of Paoli's singing. Badini as *Silvio* is fully adequate, while the smaller parts are well filled. Nothing need be said about the orchestra and chorus of La Scala, as their reputation is world wide.

Leoncavallo's beautiful opera is admirably suited for reproduction on the Victor, and while listening to the singing of the artists who have rendered these dramatic scenes, no great imagination is required to picture the various situations.

In addition to the La Scala series, which was made under the composer's direction, many other Pagliacci records are listed in their proper places.

THE ARGUMENT

During the orchestral introduction *Tonio,* in his clown costume, suddenly appears in front of the curtain and begs permission to revive the ancient Greek prologue. He then comes forward as Prologue and explains that the subject of the play is taken from real life; reminds the audience that actors are but men, with passions like their own, and that the author has endeavored to express the real feelings and sentiments of the characters he will introduce. He then orders up the curtain.

The first act shows the entrance to an Italian village. *Canio* and his troupe of strolling players, or *pagliacci,* having paraded through the village, return to their traveling theatre, followed by a noisy crowd of villagers. *Canio* announces a performance for that evening at seven, then goes with *Peppe* into the tavern. *Tonio,* the clown, remains behind ostensibly to care for the donkey, but takes advantage of his master's absence to make love to *Nedda, Canio's* wife. She repulses him scornfully, striking him with her whip, and he swears to be revenged. *Silvio,* a rich young villager, in love with *Nedda,* now joins her and begs her to fly with him. She refuses, but admits that she loves him, her confession being overheard by *Tonio,* who hurries in search of his master. *Canio* returns too late to see *Silvio,* but hears *Nedda's* parting words, "Forever I am thine!" Mad with jealousy, he demands the lover's name, and when *Nedda* refuses, tries to kill her, but is restrained by the others. *Nedda* goes to dress and *Canio* is in despair at the thought of being obliged to play while his heart is breaking.

Act II: The curtain rises on the same scene and the play is about to begin. This proves to be the usual farce in which the Clown makes love to Columbine during the absence of her husband, Punchinello, but is laughed at and resigns his pretensions, finally consenting to act as a lookout while Columbine and her accepted lover, Harlequin, dine together.

Strangely enough, this conventional farce is very like the situation in the real lives of the players, and when Punchinello (*Canio*) arrives and surprises the lovers, as the play demands, he loses his head when he hears Columbine repeat in the farce the very words he overheard her say to her real lover earlier in the day. Mad with rage, he again demands her lover's name. *Nedda* tries to save the situation by continuing the play, while the audience is delighted by such realistic acting until the intensity of *Canio's* passion begins to terrify them. The other players endeavor to silence him, but in vain. Finally, stung by his taunts, *Nedda* defies him and is stabbed, *Canio* hoping that in her death agony she will reveal the name of her lover. She falls, calling upon *Silvio,* who rushes from the crowd only to receive in turn the dagger of the outraged husband. As *Canio* is disarmed by the peasants he cries as if in a dream, *"La commedia e finita"*—(The comedy is ended).

ARRIVAL OF THE PLAYERS—ACT I

<table>
<tr><td>(Italian)</td><td>(English)</td></tr>
</table>

(Italian)	(English)
I PAGLIACCI	**THE PLAYERS**
(*Ee Pahl-yat'-chee*)	
(German)	(French)
DIE BAJAZZI	**PAILLASSE**
(*Dee Bah-yot'-si*)	(*Pah-yahss*)

DRAMATIC OPERA IN TWO ACTS

Libretto and music by Ruggiero Leoncavallo.   First performed at the Teatro dal Verme, Milan, on May 21, 1892; in London, May 19, 1893.   First New York production June 15, 1894, with Kronold, Montegriffo and Campanari.   Some famous casts of recent years at the Metropolitan and Manhattan opera: Caruso, Farrar, Stracciari—Alvarez, Scheff, Scotti—Farrar, Bars, Scotti—Cavalieri, Rousseliere, Scotti—Deveyne, Martin, Campanari—Donalda, Bassi, Sammarco, etc.

Characters in the Drama

NEDDA (*Ned'-dah*) (in the play "*Columbine*"), a strolling player,
wife of CANIO..Soprano
CANIO (*Kah'-nee-oh*) (in the play "*Pagliaccio*" [*Punchinello*]),
master of the troupe..Tenor
TONIO (*Toh'-nee-oh*) (in the play "*Taddeo*"), the clown.............Baritone
PEPPE (*Pep'-pay*) (in the play "*Harlequin*")........................Tenor
SILVIO, (*Sil'-vee-oh*) a villager...................................Baritone

Villagers and Peasants

*The scene is laid in Calabria, near Montalto, on the Feast of the Assumption.
Period, between 1865 and 1870.*

THE PROLOGUE

Leoncavallo chose a novel way to introduce his characters, and wrote this number in the midst of the orchestral prelude, when *Tonio* comes forward, like the prologue of ancient Greek tragedy, and explains that the subject of the play is taken from real life, and that the composer has devoted himself to expressing the sentiment, good or bad, but always human, of the characters he introduces.

Prologo (Prologue)

By Pasquale Amato, Baritone	(In Italian)	88326	12-inch,	$3.00
By Antonio Scotti, Baritone	(In Italian)	88029	12-inch,	3.00
By Antonio Scotti, Baritone	(In Italian)	81021	10-inch,	2.00
By Emilio de Gogórza, Baritone	(In Italian)	88176	12-inch,	3.00
By Alan Turner, Baritone	(In English)	*16157	10-inch,	.75
By Alan Turner, Baritone	(In English)	*35002	12-inch,	1.25
By Pryor's Band		31352	12-inch,	1.00
By Pryor's Band		*35158	12-inch,	1.25

Prologo (Prologue)   (Complete in two parts)

(a) Part I—Si puo ? (A Word)
   By Francesco Cigada, Baritone (In Italian)
(b) Part II—Un nido di memorie (A Song of Tender Memories)
   By Francesco Cigada, Baritone (In Italian)   *35171 12-inch, $1.25

The first part of the Prologue is in itself a miniature overture, containing the three representative themes associated with the main events of the drama to be unfolded.

The first is the motive which always accompanies the appearance of the players or *pagliacci*:

The second theme represents *Canio's* jealousy and is a sombre strain suggestive of revenge:

The third represents the guilty love of *Nedda* and *Silvio:*  and appears frequently throughout the opera, not only in the love duet, but in the last act, when *Nedda* refuses to betray her lover even with death awaiting her.

The presentation of these themes is followed by the appearance of *Tonio*, the clown, who peeps through the curtain and says:

Ladies and gentlemen!
Pardon me if alone I appear.
I am the Prologue!

He then comes in front of the curtain and explains the author's purpose, which is to present a drama from real life, showing that the actors have genuine tragedies as well as mimic ones.

Our author loves the custom of a prologue to his story,
And as he would revive for you the ancient glory,
He sends me to speak before ye!
But not to prate, as once of old,
That the tears of the actor are false, unreal,
That his sighs and the pain that is told,
He has no heart to feel!
No! our author to-night a chapter will borrow
From life with its laughter and sorrow!
Is not the actor a man with a heart like you?
So 'tis for men that our author has written,
And the story he tells you is true!

He then goes on to speak of the author's inspiration, and says:

A song of tender mem'ries
Deep in his list'ning heart one day was ringing;
And then with a trembling hand he wrote it,
And he marked the time with sighs and tears.
Come, then;
Here on the stage you shall behold us in human fashion,
And see the sad fruits of love and passion.
Hearts that weep and languish, cries of rage and anguish,
And bitter laughter!

* *Double-Faced Record—For title of opposite side see DOUBLE-FACED PAGLIACCI RECORDS, page 265.*

The beautiful *andante* which follows is the most admired portion of the aria, and is indeed a noble strain.

> Ah, think then, sweet people, when ye look on us,
> Clad in our motley and tinsel,
> For ours are human hearts, beating with passion,
> We are but men like you, for gladness or sorrow,
> 'Tis the same broad Heaven above us,
> The same wide, lonely world before us!
> Will ye hear, then, the story,
> As it unfolds itself surely and certain!
> Come, then! Ring up the curtain!

The curtain now rises, as the *pagliacci motive* reappears in the orchestra.

Opening Chorus—"Son qua!" (They're Here!)

By La Scala Chorus *(Double-faced—See page 265)* *(In Italian)* **16814** 10-inch, $0.75

COPY'T MISHKIN

SAMMARCO AS TONIO

The first scene, representing the edge of a small village in Calabria, is now revealed to the audience. The people are engaged in celebrating the Feast of the Assumption, and among the attractions offered to the crowds who have flocked to the village is the troupe of strolling players headed by *Canio*. These wandering mountebanks are common in the rural districts of Italy and are known as *pagliacci*. They take with them a small tent (usually carried in a cart drawn by a donkey), which they set up in the market places of the small villages, or anywhere that they see a prospect for the earning of a modest living.

A number of the townspeople have assembled in front of the little theatre and are awaiting the return of the clowns, who have been parading through the village to announce their arrival, as is the custom. As the curtain rises, the sound of a drum and trumpet is heard from a distance, and the villagers are full of joy at the prospect of a comedy performance. They express their excitement in a vigorous opening chorus. This is a clever bit of writing, but so difficult that it is seldom well given. The famous chorus of La Scala, however, under the leadership of Maestro Sabaino, have given this stirring number in splendid style. This oft-recurring phrase which is presented with many odd modulations, produces a peculiar and novel effect.

TONIO

> Ev - vi - va! il prin - ci - pe. ... se' dei pa - gliac - ci!
> Long life to him, the prince. .. of all pa-gliac-cios!

BOYS: Hi! They're here!
They're coming back!
Pagliaccio's there
The grown-up folks and boys
All follow after!
Their jokes and laughter
They all applaud.

WOMEN: See, there's the wagon!
My, what a fiendish din!
The Lord have mercy on us!
ALL: Welcome Pagliaccio;
Long life to him,
The prince of all pagliaccios.
You drive our cares away
With fun and laughter!

The little troupe has now come into view and the noise is redoubled. *Canio* appears at the head of his company, his wife, *Nedda*, riding in the cart drawn by a donkey, while *Tonio* and *Peppe* make hideous noises on the bass drum and cracked trumpet, which constitute the orchestra of the players. *Canio* is dressed in the traditional garb of the clown, his face smeared with flour and his cheeks adorned with patches of red. He tries to address the crowd, but the noise is tremendous. *Tonio* beats the drum furiously to silence the voices, but it is not until *Canio* has raised his hand to command attention that he is allowed to speak.

Un grande spettacolo! (A Wond'rous Performance!)

By Antonio Paoli, Tenor; Francesco Cigada, Baritone; Gaetano Pini-Corsi, Tenor; and Sig. Rosci, Baritone
(*In Italian*) 92009 12-inch, $3.00

He begins to address the peasants in this fashion:

ARRIVAL OF THE PLAYERS

> CANIO:
> A wondrous performance
> I say will be given,
> By your humble servants
> This evening at seven.
> The wrath of Pagliaccio
> Will there be presented—
> What vengeance he took,
> And the trap he invented!
> You'll witness the carcass of Tonio tremble,
> And see him dissemble and pile up the plot!
> So honor us by coming this even;
> Come all, then, at seven!

The crowd boisterously express their joy at the prospect of an evening's entertainment. *Canio* now turns to assist *Nedda* to alight from the cart, but finds *Tonio*, the Fool, there before him. Giving him a cuff on the ear, he bids him be off, and *Tonio* slinks away muttering. The boys in the crowd jeer him, saying:

> Does that suit you, Mr. Lover?

Tonio threatens the boys, who run away. He goes grumbling into the theatre, saying, aside:

> He'll pay for this ere it's over!

One of the peasants invites the players to the wine shop for a friendly glass. They accept, and *Canio* calls to *Tonio* to join them, but he replies from within: "I'm rubbing down the donkey," which causes a villager to remark, jestingly:

> A PEASANT: Careful, Pagliaccio!
> He only stays behind there
> For making love to Nedda!

Canio smiles, but knits his brow and is evidently impressed by the thought.

> CANIO: Eh! What?
> You think so?

(*He becomes serious, and signing to the peasants to come round him, he begins to address them.*)

CANIO

HARLEQUIN

Un tal gioco (Such a Game!)

By Antonio Paoli and La Scala Chorus (*In Italian*) 92010 12-inch, $3.00
By Nicola Zerola, Tenor (*In Italian*) 64206 10-inch, 1.00

The first trace of *Canio's* jealous nature is now shown, as he takes with apparent seriousness the idle joke of the peasant, and begins to warn the spectators as follows:

CANIO: Such a game, I'd have you know,
'Twere better not to play, my neighbors!
To Tonio, aye, to you all I say it!
For the stage there and life, they are different altogether!

* * * * * * * * * *

If up there, (*pointing to the theatre*)
Pagliaccio his lady should discover
With some fine fellow in her room,
He'd give the two a rating . . . or resign himself,
And take a jolly beating!

(With a sudden change of tone)

But if Nedda I really should surprise so,
What came after were a far different story!

Nedda, who is listening, is surprised and says aside: "What does he mean?" The villagers, rather puzzled at his earnestness, ask him if he is serious. With an effort he rouses himself from his gloomy mood and says lightly:

Not I—I love my wife most dearly!

COPY'T DUPONT
FARRAR AS NEDDA

(*He approaches Nedda and kisses her on the forehead.*) The sound of bagpipes (oboe) is heard in the distance, telling of the merrymaking in the village, and the church bells begin to toll the call to vespers. The people commence to disperse, and *Canio* again repeats his melodious strain of invitation:

(*He goes with several peasants into the inn.*)

Coro della campane (Chorus of the Bells)

By La Scala Chorus
(*In Italian*) *35172 12-inch, $1.25

This is the famous Bell Chorus, or "Ding Dong" Chorus, one of the most remarkable numbers in the opera. It is sung with spirit, and the chiming bells are introduced in a most effective manner. The people go off singing and the measures die away in the distance.

Ballatella, "Che volo d'angelli!" (Ye Birds Without Number!)

By Alma Gluck, Soprano   (*In Italian*)   74238 12-inch, $1.50
By Giuseppina Huguet, Soprano   (*In Italian*)   *35172 12-inch, 1.25

Nedda, left alone, is troubled by her remembrance of *Canio's* manner and wonders if he suspects her. She speaks of the fierce look he had given her, and says:

I dropt my eyes, fearful lest he should have read there
What I was secretly thinking.

But shaking off her depression, she becomes once more alive to the brightness of the day, which fills her with a strange delight. A gay tremolo in the strings announces the theme of the birds, and *Nedda* speaks of her mother, whom she said could understand their language. NEDDA: Ah, ye birds without number!
What countless voices!
What ask ye? Who knows?
My mother, she that was skillful at telling one's fortune,
Understood what they're singing,
And in my childhood, thus would she sing me.

Then follows the brilliant *Balatella* or Bird Song, beginning:

It is a most beautiful number with an exquisite accompaniment, mainly of strings. Mme. Gluck gives it here in delightful fashion, singing with dazzling brilliancy, while a very fine rendition by Mme. Huguet is offered as part of a double-faced record.

COPY'T MISHKIN

GLUCK AS NEDDA

So ben che deforme (I Know That You Hate Me)

By Giuseppina Huguet, Soprano, and Francesco Cigada, Baritone
(In Italian) *35173 12-inch, $1.25

At the close of her song *Nedda* finds that the hideous *Tonio* has been listening, and now seeing the handsome Columbine alone, begins to make love to her; but she scornfully orders him away. He persists, but his protestations are greeted with mocking laughter, and *Nedda* says insolently:

NEDDA:
There's time, if you like,
Once more to tell me this evening
When you will be acting the fool!
* * * * * * *
Just now, it is painful.

In a furious rage, *Tonio* swears she must listen to him and cries:

TONIO:
You mock me? Wretched creature!
By the cross of the Savior
You shall pay for this, and dearly!

NEDDA:
A threat, eh? Come, or I'll be calling Canio!
TONIO:
But not until I've kissed you!
(*Rushing toward her.*)

Nulla scordai! (Naught I Forget!)

By Giuseppina Huguet, Francesco Cigada, and Ernesto Badini
(Doubled with above duet) (In Italian) *35173 12-inch, $1.25

Tonio, driven almost to madness by *Nedda's* scorn and ridicule, seizes and tries to kiss her. She strikes him across the face with her whip, crying:

Oh, you would, you cur!
TONIO (*screaming*): By the Blessed Virgin of Assumption,
Nedda, I swear it,
You shall pay me for it! (*Rushes off.*)
NEDDA (*watching him*): Scorpion! at last you've shown your nature!
Tonio, the clown,
The heart of you is just as crooked as your body!

The young villager, *Silvio*, whom *Nedda* has secretly met on previous visits to the town, now jumps over the wall. *Nedda*, alarmed, cries:

SILVIO

NEDDA: Silvio! In the daytime? What folly!
SILVIO (*smiling*): I fancy it's no great risk I'm taking!
Canio I spied from afar with Peppe yonder.
Ay! at the tavern I saw them!

She tells him of *Tonio's* behavior and bids him beware, as the clown is to be feared. Her lover cheers her and laughs at her fears, and they sing the beautiful love duet, in which *Silvio* urges her to fly with him; but she is afraid and begs him not to tempt her. He persists, and reproaches her for her coldness, until finally in a passion of abandonment she yields, singing the beautiful passage which begins the record:

Then together they sing the lovely duet:

NEDDA [Overcome and yielding]
perdutamente con passione
Più mosso

Nul - la scor - dai   scon - vol   ta e tur - ba   ta.........
Naught I for - get,........ but see   with e mo - tion......

BOTH: All, all forgot!   SILVIO: Thou'lt come?
NEDDA: Look into my eyes, love,   NEDDA (*passionately*):
All is forgotten!   Aye! kiss me once more!
Then kiss me, dear!   BOTH: I love thee!

The lovers, who have cast aside all prudence and see only each other, fail to observe *Canio,* who has been warned by *Tonio* and has hurried from the tavern.

TONIO (*holding Canio back*): Now just step softly,
    And you will catch them now!
SILVIO (*disappearing over the wall*):
    To-night at midnight,
    I'll be there below!
NEDDA: 'Till to-night then,
    And forever I'll be thine!

(*She sees Canio and gives a cry of fear.*) Ah!

Aitalo Signor! (May Heaven Protect Him!)

By Antonio Paoli Tenor; Giuseppina Huguet, Soprano; Francesco Cigada, Baritone; Gaetano Pini-Corsi, Tenor (*In Italian*) 92011 12-inch, $3.00

Canio, who has not seen *Silvio,* but has heard *Nedda's* parting words, now rushes toward the wall. *Nedda* bars his way. The record begins with the melodramic music written by Leoncavallo for this exciting struggle, during which *Canio* pushes her aside and runs in pursuit of *Silvio.*

SILVIO AND NEDDA

NEDDA (*listening anxiously*): May Heaven protect him now!
CANIO (*from behind*): Scoundrel! Where hidest thou?
TONIO (*laughing cynically*): Ha! Ha! Ha!
NEDDA (*turning to Tonio with loathing*): Bravo! Well done, Tonio!
TONIO (*with fiendish satisfaction*): All that I could do!
    But I hope in the future to do better!

Canio re-enters, out of breath and completely exhausted. As he turns to *Nedda* with suppressed rage we hear again in the accompaniment that dismal theme of revenge:

which throughout the opera always accompanies the scenes of *Canio's* jealousy and passion.

CARUSO SINGING "VESTI LA GIUBBA"

CANIO:
    No one!
    That shows how well he knows that path.
    But no matter!
(*Furiously*):
    Because right now you'll tell me his name!
NEDDA (*indifferently*):
    Me?
CANIO (*in frenzy*):
    You! By God in Heaven!
    And if up to this moment I have not cut your throat,
    * * * * * * * * * *
    'Tis because I'd have you name him!
    Speak now!

Nedda proudly refuses. Filled with joy because of *Silvio's* escape, she cares not what may be her own fate. *Canio,* beside himself, rushes on her with the knife, but *Peppe* holds him back and takes away his weapon. *Tonio* comes to *Peppe's* assistance, saying:

Restrain yourself, good master,
'Tis best to sham awhile.
The fellow will come back,
You take my word for it!

They finally persuade him to restrain himself, and beg him to make ready for the play, as the audience is already assembling. *Nedda* goes into the theatre and *Canio* remains alone, his head bowed with shame and baffled revenge in his soul.

Vesti la giubba (On With the Play)

By Enrico Caruso, Tenor   88061   12-inch, $3.00
By Carlo Albani, Tenor   74097   12-inch, 1.50
By Nicola Zerola, Tenor   64169   10-inch, 1.00

We now come to the most famous of the numbers in Leoncavallo's opera, the great Lament of Pagliaccio. Its heart-breaking pathos never fails to touch the listener, when sung by such artists as the Victor offers.

The unhappy *Canio,* left alone after the exciting scene with *Nedda,* wrings his hands and cries:

CANIO:
To play! When my head's whirling with madness,
Not knowing what I'm saying or
what I'm doing!

Yet I must force myself!
I am not a man,
I'm but a Pagliaccio!

The great aria now follows, in which the unfortunate Pagliaccio describes how he must paint his face and make merry for the public while his heart is torn with jealousy.

CANIO:
The people pay you, and they must have
their fun!
If Harlequin your Columbine takes from
you,
Laugh loud, Pagliaccio!
And all will shout, well done!
* * * * * *
Laugh, Pagliaccio, for the love that is ended!
(*Sobbing*):
Laugh for the pain that is gnawing your
heart!

(*He moves slowly toward the theatre, weeping; he stops at the entrance and hesitates. Seized by a new fit of sobbing, he buries his face in his hands; then as the curtain slowly falls, rushes into the tent.*)

Caruso's Canio is still the great feature of Pagliacci, and his magnificent singing of this famous lament cannot be described—it must be heard. In all that this artist has done there is no piece of dramatic singing to equal his delivery of the reproaches of the clown, which he pours out not only on his faithless wife, but on himself and the occupation that bids him be merry when his heart is breaking. Sometimes Caruso's voice merely delights the ear—here he searches the heart; and is not merely the greatest of tenors, but is the clown himself, full of the most tragic emotion.

CANIO

ACT II

SCENE—*Same as Act I*

La Commedia (The Play) Part I, Serenata d'Ar-lecchino (Harlequin's Serenade)

By Giuseppina Huguet and Gaetano Pini-Corsi,

(*Double-faced—See page 265*) (*In Italian*) **35174 12-inch, $1.25**

Passing over the preparations for the play and the quarreling chorus of the peasants as they fight for the best seats, which is not interesting without the action, we come to the commencement of the comedy. The curtain is drawn aside, disclosing a small room with two side doors and a window at the back. *Nedda* as Columbine is discovered walking about anxiously. The tripping minuet movement which runs throughout the action of the comedy now begins.

Columbine rises and looks out of the window, saying:

Pagliaccio, my husband, till late this evening
Will not be at home.

The sound of a guitar, cleverly imitated by the violins, *pizzicato,* causes Columbine to utter a cry of joy, and the voice of Harlequin is heard out-side in the Serenade, be-ginning:

NEDDA AS COLUMBINE

HARLEQUIN (Peppe, behind scene)

O... ... Co - lom - bi - na, il te - ne - ro Ar-lec - chin
O... ... Col - um-bine, your Har - le - quin is here with you,

in which he extravagantly rhapsodizes his sweetheart.

La Commedia (The Play) Part II, E dessa! (Behold Her!)

**By Giuseppina Huguet, Soprano; Francesco Cigada, Baritone; and
Gaetano Pini-Corsi, Tenor** *(In Italian)* *35174 12-inch, $1.25

AMATO AS TONIO

Tonio as Taddeo, with his basket, now peeps through the door and says exaggeratedly, with a comical cadenza »

Moderato e sostenuto (In mock-tragic style)   (lifting his hands and the basket upwards)

É   des - sa!   Del, co-me ò   bel . . . . la!
Be - hold her!   Is - n't she   love . . . . ly!

The audience laughs in delight as *Tonio* tries to express his love by a long exaggerated sigh. *Columbine* tries to suppress him by inquiring about the chicken he had been sent for, but *Tonio* kneels, and holding up the fowl, says:

> See, we are *both* before thee kneeling!

His pretensions are cut short by Harlequin, who enters and leads him out by the ear. As he goes he gives the lovers a mock benediction, singing:

> Then I my claim surrender. Bless you, my children!

This scene is most cleverly done and the three records depicting the little farce are among the most enjoyable of the series.

Versa il filtro nella tazza sua! (Pour the Potion in His Wine, Love!)

**By Antonio Paoli, Tenor; Giuseppina Huguet, Soprano;
Francesco Cigada, Baritone; and Gaetano Pini-
Corsi, Tenor** *(In Italian)* 91073 10-inch, $2.00

**By Augusto Barbaini, Tenor; Giuseppina Huguet, Soprano; Francesco
Cigada, Baritone; and Gaetano Pini-Corsi, Tenor**
(Double-faced—See page 265) *(In Italian)* 35175 12-inch, 1.25

The lovers now partake of their feast and make merry together. Harlequin takes from his pocket a little vial, which he gives to Columbine, saying:

HARLEQUIN:
Take this little sleeping draught,
'Tis for Pagliaccio!
Give it him at bedtime,
And then away we'll fly.

COLUMBINE *(eagerly)*:
Yes, give me!

Upon the scene suddenly bursts *Tonio,* in mock alarm crying:

TONIO *(bawling loudly)*:
Be careful! Pagliaccio is here!
Trembling all over, he seeks for weapons!
He has caught you, and I shall fly to cover!

The lovers simulate the greatest alarm, at which the excited audience is highly pleased, and applaud lustily. Harlequin leaps from the window, and *Nedda* continues the scene by repeating Columbine's next lines, which by a strange chance are the very words she had spoken to *Silvio* earlier in the day »

Larghetto affettuoso (♩ = 88)
COLUM. (at the window)

A sta - not - te   E per sem - pre   io   sa   rò   tua!
Till to - night, then!   And for ev - er   I   shall be   thine!

Canio, dressed as Punchinello, now enters from the door on the right.

CANIO *(with suppressed rage)*:
Hell and damnation!
And the very same words, too!
(Recovering himself):
But, courage!
(Taking up his part):
You had a man with you!
COLUMBINE *(lightly)*:
What nonsense! You are tipsy!

PAGLIACCIO *(restraining himself with difficulty)*:
Ah, if thou wast alone here
Why these places for two?
COLUMBINE:
Taddeo was supping with me.
He's there—you scared him into hiding!
TADDEO *(from within)*:
Believe her, sir! She is faithful!
(Sneering):
Ah, they could never lie, those lips so truthful!

The audience laughs loudly, which enrages the unhappy man, and forgetting his part he turns to *Nedda* and fiercely demands the name of her lover:

CANIO: Woman, 'tis thy lover's name I want,
The wretched scoundrel from whose arms thou comest!
Oh, shameless woman!

NEDDA (*faintly, much alarmed*): Pagliaccio! Pagliaccio!

No, Pagliaccio non son! (No, Punchinello No More!)

By Enrico Caruso, Tenor
(*Italian*) 88279 12-inch, $3.00
By Antonio Paoli, Tenor
(*Italian*) 92012 12-inch, 3.00
By Nicola Zerola, Tenor
(*Italian*) 74247 12-inch, 1.50
By Augusto Barbaini, Tenor
(*Italian*) *35175 12-inch, 1.25

Throwing off entirely the mask of the player, *Canio* becomes again the jealous husband, and sings this great aria, which is second only to the *Vesti la giubba* in dramatic power.

CANIO:
No, Pagliaccio, I'm not!
If my face be white,
'Tis shame that pales it
And vengeance twists my features.

* * * * * *

I am that foolish man
Who in poverty found and
tried to save thee!
He gave a name to thee,
A burning love that was madness!
(*Falls in a chair, overwhelmed.*)

The people, while a little puzzled by such intensity, loudly applaud what they think is a piece of superb acting.

FROM "THE GREAT OPERAS" BY J. CUTHBERT HADDEN

COLUMBINE AND HARLEQUIN AT SUPPER

CANIO (*recovering himself*): All my life to thee I sacrificed with gladness!
Full of hope and believing far less in God than thee!
* * * * * * * * *
Go! Thou'rt not worth my grief,
O thou abandoned creature!
And now, with my contempt,
I'll crush thee under heel!

Caruso's rendering of this great scene is a magnificent one. The opening passage is delivered with tremendous power, as *Canio* pleads his defense, saying that he is no longer a player, but a man, and protests as a man against the wrong inflicted upon him. His passion gives place to a softer strain as he speaks of his love for *Nedda*, his faithfulness and his sacrifices for her. At the close is the intense climax, with its splendid high B flat. Other fine renditions of the air are by Paoli, Zerola and Barbaini.

Finale

By Antonio Paoli, Tenor; Giuseppina Huguet, Soprano; Francesco Cigada, Baritone; Gaetano Pini-Corsi, Tenor; Ernesto Badini, Tenor; and Chorus (*In Italian*) 92013 12-inch, $3.00

LE THÉÂTRE   THE PLAY—ACT II

The close of *Canio's* great air, "No, Pagliaccio No More!" is greeted with loud cries of "bravo" from the excited audience.

Nedda is now thoroughly alarmed, but courageously faces her husband with outward calm.

NEDDA (*coldly but seriously*):
'Tis well!
If thou think'st me vile,
Send me off, then,
Before this moment's over!

CANIO (*laughing loudly*):
Ha! Ha!
Oh, nothing better would'st thou ask,
Than to be let run to meet thy lover!
No! by Heaven, for here thou stayest,
Until thy paramour's vile name thou sayest!

Nedda, in desperation, tries to continue the play, and as the little gavotte movement is resumed in the accompaniment, she sings:

NEDDA: Oh dear, I never knew that you
Were such a fearful man, sir!
There's nothing tragic for you here.
Come now, Taddeo, answer!

The crowd begins to laugh, but is checked by *Canio's* appearance, which is alarming.

CANIO (*violently*): Ah, you defy me!
* * * * * * * *
You'll name him, or else I'll kill you!
(*Shouting*): Who was it?
NEDDA (*throwing off her mask defiantly*):
No, by my mother,
I'm faithless, or whatever you choose to call me;
(*Proudly*): But cowardly, no, never!
* * * * * * * *
I will not speak!
No, not even if you kill me.

As she sings we hear triumphantly appearing above her voice the love motive:

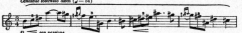

Cantabile sostenuto assai ($\quad = 54$)
p *con passione*

telling of her passion for *Silvio*, which is to endure even unto death. *Canio* now rushes toward her, but is restrained by *Tonio* and *Peppe*. *Nedda* tries to escape, but *Canio* breaks away and stabs her, crying:

CANIO: Take that!
Perhaps in death's last agony,
You will speak!

Nedda falls, and with a last faint effort calls:
"Oh, help me, Silvio."

Silvio, who has drawn his dagger, rushes to her, when *Canio* cries:
Ah, 'twas you! 'Tis well! (*Stabs him.*)
CANIO (*as if stupefied, letting fall his knife*):
The comedy is ended!

CANIO

Then once more is heard the tragic motive of jealousy and death, now thundered out by the orchestra as if rejoicing at its final triumph.

Curtain.

DOUBLE-FACED AND MISCELLANEOUS PAGLIACCI RECORDS

Prologue, Part I—Si puo By Francesco Cigada, Baritone *(In Italian)*			
Prologue, Part II—Un nido di memorie By Francesco Cigada, Baritone *(In Italian)*	35171	12-inch,	$1.25
Prologue By Alan Turner, Baritone *(In English)*			
Come into the Garden, Maud By Harold Jarvis, Tenor	35002	12-inch,	1.25
Prologue By Pryor's Band			
Flying Dutchman Fantasia By Pryor's Band	35158	12-inch,	1.25
Coro della campane By La Scala Chorus *(In Italian)*			
Che volo d'angelli By Giuseppina Huguet, Soprano *(In Italian)*	35172	12-inch,	1.25
So ben che deforme By Giuseppina Huguet, Soprano, and Francesco Cigada, Baritone *(In Italian)*			
Nulla scordai! By Giuseppina Huguet, Soprano; Francesco Cigada, Baritone; Ernesto Badini, Tenor *(In Italian)*	35173	12-inch,	1.25
La Commedia—Part I By Giuseppina Huguet, Soprano, and Gaetano Pini-Corsi, Tenor *(In Italian)*			
La Commedia—Part II By Giuseppina Huguet, Soprano; Francesco Cigada, Baritone; Gaetano Pini-Corsi, Tenor *(In Italian)*	35174	12-inch,	1.25
Versa il filtro nella tazza sua! By Augusto Barbaini, Tenor; Giuseppina Huguet, Soprano; Francesco Cigada, Baritone; Gaetano Pini-Corsi, Tenor *(In Italian)*			
No, Pagliaccio non son! By Augusto Barbaini, Tenor *(In Italian)*	35175	12-inch,	1.25
Pagliacci Selection By Pryor's Band	31799	12-inch,	1.00
Prologue By Alan Turner, Baritone *(In English)*			
Brown Eyes By Alan Turner, Baritone *(In English)*	16157	10-inch,	.75
Opening Chorus, "Son qua" By La Scala Chorus *(In Italian)*			
Trovatore—Per me ora fatale By Ernesto Caronna, Baritone, and Chorus *(In Italian)*	16814	10-inch,	.75

LE THÉÂTRE   THE COMEDY IS ENDED!

PESCATORI DI PERLE   PEARL FISHERS
(Pes-kah-toh'-ree dee Pair-laay)

OPERA IN THREE ACTS

Text by Carré and Cormon. Music by Georges Bizet. First production at the Théâtre Lyrique, Paris, September 29, 1863. First London production, entitled "Leila," at Covent Garden, April 22, 1887; and as *Pescatori di Perle,* May 18, 1889. First New York production January 11, 1896.

Characters

LEILA, a priestess...Soprano
NADIR, a pearl fisher ....Tenor
ZURGA, a chief ....Baritone
NOURABAD, high priest..Bass

Priests, Priestesses, Pearl Fishers, Women, etc.

Scene and Period : Ceylon ; barbaric period.

Les Pêcheurs de Perles, one of Bizet's earlier operas and the first one to achieve success, is a work dealing with an Oriental subject, and contains much music of charm and originality, showing traces of that dramatic force which reached its full development in *Carmen.* The character of the music, less passionate and highly colored than *Carmen,* is yet equally original and of even more striking beauty.

The story tells of the love of two Cingalese pearl fishers for the priestess *Leila,* and of the generosity of the unsuccessful rival, who helps the lovers to escape at the cost of his own life.

THE PRELUDE

The prelude is a most beautiful number, and considered one of the finest of Bizet's instrumental writings.

Preludio (Prelude)
By La Scala Orchestra
                                          *62100   10-inch, $0.75

ACT I
SCENE—*The Coast of Ceylon*

The rise of the curtain discloses a company of Cingalese pearl fishers, who, after choosing one of their number, *Zurga,* to be their chief, are enjoying themselves with games and dances. *Nadir* appears and *Zurga* recognizes him as a friend of his youth. They greet each other and speak of the days when they were rivals for the hand of a beautiful woman. *Nadir,* beginning the duet, recalls the moment when the friends first beheld the lovely *Leila.*

Del tempio al limitar (In the Depths of the Temple)
By Enrico Caruso, Tenor, and Mario Ancona, Baritone

	(*In Italian*)	89007	12-inch, $4.00
By Giorgini and Federici	(*In Italian*)	88319	12-inch, 3.00
By John McCormack and G. Mario Sammarco (*Italian*)		87082	10-inch, 2.00
By Giuseppe Acerbi and Renzo Minolfi	(*In Italian*) *68063	12-inch, 1.25

In an impressive strain he describes the scene within the Temple of Brahma:

NADIR:
In the depths of the temple
A lovely form we beheld,
That form I still can see!
ZURGA:
'Twas a vision of beauty!
NADIR:
The kneeling worshipers, astonished,
Now murmur, "The goddess comes!"
ZURGA:
She descends from the altar
And, moving near to us

Lifts her veil, revealing
A face that haunts me still
With its beauty ethereal!
NADIR:
But now her veil she drops
And, passing through the wandering crowd
She disappears.
Now a strange emotion overpowers me,
I fear to touch thy hand.
ZURGA:
A fatal love both our souls possess.

Double-Faced Record—For title of opposite side see DOUBLE-FACED PEARL FISHERS RECORDS, page 268.

They speak of their sudden realization of the fact that they had both fallen in love at sight with the priestess, and fearing their friendship was in danger, they swore never to see her again. The comrades, now pronouncing themselves entirely cured of their infatuation, pledge anew their friendship and swear to be brothers to the end.

A fisherman now enters and announces the arrival of the mysterious veiled lady who comes once a year to pray for the success of the fisheries, and whom the Ceylonese have adopted as their guardian saint. She enters and begins her prayer. *Nadir* recognizes her voice and realizes that it is the priestess *Leila*. The pearl fishers sing a chorus of appeal to *Brahma* for a blessing, in which *Leila* joins.

Brahma gran Dio (Divine Brahma!)

By Linda Brambilla, Soprano, and La Scala Chorus

(*In Italian*) *68062 12-inch, $1.25

This is a most impressive record, the lovely voice of Mme. Brambilla showing to great advantage above the choral background.

Leila goes into the temple and the people disperse. *Nadir*, left alone, is agitated by his discovery, realizing that he still loves the maiden. He recalls the memories of his first sight of her in a lovely song.

Mi par d'udir ancora (I Hear as in a Dream)

By Florencio Constantino, Tenor (*In Italian*) 74067 12-inch, $1.50

Leila reappears and the act closes with her prayer to Brahma for the good fortune of the fishermen. Just as the curtain falls she recognizes *Nadir,* and contrives to let him know that she loves him.

ACT II

SCENE—*A Ruined Temple*

As the curtain rises *Leila* and *Nourabad,* the high priest, are seen, they having sought shelter in the ruins of an ancient temple. The high priest, in a fine air, reminds *Leila* of her oath to renounce love and marriage and devote herself to the welfare of the people. She says that she will keep her promise and tells him of a vow she made when a child to a fugitive who implored her to save his life. Although his pursuers held a dagger to her breast she refused to betray him and he escaped to safety.

Siccome un di caduto (A Fugitive, One Day)

By Giuseppina Piccoletti, Soprano (*In Italian*) *68307 12-inch, $1.25

The high priest sternly recites the punishment which will overtake her should she prove false to her vow. "Shame and death be thy portion!" cries the stern priest. Left alone, the miserable woman broods over her unhappy plight. Bound by an oath which she now regrets, and conscious of her love for *Nadir,* which may mean death for them both, she sinks down in an agony of despair. *Nadir* enters and asks her to fly with him, defying Brahma and the priests. She at first repulses him, but love is finally triumphant and the lovers rapturously embrace, while a fearful storm rages, unheeded, without the ruins.

This scene is expressed by a splendid duet, two records of which are given here for a choice.

Non hai compreso un cor fedel (You Have Not Understood)

By Giuseppina Huguet, Soprano, and Fernando de Lucia,
Tenor (*In Italian*) 92054 12-inch, $3.00
By Giuseppina Piccoletti, Soprano, and Ivo Zaccari,
Tenor (*In Italian*) *68062 12-inch, 1.25

The lovers are surprised by *Nourabad,* and *Nadir* flees, closely pursued by the priests. He is captured and brought back, while *Zurga* is summoned to pronounce sentence on the guilty lovers. His friendship for *Nadir* moves him to mercy, and he spares their lives and bids them fly the country. As they go, however, the high priest tears the veil from *Leila,* and when *Zurga* realizes that it is the woman *Nadir* has sworn never to see, he is enraged and sentences them both to death.

Double-Faced Record—For title of opposite side see DOUBLE-FACED PEARL FISHERS RECORDS, page 268.

ACT III
SCENE I—*The Camp of Zurga*

Zurga is discovered alone, brooding over the impending death of his friend and the woman he loves. His mood of despair is interrupted by *Leila*, who appears at the entrance to his tent and asks him to dismiss the guards and speak with her alone. She asks mercy for *Nadir* in a dramatic aria.

Temer non so per me (I Fear Not)
By Emilia Corsi, Soprano   (*In Italian*) *63394 10-inch, $0.75

She proudly refuses to plead for her own life, but begs that he spare the friend whom he loves. *Zurga* refuses and summons the guards to conduct her to execution.

SCENE II—*The Place of Execution*

The scene shows the wild spot where the funeral pile has been erected. *Leila* and *Nadir* are led in, and are about to mount the pyre when a red glow is seen in the sky, and *Zurga* enters crying that the camp is on fire, and bids the people fly to save their children and effects. All run out except *Leila, Nadir* and *Zurga,* and the high priest, who, suspecting a plot, hides to hear what *Zurga* will say. The latter confesses that he kindled the fire in order to save the lovers. Unfastening their chains, he bids them escape, while *Nourabad* runs to warn the Indians, and *Leila* and *Nadir,* beginning the great trio, voice their gratitude.

Terzetto finale—Fascino etereo
By Linda Brambilla, Soprano; Giuseppe Acerbi, Tenor;
Francesco Cigada, Baritone   (*In Italian*) *68063 12-inch, $1.25

The lovers praise the generosity and greatness of *Zurga,* who for the sake of friendship has committed an act which may cost him his own life. He bids them fly at once, and they go as the voices of the enraged Indians are heard returning for vengeance. *Nourabad* denounces *Zurga* for the escape of the victims and for the destruction of the camp, and he is forced to mount the funeral pyre. As the flames mount about him he cries:

ZURGA:
Farewell, my friend!
Farewell, my Leila!
For thee I give my life!

As *Zurga* dies a fiery glow reveals that the forest is ablaze, and all prostrate themselves, fearing the displeasure of Brahma. The curtain falls as the flames envelop the stage.

DOUBLE-FACED AND MISCELLANEOUS PEARL FISHERS SELECTIONS

Del tempio al limitar (In the Depths of the Temple) By Giuseppe Acerbi and Renzo Minolfi (*In Italian*) Terzetto finale—Fascino etereo By Linda Brambilla, Soprano; Giuseppe Acerbi, Tenor; Francesco Cigada, Baritone (*In Italian*)	68063	12-inch, $1.25
Non hai compreso un cor fedel (You Have Not Understood) By Giuseppina Piccoletti, Soprano, and Ivo Zaccari, Tenor (*In Italian*) Brahma gran Dio (Divine Brahma!) By Lina Brambilla, Soprano, and La Scala Chorus (*In Italian*)	68062	12-inch, 1.25
Siccome un di (A Fugitive, One Day) By Giuseppina Piccoletti, Soprano (*In Italian*) Hermes—S'io t'amo By Melis and Taccani (*In Italian*)	68307	12-inch, 1.25
Pearl Fishers Selection Sousa's Band Spinning Wheel (Spindler) Pryor's Band	35033	12-inch, 1.25
Preludio (Prelude) By La Scala Orchestra Ebrea—Rachele allor che Iddio By Gino Martinez-Patti, Tenor (*In Italian*)	62100	10-inch, .75
Temer non so per me (I Fear Not) By Emilia Corsi, Soprano (*In Italian*) Jana—Si dannato morro By Taccani (*In Italian*)	63394	10-inch, .75

---

*Double-Faced Records—For title of opposite side see above list.

(Italian) (French) (English)
IL PROFETA   LE PROPHÈTE   THE PROPHET
(Eel Pro-fay'-tah) *(Leh Proh-fayt')*

OPERA IN FIVE ACTS

Text by Scribe. Music by Giacomo Meyerbeer. First presented in Paris, April 16, 1849. First London production July 24, 1849. First New York production November 25, 1854. Revived at the Manhattan Opera in 1909 with d'Alvarez, Lucas and Walter-Villa.

Characters

JOHN OF LEYDEN, *(Ly'-den)* the Prophet, chosen leader of the Anabaptists. . Tenor
BERTHA, his sweetheart. . . . . Soprano
FIDÈS, *(Fee'-dayz)* mother of John of Leyden . . . . Mezzo-Soprano
COUNT OBERTHAL, ruler of the domain about Dordrecht. . . . . Bass
ZACHARIAH, ⎫ . . . . ⎧Bass
JONAS, ⎬three Anabaptist preachers. . . . . ⎨Tenor
MATHISEN, ⎭ . . . . ⎩Bass

Nobles, Citizens, Peasants, Soldiers, Prisoners.

Scene and Period: Holland and Germany; in 1543, at the time of the Anabaptist uprising.

COPY'T DUPONT

ALVAREZ AS THE PROPHET

Meyerbeer's great work is certainly entitled to be called a grand opera, for it is grand to the utmost in theme, character and scenes; and with its brilliant and impressive music, at the time of its production sixty years ago was a model of its kind, as opera-goers demanded melodramatic action, tuneful music and opportunity for ballet; and all these requirements are fully met with in Le Prophète.

The plot is based on the Anabaptist fanaticism of the sixteenth century, which agitated a large part of Germany and Holland, and the leader of which was one Bockelson, commonly called John of Leyden.

ACT I

SCENE—*A Suburb of Dordrecht, Holland*

The story furnished by the librettists describes *John* as the son of the widow *Fidès,* an innkeeper of Leyden. At the opening of the opera he is about to wed *Bertha,* an orphan. She, being a vassal of the *Count Oberthal,* is obliged to ask his permission before marrying, and goes with *Fidès, John's* mother to beg the Count's consent. The Count, struck with the young girl's beauty, covets her for himself, refuses his consent and orders *Fidès* and *Bertha* into the castle.

ACT II

SCENE—*The Inn of John in the Suburbs of Leyden*

Three Anabaptists enter and being struck with the resemblance of *John* to the portrait of the guardian saint, *David,* at Munster, they try to induce him to become their leader. He refuses, but tells them of a strange dream he has had.

> JOHN: Under the vast dome of a splendid temple
> I stood—the people at my feet were prostrate—
> The royal coronal adorn'd my brow!

The Anabaptists declare that Heaven has spoken in the dream, and promise that he shall yet be a ruler; but *John's* thoughts turn to his beloved *Bertha,* and in this beautiful *Pastorale* he tells them that another and sweeter life calls to him.

© DUPONT

Schumann-Heink as Fidès

Pastorale (There's a Sweeter Empire)

By Leo Slezak, Tenor   *(In German)*   **64112**   10-inch $1.00

Slezak, whose *John* is one of his greatest rôles, sings this lovely romanza with beautiful expression.

JOHN:
Oh, there's a sweeter empire, far,
Which long has been my guiding star;
Oh, thou my joy, my greatest gain,
If in thy faithful heart I reign!
For me, the proudest kingdom,

Less than this thatch'd roof
My hopes would bless,
Sweet home of calm felicity,
Where I would gladly live and die,
Where Bertha will forever prove
Alike my bosom's queen and love!

Bertha, who has escaped from the castle, now runs in, asking *John* to save her. She is concealed by him as the Count's soldiers enter and threaten to kill *Fidès* unless *John* delivers up the maiden. To save his mother's life he is forced to yield, and sees his bride carried off to become the Count's mistress.

Fidès, in her gratitude, sings this most dramatic and intense of Meyerbeer's airs, which has attained a world-wide popularity.

Ah, mon fils! (Ah, My Son!)

By Louise Homer, Contralto   *(In French)*   **88284**   12-inch, $3.00
By Ernestine Schumann-Heink, Contralto   *(In French)*   **88187**   12-inch, 3.00

FIDES:
Ah, my son! Blessed be thou!
Thy loving mother to thee was dearer
Than was Bertha, who claim'd thy heart!
Ah, my son! For thou, alas,
Thou dost give for thy mother more than life,
For thou giv'st all the joy of thy soul!
Ah, my son! now to heav'n my pray'r ascends
  for thee;   <small>From Operatic Anthology, by permission of</small>
My son, blessed be forever more!   <small>G. Schirmer. (Copy't 1899.)</small>

The part of *Fidès*, the most interesting in the opera, is one of Mme. Schumann-Heink's great successes, and the *Ah, mon fils*, a dramatic aria full of real passion, she sings with exquisite tenderness.

This rôle being originally written for a soprano, requires a voice of wide compass and great power. Mme. Homer's voice not only possesses these qualities, but is brilliant in the higher register and full and musical in the lower, and she sings this wonderful music just as Meyerbeer wrote it, delivering the beautiful words with real pathos.

John, left by his mother to bitter thoughts, hears the Anabaptists in the distance, and resolves to join them as a means of vengeance on the Count. The compact is soon made and they depart, leaving some blood-stained garments to lead *Fidès* to believe *John* has been slain by the Count's assassins.

ACT III

SCENE—*Camp of Anabaptists in the Westphalia Forest*

The city of Munster is about to be besieged by the rebels, and before proceeding to the charge, *John,* now the *Prophet,* and in command of the rebels, makes them kneel and pray for victory. They chant the *Miserere,* and *John* sings this noble *Inno* or hymn.

Re del cielo e dei beati (Triumphal Hymn, "King of Heaven")

By Francesco Tamagno, Tenor *(Piano acc.)*   *(In Italian)*   **95005**   10-inch, $5.00
By Antonio Paoli, Tenor, and La Scala Chorus   *(Italian)*   **91080**   10-inch, 2.00
By Luigi Colazza, Tenor *(Double-faced—See p. 273)*   *(Italian)*   **16578**   10-inch, .75

JOHN:
King of Heaven and of the angels,
I will praise Thee,
Like David, Thy servant.
A voice I heard—"Array thyself,
And safely on I will guide thee."
Praise to the Omnipotent!
Yes, victory is on our side,

Let's unfurl the sacred flag,
He whom we serve is Lord
Of Heaven and earth.
Let's sing and march away.
The eye of Heaven will watch over us,
A supreme power will guide us!
With songs of joy—with shouts of glory—
On—on to Munster!

Three renditions of this inspiring number are presented. Tamagno, who was perhaps the most famous of all *Prophets*, sings the air gloriously, while other fine records are furnished by Colazza and Paoli, the latter being assisted by La Scala Chorus.

ACT IV
SCENE I—*A Public Square in Munster*

The insurgents have captured the city. The *Prophet* is received with mixed feelings, some denouncing him as an impostor. *Fidès,* reduce to beggary, meets *Bertha,* who had escaped from the Count and come to Munster to seek *John.* *Fidès* tells her *John* is dead, and *Bertha,* thinking the *Prophet* is responsible, swears to have vengeance.

SCENE II—*The Munster Cathedral*

This magnificent cathedral scene is one of Meyerbeer's most brilliant compositions. It forms a striking contrast to the rest of the opera, so gloomy with religious and political fanaticism, and as a piece of glittering pageantry with gorgeous decoration, pealing bells, solemn chants, and the stately Coronation March, has seldom been equaled.

Coronation March
By Arthur Pryor's Band
31503   12-inch, $1.00
By Garde Republicaine Band
4115   10-inch,   .60

The great symphonic march which occurs in this scene is by far the most striking instrumental number in Meyerbeer's opera. It is brilliant and powerful, with superb instrumentation, and even without the dramatic setting in which it is played in Prophète, always produces a marked effect on the listener.

Of the performance of this noble and stately march by Pryor's Band, we can only say that it is superb in every respect, and the record has a volume

JOHN DENYING HIS MOTHER—ACT IV

of tone which makes one marvel that it all could come from the minute disc vibrations.

As *John* passes into the church, *Fidès* sees him, and in a transport of joy greets him as her son. He declares she is mad, knowing it is death to both if he acknowledges her. She finally realizes the situation, confesses that she is mistaken, and is led away to prison.

ACT V
SCENE I—*The Crypt of the Palace at Munster*

The first scene takes place in the prison vaults beneath the palace, where *Fidès,* feeling certain that *John* will contrive to see her, patiently awaits his coming. She at first denounces him as an ungrateful son, then, repenting, prays that Heaven may soften his heart and lead him to repent.

Prison Scene, Part I
By Ernestine Schumann-Heink, Contralto   (*In French*)   **88094**   12-inch, $3.00

Fidès (*alone*):

O! my cruel destiny! Whither have you led me?
What, the walls of a prison! they arrest my footsteps.
I am no longer free.
Bertha swore my son's death, he denied his mother;
On his head let the wrath of Heaven fall!

(*Her wrath subsides.*)
Though thou hast abandoned me,
But my heart is disarmed,
Thy mother pardons thee.
Yes, I am still a mother.
I have given my cares that thou may'st be happy,
Now I would give my life,
And my soul exalted, will wait for thee in heaven!

An officer enters and announces the arrival of the Prophet.

Prison Scene, Part II
By Ernestine Schumann-Heink, Contralto   (*In French*)   **88095**   12-inch, $3.00

DU GUY, PARIS   JOHN THE PROPHET

Fidès then begins the second part of her great scene.

FIDÈS (*joyfully*):
He comes!
I shall see him, delightful hope!
Oh, truth! daughter of heaven,
May thy flame, like lightning,
Strike the soul of an ungrateful son.
Celestial flame restore to him calmness!
Restore, bless'd Heaven, his guardian angel!
Immortal grace, Oh! conq'ring come;
With thy pure love his heart reprove;
Tho' he be guilty, save him now
From that dark abyss which threatens to
   engulf him;
Let thy light pierce this ingrate son,
Conscience riv'n, his soul soften,
Like brass in furnace fierce,
That he may ascend and reign in Heav'n!

When *John* enters, *Fidès* denounces the bloody deeds of the Anabaptists and calls on her son to repent and renounce his false robes.

FIDES:
But thou, whom the world detests,
Yes, thou, braving Heaven's behests;
Thou, whose fell hand is reeking with blood;
Go thou, my son no longer now!
Far from my heart, far from my eyes—
Blood-stain'd, go!

John confesses his sins and pleads for forgiveness, finally kneeling and receiving her blessing, just as a faithful officer enters and informs *John* that the Anabaptists are plotting to deliver him to the Emperor's forces, which are marching on the city.

Bertha enters through a secret passage, revealed to her by her grandfather, who was once keeper of the palace. She has resolved to blow up the palace and the false Prophet, and is horrified to learn that *John* is the *Prophet*. She denounces him for his crimes, and declaring she has no longer reason to live, stabs herself.

John, in despair, resolves to die with his enemies, and sending away his mother, plans to have the palace set on fire, and goes to the banquet hall.

SCENE II—*The Great Hall of the Palace*

After the Emperor's forces have entered, crying, "Death to the Prophet," *John* orders the gates closed. An explosion occurs and the palace falls, carrying down to death *John* and all his enemies.

OBERTHAL:
You are my prisoner!
JOHN:
Nay, ye are all *my* captives!
(*An explosion takes place, the walls fall and flames spread on every side.*)
JOHN (*to Gione and Oberthal*):
Thou, traitor! and thou, tyrant! shalt perish
   with me;
Justice has sealed our doom;
I am the instrument,
We, all guilty, are all punished!

(*A woman with dishevelled hair rushes through the ruins into John's arms. He recognizes his mother.*)
JOHN:
My mother!
FIDÈS:
Yes, receive my pardon; I will die with thee!
FIDÈS AND JOHN:
Welcome, sacred flame!
To yon celestial sphere may our souls take
   flight!
Adieu!
(*As the flames mount about them the curtain falls.*)

DOUBLE-FACED LE PROPHÈTE RECORDS

{ Fantasie	By Pryor's Band }	35125	12-inch,	$1.25
{ *Barber of Seville Selection*	By Pryor's Band }			
{ Re del cielo (King of Heaven)	By Luigi Colazza, Tenor }	16578	10-inch,	.75
{ *William Tell Ballet Music—Part III*	By Pryor's Band }			

(Italian)   (English)
I PURITANI   THE PURITANS
(*Ee Poo-ree-tah'-nee*)

OPERA IN THREE ACTS

Book by Count Pepoli; music by Vincenzo Bellini. First presented at the *Théâtre Italien*, Paris, January 25, 1835, with a famous cast—Grisi, Rubini, Tamburini and Lablache. First London producton, King's Theatre, May 21, 1835, under the title of *Puritani ed i Cavalieri*. First New York production, February 3, 1844. Revived in 1906 at the Manhattan Opera, with Pinkert, Bonci and Arimondi.

Characters

LORD GAUTIER WALTON, Puritan ....Bass
SIR GEORGE, Puritan ....Bass
LORD ARTHUR TALBOT, Cavalier.................................Bass
SIR RICHARD FORTH, Puritan ....Baritone
SIR BRUNO ROBERTSON, Puritan ....Tenor
HENRIETTA OF FRANCE, widow of Charles I....................Soprano
ELVIRA, daughter of Lord Walton.............................Soprano

Chorus of Puritans, Soldiers of Cromwell, Heralds and Men-at-Arms of Lord Arthur, Countrymen and Women, Damsels, Pages and Servants.

Scene and Period: England in the neighborhood of Plymouth, in the period preceding the impeachment and execution of Charles II by Parliament.

Previous to Mr. Hammerstein's revival in 1906, *Puritani* had not been given in America since the production of 1883, with Gerster as *Elvira*. This is not strange, as the opera on the whole is somewhat dreary, only the few numbers the Victor has collected being really worth hearing.

The plot is rather a foolish one: the libretto being one of the poorest ever written for Bellini, but the music is delightful and fascinating. However, we will briefly sketch the story, as it will add to the enjoyment of the lovely melodies of Bellini which the Victor has recorded. The translation is a very unsatisfactory one, but a few quotations are given.

The action occurs in England in the time of the Stuarts, during the civil war between the Royalists and the Puritans. *Lord Walton*, the Puritan Governor-General, has a daughter *Elvira*, whom he wishes to marry to *Richard Forth*, a Puritan colonel, but the young girl loves an enemy, *Lord Arthur*.

ACT I

SCENE I—*Exterior of a Fortress near Plymouth*

At the beginning of Act I, *Forth*, learning that *Elvira* loves *Arthur*, and that her father refuses to force her into an unwelcome marriage, is disconsolate and gives vent to his feeling in a famous air:

Ah per sempre (To Me Forever Lost)

By Mario Ancona, Baritone   (*In Italian*)   87014 10-inch, $2.00

given here by Signor Ancona, whose success in this part at the Manhattan revival is well remembered.

FORTH:
Ah! to me forever lost,
Flow'r of love, and hope the dearest!
Life, to me thou now appearest,
Gloomy and with tempests cross'd.
Oh, happy and lovely dream of peace and joy!
Oh, change thou my fate, or change my heart!
Ah, what a keen torment, in the day of grief,
Becomes the memory of a vanish'd love!

SCENE II—*Elvira's Room in the Castle*

The next scene shows *Elvira's* apartment, where her uncle, *Sir George,* in a fine air, tells her that he has persuaded her father to consent to her marriage with *Arthur.* This is sung here by de Segurola and issued as a double-faced record, the opposite selection being the *Infelice* from *Ernani.*

Sorgea la notte (The Night Was Growing Dark)

By A. Perelló de Segurola, Bass   *(In Italian)*   **55007**   **12-inch, $1.50**

COPY'T MISHKIN

ANCONA AS SIR RICHARD

The night was growing dark,
And Heav'n and earth were silent,—
Favorable the sad hour,
Thy pray'rs gave courage to my soul,
And to thy sire I went.

Thus I began,—"My brother"—
"Your angel-like Elvira
Is for the valiant Arthur pining—
Should she another wed,
Oh, wretched one! she dies!"

Said thy father
"She is to Richard promised!"
"Thy unhappy child," repeated I, "will die."
"Oh! say not so," he cried,
"I must yield, let Elvira live,—
Ah! may she be happy—
Let her live in love!"

Elvira is overjoyed, and expresses her gratitude. Trumpets are now heard, and *Elvira's* surprise is complete when *Lord Arthur* arrives, attended by squires and pages, and bearing nuptial presents, prominent among which is a splendid white veil, soon to play an important part in the events to come.

Shortly after his arrival *Arthur* discovers that the widow of *Charles I* is in the castle under sentence of death, and his sense of duty toward the late Queen impels him to contrive her escape by concealing her in *Elvira's* veil, the guards thinking it is the bride. The escape is soon discovered and *Elvira,* supposing that her lover has deserted her on the eve of her bridal day, becomes insane. All denounce *Arthur* and swear to be revenged.

ACT II

SCENE—*The Puritan Camp*

Act II shows the camp of the Puritan forces. *Sir George* announces that Parliament has condemned *Arthur* to death for aiding in the escape of the late Queen. *Elvira* enters, demented, and sings her famous air, much like the Mad Scene in Lucia.

Qui la voce (In Sweetest Accents)

By Marcella Sembrich, Soprano   *(In Italian)*   **88105**   **12-inch, $3.00**

She recalls her first meeting with *Arthur* and repeats the vows he swore.

ELVIRA:
It was here in accents sweetest,
He would call me—he calls no more!
Here affection swore he to cherish,
That dream so happy, alas! is o'er!
We no more shall be united,
I'm in sorrow doomed to sigh,
Oh, to hope once more restore me,
Or in pity let me die!
(*Her mood changes.*)
Yes,—my father: thou call'st me to the temple?
'Tis no dream, my Arthur, oh, my love!
Ah, thou art smiling—thy tears thou driest,
Fond Hymen guiding, I quickly follow!
Then dancing and singing,
All nuptial feasts providing.
(*Dancing toward Richard, whom she takes by the hand.*)
And surely you will dance with me—
Come to the altar.

Elvira's uncle, hoping that the sight of her lover will restore her reason, begs *Sir Richard* to pardon the young man. *Richard* consents, provided he returns helpless and in peril, but if he comes bearing arms against his country he shall die. *Sir George* agrees to this, and in the splendid *Sound the Trumpet* they pledge themselves to fight together for their country.

Suoni la tromba (Sound the Trumpet)

By Mario Ancona, Baritone, and Marcel Journet, Bass

(*In Italian*)   88500   12-inch, $3.00

This favorite duet, often sung in concert, has been aptly described as a "stentorian" number. It is undeniedly a most vigorous piece of declamation, and if the loyalty of *Sir George* and *Sir Richard* can be judged by the vigor of the usual rendition, they are loyal indeed!

> SIR RICHARD AND SIR GEORGE:
> Sound, sound the trumpet loudly!
> Bravely we'll meet the foemen,
> 'Tis sweet affronting death!
> Bold love of country aiding.
> The victor's wreath unfading,
> Will unto us be proudly
> Restor'd by Love and Faith!
> Morn! rising on a nation,
> Whose only trust is freedom—
> Will bring us eternal fame!
> Earth's tyrants who dissemble,
> At the war-message tremble,
> Midst the world's execration
> They sink in endless shame!

The Puritans then renew their pledge as to *Arthur,* saying:

> SIR GEORGE:
> All is now concluded,
> If Arthur is defenceless—
> RICHARD:
> He'll find support and succor.
> SIR GEORGE:
> If he in arms returns—
> RICHARD:
> He comes to shame and vengeance!

ACT III

SCENE—*A Garden near Elvira's House*

The rise of the curtain discloses *Arthur,* who is fleeing from the enemy, and has come to the castle in the hope of seeing *Elvira* once more before he leaves England forever. She comes from the castle and at the sight of *Arthur* her reason suddenly returns. The lovers are reconciled after *Arthur* explains that it was in the service of his Queen that he had fled from the castle. They sing a lovely duet:

Vieni fra queste braccia (Come to My Arms)

By Maria Galvany, Soprano, and Francesco Marconi, Tenor

(*In Italian*)   89046   12-inch, $4.00

Forgetting their present danger, they think only of their love and that they are in each other's arms again.

> ARTHUR:
> Come, come to my arms,
> Thou my life's sole delight!
> And thus press'd to my heart,
> We'll no more disunite!
> Thrill'd with anxious love and fear,
> On thee I call—for thee I sigh;—
> Come, and say the love is dear
> That soareth to boundless height!

The sound of a drum is heard, and *Elvira* again becomes delirious, which so alarms *Arthur* that he thinks not of escape and is captured by the Puritan forces. The sentence of death is read to him and he is being led to his execution, when a messenger arrives from *Cromwell* saying that the *Stuarts* were defeated and a pardon had been granted to all captives. *Elvira's* reason returns, and the lovers are united, no more to part.

(Curtain)

(Italian)
REGINA DI SABA
(Ray-gee'-nah dee Sah'-bah)

(English)
QUEEN OF SHEBA

OPERA IN FOUR ACTS

Text by Mosenthal, founded upon the Biblical mention of the visit of the Queen of Sheba to Solomon. Music by Goldmark. First production 1875, in Vienna. In New York 1885, with Lehmann and Fischer. Revived in 1905, with Walker, Rappold, Knote and Van Rooy.

Characters

KING SOLOMON . . . . Baritone
HIGH PRIEST . . . . Bass
SULAMITH, his daughter . . . . Soprano
ASSAD, Solomon's favorite . . . . Tenor
QUEEN OF SHEBA . . . . Mezzo-Soprano
ASTAROTH, her slave (a Moor) . . . . Soprano

Priests, Singers, Harpists, Bodyguards, Women of the Harem, People.

Scene : Jerusalem and vicinity.

Goldmark's opera, which was his first successful work, was revived on a sumptuous scale by the Metropolitan Company a few years ago, but since that time the only opportunity opera-lovers have had of hearing the beautiful airs has been that offered by their Victors.

The plot tells of the struggle of *Assad,* a courtier of *Solomon,* against fleshly temptation. and of his final victory which involves the sacrifice of the happiness of his betrothed, *Sulamith.*

For this text Goldmark furnished some of the most beautiful and sensuous music in the entire range of opera.

The wisdom and fame of *Solomon* having reached even distant Arabia, the *Queen of Sheba* decides to visit him, and a favorite courtier, *Assad,* has been sent to meet her and escort her to the city. When *Assad* arrives with the Queen, his betrothed, *Sulamith,* is astonished to find him pale and embarrassed, and trying to avoid her. *Assad* afterward confesses to *Solomon* that he had met a beautiful woman at Lebanon and had fallen in love with her. When the *Queen of Sheba* arrives and removes her veil, *Assad* is astounded to recognize in her the mysterious woman who had captured his senses. Involuntarily he rushes toward her, but she coldly repulses him and passes on with the King.

In Act II the Queen discovers that she loves *Assad,* and seeing him in the garden, bids her maid attract his attention with a weird Oriental song. *Assad* starts when he hears the mysterious air, as it seems to bring back memories of the night at Lebanon. He sings his beautiful air, *Magic Tones.*

Magiche note (Magic Tones !)

By Enrico Caruso, Tenor	*(In Italian)*	87041	10-inch, $2.00
By Leo Slezak, Tenor	*(In German)*	64115	10-inch, 1.00

A lovely melody, sung at first in *mezzo-voce,* develops gradually until the intense and passionate climax is reached.

The Queen and *Assad* soon meet and confess their love for each other, but are interrupted by the arrival of the night guard.

In the next scene the Court assembles for the wedding of *Sulamith* and *Assad,* but *Assad* insults his bride and declares his love for the Queen. He is banished from Jerusalem and finally dies in the arms of *Sulamith,* who is crossing the desert on her way to a convent.

THE THEFT OF THE RHINEGOLD

(German)   (English)

DAS RHEINGOLD   THE RHINEGOLD
(*Dahss Rine'-gold*)

MUSIC DRAMA IN FOUR SCENES

Prelude to the Trilogy : "The Nibelungs' Ring"
(*Nee'-bel-oong*)

Words and music by Richard Wagner. First produced at Munich, September 22, 1869.
First American production at New York, January 4, 1888.

Characters

WOTAN, (*Vo'-tahn*)	⎫	Baritone
DONNER,		Bass
FRÖH,	Gods	Tenor
LOGI, (*Low'-jee*)	⎭	Tenor
FASOLT,	⎱ Giants	Bass
FAFNER,	⎰	Bass
ALBERICH, (*Ahl'-ber-ish*)	⎱ Nibelungs (Gnomes)	Baritone
MIME, (*Mee'-mee*)	⎰	Tenor
FRICKA, (*Free'-kah*)	⎫	Soprano
FREIA, (*Free'-ah*)	Goddesses	Soprano
ERDA, (*Ehr'-dah*)	⎭	Contralto
WOGLINDE,	⎫	Soprano
WELLGUNDE,	Nymphs of the Rhine	Soprano
FLOSSHILDE,	⎭	Contralto

Rheingold is not a "society" opera. Played in complete darkness and with no inter-missions during the two hours required for its presentation, it is a work only for real music-lovers who understand something of the story and appreciate Wagner's wonderful music.

This first part of the *Ring* is an introduction to the *Trilogy* proper, and a full under-standing of its incidents is necessary to properly appreciate the other *Ring* operas.

SCENE I—*The Bottom of the Rhine*

The stage is in semi-darkness, representing the murky depths of the Rhine, and the light glimmering on the surface of the water above shows but faintly the three Rhine maidens guarding the *Rhinegold*.

They sing their quaint songs as they float about the rock which conceals the treasure.

MOTIVE OF THE RHINE MAIDENS

Alberich, prince of the *Nibelungs,* a strange race of dwarfs who dwell deep in the earth, observes the beauty of the maidens and tries to make love to them. They laugh at him and evade with ease his clumsy endeavors to catch them. Suddenly, as the sun rises, the gleam of the *Rhinegold* is seen. *Alberich,* dazzled by the splendor of this glow, asks what it is, and the maidens foolishly inform him that whoever can secure this treasure and form it into a ring can become lord of all the world. One condition, however, is that the possessor cannot wield this power unless he renounces forever the joys of love.

Alberich, having failed in his amorous attempts towards the *Naiads,* now conceives an ambition for power. He cries, "Then love I renounce forever," and swimming to the rock, he tears the gold from its place and flees, while from the complete darkness which ensues comes the dwarf's mocking laughter and the wailing of the maidens who are moaning for their lost treasure.

FROM AN OLD PRINT

THEFT OF THE RHINEGOLD—SCENE I

SCENE II—*A Mountain Top, Showing the Castle of Walhalla*

During this darkness the scene changes and as the stage becomes lighter we see *Walhalla,* the abode of the gods, a wonderful castle built for *Wotan* by the giants. *Wotan* and his wife are lying asleep on a flowery bank, but soon wake and see the castle which has been built while they slept. *Wotan* is overjoyed at the glorious sight, but the more practical *Fricka* reminds him of the price which he had agreed to pay the giants for this godly dwelling; this being the surrender of *Freia,* goddess of youth and beauty. *Wotan* tells her that he never intended to keep his agreement, the god *Loge* having promised to show him a way to evade payment.

Freia now hastily enters, closely pursued by the giants *Fasolt* and *Fafner,* who call upon *Wotan* to deliver the goddess to them as agreed. *Wotan* repudiates his promise, saying that it was made only in jest.

WOTAN:
How sly to take for truth
What only in sport we had settled!
This beauteous goddess, light and bright,
What use to you are her charms?

Fröh and *Donner, Fricka's* brothers, enter, also *Loge,* and a long argument ensues, *Wotan* finally realizing that he must give up *Freia* to the giants. *Loge,* however, tells them of the *Rhinegold,* saying that if this treasure could be stolen from *Alberich* by *Wotan,* it might be accepted by the giants in place of *Freia.* *Wotan* refuses to entertain this plan and the giants seize *Freia* and carry her off, declaring that if the *Rhinegold* is not in their hands by night the original bargain must stand, and *Freia* be lost to the gods forever.

Left alone, the gods realize the serious

PHOTO HOFFERT   FREIA AND THE GIANTS

predicament they are in, especially as it is seen that, deprived of their youth goddess, they are suddenly aging. *Wotan* thereupon decides to secure the *Nibelungs'* gold, and goes with *Loge* in search of *Alberich.* A vapor arises from the earth, concealing the stage, and when it disappears the scene has changed.

SCENE III—*Alberich's Cave*

Alberich, since he has acquired the *Rhinegold,* has become more arrogant and cruel than ever, and compels *Mime* and the other *Nibelungs* to continually toil and slave to bring him in more gold. At the beginning of the scene he is berating *Mime* for loitering over his task of making a *Tarnhelm,* or magic cap, fashioned from the *Rhinegold,* and which gives the wearer the power to become invisible. *Wotan* and *Loge* now enter on this scene and are rudely greeted by *Alberich,* who demands their business, and holding out the *Ring* bids them tremble at his power. They at first craftily flatter him, but he is surly and says that naught but envy could have brought them here. *Wotan* is angry and is about to voice his wrath when the crafty *Loge* makes him a sign to be quiet and begins to taunt *Alberich,* doubting his power. *Alberich* is so enraged that he offers to change himself into any shape required to prove the magic of the *Tarnhelm,* and immediately becomes a huge dragon. *Loge* affects extreme terror, at which *Alberich* laughs and resumes his human shape again. The god then cunningly asks him to change to a toad, which shape he has no sooner assumed than *Loge* puts his foot on the toad and seizes the *Tarnhelm,* thus robbing *Alberich* of his power. His natural form returns and they bind him and start for the upper earth. The scene changes again to the mountain summit.

SCENE IV—*Same as Scene II*

Wotan and *Loge* enter, dragging the helpless *Alberich,* who is beside himself with rage. They demand that he give them his hoarded store of gold as the price of his freedom. He reluctantly obeys and summons the *Nibelungs,* who instantly swarm up from below carrying the hoard. He then asks to be set free, but *Wotan* demands also the Ring. *Alberich* is horrified, but is finally compelled to add it to the pile of gold. He then sings his bitter and ironical air, *Bin ich nun frei?*

Bin ich nun frei? (Am I Now Free?)
By Otto Goritz, Baritone

(*In German*) 64203 10-inch, $1.00

He lays a frightful curse on the Ring, predicting that it will bring misery and death to each possessor until it is restored to him again.

ALBERICH (*with bitter irony*):
Am I now free?—
Really free?
Then listen, friends,
To my freedom's first salute!—
As at first by my curse 'twas reached,
Henceforth cursed be this ring!
Gold which gave me measureless might,
Now may its magic deal each owner death!
No man shall e'er own it in mirth,
And to gladden no life shall its luster gleam.
May care consume each several possessor,
And envy gnaw him who neareth it not!
All shall lust after its delights,
But none shall employ them to profit him.
To its master giving no gain,
Aye the murd'rer's brand it shall bring.
To death he is fated,
Its fear on his fancy shall feed;
Though long he live shall he languish each
　　day,
The treasure's lord and the treasure's slave:
Till within my hand I in triumph once more
　　behold it!—
So—stirred by the hardest need,
The Nibelung blesses his ring!—
I give it thee,—guard it with care—
But my curse canst thou not flee!

PAINTED BY ECHTER

THE CAPTURE OF ALBERICH—SCENE III

PAINTED BY MAKART   BATTLE OF THE GIANTS—SCENE IV

He vanishes and *Wotan*, who has paid little attention to his cursing, dons the Ring, gazing at it in admiration. The giants now return for their pay, and demand that enough gold shall be piled around *Freia* to hide her completely from sight. This is done, but when all the gold is piled up *Fafner* says there is still one small crevice visible, and insists that it be filled with the Ring. *Wotan* refuses, and the giants are about to seize *Freia* again, when *Erda*, the earth goddess, rises and delivers her appeal to *Wotan*.

Weiche, Wotan, weiche! (Waver, Wotan)

By Ernestine Schumann-Heink, Contralto   (*In German*)   88092   12-inch, $3.00

(*Wotan's* responses are sung by Mr. Witherspoon)

She warns him solemnly that the Ring is cursed and charges him to give it up.

ERDA (*stretching her hand*):
Waver, Wotan, waver!
Quit the Ring accursed!
(*She continues her solemn warning*)
Ruin and dismalest downfall wait thee in its wealth.
WOTAN:
Who speaks such menacing words?

COPY'T DUPONT
HOMER AS ERDA

ERDA:
Whatever was, was I; what is, as well;
What ages shall work—all I show;
The endless world's All-wise one, Erda, opens thine eyes.
Three, the daughters born to me
E'er the world was made; all I notice
Nightly thou know'st from the Nornir.
But hither in dire danger haste I to thy help.
Hear me! Hear me! Hear me!
All that exists, endeth!
A dismal day dawns for the Æsir:
O render wisely the ring!
(*She begins to sink slowly into the earth.*)
WOTAN:
A secret spell speaks in thy words:
Wait and impart more wisdom.
ERDA (*disappearing*):
I've warned thee now; thou wott'st enough;
Pause and ponder truth!
(*She completely disappears.*)

Mme. Schumann-Heink sings this powerful number with dignity and dramatic force.

Wotan at last yields and throws the Ring on the heap of gold. The giants, as if to prove the curse, immediately begin to quarrel about its possession, and *Fasolt* is killed by *Fafner*; after which the murderer coolly proceeds to collect the gold and then departs.

Donner, the god of thunder, now calls up a storm and causes a rainbow bridge to form, making a passage to the castle. As the gods proceed across the bridge to *Walhalla* the voices of the Rhine maidens can be heard from below, still bewailing the loss of their gold.

RHINE-NYMPHS (*from below*):
Rhinegold! Rarest gold!
O might but again

In the wave thy pure magic wake!
What is of worth dwells but in the waters!
Base and bad those who are throned above.

(*As the gods slowly cross the bridge to the castle, the curtain falls.*)

MONTERONE DENOUNCES THE JESTER—ACT I

RIGOLETTO

OPERA IN THREE ACTS

Text by Piave, adapted from Victor Hugo's drama *Le Roi s'Amuse*. Music by Giuseppe Verdi. First produced in Venice, March 11, 1851. First London production at Covent Garden, May 14, 1853; at the *Italiens*, Paris, January 19, 1857. First New York production November 2, 1857.

Characters

RIGOLETTO, a hunchback, jester to the Duke.....................Baritone
DUKE OF MANTUA, a titled profligate ....Tenor
GILDA, (*Jeel'-dah*) daughter of Rigoletto..........................Soprano
SPARAFUCILE, (*Spahr-ah-foo-cheel'*) a hired assassin ....Bass
MADDALENA, (*Mad-dah-lay'-nah*) his sister ....Contralto
COUNT MONTERONE (*Mon-ter-oh'-nay*) ....Baritone
COUNT CEPRANO...Bass
Courtiers, pages, servants.

Scene and Period: Mantua and vicinity; sixteenth century.

The story tells of the gay and unprincipled *Duke of Mantua*, who is assisted in his crimes by his jester, *Rigoletto*, a hunchback. The father of one of the *Duke's* victims is mocked by *Rigoletto* and launches upon him a father's awful curse, which stuns and sobers the jester, as he, too, has a daughter, *Gilda*, unknown to the court.

On his way home *Rigoletto* meets a professional assassin, *Sparafucile*, who offers, for a price, to kill any enemy he may have. *Rigoletto* says he may need him later. The *Duke*, in the guise of a young student, has already met *Gilda*, not knowing who she is, and the young girl has fallen in love with him. When *Rigoletto* has left the house the *Duke's* courtiers abduct *Gilda* and take her to the Palace. The father's rage is terrible to witness, and he goes to the Palace, but too late to save his daughter. She pleads for the *Duke's* life, but *Rigoletto* swears to kill him, and arranges with the assassin, *Sparafucile*, to accomplish the deed. The *Duke* is lured to a lonely inn by *Sparafucile's* attractive sister, *Maddalena*, and is about to be murdered when *Maddalena*, who has taken a fancy to him, begs for his life. *Sparafucile* consents provided a substitute should happen along before midnight. *Gilda*,

SETTING OF ACT I AT THE METROPOLITAN

whom *Rigoletto* had brought hither (disguised as a page) in order that she might witness the fickleness of her lover, has been listening to the conversation, and now resolves to save the *Duke's* life at the cost of her own. She enters the hut, is stabbed by *Sparafucile*, who delivers the body to *Rigoletto* according to agreement. *Rigoletto* is about to cast the body into the river when he hears the *Duke's* voice in the distance. The wretched man opens the sack, sees his daughter and falls senseless on her body.

ACT I

SCENE I—*Ballroom in the Duke's Palace*

As a fête is in progress in the ducal residence, the *Duke* confides to one of his courtiers that he is about to make a new conquest. For some months he has seen a young and beautiful girl at church, but knows nothing of her except that she is visited often by a man who is supposed to be her lover. The *Duke* then sings his first air, *Questo o quella*.

Questa o quella ('Mid the Fair Throng)

By Enrico Caruso, Tenor	(*In Italian*) 87018	10-inch, $2.00
By Florencio Constantino, Tenor	(*In Italian*) 64069	10-inch, 1.00

This melodious number is perhaps the best of the *Duke's* solos, though usually cast somewhat in the background by the popular *La donna e mobile*. In it the *Duke* announces himself as a man of pleasure, sets forth his code of morals, and boasts of his conquests.

DUKE:
'Mid the fair throng that sparkle around me,
　Not one o'er my heart holds sway;
Though a sweet smile one moment may
　　charm me,
　A glance from some bright eye its spell
　　drives away.
All alike may attract, each in turn may please;
　Now with one I may trifle and play,
Then another may sport with and tease—
　Yet all my heart to enslave their wiles
　　display.

As a dove flies, alarm'd, to seek shelter,
　Pursued by some vulture, to bear it aloft
　　in flight,
Thus do I fly from constancy's fetter:
　E'en women's spells I shun—all their efforts
　　I slight.
A husband that's jealous I scorn and despise,
And I laugh at and heed not a lover's sighs;
If a fair one take my heart by surprise,
I heed not scornful tongues or prying eyes.

Caruso's interpretation of the *Duke* is quite different from the one to which opera-goers have been accustomed. He does not picture *Mantua* as a deliberate villain, a fiend in human guise, but as a light-hearted, careless and irresponsible devotee of pleasure,—so attractive that the infatuation of *Gilda* seems wholly natural. This air is always sung by the tenor with perfect ease and extreme brilliancy, and the record is a superb one, not surpassed by any in his list.

Constantino has made a great success as the *Duke,* both at the Manhattan Opera and in Boston during the past season. He sings this gay air with grace and abandon.

After making another enemy in the person of the *Count Ceprano,* by his marked attention to the latter's wife, the *Duke* departs. *Marullo* enters and eagerly announces to the courtiers a rich discovery. *Rigoletto,* the *Duke's* jester, is in love! The courtiers refuse to believe this, as *Rigoletto* is known as a confirmed woman-hater. *Marullo* insists that the jester makes frequent visits to a young girl. The nobles, who all hate *Rigoletto* for his cruel tongue, are eager to turn this knowledge into a means of revenge, and agree to meet *Ceprano* the next evening for a rare adventure.

The voice of the aged *Count Monterone,* whose daughter is one of the recent victims of the *Duke,* is now heard outside demanding admittance. He throws aside the guards who seek to stop him, and entering, denounces the *Duke* for his crimes.

Ch'io le parli (I Will Speak to Him)

By Francesco Cigada, Baritone; Aristodemo Sillich, Bass; La Scala Chorus
(*In Italian*) *68190 12-inch, $1.25

HALL

SPARAFUCILE OFFERS HIS SERVICES
ACT I, SCENE II

Rigoletto ridicules and mocks the old man, who calls him a "vile buffoon," and then, in an awful rage, utters so terrible a curse upon him,—the curse of a father,—that all are horrified.

Rigoletto is stunned and sobered by this terrible malediction, for he, too, has a daughter, unknown to the court, and love for his child and respect for her dead mother are the sole redeeming traits in his cruel nature.

Monterone is removed by the guards, and the scene changes to the street in front of *Rigoletto's* house.

SCENE II—*A Street; Rigoletto's Cottage on one side, opposite the Palace of Count Ceprano*

The jester enters, brooding with superstitious fear over the curse which had been laid upon him. He is accosted by *Sparafucile,* a professional assassin, who offers to rid him of an enemy if he has one. *Rigoletto* looks at him thoughtfully and says that if he has need of his services he will inform him. *Sparafucile* departs and *Rigoletto* delivers his famous monologue.

Monologo—Pari siamo (We Are Equal)

By Mario Sammarco, Baritone	(*In Italian*)	88320	12-inch, $3.00
By Antonio Scotti, Baritone	(*In Italian*)	88032	12-inch, 3.00
By Emilio de Gogorza, Baritone	(*In Italian*)	88179	12-inch, 3.00
By Titta Ruffo, Baritone	(*In Italian*)	92041	12-inch, 3.00
By Ernesto Badini, Baritone	(*In Italian*)	*45032	10-inch, 1.00

He looks at the retreating form of the bravo and says:

RIGOLETTO:
Yon assassin is my equal—
He stabs in darkness,
While I with a tongue of malice
Stab men by daylight!
(*He thinks of Monterone's curse.*)
He laid a father's curse on me. . . .
(*Continuing in a burst of rage.*)
Oh hideous fate! Cruel nature!
Thou hast doom'd me to a life of torment.
I must jest, I must laugh,
And be their laughing stock!
Yonder the Duke, my master,
Youthful and brilliant, rich and handsome,

Tells me, between sleeping and waking:
"Come, buffoon, I would laugh now!"
Oh shame, I must obey him!
Oh life accursed! How I hate ye,
Race of vile and fawning courtiers!
'Tis my only joy to taunt ye!
For if I am vile, 'tis to your vice I owe it!
(*He thinks of his home and daughter.*)
In that blest abode my nature changes!
(*Again he remembers the curse.*)
How heavy was that old man's curse!
Still I hear it; 'tis ringing in my ears!
My soul is troubled—fear I some misfortune?
Ah, no, this is folly!

---

* *Double-Faced Record—For title of opposite side see DOUBLE-FACED RIGOLETTO RECORDS, page 294.*

COPY'T MISHKIN

SAMMARCO AS RIGOLETTO

Five records of this great number are here presented, sung by famous exponents of the part of *Rigoletto*.

The jester enters the court-yard and is affectionately greeted by *Gilda*, who comes from the house. She notes his anxious looks and begs him to confide in her. She asks him about her mother, whom she but dimly remembers. *Rigoletto* avoids her question and sings a pathetic air:

Deh non parlare al misero (Recall Not the Past)

By Antonio Scotti, Baritone

(*In Italian*) 85031 12-inch, $3.00

in which he begs her to refrain from questions regarding their past life.

He embraces her tenderly, then, recalling the curse, solemnly enjoins her to keep within the house and never venture into the town. *Gilda* says she has only been to Mass each Sunday, but does not tell him of the student with whom she had exchanged fond glances. *Rigoletto* summons the maid, *Giovanna*, and questions her, beginning a lovely duet, full of pathos.

Veglia o donna (Safely Guard This Tender Blossom)

By Maria Galvany, Soprano, and Titta Ruffo, Baritone

(*In Italian*) 91500 10-inch, $3.00

He warns the maid to always closely guard her mistress from any danger which may threaten.

RIGOLETTO:
Safely guard this tender blossom,
Which to thee I now confide;
In her guileless heart and bosom
May no thought of ill betide;
From the arts of vice protect her,
May its snares be laid in vain;
Her father will from thee expect her
Safely brought to him again.

GILDA:
Ah! such fear for me revealing,
Father dear, why thus display?
One from whom there's no concealing
Guides me ever on my way
From on high my mother's spirit
Leads me on with tender care;
While this heart bears life within it,
'Twill defy each artful snare!

Rigoletto bids his daughter a tender farewell and takes his departure. The *Duke*, again dressed as a student, now enters, having previously purchased the silence of *Giovanna*.

Gilda is alarmed, not thinking her innocent flirtation in the church would lead to this, and bids him begone, but he reassures her, beginning a fine duet.

E il sol dell' anima (Love is the Sun)

By Giuseppina Huguet, Soprano, and Fernando de Lucia, Tenor

(*In Italian*) 92056 12-inch, $3.00

By Alice Nielsen, Soprano, and Florencio Constantino, Tenor

(*In Italian*) 74063 12-inch, 1.50

He soothes her fears, telling her he loves her with a pure devotion.

DUKE:
Love is the sun by which passion is lighted,
Happy the mortal who feels its power;
Each pleasure once priz'd without it seems blighted;
With it we heed not what fate may shower.
Feeling celestial, no joy terrestrial
Ever to me can such sweet joys impart.
Ah! may no blight ever this heart from thee sever;
Rest in my bosom, ne'er to depart!

Footsteps are now heard, and after a tender farewell he leaves, after telling her that his name is Walter Malde.

Gilda remains pensively gazing at the gate through which the pretended student has departed. In rapturous soliloquy she sings:

COPY'T DUPONT

ABOTT AS GILDA

ACT I, SCENE II

GILDA:
Walter Malde! That romantic name!
Already it is on my heart engraven!

Walter, I love thee,
Ev'ry fond, tender thought for thee I cherish!

Caro nome (Dearest Name)

By Luisa Tetrazzini, Soprano	(*In Italian*)	88295	12-inch,	$3.00
By Marcella Sembrich, Soprano	(*In Italian*)	88017	12-inch,	3.00
By Nellie Melba, Soprano	(*In Italian*)	88078	12-inch,	3.00
By Bessie Abott, Soprano	(*In Italian*)	88050	12-inch,	3.00
By Graziella Pareto, Soprano	(*In Italian*)	76007	12-inch,	2.00
By Edith Helena, Soprano	(*In English*)	*35067	12-inch,	1.25
By Marie Michailowa, Soprano	(*In Russian*)	61141	10-inch,	1.00

Then the lovely air, Caro Nome, begins.

GILDA:
Carv'd upon my inmost heart
Is that name forevermore
Ne'er again from thence to part,
Name of love that I adore,
Thou to me are ever near,
Ev'ry thought to thee will fly,
Life for thee alone is dear,
Thine shall be my parting sigh!
(*Gilda enters the house, but reappears on the
balcony.*)
Oh, dearest name!
Oh name beloved!

(*She disappears, but can be heard from
within.*)
Oh! name beloved!
Dear name, within this breast,
Thy mem'ry will remain!
My love for thee confess'd,
No power can restrain!
Carved upon my inmost heart
Is that name for evermore.
Thine shall be my parting sigh,
Oh Walter mine!

This delightful song, with its grace, delicacy and coloring, has never been surpassed and the scoring for orchestra, especially in Verdi's use of the wood-wind, is admirable.

Melba's rendition is worthy of so exquisite a number, and she has surpassed herself here. The ease with which she sings is wonderful, and her voice shows in an unusual degree that luscious smoothness, golden purity and perfect equality for which it is noted.

The character of *Gilda* is represented by Mme. Sembrich with genuine simplicity, yet with truly impassioned feeling where occasion calls for it; as in this tuneful "Caro nome," when the young girl in soliloquy dwells with rapture on the name of the pretended student, Walter Malde, who has secretly won her heart. Nothing could be more perfect in its way than Mme. Sembrich's singing of this beautiful number.

Tetrazzini's delivery of this lovely air is marked by surpassing beauty of tone, the roulades, trills and staccatos in the concluding portion being poured out lavishly and with the utmost ease and fluency. Other adequate renditions, at lower prices, are also listed above.

* *Double-Faced Record—For title of opposite side see DOUBLE-FACED RIGOLETTO RECORDS, page 294.*

Night has now fallen and the courtiers, led by *Ceprano*, enter, wearing masks. *Rigoletto* returns and is much alarmed to see them in this neighborhood, but his fears are allayed when they announce that they have come to carry off *Ceprano's* wife, as he is well aware that the *Duke* has had designs on that lady for some time past. He tells them *Ceprano's* palace is on the opposite side and offers to help them. They insist that he must be disguised and contrive to give him a mask which covers his eyes and ears, and lead him in a circle back to his own balcony, giving him a ladder to hold. *Gilda* is seized, her mouth gagged with a handkerchief, and she is carried away.

PHOTO BERT

THE ABDUCTION OF GILDA

Rigoletto, suddenly finding himself alone, becomes suspicious, tears off his mask and finds himself at his own balcony. Frantic with fear he rushes in, finds his daughter gone, and falls in a swoon as the curtain descends.

ACT II
SCENE—*A Hall in the Duke's Palace*

The courtiers enter and tell the *Duke* that they have captured *Rigoletto's* mistress. He expresses his appreciation of the adventure, not knowing they had abducted the young girl he had just left, and asks for particulars. They sing their chorus, *Scorrendo unite,*

Scorrendo unite remota via (On Mischief Bent)
By New York Grand Opera Chorus   (*In Italian*)   64049   10-inch, $1.00

which gives the details of the huge joke they have played on *Rigoletto* by making him assist in the capture of his own mistress.

COURTIERS:
Unto a lonely abode directed,
When shades of evening were falling fast,
By dark'ning shadows we were protected
Until our game we spied at last;
With timid footsteps the scarce came nigh us,
We were preparing our prey to seize
When Rigoletto just then came by us,
With angry brow and ill at ease.
And that the joke might be all the madder,
We said Ceprano's wife should be our prey,

We then desir'd him to hold the ladder;
His eyes were bandag'd, he did obey.
We swiftly mounted to the room, and found her,
The startled beauty we bore away!
DUKE (*aside*):
Wondrous! it must be my love, my lost one!
COURTIERS:
When he discover'd how we'd fooled him,
No doubt he curs'd till break of day!

When the *Duke* learns that *Gilda* is in an adjoining room he joyfully goes to her, saying that her fears will be soothed when she discovers he is the *Walter Malde* she loves.

Then occurs one of the most dramatic scenes in the opera, and the greatest opportunity for *Rigoletto*. This scene has been recorded in its entirety by Amato, one of the greatest of *Rigolettos*, assisted by Bada, Setti and the Metropolitan Chorus.

Povero Rigoletto! (Poor Rigoletto!)
By Pasquale Amato, Baritone, with Bada, Setti and Metropolitan
Chorus   *In Italian*   88340   12 $3.00

Rigoletto's voice is now heard outside, singing a careless air. He enters, affecting indifference, but trying to find some clue to *Gilda's* whereabouts. A page enters with a message for the *Duke* and the courtiers tell him their master cannot be disturbed. *Rigoletto* listens, his fears becoming confirmed, and he exclaims:

RIGOLETTO:
Ah, she must be here then!
In yonder chamber!
COURTIERS: (*affecting surprise*): Who?

RIGOLETTO:
The maid whom you last night
From my roof carried hither.
Ah, she is there, I know it!

| COURTIERS: If a sweetheart you've lost, | RIGOLETTO: |
| | Yes, my daughter! |

COURTIERS: If a sweetheart you've lost,
Go somewhere else to seek her!
RIGOLETTO (*with terrible emphasis*):
Give me my daughter!
COURTIERS (*in astonishment*):
What, his daughter!

RIGOLETTO:
Yes, my daughter!
(*Rushes toward the door, but the courtiers bar his passage and a terrible struggle occurs.*)
She is there! stand back, I tell ye!

His rage, now terrible to witness, is expressed in the second part, *Cortigiani, vil razza.*

Cortigiani, vil razza dannata (Vile Race of Courtiers)

By Pasquale Amato, Baritone	(*In Italian*)	88341	12-inch, $3.00
By G. Mario Sammarco, Baritone	(*In Italian*)	88315	12-inch, 3.00
By Titta Ruffo, Baritone, and La Scala Chorus	(*Italian*)	92066	12-inch, 3.00
By Emilio Sagi-Barba, Baritone	(*In Spanish*)	74161	12-inch, 1.50
By Renzo Minolfi, Baritone (*Double-faced—See page 294*)		16573	10-inch, .75

He at first denounces them as abductors and assassins, then breaking down, asks for pity.

RIGOLETTO:
Race of courtiers, vile rabble detested,
Have ye sold her, whose peace ye molested?
Gold and favor will buy ye, I know it—
E'en the treasure that nought can restore.
Ah, where is she? do not rouse me to madness—
Though unarm'd, of my vengeance beware ye;
For the blood of some traitor I'll pour!
(*Again making for the door, and again interrupted.*)
Let me enter, ye assassins, stand back!
That door I must enter!
(*He struggles again with the courtiers but is repulsed and gives up in despair.*)
Ah, I see it—all against me—have pity!

(*He weeps.*)
Ah, I weep before ye, Marullo, so kindless?
Others' grief never yet saw these mindless,
Tell, oh tell where my child they have hidden,
Marullo, have pity,
Say the word where my daughter is hidden!
Is't there?—say in pity—thou'rt silent! alas!
(*In tears.*)
Oh, my lords, will ye have no compassion
On a father's despairing intercession?
Give me back my belov'd only daughter,
Dearer far than my life, give her back, I implore!
Have pity, oh give me back my child,
In pity, oh hear me implore!

This affecting scene is ended by *Gilda,* who now enters, in tears, and embraces her father.

RIGOLETTO (*overjoyed*):
Gilda, my daughter!
My lost one—my treasure!
My lords, she is all I cherish.
Now we need fear nothing,
Angel, I've found thee!
Come tell me, 'twas but jesting?
(*To the courtiers.*)
I who was weeping rejoice now.
(*To Gilda.*)
But why art thou weeping?

GILDA (*hiding her face*):
Dishonor, oh my father!
RIGOLETTO: Horror! what say'st thou?
GILDA:
Father, oh hide me from ev'ry eye but thine!
RIGOLETTO (*imperiously, to the courtiers*):
Hence, I command, and leave us!
If the worthless duke ye serve dares approach,
I forbid him to enter!
Say that, I charge ye!

The courtiers, somewhat ashamed at the turn of affairs, obey, and *Gilda* begins her pitiful confession.

Tutte le feste al tempio (On Every Festal Morning)

By Marcella Sembrich, Soprano, and G. Mario Sammarco, Baritone			
	(*In Italian*)	89042	12-inch, $4.00
By Olimpia Boronat, Soprano	(*In Italian*)	88242	12-inch, 3.00
By Laura Mellerio, Soprano, and Ernesto Badini, Baritone			
	(*In Italian*)	*45000	10-inch, 1.00
By Giuseppina Huguet, Soprano	(*In Italian*)	*62083	10-inch, .75

GILDA:
On ev'ry festal morning
Near to the holy altar,
I saw a youth observing me,
Beneath whose gaze mine did falter,
Though not a word he said to me,
My heart his meaning well did know!
When twilight shades were darkening,
Last night he stood before me,
Fondly he vow'd to love me,
And I gave him my vow for vow.
RIGOLETTO (*despairingly*):
Ah! that thou be spared my infamy
I've wearied Heaven with praying,
That every good may light on thee
Far from the world's betraying,

Ah, in my hopeless misery,
My saint I have enshrined thee,
In horror and anguish here I must find thee,
Thy future all turned to woe!
(*To Gilda.*)
Daughter come, let me comfort thee in thy sorrow—
GILDA:
Father!
RIGOLETTO:
Weep here, weep, on my heart thy tears may flow.
GILDA:
Father, in thee an angel doth comfort bestow.

* Double-Faced Record—For title of opposite side see DOUBLE-FACED RIGOLETTO RECORDS, page 294.

Piangi fanciulla (Weep, My Child)

By Maria Galvany, Soprano, and Titta Ruffo, Baritone
(*In Italian*) 92502 12-inch, $4.00

By A. Cassani, Soprano, and F. Federici, Baritone
(*In Italian*) *45032 10-inch, 1.00

The *Count Monterone* now passes through the hall under guard. He pauses before the *Duke's* portrait and exclaims:

> MONTERONE:
> Oh, then, 'twas in vain in my anger I cursed
>   thee!
> No thunder from Heaven yet hath burst down
>   to strike thee.
> With pleasure triumphant thy days yet are
>   crowned.
> (*Exit, guarded.*)

Rigoletto, gazing after *Monterone*, grimly says that vengeance will not be long delayed.

Si vendetta (Yes, My Vengeance)

By Maria Galvany, Soprano, and Titta Ruffo, Baritone
(*In Italian*) 91501 10-inch, $3.00

By Laura Mellerio, Soprano, and Ernesto Badini, Baritone
(*In Italian*) *45000 10-inch, 1.00

He in turn gazes on the *Duke's* portrait and sings fiercely:

RIGOLETTO:
But 'twill not be long thus, the avenger is
  nigh.
(*Impetuously.*)
Yes, my vengeance hath doomed thee.
Heartless fiend, 'tis my sole consolation,
That ere the flames of Hell entomb thee,
Thou shalt feel a father's wrath.
GILDA:
Oh my father, a joy ferocious
In thy words doth tell of danger—
RIGOLETTO:
To vengeance!

GILDA (*timidly*):
Heav'n doth know his crime atrocious,
Oh, might I avert its wrath—
RIGOLETTO:
To vengeance!
GILDA:
(In my heart there's nought of anger.)
RIGOLETTO:
Yes, to vengeance fierce I doom thee—
Thou shalt feel a father's wrath!
GILDA:
Oh, forgive him!
Ah, might I avert the wrath of Heaven!
(*They depart.*)

SPARAFUCILE'S DEN—ACT III

---

* *Double-Faced Record—For title of opposite side see DOUBLE-FACED RIGOLETTO RECORDS, page 294.*

ACT III

SCENE I—*A Lonely Spot on the River Mincio. A House, Half in Ruins, at one Side. The front of the house, open to the spectator, shows a rustic inn on the ground floor; a broken staircase leads from this to a loft, where stands a rough couch. On the side towards the street is a door, and a low wall extends backwards from the house. The Mincio is seen in the background, behind a ruined parapet; beyond, the towers of Mantua. It is night. Sparafucile in the house, seated by a table polishing his belt, unconscious of what is spoken outside.*

Rigoletto and *Gilda,* the latter in male attire, now approach the inn. *Rigoletto* pityingly asks his daughter if she still can love the *Duke.* She confesses that she does, and he exclaims:

RIGOLETTO:
Thou lov'st him?
GILDA:
Always.
RIGOLETTO:
Still to love him is mere infatuation.
GILDA:
I love him.
RIGOLETTO:
Ah, tender heart of woman!
Oh, base despoiler!
Thou my child shalt yet have vengeance.

GILDA:
Nay, rather pity.
RIGOLETTO:
And if I could convince thee that he is worthless, wouldst thou still then love him?
GILDA:
Perhaps. Ah, he does love me!
RIGOLETTO (*leads her towards the house to look through a fissure in the wall*):
Come here, and look within.

She does so, and is startled to see the *Duke,* who comes in disguised as a soldier, demand some wine and sing his famous *La donna e mobile.*

La donna e mobile (Woman is Fickle)

By Enrico Caruso, Tenor	(*In Italian*) 87017	10-inch, $2.00
By Florencio Constantino, Tenor	(*In Italian*) 64072	10-inch, 1.00
By Giuseppe Acerbi, Tenor	(*In Italian*) *62083	10-inch, .75

This familiar canzone, beginning

La don-na è mo-bi - le qual piu-ma al ven - to, mu-ta d'ac - cen - to e di pen sie - ro
Wom-an is fick - le, false al-to-geth-er, Mov'd like the fea-ther borne by the bree-zes

is perhaps the best known of all the airs of the opera. Its spontaneous melody pictures the gay, irresponsible character of the young noble who thus sings of changeable womankind.

DUKE:
Woman is fickle, false altogether,
  Moves like a feather borne on the breezes;
Woman with guiling smile will e'er deceive you,
  Often can grieve you, yet e'er she pleases,
Her heart's unfeeling, false altogether;
  Moves like a feather borne on the breeze,
  Borne on the breeze, borne on the breeze!
Wretched the dupe is, who when she looks kindly,
  Trusts to her blindly. Thus life is wasted!
Yet he must surely be dull beyond measure,
  Who of love's pleasure never has tasted.
Woman is fickle, false altogether,
  Moves like a feather, borne on the breeze!

Caruso delivers the gay air with an ease and abandon which are infectious, and sings the difficult cadenza in the second verse with unusual effectiveness.

Other renditions are given at varying prices.

---

* Double-Faced Record—For title of opposite side see DOUBLE-FACED RIGOLETTO RECORDS, page 294.

CONSTANTINO AS THE DUKE—ACT III

At the close of the *Duke's* song *Sparafucile* enters with the wine. He knocks twice on the ceiling and a young girl comes down. The *Duke* tries to embrace her but she laughingly escapes him. Now occurs the great Quartet, one of the most famous of concerted pieces.

Quartet—Bella figlia dell'amore (Fairest Daughter of the Graces)

By Bessie Abott, Soprano; Louise Homer, Contralto; Enrico Caruso, Tenor; Antonio Scotti, Baritone
(*In Italian*) 96000 12-inch, $6.00

By Marcella Sembrich, Soprano; Mme. Severina, Contralto; Enrico Caruso, Tenor; Antonio Scotti, Baritone
(*In Italian*) 96001 12-inch, 6.00

By Giuseppina Huguet, Soprano; Emma Zaccaria, Mezzo-Soprano; Carmelo Lanzirotti, Tenor; Francesco Cigada, Baritone
(*In Italian*) *68067, 12-inch, 1.25

By Giuseppina Huguet Soprano; Emma Zaccaria, Mezzo-Soprano; Carmelo Lanzirotti, Tenor; Francesco Cigada, Baritone
(*In Italian*) 58359 12-inch, 1.00

By Arthur Pryor's Band   31471 12-inch, 1.00
By Arthur Pryor's Band   *16276 10-inch, .75

Among the musical gems with which the score of Rigoletto abounds, none is so well known and universally admired as this fine number, sung by the *Duke, Gilda, Maddalena* and *Rigoletto*. It is undoubtedly the most brilliant and musically of all Verdi's concerted pieces, and the contrasting emotions—the tender addresses and coquetry on the one side, and the heart-broken sobs of *Gilda* and the cries for vengeance of her father on the other—are pictured with the hand of a genius.

No less than four records of this great number, at varying prices, also two instrumental renditions, are offered by the Victor. The singers who have been engaged for these records are all noted for their artistic interpretations of the characters represented. Caruso's *Duke*, with its glorious outpourings of luscious voice in the lovely airs; Sembrich's perfect portrayal with its wonderful vocalization; Abott's girlish and brilliantly sung impersonation; Homer's *Maddalena*, which is fascinating enough to attract any Duke, and whose one vocal opportunity occurs here; Scotti's truly wonderful and superbly sung *Jester*, one of the most powerful impersonations on the operatic stage—all these are familiar and admired portrayals; while the artists who render the low-priced record are all well-known and competent singers.

PHOTO HALL   THE QUARTET—ACT III

The situation at the opening of the act is a most dramatic one. The *Duke*, gay and careless, is making love to *Maddalena* in the inn of *Sparafucile*, the bandit, all unconscious that the assassin hired by *Rigoletto* is waiting for his opportunity.

He sings, beginning the quartet:

COPY'T DUPON.

HOMER AS MADDALENA

DUKE:
Fairest daughter of the graces,
I thy humble slave implore thee,
With one tender word to joy restore me,
End the pangs, the pangs of unrequited love.
Of my anguish see the traces,
Thee I treasure all above.
With one tender word to joy restore me,
End the pangs, the pangs of unrequited love!

MADDALENA (*repulsing him*):
I appreciate you rightly,
All you say is but to flatter.
Ah, I laugh to think how many
Yet your tender tale may move!

Rigoletto, who desires to prove to *Gilda* that her lover is false, bids her look through the window of the inn at the scene within. The unhappy girl, convinced, exclaims:

GILDA:
Ah, to speak of love thus lightly!
Words like these to me were spoken,
He is false; my heart is broken!

RIGOLETTO:
Silence, thy tears will not avail thee,
It were baseness to regret him!
Thou must shun him and forget him.
(*With fierce joy.*)
Thy avenger I will prove
The strength to punish will not fail me
That I vow to every power that rules above!

The blending of the four voices is marvelous in its smoothness, and the manner in which every syllable and every note of the difficult music is brought out, is most remarkable. The sales of these wonderful reproductions have been enormous, and copies of the records have made their way to every part of the world, and are in the collections of music lovers everywhere.

The *Duke* now goes to his bedroom and is soon asleep. *Rigoletto* bids his daughter go to Verona with all speed and he will meet her there. She reluctantly departs and *Rigoletto* pays *Sparafucile* half his price, the remainder to be paid on the delivery of the body of the *Duke* at midnight. *Rigoletto* goes away just as *Gilda,* who has disobeyed her father, returns and tries to see what is going on inside the house. *Sparafucile* enters the house and *Maddalena,* who has taken a fancy to the *Duke,* begs her brother to spare his life, delicately suggesting that he kill *Rigoletto* and take the money from him. *Sparafucile* is indignant and protests that he has never yet failed in his duty to his employers. *Maddalena* pleads with him and he finally says if another guest should enter he will kill him instead of the *Duke*.

PHOTO BERT

GILDA FINDS HER LOVER FALSE

During this dramatic scene a storm is raging, and in addition to the stage effects of thunder and lightning Verdi has used the effective device of the chorus humming in chromatic thirds to illustrate the moaning of the wind. This scene is given here in a wonderfully impressive record by Brambilla, Cappiello and Sillich, assisted by La Scala Chorus.

Tempesta—Somiglia un Apollo (He's Fair as Apollo)

By Linda Brambilla, Soprano; Maria Cappiello, Mezzo-Soprano; Aristodemo Sillich, Bass; and La Scala Chorus (*In Italian*) *68190 12-inch, $1.25

Gilda hears this terrible agreement and the broken-hearted girl resolves to sacrifice her own life to save that of her false lover. She knocks at the door, is seized and stabbed by the bandit and her body wrapped in a sack. *Rigoletto* soon returns, pays the remainder of the price agreed upon, and receives the body. *Sparafucile*, fearing that *Rigoletto* will discover the substitution, offers to throw the body into the river. The Jester says he will do it himself and bids the bravo depart.

Left alone, the Jester gazes on the body with a horrible satisfaction, saying:

RIGOLETTO:
He is there, pow'rless! Ah, I must see him!
Nay, 'twere folly! 'tis he surely! I feel his
   spurs here.
Look on me now ye courtiers!
Look here and tremble,
Here the buffoon is monarch!

Yes, my foot is upon him!
My grief has vanish'd,
'Tis turned to joy triumphant;
Thy tomb shall be the waters,
This coarse sack thy shroud and grave cloth!
Away, now!

He is about to drag the sack towards the river, when he hears the voice of the *Duke* leaving the inn on the opposite side.

DUKE:
Woman is fickle, false altogether, etc.
RIGOLETTO (*tearing his hair*):
That voice! Am I mad? What fiend deludes
   me?
No, no, no! here I hold him!
(*Calling to the house.*)
Hola, thou thief, thou bandit!
(*The Duke's voice dies in the distance.*)
Then whom have I within here?
I tremble—the form is human!
(*With utmost horror, recognizing Gilda.*)
My daughter, oh, Heav'n, my daughter!
Ah, no! Not my daughter! She is in Verona!
'Twas a dream!

Then begins the wonderful final duet, a fitting end to such a noble and powerful work, and a number which is unfortunately omitted in American performances of the opera. However, the Victor owner, more fortunate than the opera-goer, may hear it at his pleasure.

Lassù in cielo (In Heaven Above)

By Graziella Pareto, Soprano, and Titta Ruffo, Baritone
(*In Italian*) 92506 12-inch, $4.00
By Giuseppina Huguet, Soprano, and Renzo Minolfi, Baritone
(*In Italian*) *68067 12-inch, 1.25

RIGOLETTO:
'Tis Gilda!
(*Kneeling.*)
Child of sorrow! my angel, look on thy father!

The assassin deceived me. Hola!
(*Knocks desperately on the door of the house.*)
No answer! despair! my daughter! my Gilda!
Oh, my daughter!

The young girl, who is not yet dead, opens her eyes and cries feebly:

GILDA:
Ah, who calls me?
RIGOLETTO:
Ah, she hears me! She lives then!
Oh, thou, my heart's only treasure,
Behold thy father despairing!
GILDA:
Dearest father!
RIGOLETTO:
Who was't that struck thee?
GILDA:
Oh, my father, for him that I cherish,
I deceived thee, and for him I perish.

RIGOLETTO:
Heaven's avenging wrath has undone me,
Must I lose all on earth that was left me!
(*To Gilda.*)
Turn thine eyes, oh my angel, upon me,
Speak, oh speak to me, who hath bereft me?
GILDA:
Father, oh ask not,
Bless thy daughter and forgive her.
From yonder sky, with the blest angels flying,
Comes my mother to welcome me home!

* *Double-Faced Record—For title of opposite side see* DOUBLE-FACED RIGOLETTO RECORDS, *page 294.*

RIGOLETTO:
Child, in pity, oh speak not of dying;
Stay thou to bless me, oh leave me not alone.
GILDA (*feebly*):
There we wait, my father, for thee!
RIGOLETTO:
Ah, no, no, leave me not!
Live, my child.
Canst thou leave me alone, despairing to
mourn?

GILDA:
Ah, no—forgive my betrayer, my father, for-
give him.
From yonder sky—there we wait—my father,
for— (*She dies.*)
RIGOLETTO:
Gilda! my Gilda! I've lost her!
(*He recalls the curse.*)
Ah! 'twas a father cursed me!
(*Tears his hair and falls senseless on the body
of Gilda.*)

(*Curtain*)

DOUBLE-FACED RIGOLETTO RECORDS

Ch 'io le parli (I Will Speak to Him)
    By Cigada, Sillich, and La Scala Chorus (*In Italian*)
Tempesta—Somiglia un Apollo (He's Fair as Apollo)
    By Linda Brambilla, Maria Cappiello, Aristodemo Sillich,
    and La Scala Chorus (*In Italian*)
	68190	12-inch,	$1.25

Caro nome (Dearest Name) By Edith Helena (*English*) Sonnambula—*Ah, non giunge* By Edith Helena (*English*)	35067	12-inch,	1.25

Quartet—Bella figlia dell' amore (Fairest Daughter of the
    Graces) By Giuseppina Huguet, Emma Zaccaria, Carmelo
    Lanzirotti, and Francesco Cigada (*In Italian*)
Lassù in cielo (In Heaven Above) By Giuseppina
    Huguet, Soprano, and Renzo Minolfi, Baritone (*In Italian*)
	68067	12-inch,	1.25

Monologo—Pari siamo By Ernesto Badini (*In Italian*) Piangi fanciulla By Cassani and Federici (*In Italian*)	45032	10-inch,	1.00

Tutte le feste al tempio (On Every Festal Morning)
    By Laura Mellerio and Ernesto Badini (*In Italian*)
Si vendetta (Yes, My Vengeance)
    By Laura Mellerio and Ernesto Badini (*In Italian*)
	45000	10-inch,	1.00

Cortigiani, vil razza dannata (Vile Race of Courtiers) By Renzo Minolfi, Baritone (*In Italian*) *Lakme—Fantaisie aux divins* By M. Rocca, Tenor (*In French*)	16573	10-inch,	.75
Tutte le feste al tempio (On Every Festal Morning) By Giuseppina Huguet, Soprano (*In Italian*) La donna e mobile By Giuseppe Acerbi, Tenor (*Italian*)	62083	10-inch,	.75
Rigoletto Quartet By Arthur Pryor's Band *Peacemaker March* By Arthur Pryor's Band	16276	10-inch,	.75

GILDA'S DESPAIR—ACT II

ROBERTO IL DIAVOLO
(Roh-behr-toh eel Dee-ah'-voh-loh)

(French)   (English)

ROBERT LE DIABLE   ROBERT THE DEVIL
(Roh-behr-leh Dee-ah'-bl)

OPERA IN FIVE ACTS

Words by Scribe and Delavigne; music by Giacomo Meyerbeer. First presented at the Académie, Paris, November 21, 1831. In London, and in English, imperfectly, as The Demon, or the Mystic Branch, at Drury Lane, February 20, 1832; and as The Fiend Father, or Robert of Normandy, at Covent Garden the day following; as Robert the Devil at Drury Lane, March 1, 1845. In French at Her Majesty's Theatre, June 11, 1832. In Italian at Her Majesty's Theatre, May 4, 1847 (first appearance of Jenny Lind and Staudigl).

CAST

ROBERT, Duke of Normandy......................................Tenor
BERTRAM, the Unknown ....Bass
RAMBALDO, a minstrel..Tenor
ISABELLA, Princess of Sicily...................................Soprano
ALICE, foster sister of Robert..................................Soprano

Knights, Courtiers, Heralds, Pilgrims, Peasants, Chaplains, Priests, Nuns, etc.

OLD PRINT   ALICE AND BERTRAM—ACT II

Although Meyerbeer had produced several operas, mostly unsuccessful, it was not until the production of Robert le Diable in 1831 that the genius of the composer became known. The opera met with an unparalleled success and really made the fortune of the Paris Opéra with its splendid scenic effects, brilliant instrumentation, vigorous recitative and its heroic and partly legendary story.

Robert, Duke of Normandy, who was called *Robert the Devil* because of his courage in battle and his successes in love, is banished by his subjects and goes to Sicily, where he continues to struggle with an Evil Spirit, which seems to tempt him to every kind of excess. *Alice,* his foster sister, suspects that his supposed friend *Bertram,* is in reality this evil influence. At the close of Act I *Robert,* led on by *Bertram,* gambles away all his possessions, and failing to attend the Tournament, loses the honor of a knight and greatly displeases the *Lady Isabella,* whom he loves.

The second act shows the entrance to the Cavern of Satan, wherein a company of Evil Spirits are collected, and where occurs the great scene for *Bertram* and the chorus of fiends.

Valse Infernal, "Ecco una nuova preda" (I Have Well Spread My Toils)

By Marcel Journet, Bass, and Metropolitan Opera Chorus

(*In French*) 74282 12-inch, $1.50

Bertram promises the Demons that he will complete the ruin of *Robert* and the fiends rejoice at the prospect of adding another soul to their company.

BERTRAM:
I have well spread my toils, another soul to capture!
One more gained! glorious conquest,
At which demons must rejoice!
(*A subterraneous noise is heard; darkness falls. Bertram, under the control of the evil one, feels an unholy joy.*)
King of fallen angels! ruler mine! * * *
He is here! * * * He awaits me! * * *
I hear the noise

Of their infernal joy * * * the fallen spirits seek
To drown their remorse in hellish mirth!
INFERNAL CHORUS (*from the cavern*):
Ye demons, who Heaven and its laws defy,
The sound of your revels now mounts to the sky,
Your voices lift high!
Praise the master who reigns over us,
Sing aloud in lusty chorus!
Praise the Master, yes praise!

Journet gives an impressive rendering of the utterances of the fiend, *Bertram*, while the chorus of demons, supposed to proceed from the Cavern of Satan, is strikingly sung by the Opera Chorus.

Alice, who has come to the vicinity of the cave to meet her lover, overhears this infernal bargain and determines to save him. *Robert*, dejected over the loss of his honor and wealth, meets *Bertram*, who promises that all shall be restored to him if he will have the courage to visit the ruined abbey and secure a magic branch, which can give wealth, power and immortality.

The next scene shows the ruins, where *Bertram* invokes the aid of the buried nuns in completing the downfall of *Robert*. This famous invocation is sung here by Plançon with spirit and power.

Invocation—Nonnes, qui reposez (Ye Slumb'ring Nuns)

By Pol Plançon, Baritone   (*In French*) 85125 12-inch, $3.00

Bertram speaks of the founding of the convent and of the false nuns who lie buried here, and calls upon them to arise.

BERTRAM:
Here then are the nuns of the ancient monastery,
To Heaven's cause bequeathed by St. Rosalie,
Here lie buried the false daughters

Whose unholy devotion was offered to other gods.
Nuns, who beneath this cold stone repose,
For an hour forsake your sepulcher beds,
King of Hell, it is I who calls you.

THE RUINED ABBEY—ACT III

The spectres arise, and when *Robert* appears they dance around him and lead him to the grave of *St. Rosalie*, where he is shown the magic branch. Overcoming his fears, he grasps it, and by its power defeats the multitude of demons who arise from the infernal regions to prevent his escape.

In the next scene *Robert* uses the branch to become invisible, and goes to *Lady Isabella's* room to carry her off. In this scene occurs the famous air for *Isabella*, "Oh, Robert, My Beloved," part of which will be found in this selection by Pryor.

Selection, including "Oh, Robert, My Beloved"

By Arthur Pryor's Band (*Double-faced*)   35064 12-inch, $1.25

Moved by her entreaties, he yields to the promptings of his good angel and breaks the branch, thus destroying the spell.

In the last act *Bertram* renews his efforts to induce *Robert* to sign an eternal contract. Tired of life, he is about to yield when *Alice* appears and tells him of the last words of his mother, warning him against the *Fiend*, who is in reality *Robert's* father. The clock strikes twelve, and the baffled *Fiend* disappears, while the cathedral door opens showing the *Princess* waiting for the reformed *Robert*.

LE ROI DE LAHORE

(Le Rwah deh Lah-howr')

(English)

THE KING OF LAHORE

OPERA IN FIVE ACTS

Libretto by Louis Gallet; music by Jules Massenet. First production at the Grand Opéra, Paris, April 27, 1877; and at Covent Garden, Royal Italian Opera, June 28, 1879.

Cast

ALIM, King of Lahore	Tenor
SCINDIA, his minister	Baritone
TIMUR, a priest	Bass
INDRA	Bass
SITA	Soprano
KALED, confidant of the King	Mezzo-Soprano

Time and Place: India; the eleventh century, during the incursion of the Mohammedans.

This early work of Massenet's is founded upon an Indian subject, and deals with the Mussulman invasion. It is noted for its brilliant ballet, illustrative of an Indian paradise.

Sita, niece of the high priest, *Timur,* is beloved by *Alim,* King of Lahore. His rival, *Scindia,* accuses her of profaning the Temple and she is condemned to death, but is saved by the King, who asks her hand in marriage.

In the second act *Alim,* at war with the Mussulmans, is betrayed to the enemy by *Scindia,* and is killed in battle, while *Scindia* seizes his throne and carries away *Sita.*

Alim is transported to the celestial realm of India, but is not contented, and begs the divinities to allow him to return to earth. His request is granted on condition that he does not resume his rank and returns to India when *Sita* dies. On his return he finds that *Scindia* has secured the throne and forced *Sita* to become his wife. *Alim* declares himself, but *Scindia* denounces him as an impostor. *Alim* is obliged to flee, but *Sita* goes with him, and when they are about to be captured she kills herself. *Alim,* in fulfillment of his vow, also dies, and the lovers are united in celestial India.

Promesse di mon avenir (Oh, Promise of a Joy Divine)

By Emilio de Gogorza, Baritone   (*In French*)   88172   12-inch, $3.00

The most famous of the numbers is of course this superb air for baritone in the fourth act, which La Salle sung in the first production with great success. A portion of the fine translation by Dudley Buck, from the Schirmer "Operatic Anthology" (Copy't G. Schirmer), is given here by permission.

SCINDIA:
The Sultan's barb'rous horde, who had so
  gladly riven
From us fair Lahore,
By our own might have from the field been
  driven.
From care my people free,
  Loudly sound forth my praises!

O promise fair of joy divine, Sita,
Thou dream of all my life,
O beauty torn from me by strife,
At last, thou shalt be mine! O Sita!
O fair one, charm my loving heart,
And ne'er again from me depart!

* * * * * * * * * *
Sita, my queen thou soon shalt be!
To thee the world its glory offers,
To thee a king his crown now proffers;
Come, Sita, O come! ah! be mine!

A fine rendition of this air is given here by Mr. de Gogorza, whose beautiful voice and perfect French diction are well exhibited.

Farrar as Juliet

ROMÉO ET JULIETTE   ROMEO AND JULIET
(French)   (English)

(Roh'-may-oh ay Joo-lee-et')

OPERA IN FIVE ACTS

Words by Barbier and Carré, after Shakespeare's drama.   Music by Charles Gounod. First produced at the *Théâtre Lyrique*, Paris, April 27, 1867.   First London production July 11, 1867.   Presented in America, 1868, with Minnie Hauk.

Some famous American productions occurred in 1890, with Patti, Ravelli, del Puente and Fabri; in 1891, with Eames (début), the de Reszkes and Capoul; in 1898, with Melba, Saleza, de Reszke and Plançon; and more recently with Farrar as *Juliet.*

Characters

JULIET, *(Joo-lee-et')* daughter of Capulet ....Soprano
STEPHANO, *(Stef'-ah-noh)* page to Romeo.........................Soprano
GERTRUDE, Juliet's nurse ....Mezzo-Soprano
ROMEO ....Tenor
TYBALT, *(Tee-bahl')* Capulet's nephew ....Tenor
BENVOLIO, *(Ben-vo'-lee-oh)* friend of Romeo...........................Tenor
MERCUTIO, *(Mer-kew'-shee-oh)* friend of Romeo ....Baritone
PARIS, *(Pah-ree')* Capulet's kinsman ....Baritone
GREGORIO, Capulet's kinsman ..:............................Baritone
CAPULET, *(Cap-u-leh')* a Veronese noble ....Basso-Cantante
FRIAR LAURENCE.......................................Bass
THE DUKE OF VERONA ....Bass

Guests; Relatives and Retainers of the Capulets and Montagues.

The action takes place at Verona.

PHOTO LARCHER   THE LOVERS' FIRST MEETING

Romeo and Juliet overflows with charming music, Gounod having written for the lovers some of the most emotional passages ever composed, and the opera has even been called "a love duet with occasional interruptions." It is of course not another Faust,—no composer could write two such works,—but it is a most beautiful setting of the story of the ill-fated Italian lovers, which will always be listened to with pleasure.

Several of the Shakespearean personages have been omitted from the opera cast by the librettists, and a new character, that of the page *Stephano*, has been added.

ACT I

SCENE—*Ballroom in Capulet's House, Verona*

The curtain rises on a scene of festivity. *Capulet*, a Veronese noble, is giving a masked fête in honor of his daughter *Juliet's* entrance into society.

Juliet is presented to the guests by her father, and *Capulet* calls on his guests to make merry in a rousing air.

Couplets de Capulet (Capulet's Air)

By Pol Plançon, Bass *(Piano acc.)*
(In French) **81035** 10-inch, **$2.00**

When the guests have gone to the banquet hall, *Juliet* lingers behind and gives expression to her girlish joy in the famous waltz.

Valse (Juliet's Waltz Song)

By Louise Tetrazzini, Soprano
(In Italian) **88302** 12-inch, **$3.00**
By Emma Eames, Soprano
(In French) **88011** 12-inch, **3.00**
By Blanche Arral, Soprano
(In French) **74151** 12-inch, **1.50**

COPY'T DUPONT

FARRAR AS JULIET

It is maintained by some critics that this waltz is too showy and brilliantly effective to be sung by a modest young girl at her first ball. However, Gounod has written such an uncommonly pretty waltz of exquisite melody, that most hearers are too delighted to inquire very closely into questions of dramatic fitness.

JULIET:

Song, jest, perfume and dances.	Sprites from fairyland olden,
Smiles, vows, love-laden glances	On me now bend.
All that spells or entrances	Forever would this gladness
In one charm blend	Shine on me brightly as now,
As in fair dreams enfolden	Would that never age or sadness
Born of fantasy golden,	Threw their shade o'er my brow!

Three records of this delicate waltz, with its ear-haunting melody, are offered for a selection. Mme. Tetrazzini gives it with much animation, its difficult requirements being met with a perfect ease and grace.

Mme. Eames, whose *Juliet* is remembered with pleasure, sings the number with much charm; while a lower-priced rendition is contributed by Mme. Arral.

Juliet is about to leave the room when *Romeo* enters, having ventured masked into the house of his enemy. He is much impressed with her beauty and grace, and contriving to speak with her, asks her to remain a moment. They sing the first of their duets, the opening portion of which is full of airy repartee. As the number progresses a mysterious attraction seems to draw the youth and maiden toward each other, and the duet becomes an impassioned love scene.

Ange adorable (Lovely Angel)

By Alice Nielsen and Florencio Constantino *(In French)* **74108** 12-inch, **$1.50**

ROMEO:
Angel that wearest graces the fairest,
Forgive, if to touch I dare,
The marble whiteness of thy hand
That Heav'n hath formed so fair!
Claim, then, unsparing, that for my daring
I one soft kiss be fined.
Kiss, that effaces unworthy traces,
This hand hath left behind.
JULIET:
Thy hand, good pilgrim, this fine but wrongeth
For thou dost blame it o'ermuch,
To pure devotion surely belongeth,
Saintly palm that thou may'st touch.
Hands there are, sacred to pilgrim's greeting,

But, ah me! I not such as this,
Palm unto palm, not red lips meeting,
Is a holy palmer's kiss!
ROMEO:
To palmer and to saint, have not lips too
been given?
JULIET:
Yes; but only for prayer!
ROMEO:
Then grant my pray'r, dear saint, or faith
may else be driven,
Unto deepest despair!
JULIET:
Know, the saints ne'er are moved,
And if they grant a pray'r, 'tis for the
prayer's sake!

ABOTT AS JULIET

ROMEO:
Then move not, sweetest saint,
Whilst the effect of my pray'r, from thy lips
(*He kisses her*)
I shall take!
JULIET:
Ah! now my lips from thine burning,
Have the sin that they have taken!
ROMEO:
O give that sin back again,
To my lips their fault returning.
JULIET:
No, not again! No, not again!
ROMEO:
O give the sin to me again!

Tybalt, a hot-headed member of the *Capulet* family, recognizes *Romeo* through his mask, and threatens to kill him for his presumption in coming to the house of his enemies. *Capulet* restrains *Tybalt* and the dancing recommences as the curtain falls.

ACT II

SCENE—*Capulet's Garden; Juliet's Apartments Above*

This balcony scene is taken almost literally from Shakespeare, about the only variation being the entrance of *Gregorio* and the servants, which serves merely to divide the long love duet into two parts.

Romeo appears, and gazing at the balcony, sings his lovely serenade.

Ah! leve toi soleil (Arise, Fairest Sun)

By Charles Dalmores, Tenor
(*In French*) 85121 12-inch, $3.00
By Leo Slezak, Tenor
(*In German*) 61204 10-inch, 1.00

ROMEO:
Rise, fairest sun in heaven!
Quench the stars with thy brightness,
That o'er the vault at even
Shine with a feeble lightness,
Oh! rise again! Oh! rise again!
And banish night's dark shades.
She is watching. ah! ever untwining
From their bonds her tresses shining!
Now she speaketh. Ah! how charming!
By her beauty's brilliant ray,
As burneth, ashamed and jaded,
A lamp by the light of day!
At her window, on her fair hand,
See now she leaneth her cheek.
On that hand, were I a glove,
That I might touch that cheek!

Juliet appears on the balcony and *Romeo* conceals himself. She speaks to the stars of her new-found happiness.

JULIET:
Ah, me—and still I love him!
Romeo, why art thou Romeo?
Doff then thy name, for it is no part,
My love, of thee! What rose we call
By other name would smell as sweetly:
Thou'rt no foe, 'tis thy name!

THE BALCONY SCENE

A long scene between the lovers is interrupted by *Gregorio* and some retainers, who are searching for *Romeo*. He conceals himself, and on their departure the duet is resumed.

Ne fuis encore (Linger Yet a Moment)

By Alice Nielsen, Soprano, and Florencio Constantino, Tenor

(In French) **64091** 10-inch, **$1.00**

ROMEO AND JULIET:
  Ah! go not yet, but stay thee!
  Let me once more kiss thy dear hand, I pray
    thee!
JULIET:
  Silence! a step is near us.
  Someone I fear will hear us,
  Let me at least take my hand from thy keep-
    ing.
      Good night, love.
ROMEO:
  Good night, love.
BOTH:
  Good night! Dearest, this fond good night
    is such sweet sorrow
  That I would say good night, till it be dawn!
ROMEO:
  Soft be thy repose till morning!
  On thine eyes slumber dwell, and sweet peace
  In thy bosom: would I were sleep and peace
    So sweet to rest!

FROM THE PAINTING BY PAPPERITZ

ROMEO AND JULIET

ACT III

SCENE I—*The Cell of Friar Laurence*

Romeo and *Juliet* meet by appointment in the Friar's cell to ask him to marry them. He at first protests but finally consents, hoping the union will bring the rival houses together in friendship. The marriage takes place, and *Juliet* returns home with her nurse.

SCENE II—*A Street in Verona*

Stephano enters, seeking his master. Observing the residence of *Capulet,* he decides to sing a song, thinking *Romeo* may still be lingering near the house. A fine rendition of this air has been given by Rita Fornia.

Chanson de Stephano (Page Song)
By Rita Fornia, Soprano

(In French) **74211** 12-inch, **$1.50**

PHOTO LARCHER

FRIAR LAURENCE AND ROMEO

This brilliant young soprano, who has just been engaged by the Victor, has made an especial success at the Metropolitan in this rôle, her fresh and youthful voice being admirably suited to the music of the Page, while in the recent revival of Romeo her singing of *Stephano's* air was pronounced one of the best features of the performance.

Gregorio appears, angry at being waked up, and scolds the noisy youth, finally recognizing him as the companion of *Romeo* on the previous night. They fight, but are interrupted by *Mercutio* and *Tybalt,* who begin to quarrel with *Gregorio*. *Romeo* enters and tries to act as peacemaker, but is insulted and forced to fight, killing *Tybalt*. The action comes to the ears of the

Duke of Verona, who happens to be passing with his suite, and he banishes Romeo from the kingdom. The unhappy youth yields to the decree, but secretly vows to see Juliet again.

ACT IV
SCENE—Juliet's Room

Romeo has made his way into Capulet's house at imminent risk of death, and has penetrated to the room of his bride. As the curtain rises he is taking leave of her, and in another exquisite duet she begs him not to go. He finally departs after a tender farewell, just as Capulet and Friar Laurence enter to tell her that it was Tybalt's dying wish that she should marry Paris. Left alone with the good priest she tells him she will die rather than be separated from Romeo. The Friar tells her to have patience, as he has a plan by which they are to be reunited. He then gives Juliet a potion, commanding her to drink it when her marriage with Paris seems imminent, and tells her she will go into a death-like trance. He continues:

FRIAR LAURENCE:
Loud will they raise the sound of lamentation,
"Juliet is dead! Juliet is dead!" For so
Shall they deem thee reposing. But
The angels above will reply, "She but sleeps!"
For two-and-forty hours thou shalt lie in
    death's seeming,
And then, to life awaking as from a pleasant
    dreaming,
From the ancient vault thou shalt haste away;
Thy husband shall be there, in the night to
    watch o'er thee!

The good priest leaves her and shortly afterward, seeing her father and Paris approaching, she drinks the contents of the phial, and growing faint, apparently expires in Capulet's arms.

ACT V
SCENE—The Tomb of Juliet

The curtain rises, showing the silent vault of the Capulets, where Juliet is lying on the bier still in her trance. Romeo, who has failed to receive Friar Laurence's message, and believes Juliet is dead, now forces the door open with an iron bar and enters.

He sees his bride apparently dead, and flings himself on her body. After a mournful air in which he bids her farewell, he drinks poison, but is soon startled to see signs of life in the body of Juliet. Forgetting the poison he had taken, he embraces her joyfully and they sing their final duet:

COPY'T MISHKIN
CONSTANTINO AS ROMEO

JULIET:
Ah! methought that I heard
Tones that I lov'd, soft falling!
ROMEO:
'Tis I! Romeo—thine own—
Who thy slumbers have stirr'd,
Led by my heart alone,
Thee, my bride, unto love
And the fair world recalling!
(Juliet falls into his arms.)

Suddenly remembering the fatal draught, Romeo cries out in horror:

ROMEO:
Alas! I believed thee dead, love, and—
I drank of this draught!
(Shows the phial.)
JULIET:
Of that draught! It is death!
(Taking the phial.)
Ah! thou churl
To drink all! No friendly drop thou'st
left me,
So I may die with thee!
(She flings the phial away, then remember-
ing the dagger, draws it out.)
Ah! here's my dagger still!

ROMEO:
Come, let's fly hence!
JULIET:
Happy dawn!
ROMEO AND JULIET:
Come, the world is all before us,
two hearts, yet one!
Grant that our love—
Be now and ever
Holy and pure, till our life shall end.

Now, happy dagger, behold thy sheath!
(She stabs herself. With a supreme effort
Romeo half raises himself to prevent her.)
ROMEO:
Hold! Hold thy hand!
JULIET:
Ah, happy moment.
My soul now with rapture is swelling,
Thus to die, love, with thee.
(She lets fall the dagger.)
Yet one embrace! I love thee!
(They half rise in each other's arms.)
O heav'n grant us thy grace!
(They die.)

MISCELLANEOUS ROMEO RECORDS
Selection from the Opera
By Pryor's Orchestra

31353 12-inch, $1.00

(French)
SAMSON ET DALILA
(Sahm'-sahn' ay Dah'-lee-lah')

(English)
SAMSON AND DELILAH

OPERA IN THREE ACTS

Text by Ferdinand Lemaire; music by Camille Saint-Saëns (*Sahn'-Sahnz'*). First production at Weimar, under Liszt, December 2, 1877. In France at Rouen, 1890. Performed at Covent Garden, in concert form, September 25, 1893. First American production February, 1895, with Tamagno and Mantelli (one performance only). Revived by Oscar Hammerstein, November 13, 1908.

Cast of Characters

DELILAH .... Mezzo-Soprano
SAMSON .... Tenor
HIGH PRIEST OF DAGON .... Baritone
ABIMELECH, Satrap of Gaza .... First Bass
AN OLD HEBREW .... Second Bass
PHILISTINE MESSENGER .... Tenor
FIRST PHILISTINE .... Tenor
SECOND PHILISTINE .... Bass

Chorus of Hebrews and Philistines.

Time and Place: 1150 B. C.; Gaza in Palestine.

Camille Saint-Saëns has been for two generations the foremost figure in music in France. Poet, astronomer, traveler, excelling in every branch of the art of music, he is undoubtedly the most versatile musician of our time. He has held a commanding position on the concert stage since 1846, when at the age of ten he gave a concert in Paris. On October 15, 1906, he played one of his own concertos at the Philharmonic concert in Berlin. Sixty years before the public! In all the history of music there is no more wonderful career than that of the composer of Samson, who a few years ago visited America for the first time.

Samson et Dalila may be called a biblical opera, almost an oratorio, and the polished beauty and grace of this great composition has caused it to be pronounced Saint-Saëns' masterpiece. The religious and militant flavor of the Jewish nation is finely expressed in the score, and the exquisite love music is more or less familiar by its frequent performance on the concert stage.

ACT I

SCENE—*A Public Square in Gaza*

The opera has no overture. The first scene shows a square in the city of Gaza, where a crowd of Hebrews are lamenting their misfortunes, telling of the destruction of their cities and the profanation of their altars by the Gentiles.
Samson speaks to the people and bids them take courage.

COPY'T DUPONT

TAMAGNO AS SAMSON

COPY'T MISHKIN

DALMORES AS SAMSON

Figlia miei v'arrestate (Pause, My Brothers)

By Charles Dalmores, Tenor
(*In French*) **87087** 10-inch, $2.00
By Antonio Paoli, Tenor
(*In Italian*) **91078** 10-inch, 2.00
By Nicola Zerola **64173** 10-inch, 1.00

SAMSON (*coming out from the throng*):
Let us pause, O my brothers,
And bless the holy name of the God of our
fathers!
For now the hour is here when pardon shall
be spoken.
Yes, a voice in my heart is the token.
'Tis the voice of the Lord, who by my mouth
thus speaketh.
Our prayers to him have risen,
And liberty is ours.
Brothers! we'll break from bondage!
Our altars raise once more
To our God, as before!

The Hebrews are cheered by *Samson's* words, but their mood soon changes when a number of Philistines enter and revile them. A fight occurs, and *Samson* wounds *Abimelech*. The High Priest of Dagon comes out of the Temple and curses *Samson*.

From the Temple now comes *Delilah*, followed by the Priestesses of Dagon, bearing flowers and singing of Spring. *Delilah* speaks to *Samson* and invites him to the valley where she dwells. He prays for strength to resist her fascinations, but in spite of himself he is forced to look at her as she dances with the maidens. As the young girls dance *Delilah* sings to *Samson* the lovely *Song of Spring*.

Printemps qui commence (Delilah's Song of Spring)

By Gerville-Réache, Contralto (*In French*) **88244** 12-inch, $3.00

DELILAH:
Spring voices are singing,
Bright hope they are bringing,
All hearts making glad.
And gone sorrow's traces,
The soft air effaces
All days that are sad.
The earth glad and beaming,
With freshness is teeming.

In vain all my beauty!
I weep my poor fate!
(*She gazes fondly at Samson.*)
When night is descending,
With love all unending,
Bewailing my fate,
For him will I wait.
Till fond love returning,
In his bosom burning
May enforce his return!

Samson shows by his hesitation and troubled bearing that *Delilah* has shaken his resolutions, and as the curtain falls he is gazing at her, fascinated.

ACT II
SCENE—*Delilah's Home in the Valley of Soreck*

Delilah, richly attired, is awaiting the coming of *Samson,* and muses on her coming triumph over his affections, and the plot to secure his downfall. In a fine air she calls on Love to aid her.

Amour viens aider (Love, Lend Me Thy Might)

By Louise Homer, Contralto (*In French*) **88201** 12-inch, $3.00

DELILAH:
O Love! in my weakness give power!
Poison Samson's brave heart for me!
'Neath my soft sway may he be vanquished;
Tomorrow let him captive be!
Ev'ry thought of me he would banish,
And from his tribe he would swerve,

Could he only drive out the passion
That remembrance doth now preserve.
But he is under my dominion;
In vain his people may entreat.
'Tis I alone that can hold him—
I'll have him captive at my feet!

After a scene between *Delilah* and *Dagon,* who urges her not to fail in her purpose, *Samson* arrives, impelled by a power he cannot resist.

Delilah greets him tenderly, and when he bitterly reproaches himself for his weakness, she sings that wonderfully beautiful song of love and passion.

NOTE.—Text on this page from Ditson Edition by permission. Copy't 1895, Oliver Ditson Co.

COPY'T MISHKIN

GERVILLE-RÉACHE AS DALILA

Mon coeur s'ouvre a ta voix (My Heart at Thy Sweet Voice)

By Louise Homer, Contralto
(In French) 88199 12-inch, $3.00
By Schumann-Heink, Contralto
(In German) 88190 12-inch, 3.00
By Jeanne Gerville-Réache, Contralto
(In French) 88184 12-inch, 3.00
By Elsie Baker, Contralto
(In English) *16192 10-inch, .75

This lovely air of *Delilah*, perhaps the most beautiful contralto air ever written, and the most familiar of the numbers in the opera, is in the repertoire of almost every contralto.

This quotation from the effective translation by Nathan Haskell Dole is from the Schirmer libretto. (Copyright 1892, G. Schirmer.)

DELILAH:
My heart at thy sweet voice opens wide like the flower
Which the morn's kisses waken!
But, that I may rejoice, that my tears no more shower,
Tell thy love still unshaken!
O, say thou wilt not now leave Delilah again!
Repeat thine accents tender, ev'ry passionate vow,
O thou dearest of men!

Four records of this well-known air are listed here. Mme. Schumann-Heink sings it in a manner which displays her rich, melodious contralto, and she delivers the lovely music with warmth and feeling; while it is sung by Mme. Homer with an intensity of sentiment and a beauty almost incomparable. Mme. Gerville-Réache's performance of *Delilah* was one of the sensations of the late Hammerstein season, her rendition of *Delilah's* song being particularly admired; while a record in English is contributed by Miss Baker.

Delilah now asks that *Samson* confide to her the secret plans of the Hebrews, and when he refuses she calls the Philistines, who are concealed, and *Samson* is overpowered.

ACT III

SCENE I—*A Prison at Gaza*

Samson is shown in chains, blinded and shorn of his hair. As he slowly and painfully pushes a heavy mill which is grinding corn, he calls on Heaven to forgive his offence. A file of guards enter and conduct him to the Temple.

SCENE II—*A Magnificent Hall in the Temple of Dagon*

The High Priests and Philistines, with *Delilah* and the Philistine maidens, are rejoicing over the downfall of their enemies. The music of the opening chorus and the Bachanal has been given here in a fine record by a famous Spanish band.

Coro y Bacanal (Chorus and Bachanal)

By Banda Real de Alabarderos de Madrid   *62660 10-inch, $0.75

They have sent for *Samson* to make sport of him. *Delilah* approaches him and taunts him with his weakness. He bows his head in prayer, and when they have wearied of their sport *Samson* asks the page to lead him to the great pillars which support the Temple. He offers a last prayer to God for strength to overcome his enemies, then, straining at the pillars, he overthrows them. The Temple falls amid the shrieks and groans of the people.

DOUBLE-FACED SAMSON AND DELILAH RECORDS

{My Heart at Thy Sweet Voice	By Elsie Baker (In English)}	
{ Manon—Laughing Song	By Edith Helena (In English)}	16192 10-inch, $0.75
{Chorus and Bachanal	By Banda Real de Alabarderos}	
{ Minuet from 2nd Symphony (Haydn)	By Banda Real}	62660 10-inch, .75

*Double-Faced Record—For title of opposite side see above list.

(Italian)

SEMIRAMIDE

TRAGIC OPERA IN TWO ACTS

Text by Rossi; music by Gioachino Antonio Rossini. It is founded on Voltaire's tragedy *Semiramis*. First produced at the Fenice Theatre, Venice, February 3, 1823; in London at the King's Theatre, July 15, 1824. In French, as *Semiramis*, it appeared in Paris, July 9, 1860. First American production occurred in New York, April 25, 1826. Some notable American revivals were in 1855 with Grisi and Vestvalli; in 1890 with Adelina Patti as *Semiramide;* and in 1894 with Melba and Scalchi.

Cast of Characters

SEMIRAMIDE, or SEMIRAMIS, Queen of Babylon....Soprano
ARSACES, commander in the Assyrian army, afterward the son of Ninus and heir to the throne..Contralto
THE GHOST OF NINUS............................Bass
OROE, chief of the Magi...........................Bass
ASSUR, a Prince of the blood royal.................Bass
AZEMA, Princess of the blood royal..............Soprano
IDRENUS, of the royal household...................Tenor
MITRANES, of the royal household...............Baritone
Magi, Guards, Satraps, Slaves

FROM HARPER'S WEEKLY, 1855
GRISI AS SEMIRAMIDE

Semiramide is perhaps the finest of Rossini's serious operas, but although it was a great success in its day, its splendid overture and the brilliant *Bel raggio* are about the only reminders of it which remain.

The story is based on the classic subject of the murder of *Agamemnon* by his wife, called *Semiramis* in the Babylonian version. It is a work which the composer completed in the astonishingly short time of one month, but which shows his art at its ripest.

The action takes place in Babylon; *Semiramide,* the Queen, assisted by her lover *Assur,* has murdered her husband, *King Ninus,* who, in the second act, rises in spirit from the tomb and prophesies the Queen's downfall.

Overture

By Police Band of Mexico City	*35167	12-inch, $1.25
By Police Band of Mexico City	31676	12-inch, 1.00
By Arthur Pryor's Band	31527	12-inch, 1.00

The overture opens with an unusually brilliant introduction, followed by a beautiful chorale for brass which is one of the most admired portions of the work. The familiar melody which forms the principal theme of the overture then appears as a clarinet passage. It begins:

The finale is rather long drawn out for modern ears, but is a fine example of its kind, and the overture is a most showy one, very popular on band and orchestra programs. Three splendid records of this famous number are presented here, and a comparison of the playing of these two great organizations is most interesting.

* Double-Faced Record—For title of opposite side see next page.

The *Bel raggio*, a favorite cavatina with all prima donnas, and a brilliant and imposing air, occurs in the first act. The scene shows the Temple of Belus, where a religious festival is in progress. *Semiramide* is about to announce an heir to the throne and has secretly determined to elect *Arsaces*, a young warrior, with whom she has fallen in love, unaware that he is in reality her own son.

Bel raggio lusinghier (Bright Gleam of Hope)

By Marcella Sembrich, Soprano
(*In Italian*) 88141 12-inch, $3.00

SEMIRAMIDE:
Here hope's consoling ray
Bids sorrow hence away,
And joy calls from above!
Arsaces to my love soon will return dejected,
But ere while with grief I dropp'd my head,
Now once more beams my smile!
Hence all my doubts have fled,
No more I feel the sway of grief and anguish
   dread!
Yes! now hope's consoling ray
Bids dark sorrow hence away,
And calls down joy from above,
Awhile in this breast to stay.
Arsaces will return!
Vision enchanting, my spirit haunting,
With fond emotion thou fill'st my heart,
Ah, bright smiles the morn
When dark waves of sorrow
Like some wild ocean sink and depart!

FROM HARPER'S WEEKLY
ALBONI AS ARSACES

Rossini, who objected to the ornamentation of his music by famous singers, is said to have written this air in so elaborate a fashion as to make further additions impossible. But even as left by Rossini, *Bel raggio* is not sufficiently elaborate to show the skill of a Sembrich, and the additions with which the *diva* has embellished it not only make it more dazzling, but belong also to the true spirit of the air. Thus the inspiring declamatory passages, with their brilliant runs, receive a lavish addition of the singer's splendid high notes, notably the high B on the *alfin perme brillo,* and the astonishing arpeggio up to C sharp on the *dal mio pensier* which follows. The ensuing *cantabile* is sung with all the *legato* and grace which it requires, its principal figure being also additionally embellished.

FROM HARPER'S WEEKLY
TAMBURINI AS ASSUR

DOUBLE-FACED SEMIRAMIDE RECORD

$$\left\{\begin{array}{l}\text{Overture \quad By Police Band of} \\ \text{\quad Mexico City} \\ \text{Marche Slave (Op. 31)} \\ \text{\quad By Arthur Pryor's Band}\end{array}\right\}\ \text{35167 \ 12-inch, \$1.25}$$

SIEGFRIED

(Seeg'-freed)

MUSIC DRAMA IN THREE ACTS

Second Opera of the Rhinegold Trilogy

Words and music by Wagner. First produced at Bayreuth, August 16, 1876. It was given in French at Brussels, June 12, 1891, and subsequently at the Opéra in Paris. In London (in English) by the Carl Rosa Company, in 1898. First American production in New York, February 1, 1888.

Characters

SIEGFRIED...Tenor
MIME (*Mee'-mee*)...Tenor
THE WANDERER (WOTAN)..Baritone
ALBERIC (*Ahl'-ber-ik*)..Baritone
FAFNER (*Faf'-ner*)..Bass
ERDA (*Ehr'-dah*)..Contralto
BRÜNNHILDE (*Broon-hil'-dah*)....................................Mezzo-Soprano

There is little of tragedy and much of lightness and the joy of youth and love in this most beautiful of the Ring Cycle, which tells of the young *Siegfried,*—impetuous, brave, joyful and handsome; and *Brünnhilde,* the god-like maid—unselfish, lovely, innocent, who finds she is but a woman after all.

After *Sieglinde* had been saved from the wrath of *Wotan* by *Brünnhilde* (related in the last part of *Walküre*), she wanders through the forest and dies in giving birth to the child *Siegfried,* who is found and brought up by *Mime,* the *Niblung.*

In the first two acts of Siegfried the hero is shown in his forest home, where he forges the sword with which he slays the dragon. Having accidentally tasted the dragon's blood, he becomes able to understand the language of the birds, which tells him of *Brünnhilde,* the fair maiden who sleeps on the fire-encircled rock. He follows the guidance of one of the birds, cuts through the spear of *Wotan,* who endeavors to stop him, and penetrates the flames. On the top of the rock he beholds the sleeping *Valkyrie* covered with her shield. He removes the armor, and *Brünnhilde* lies before him in soft, womanly garments. She is the first woman he has ever seen, and he kneels down and kisses her long and fervently. He then starts up in alarm; *Brünnhilde* has opened her eyes. He looks at her in wonder, and both remain for some time gazing at each other. She recognizes him as *Siegfried,* and hails him as the hero who is to save the world. This part of the trilogy ends in a splendid duet.

PANEL BY BRAUNE

SIEGFRIED AND THE SWORD

COPY'T DUPONT

REISS AS MIME

ACT I

SCENE—*A Forest. At One Side a Cave*

Mime, the *Niblung,* brother of *Alberic,* found *Sieglinde* in the forest after she had escaped from *Wotan,* and brought up her child, knowing that it was *Siegfried,* who was destined to kill *Fafner* and regain the Ring. The opera opens with an air by *Mime,* who is discovered at the anvil in his forest smithy trying to forge a sword for *Siegfried.*

Siegfried and the Dragon

Zwangvolle Plage! (Heartbreaking Bondage)

By Albert Reiss, Tenor
(*In German*) 74235 12-inch, $1.50

Mr. Reiss' wonderful character study of *Mime*, the dwarf, has been one of the most impressive features of the Metropolitan performances during the past few years. His impersonation gains each year in the sardonic and malignant side of *Mime's* nature, but is always amusing, nevertheless. The artist's portrayal, dramatically and vocally, leaves nothing to be desired, and in the episodes where the dwarf is most abject and fawningly malicious he is superb.

Siegfried, in forest dress, with a horn around his neck, bursts impetuously from the woods. He is driving a great bear and urges it with merry roughness towards *Mime*, who drops the sword in terror and hides behind the forge. Taking pity on the frightened dwarf, *Siegfried* drives the bear back into the wood, and seeing the sword, breaks it over the anvil, as he has broken all of the others. He questions *Mime* about his childhood, and the dwarf tells him reluctantly about his mother and about the sword his father had broken in his last fight. *Siegfried* demands that *Mime* shall mend his father's sword without delay, and goes back into the forest.

PAINTED BY ECHTER

SIEGFRIED, MIME AND THE BEAR—ACT I

Wotan now enters and in answer to *Mime's* questions says he is the *Wanderer*, and speaks to *Mime* of the sword, telling him that only he who knows no fear will be able to forge the broken weapon. After the *Wanderer* has departed, *Siegfried* returns, and *Mime*, who is now beginning to be afraid of the youth, tells him that it was his mother's wish that he should learn fear. "What is this fear?" says *Siegfried*, and *Mime* attemps to describe it.

MIME: Feltest thou ne'er in forest dark,
At gloaming hour in gloomy spots,
Feltest thou then, no grisly gruesomeness grow
o'er thy fancy?
Balefullest shudders shake thy whole body,
All thy senses sink and forsake thee,
In thy breast bursting and big
Beat thy hammering heart?

PHOTO HOFFERT

MIME AT THE ANVIL—ACT I

Siegfried regretfully admits that he has never felt any such sensation. *Mimi*, in despair, then tells him of the Dragon which dwells near by. *Siegfried* eagerly asks *Mime* to conduct him hither, but says he must have his sword mended first, and, when *Mime* refuses, he forges it himself. When it is finished, to try the blade, he strikes the anvil a mighty blow and splits it in half, while *Mime* falls on the ground in extreme terror. *Siegfried* brandishes the sword and shouts with glee as the curtain falls.

ACT II

SCENE—*The Dragon's Cave in the Forest*

Fafner, who has changed himself into a dragon, the better to guard his gold, dwells within a cave, keeping constant watch. *Alberic* is spying near by, hoping to regain the treasure by killing the hero whom he knows will overcome the Dragon. The *Wanderer* enters and warns *Alberic* of the approach of *Siegfried*. *Alberic* wakes the Dragon and offers to save its life in return for the Ring. *Fafner* contemptuously refuses, and makes light of the hero's prowess. *Wotan* departs, laughing at the discomfited *Alberic*, who hides as *Siegfried* and *Mime* approach. The latter is still trying to terrorize *Siegfried* with awful descriptions of the Dragon, but *Siegfried* laughs at him and finally drives him away.

The young hero, left alone, sits down under a tree and meditates about his mother, whom he pictures as gentle and beautiful. His dreaming is ended by the song of the birds, and he regrets that he cannot understand their language. He answers their song with a blast of his horn, which disturbs *Fafner* and the Dragon utters an awful roar, which, however, only makes the youth laugh. The Dragon rushes upon him, but *Siegfried* jumps aside and buries his faithful sword in the reptile's heart.

Having accidentally tasted of the Dragon's blood by carrying his stained hand to his lips, he finds to his astonishment that he is able to understand the song of the bird, which tells him to go into the cave and secure the Ring. *Siegfried* thanks the warbler and goes into the cavern. *Mime* comes back and, seeing the dead *Fafner,* is about to enter the cave when *Alberic* stops him and a heated argument occurs. This scene has been given for the Victor by two celebrated impersonators of these rôles, Goritz and Reiss.

Wohin schleichst du? (Whither Slinkest Thou?)

By Otto Goritz, Baritone, and Albert Reiss, Tenor

(In German)   64215   10-inch, $1.00

HOFFERT

KRAUS AS SIEGFRIED

ALBERIC:
Wither slinkest thou, hasty and sly, slippery scamp?
MIME:
Accursed brother, what brings thee here? I bid thee hence.
ALBERIC:
Graspest thou, rogue, towards my gold? Dost lust for my goods?
MIME:
Yield the position! This station is mine. What stirrest thou here?
ALBERIC:
Startled art thou from stealthy concerns, that I've disturbed?

SIEGFRIED

MIME:
What I have shaped with shrewdest toil' shall not be shaken.
ALBERIC:
Was't thou that robbed the golden Ring from the Rhine?
Or charged it with great and choice enchantment around?
MIME:
Who formed the Tarnhelm which to all forms can turn?
By thee 'twas wanted; its worker wert thou too?
ALBERIC:
What couldst thou ere, fool,
By thyself have fancied and fashioned?
The magic Ring made the dwarf meet for the task.
MIME:
Where now is thy Ring?
The giants have robbed thee, thou recreant!
What thou hast lost, by my lore, belike, I will gain.
ALBERIC:
By the boy's exploit
Shalt thou, booby, be bettered?
Thou shalt have it not,
For its holder in truth is he.
MIME:
I nourished him,
And his nurse now shall he pay:
For toil and woe long while have I waited reward.
ALBERIC:
For a bantling's keep
Would this beggarly, niggardly boor,
Bold and blustering,
Be well nigh as a king?
To rankest of doge booteth the ring
Far rather than thee:
Never, thou rogue, shall reach thee the magic round!
MIME:
Then hold it still and heed it well,
Thy hoarded Ring.
Be thou head, and yet hail me as a brother!
For my own Tarnhelm,
Excellent toy, I'll tender it thee!
'Twill boot us twain,
Twin we the booty like this.

ALBERIC (*laughing scornfully*):
  Twin it with thee?
  And the Tarnhelm too?
  How sly thou art!
  Safe I'd sleep then
  Never from thy ensnarings.
MIME (*beside himself*):
  Wilt not bargain? Wilt not barter?
  Bare must I go, gaining no boon?
  Giv'st thou to me no booty?
ALBERIC:
  Not an atom, not e'en a nail's worth:
  All I deny thee.
MIME (*furiously*):
  In the Ring and Tarnhelm
  Ne'er shalt thou triumph!
  Nought talk we of shares!
  Unto thee I'll call
  For Siegfried to come;
  With his carving sword
  The caustic boy
  Shall crush thee, brother of mine!

ALBERIC:
  Turn thy head round;—
  From the cavern toward us he comes.
MIME:
  Trivial toys have tempted him there.
ALBERIC:
  The Tarnhelm he holds!—
MIME:
  Aye, and the Ring!—
ALBERIC:
  A curse!—the Ring!—
MIME (*with an evil laugh*):
  Let him the Ring to thee render!
  I ween full soon I shall win it.
  (*He slips back into the wood.*)
ALBERIC:
  And yet to its lord
  Shall it alone be delivered!
  (*He disappears in the cleft.*)

They hide themselves as *Siegfried* comes from the cave with the Ring, the value of which he does not yet comprehend. The bird's voice is again heard explaining its history, and revealing the intended treachery of *Mime*. When the dwarf approaches, *Siegfried* is able, by the magic of the Ring, to read his thoughts. Horrified to learn that *Mime* is planning to kill him, he strikes down the dwarf and throws his corpse in the cave, rolling the body of the Dragon before the entrance.

Wearying of his adventures *Siegfried* reclines under the tree and asks the bird to sing again. This time the songster reveals to him that *Brünnhilde* lies sleeping, waiting for the hero who is able to reach the fire-encircled spot.

THE BIRD:
  Hey! Siegfried has slain now the sinister
    dwarf!
  I wot for him now a glorious wife.
  In guarded fastness she sleeps,
  Fire doth emborder the spot:
  O'erstepped he the blaze,
  Waked he the bride,
  Brünnhilde then would be his!
SIEGFREID (*starting impetuously to his feet*):
  O lovely song! Sweetest delight!
  How burns its sense my suffering breast!
  But once more say to me, lovely singer,—
  May I the furnace then break through?
  And waken the marvelous bride?
THE BIRD:
  The bride is won,
  Brünnhilde awaked by faint-heart ne'er:
  But by him who knows not fear.

CAUTIN-BERGER

MIME

He laughs with delight, saying, "Why, this stupid lad who knows not fear,—it is I!" and follows the bird, who flies ahead to guide him to *Brünnhilde's* fiery couch.

ACT III

SCENE—*A Wild Region at the Foot of a Rocky Mountain*

The act opens with a long scene between *Erda* and *Wotan*. The god summons his earth goddess wife and tries to consult her regarding the coming deliverance of the world through *Siegfried* and *Brünnhilde*. The goddess, however, is confused and bewildered by *Wotan's* eager questions and fails to give counsel, asking only to be allowed to return to her sleep. *Wotan*, wearying of the struggle against fate, renounces his sway over the world, realizing that the era of love must supplant the rule of the gods.

Siegfried approaches and *Wotan* attempts to bar his way as a final trial of his courage. The youth, however, makes short work of the weary god, shatters his spear at a single stroke, and continues on his way singing:

SIEGFRIED:
  Ha! Heavenly glow! brightening glare!
  Roads are now opening radiantly round me!
  In fire will I bathe,

  Through fire will I fare to my bride!
  Oho! Oho! Aha! Aha! Gaily! Gaily!
  Soon greets me a glorious friend!

OLD PRINT   BRÜNNHILDE'S FIERY COUCH

As the hero plunges fearlessly through the fire the flames gradually abate, and when he reaches the sleeping *Brünnhilde* they die out completely. *Siegfried* approaches the unconscious maiden with awe and removes her helmet. He is speechless with admiration, and naively asks if the strange emotion which he feels can be fear. Finally, when he presses an ardent kiss on her lips she awakes and greets him joyfully as the hero *Siegfried* who is to save the world. After a long scene in which *Siegfried's* ardent wooing is gently repressed by *Brünnhilde*, he finally seizes her in his arms. Frightened, she repulses him, crying:

BRÜNNHILDE:
No god e'en has touched me!
As a maiden ever heroes revered me:
Virgin I hied from Valhalla!—

Woe's me! Woe's me!
Woe for the shame, the shunless disgrace!
My wak'ning hero deals me this wound!

Siegfried pleads his love and asks her to be his bride, but she begs him to spare her in a wonderful plea, *Deathless Was I*, sung here by Mme. Gadski.

Ewig war Ich   (Deathless Was I)   (Brünnhilde's Appeal to Siegfried)

By Johanna Gadski, Soprano
(*In German*)   88186   12-inch, $3.00

BRÜNNHILDE:
Deathless was I, deathless am I,
Deathless to sweet sway of affection—
But deathless for thy good!
O Siegfried, happiest hope of the world!
Life of the universe! Lordliest hero!
Leave me in peace!
Press not upon me thy ardent reproaches!
Master me not with thy conquering might!
Saw'st e'er thy face in crystal floods?
Did it not gladden thy glance?
When into wavelets the water was roused,
The brook's glassy surface broken and flawed,
Thy face saw'st thou no more:
Nought but ripples swirling round!
So disturb me no more, trouble me not:
Ever then thou wilt shine
In me an image reflected,
Fair and lovely, my lord!—
O Siegfried! Siegfried! Light of my soul!
Destroy not thy faithful slave!

SIEGFRIED

But the impetuous hero resumes his wooing, and love finally conquers the god-like maiden. She laughs in a transport of love, exclaiming:

BRÜNNHILDE:
O high-minded boy! O blossoming hero!
Thou babe of prowess,
Past all that breathe!
Gladly love do I glow with,
Gladly yield to thee blindly,

Gladly glide to destruction,
Gladly go down to death!
Far hence, Walhall' lofty and vast,
Let fall thy structure of stately tow'rs;
Farewell, grandeur and pride of gods!

and throws herself into *Siegfried's* arms as the curtain falls.

MISCELLANEOUS SIEGFRIED RECORDS

Siegfried Fantasie   By Sousa's Band   31621   12-inch, $1.00

A superb record of some of the most famous portions of Wagner's great music drama, including several of the *leit motive*—*Siegfried's Hunting Call*, *The Sword*, *The Bird*, and *Casting of the Steel*, with part of *Siegfried's* wonderful *Song of the Forge*.

LANDE

THE SLEEP-WALKING SCENE—ACT III, SCENE II

(Italian)   (English)

LA SONNAMBULA—THE SOMNAMBULIST

(Lah Son-nahm'-bu-lah)

OPERA IN THREE ACTS

Libretto by Felice Romani; music by Vincenzo Bellini. Produced at the *Teatro Carcano,* Milan, March 6, 1831; Paris, October 28, 1831; and at the King's Theatre, London, July 28th of the same year. At Drury Lane in English, under the Italian title, May 1, 1833. First performance in New York, in English, at the Park Theatre, November 13, 1835, with Brough, Richings, and Mr. and Mrs. Wood. First performance in Italian in New York, Palmo's Opera Company, May 11, 1844. Revived in 1905 at the Metropolitan with Caruso, Sembrich and Plançon; at the Manhattan Opera, 1909, with Tetrazzini, Trentini, Parola and de Segurola.

Characters

COUNT RUDOLPH, lord of the village .... Bass
TERESA, milleress.. Mezzo-Soprano
AMINA, orphan adopted by Teresa, betrothed to Elvino............ Soprano
ELVINO, wealthy peasant... Tenor
LISA, inn-keeper, in love with Elvino........................... Soprano
ALESSIO, peasant, in love with Lisa............................... Bass
A NOTARY .... Tenor

Peasants and Peasant Women.

The scene is laid in a Swiss village.

How our grandfathers and grandmothers doted on this fine old opera by Bellini! In the '30's it was a novelty by a young and gifted composer; by 1850 it was part of every opera season and shone through a halo of great casts—Malibran, Pasta, Jenny Lind, Gerster, Campanini, Grisi—and in the '60's and '70's it continued to be popular. Then came the Wagnerian era, and the pretty little pastoral work was all but forgotten.

Now, however, Italian opera of the old-fashioned kind has begun to be appreciated once more, and even the Wagnerites admit that there may be some pleasure in witnessing this charming little opera.

ACT I

SCENE—*A Village Green*

The peasants are making merry in honor of the marriage of *Amina* and *Elvino*. *Lisa,* the hostess of the inn, enters and gives way to bitter reflections. She also loves *Elvino,* and her jealousy finds expression in a melodious air, *Sounds So Joyful*. *Alessio,* a villager who fancies *Lisa,* tries to console her, but she repulses him. *Amina* and her friends enter, followed soon after by *Elvino,* and the marriage contract is signed. *Elvino* places the ring on his bride's finger, and they sing a charming duet, *Take Now This Ring*.

Prendi l'anel ti dono (Take Now This Ring)

By Maria Galvany, Soprano, and Fernando De Lucia, Tenor
    (Piano accompaniment) *(In Italian)* 89045 12-inch, $4.00
By Emilio Perea, Tenor   *(In Italian)* *62092 10-inch, .75

Two renditions of this number, at widely varying prices, are given here, the latter including only *Elvino's* solo at the beginning of the duet. The words are not given, being merely a succession of flowery phrases to which Bellini has written his delightful melodies.

The nuptial celebration is interrupted by the sound of horses' hoofs, and a handsome and distinguished stranger enters, inquires the way to the castle, and learning that it is some distance, decides to remain at the inn. He looks around him, appearing to recognize the scene, and sings his fine air, *Vi ravviso*.

Vi ravviso (As I View These Scenes)

By Antonio Scotti, Baritone   *(In Italian)* 88028 12-inch, $3.00
By Antonio Scotti, Baritone   *(In Italian)* 87034 10-inch, 2.00
By Perello de Segurola, Bass   *(In Italian)* *62092 10-inch, .75

COUNT:
As I view the scene, how familiar that mill-
 stream, yon fountain, those meadows!
Oh remembrance of scenes long vanish'd,
Soft enchantment long lost and banish'd,

Where my childhood serenely glided,
Where the joyous moments flew;
Oh how peaceful have ye abided,
While those days nought can renew!

Two versions of this noble air are given here—one by Scotti, whose *Rudolph* is always a fine impersonation; and a lower-priced rendition by de Segurola, who sang the character at the Manhattan when the opera was revived for Tetrazzini.

The stranger inquires the reason for the festivities, and is presented to the pretty bride, in whom he is much interested. He tells the peasants that in his childhood he lived with the lord of the castle, and now brings news of the lord's only son, who disappeared some years since.

Amina's mother, *Teresa,* now says that as night is falling they must go within, as the phantom may appear. The stranger is told that a spectre has been often seen of late, and he scoffs at the tale, but the peasants, in an effective chorus, describe the appearance of the ghost.

Ah! fosco ciel! (When Daylight's Going)

By La Scala Chorus   *(In Italian)* *62642 10-inch, $0.75

CHORUS:
When dusky nightfall doth shroud the sun-
 beam,
And half repulses the timid moonbeam,
When thunder boometh; where distance loom-
 eth;
Floating on mist, a shade appears;
In filmy mantle of pallid whiteness,
The eye once gentle now glaring brightness,
Like cloud o'er Heaven by tempest driven,
Plainly confest the phantom wears!
RUDOLPH:
You are all dreaming; 'tis some creation
Of mere gossips, to frighten youth.

CHORUS:
Ah, no such folly in our relation;
We all have seen it, in very truth.
And wheresoever its pathway falleth
A hideous silence all things appalleth;
No leaflet trembles, no zephyr rambles,
As 'twere a frost the brook congeals.
The fiercest watchdog can nought but cower,
A mute true witness of its fell power.
The screech-owl shrieking, her haunt seeking,
Far from the ghost her dark wing wheels.
RUDOLPH:
'Tis fright for youth. I will discover
What hidden mystery your tale conceals.

The stranger now desires to retire and is shown to his room. *Amina* and *Elvino* remain, and the latter reproaches his bride for her interest in the guest; but at the sight of her tears he repents his suspicions, and the act closes with a duet by the reconciled lovers.

---

* *Double-Faced Record—For title of opposite side see list on page 318.*

ACT II

SCENE—*The Apartment of the Stranger*

The guest muses that he might have done worse than stop at this little inn—the people are courteous, the women pretty, and the accommodations good. *Lisa* enters and asks if he is comfortable, calling him "my lord," the villagers having suspected that he is the *Count Rudolph.*

The Count, although somewhat annoyed that his identity is revealed, takes it good-naturedly, and even flirts a little with the buxom landlady. She coyly runs away, dropping her veil as she does so.

Amina now appears at the window, walking in her sleep. She unlatches the casement and steps into the room, saying in her sleep, "Elvino, dost thou remain jealous? I love but thee." The Count is at first astonished, but soon sees that the young girl is asleep. Just here *Lisa* peeps into the room, and seeing *Amina,* runs off scandalized. *Amina,* in her dream, again goes through the marriage ceremony, and entreats *Elvino* to believe that she loves him, finally throwing herself on the bed in a deep sleep. The Count is somewhat puzzled at the situation, and finally deciding to leave the young girl in possession of the room, goes out by the window.

Elvino and the villagers, who have been summoned by *Lisa,* now enter and are astonished to see *Amina* asleep in the Count's room. She wakes at the noise, bewildered, and runs to *Elvino,* who repulses her roughly. She is met with cold looks on every hand, and sinks down in despair, crying bitterly. Rousing herself, she begins the duet, *D'un pensiero.*

D'un pensiero (Hear Me Swear, Then)

By Giuseppina Huguet, Soprano; Aristodemo Giorgini, Tenor; and Chorus   (*In Italian*)   88255   12-inch, $3.00

AMINA:
Not in thought's remotest dreaming,
Was a crime by me intended;
Is the little faith now granted,
Fit return for so much love?

ELVINO:
Heav'n forgive ye, this guilt redeeming;
May thy breast be ne'er thus rended;
With what love my soul was haunted,
Let these burning tear-drops prove!

Finding all turned against her except her mother, she runs to the maternal arms, while *Elvino* rushes from the room. The curtain falls.

ACT III

SCENE I—*A Shady Valley near the Castle*

Amina and *Teresa* enter on their way to the castle to plead with the Count to clear the girl's good name. Seeing *Elvino,* *Amina* makes another effort to convince him she is still true, but he reproaches her bitterly, takes the ring from her finger, and rushes away.

SCENE II—*A Street in the Village. Teresa's mill on the left*

The villagers enter and inform *Lisa* that *Elvino* has transferred his affections to her. He enters and confirms the good news, and they go toward the church. The Count stops them, and assures *Elvino* that *Amina* is the victim of a dreadful misunderstanding. *Elvino* refuses to listen to him and bids *Lisa* follow him to the church, but they are again interrupted by *Teresa,* who has learned of the proposed marriage, and now shows *Lisa's* veil which she had found in the Count's room. "Deceived again," cries *Elvino,* and asks if any of these women are to be trusted.

Rudolph assures him again that *Amina* is guiltless, and *Elvino* desperately says, "But where is the proof?" "There," cries the Count, suddenly pointing to *Amina,* who in her night dress comes from a window in the mill roof, carrying a lamp. All watch her breathlessly, fearing to wake her lest she fall. She climbs down to the bridge over the wheel, and descends the stairs.

AMINA (*advancing, still in her sleep, to the middle of the stage*):
Oh, were I but permitted
Only once more to see him,
Ere that another he doth lead to the altar!
RUDOLPH (*to Elvino*):
Hear her—
TERESA:
She is thinking, speaking of thee!

(*Amina, clasping her hands on her bosom, takes from it the flowers given her by Elvino in the first Act.*)
AMINA:
Sweet flowers, tenderest emblems,
Pledging his passion, from ye ne'er will I sever.
Still let me kiss you—
But your bloom is fled forever!

The first of the two lovely airs for *Amina* in this act now occurs.

Ah! non credea mirarti (Could I Believe)

By Luisa Tetrazzini, Soprano	(*In Italian*) 88305	12-inch, $3.00
By Graziella Pareto, Soprano	(*In Italian*) 76003	12-inch, 2.00

Perhaps the most effective part of the opera lies in this sleep-walking scene, when *Amina*, in a state of somnambulism, walks along the roof of the building, and finally climbs down to the ground. This act establishes her innocence, and clears up a mystery which had caused her good character to be doubted.

Ah! non credea is sung by the sleeper as she descends from her dangerous position, while her lover and friends watch in terror, fearing to awaken her. It opens with a beautiful *cantabile* in the key of A minor, its pathos being fully in keeping with the plight of *Amina*, who, being discarded by her lover and doubted by her friends, weeps over her short-lived love and happiness. At the words "*Potrio novel vigore*," the pathetic note gives place to a more ardent emotion, as hope is mingled with her despair.

Regarding the flowers which her lover had given her, and which are now faded, she exclaims:

AMINA:
Ah! must ye fade, sweet flowers,
   Forsaken by sunlight and showers,
   As transient as lover's emotion
   That lives and withers in one short day!

But tho' no sunshine o'er ye,
   These tears might yet restore ye,
   But' estranged devotion
   No mourner's tears have power to stay!
—From the Ditson Edition.

The singer's aim has been to illustrate the simple charm of the character of *Amina* and the pathos of the scene, rather than exhibit brilliance of ornament. The cadenza at the close, although typical of Tetrazzini's marvelous powers of execution, is well subordinated to the character of the song, and pleases as much by its delicate beauty as by its amazing technical perfection.

Elvino can restrain himself no longer, and rushes to *Amina*, who wakes, and seeing *Elvino* on his knees before her, utters a cry of delight and falls in his arms.

The opera then closes with the joyous, bird-like air, *Ah! non giunge*, which is a fitting close to this charming work, with its graceful and tender music and peaceful pastoral scenes. In *Amina*, Mme. Tetrazzini finds a most congenial rôle, and for her sake alone Sonnambula would always be worth hearing. She has the voice, style and technical skill to make such music as this captivating; while Sembrich's impersonation of the ingenuous village beauty, who is all liveliness and joy, leaves nothing to be desired. Hers is a graceful and natural impersonation, and the delightful sleep-walking scene is given with a delicacy which is admirable.

Ah non giunge (Oh Recall Not One Earthly Sorrow)

By Luisa Tetrazzini, Soprano	(*In Italian*) 88313	12-inch, $3.00
By Marcella Sembrich, Soprano	(*In Italian*) 88027	12-inch, 3.00

AMINA:
Do not mingle one human feeling
   With the rapture o'er each sense stealing;
   See these tributes, to me revealing
   My Elvino, true to love.

Ah, embrace me, and thus forgiving,
   Each a pardon is now receiving;
   On this bright earth, while we are living,
   Let us form here a heaven of love!

(*Curtain.*)

DOUBLE-FACED AND MISCELLANEOUS SONNAMBULA RECORDS

Vi ravviso (As I View These Scenes)			
By Perello de Segurola, Bass	(*In Italian*)	62092 10-inch, $0.75
Prendi l'anel ti dono (Take Now This Ring)			
By Emilio Perea, Tenor	(*In Italian*)	
Ah! fosco ciel! (When Daylight's Going)			
By La Scala Chorus	(*In Italian*)	62642 10-inch, .75
Lohengrin—Coro Nuziale By La Scala Chorus	(*In Italian*)	

(French)
CONTES D'HOFFMAN
(*Cont Doff'-man*)

(English)
TALES OF HOFFMAN

(German)
HOFFMAN'S ERZÄHLUNGEN
(*Air-tsay'-loong-en*)

OPERA IN THREE ACTS
WITH PROLOGUE AND EPILOGUE

Text by Jules Barbier. Music by Offenbach. First performance in Paris, February 10, 1881. First United States production October 16, 1882, at Fifth Avenue Theatre. Revived at the Manhattan Opera House, New York, November 27, 1907.

Cast

THE POET HOFFMAN	Tenor
NICLAUS, his friend	Soprano
OLYMPIA, GIULIETTA, ANTONIA, STELLA, the various ladies with whom Hoffman falls in love	Sopranos
COPPELIUS, DAPERTUTTO, MIRACLE, his opponents. (These three rôles are usually sung by the same artist)	Baritone
LUTHER, an innkeeper	Bass
SCHLEMIL, Giulietta's admirer	Bass
SPALANZANI, an apothecary	Tenor
COUNCILLOR CRESPEL, father of Antonia	Bass

Offenbach's delightful and fantastic *opéra comique*, first produced at Paris in 1881, has been a success wherever performed, although it was tabooed in Germany for many years after the disastrous fire at the Ring Theatre in Berlin, which occurred during the presentation of the opera at that house. Its American successes are familiar to opera-goers, especially the brilliant and altogether admirable Hammerstein production, which drew large and delighted audiences for several years.

THE PROLOGUE

This introductory scene occurs in Nuremberg at Luther's tavern, a popular student resort. *Hoffman*, the favorite of all, enters with his friend *Nicholas* and joins in the merry-making. In response to calls for a song, *Hoffman* sings the *Ballad of Klein-Zach*, and then volunteers to relate his three love affairs. This proposal is greeted with enthusiasm, and as *Hoffman* begins by saying "The name of my first was Olympia," the curtain falls. When it rises, the first tale of *Hoffman* is seen in actual performance.

PROLOGUE—THE LEGEND OF KLEINSACK

319

ACT I

Spalanzani, a wealthy man with a mania for automatons, has perfected a marvelous mechanical figure of a young girl which he calls Olympia, pretending it is his daughter. Hoffman and Nicholas call upon him, and during Spalanzani's absence, Hoffman discovers Olympia, and falls in love at sight. Unable to take his eyes from the doll-like perfection of the figure, he expresses his infatuation in a beautiful air.

COPY'T MISHKIN

THE MECHANICAL DOLL—ACT I

C'est elle ('Tis She!)

By Charles Dalmores, Tenor
(In French) **87089 10-inch, $2.00**

COPY'T MISHKIN

DALMORES AS HOFFMAN

Dalmores makes a great success in the part of Hoffman. This rôle calls for a handsome appearance, a gallant bearing, and enduring vocal powers, and this tenor fills these requirements admirably. He sings this beautiful air with graceful fluency and much warmth of tone.

Nicholas tries in vain to prevent his friend from making a fool of himself, but Hoffman, owing to the magic glasses Spalanzani has induced him to wear, sees only a lovely woman instead of an automaton; but is undeceived when he dances with the figure and she falls to pieces before his astonished eyes.

ACT II

This adventure concerns the Lady Giulietta, who resides in Venice. Among her many friends are Hermann and Nathanael, and the latter, fearing the power of the lovely coquette, tries to get Hermann away, but he insists that he is proof against her fascinations. Dapertutto, the real lover of the lady, hearing this boast, induces Giulietta to try her arts on the young man. She succeeds, and Hoffman, madly in love, challenges Giulietta's protector, Schlemil, and kills him in a duel. Hoffman rushes back to his charmer's residence only to find that she has fled with her chosen admirer.

This second tale introduces that lovely gem, the Barcarolle, with its languorous, fascinating rhythm and charming melody.

Barcarolle—Belle Nuit (Oh, Night of Love)

By Geraldine Farrar and Antonio Scotti	(In Italian)	87502	10-inch, $3.00
By Mr. and Mrs. Wheeler (Double-Faced—See p. 321) (English)		16827	10-inch, .75
By the Victor Orchestra, with duet for two violins		5333	10-inch, .60
By the Vienna Quartet		5754	10-inch, .60

This popular Offenbach number, which is given as a duet in the Venetian scene and afterwards as an instrumental intermezzo, is one of the best known examples of the barcarolle. As the name implies, it was originally a song or chant used by the Venetian gondoliers.

The music, in 6-8 time, portrays admirably the swaying of the boat

and its dreamy melancholy suggests the calm of a perfect moonlight night. Mr. Scotti and Miss Farrar have sung it delightfully, their voices blending in the lovely serenade with charming effect. The instrumental renditions are exquisitely played with a graceful lightsomeness wholly pleasing, while those who prefer a vocal record at a popular price will find the rendition by the Wheelers a very fine one.

O Night of Love

Beauteous night, O night of love,
Smile thou on our enchantment;
Radiant night, with stars above,
O beauteous night of love!
Fleeting time doth ne'er return
But bears on wings our dreaming,

Far away where we may yearn,
For time doth ne'er return.
Sweet zephyrs aglow,
Shed on us thy caresses—
Night of love, O night of love!

From Ditson Edition—Cop't 1909.

In this act is also the air sung by *Dapertutto* to the sparkling diamond, which he says never yet failed to tempt a woman.

Air de Dapertutto (Dapertutto's Air)

By Marcel Journet, Bass　　　　　　　(*In French*)　74103　12-inch, $1.50

Journet delivers this song of the swaggering, garrulous Venetian bravo with much spirit.

ACT III

The third adventure of *Hoffman* introduces us to an humble German home where *Antonia,* a young singer, has become the victim of consumption. She is forbidden to sing by her father, but a *Dr. Miracle,* who is the secret enemy of the family, Svengali-like, urges her on, and *Hoffman,* who knows nothing of the poor girl's affliction, sees her literally sing herself to death, and she dies in his arms.

THE EPILOGUE

The epilogue shows again the tavern of the prologue, where *Hoffman* is apparently just concluding his third tale. Having tried three kinds of love—the love that is inspired by mere beauty, the sensuous love, and the affection that springs from the heart—he says he has learned his lesson, and will henceforth devote himself to art, the only mistress who will prove faithful. He bids farewell to another of his flames, *Stella,* an opera singer, and as the curtain falls is left alone, dreaming, while the Muse appears and bids him follow her.

DOUBLE-FACED AND MISCELLANEOUS HOFFMAN RECORDS

Contes d'Hoffman Selection　　　By Victor Concert Orch.　31820　12-inch, $1.00
{Barcarolle—O, Night of Love!　By Mr. and Mrs. Wheeler}16827　10-inch,　.75
{ *Fatinitza Selection* (*von Suppe*)　　*By Pryor's Band*}

LE THÉÂTRE

TALES OF HOFFMAN—ACT III—THE BARCAROLLE

FROM A PAINTING BY KNIELE

TANNHÄUSER AND VENUS

(German)

TANNHÄUSER

(*Tahn'-hoy-zer*)

ROMANTIC OPERA IN THREE ACTS

Words and music by Richard Wagner. First presented at the Royal Opera, Dresden, October 20, 1845; at the Grand Opera, Paris, March 13, 1861. First London production at Covent Garden, in Italian, May 6, 1876. First performance in English took place at Her Majesty's Theatre, February 14, 1882. First New York production April 4, 1859.

Characters

HERMANN, Landgrave of Thuringia	Bass
TANNHÄUSER	Tenor
WOLFRAM VON ESCHENBACH	Baritone
WALTHER VON DER VOGELWEIDE ⎱ Minstrel Knights	Tenor
BITEROLF	Bass
HEINRICH DER SCHREIBER	Tenor
REINMAR VON ZWETER	Bass
ELIZABETH, Niece of the Landgrave	Soprano
VENUS	Soprano
A Young Shepherd	Soprano
Four Noble Pages	Soprano and Alto

Chorus of Thuringian Nobles and Knights, Ladies, Elder and Younger Pilgrims, and Sirens, Naïads, Nymphs and Bacchantes.

Scene and Period: Vicinity of Eisenach; beginning of the thirteenth century.

THE STORY

There are a great many people who love to go to the opera, but who do not care for Wagner's Ring Operas, with their Teutonic myths and legends, and their long and sometimes undeniably tedious scenes. But *Tannhäuser*, with its poetry, romance and passion, and above all its characters, who are real human beings and not mysterious mythological gods, goddesses and heroes, appeals strongly to these opera-goers.

To show the wonderful vogue of this work, it is estimated that more than one thousand performances of the opera take place annually throughout the world.

The story is quite familiar, but the chief events will be noted here in brief. It tells of conflict between two kinds of love: true love of the highest human kind as distinguished from mere sensuous passion; and relates how the higher and purer love triumphed in the end.

Tannhäuser, a knight and minstrel, in an evil moment, succumbs to the wiles of *Venus* and dwells for a year in the Venusberg. Tiring of these monotonous delights, he leaves the goddess and returns to his home, where he is warmly received and told that the fair *Elizabeth*, niece of

FIRST PROGRAM OF TANNHÄUSER, 1845

the *Landgrave*, still mourns for him. He is urged to compete in the Tournament of Song not far distant, the prize being the hand of *Elizabeth*. The theme of the contest is The Nature of Love, and when *Tannhäuser's* turn arrives the evil influence of the Venusberg is apparent when he delivers a wild and profane eulogy of passion. Outraged by this insult the minstrels draw their swords to slay him. Coming to his senses, too late, he repents, and when a company of Pilgrims pass on their way to Rome, he joins them to seek pardon for his sin. In the last act we see *Elizabeth*, weary and worn, supported by the noble *Wolfram*, who

LANDE

SETTING OF ACT III AT THE METROPOLITAN

323

also loves her, watching for the Pilgrims to return, but *Tannhäuser* is not among them. *Elizabeth* is overcome with disappointment and feebly returns to her home.

Tannhäuser now appears, in a wretched plight, on his way to re-enter the Hill of Venus. He tells *Wolfram* that he appealed to the Pope for pardon, but was told that his redemption was as impossible as that the Pope's staff should put forth leaves. *Wolfram's* remonstrances are in vain, and *Tannhäuser* is about to invoke the goddess, when a chant is heard and he Pilgrims appear, announcing that the Pope's staff had blossomed as a sign that the sinner was forgiven. *Tannhäuser* kneels in prayer as the mourners pass with the body of *Elizabeth*, who, overcome by her bitter disappointment, had suddenly passed away.

The Overture

Overture—Part I
By Arthur Pryor's Band   31382   12-inch, $1.00

Overture—Part II
By Arthur Pryor's Band   31383   12-inch,   1.00

This overture, with its sombre opening chorus, its weird music of the Venus Mount, and the final return of the penitents, when the chant is accompanied by a striking variation for clarinets, is one of the greatest works of Wagner. It has become quite familiar by its frequent repetitions in orchestra and military band concerts, and no concert piece is more admired.

The overture depicts the struggle between good and evil, and as Liszt has said, is a poem on the same subject as the opera and equally comprehensive.

The sombre religious motive appears first:

beginning softly and gradually swelling to a *fortissimo*. Then, as it is dying away, it is suddenly interrupted by the Venusberg motive:

with its rising tide of sensual sounds. This motive continues with terrible persistence, leading into *Tannhäuser's* hymn to *Venus,* after which the enchanting Venus motive returns and is developed with various changes. The tide now changes again and the majestic pilgrim theme predominates, finally reaching a climax in the final hymn of triumph.

ACT I

SCENE I—*The Hill of Venus—Nymphs, Sirens, Naïads and Bacchantes dancing or reclining on mossy banks*

The rising of the curtain discloses *Venus* reclining on a couch gazing tenderly at *Tannhäuser,* who is in a dejected attitude. The goddess asks him why he is melancholy, and he tells her he is weary of pleasure and would see the earth again. She reproves him fondly:

VENUS:

What! art thou wav'ring? Why these vain lamentings?
Canst thou so soon weary of the blisses
That love immortal hath cast 'round thee?
Can it be—dost thou now repent that thou'rt divine?
Hast thou soon forgotten how thy heart was mourning,

Till by me thou wert consoled?
My minstrel, come, let not thy harp be silent;
Recall the rapture—sing the praise and bliss of love
In tones that won for thee love's self to be thy slave!
Of love sing only, for her treasures are all thine!

He rouses himself and sings the *Praise to Venus,* but it is a forced effort, and throwing down his harp he exclaims:

TANNHAUSER:

For earth I'm yearning,
In thy soft chains with shame I'm burning,
'Tis freedom I must win or die—
For freedom I can all defy;

To strife or glory forth I go,
Come life or death, come joy or woe,
No more in bondage will I sigh!
Oh queen, beloved goddess, let me fly!

Venus in a rage, then tells him to go if he will, but predicts his return and disappears with all her train, while the scene instantly changes.

SCENE II—*A Valley*

Tannhäuser suddenly finds himself in a beautiful valley near the Wartburg. On the peaceful scene there break in the notes of a shepherd's pipe, and tinkling sheep bells sound from the heights. A company of Pilgrims pass, singing their chant, while the little shepherd pauses in his lay, and begs them utter a prayer for him in Rome.

A fine rendition of the music of this inspiring chorus is given here by Pryor's Band.

Pilgrims' Chorus

By Pryor's Band
By Pryor's Band   (*Double-faced—See page 330*)

31160 12-inch, $1.00
16537 10-inch,   .75

TANNHAUSER (*kneeling in ecstasy*):

Almighty, praise to Thee!
Great are the marvels of Thy mercy!
Oh, see my heart by guilt oppress'd—

I faint, I sink beneath the burden!
Nor will I cease, nor will I rest,
Till heav'nly mercy grant me pardon!

The *Landgrave* and several minstrels now enter, and seeing a knight kneeling in prayer, accost him. They are amazed and delighted to see that it is the long lost *Henry,* their brother knight. They question him, but he gives evasive replies:

TANNHAUSER:

In strange and distant realms I wandered far,
Where neither peace nor rest was ever found.
Ask not! at enmity I am with none;
We meet as friends—let me in peace depart!

PHOTO BENQUE

RENAUD AS WOLFRAM

The Knights urge him to return with them, and speak the name of *Elizabeth.* *Tannhäuser* joyfully exclaims:

TANNHAUSER:

Elizabeth! oh, Heaven!
That name ador'd once more I hear!

Wolfram then tells him that he is beloved by the *Landgrave's* fair niece.

WOLFRAM:

When for the palm in song we were contending,
And oft thy conq'ring strain the wreath had won,
Our songs anon thy victory, suspending,
One glorious prize was won by thee alone!
Was't magic, or a pow'r divine,
That wrought thro' thee the wondrous sign,
Thy harp and song in blissful hour
Enthrall'd of royal maids the flower!
For ah, when thou in scorn hadst left us,
Her heart was closed to joy and song,
Of her sweet presence she bereft us,
For thee in vain she wearied long.
Oh! minstrel bold, return and rest thee,
Once more awake the joyous strain!
Cast off the burden that oppress'd thee,
And her fair star will shine again!

Tannhäuser joyfully consents to return and promises to compete in the forthcoming Tournament of Song, the prize for which is to be the hand of *Elizabeth.* The remainder of the hunting train of the *Landgrave* now arrives, and as *Tannhäuser* is being greeted by his friends, the curtain falls.

ACT II

SCENE—*The Great Hall in the Wartburg*

Elizabeth enters, full of joy over the return of *Tannhäuser*, and greets the Hall in a noble song.

Dich, theure Halle (Hail, Hall of Song)

By Johanna Gadski, Soprano
(*In German*) 88057 12-inch, $3.00

By Louise Voigt, Soprano
(*German*) 31849 12-inch, 1.00

ELIZABETH:
    Oh, hall of song, I give thee greeting!
    All hail to thee, thou hallowed place!
    'Twas here that dream so sweet and fleeting,
    Upon my heart his song did trace.
    But since by him forsaken
    A desert thou dost seem—
    Thy echoes only waken
    Remembrance of a dream.
    But now the flame of hope is lighted,
    Thy vault shall ring with glorious war;
    For he whose strains my soul delighted
    No longer roams afar!

Mme. Gadski, whose superb impersonation of *Elizabeth*, replete with tenderness and vocal charm, is a familiar one to opera-goers, sings this glorious air in a surpassingly beautiful fashion, while a splendid rendition, at a lower price, is given by Miss Voigt.

Tannhäuser enters and kneels at the feet of *Elizabeth*, who in blushing confusion bids him rise. With that frankness which seems characteristic of Wagner's heroines, the young girl makes no secret of her partiality for the Knight, and a long scene between the lovers ensues, interrupted by the entrance of the *Landgrave*, who greets *Tannhäuser* cordially and welcomes him to the contest.

BRAND, BAYREUTH
THE HALL OF SONG—ACT II

The Knights and Ladies now assemble to the strains of the noble *Fest March,* given here in splendid fashion by Sousa's Band.

Fest March

By Sousa's Band   **31423 12-inch, $1.00**
By Sousa's Band *(Double-faced—See page 330)* **16514 10-inch, .75**

When the company is seated, the *Landgrave* rises and makes the address of welcome.

LANDGRAVE:

Minstrels assembled here, I give you greeting,
Full oft within these walls your lays have
 sounded;
In veiled wisdom, or in mirthful measures
They ever gladdened every list'ning heart.
And though the sword of strife was loosed
 in battle,
Drawn to maintain our German land secure,
Unto the harp be equal praise and glory!
The tender graces of the homestead,
The faith in what is good and gracious—
For these you fought with word and voice;
The meed of praise for this is due.
Your strains inspiring, then, once more
 attune,
Now that the gallant minstrel hath returned,
Who from our land too long was parted.

To what we owe his presence here amongst us
In strange, mysterious darkness still is
 wrapp'd;
The magic power of song shall now reveal it,
Therefore hear now the song you all shall
 sing.
Say, what is love? by what signs shall we
 know it?
This be your theme. Who so most nobly
 this can tell,
Him shall the Princess give the prize.
He may demand the fairest guerdon:
I vouch that whatsoe'er he ask is granted.
Up, then, arouse ye—sing, oh, gallant min-
 strels!
Attune your harps to love—great is the prize.
Ere ye begin, let all receive our thanks!

Four pages, who have drawn lots from a gold cup, now announce that *Wolfram* is to begin the contest. He rises and delivers his *Eulogy of Love.*

Wolfram's Ansprache (Wolfram's Eulogy of Love)

By Otto Goritz, Baritone   *(In German)* **74215 12-inch, $1.50**

The singer gives his conception of love, which he describes as pure and ethereal, comparing it to a crystal spring.

WOLFRAM:

Gazing around upon this fair assembly,
How doth the heart expand to see the scene!
These gallant heroes, valiant, wise and gentle—
A stately forest soaring fresh and green.
And blooming by their side in sweet perfec-
 tion,
I see a wreath of dames and maidens fair;
Their blended glories dazzle the beholder—
My song is mute before this vision rare!
I raised my eyes to one whose starry splendor
In this bright heaven with mild effulgence
 beams,
And gazing on that pure and tender radiance,

My heart was sunk in prayerful holy dreams.
And lo! the source of all delights and power
Was then unto my listening soul revealed,
From whose unfathomed depths all joy doth
 shower—
The tender balm in which all grief is healed.
Oh, may I never dim its limpid waters,
Or rashly trouble them with wild desires!
I worship thee kneeling, with soul devoted:
To live and die for thee my heart aspires!
(After a pause.)
I know not if these feeble words can render
What I have felt of love both true and tender.

Tannhäuser, who has shown signs of impatience during this recital, now jumps to his feet, flushed and eager, while the company looks at him in astonishment.

TANNHAUSER:

Oh, minstrel, if 'tis thus thou singest,
Thou ne'er hast known or tasted love!
If thou desire an unapproached perfection—
Behold the stars—adore their bright reflec-
 tion—
They were not made to be belov'd:

(Ardently.)
But what can yield to soft caresses,
And, fram'd with me in mortal mould
Gentle persuasion's rule confesses,
And in these arms I may unfold—
This is for joy, and knows no measure,
For love's fulfillment is its pleasure!

At this definition of love, strange for such an occasion, *Biterolf,* a hotheaded Knight, rises and challenges *Tannhäuser,* who excitedly retorts that such a grim wolf as *Biterolf* can know nothing of the delights of love! He then, in wild exultation, sings his blasphemous *Praise of Venus,* saying

TANNHAUSER:
Dull mortals, who of love have never tasted
Go forth! Venus alone can show ye love!

At this the Knights rush toward him with drawn swords, exclaiming:

KNIGHTS:
Ye all have heard,
His mouth hath confess'd
That he hath shared the joys of Hell,

In Venus' dark abode that dwell,
Disown him—curse him—banish him!
Or let his traitor life-blood flow!

Elizabeth throws herself in front of the unhappy *Tannhäuser,* who stands as if in a trance. She begs for his life in a touching plea.

ELIZABETH:
Away from him! 'Tis not for you to judge him!
Shame on you! He is one against you all!
I pray for him—spare him, oh, I implore ye!
Let not the hope of pardon be denied!
To life renew'd his sinking faith restore ye.
Think that for him, too, once the Saviour died!
Oh, let a spotless maid your grace implore!
Let Heav'n declare through me what is its will—
The erring mortal, who hath fallen
Within the weary toils of sin,
How dare ye close the heav'nly portal!
On me, a maiden young and tender,
Yon knight hath struck a cruel blow—
I, who so deeply, truly loved him,
Am hurl'd in dark abyss of woe!

The *Landgrave* pronounces judgment and declares *Tannhäuser* banished, suggesting that he join the band of Pilgrims about to start for Rome. In the distance is heard the Pilgrims' chant, and the strains seem to bring the erring knight to his senses. He cries: "To Rome," and dashes from the hall.

ACT III
SCENE—*The Valley beneath the Wartburg—at one side a Shrine*

As the curtain rises *Elizabeth* is seen kneeling at the shrine in prayer. *Wolfram* comes down by the path, and observing her, sadly notices her changed appearance, and muses of his own hopeless love. The song of the Pilgrims is heard in the distance, and *Elizabeth* eagerly rises and scans the approaching band. *Tannhäuser* is not among them, and the despairing maiden kneels again at the shrine, and offers her prayer to the Virgin.

Elizabeth's Gebet (Elizabeth's Prayer)
By Geraldine Farrar, Soprano　　　　(*In German*)　　88053　12-inch,　$3.00
By Elizabeth Wheeler, Soprano　　　(*In English*)　*35096　12-inch,　1.25

HOFFERT
ELIZABETH AT THE SHRINE

This prayer of the sainted *Elizabeth* is one of the most beautiful and touching of the master's compositions. "He will return no more!" cries the unhappy girl, and falls on her knees.

ELIZABETH:
Oh, blessed Virgin, hear my prayer!
Thou star of glory, look on me!
Here in the dust I bend before thee
Now from this earth, oh, set me free!
Let me, a maiden pure and white,
Enter into thy kingdom bright!
If vain desires and earthly longing
Have turn'd my heart from thee away,
The sinful hopes within me thronging,
Before thy blessed feet I lay;
I'll wrestle with the love I cherish'd,
Until in death its flame hath perish'd.
If of my sin thou will not shrive me,
Yet in this hour, oh grant thy aid!
Till thy eternal peace thou give me,
I vow to live and die thy maid.
And on thy bounty I will call,
That heav'nly grace on him may fall!

She remains for a long time in prayerful rapture; as she slowly rises she glances at *Wolfram,* who is approaching. She bids him by gesture not to speak to her, but he asks that he may escort her.

WOLFRAM:
O royal maid, shall I not guide thee homeward?

Elizabeth again expresses to him by gesture that she thanks him from her heart for his faithful love; her way, however, leads to Heaven, where she has a high purpose to fulfill; she wishes him not to accompany or follow her now. She slowly ascends the height and disappears gradually from view.

Wolfram gazes sadly after her for a long time, then seats himself at the foot of the hill, begins to play upon his harp, and finally sings the noble and beautiful ode to the evening star.

O du mein holder Abendstern (Song to the Evening Star)

By Emilio de Gogorza, Baritone	(In German)	88154	12-inch,	$3.00
By Marcel Journet, Bass	(In German)	74006	12-inch,	1.50
By Reinald Werrenrath, Baritone	(In German)	*35160	12-inch,	1.25
By Reinald Werrenrath, Baritone	(In German)	31462	12-inch,	1.00
By Victor Sorlin, 'Cellist		*16813	10-inch,	.75
By Alan Turner, Baritone	(In English)	5336	10-inch,	.60
By Victor Sorlin, 'Cellist		5412	10-inch,	.60

O douce étoile (Song to the Evening Star)

By Maurice Renaud, Baritone	(In French)	91067	10-inch,	$2.00

WOLFRAM:

Like Death's dark shadow, Night her gloom
    extendeth,
Her sable wing o'er all the vale she bendeth;
The soul that longs to tread yon path of light,
Yet dreads to pass the gate of Fear and Night,
I look on thee, oh, star in Heaven the fairest,
Thy gentle beam thro' trackless space thou
    bearest;
The hour of darkness is by thee made bright,
Thou lead'st us upward by pure light.
O ev'ning star; thy holy light
Was ne'er so welcome to my sight,
With glowing heart, that ne'er disclos'd;
Greet her when she in thy light reposed;
When parting from this vale a vision,
She rises to an angel's mission.
*(He continues to play, his eyes raised to
Heaven.)*

Tannhäuser now appears, wearing a ragged Pilgrim's dress, his face pale and drawn, and supporting himself with difficulty by means of a staff. *Wolfram* greets him with emotion and learns that he is still unforgiven and has resolved to re-enter the Venusberg.

The unhappy *Tannhäuser* tells of the *Pope's* refusal of a pardon:

TANNHÄUSER:

Rome I gained at last; with tears imploring,
I knelt before the rood in faith adoring.
When daylight broke, the silv'ry bells were
    pealing;
Through vaulted roof a song divine was
    stealing;
A cry of joy breaks forth from thousand
    voices—
The hope of pardon ev'ry heart rejoices.
I told what mad desires my soul had dark-
    ened,
By sinful earthly pleasure long enslav'd—
To me it seem'd that he in mercy harken'd—
A gracious word in dust and tears I crav'd.
Then he who thus I prayed replied:
"If thou hast shared the joys of Hell
If thou unholy flames hast nurs'd
That in the hill of Venus dwell,
Thou art forever more accurs'd!
And as this barren staff I hold
Ne'er will put forth a flower or leaf,
Thus shalt thou never more behold
Salvation or thy sin's relief!"

FROM A PAINTING BY KAULBACH

THE DEATH OF ELIZABETH

* *Double-Faced Record—For title of opposite side see DOUBLE-FACED TANNHÄUSER RECORDS, page 330.*

Wolfram, in horror, urges him to remain, but *Tannhäuser* refuses until *Wolfram* mentions the name of *Elizabeth*. The unhappy man, in sudden repentance, sinks to his knees, while in the distance is seen a company of minstrels bearing the body of *Elizabeth*, who has passed away. As the procession approaches, a company of Pilgrims enter and announce that the staff of the Pope had put forth green leaves as a sign that *Tannhäuser* was pardoned. The *Minstrel*, supported by *Wolfram*, gazes on the saintly face of the dead *Elizabeth*, then expires, while the Pilgrims and minstrels with great emotion exclaim:

The Lord Himself now thy bondage hath riven—
Go, enter in with the blest in His Heaven!

Curtain

DOUBLE-FACED AND MISCELLANEOUS TANNHAUSER RECORDS

Elizabeth's Prayer — By Elizabeth Wheeler, Soprano *A Night in Venice* *By Elizabeth Wheeler, Soprano, and William Wheeler, Tenor*	35096	12-inch,	$1.25
O du mein holder Abendstern (Evening Star) *(In German)* By Reinald Werrenrath, Baritone *Treue Liebe—Ach, wie ist's moglich dann* *(In German) By Emil Muench, Tenor*	35160	12-inch,	1.25
Overture—Part I — By La Scala Orchestra Overture—Part II — By La Scala Orchestra	68205	12-inch,	1.25
Fest March — By Sousa's Band *La Marseillaise—National Air of France* — By Sousa's Band	16514	10-inch,	.75
The Evening Star — By Victor Sorlin, 'Cellist *Last Rose of Summer* — *By Elizabeth Wheeler, Soprano*	16813	10-inch,	.75
Pilgrims' Chorus — By Pryor's Band *Lohengrin—Coro delle nozze (Bridal Chorus)* *(In Italian) By La Scala Chorus*	16537	10-inch,	.75

BYRON

THE REDEMPTION OF TANNHÄUSER

(Italian)

TOSCA

(*Toss'-kah*)

OPERA IN THREE ACTS

Text by Illica and Giacosa after Sardou's drama. Music by Giacomo Puccini. First produced at the Constanzi Theatre, Rome, in January, 1900. First London production July 12, 1900. First American production February 4, 1901, at the Metropolitan, the cast including Ternina, Cremonini, Scotti and Gilibert. Also produced in English by Henry W. Savage.

Characters

FLORIA TOSCA, (*Floh'-ree-ah Toss'-kah*) a celebrated singer	Soprano
MARIO CAVARADOSSI, (*Mah'-ree-oh Cav-a-rah-doss'-ee*) a painter	Tenor
BARON SCARPIA, (*Scar'-pee-ah*) chief of the police	Baritone
CESARE ANGELOTTI, (*See-zahr'-ay Ahn-jel-lot'-tee*)	Bass
A SACRISTAN	Baritone
SPOLETTA, (*Spo-let'-tah*) a police agent	Tenor
SCIARRONE, a gendarme	Bass
A JAILOR	Bass

Judge, Cardinal, Officer, Sergeant, Soldiers, Police Agents, Ladies, Nobles, Citizens.

Scene and Period: Rome, June, 1800.

The Story

Tosca is Puccini's fifth opera, and by far the most popular, next to Mme. Butterfly, which probably holds first place in the affections of opera-goers. The opera is a remarkable example of Puccini's skill in adjusting both instrumental and voice effects to the sense of the story, interpreting both the characters and the situations.

The plot is gloomy and intensely tragic, following closely the Sardou melodrama, but is relieved somewhat by the beauty of the musical setting, which confirmed Puccini's place in the first rank of modern operatic composers. The three acts of the opera are crowded with sensational events and highly dramatic situations.

The work has neither introduction nor overture. The first scene occurs in the church of *San Andrea*, where the painter, *Mario Cavaradossi*, is at work on the mural decorations. Here he has been accustomed to meet his fiancée, the beautiful *Floria Tosca*, a singer. While awaiting her, he contemplates the Magdalene he is at work on, the face being that of the unknown beauty who had frequently prayed at the altar.

Suddenly a political refugee, *Angelotti*, who has just escaped from the castle, appears, recognizes his friend *Cavaradossi*, and asks his assistance. The painter gives him food and sends him to his (*Cavaradossi's*) villa, just as *Tosca* arrives. Her lover's confused manner arouses her curiosity, and when she sees the likeness on the easel, she is jealous. He soothes her, and after her departure hurries out to guide *Angelotti*, a cannon shot from the castle meanwhile announcing the escape of the fugitive.

Scarpia and his police enter in search of the prisoner, who has been traced to the church. *Cavaradossi* is suspected as an accomplice, and *Scarpia*, who is secretly in love with *Tosca*, plans his ruin, with a view to removing from his path a dangerous rival.

PHOTO MANUEL

FARRAR AS TOSCA

In the second act *Scarpia*, putting into execution his schemes, orders *Mario's* arrest, and when the painter is brought in, sends for *Tosca* and contrives that she shall hear the cries of her lover as he is being tortured to induce him to reveal *Angelotti's* hiding place. Unable to endure *Mario's* agony, she tells *Scarpia* where the refugee is concealed. *Mario* is sent to prison, and *Scarpia* tells *Tosca* that unless she looks with favor on him, her lover shall die within an hour. To save his life she consents, but demands that they be allowed to depart in safety the next day. A mock execution is planned by *Scarpia,* who writes out a pass for the lovers. As he gives it to *Tosca,* she stabs him and runs to *Mario* with the release.

In Act III the mock execution takes place as planned, but through *Scarpia's* treachery, it proves to be a real one, and *Mario* is killed. *Tosca* afterwards throws herself from the castle parapet as they attempt to arrest her for *Scarpia's* murder.

ACT I

SCENE—*Interior of the Church of St. Andrea*

Mario Cavaradossi, the painter, enters the church, where he has been at work on a Madonna. As he uncovers the portrait, the Sacristan, who is assisting *Mario*, is surprised to discover in the face of the painting the unknown beauty whom he had noticed

COPY'T DUPONT

CARUSO AS MARIO—ACT I

of late in the church. *Mario* smilingly confesses that while she had prayed he had stolen her likeness for his Madonna. Then taking out a miniature of his betrothed, *Tosca,* he sings a lovely air in which he compares her dark beauty with the fair tresses and blue eyes of the unknown worshipper, calling it "a strange but harmonious contrast."

Recondita armonia (Strange Harmony)
By Enrico Caruso, Tenor   (*In Italian*)   **87043 10-inch, $2.00**

His musings are interrupted by the hurried entrance of a man in prison garb, panting with fear and fatigue, whom *Mario* recognizes as an old friend, *Angelotti*, a political prisoner. *Mario*, in response to his friend's appeal for assistance, hastily closes the outer door, and conceals *Angelotti* in the chapel, just as *Tosca's* voice is heard impatiently demanding admittance.

He admits her, but is anxious and ill at ease, fearing to intrust even *Tosca* with so dangerous a secret, but she notices his preoccupation and is somewhat piqued because he is not as attentive as usual. She is at first jealous and asks him if he is thinking of another woman; but soon repents, and in the charming love scene which follows endeavors to smooth his brow by planning an excursion for the morrow.

LE THÉÂTRE   TOSCA AND MARIO IN THE CHURCH—ACT I

EAMES AS TOSCA

Ora stammi a sentir (Now Listen to Me)

By Geraldine Farrar, Soprano
(*In Italian*) 88287 12-inch, $3.00

She sings of the delights of the proposed visit to the villa, and the romantic forest where they will wander and forget the cares and troubles of their professional life.

He listens but seems absent-minded, and she continues her recital of the joys of their secluded little retreat among the hills. *Mario* says she is an enchantress, and in this duet they exchange anew their vows of love.

Non la sospiri la nostra casetta (Our Cottage Secluded)

By Ruszcowska, Soprano; Cunego, Tenor
(*In Italian*) 88272 12-inch, $3.00

Tòsca now perceives the Madonna and recognizes the face as that of the *Attavanti*, sister of *Angelotti*. Her jealousy revives, and she declares that *Mario* has fallen in love with the blue eyes. Beginning another duet, he swears that none but *Tosca's* eyes are beautiful to him.

Qual occhio al mondo (No Eyes on Earth)

By Elena Ruszcowska and Egidio Cunego
(*In Italian*) 88273 12-inch, $3.00

Mario promises to meet her at the stage door that evening, and she bids her lover a tender farewell and departs.

The painter hurries to the chapel and bids *Angelotti* escape, showing him the path to the villa, where he will be safe. A cannon shot from the fortress tells that the escape of the prisoner has been discovered.

He is no sooner gone than the Sacristan and choir enter, followed soon after by *Scarpia* and his police, who have traced *Angelotti* to the church. The *Attavanti's* fan and *Mario's* empty basket are found in the chapel, and when the Sacristan says it should contain the painter's lunch, *Scarpia* suspects *Mario* of aiding the prisoner.

Tosca now returns, still doubting her lover, and *Scarpia*, divining the state of affairs, decides to add fuel to the flame of jealousy. He approaches her respectfully and sings his first air, *Divine Tosca*.

Tosca Divina (Divine Tosca!)

By Gustav Berle-Resky, Baritone
(*In Italian*) *16745 10-inch, $0.75

He praises her noble character and devout habits. She is inattentive and scarcely hears him, until he insinuatingly says that she is not like other women who come here to meet their lovers. She asks him what he means and *Scarpia* shows her the fan which he had found in the church. *Tosca* is now convinced that *Mario* has been deceiving her, and in a jealous rage she leaves the church, weeping.

Te Deum

By Giuseppe Magge, Bass, and La Scala Chorus (*In Italian*) *55008 12-inch, $1.50

MARTIN AS MARIO—ACT I

---

* *Double-Faced Record—For title of opposite side see* DOUBLE-FACED TOSCA RECORDS, *page 337.*

The act closes with a *Te Deum,* sung in celebration of the defeat of Bonaparte, and the scene at the fall of the curtain is a most impressive one, the solemn strains of the service sounding through the church, while *Scarpia* kneels, apparently in reverence, but secretly plotting his diabolical crimes.

ACT II

SCENE—*A Room in Scarpia's Apartments in the Farnese Palace*

When the curtain rises *Scarpia* is shown at his supper, restless and agitated, awaiting the report of his police, who have been sent to arrest *Mario* and *Angelotti.* Hearing *Tosca's* voice in the apartments of the Queen below, where she is singing at a *soiree,* he sends her a note saying he has news of

CLICHE BOYER   THE TORTURE—ACT II

her lover. He is certain she will come for *Mario's* sake, and sure that his plans will succeed. He then sings his celebrated soliloquy. *Scarpia* loves such a conquest as this— no tender vows in the moonlight for him! He prefers taking what he desires by force, then when wearied he is ready for further conquest. This, in short, is his creed— God has created divers wines and many types of beauty— he prefers to enjoy as many of them as possible!

Mario is brought in by the police, who report that *Angelotti* cannot be found. *Scarpia* is furious, and tries to force *Mario* to reveal the hiding place of the fugitive; but he refuses to speak, and is ordered into the torture chamber adjoining. *Tosca* comes in answer to *Scarpia's* summons and is told that *Mario* is being tortured into a confession. Unable to bear the sound of his groans, she reveals the hiding place of *Angelotti.*

Scarpia, in triumph, orders the torture to cease, but sends *Mario* to prison, telling him he must die. *Tosca* tries to go with him but is forced to remain.

Then begins the great scene of the opera, which *Scarpia* begins by offering to save *Mario's* life. She scornfully asks him his price, and he proposes that *Tosca* shall accept his attentions in order to save her lover's life. He then sings his famous *Cantabile,* given here in two parts.

Cantabile Scarpia (Venal, My Enemies Call Me)
By Antonio Scotti, Baritone 88122 12-inch, $3.00

Gia mi struggea   (You Have Scorned Me)
(Last Part of Cantabile)
By Ernesto Badini (*In Italian*) 45016 10-in., $1.00

He tells her that he has long loved her and had sworn to possess her. She scorns him, but when he tells her that *Mario* shall die in an hour and exults in his power, her spirit is broken, and weeping for shame, she sings that loveliest and most pathetic of airs, *Vissi d'arte.*

PHOTO GARO

SCOTTI AS SCARPIA

Vissi d'arte e d'amor   (Love and Music)

By Nellie Melba, Soprano	(*In Italian*)	88075	12-inch,	$3.00
By Geraldine Farrar, Soprano	(*In Italian*)	88192	12-inch,	3.00
By Emma Eames, Soprano	(*In Italian*)	88010	12-inch,	3.00
By Lucille Marcell, Soprano	(*In Italian*)	76018	12-inch,	2.00
By Maria Bronzoni, Soprano	(*In Italian*)	45017	10-inch,	1.00

TOSCA SECURING THE DAGGER

One of the most interesting comparisons to be found in the Victor's opera list is in a hearing of these five renditions, by five famous *Toscas*—Melba, the Australian; Farrar and Eames, the Americans; Marcell, the Frenchwoman; and Bronzoni, the Italian, the latter record being doubled with *Mario's* 3d Act air.

This highly impassioned number is given its full dramatic value by Mme. Melba, whose performance of the ill-fated *Floria Tosca* is always an impressive one.

Farrar, in her rendition, delivers this touching appeal of the unfortunate *Tosca* with much pathos and simplicity. It is probably the most perfect and beautiful of all the Farrar records.

The air is also a fine test of Mme. Eames' dramatic ability, and this scene is one in which she has made one of her greatest triumphs.

The unhappy woman asks what she has done that Heaven should forsake her. *Scarpia,* who is watching her intently, calls her attention to the sound of drums, summoning the escort for the condemned prisoners, and demands her answer. She yields, bowing her head for shame. *Scarpia* is overjoyed, and when she insists that *Mario* shall be set free he consents, but says a mock execution is necessary.

It is agreed that after this pretended execution, *Mario* shall have his liberty, but *Tosca* demands a safe escape from the country for them both. While *Scarpia* is writing the document, *Tosca* contrives to secure the dagger from the table, and as *Scarpia* approaches to give it to her and then take her in his arms, she stabs him, crying that thus she gives him the kiss he desired. In a prolonged and highly dramatic scene she takes the paper from *Scarpia's* dead fingers, then washes her hands in a bowl on the table, places the two candles at the dead man's head and the cross on his bosom, then goes out, turning for a last look at the lifeless body as the curtain falls.

LE THEATRE

THE MURDER OF SCARPIA—ACT II

ACT III

(A terrace of San Angelo Castle, outside the prison cell of Cavaradossi. View of Rome by night)

The music of the opening act is most effective, with its accompaniment of pealing church bells, and it is splendidly played by Mr. Pryor in the *Tosca Selection.* This entire prelude is also given by an Italian orchestra under the direction of Sabaino, doubled with the Te Deum of Act I.

Prelude

By Italian Orchestra, M. Sabaino, Director

55008 12-inch, $1.50

Mario is brought out from his cell, is shown the official death warrant, and told he has but one hour to live. He asks permission to write a note to *Tosca,* and is given paper and pen. He begins to write, but engrossed with memories of the past, he pauses and sings passionately of his loved one, whom he expects never to see again.

MARIO AND TOSCA—ACT III

CLICHÉ BOYER

THE EXECUTION—ACT III

E lucevan le stelle (The Stars Were Shining)

By Enrico Caruso, Tenor	(*Piano acc.*)	(*In Italian*)	87044	10-inch, $2.00
By Riccardo Martin, Tenor		(*In Italian*)	87050	10-inch, 2.00
By Franco de Gregorio, Tenor		(*In Italian*)	45017	10-inch, 1.00

Mario at first recalls their former meetings on starlight nights in quiet gardens; then, feeling the bitter regret of loss of life and all that he holds dear, the voice rises in passages of tragical import and power as the air proceeds. The regret, the grief and the hopelessness of the situation are depicted by Caruso with intense pathos, the air closing with a sob—an effect by which this singer can effectively express the extremity of passionate grief.

In Martin's rendition this tenor is at his best, singing the lovely Puccini music with much beauty of tone. The de Gregorio record is a double-faced one, being paired with Mme. Bronzoni's *Vissi d'arte*.

Tosca now enters, and joyfully telling *Mario* he is to be free, shows him the safe conduct, telling him how she has killed *Scarpia*. He gazes at her with compassion and regrets that these hands—such tender and beautiful hands—should be compelled to foul themselves with a scoundrel's blood. She then explains that a mock execution has been arranged, and instructs him to fall down when the volley is fired, and when the soldiers are gone they are to escape together.

In a beautiful duet, recorded here in two parts, they rejoice in their hopes for the future.

Amaro sol per te m'era il morire (The Bitterness of Death)

By Elena Ruszcowska, Soprano, and Egidio Cunego, Tenor

(*In Italian*) 88274 12-inch, $3.00

Trionfa di nuova speme

By Elena Ruszcowska and Egidio Cunego   (*In Italian*) 87069 10-inch, 2.00

The squad of soldiers now enter and the pretended execution takes place as planned; the shots are fired and *Mario* falls as if dead. *Tosca* waits till the firing party is gone, whispering to her lover not to get up until the footsteps have died away. *"Now, Mario, all is safe,"* she cries, but is astounded that he does not obey her. She rushes to him, only to find that *Scarpia* had added another piece of treachery to his long list, having secretly ordered *Mario* to be killed. She throws herself on his body in an agony of grief.

Spoletta and soldiers now come running in and announce the murder of *Scarpia*; but when they attempt to arrest *Tosca* she leaps from the castle wall and is killed.

DOUBLE-FACED AND MISCELLANEOUS TOSCA RECORDS

{ Te Deum   By Giuseppe Maggi and Chorus   (*In Italian*) }
{ Preludio—*Atto III*   By Italian Orchestra }   55008   12-inch, $1.50

{ Tosca Selection   By Pryor's Band }
{   *Manon Lescaut Intermezzo*   By Pryor's Band }   35003   12-inch,   1.25

{ Già mi struggea   By Ernesto Badini, Baritone   (*In Italian*) }
{   Manon Lescaut—Donna non vidi mai   (*Puccini*) }
{   By Egidio Cunego, Tenor   (*In Italian*) }   45016   10-inch,   1.00

{ Vissi d'arte   By Maria Bronzoni, Soprano   (*In Italian*) }
{ E lucevan le stelle   By De Gregorio, Soprano   (*In Italian*) }   45017   10-inch,   1.00

{ Tosca—*Tosca Divina*   By Berl-Resky, Baritone   (*In Italian*) }
{   Preghiera—*Alla mente confusa*   (*Tosti*) }
{   By Gustav Berl-Resky, Baritone   (*In Italian*) }   16745   10-inch,   .75

THE TE DEUM, FINALE—ACT I

Melba

LA TRAVIATA

(Lah Trah-vee-ah'-tah)

OPERA IN THREE ACTS

Text by Piave, founded on Dumas' "Lady of the Camelias," but the period is changed to the time of Louis XIV. Score by Giuseppe Verdi. First presented in Venice, March 6, 1853. First London production May 24, 1856. First New York production December 3, 1856.

Characters of the Opera

VIOLETTA VALERY, a courtesan..................................Soprano
FLORA, friend of Violetta.....................................Mezzo-Soprano
ANNINA, confidante of Violetta................................Soprano
ALFREDO GERMONT, *(Zher-maw)* lover of Violetta ....Tenor
GIORGIO GERMONT, his father...................................Baritone
GASTONE, Viscount of Letorieres...............................Tenor
BARON DOUPHOL, a rival of Alfred..............................Baritone
DOCTOR GRENVIL, a physician...................................Bass
GIUSEPPE, servant to Violetta.................................Tenor

Chorus of Ladies and Gentlemen, friends of Violetta and Flora.
Mute Personages: Matadors, Picadors, Gypsies, Servants, Masks, etc.

Scene and Period: Paris and environs, about the year 1700.

Verdi's La Traviata is based upon a well-known play by Alexandre Dumas, *La Dame aux camelias*, familiar in its dramatic form as *Camille*. It is one of the most beautiful works of its class, and is full of lovely melodies; while the story of the unfortunate *Violetta* has caused many tears to be shed by sympathetic listeners.

FRANCESCO PÍAVE
(1810-1876)
LIBRETTIST OF
TRAVIATA

VERDI AT THE TIME OF THE FIRST TRAVIATA PRODUCTION

The opera met with but indifferent success at its first production. Several ludicrous incidents aroused the laughter of the audience, the climax being reached when the *Violetta* (Mme. Donatelli), who happened to be very stout, declaimed in feeble accents that she was dying of consumption! This was too much for the Venetian sense of humor, and the house exploded with mirth, utterly spoiling the final scene.

The opera was then revised, eighteenth century costumes and settings being substituted for the modern ones first used; and the new version was produced in various cities with success, the London season being particularly brilliant.

The plot, being quite familiar, will be but briefly sketched here. *Violetta*, a courtesan of Paris, is holding a brilliant revel in her home. Among the guests is a young man from Provence, *Alfred*, who is in love with *Violetta*, and after much persuasion, the spoiled beauty agrees to leave her gay life and retire with him to an humble apartment near Paris. After a few brief months of happiness, the lovers are discovered by *Alfred's* father, who pleads with *Violetta* to release his son from her promises. She yields for his sake, and resumes her former life in Paris. *Alfred*, not knowing the real cause of her desertion, seeks her out and publicly insults her. Too late he discovers the sacrifice *Violetta* has made, and when he returns, full of remorse, he finds her dying of consumption, and she expires in his arms.

Prelude to Act I

By La Scala Orchestra   *68027   12-inch, $1.25

The prelude, one of the loveliest bits in the opera, is played in fine style by the famous orchestra of La Scala.

Double-Faced Record—For title of opposite side see DOUBLE-FACED LA TRAVIATA RECORDS, page 344.

ACT I

SCENE—*Drawing-room in the House of Violetta*

A gay revel is in progress at the house of *Violetta*, and the act opens with a lively chorus, followed by a rousing drinking song, given by *Alfred*, in which *Violetta* joins.

Libiam nei lieti calici   (A Bumper We'll Drain)

By Amelia Rizzini, Soprano; Emilio Perea, Tenor; and La Scala Chorus   *(In Italian)* *62415 10-inch, $0.75

ALFRED:
A bumper we'll drain from the wine-cup flowing,
That fresh charms to beauty is lending,
O'er fleeting moments, so quickly ending,
Gay pleasure alone should reign.

VIOLETTA:
Enjoy the hour, for rapidly
The joys of life are flying—
Like summer flow'rets dying—
Improve them while we may!
The present with fervor invites us.
Its flattering call obey.

CHORUS:
Enjoy then the wine-cup with songs of pleasure
That make night so cheerful and smiling,
In this charming paradise, beguiling,
That scarcely we heed the day.

The dance commences, and all go into the ballroom except *Violetta* and *Alfred*, who remain for a charming love scene. In a beautiful duet the lovers speak of their first meeting.

Un di felice   (Rapturous Moment)

By Marie A. Michailowa, Soprano, and A. M. Davidow, Tenor   *(In Russian)* 61138 10-inch, $1.00
By Emma Trentini, Soprano, and Gino Martinez-Patti, Tenor   *(In Italian)* *62067 10-inch, .75

Alfred now bids her a tender farewell and takes his departure, and *Violetta* sings her great air, one of the most brilliant of all coloroture numbers.

{ Ah, fors' è lui (The One of Whom I Dreamed)
{ Sempre libera (The Round of Pleasure)

By Luisa Tetrazzini, Soprano	*(In Italian)*	88293	12-inch, $3.00
By Marcella Sembrich, Soprano	*(In Italian)*	88018	12-inch, 3.00
By Nellie Melba, Soprano	*(In Italian)*	88064	12-inch, 3.00
By Blanche Arral, Soprano	*(In French)*	74132	12-inch, 1.50
By Giuseppina Huguet, Soprano (Part I)	*(In Italian)*	*62084	10-inch, .75
By Giuseppina Huguet, Soprano, and Pietro Lara, Tenor (Part II)	*(In Italian)*	*62084	10-inch, .75

The aria occurs at the close of the act. *Violetta*, wonderstruck at finding herself the object of a pure love, begins the soliloquy, *E strano*, saying:

How wondrous!
His words deep within my heart are graven!
No love of mortal yet hath moved me.

Shall I dare disdain it,
And choose the empty follies that now surround me?

She then sings the plaintive air, *Ah, fors' è lui*, and gives herself up to the spell of awakening love:

VIOLETTA:
Ah, was it he my heart foretold, when in the throng of pleasure,
Oft have I joy'd to shadow forth one whom alone I'd treasure.
He who with watchful tenderness guarded my waning powers,

Strewing my way with flowers,
Waking my heart to love!
Ah, now I feel that 'tis love and love alone,
Sole breath of all in the life, the life universal,
Mysterious power, guiding the fate of mortals,
Sorrow and sweetness of this poor earth.

The animated last movement follows, as the unhappy woman shakes off the illusion and once more vows to devote her life to pleasure.

Double-Faced Record—For title of opposite side see DOUBLE-FACED LA TRAVIATA RECORDS, page 344.

What folly! what folly!
For me there's no returning!
In ev'ry fierce and wild delight,
I'll steep my sense and die!
I'll fulfill the round of pleasure,
Joying, toying from flower to flower,
I will drain a brimming measure from the cup
    of rosy joy.
Never weary, each dawning morrow
Flies to bear me some new rapture
Ever fresh delights I'll borrow,
I will banish all annoy!

The Victor owner has no fewer than five renditions of this great air to choose from and is likely to be embarrassed in his attempt to choose the best, but will probably compromise by selecting two or more of them.

Melba's singing of this air, which is one of the supremely beautiful songs that stand out strongly among much that is commonplace in compositions of its class, is marked not only by great brilliancy, but by dramatic fervor, and she makes a marked contrast between the sadness of the prelude and the forced gayety of the finale.

It is a fact worthy of note in connection with Melba's rendition that both portions of the aria (formerly issued in two parts) now are included in one record.

Mme. Tetrazzini chose this opera for her first appearance both in London and New York, and the

PHOTO CLERKE, LONDON

MELBA AS VIOLETTA

choice was an admirable one, as Verdi's work exhibits all the soprano's fine qualities—not only her wonderful coloratura but the warmth and color which she possesses in a high degree.

Many operatic sopranos regard the part of *Violetta* merely as a background for a vocal display. Tetrazzini on the other hand, while not neglecting the opportunities for coloratura, brings to the part a human tenderness and a pathos which are most affecting. Her rendering of this familiar *Ah, fors' è lui* is a most musical one, with its astonishing feats of execution; and the ease with which she trills an E *in alt* can only be described as amazing.

Mme. Sembrich in her turn fully realizes the composer's ideal in the presentation of this florid and ornamental air, and seldom has a more vital and satisfying rendition been heard than that of this mistress of vocal art. She sings it with such purity and mellowness of voice and such a brilliancy of vocalization that we can but wonder at the perfection of art which makes such a record possible.

Other lower-priced, but nevertheless very fine renderings, are provided by Mme. Arral and Mme. Huguet—these records, however, including only part of the air.

ACT II

SCENE—*Interior of a Country House near Paris*

Alfred enters and soliloquizes upon his new-found happiness.

ALFRED:
    Three months have already flown
    Since my belov'd Violetta
    Left for me her riches and admirers.
    Yet now contented in this retreat, so quiet
    She forgets all for me.

He then sings his *Dei miei bollenti.*

COPY'T MISHKIN

CONSTANTINO AS ALFRED
(ACT II, SCENE I)

Dei miei bollenti spiriti (Wild My Dream of Youth)

By Aristodemo Giorgini, Tenor

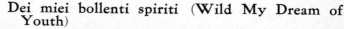

(*In Italian*) 76011 12-inch, $2.00

COPY'T MISHKIN
CONSTANTINO
AS ALFRED
(ACT II, SCENE II)

By Florencio Constantino, Tenor
(In Italian) 74083 12-inch, $1.50
By Emilio Perea, Tenor
(In Italian) *68156 12-inch, 1.25
By Alberto Amadi, Tenor
(In Italian) *63314 10-inch, .75

ALFRED:
Fever'd and wild my dream of youth,
No star on high to guide me,
She shone on me with ray benign,
And trouble fled away!
When low she whisper'd: "Live for me, on
    earth I love but thee,"
Ah, since that bright, that blessed day,
In Heaven, 'mid joys celestial,
In Heaven I seem to be!

Alfred learns from *Violetta's* faithful maid that she has been obliged to sell her jewels for their support. He is much ashamed and leaves for Paris to secure some money.

Violetta returns and is surprised at *Alfred's* sudden departure. A visitor is announced, who proves to be *Germont,* the father of *Alfred.* He has been greatly distressed at his son's entanglement, and comes to beg *Violetta* to release the young man from his promises. She is much moved, and her bearing makes a favorable impression on *Germont,* especially when he learns that she has sold her property for *Alfred's* sake.

Pura siccome un angelo (Pure as an Angel)

By G. Battaglioli, Soprano, and Ernesto Badini,
Baritone (In Italian) *45001 10-inch, $1.00
By Renzo Minolfi, Baritone (In Italian) *62415 10-inch, .75

Non sapete (Ah, You Know Not)

By Ernesto Badini, Baritone (In Italian) *45028 10-inch, $1.00

In this air *Germont* pleads for his own daughter, whose engagement to a youth of Provence will be broken if *Alfred* does not return home. *Violetta* at first refuses, saying that her love for *Alfred* is above all other considerations, but when *Germont* says:

Be to my home and lov'd ones   While yet there may be time.
Our angel, good, consoling.   'Tis Heav'n itself that bids me speak,
Violetta, oh, consider well   These words in faith sublime!

she finally yields, agreeing to leave *Alfred* forever, and they sing a melodious duet:

Dite alla giovine (Say to Thy Daughter)

By Maria Galvany, Soprano, and Titta Ruffo, Baritone
(In Italian) 92503 12-inch, $4.00

Germont expresses his gratitude, embraces the weeping *Violetta* and departs, while the unhappy woman writes to *Alfred* of her decision and returns to Paris.

When the young man returns he is driven to despair by *Violetta's* note, and repulses his father, who pleads with him to return. *Germont* then sings his most beautiful number, the *Di Provenza.*

Di Provenza il mar (Thy Home in Fair Provence)

By G. Mario Sammarco, Baritone (In Italian) 88314 12-inch, $3.00
By Mario Ancona, Baritone (In Italian) 87006 10-inch, 2.00
By Giuseppe Campanari, Baritone (In Italian) 81071 10-inch, 2.00
By Ernesto Badini, Baritone (In Italian) *45001 10-inch, 1.00

In this touching appeal he asks his son to return to his home in Provence and to his father's heart.

Sammarco sings the number with a wealth of tenderness and expression, revealing a smooth, rich and resonant baritone which is good to hear, while a fine rendition by Ancona and a popular-priced record by Badini are also offered.

Double-Faced Record—For title of opposite side see DOUBLE-FACED LA TRAVIATA RECORDS, page 344.

GERMONT:
From fair Provence's soil and sea,
Who hath won thy heart away?
From thy native sunny clime,
What strange fate caus'd thee to stray?
Oh, remember in thy woe
All the joy that waits for thee,
All the peace thy heart would know,
Only there, still found may be.
Ah, thy father old and worn,
What he felt thou ne'er canst know,
In thine absence, so forlorn
Seem'd his home, with grief and woe.
But I find thee now again,
If my hope doth not mislead,
If yet honor doth remain
With its voice not mute or dead,
Heav'n sends me aid!

Alfred refuses to yield to his father's plea, and departs for Paris in search of *Violetta*.

SCENE II—*A Richly Furnished Salon in Flora's Palace. On the Right a Gaming Table*

FARRAR AS VIOLETTA—ACT III

As the curtain rises *Flora* and her friends are discussing the separation of the lovers and *Flora* says she expects *Violetta* will soon arrive with the *Baron*. *Alfred* enters, and remarking with assumed indifference that he knows nothing of *Violetta's* whereabouts, begins to gamble and wins heavily. The *Baron* appears, accompanied by *Violetta*, who is agitated at the sight of *Alfred*, but he pretends not to see her and challenges the *Baron* to a game, again winning large amounts. Supper is announced and all leave the room except *Violetta* and *Alfred*, who linger behind. He charges her with her falseness, and, in furtherance of the promise made to *Germont*, she pretends to him that she loves the *Baron*. *Alfred* then loses all control over himself, and throwing open the doors, he calls to the guests to re-enter.

Questa donna conoscete (Know Ye All This Woman?)

By Alberto Amadi, Tenor   (*In Italian*) *63314   10-inch, $0.75

Pointing to *Violetta*, *Alfred* cries wildly:

ALFRED:
All she possess'd, this woman here,
Hath for my love expended.
I, blindly, basely, wretchedly,
This to accept, condescended.

But there is time to purge me yet
From stains that shame, confound me.
Bear witness all around me
That here I pay the debt!

and completes the insult by throwing at her feet the money he had just won.

At this moment *Alfred's* father, *Germont*, enters, and is horrified at the scene which confronts him. Then follows the splendid finale, one of the greatest of Verdi's concerted numbers.

Alfredo, di questo core (Alfred, Thou Knowest Not)

By Giuseppina Huguet, Soprano; G. Pini-Corsi, Tenor; Ernesto
Badini, Baritone; and Chorus   (*In Italian*) *58392   12-inch, $1.00

The emotions of the various characters are expressed by the librettist as follows:

GUESTS:
Oh, to what baseness thy passions have led
To wound thus fatally one who has loved thee!
GERMONT:
Of scorn most worthy himself doth render
Who wounds in anger a woman tender!
My son, where is he? No more I see him;
In thee, Alfred, I seek him; but in vain!
ALFRED (*aside*):
Ah! yes, 'twas shameful! a deed abhorrent!
A jealous fury—love's madd'ning torrent.
But now that fury is all expended,
Remorse and horror to me remain.

BARON:
This shameful insult against this lady
Offends all present; behold me ready
To punish the outrage!
VIOLETTA (*reviving*):
Ah, lov'd Alfredo, this heart's devotion
Thou canst not fathom yet—its fond emotion!
When, hereafter the truth comes o'er thee
May Heaven in pity then spare thee remorse!
(*Germont goes out supporting Alfred, who is almost in a state of collapse. The fainting Violetta is led away by her friends, and the guests begin to disperse as the curtain falls.*)

Double-Faced Record—For title of opposite side see DOUBLE-FACED LA TRAVIATA RECORDS, page 344.

ACT III

(Violetta's apartment. She is asleep on the couch, while her maid dozes by the fire)

As the curtain rises the doctor's knock is heard, and *Dr. Grenvil, Violetta's* physician, enters and attends his patient, afterwards telling the maid that she has not long to live. Left alone, *Violetta* reads again a letter she has received from *Germont.*

"*Thou hast kept thy promise. The duel took place and the Baron was wounded, but is improving. Alfredo is in foreign countries. Your sacrifice has been revealed to him by me, and he will return to you for pardon. Haste to recover; thou deserveth a bright future.*"

Giorgio Germont

"Alas, it is too late," she exclaims, and sings her beautiful and pathetic "Farewell."

Addio del passato (Farewell to the Bright Visions)

By Alice Nielsen, Soprano (*In Italian*) 64068 10-inch, $1.00
By Marie Michailowa, Soprano (*In Russian*) 61178 10-inch, 1.00

VIOLETTA:

Farewell to the bright visions I once fondly cherish'd,
Already the roses that deck'd me have perish'd;
The love of Alfredo is lost, past regaining,
That cheer'd me when fainting, my spirit sustaining.

Pity the stray one, and send her consolation,
Oh, pardon her transgressions, and send her salvation.
The sorrows and enjoyments of life will soon be over,
The dark tomb in oblivion this mortal form will cover!

Alfred now enters, filled with remorse, and asks forgiveness, which is freely granted; and *Violetta,* forgetting her illness, plans with *Alfred* to leave Paris forever. They sing this melodious duet, "Gay Paris We'll Leave With Gladness."

Parigi o cara (Far from Gay Paris)

By Alice Nielsen and Florencio Constantino (*Italian*) 74075 12-inch, $1.50
By Amelia Rizzini, Soprano, and Emilio Perea, Tenor *62067 10-inch, .75

At the close of the duet *Violetta's* overtaxed strength gives way, and she collapses in her lover's arms. He notices for the first time her paleness, and is much alarmed, sending the maid to call the doctor. *Dr. Grenvil* soon enters, accompanied by *Germont,* and after an affecting scene, in which *Germont* blames himself for all that has occurred, *Violetta* expires, and the curtain falls on a sorrowful tableau.

DOUBLE-FACED AND MISCELLANEOUS TRAVIATA RECORDS

Prelude	By La Scala Orchestra	68027	12-inch, $1.25
L'Africana—Marcia Indiana	By La Scala Orchestra		
Traviata Selection	By Pryor's Band	35076	12-inch, 1.25
Trovatore Selection	By Pryor's Band		
Alfredo, di questo core	By Huguet, Pini-Corsi and Badini	68070	12-inch, 1.25
Ruy Blas—O dolce volutta	By Grisi and Lara (*In Italian*)		
Dei miei bollente (Wild My Dream)	By Perea (*In Italian*)	68156	12-inch, 1.25
Ernani—Ferma crudele	By Bernacchi, Colazza and de Luna		
Non sapete (Ah, You Know Not)	By Ernesto Badini	45028	10-inch, 1.00
Manon—Gavotta	By Giuseppina Huguet (*In Italian*)		
Di Provenza il mar	By Ernesto Badini (*In Italian*)	45001	10-inch, 1.00
Pura siccome un angelo	By Battaglioli and Badini (*In Italian*)		
Ah, fors' è lui	By Giuseppina Huguet (*In Italian*)	62084	10-inch, .75
Sempre libera	By Huguet and Lara (*In Italian*)		
Un di felice, eterea	By Trentini and Martinez-Patti		
Parigi o cara	By Amelia Rizzini, Soprano, and	62067	10-inch, .75
Emilio Perea, Tenor	(*In Italian*)		
Pura siccome un angelo	By Renzo Minolfi (*In Italian*)		
Libiam nei lieti calici (A Bumper We'll Drain)		62415	10-inch, .75
	By Rizzini, Perea and Chorus (*In Italian*)		
Dei miei bollenti spiriti	By Alberto Amadi (*In Italian*)	63314	10-inch, .75
Questa donna conoscete	By Alberto Amadi (*In Italian*)		

* *Double-Faced Record—For title of opposite side see above list.*

SCENES FROM TRISTAN

TRISTAN UND ISOLDE
(Tris'-tahn oondt Ees-sol'-deh)

(Italian)

TRISTANO E ISOTTA
(Trees-tah'-noh ay Ees-sot'-tah)

(English)

TRISTAN AND ISOLDE
(Tris-tan and Iss-ol'-dih)

OPERA IN THREE ACTS

Words and music by Richard Wagner, the plot being derived from an old Celtic poem of the same name, written by Gottfried of Strasburg, who flourished in the thirteenth century—though Wagner has changed the narrative sufficiently to make it his own. *Tristan* is one of the most popular of legendary heroes and has been treated of by numerous writers, among them Tennyson, Matthew Arnold and Swinburne.

Wagner's *Tristan und Isolde* was first presented in Munich, June 10, 1865. First London production June 20, 1882. First American performance in New York, December 1, 1885.

Gadski as Isolde

Characters

TRISTAN, a Cornish knight, nephew of King Mark..Tenor
KING MARK of Cornwall.........................Bass
ISOLDE, Princess of Ireland....................Soprano
KURVENAL, Tristan's devoted servant..........Baritone
MELOT, (*May'-lot*) one of King Mark's courtiers....Tenor
BRANGÄNE, (*Bran-gay'-neh*) Isolde's friend and
    attendant..............................Soprano
A SHEPHERD................................Tenor
A STEERSMAN ....Baritone
A SAILOR LAD..............................Tenor
  Chorus of Sailors, Knights, Esquires and Men-at-Arms.

ORIGINAL PROGRAM OF TRISTAN, MUNICH, 1865

Although completed in 1859, Tristan was not produced until six years later. Through the strenuous efforts of King Ludwig II of Bavaria, it was ultimately brought out in Munich with distinct artistic success—Schnorr, the tenor, scoring brilliantly in the rôle of *Tristan*. Previous to this time, however, it had been underlined for performance in Vienna, but was abandoned after fifty-seven rehearsals.

The opera did not find its way to America until it was more than twenty years old, but since that time has grown steadily in popularity. Some notable productions occurred in 1895 with Sucher, Alvary, Brema and Fischer; in 1896 with the De Reszkes, Nordica and Brema; in 1901 with Ternina and Van Dyke; and in 1910 with Fremstad, Knote, Homer and Van Rooy, this being Gustave Mahler's American début as a conductor.

This great drama of love and hatred, with its wonderful music, is now quite generally admitted to be the finest of the master's operas. Written at the time of Wagner's own love affair (with Mathilde Wesendonck), it is supposed that he sought to emphasize the fact that love cannot always be bound by conventions.

This wonderful tragedy of love and fate requires for its adequate production artists who cannot only act with intelligence, but who are able to make the music itself express the tremendous tide of human passion, from fiercest hate to fiercest love, which sweeps through the opera. Such an artist is Gadski, whose *Isolde* is one of the greatest impersonations of recent years. She is in every way the embodiment of Wagner's heroine, and sings this wonderful music with great skill, making it express in turn tenderness, disdain, scorn and passion.

KURVENAL

Two numbers from the opera have been sung for the Victor by Mme. Gadski, and will be considered in their proper places in the story briefly sketched here.

Tristan, a Cornish knight, has a quarrel with *Morold*, an Irish chieftain who had been sent to collect tribute, and kills him; and after the custom of the time, sends back his head, which is given to his affianced, an Irish princess, *Isolde*. *Tristan* himself had received a dangerous wound which fails to heal, and he resolves to assume the name of *Tantris* and seek the assistance of *Isolde*, who is famed for her knowledge of the art of healing. *Isolde*, however, recognizes him by a notch in his sword, which fits exactly a piece of metal she had extracted from the head of *Morold*. She plans to kill him, but falls in love instead, while he merely sees in her a good wife for his uncle, *King Mark*.

347

Preludio (Prelude)

By La Scala Orchestra   68210   12-inch, $1.25

COPY'T DUPONT

VAN DYCK AS TRISTAN

The first act shows the deck of the ship which is conveying *Isolde* and *Tristan* to Cornwall, she having accepted *King Mark's* proposal, made through his nephew. During the voyage, however, the refusal of *Tristan* to see her, the exultation of the sailors over the killing of *Morold* (which freed Cornwall from its subjection to *Isolde's* royal father), and detestation of the loveless marriage she is about to contract, infuriate the Princess, and she resolves to die and drag *Tristan* down to death with her. She tells *Tristan* she is aware of his crime in killing her lover, and demands vengeance. He admits her right to kill him and offers his sword, but she bids her maid, *Brangäne,* prepare two cups of poison from her casket. *Brangäne,* unwilling to see her mistress die, secretly substitutes for the poison a love potion, the effect of which is immediate, and the lovers sink into each other's arms just as the ship approaches the shore and the King arrives to claim his bride.

Act II takes place in the garden outside *Isolde's* chamber. The King has gone on a hunting expedition, but *Brangäne* fears that it is merely a ruse, and thinks the King's courtier, *Melot,* suspects the true state of affairs. *Brangäne* then confesses that she intentionally substituted the philtre for the poisoned cup intended for *Tristan.*

BRAGÄNE:
  Fatal folly!
  The fell pow'r of that potion!
  That I framed
  A fraud for once
  Thy orders to oppose!
	Had I been deaf and blind,
	Thy work were then thy death!
	But thy distress,
	Thy distraction of grief,
	My work has contrived them,
	I own it!

This confession meets with but faint reproaches from *Isolde,* who gives herself up wholly to the intoxication of the potion, and sings with growing exaltation:

Dein Werk (Thy Act)

By Johanna Gadski, Soprano
(*In German*)   88165   12-inch, $3.00

ISOLDE:
  Thy act?
  O foolish girl!
  Love's goddess dost thou not know?
  The witch whose will the world obeys;
  Life and death she holds in her hands,
  She waketh hate into love!
  The work of death
  I took into my own hands;
  Love's goddess saw
  And gave her good commands.
  Planning our fate in her own way.
  How she may bend it, how she may end it,
  Still hers am I solely;
  What she may make me, whereso'er take me
  So let me obey her wholly!

COPY'T DUPONT

GADSKI AS ISOLDE

Refusing to heed *Brangäne's* warning, *Isolde* gives the signal for *Tristan's* coming by extinguishing the torch. He appears, and a long love scene ensues, interrupted by the return of the King, who surprises the lovers in a fond embrace. *Mark* bitterly reproaches his nephew, and *Melot,* shouting "treason," stabs *Tristan,* inflicting a fatal wound.

The third act shows *Tristan* dying of the wound at his castle in *Bretagne,* whither he has been carried by his faithful servant, *Kurvenal,* who has sent for *Isolde,* knowing that she alone can cure his master's wound by means of her healing arts.

Despairing of her coming, *Tristan* in his delirium tears off his bandages and is at the point of death when *Isolde* arrives, and dies in her arms. *King Mark* and his courtiers, closely pursuing *Isolde,* now arrive and are attacked by *Kurvenal,* who kills *Melot* and is himself slain by *Mark's* soldiers. *Mark,* seeing *Tristan* dead and *Isolde* senseless on his

body, repents his rage and gives way to grief. *Isolde* revives, and when she realizes that *Tristan* is dead, her grief bursts forth in the heartrending *Love-Death motive:*

THE LOVE DEATH:

So stur ben wir, um un ge trennt,

Then she sings this wondrous death song, so full of touching sadness and inexpressible sweetness, and expires upon the body of *Tristan.*

Isolde's Liebestod (Isolde's Love-Death)

By Johanna Gadski, Soprano
(*In German*) 88058 12-inch, $3.00
By La Scala Orchestra (*Double-faced—See below*)
68210 12-inch, 1.25

COPY'T DUPONT

JEAN DE RESZKE
AS TRISTAN

PANEL BY STASSEN   ISOLDE'S LIEBESTOD

ISOLDE (*unconscious of all around her, turning her eyes with rising inspiration on Tristan's body*):
Mild and softly he is smiling;
How his eyelids sweetly open!
See, oh comrades, see you not
How he beameth ever brighter—
How he rises ever radiant
Steeped in starlight, borne above?
See you not how his heart
With lion zest, calmly happy
Beats in his breast?
From his lips in Heavenly rest,
Sweetest breath he softly sends.
Harken, friends!
Hear and feel ye not?
Is it I alone am hearing
Strains so tender and endearing?
Passion swelling, all things telling,
Gently bounding, from him sounding,
In me pushes, upward rushes.
Trumpet tone that round me gushes.
Brighter growing, o'er me flowing,
Are these breezes airy pillows?
Are they balmy beauteous billows?
How they rise and gleam and glisten!
Shall I breathe them? Shall I listen?
Shall I sip them, dive within them?
To my panting breathing win them?
In the breezes around, in the harmony sound,
In the world's driving whirlwind be drown'd—
And, sinking, be drinking—
In a kiss, highest bliss!
(*Isolde sinks, as if transfigured, in Brängane's arms upon Tristan's body. Profound emotion and grief of the bystanders. Mark invokes a blessing on the dead. Curtain.*)

DOUBLE-FACED TRISTAN AND ISOLDE RECORD

{Prelude
{Isolde's Love-Death

By La Scala Orchestra}
By La Scala Orchestra} 68210 12-inch, $1.25

IL TROVATORE—FIRST SCENE

(Italian)   (English)
IL TROVATORE   THE TROUBADOUR
(*Eel Troh-va-toh'-reh*)

OPERA IN FOUR ACTS

Words by Salvatore Cammanaro, the story being suggested by a Spanish drama of the same name. Music by Giuseppe Verdi. Produced at the Teatro Apollo, Rome, January 19, 1853; at the *Théâtre des Italiens*, Paris, December 23, 1854; at the *Opéra*, Paris, as *Le Trouvère*, January 12, 1857; at Covent Garden, London, May 17, 1885; in English as *The Gypsy's Vengeance*, Drury Lane, March 24, 1856. First New York production May 17, 1855.

Characters

LEONORA,(*Lee-oh-noh'-rah*)a noble lady of the Court of an Aragon Princess..Soprano
AZUCENA, (*Ahz-you-say'-nah*) a wandering Biscayan gypsy.......Mezzo-Soprano
INEZ, (*Ee'-nez*) attendant of Leonora..............................Soprano
MANRICO, (*Man-ree'-koh*) a young chieftain under the Prince of Biscay,
    of mysterious birth, and in reality a brother of Count di Luna......Tenor
COUNT DI LUNA, (*dee Loo'-nah*) a powerful young noble of the Prince
    of Arragon..Baritone
FERRANDO, a captain of the guard and under di Luna................Bass
RUIZ, a soldier in Manrico's service................................Tenor
AN OLD GYPSY..Baritone

Also a Messenger, a Jailer, Soldiers, Nuns, Gypsies, Attendants, etc.

Scene and Period: Biscay and Aragon; fifteenth century.

ACT I
SCENE I—*Vestibule in Aliaferia Palace*

As befits a tragic work, *Il Trovatore* opens in an atmosphere of romance and mystery. The retainers of *Count di Luna* await the arrival of their master, and to beguile the time *Ferrando* relates the history of the Count's childhood and the loss of his brother.

Abbietta zingara (Swarthy and Threatening)

By Torres de Luna, Bass, and La Scala Chorus

(*In Italian*) *62416 10-inch, $0.75

The brother, as an infant, came under the evil eye of a witch, who was seized and condemned to the stake. This witch had a daughter, who determined to avenge her mother's fate, with the result that the Count's younger son disappeared; and after the witch's burning there was discovered upon the pile of charred embers the bones of a child. This story is told in the *Abbietta* to a fierce rhythmical tune, expressing all shades of horror.

FERRANDO:
With two sons, heirs of fortune and affection,
Liv'd the Count in enjoyment;
Watching the younger for his safe protection
A good nurse found employment.
One morning, as the dawn's first rays were
    shining,
From her pillow she rose,—
Who was found, think ye, near the child
    reclining?
(*Impressively.*)
Sat there a gypsy-hag, witch-like appearing;
Of her dark mysteries, strange symbols
    wearing.
O'er the babe sleeping—with fierce looks
    bending,
Gaz'd she upon him, black deeds intending!

Horror profound seized the nurse at that
    dark vision;
And the dark intruder was soon expelled.
Soon they found the child was failing,
Coming darkness appall'd him,
The hag's dark spell enthrall'd him!
(*All appear horrified.*)
Sought they the gypsy, on all sides turning,
Seiz'd and condemn'd her to death by burning.
One child, accursed, left she remaining,
Quick to avenge her, no means disdaining;
Thus she accomplished her dark retribution!
Lost was the Count's child; search unavailing,
But on the site of the hag's execution
They found, 'mid the embers,
The bones of a young infant,
Half consumed and burning!

In the second part *Ferrando* concludes his narrative, which is mingled with the comments of the listeners, who tell of the reputed appearance of the witch in ghostly shape.

Sull' orlo dei tetti (As a Vampire You May See Her)

By Torres de Luna, Bass, and La Scala Chorus

(*In Italian*) *16655 10-inch, $0.75

To the voice of the narrator is added the awe-stricken whispers of the chorus, which afterwards swell into a cry of fierce denunciation. The foreboding bell and an instrumental diminuendo complete the picture, which makes a fitting conclusion to a gruesome story.

The clock strikes twelve, and with cries of "Cursed be the witch infernal!" the retainers disperse.

SCENE II—*The Gardens of the Palace*

The fair *Leonora* now appears with her faithful companion, *Inez.* She confides to *Inez* her interest in the unknown knight whom she had first seen at the Tournament, and sings her first number.

LANDE

IL TROVATORE—ACT I, SCENE II

Tacea la notte placida (My Heart is His Alone)

By Celestina Boninsegna, Soprano	(*In Italian*)	92026	12-inch, $3.00
By Gina Viafora, Soprano	(*In Italian*)	74116	12-inch, 1.50
By Lucia Crestani, Soprano	(*In Italian*)	*16655	10-inch, .75

In this wistful air, so unlike the weird music preceding it, she speaks of the *Troubadour* who serenades her nightly, and of the feelings which have been inspired in her breast by his song.

Double-Faced Record—For title of opposite side see DOUBLE-FACED IL TROVATORE RECORDS, page 360.

LEONORA:
How calm, how placid, was the night!
The cloudless sky, how clear, how bright!
The moon in splendor shed her light,
And all was hushed in peace around!
Suddenly, on the midnight air,

In tones so sweet and thrilling,
Breathing to Heav'n an earnest pray'r,
My heart with deep joy filling,
I heard a voice oft heard before,
My long-loved knightly Troubadour!

The ladies go into the house just as the *Count,* who is also wooing the fair *Leonora,* appears to watch under her window. He has barely taken his station when the lovely song of the *Troubadour* is heard:

Deserto sulla terra (Naught on Earth is Left Me)

By Carlo Albani, Tenor   (*In Italian*) 64081 10-inch, $1.00
By Nicola Zerola, Tenor   (*In Italian*) 64172 10-inch, 1.00

In this beautiful serenade, one of the gems of the opera, the *Troubadour* sings of his lonely life and the one hope that remains to him.

MANRICO:
Lonely on earth abiding,
Warring 'gainst fate's cruel chiding,
Hope doth one heart implore,
To love the Troubadour!

The Count is filled with rage as *Manrico* appears and confesses his love in song, and when *Leonora* comes forth to greet her lover, the anger of *di Luna* bursts in a storm upon them both, in the strain with which this number opens.

Di geloso amor sprezzato (Now My Vengeance)

By Antonio Paoli, Tenor; Clara Joanna, Soprano; Francesco
    Cigada, Baritone   (*In Italian*) 91082 10-inch, $2.00
By Maria Bernacchi, Soprano; Luigi Colazza, Tenor; Ernesto
    Caronna, Baritone   (*In Italian*) *16808 10-inch, .75

Manrico defies him and they agree to fight to the death. *Leonora* implores her lover to stay, but is unable to restrain the jealous passion which inspires the rivals, and after the powerful and exciting trio they rush out with drawn swords, while *Leonora* falls senseless.

ACT II

SCENE I—*A Gypsy Camp in the Biscay Mountains*

We are now in the gypsy encampment at early morning, as the shadows of night are passing away before the dawn. The men are beginning work, and in this, the famous *Anvil Chorus,* they hammer as they sing.

COPY'T MISHKIN
ZEROLA AS MANRICO

La zingarella (Anvil Chorus)

By La Scala Chorus   (*In Italian*) *62418 10-inch, $0.75
By Victor Male Chorus   (*In English*) 1258 10-inch, .60
By Victor Orchestra   2146 10-inch, .60

The swinging tune is accompanied by the ring of blows on the anvil, and the rough voices of the men and the sound of the hammers make a truly impressive musical picture.

CHORUS OF GYPSIES:
See how the shadows of night are flying!
Morn breaketh, Heav'n's glorious arch unveiling;
Like a young widow, who, weary of sighing,
Lays by her garments of sorrow and wailing.
Rouse up, to labor!
Take each his hammer.

MEN:
Who makes the gypsy's, a life with pleasure
laden?

WOMEN:
Who makes the gypsy's, a life with pleasure
laden, who?

ALL:
The gypsy maiden!
See how the sunlight, radiantly glowing,
Borrows new beams from our wine cups o'erflowing!
Resume our labor! Take each his hammer!
Who makes the gypsy's life, etc.

Double-Faced Record—For title of opposite side see DOUBLE-FACED IL TROVATORE RECORDS, page 360.

Azucena, the gypsy, who now appears, proves to be none other than the witch's daughter spoken of in the first act. In the highly dramatic song allotted to her she relates to *Manrico* the dreadful story of the death of her mother, who had been burned at the stake as a witch by the father of the present *Count di Luna.*

Stride la vampa (Fierce Flames Are Soaring)

By Louise Homer, Contralto
   (*In Italian*)   87033   10-inch, $2.00
By Jeanne Gerville-Réache,
  Contralto (*In Italian*)   87065   10-inch, 2.00
By Lina Mileri, Contralto
   (*In Italian*)   *16808   10-inch, .75

COPY'T McINTOSH

HOMER AS AZUCENA

In the aria she mentally lives again through the scene of her mother's execution, each horrible detail of which is indelibly imprinted upon her memory.

This wild contralto air in the minor, with its deep, rich, and ever-changing tones, is well suited to so grim a recital.

Upward the flames roll; the crowd presses fiercely on,
Rush to the burning with seeming gladness;
Loud cries of pleasure from all sides re-echoing!
By guards surrounded—forth comes a woman!
While, o'er them shining, with wild, unearthly glare,
Dark wreaths of flame curl, ascending to heaven!
Upward the flames roll! on comes the victim still;

Robed in dark garments, ungirt, unsandal'd;
Fierce cries of vengeance from that dark crowd arise;
Echo repeats them from mountain to mountain.
O'er them reflecting, with wild, unearthly glare.
Dark wreaths of flame curl, ascending to heaven!

The two renditions of this thrilling air, by Mme. Homer and Mme. Gerville-Réache, are most dramatic and impressive ones; while an excellent lower-priced record is furnished by Mme. Mileri.

Questioned by *Manrico, Azucena* tells him the story of her past. In obedience to her mother's last cry for vengeance, she stole the Count's young child, and threw it on the flames where her mother was consumed. But she soon discovered that in her frenzy she had destroyed her own infant, and preserved the child of the noble. Wild as was the previous air, this proves a still more dramatic setting of the conclusion of the story. The orchestral accompaniment crashes, wails and sobs, the voice rises and falls in hatred or terror, until at last the gypsy sinks exhausted with the stress of emotion that her tale has excited.

Condotta ell'era in ceppi (In Chains to Her Doom They Dragged Her)

By Lina Mileri, Contralto   (*In Italian*)   *35176   12-inch, $1.25

The story has set *Manrico* thinking. "If your son perished," he asks, "whose child am I?" But the gypsy, with a born instinct for dissimulation, avoids the question, still claiming him as her son. She reminds him of the almost fatal wounds received in an attack from the *Count di Luna* and his men, from which she had nursed him back to life.

Mal reggendo all'aspro assalto (At My Mercy Lay the Foe)

By Louise Homer, Contralto, and Enrico Caruso, Tenor
      (*In Italian*)   89049   12-inch, $4.00
By Clotilde Esposito, Contralto, and Luigi Colazza, Tenor
      (*In Italian*)   *16550   10-inch, .75

In the opening strain of this air, *Manrico* tells of his single combat with the *Count,* in which by an irresistible impulse, after felling his antagonist to earth, he spared the noble's life. The voice of the gypsy then bids him never again to allow their enemy to escape, but to unhesitatingly administer the death-blow. *Manrico's* story of the duel is expressed by a

* Double-Faced Record—For title of opposite side see DOUBLE-FACED IL TROVATORE RECORDS, pages 359 and 360.

LANDE

THE CONVENT NEAR CASTELLOR—ACT II

bold martial air, the gypsy's incitements to vengeance being heard at the same time, leading to the vigorous climax of the duet.

SCENE II—*The Cloisters of a Convent*

In this scene we return to the fortunes of the *Count* and *Leonora*. She, believing the *Troubadour* to have been killed, presumably in a recent duel with his rival, has determined to enter a convent. *Di Luna* appears in front of the convent with the intention of carrying her away before the ceremony shall have taken place, and sings his famous air, "Il balen."

Il balen del suo sorriso (The Tempest of the Heart)

By Emilio de Gogorza, Baritone	(*In Italian*)	88175 12-inch, $3.00
By Francesco Cigada, Baritone	(*In Italian*)	*16812 10-inch, .75
By Alan Turner, Baritone	(*In English*)	*16521 10-inch, .75

This solo almost wins the *Count* our sympathy, in spite of ourselves, so genuine and heartfelt an expression of the tender passion it is.

COUNT:
Of her smile, the radiant gleaming
  Pales the starlight's brightest reflection,
While her face with beauty beaming,
  Brings me fresh ardor, lends to my affection.

Ah! this love within me burning,
  More than words shall plead on my part,
Her bright glances on me turning,
  Calm the tempest in my heart!

The convent bell is heard tolling as a signal for the final rites which make *Leonora* a nun. The *Count*, in a burst of passion, declares they must seize her before she reaches the altar.

Per me ora fatale (This Passion That Inspires Me)

By Ernesto Caronna, Baritone   (*In Italian*) *16814 10-inch, $0.75

This declaration is expressed in a vigorous air.

COUNT (*furiously*):
Oh, hour of fate to me,
Hasten thy lagging moments.
The joy that I anticipate
Is of more than mortal worth!

No rival can I have;
No one dare my love to thwart!
For me hath fate design'd her,
And to me she shall belong!

They conceal themselves among the trees as the chant of the nuns is heard.

Ah! se l'error t'ingombra ('Mid the Shades of Error)

By Francesco Cigada, Baritone, and La Scala Chorus
    (*In Italian*) *16550 10-inch, $0.75

They sing of the coming retirement of *Leonora* from the world, while from their place of concealment the *Count* and his retainers speak of their coming triumph.

CHORUS OF NUNS:
Ah! when the shades of night,
Oh, daughter of Eve, shall close on thee,
Then wilt thou know that life
Is but a shadow, a fleeting dream;—
Yes, like the passing of a shadow
Are all our earthly hopes!

Come, then, and let this mystic veil
From human eye enshroud thee;
Hence let care and worldly thought
For evermore be banish'd.
To Heaven now turn thee, and Heaven
Will open to receive thee!

* *Double-Faced Record—For title of opposite side see DOUBLE-FACED IL TROVATORE RECORDS, page 360.*

COUNT:
> Triumphant hour impending,
> Thy moments urge with speed elating,
> The joy my heart's awaiting,
> Is not of mortal birth,
> In vain doth Heaven, contending
> With rival claims, oppose me,
> If once these arms enclose thee,
> No power in heav'n or earth,
> No pow'r shall tear thee from me!

FERRANDO AND RETAINERS:
> How bold! Let's go—conceal ourselves
> Amid the shades in haste.
> How bold!—Come on—and silence keep,
> The prize he soon will hold!

As the nuns appear, conducting the penitent, the Count's retainers rush out and seize *Leonora.*

The calculations of *di Luna* are once more upset, for just as he interrupts the ceremony, *Manrico* unexpectedly appears. *Leonora,* overjoyed to find her lover still living, begins the great trio.

E deggio e posso crederlo (Oh, Blessed Vision)

By Maria Grisi, Soprano; Remo Sangiorgi, Tenor; Francesco Cigada, Baritone; La Scala Chorus
(*In Italian*) *35176 12-inch, $1.25

Leonora foregoes her religious vows, and the lovers, for the time united, make their escape, to the chagrin of the baffled Count, while his men are defeated by *Manrico's* followers.

COPY'T DUPONT

MARTIN AS MANRICO

ACT III

SCENE I—*The Camp of di Luna*

Squilli echeggi la tromba (Soldiers' Chorus)

By New York Grand Opera Chorus (*In Italian*) 64050 10-inch, $1.00

Act III opens with the chorus of *di Luna's* men—called the *Soldiers' Chorus.* In spite of the wealth of melody already heard in this work, here is yet another marvelous number, which works up to a powerful climax, and then dies away softly, as these *Trovatore* choruses so frequently do.

Giorni poveri vivea (In Despair I Seek My Son)

By Ida Mamelli, Soprano; Renzo Minolfi, Baritone; Cesare Preve, Baritone; La Scala Chorus (*In Italian*) *35177 12-inch, $1.25

A scouting party from the Count's troops have fallen in with *Azucena,* and now bring her to the Count as a possible spy. Inquiries as to her past immediately connect her with the episode of the Count's childhood, and *Ferrando* declares her to be the murderess of *di Luna's* lost brother. *Azucena* in her extremity, cries out the name of *Manrico,* and the Count, finding she claims the *Troubadour* as her son, vows upon her a double vengeance, and she is bound and dragged away. The gypsy's pleading, the Count's threatening anger and triumph, with the accompanying chorus, combine to make a moving and dramatic *ensemble.*

SCENE II—*Manrico's Castle*

The scene changes to the castle wherein *Manrico* and *Leonora* are at last enjoying a brief honeymoon, though in expectation of an attack from the baffled *Count di Luna.* Here *Manrico* sings a tender and affectionate farewell to his beloved ere he departs to repel his rival's assault.

Ah, si ben mio (The Vows We Fondly Plighted)

By Enrico Caruso, Tenor	(*In Italian*)	88121	12-inch,	$3.00
By Charles Dalmores, Tenor	(*In Italian*)	85123	12-inch,	3.00
By Giorgio Malesci, Tenor	(*In Italian*)	*16809	10-inch,	.75

* *Double-Faced Record—For title of opposite side see DOUBLE-FACED IL TROVATORE RECORDS, pages 359 and 360.*

SLEZAK AS MANRICO

This beautiful lyrical number is a delightful relief after so much that is forcible and dramatic.

MANRICO:
'Tis love, sublime emotion, at such a moment
Bids thy heart still be hopeful.
Ah! love; how blest our life will be
Our fond desires attaining,
My soul shall win fresh ardor,
My arm new courage gaining.
But, if, upon the fatal page
Of destiny impending,
I'm doom'd among the slain to fall,
'Gainst hostile arms contending,
In life's last hour, with fainting breath,
My thoughts will turn to thee.
Preceding thee to Heaven, will death
Alone appear to me!

Quietness soon departs, for the news comes that the attacking party have captured *Azucena*, and are piling up faggots around the stake at which she is to be burnt. Maddened at the approaching outrage upon one whom he believes to be his mother, *Manrico* prepares to rush to her assistance. The air with chorus which forms the climax to this scene is full of martial fire.

Di quella pira (Tremble Ye Tyrants)

By Francesco Tamagno, Tenor

	(*In Italian*)	95006	10-inch,	$5.00

By Antonio Paoli, Tenor, and La Scala Chorus

	(*In Italian*)	92032	12-inch,	3.00

By Enrico Caruso, Tenor (*In Italian*) 87001 10-inch, 2.00
By Nicola Zerola, Tenor (*In Italian*) 64170 10-inch, 1.00
By Giovanni Valls, Tenor, and La Scala Chorus (*In Italian*) *16809 10-inch, .75

It is led up to by a very powerful introductory passage, and the high notes at the end, delivered in robust tones, never fail of their effect.

MANRICO:
Ah! sight of horror! See that pile blazing—
Demons of fury round it stand gazing!
Madness inspiring, Hate now is raging—
Tremble, for vengeance on you shall fall.

Oh! mother dearest, though love may claim me,
Danger, too, threaten, yet will I save thee;
From flames consuming thy form shall snatch'd be,
Or with thee, mother, I too will fall!

Caruso's singing of this number is absolutely electrifying in its effect on the listener, the two famous high C's being easily taken and with the full power of his great voice.

Tamagno's *Manrico* was a figure of noble proportions, and he endowed it with all his splendid vitality. Such a high C had never before been heard, and it electrified the audiences. The record of *Di quella pira* is a faithful reproduction of the great singer's rendition of the famous aria. Paoli, the famous Milan tenor, also gives a vigorous performance of this great air.

Other fine renditions, at a lower price, are given by Zerola and by Signor Valls, assisted by La Scala Chorus.

THE RAMPARTS OF ALIAFERIA—ACT IV

* Double-Faced Record—For title of opposite side see DOUBLE-FACED IL TROVATORE RECORDS, page 360.

ACT IV

SCENE I—*Exterior of the Palace of Aliaferia*

The last act brings us outside the palace of *Aliaferia,* wherein *Manrico,* defeated by *di Luna's* men, and the gyspy, are confined in the dungeons. Hither *Leonora* has wended her way to be near her lover, and she now sings the plaintive *D'amor.*

D'amor sull' ali rosee (Love, Fly on Rosy Pinions)

By Lucia Crestani, Soprano   (*In Italian*) *16810 10-inch, $0.75

This sad but melodious air reveals her heartfelt grief for the sorrows which she cannot relieve.

LEONORA:

In this dark hour of midnight
I hover round thee, my love!
Ye moaning breezes round me playing,
In pity aid me, my sighs to him conveying!
On rosy wings of love depart,
Bearing my heart's sad wailing,
Visit the prisoner's lonely cell,

Console his spirit failing.
Let hope's soft whispers wreathing
Around him, comfort breathing,
Recall to his fond remembrance
Sweet visions of his love;
But, let no accent reveal to him
The sorrows, the griefs my heart doth move!

And now comes Verdi's most famous operatic scene, the great *Miserere.*

Miserere (I Have Sighed to Rest Me)

By Enrico Caruso, Tenor; Frances Alda, Soprano;
Chorus of the Metropolitan Opera   (*In Italian*) 89030 12-inch, $4.00
By Ida Giacomelli, Soprano; Gino Martinez-Patti,
Tenor; La Scala Chorus   (*In Italian*) 58366 12-inch, 1.00
By Elise Stevenson, Soprano; Harry Macdonough,
Tenor; Victor Male Chorus   (*In English*) 31703 12-inch, 1.00
By Elise Stevenson, Soprano; Harry Macdonough,
Tenor; Victor Male Chorus   (*In English*) *16013 10-inch,   .75
By Arthur Pryor and Emile Keneke (*Trombone-Cornet*) *16371 10-inch,   .75
By Walter Rogers and Arthur Pryor (*Cornet-Trombone*) *16794 10-inch,   .75
By Walter Rogers and Arthur Pryor (*Cornet-Trombone*) 4513 10-inch,   .60

Leonora is terror-stricken at the solemn tolling of a deep-toned bell and the mournful chorus of priests chanting for the soul of a doomed prisoner.

CAMPANINI AS MANRICO

PRIESTS:

Pray that peace may attend a soul departing,
Whither no care or thought of earth can follow;
Heav'nly mercy allays the pangs of parting,
Look up beyond this life's delusions hollow.

Then follows an impressive series of chords in the orchestra, leading to a sobbing lament of *Leonora.*

LEONORA:

What voices of terror! For whom are they praying?
With omens of fear unknown, they darken the air,
New horrors assail me, my senses are straying,
My vision is dim, is it death that is near?

In upon this there breaks the beautiful air of the *Troubadour,* sung within the prison, followed by a joyful cry of devotion from his beloved.

MANRICO:

Ah! I have sighed to rest me; deep in the quiet grave—
Sighed to rest me, but all in vain I crave.
Oh fare thee well, my Leonora, fare thee well!

These fragments, first given separately, are next combined and heard together, forming a most impressive scene of touching beauty, for which the opera of *Il Trovatore* will ever be remembered.

* *Double-Faced Record—For title of opposite side see DOUBLE-FACED IL TROVATORE RECORDS, page 360.*

The entrance of *di Luna* brings from *Leonora* a prayer for mercy for the prisoner. The appeal is unheeded, or rather it appears to increase the triumph which belongs to the *Count's* vengeance. The appeal of the unhappy woman and the fierce joy of the gratified noble are powerfully expressed in this magnificent duet.

Mira d'acerbe lagrime (Oh, Let My Tears Implore Thee)

By Emma Eames, Soprano, and Emilio de Gogorza, Baritone

       (*In Italian*)   89022 12-inch, $4.00

By Celestina Boninsegna, Soprano, and Francesco Cigada, Baritone

       (*In Italian*)   91077 10-inch. 2.00

By Maria Bernacchi, Soprano, and Ernesto Caronna, Tenor

       (*In Italian*) *16810 10-inch, .75

In the extremity of despair, *Leonora* makes one last effort. If the *Count* will spare the one she loves, she will consent to become *di Luna's* wife. She swears to perform her promise, at the same time intending to take poison as soon as *Manrico* is free. *Di Luna's* wrath is now changed into joy, while *Leonora,* forgetting her own fate, is filled with happiness at the thought of the *Troubadour's* release. This situation gives opportunity for another wonderful duet of a most thrilling character.

Vivra! Contende il giubilo (Oh, Joy, He's Saved)

By Celestina Boninsegna, Soprano, and Francesco Cigada, Baritone

       (*In Italian*)   91071 10-inch, $2.00

By Angela de Angelis, Soprano, and Francesco Cigada, Baritone

       (*In Italian*) *16811 10-inch, .75

In this number the *Count* expresses his rapture at the success of his conquest, while *Leonora* exclaims, aside: "Thou shalt possess but a lifeless bride." As the scene changes they enter the tower to secure the release of *Manrico.*

SCENE II—*The Prison Cell of Manrico*

Yet a third duet—the famous *Home to Our Mountains.* The scene has changed to the prison interior, where *Azucena* and *Manrico* are together, and the gypsy, with the second-sight of her race, predicts her approaching end.

Ai nostri monti (Home to Our Mountains)

By Louise Homer, Contralto, and Enrico Caruso, Tenor

       (*In Italian*)   89018 12-inch, $4.00

By Corinne Morgan, Contralto, and Harry Macdonough, Tenor

       (*In English*) *35118 12-inch, 1.25

By Corinne Morgan, Contralto, and Harry Macdonough, Tenor

       (*In English*)   31555 12-inch, 1.00

By Clotilde Esposito, Soprano, and Luigi Colazza, Tenor

       (*In Italian*) *16811 10-inch, .75

By Corinne Morgan, Contralto, and Harry Macdonough, Tenor

       (*In English*) *16407 10-inch, .75

This familiar duet is considered by many to be the gem of Verdi's opera, and especially when given by such artists as Caruso and Homer, it is doubly enjoyable.

Manrico is watching over the couch of *Azucena,* whose strength is exhausted, and who is full of vague terrors; and he endeavors to soothe her fears.

MANRICO:
If any love remains in thy bosom,
If thou art yet my mother, oh, hear me!
Seek thy terrors to number,
And gain repose from thy sorrows in soothing
  slumber.

AZUCENA:
Yes, I am grief-worn and fain would rest me.
But more than grief have sad dreams
  oppressed me;
Should that dread vision rise in slumber
Rouse me! its horrors may then depart.

MANRICO:
Rest thee, oh mother! I'll watch o'er thee,
Sleep may restore sweet peace to thy heart.

A fierce and avenging gypsy no longer, but a broken woman whose consuming passions of remorse and revenge have died away, she dreams of the happy days gone by.

---

* *Double-Faced Record*—*For title of opposite side see* DOUBLE-FACED IL TROVATORE RECORDS, *pages 359 and 360.*

AZUCENA (*dreaming*): Home to our mountains, let us return, love,
There in thy young days peace had its reign:
There shall thy song fall on my slumbers,
There shall thy lute, make me joyous again.
MANRICO: Rest thee, my mother, kneeling beside thee,
I will pour forth my troubadour lay.
AZUCENA: O sing and wake now thy sweet lute's soft
numbers,
Lull me to rest, charm my sorrows away.
BOTH: Lull { me / thee } to rest!

Caruso sings this beautiful scene with that tenderness of voice which he can assume when he will; while Mme. Homer delivers *Azucena's* music with exceptional purity and charm. Altogether one of the most beautiful records in the Red Seal List.

Matters now move swiftly to a climax. *Leonora* arrives on the scene, bringing *Manrico* the news of his freedom. The joy of meeting is all too soon destroyed when the prisoner finds his liberty to have been purchased at the cost of a happiness which is to him dearer than life itself. He accuses *Leonora* of betraying his love.

Ha quest' infame (Thou Hast Sold Thyself)

By Ida Giacomelli, Soprano; Lina Mileri, Contralto; Gino
Martinez-Patti, Tenor   (*In Italian*) *35177 12-inch, $1.25

Here *Azucena*, who cares nothing for his passion, counsels flight. This gives the elements of the closing trio: *Manrico's* reproaches, *Leonora's* ineffectual protestations, and the gypsy's voice through all, singing dreamily of her mountain home. With these mingled voices dying away into soft peaceful harmonies the musical portion of the opera draws to a close.

MANRICO:
Thou giv'st me life? No! I scorn it!
Whence comes this power? what price has
bought it?
Thou wilt not speak? oh, dark suspicion!

'Twas from my rival thou purchased thy
mission!
Ah! thou hast sold him thy heart's affection!
Barter'd a love once devoted to me!

Leonora, who had already taken the poison, now sinks dying at *Manrico's* feet, and he pleads forgiveness as he learns the truth. *Di Luna* now enters, and furious at finding himself cheated of his promised bride, orders the *Troubadour* to instant execution. *Manrico* is taken out by the guards and beheaded.

At the moment of his death, the gypsy awakes, and not seeing *Manrico*, realizes that he has gone to his execution. She drags the *Count* to the window and cries to him: "You have killed your brother!" *Di Luna* utters a wild cry of remorse and falls senseless as the curtain slowly descends.

DOUBLE-FACED AND MISCELLANEOUS TROVATORE RECORDS

{ Condotta ell'era in ceppi (In Chains to Her Doom)
By Lina Mileri, Contralto (*In Italian*)
E deggio e posso crederlo (Oh, Blessed Vision) By } 35176 12-inch, $1.25
Maria Grisi, Soprano; Remo Sangiorgi, Tenor; Francesco
Cigada, Baritone; La Scala Chorus   (*In Italian*)

{ Giorni poveri vivea (In Despair I Seek My Son) By
Ida Mamelli, Soprano; Renzo Minolfi, Baritone; Cesare
Preve, Baritone; La Scala Chorus   (*In Italian*)
Ha quest' infame (Ah, Thou Hast Sold Thyself) By } 35177 12-inch, 1.25
Ida Giacomelli, Soprano; Lina Mileri, Contralto; Gino
Martinez-Patti, Tenor   (*In Italian*)

{ Ai nostri monti (Home to Our Mountains) By Corinne
Morgan and Harry Macdonough   (*In English*) } 35118 12-inch, 1.25
Huguenots—Selection, Act IV   By Sousa's Band

{ Trovatore Selection   By Arthur Pryor's Band } 35076 12-inch, 1.25
Traviata Selection   By Arthur Pryor's Band

* Double-Faced Record—For title of opposite side see above list.

Abbietta zingara (Swarthy and Threatening)　By Torres
　de Luna, Bass, and La Scala Chorus　　　(In Italian)
Sull' orlo dei tetti (As a Vampire You May See Her)　62416　10-inch, $0.75
　　By Torres de Luna and La Scala Chorus　(In Italian)

Sull' orlo dei tetti (As a Vampire You May See Her)
　　By Torres de Luna and La Scala Chorus　(In Italian)
Tacea la notte placida (My Heart is His Alone)　16655　10-inch, .75
　　By Lucia Crestani, Soprano　(In Italian)

Di geloso amor sprezzato (Now My Vengeance)
　By Bernacchi, Soprano; Colazza, Tenor; and Caronna,
　Baritone　　　　　　　　　　　　　(In Italian)　16808　10-inch, .75
Stride la vampa (Fierce Flames Are Soaring)
　　By Lina Mileri, Contralto　(In Italian)

Mal reggendo all'aspro assalto (At My Mercy Lay the
　Foe)　By Clotilde Esposito and Luigi Colazza　(In Italian)
Ah! se le error t' ingombra ('Mid the Shades of Error)　16550　10-inch, .75
　　By Francesco Cigada and Chorus　(In Italian)

Il balen del suo sorriso (The Tempest of the Heart)
　　By Francesco Cigada, Baritone　(In Italian)　16812　10-inch, .75
　Martha—Porter Song　　By Carlos Francisco　(In Italian)

Il balen del suo sorriso (The Tempest of the Heart)
　　By Alan Turner, Baritone　(In English)　16521　10-inch, .75
　Carmen—Toreador Song　　By Alan Turner　(In English)

Per me ora fatale (This Passion That Inspires Me)
　　By Ernesto Caronna, Baritone　(In Italian)
　　　　　　　　　　　　　　　　　16814　10-inch, .75
　Pagliacci—Opening Chorus, Son qua
　　　　　　　　By La Scala Chorus　(In Italian)

Ah, si ben mio (The Vows We Fondly Plighted)
　　By Georgio Malesci, Tenor　(In Italian)
Di quella pira (Tremble Ye Tyrants)　By Giovanni　16809　10-inch, .75
　Vals, Tenor, and La Scala Chorus　　　(In Italian)

D'amor sull ali rosee (Love, Fly on Rosy Pinions)
　　By Lucia Crestani, Soprano　(In Italian)
Mira d'acerbi lagrime (Oh, Let My Tears Implore Thee)　16810　10-inch, .75
　　By Maria Bernacchi and Ernesto Caronna　(In Italian)

Miserere　By Elise Stevenson, Soprano, and Harry Mac-
　donough, Tenor　　　　　　　　　　(In English)
　I Would That My Love　By Elise Stevenson, Soprano, and　16013　10-inch, .75
　Harry Macdonough, Tenor　　　　　(In English)

Miserere　　By Pryor and Keneke　(Trombone-Cornet)
　Spring Song　(Mendelssohn)　　By Victor String Quartet　16371　10-inch, .75

Miserere　　By Rogers and Pryor　(Cornet-Trombone)
　Chant sans paroles　(Tschaikowsky)　By Vienna String Quartet　16794　10-inch, .75

Vivra! contende il giubilo (Oh, Joy, He's Saved)　By
　Angela de Angelis and Francesco Cigada　(In Italian)
Ai nostri monti (Home to Our Mountains)　By Clotilde　16811　10-inch, .75
　Esposito, Soprano, and Luigi Colazza, Tenor　(In Italian)

Ai nostri monti (Home to Our Mountains)　By Corinne
　Morgan, Contralto, and Harry Macdonough, Tenor
　　　　　　　　　　　　　　　　　(In English)　16407　10-inch, .75
　Bohemian Girl—Heart Bow'd Down
　　　　　　　By Alan Turner, Baritone　(In English)

Di geloso amor sprezzato　(Now My Vengeance)
　By Maria Bernacchi, Soprano; Luigi Colazza, Tenor;
　　and Ernesto Caronna, Baritone　　(In Italian)　62418　10-inch, .75
La zingarella　(Anvil Chorus)
　　　　　　By La Scala Chorus　(In Italian)

(German)
DIE WALKÜRE
(Dee Vahl-keu'-ri)

(French)
LA VALKYRIE
(Lah Val-kee'-ri)

(English)
THE VALKYRIE
(Vahl-kee'-ree)

MUSIC-DRAMA IN THREE ACTS

Text and music by Richard Wagner. First presented in Munich in 1870. First New York production at the Academy of Music, April 2, 1877.

Characters

SIEGMUND *(Seeg'-moond)* ....Tenor
HUNDING *(Hoond'-ing)* ....Bass
WOTAN *(Voh'-tahn)* ....Baritone
SIEGLINDE *(Seeg-lin'-duh)* ....Soprano
BRÜNNHILDE *(Broon-heel'-duh)* ....Soprano
FRICKA *(Frik'-ah)* ....Soprano
VALKYRIES—Gerhilda, Ortlinda, Valtrauta, Sverleita, Helmviga, Siegruna, Grimgerda, Rossvisa.

Walküre is the second in the series of music-dramas composing the *Niebelung Ring,* and from a popular standpoint perhaps the most melodious and pleasing. The story is beautiful and compelling, the situations by turn thrilling and pathetic, while the glorious music written by the master to accompany the adventures of his mythical personages is easily understood and appreciated by the average listener.

A perusal of the preceding description of the story of the *Niebelung* in *Rhinegold* (page 279) will help the reader to understand more fully the Victor synopsis of *Walküre.*

Wotan has been warned by *Erda,* the *Earth Goddess,* that if *Alberich* regains the *Ring* the gods must perish. Brooding over this impending fate, *Wotan* descends to earth and weds the goddess; this union resulting in nine splendid daughters, the *Walküre,* who are to aid in the salvation of the gods. Riding forth each day among the tumult and the strife which prevail on the earth as a result of the Curse of the Ring, they carry to *Walhalla,* on their flying horses, the bravest of the warriors who fall in battle. These revived heroes keep themselves ready to defend *Walhalla* from the *Niebelungs.* But in order to regain the Ring, a brave hero is necessary, who shall be free from the universal curse and who can take it from Fafner, now changed into a dragon the better to guard the treasure. With this in mind *Wotan* visits the earth again and weds a mortal who bears him twins, *Siegmund* and *Sieglinde.*

While these children are quite young, the brutal *Hunding* finds their cottage, burns it, kills the mother and carries off *Sieglinde,* whom he afterward forces to become his bride.

The father and son return and swear vengeance on *Hunding.* *Wotan* (known as *Volse* on earth) returns to *Walhalla,* leaving the young *Siegmund* to fight alone and become a self-reliant hero. This is the situation when the action begins.

ACT I

SCENE I—*Interior of Hunding's Hut in the Forest—a Large Tree rises through the Roof*

The prelude represents a fearful storm in the forest, in

FIRST ACT SCENE—BAYREUTH

Brünnhilde Bearing a Wounded Warrior to Walhalla

the midst of which *Siegmund* rushes in exhausted, and falls by the fire. *Sieglinde* gives him refreshment and feels drawn to him by some strange attraction. While they are conversing, *Hunding* enters, and after questioning the stranger, recognizes in him his mortal enemy. He says, "Thou shalt have shelter from the storm to-night, but to-morrow thou diest!" and goes to his room, bidding *Sieglinde* prepare his evening drink. She does so but puts a drug in it to make him sleep soundly, and returns to *Siegmund*, unable to control her interest in the mysterious youth who has so strangely affected her.

Then occurs the lovely *Liebeslied*, the gem of this beautiful first act.

Siegmund's Liebeslied (Siegmund's Love Song)

By Riccardo Martin, Tenor
(*In German*)   88276   12-inch, $3.00

By George Hamlin, Tenor
(*In German*)   74111   12-inch, 1.50

The hut, which has been in semi-darkness, is suddenly illuminated by the blowing open of the great door at the back, and without can be seen the beauty of the spring night after the storm. The full moon shines in upon them, so that they see each other clearly for the first time. *Siegmund*, in ecstasy, rhapsodizes Spring and Love:

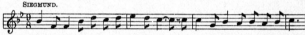

SIEGMUND.

Win - ter stür - me wi - chen dem Won-ne-mond, in mil - dem Lich - te leuchtet der Lenz.
Winter storms have waned, to the winsome moon, In mild as-cen-dance smileth the Spring.

VAN DYCK AS SIEGMUND

He takes her hand, seats her beside him on the rude bench, and continues:

SIEGMUND:
With balmy breezes, soft and soothing,
Wonders weaving, on he wends,
Through wood and meadow wafts his breathing,
Wide and lustrous laughs his eye;
In songs of birds his silv'ry voice resounds,
Wondrous fragrance he outbreathes;
From his living blood the loveliest flowers are blooming
Leaf and spray spring forth at his voice.
With gentle sceptre's sway he ruleth the world;
Winter and storm wane as his strength awakes:
By dint of his hardy striving
The stoutest doors he is cleaving,
Which, stubborn and strong, once held us from him!
To greet his sister swiftly he flies;
Thus Love the spring hath allured.
Within our bosoms Love lay asleep
That now laughs out to the light
The bride and the sister is freed by the brother;
Destroyed the walls that held them apart;
Joyous meet now the youthful pair;
United are Love and Spring.

SIEGMUND AND SIEGLINDE

Although the true charm of this poetry can be realized best by those on intimate terms with the German tongue, this excellent translation from the Ditson *Wagner Lyrics for Tenor* will add to the enjoyment of the record.

Sieglinde then tells *Siegmund* the story of the Sword—how at her wedding a stranger had suddenly appeared and thrust into the trunk of the tree a magic sword which should belong only to him who could take it out. The stranger had secretly told *Sieglinde* that no one but *Siegmund* would have power to remove it.

Siegmund rises eagerly, and going to the tree withdraws the sword with a mighty effort. The reunited brother and sister embrace each other and agree to fly from the power of

Hunding. The curtain falls as they pass out into the moonlit forest.

The love scenes between *Sieglinde* and *Siegmund* should be considered in their allegorical and poetical sense, and not judged by modern ethical standards. Wagner intended this episode to represent the union of Love and Spring.

ACT II

SCENE I—*A Wild and Rocky Pass*

Wotan and his favorite *Valkyrie* daughter, *Brünnhilde*, are discovered in full armor. He tells her to go to the rescue of the *Volsung* (*Siegmund*), whom *Hunding* is pursuing.

> WOTAN: Make ready thy steed, warrior maid,
> Soon will come battle and strife;
> Brünnhilde, haste to the field,
> Give aid to Volsung to-day!

The *Valkyrie* eagerly prepares for her flight, and sings her famous *Battle Cry.*

Ho, yo, to, ho! (Brünnhilde's Battle Cry)

By Johanna Gadski, Soprano
(*In German*) 87002 10-inch, $2.00

COPY'T DUPONT

GADSKI AS BRÜNNHILDE

Gadski is always a statuesquely beautiful *Brünnhilde*, and her voice glorifies this music, in which many persons, insensible to the poetic depth and power of the story, hear only noisy declamation. In this first scene especially, she brings into beautiful relief the joyful nature of the *Valkyrie*, and her cries are full of eager, happy vitality. Some idea of the difficult nature of this famous *Battle Cry* may be had from these few measures

Ho - yo - to ho. . . .   Ho - yo - to ho . . .   Ho - yo - to - ho. . . .

THE RESCUE OF SIEGLINDE

Mme. Gadski, however, surmounts these difficulties with ease, and the aria is a really wonderful specimen of both singing and recording.

> BRÜNNHILDE:
> Ho-yo-to-ho! Ho-yo-to-ho! Hei-aha!
> But listen, father! care for thyself;
> For a storm o'er thee will break;
> Fricka, thy busy wife, approacheth in her
> ram-impelled car.
> Ha! how she swings her golden whip!
> The frighten'd goats are fainting with fear,
> Wheels rattling and rolling whirl her here to
> the fight.
> At such a time away I would be,
> Tho' my delight is in scenes of war!
> Take heed that defeat be not thine,
> For now I must leave thee to fate!

Brünnhilde is right—*Wotan* is in for a scolding, as *Fricka* now appears in an extremely bad humor. *Hunding* has appealed to her, the guardian of marriage, for help, and she insists that *Siegmund* be punished. *Wotan* protests that this true love romance should not be interfered with, but the wrathful wife reminds him that the whole difficulty is but the result of his own infidelity, and he is finally forced to swear that *Siegmund* shall be punished.

Fricka then triumphantly calls to *Brünnhilde* that *Wotan* has further instructions for her. *Brünnhilde* finds her father in deep dejection, and when she questions him he confides to her his efforts to find a hero who shall banish the curse, but says his quest has been in vain. He bids her see that victory goes to *Hunding.* She protests, but he sternly commands obedience and leaves her.

Siegmund and *Sieglinde* now appear, fleeing from the wrath of *Hunding.* *Sieglinde's* strength has failed her, and she falls down exhausted. *Brünnhilde* comes to the lovers and tells *Siegmund* he must die. He scorns her prophecy and says his sword will not fail him. *Hunding's* voice is now heard, and in a sudden wave of sympathy *Brünnhilde* resolves to defend the young lovers.

Siegmund rushes to meet *Hunding,* and amid flashes of lightning the warriors can be seen in deadly combat, while *Brünnhilde* is visible flying above *Siegmund* and protecting him. *Wotan,* seeing the situation, then appears and causes *Siegmund* to fall by his opponent's sword.

Brünnhilde retreats in terror from her father's wrath, and runs to protect *Sieglinde.* She lifts the helpless maiden on her horse and they disappear.

ACT III
SCENE I—*The Summit of a Rocky Mountain*

The act opens with the wonderful *Ride of the Valkyries,* one of the most striking of all the master's compositions. This is graphically pictured in the splendid Fantasia by Pryor's Band, and in the La Scala record.

THE DEATH OF SIEGMUND

Cavalcata (Ride of the Valkyries)
By La Scala Orchestra   (*Double-faced, see page 369*)   62693   10-inch, $0.75

Fantasie (Including Ride of the Valkyries)
By Arthur Pryor's Band   31333   12-inch,   1.00

The Fantasie contains some of the finest portions of this second opera of the Niebelungen Ring. At first we hear the motive of *The Sword*

by full band, followed by the tumultuous *Ride of the Valkyries,* one of the most tremendous compositions in existence. The wild shouts of the goddesses as they ride their winged steeds through the air to the Rock, the warlike cries of *Brünnhilde* and the neighing of the war horses are splendidly portrayed.

A skillful modulation brings us to the last act, and a part of the great scene between *Wotan* and *Brünnhilde* is given, beginning with the wonderful *Siegfried, Guardian of the Sword* theme

on the trombone and which is repeated magnificently by the basses in another key.

The closing line of Wotan's Farewell, *So küsst er die Gottheit von dir* ("with a kiss I divest thee of godhead"), is heard on the cornet, followed by the Fire Music, an exquisite blending of the two fire *motive* with *Brünnhilde's Sleep.*

The *Valkyries* see *Brünnhilde* flying toward them, evidently in great distress. She alights

COPY'T DUPONT

VAN ROOY AS WOTAN

and asks her sisters to shield her from the wrath of *Wotan*, who is riding in pursuit; but they dare not help her. She then bids *Sieglinde* flee alone, telling her that she is destined to bear a son who shall be the hero *Siegfried*.

BRÜNNHILDE:
Fly then swiftly, and speed to the east!
Bravely determine all trials to bear.
Hunger and thirst, thorns and hard ways,
Smile through all pain while suffering pangs!
This only heed and hold it ever:
The highest hero of worlds hidest thou,
O wife,
In sheltering shrine!
(*She produces the pieces of Siegmund's sword from under her breastplate and hands them to Sieglinde.*)
For him keep these shreds of shattered sword-blade;
From his father's death-field by fortune I saved them:
Anon renewed this sword shall he swing;
And now his name I declare—Siegfried, of vict'ry the son!

SIEGLINDE:
O marvelous sayings! maiden divine!
What comfort o'er my mind thou hast cast!
For his sake I live and save this belov'd one!
May my blessing frame future reward!
Fare thee well! Be Sieglinde's sorrow thy weal!
(*She hastens away. The rocky peak is enveloped in black thunder-clouds; a fearful tempest roars up from the back; between the peals of thunder Wotan's voice is heard.*)

The *Valkyries* hurriedly conceal *Brünnhilde* in their midst as *Wotan* springs from his horse in a furious rage.

WOTAN:
Where is Brünnhilde? Where the rebellious one?
Dare ye to veil her from Wotan's vengeance?
(*Brünnhilde comes out from the group and faces her father, saying*):

BRÜNNHILDE:
Here stand I, father, to suffer my sentence!

WOTAN:
I sentence thee not; thou hast shaped the stroke for thyself.
Wish-maid art thou no more.
One time a Valkyrie wert thou,
Remain henceforth but merely thyself!

BRÜNNHILDE (*violently startled*):
Thou disownest me? Thine aim I divine!

WOTAN:
From heavenly clans art thou excluded,
Bann'd, degraded from thy blessed degree;
For broken now is our bond; exiled for aye
Art thou banished from bliss.

He then tells her that she must be put in a deep sleep, and shall be wakened by the first man who passes. She pleads with him in a beautiful appeal.

Brünnhilde's Bitte (Brünnhilde's Appeal to Wotan)

By Johanna Gadski, Soprano
(*In German*) 88183 12-inch, $3.00

PHOTO BERT

JOURNET AS WOTAN

Wotan's Farewell

WOTAN INVOKING THE FIRE GOD

BRÜNNHILDE:
Was it so shameful, what I have done,
That for my deed I so shamefully am
scourged?
Was it so base to warp thy command, that
thou
For me such debasement must shape?
Was't such dishonor what I have wrought

That it should rob me of honor for aye?
O speak, father! see me before thee: soften
thy wrath;
Wreak not thine ire, but make to me clear
the mortal
Guilt that with cruel firmness compels thee to
Cast off thy favorite child!

Wotan, deeply moved, softens his stern decree, and consents that she shall be won only by a great hero who can brave the flames with which she is to be surrounded. He then bids her farewell in the splendid *Abschied*.

Wotan's Farewell

WOTAN:
Farewell, my brave and beautiful child!
Thou once the light and life of my heart!
Farewell! Farewell! Farewell!
Loth I must leave thee; no more in love
May I grant thee my greeting;
Henceforth my maid no more with me rideth,
Nor waiteth wine to reach me!
When I relinquish thee, my beloved one,
Thou laughing delight of my eyes,

Thy bed shall be lit with torches more brilliant
Than ever for bridal have burned!
Fiery gleams shall girdle the fell,
With terrible scorchings scaring the timid,
Who, cowed, may cross not Brünnhilde's
couch
For one alone freeth the bride;
One freer than I; the God!

Brünnhilde sinks, wrapt and transfigured, on *Wotan's* breast; he holds her in a long embrace. She throws her head back again and gazes with solemn emotion into her father's eyes.

WOTAN:
Those eyes so lustrous and clear,
Which oft in love I have kissed,
When warlike longings won my lauding,
Or when with lisping of heroes leal thy
honied lips were inspired;
Those effulgent, glorious eyes,
Whose flash my gloom oft dispelled,
When hopeless cravings my heart discouraged,

Or when my wishes t'wart wordly pleasure
from wild warfare were turning—
Their lustrous gaze lights on me now as my
lips imprint this last farewell!
On happier mortal here shall they beam;
The grief-suffering god may never henceforth
behold them!
Now heart-torn, he gives thee his kiss,
And taketh thy godhood away!

He imprints a long kiss on her eyes; she sinks back in his arms with closed eyes, her powers gently departing. He tenderly helps her to lie upon a low mossy lounge, closes her helmet and completely covers her with the great steel shield of the *Valkyrie.* He slowly moves away, then directs the point of his spear toward a huge stone, and summons the *God of Fire.*

WOTAN:
Loki, hear! Listen and heed!
Appear, wavering spirit, and spread me thy
Fire round this fell!
Loki! Loki! Appear!

A stream of fire issues from the stone, which swells to an ever brightening glow of flame; bright flames surround *Wotan,* leaping wildly.

A FAMOUS GROUP OF VALKYRIES AT BAYREUTH

Magic Fire Spell (Feuerzauber) (Transcription by Brassin)

By Alfred Grünfeld, Pianist
58006 12-inch, $1.00

The leave-taking and the breaking out of the flames are musically pictured in one of those marvelous bits of writing which only Wagner could produce, and this beautiful transcription is artistically played here by Herr Grünfeld. The record begins with the passage just preceding *Wotan's* summons to *Loge.*

Then follows a long modulation ending in E major, when the fire motive

MATERNA AS BRÜNNHILDE
(BAYREUTH, 1876)

begins and continues with all its varied changes and modulations to the close of the opera.

Wotan directs, with his spear, the fiery flood to encircle the rocks.

WOTAN: He who my spear in spirit feareth,
Ne'er springs through this fiery bar!

He casts a last look on *Brünnhilde* and disappears through the fire.

(*The curtain falls.*)

DOUBLE-FACED WALKÜRE RECORD

{ Cavalcata (Ride of the Valkyries) By La Scala Orchestra }
{ Lohengrin—Prelude, Act III By La Scala Orchestra } 62693 10-inch, $0.75

(French)

GUILLAUME TELL
(Jee-yaum Tell)

(Italian)

GUGLIELMO TELL
(Gool-yel'-mo Tell)

(English)

WILLIAM TELL

OPERA IN FOUR ACTS

Words by Etienne Jouy, Hippolyte Bis and Armand Marast, taken from Schiller's drama of the same name. Music by Gioachino Rossini. First presented at the *Académie*, Paris, August 3, 1829. First London production, in English, at Drury Lane, 1830, and in Italian at Her Majesty's, 1839.

Characters

WILLIAM TELL,	} Swiss Patriots {	Bass
ARNOLD, suitor of Matilda,		Tenor
WALTER FÜRST,		Bass

MELCTHAL, Arnold's father . . . . Bass
GESSLER, Governor of Schwitz and Uri . . . . . Bass
RUDOLPH, Captain of Gessler's bodyguard . Tenor
RUODI, a fisherman . . . . Tenor
LEUTHOLD, a shepherd . . . . Bass
MATILDA, daughter of Gessler . . . . Soprano
HEDWIGA, Tell's wife . . . . Soprano
JEMMY, Tell's son . . . . Soprano

Chorus of Peasants of the Three Cantons;
Knights, Pages and Ladies of the train
of Matilda; Hunters, Soldiers and
Guards of Gessler.

Scene and Period : Switzerland ; thirteenth century.

THE PLOT

The story of *Tell*, the distinguished patriot, and chief instrument of the revolution which delivered the Swiss cantons from the German yoke in 1207, has been taken by Rossini for the theme of one of his most admired operas, the dramatic interest being heightened by the introduction of love scenes and other episodes.

In the libretto by Jouy and Marast *Gessler* is endowed with a beautiful and amiable daughter, *Matilda*, who has been saved from a watery grave by *Arnold*, son of *Melcthal*, the patriarch of the country, and a determined opponent of the tyrannies of *Gessler*. As a matter of course, mutual attachment ensues, and leads to the troubles which might have been expected from so ill-sorted a connection.

At the opening of the opera we learn that an agent of *Gessler's* has attempted an outrage on the daughter of a herdsman, and been slain by her father, *Leuthold*. Obliged to fly the country after this act of vengeance, it becomes necessary to cross Lake Lucerne while the weather is so adverse that none of the boatmen will row the old man across the tempestuous waters. *William Tell* finally undertakes the rescue, and by so doing incurs the mortal hatred of *Gessler*.

As time progresses, the people become more and more disaffected; and the father of *Arnold,* suspected of inciting them to acts of insubordination, is seized by *Gessler* and executed. The son's feelings are thus subjected to a severe conflict between his love for *Matilda, Gessler's* daughter, his duty to his country, and his desire to avenge his father's death. He, however, renounces his love, and joins the band of patriots now marshaled under *William Tell.* Events are brought to a climax by *Gessler* causing a cap to be elevated on a pole, and requiring all passers-by to bow to it. *Tell* firmly refuses to do so, and is thereupon subjected to the ordeal of the apple, being required, under pain of death, to shoot at an apple placed on the head of his son. Although the distance was considerable, he was able to strike the apple off without injuring the child. The tyrant, perceiving another arrow concealed under *Tell's* cloak, asks him for what purpose it was intended. To which he boldly replies, "To have shot you to the heart, if I had killed my son!" The enraged governor orders him to be hanged; but the Swiss, animated by such fortitude and patriotism, flew to arms, attacked and vanquished *Gessler,* who was shot by *Tell. Matilda* and *Arnold* were united, and the independence of the country was assured.

CAUTIN-BERGER

THE TYRANT GESSLER

OVERTURE

This great overture, which Berlioz has called a symphony in four parts, is a fitting prelude to such a noble and serious work, and is full of beautiful contrasts.

The first movement is reposeful, expressing the solitude of Nature, and is followed by the contrasting *Storm*, a majestic and awe-inspiring tone picture. To the *Storm* succeeds a beautiful pastoral with a delicious melody for the English horn, and as Berlioz says, "with the gamboling of the flute above this calm chant producing a charming freshness and gayety." As the last notes of the melody die away, the trumpets enter with a brilliant fanfare on the splendid finale, a fitting climax to a great work.

Part I—At Dawn
By Pryor's Band 31218 12-inch, $1.00

Part II—The Storm
By Pryor's Band 31219 12-inch, 1.00

Part III—The Calm
By Pryor's Band 31220 12-inch, 1.00

Part IV—Finale
By Pryor's Band 31221 12-inch, 1.00

Note.—This series is also issued in Double-Faced form.—See page 375.

ACT I

SCENE—*A Village in the Canton of Uri*

The curtain rises on a peaceful scene, showing a charming village with the house of *William Tell* in the foreground. *Tell* and his family are engaged in rural occupations, and the fishermen, while they prepare to put out the boats, sing a lovely *barcarolle*.

Accours dans ma nacelle (Come, Love, in My Boat)
M. Regis, Tenor (*In French*) *45026 10-inch, $1.00

FISHERMEN:
Come hither, my dearest love!
In my little boat embark;
Ah! hither come, and with thy smile
My loving heart rejoice.
Though leave I must, Eliza, dear,
Do not let me alone depart;
See how the shining sky above
A brilliant day doth augur.
Gentle as the bending rosebud,
Born in the morning's early dew,
Heaven's threaten'd tempests wild
Will thy presence, love, appease;
When by your side I'm seated,
What new life my soul receives!
There's a Providence above us
Our heart's affections will protect.

OPERA ARCHIVES   FIRST ACT SCENE

A horn sounds as the signal for the beginning of the annual Shepherds' Festival, at which three marriages are to be celebrated by *Melcthal*, the patriarch of the village. *Arnold, Melcthal's* son, is saddened at the signal, thinking of his own love, *Matilda*, who is the daughter of the tyrant *Gessler*.

Tell confides to *Arnold* some of his plans for overthrowing the power of *Gessler*, and asks *Arnold* to assist.

*Double-Faced Record—For title of opposite side see DOUBLE-FACED WILLIAM TELL RECORDS, page 375.

Chè finger tanto invano (Vain is the Attempt!)

By Antonio Paoli, Tenor, and Francesco Cigada, Baritone

(*In Italian*) **92048 12-inch, $3.00**

ARNOLD:
(Ah! vain is all dissembling.)
While the tyrant's yoke continues,
My heart is o'erwhelm'd with grief.
What dost thou desire?
TELL:
To recall you, Arnold, to your duty.
ARNOLD:
Ah! Matilda, dearly do I love thee;
But from my heart the passion I must root,
If my country and my honor so demand.
TELL (*aside*):
If to us unfaithful he has been,
His grief his repentance doth attest.
(*To Arnold*):
We have no need for doubt or fear—
If true to ourselves, we must conquer.

ARNOLD:
What power do we possess?
TELL:
Strength enough has he who doubts not.
If our valor fail us not,
The tyrant will surely fall.
ARNOLD:
But, if conquer'd, where our refuge?
TELL:
In the tomb!
ARNOLD:
And who will avenge our fall?
TELL:
Heaven!
ARNOLD:
When the hour of danger comes,
Faithfully I will stand by you.

The young man hesitates between duty to his country and his love for the tyrant's daughter, but finally casts his lot with *Tell*, and goes to bid a last farewell to *Matilda*.

The festival now begins, but is interrupted at intervals by the sound of hunting horns, showing that *Gessler* and his huntsmen are in the mountains near by. The young couples are wedded, and all are rejoicing in their happiness when the festival is rudely interrupted by *Leuthold*, a shepherd, who rushes in crying, "Save me from the tyrant." He explains that one of *Gessler's* officers had abducted his daughter, and to rescue her he had killed the villain. He begs the fishermen to row him across the lake to safety. They refuse, not daring to offend the tyrant, and because of the storm which is raging. *Tell* appears, rushes to the boat with *Leuthold* and puts out on the raging lake just as the soldiers of *Gessler* appear. Baffled of their revenge, they burn the village, devastate the fields, and strike down the aged *Melcthal*.

ACT II

SCENE—*A deep valley in the Alps. On the left the Lake of the Four Cantons.   Twilight*

Matilda appears and muses upon her love for *Arnold*. Her lover now joins her, and an effective love scene ensues, which is interrupted by the approach of *Tell* and *Walter*, and *Matilda* departs. *Tell* has seen the young man talking to the daughter of his mortal enemy, and accuses him of being false to the Swiss. *Arnold* confesses that he loves *Matilda*, but says he will renounce her if his country demands the sacrifice.

They then break to *Arnold* the news that *Gessler* has put his father to death, and feelings of vengeance drive from his mind all thought of *Matilda*. In a fine trio the three patriots call upon Heaven to aid their righteous cause.

Troncar suoi di (His Life Basely Taken)

By Antonio Paoli, Tenor; Francesco Cigada, Baritone; Aristodemo
Sillich, Bass

(*In Italian*) **92051 12-inch, $3.00**

ARNOLD:
His life the tyrant wickedly hath taken,
And yet my sabre in its sheath reposeth;
Alas! my father his son's aid was needing,
While I Helvetia was e'en then betraying.
Heavens! never again shall I behold him!
TRIO:
May glory our hearts with courage exalt

Our cause propitious Heaven will aid;
The shade of your father our souls will inspire!
Vengeance it calls for, and not lamentation;
Although departed, he doth seem to say,
Happy in his destiny hath he been;
His remains a martyr's tomb shall hallow,
Of virtue such as his the fit recompense.

Berlioz writes of his attempt to analyze this great trio: "What! Analyze the awful despair of a son who learns his father is brutally slain? Note the details of a flute or second violin passage! No,—I can only cry, 'Wonderful, superb, heart-rending!'"

The men of the cantons now assemble, and in a splendid finale swear to conquer or die.

Domo, o ciel, da uno straniero (By a Vile Foreigner Subdued)

By Nestore Della Torre, Baritone   (*In Italian*) **76013 12-inch, $2.00**

The curtain falls to a magnificent outburst of patriotism, "To arms! To arms!"

ACT III

SCENE—*The Grand Square of Altorf—Gessler's Castle in the background. In the Foreground a Pole surmounted by a Cap*

Gessler and his barons are seated on a throne at one side of the Square, while various amusements are given for their entertainment. It is here that the superb ballet, one of the most beautiful ever composed, is introduced. This has been recorded in three parts, by Pryor's Band.

{William Tell Ballet Music—Part I	By Pryor's Band}	*35042 12-inch, $1.25
{William Tell Ballet Music—Part II	By Pryor's Band}	
William Tell Ballet Music—Part III	By Pryor's Band	*16578 10-inch, .75

The band, under Mr. Pryor's masterly baton, has played this brilliant music in a manner which brings out all its beauties.

Gessler, who, with much satisfaction, has been watching the populace bow to the cap which he has had placed on a pole as a symbol of his authority, suddenly notices that *Tell* and his son fail to pay honor to the standard. He orders them seized and brought before him, and when he is told that *Tell* is the man who aided *Leuthold* to escape, his rage is intensified. He asks if the boy is *Tell's* son, and when *Tell* replies, "My only son," a fiendish idea strikes the tyrant. He orders *Tell* to shoot an apple from the boy's head on pain of instant death for both. *Tell* refuses, but *Jemmy* urges his father to obey, saying, "Father, remember your skill! Fear not, I will not move!"

Tell embraces his boy, and selecting an arrow, manages to conceal another in his coat. He casts a fierce look at the tyrant, then aims with care and strikes the apple fairly in the centre. When he realizes *Jemmy* is safe, *Tell* faints and the concealed arrow is discovered. "For whom was the second arrow?" demands *Gessler.* "For you, tyrant, if I had harmed my child!"

Gessler then orders both put to death, but *Matilda,* who has entered, demands the life of the boy and takes him under her protection. *Tell* is taken to prison amid the curses of the Swiss.

GORITZ AS WILLIAM TELL

ACT IV

SCENE—*The Ruined Village of Act I. At the Right the partially burned Cottage of Melcthal*

Arnold, who knows nothing of the capture of *Tell,* has come to his native village to bid farewell to the home of his boyhood. He gazes at the desolate cottage and sings his charming and pathetic air, *Oh, Blessed Abode.*

O muto asil (Oh, Blessed Abode)

By Francesco Tamagno, Tenor	(*In Italian*)	95009	10-inch, $5.00
By M. Gautier, Tenor	(*In French*)	*45007	10-inch, 1.00
By Leon Beyle, Tenor	(*In French*)	*45026	10-inch, 1.00

This number is one of the most effective of those allotted to *Arnold.* It begins with the beautiful passage

O mu - to a - sil del pian to do - ve io sor - ti - va il df.
Oh! bless'd a - bode, with - in whose walls mine eyes first saw the light,

This aria is reposeful and offers a fine contrast to the tumult of the last scene.

ARNOLD:

Oh! bless'd abode, within whose walls
  Mine eyes first saw the light,
Once so belov'd, yet now thy halls,
  Bring mis'ry to my aching sight.

In vain I call; no father's greeting,
Which fancy now to me's repeating,
Will e'er again these ears be meeting,
Then home once lov'd, forevermore, farewell!

Tamagno brought all his strength and vitality to the part of *Arnold,* singing it superbly, and this fine air is given with wonderfully truthful and impressive declamation.

A company of Swiss patriots enter hurriedly and tell *Arnold* of the events at Altorf. He calls on them to follow him to the rescue of *Tell,* and departs in the direction of the capital.

Double-Faced Record—For title of opposite side see DOUBLE-FACED WILLIAM TELL RECORDS, page 375.

PAINTED BY KAULBACH

WILLIAM TELL'S FLIGHT

SCENE II—*Lake of Four Cantons.*
A Storm is Gathering

Tell's wife is resting here on her way
to demand of *Gessler* her husband and son.
She hears her son's voice and is overjoyed
to see him brought to her by *Matilda.* She
clasps him in her arms, and anxiously inquires for her husband. *Matilda* says that
Tell has been removed from Altdorf Prison,
and taken across the lake. She has no
sooner spoken than *Tell* appears, having
escaped from the boat and sent an arrow
through the tyrant's heart. *Arnold* and the
patriots appear, rejoicing that *Gessler* has
been slain and that the Swiss are free once
more.

The storm breaks, and as if to announce liberty to Switzerland the sun
bursts forth, revealing the glittering, snowy
peaks of the Alps in all their dazzling
beauty. An invocation to Freedom comes
from every throat:

TELL:
Let us invoke, with hearts devout,
Thee, oh Freedom, to sway each heart!
Thou gav'st us pow'r to strike and conquer,
Do thou ne'er depart!
ALL:
Thou gav'st us pow'r to strike and conquer!
We are free, do thou ne'er depart!

DOUBLE-FACED AND MISCELLANEOUS WILLIAM TELL RECORDS

{Overture, Part I—At Dawn {Overture, Part II—The Storm	By Pryor's Band} By Pryor's Band}	16380	10-inch,	$0.75
{Overture, Part III—The Calm {Overture, Part IV—Finale	By Pryor's Band} By Pryor's Band}	16381	10-inch,	.75
{Overture, Part I—At Dawn {Overture, Part II—The Storm	By Pryor's Band} By Pryor's Band}	35120	12-inch,	1.25
{Overture, Part III—The Calm {Overture, Part IV—Finale	By Pryor's Band} By Pryor's Band}	35121	12-inch,	1.25
{Ballet Music, Part I {Ballet Music, Part II	By Pryor's Band} By Pryor's Band}	35042	12-inch,	1.25
{Ballet Music, Part III { Profeta—Re del cielo By Luigi Colazza, Tenor	By Pryor's Band} (In Italian)}	16578	10-inch,	.75
{Asile hereditaire (Oh! Blessed Abode) { By M. Gautier, Tenor { Les Huguenots—Plus blanche (Meyerbeer) { By M. Gautier, Tenor	 (In French)} (In French)}	45007	10-inch,	1.00
{Accours dans ma nacelle—Barcarola (Come, Love, In My { Boat) By M. Regis, Tenor {Asile hereditaire (Oh! Blessed Abode) { By Leon Beyle, Tenor	 (In French)} (In French)}	45026	10-inch,	1.00